Footprint
Tunisia
Handbook
Justin McGuinness

Minarets, so beautiful above the souks,
Cries in stone soaring from heart of Orient,
Mystic sentinels against the smiling sky,
White towers lying in wait for shivers of hope.

Mario Scalesi, *Poèmes d'Orient*
(Tunis, Ed. Saliba, 1935)

3rd edition

Tunisia Handbook
3rd edition
© Footprint Handbooks Ltd
October 2002

Published by Footprint Handbooks
6 Riverside Court
Lower Bristol Road
Bath BA2 3DZ. England
T +44 (0)1225 469141
F +44 (0)1225 469461
Email discover@footprintbooks.com
Web www.footprintbooks.com

ISBN 1 903471 28 1
CIP DATA: A catalogue record for this
book is available from the British Library

Distributed in the USA by
Publishers Group West

Neither the black and white nor
coloured maps are intended to have any
political significance.

Every effort has been made to ensure
that the facts in this Handbook are
accurate. However, travellers should still
obtain advice from consulates, airlines
etc about current travel and visa
requirements before travelling. The
authors and publishers cannot accept
responsibility for any loss, injury or
inconvenience however caused.

Credits

Series editors
Patrick Dawson and Rachel Fielding

Editorial
Editor: Tim Jollands
Maps: Sarah Sorensen

Production
Page layout: Emma Bryers
Typesetting: Davina Rungasamy
Maps: Leona Bailey, Claire Benison
and Robert Lunn
Colour maps: Kevin Feeney
Cover: Camilla Ford

Design
Mytton Williams

Photography
Front cover: Art Directors and Trip
Back cover: Impact Photo Library
Inside colour section:
James Davis Travel Photography:
page 8 (top left), page 11 (top left)
Eye Ubiquitous/David Forman:
page 8 (centre)
gettyone Stone: page 14 (top right)
Robert Harding Picture Library: page 4;
David Poole page 1; M Short page 11
(bottom)
Patrick Syder Images: page 11 (centre)
The Travel Library/Steve Day: page 8
(top right and bottom), pages 12-13,
page 16
Art Directors and Trip: H Rogers page 11
(top right), page 14 (centre and top left);
M Taylor page 7; B Turner page 14
(bottom)

Print
Manufactured in Italy by LEGOPRINT

Tunisia

Mediterranean Sea

Bizerte
Menzel Bourguiba
Lac Ichkeul
Kalaât el Andalous
Sidi Daoud
El Haouaria
Kerkouane
Mateur
Utique
Kélibia
Carthage
Gulf of Tunis
Tabarka
Aïn Draham
Hammam Bourguiba
Béja
Djebba
TUNIS
Korbous
El Feidja
Bulla Regia
Aïn Tuonga
Medjez-el-Bab
Nabeul
Chemtou
Jendouba
Dougga
Zaghouan
Hammamet
Mustis
Thuburbo Majus
Gulf of Hammamet
Le Kef
Medeina
Makthar
Port el Kantaoui
Sousse
Monastir
Uzitta
Kairouan
Sebkha Sidi el Hani
Mahdia
Haïdra
Sbiba
Kaserine
El Djem
Sbeïtla
Botria
Chaâmbi
Thélepte
Sfax
Thyna
El Kantara
Moularès
Gafsa
Bou Hedma
Metlaoui
Chott el Rharsa
Tozeur
Nefta
Chott el Djerid (Salt Lake)
Chott el Fejej
Gabès
Houmt Souk
Isle of Djerba
Zarat
Djorf
Meninx
Tritonis Lacus
Kebili
Bou Ghrara
Zarzis
Matmata
Ras Ajdir
Douz
Medenine

ALGERIA

Ksar Ghilane
Tataouine

N

0 km 50
0 miles 50

Remada

Dehiba

Lorzot
LIBYA

Borj Jenein

Bir Zhar

See colour maps at back of book

M'Chiguig

Dougga Archaeological site/town

Chaâmbi National park

Contents

Left Souk Echaouachia, the chechia makers' souk, in Tunis's médina

11

Right Sidi Bou Said, 'bird cage' village, as typically Mediterranean in feel as a Greek island

A foot in the door

Right Pillared cloisters of the Great Mosque of Okba Ibn Nafi, Kairouan, spiritual and religious capital of Tunisia
Below Hammamet fishermen going about their evening ritual

Above Remote but well worth the visit, Sbeïtla is one of the best preserved Roman cities in North Africa, remarkable for its dramatic temples
Right Berber women and child at Guermessa, a hillcrest village accessible from Tatouine in Tunisia's southeast corner

Highlights

Tunisia is a country where the shores of exotica begin. Mediterranean whitewashed villages, beaches of fine sand and palm trees meet souks, caftans and copper trays, deserts and Roman ruins fit for a sword-and-sandal epic. But this is also arguably the Arab world's most forward-looking state, 'a Mediterranean tiger' economy. This blend of old and new is both a product of tourism and a reason for it – the country's great classical set-peices are as much of a pull as its coastline or the arid expanses of the Great South.

Tunisia is a land of ancient dramas, the country that saw despairing Queen Dido throw **Imperial Africa** herself on a pyre and Jugurtha, now a hero for the Imazighen, fight his wars; from this corner of North Africa, Hannibal set out with his elephants, heading for victories over Rome. But after years of conflict, Rome won over Carthage, and a new province, Africa, was created. It was to become one of the richest in the empire, exporting wheat, olive oil, wine and wild beasts. Carthage was also a centre of early Christianity, conquered by the Vandals, reoccupied by the vainglorious Byzantines and then, in the seventh century, taken by invading Arab-Muslim armies, and renamed *Ifrikiya* in the process.

Of all these empires, much has survived: Punic Kerkouane, hilltop Dougga, contemplating a valley of gentle farmland, the gold-stone temples of Sbeïtla, remote Haïdra with its Byzantine fortress, and the great coliseum of El Djem, once a place of spectacular carnage, now the setting for an occasional summer concert.

Rather like its northern neighbour Sicily, Tunisia has a strategic location, right at the **Arab Ifrikiya** heart of the Mediterranean. The northernmost point of Africa is in Tunisia, a fact not lost on the area's frequent invaders. The area had a distinctly tumultuous history from the eighth century onwards, with first the various Arab dynasties and the Normans, and later the Ottomans and Habsburgs, competing for power. Kairouan was the first Muslim power centre in North Africa, and its great ochre mosque is one of the finest in all Islam. From the late 15th century, Tunis was an Ottoman provincial capital and the Turks left a heritage of mosques (such as the pointy towered Hanefite mosques in Tunis) and fortifications.

In the 19th century, North Africa was the object of European colonial designs. Tunisia **Colonial** was to come under French rule in 1881, remaining so until 1956. The French built **heritage** pleasant, spacious cities, filled with buildings from the neo-Moorish, Art Deco, Functionalist and Modern movements. Much of this architecture still survives today, especially in Tunis, Bizerte and Sfax.

The potential of the new protectorate in terms of its natural assets was also exploited by the **Coasts, hills** colonial rulers: tourism soon developed and has grown steadily since the late 19th century. **& deserts** A couple of hours' flight from Europe are hills covered in evergreen forest, open steppe lands and great salt lakes. There is a remote and rocky northern coast and a gentle east-facing coast of sandy beaches, which provides swimming, suntans and thalassotherapy. Near the Libyan border sits the sleepy holiday island of Djerba. Here the traditional whitewashed farmstead or menzil, surrounded by peaceful olive groves, has been a model for the better hotels. But the real treasure of southern Tunisia is the landscape. Marred in places by the ever expanding concrete towns, it is best taken in 'road movie' spirit. Here you can pass through the places oft used as backdrops in the movies. For those with a geographical bent, there is a full range of arid environments, from craggy hills and stone plains to dunes and oases. Note too that you don't need to be Lawrence of Arabia to get around the South. New roads have put these previously inaccessible places within easy reach of bus and car.

Modern Tunisia

For some Tunisia compares well with, say, Greece or Portugal in the 1970s, rather than certain Middle Eastern states. The closeness to Europe is reflected in social attitudes: with advanced legislation on women's status and a strong middle class, Tunisians consider themselves the most advanced people in the Arab World. If the present rate of development can be maintained, this will be one of the most interesting Arab countries to watch over the next ten years. Will it eventually apply for membership of the European Union, as both Morocco and Turkey have in the past? Close economic ties with Europe may eventually imply far-reaching political changes as well.

Reform & development For the moment, Tunisia is busy with a major structural reform programme, privatizing industry and developing business-friendly institutions. The difficulty lies in keeping the right balance between economic growth and social stability, ensuring that local businesses do not go under as international competition arrives. State policy has a reassuring old-style social-democrat feel: everyone is to get a slice of the increasingly prosperous national cake. Remote rural communities, where life is structured still by the rains and the Muslim year, now have phones, electricity and drinking water. Relatives settled abroad, mainly in France and Italy, are an important source of income. (The élite is French speaking – but likes to feel it has tradition.) Women work in all sectors of the economy, the business community has mobile phones and the internet – but Ramadan, the Muslim month of fasting, is taken very seriously. Tunisians are very much family people, with a deep love of children, immediately noticeable when travelling with children.

A young country Perhaps the word 'youth' best sums up early 21st century Tunisia. This is a young – and surprising – country. None of the clichés about Arab lands seem to fit. The women aren't veiled, there is an upbeat air of prosperity. Visitors generally start in one of the east coast resorts, pleasant, clean, where beaches are beautiful and sunshine reliable. Street crime is extremely rare, getting around on public transport is easy. But if you take time to get away from the hotel complex, you may explore teeming cities. Look out for small souk restaurants, markets fragrant with fresh produce. Listen out for music – the cassette stalls are piled high with sounds unfamiliar. In summer, you might get to an open-air concert by an Algerian *raï* singer or a gaudy Lebanese starlet, packed with an enthusiastic, vocal crowd. Or you might find yourself embroiled in a wedding, a big family affair with bride and groom perched on gilded thrones, the women decked out in Oriental splendour and a noisy six-piece traditional orchestra. Such weddings are time for noisy family reunions; the relatives are back from Europe and conversations race along in Franco-Arabe. On a cultural level, Tunisia is home to the Arab world's most interesting cinema and avant-garde theatre.

Glassy seas & birds of prey But perhaps Tunisia is at its best in the density of close detail. There are the great set-piece sights – the amphitheatre of El Djem, magnificent Dougga, the dunes of Douz – it is true, but you need to be attentive to the fine grain: dusty-red skeins of peppers drying against a whitewashed wall; alleys of olive trees and the wind shifting the silvery leaves in a vast landscape; birds of prey riding the air currents off Jugurtha's Citadel; sunlight through latticework patterning tiles and marble; the honey-tobacco gurgling of a water pipe; warm smells of tabouna bread or fish frying; the glass-clear sea at Kélibia … For some, Tunisia is the most typical corner of the Mediterranean – more Mediterranean than even a Greek island or the Iberian coast. Happily, even in the face of the development of its tourist industry, it manages to maintain a homely feel, at ease with its contradictions like a sprawling old family. People still have time for you, and no doubt you will be made welcome in a way no longer possible in hectic, career-driven Europe.

Left *Nabeul's Friday market. Once noted for their rush-mat making, supplying hsur to mosques, Nabeulian weavers have found new outlets for their craft, making floor mats for sale to tourists*
Below *Baker at Nefta*

Above *Interior of the Synagogue of El Ghriba, Djerba*
Left *A typically decorative window in a carpet shop in Kairouan's médina*
Next page *The weekly market at Douz, where each year in December the Festival of the Desert takes place*

Right Seasonal nomad migrations are now
a thing of the past but tourists can trek by
camel to seek the white dunes of Nefzaoua
Below The low-lying region of salt lakes, the
Chott el Djerid, beyond which lies the Sahara

Above Ghorfas used to store grain line a
courtyard at Ksar Ouled Soltane, one of the
best preserved ksour in Tunisia
Right The citadel village of Chenini,
its white mosque glinting high above the
arid plain
Next page The Cap Bon Peninsula, farming
heartland of Tunisia

Le Grand Sud

The southern third of Tunisia, that pointy triangle of land running down into the desert between Algeria and Libya, was negotiated and defined by French and Ottoman functionaries in the 19th century. Its dune deserts and salt flats, bone arid hills and occasional oases were tribal land, a region of seasonal migrations ever ripe for conflict with central powers. In early times the caravans had brought slaves up from Africa, the oases paid occasional taxes to the Bey. For the French, it was administered as part of the Great Saharan Territories, a place for an unknown officer to build a bold career. It was not 'la Tunisie utile' and beyond it lay the colossal expanses of the Sahara.

Ancient ksours & citadels

The visitor to Djerba will find a fine patch of the pre-Sahara in easy striking distance. Around Tataouine, 'the springs' in Amazigh, are hilly landscapes and some of Tunisia's most interesting vernacular building. On rocky crests and contours are the villages of Chenini, Douiret and Guermessa. You also have the ksours, fortified granaries on the plain and, a new plus, a Jurassic trail, complete with the occasional replica dinosaur perched up at a strategic viewpoint. Also within a long day trip visit from Djerba is the once obscure underground village of Matmata, now endlessly visited for its minor role in an exotic bar scene in the first *Star Wars* film.

Land of the date palm

Heading southwest from the Sahel holiday towns, Gafsa is Tunisia's northernmost inland oasis town. Its backdrop of arid hills are a foretaste of the landscapes to come. Further south, civilization's hold over nature becomes more shaky. Once upon a time, life in the oases of Tozeur, Nefza and Kebili depended solely on spring water, pack animals, and the fruitful, protective palm tree. No wonder that 'El Djerid', 'palm' in Arabic, is the name for the region around Tozeur.

Hill villages & phosphate towns

A day-trip from the Djerid lie the mountain oases of Chebika, Tamerza and Midès. Immortalized by anthropologists, Chebika looks westwards across the plain. Tamerza has been restored to a tasteful level of decay, best viewed from the upmarket hotel across the *oued*. At Midès, the abandoned village overlooks a deep gorge. In the nearby oasis, market gardens grow under the palms. To the east are the tough, dusty phosphate towns of Redeyef and Moularès, major wealth generators for Tunisia in the days before tourism.

Across salt flats to the dunes at Douz

Crossing the Chott el Djerid used to be a risky business. While in earlier days, camel caravans were swallowed in the great salt waste, today the four-wheel drive vehicles belt across. South of the salt flats, you are in the Nefzaoua, out on the eastern edge of the Grand Erg Oriental, dune desert fit for heroic films. The oases appear as tiny spots of green in a white sand waste – a 'leopard skin' in local poetry. The best way to explore it? On camel back. From settlements like Zaâfrane it is possible to head off with a local guide to spend a few nights out in the white dunes.

Change in the Desert

Across the Deep South, the old ways have largely gone. Today, the pure nomad lifestyle is very much a thing of the past. The attractions of a settled life are too great. Although you can still see old-style oasis cultivation, the region has vast new agri-business palm plantations. In the 1990s mass tourism arrived in the oases and troglodyte settlements. No doubt the citadel villages will be next. At the main sights, you are as likely to see tourists, decked out in mock-Touareg dress, as you are to see nomad tents. Although the desert lifestyle of the M'razig and the Adhara, perfectly adapted to a harsh environment, did not survive the 20th century unadulterated, it could yet provide the basis for a new, ecologically friendly tourism based in the local communities.

Essentials

2

Essentials

Planning your trip

Where to go

Tunisia is a small country, with short distances between the main tourist areas and sights, so the traveller can see a lot in a two-week trip. To make the most of your time, some careful planning is not a bad thing. What can you expect to see, without pushing yourself too hard, within the time you have for your trip? Rather than try to take in a maximum of towns and places, perhaps it is better to try to get to know a couple of places really well. Off the beaten track, Tunisia has some surprises – and for those with time, and a visa (obtained well in advance), an excursion into neighbouring western Libya is now becoming a real possibility.

Traditionally, Tunisia was one of the more unusual cheap package destinations. Its selling point was beaches, sun and 'a touch of the exotic'. Well-run three-star hotels catered for the needs of the mass market, resort towns Hammamet, close to Tunis, and Sousse-Monastir were the destinations. In the late 1980s, the Tunisian authorities woke up to the fact that the typical tourist was spending little in the country and tour operators were making all the profits, and since then there has been a bid to develop more upmarket tourism and certain niche areas like golf, thalassotherapy and 'desert safaris'. In fact, the country really does have a lot to offer beyond the resort towns. Travelling by hire car or by *louage* (the ubiquitous inter-city shared taxis) will enable you to see a lot in a short space of time.

Tunisia's cities are concentrated on its eastern coastline. If you have bought a package, you will fly into Tunis-Carthage airport (for **Hammamet**) or Skanès-Monastir (for **Sousse**, **Mahdia** and **Monastir**). There are clean, safe, sandy beaches at these resorts and the shallow waters are perfect for kids. Both Tunis and Sousse have well preserved *médinas*, as the old walled towns are known, and the striking old city of **Kairouan** as well as the **Cap Bon** region are within easy distance of both cities. In the interior, there are some of the most spectacular Roman sites, which can be taken in as organized day excursions from the resorts.

So how should you go to Tunisia? Apart from doing flight only and arranging accommodation yourself, the cheap package is one of the best options. A sufficiently cheap package will give you a base in a resort from which you can travel out to other areas, spending nights away in places of interest. Note that Tunisia, while very reasonable in price terms when compared with Western Europe, is not a cheap destination.

For people who want interesting sites to visit – and whose kids want a beach – Tunisia is a good compromise destination. Teenagers and 20-somethings looking for clubs will find it a little tame, however. Out of season, reasonable prices make Tunisian resorts a good destination for senior travellers seeking to escape the winter grey of northern Europe. Backpackers on a very tight budget will need to plan their money carefully. While upscale travellers will not (as yet) find chic hotels with very high standards of service, for the independent traveller prepared to make an effort, Tunisia has a lot of cultural interest.

Ancient sites To explore the **Roman sites**, you would be best to hire a car, however. Inland from Tunis is **Dougga**, perhaps the most beautiful site, **Bulla Regia** and its underground villas and marble quarry town of **Chemtou**, which has the best museum in the country (after the Bardo in Tunis with its enormous collection of mosaics). Although these sites can be covered by public transport, the advantage of three days' car hire is that it allows you to take in lots of minor places. Close to Hammamet is **Zaghouan** and its mountain, and the **hillcrest villages** of Jeradou, Takrouna and Zriba. Heading west for Dougga, is Andalusian Testour. If you opted to overnight in **Le Kef**, you could cover places on the western border, including the remote plateau of **Kalaât Senan**, and Roman cities **Haïdra** and **Sbeïtla**. South of Sousse is the spectacular amphitheatre of **El Djem**.

Essentials

Desert tourism	Tunisia's other big selling point is the **desert**. Although there are organized trips, which can work out cheap for a group, there is no problem getting to the southern areas by public transport. Basically, there are four areas to visit: the **Djerid** and the **Nefzaoua**, the **Matmatas** and the **Tataouine region**. The Djerid centres on the oasis town of Tozeur; close by is Nefta and the hill villages of Chebika, Midès and Tamerza. The Nefzaoua, south of the Djerid across a great salt flat, has the best dunes, near Douz and Zaâfrane. A new road links Douz to the Matmata region, famed for its underground houses. Tataouine, a couple of hours south of Djerba, has rock desert and a set of Berber villages perched up in the hills, Chenini, Douiret and Guermessa.
Newer beach-holiday destinations	In its effort to diversify its tourist industry, Tunisia has invested heavily in the southern island of **Djerba**, and on a more modest scale in **Tabarka**, a tiny harbour town up in the northwest near the Algerian frontier. Djerba is said to be where Odysseus stopped off for a spot of lotus-eating. The island, flat, planted with palms and olives, ringed with splendid beaches, is great for anyone with a desperate need to slow down and relax, although some would say now rather over-developed. (The energetic could bicycle round the interior, looking at mosques and villages.) Tabarka, once a winter haunt of wild-boar hunters, now has a golf course and beach hotels. Further east, all along the north coast, are beautiful unspoiled beaches at places like Sidi Mechrig and Cap Serrat, and, moving closer to Bizerte, Ras Angela and Aïn Dammous.
Specialist & eccentric interests	Tunisia has a lot of quirkier things to interest the visitor too: birdwatching at Haouaria during the annual migrations, the old city centres with their heritage of 19th- and 20th-century architecture, *hammams* (Turkish baths) and cafés with hubbly-bubbly pipes, tonnes of kitsch in the tourist bazaars, fashion horrors at the *friperie*, the big second-hand clothes souks. Although vegetarians will have a hard time, meat eaters will be spoiled at roadside *mechoui* (barbecue) restaurants. In summer, you might find your way into a Tunisian wedding. Tunisians are a sociable and interesting lot and generally at ease in European languages.
A week's holiday	In a sightseeing filled week, you could easily cover the main archaeological sites of **northern and central Tunisia**, perhaps with a day on the beach, if you travel in late spring or summer. You would overnight in Tunis (two nights), Le Kef (two nights), Kairouan (one night) and perhaps Sousse (one night), before heading back to Tunis. A more relaxing option might be to base yourself in Tunis or Hammamet and mix days in town/on the beach with long day trips out to sites like Dougga or El Djem. Another thought for a week's break would be to fly into Djerba or (possibly) Tozeur, and from there do a driving tour of **the desert South**, possibly combined with a day or two on the beach on Djerba.
Two-week holiday	The best way to discover the desert is really to take a camel safari from Douz. On a fortnight's holiday, four or five nights in the desert would leave you plenty of days to plan a driving tour to the country's other sights, possibly focusing on a specific region or theme (Roman towns of the interior? Islamic cities?).
Three-week holiday	With three weeks, you would easily be able to cover the main towns and archaeological sites and still have time left over for a spot of unwinding at the beach – or to really discover one of the less visited (by tourists) regions. Le Kef or Makthar/La Kessera might be rewarding. Actually spending time in places like Kebili or Tozeur, southern oasis towns which are normally just overnights on the four-wheel drive circuit, might be interesting if you meet the right people. Or you could take a full up-market thalassotherapy cure in some five-star hotel – or rub shoulders with everyday Tunisia on holiday at the hot-water springs of places like Hammam Zriba or Korbous.

Another option, really for archaeology buffs, would be to combine Roman Tunisia with an excursion over the frontier into western Libya. Tripoli, Libya's main city, has a magnificent museum to rival the Bardo in Tunis, and the sites of Sabratha and Leptis Magna are as spectacular as Dougga in Tunisia. Transport from Djerba (or indeed any Tunisian city) to Libya is no problem. The difficulty is obtaining the visa.

Across the Libyan frontier?
See Footprint Handbook to Libya by James Azema for further details

In 2001, Tunis was much touted in the quality British press as a possible weekend destination. If you could leave a northern European city on a Thursday evening, returning on the last flight on Sunday, you could have a very pleasant couple of days in Tunis. The first rather leisurely day would be spent doing Tunis itself (the great Musée du Bardo, plus the old town or médina) while day two would be devoted to the sites of the Banlieue Nord, basically the remains of Carthage and the desperately picturesque village of Sidi Bou Saïd.

Tunis city-break

Essentials

When to go

Though Tunisia is a good destination all year round, spring, early summer and autumn are undoubtedly the best times to go if you are aiming to explore the more out of the way places, médinas and Roman sites. At these times of year, you have the advantages of pleasant weather, longer days, and cheaper resort-hotel rates. July and August can be extremely hot, making urban tourism a painful, sweaty experience. The main coastal resorts are extremely crowded at these times of year. If you travel in winter, you have the disadvantage of shorter days, often rainy in the north. Nevertheless, Djerba (and Hammamet to a lesser extent) have superb microclimates which produce balmy winter days. Note that, for the beach, Tabarka is really a summer-only sort of place, there being rough sea and wind at other times. The desert is not a summer destination, especially if you are going to bivouac.

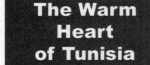
Tours and tour operators

Andante Travel, Grange Cottage, Winterbourne Dauntsey, Salisbury, Wilts, SP4 6ER, T01980-610555 (art and archaeology). *Branta Holidays*, 7 Wingfield St, London SE15 4LN, T020-7634 4812 (birdwatching winter visitors on Lake Ichkeul and Tozeur). Discovery Cruises, 47 St Johns Wood High St, London NW8 7NJ, T020-7586 7191 (sailing from Athens). *Explore Worldwide*, 1 Frederick St, Aldershot, Hants, T01252-319448 (offer interesting excursions to the ancient sites and into the mountains). *Medward Travel*, 304 Old Brompton Rd, London, SW5 9JF, T020-7373 4411, F020-7244 8174 (for individual requirements). *Prospect Music and Art Tours*, 454 Chiswick High Rd, London W4 5TT, T0181-9952151 (accompanied tours with experts in art and art history, archaeology and architecture). *Martin Randall Travel*,

UK & Ireland

Essentials

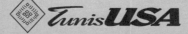

10 Barley Mow Passage, Chiswick, London W4 4PH, T020-8994 6477 (Roman and Islamic cities). *Regency Cruises*, 2 Telfords Yard, 6 The Highway, London E1 9BQ, T01473-292222 (sailing from Nice). *Wigmore Holidays*, 122 Wigmore St, London W1H 9FE, T020-7486 4425, F020-7486 3559 (specialize in fly-drive and tailor-made travel as well as breaks in Tunis and beach resorts, not cheap).

North America *Sarah Tours*, 3600 Surrey Drive, Alexandria, VA 22307, T1-800-267-0036, T703-619-0777, F703-619-9399, www.sarahtours.com Specializes in cultural tours. *TunisUSA*, 155 E. Lancaster Av, Wayne, PA 19087, T610-995-2788, F610-964-0438, Toll free T1-800-474-5500, info@TunisUSA.com, www.TunisUSA.com Specialists in Tunisian and Turkish travel.

Finding out more

Tunisian tourist boards The **ONTT** (Organisation Nationale du Tourisme Tunisien or Tunisian National Tourist Board) has a number of offices overseas, as follows: **Austria** 1010 Wien Opernring 1, Stiege R. Tür 109, Vienna, T1-5853480, F1-5853418, tunesien@magnet.at **Belgium** Office National du Tourisme Tunisien, Galerie Ravenstein 60, 1000 Bruxelles, T2-5111142, F2-5113600, tourismetunisien@skynet.be **Canada** Tunisian Tourist Office, 1253 McGill College, Bureau # 655 Montreal, Quebec H3 B2 Y5, T514-3971182, F514-3971647, tunisinfo@qc.aira.com **France** Office National du Tourisme Tunisien, 32 Avenue de l'Opéra, 75002 Paris, T1-47427267, F1-47425268, ontt@wanadoo.fr **Germany** Fremdenverkehrsamt Tunesien, Kurfuerstendamm 171, 10707 Berlin, T30-8850457, F30-8852198. **Greece** Tunisian National Tourism Office, Tunisian Embassy. Anthen 2, Palais Psychico 15452, Athens T1-6717590, F1-6713432. **Italy** Ente Nazionale Tunisino Per il Turismo, Via Calabria 25, 00187 Roma, T6-42010149, F6-42010151. **Japan** Embassy of Tunisia, Tourism Office, 29-2 Ichibancho 0 Chlyoda-Ku, Tokyo 102, T3-2627716. **Netherlands** Tunesisch National Verkeersbureau, Muntplein 2111, 1012 WR, Amsterdam, T20-622 4971, F2-638 3579, info@worldonline.nl **Russia** Embassy of Tunisia, 28/1, Katchalova, Moscow, T095-2029504, F095-7378815, tunisia@orc.ru **Spain** Oficina Nacional del Turismo Tunesino, Plaza de Espana 18, Torre de Madrid 28008, Planta 4 Oficina 1, Madrid, T1-5481435, F1-5483705, tunezturismo@mad.servicom.es **Sweden** Tunisiska Statens Turistbyra, Stureplan 15, 11145 Stockholm, T8-6780645, F8-6781905, tst@swipnet.se **Switzerland** Tunesisches Fremdenverkehrsburo, 69 Bahnhofstrasse, 8001 Zurich,T1-2114830, F1-2121353, fmami@tunisie.ch **UK** Tunisian National Tourist Office, 77-A Wigmore Street, London W1H 9LJ, T020-7224 5598/6201, F020-7224 4053, tntlondon@aol.com **USA** c/o Embassy of Tunisia, 1515 Massachussets, Avenue Washington DC 20005, T202-8621850, F202-8621858, ezzedine@ix.netcom.com

Tunisia on the web A few sites to give you some background on Tunisia. More can obviously be found by typing 'Tunisian tourism' or, for Francophones, 'Tunisie tourisme', in your favourite search engine. In Tunisia, a full list of the more official websites can be found on the information pages of *La Presse* newspaper.

www.tourismtunisia.com Official website of the **ONTT**, the Tunisian Tourist Board.
www.pagesjaunes.com.tn The Tunisian Yellow Pages.
www.tunisair.com The national airline's site. For ferries, type in *Compagnie tunisiene de navigation* or Tunisia ferries and something may pop up. At the time of going to press, neither the *SNCFT* (railways) nor the *SNTRI* (national bus company) had websites.
www.Tunisia.com General and historical information.
www.tunisiaonline.com More of the same.

www.ahlan.tourism.tn The country region by region, with hotel listings and some suggestions for tours.

www.abcsone.com/tunisie/asp Some useful information on tourist-oriented areas. Links to other sites of interest.

www.tunisie.online.fr For Francophones, has links to some useful sites.

www.ign.fr Website of the **Institut géographique français** which might be able to help you with the thorny question of obtaining decent maps of Tunisia.

www.menic.utexas.edu/menic/countries/tunisia Academic site with useful links.

www.touristic-guide.com Information on the regions most visited by tourists.

Tunisian news media www.tunisie.com/LaPresse Information from Tunisia's leading official French language newspaper.

www.tunisiatv.com and **www.radiotunis.com** Information from the *ERTT*, the country's national broadcasting organization.

Arab/North Africa-oriented sites www.arab.net

www.imarabe.org Site of the Paris-based Institut du monde arabe.

www.north-africa.com Weekly analysis on economics, politics and business. Subscriber service.

www.marweb.com/tunisie French-language search-engine focusing on the Maghreb (North Africa), with lots of links to other sites, many in English.

www.kubbar.com One of the best sources of Arabic music on the web.

Language

See Footnotes, page 485, for a list of useful Arabic and French words

Arabic is the official language in Tunisia. The language has a formal, written form derived from the Arabic of the religious texts, and a spoken form. The two differ almost as much as medieval English and modern English. French is widely spoken in Tunisia, especially in the north and the eastern coastal towns. The spread of education and in particular access to satellite television mean that the language is widely understood at a basic level, even if it is not spoken. Older people will know very little French. Many Tunisians understand some Italian, a legacy of the days when the only foreign TV channel available was RAI Uno, and English and German are widely understood as well, in particular in tourist areas. Germany generally provides Tunisia with the largest foreign visitor contingent. Hotel staff are generally proficient in English, French and German. Do not expect too much, however, and be prepared to communicate in a mixture of broken French and English. Tunisians have no problems with this – Franco-Arabe, a sort of mixed language where educated speakers happily switch back and forth between French and Arabic, is the local answer to language needs in many situations. Throwing in the odd word you've picked up in Tunisian can help communication along, too.

Disabled travellers

Tunisia cannot be said to be a very easy country to get around for those with disabilities. Nevertheless, there seems to be a growing awareness of disability issues, and the newer hotels have wheelchair ramps. Trains can be difficult to get onto – you have to climb up into the train. Tunis-Carthage airport now has satellite buildings, so you get off the plane directly into the airport and can go by wheelchair from plane to customs. (Not all planes use the satellites, however.) Other airports are more tricky, using buses to take passengers to and from the planes.

General holiday and travel information for disabled people in the UK is provided by the **Holiday Care Service**, T01293-774535, and **Tripscope**, T08457-585641. For those with access to the internet, a Global Access – Disabled Travel Network Site is www.geocities.com/Paris/1502/ It is dedicated to providing travel information for 'disabled adventurers' and includes a number of reviews and tips from members of the public. You might also want to read *Nothing Ventured*, edited by **Alison Walsh** (Harper Collins), which gives personal accounts of worldwide journeys by disabled travellers, plus advice and listings.

Gay and lesbian travellers

In Tunisia, men may wear jasmine bouquets lodged jauntily behind the ear, or walk hand in hand down the street. (Some of the women in country areas are tatooed and tough.) However, such signs must be seen in context.

Though there is no public perception of what a Tunisian lesbian might look like, gay visitors have long been a feature of the Tunisian tourist scene, although at a discrete level. (French and Italian A-gays have tasteful homes in Hammamet and Sidi Bou Saïd.) There are no gay areas or bars (although your average bloke-filled city bar might look like one) and no commercial 'scene' under the dictatorship of the rainbow flag. In city centres, Tunisians tend to stare a lot. This does not necessarily mean anything more than curiosity, and ready familiarity does not mean a gay interest.

Tunisia is not a homophobic place, provided a 'decent' façade is preserved. Single men may find themselves propositioned.

Regarding Aids (*le Sida*), Tunisia has very low incidence. People are on the whole well informed thanks to French television. The country also has several associations working to inform the public about Aids.

For more information on the gay community city of North African origin in France, contact **Kelma** (lit: 'word', as in 'word of honour') on their website at www.kelma.org

Student travellers

Prices in Tunisia are very reasonable when compared with Europe but there is no system of student discounts in operation.

Women travellers

Women travelling alone face greater difficulties than men or couples. Though young Tunisian women travel between towns for work or study without any problems, in more traditional country areas young Muslim women rarely travel without a male relative or older female. Thanks to satellite TV, Tunisians are more aware of Western mores than before, and the generation in its early 20s seems more emancipated.

Some women get pestered, others don't, and pestering seems to be more related to how you hold yourself, than your clothes. Main pestering areas will be souks and town centres. Dress modestly, the less bare flesh the better, although young Tunisian women can be seen wearing the latest tightest fashions in up-scale shopping areas. Certain nationalities seem to cope better with ridiculous macho egos – Italians, for example, perhaps because the hassle can be even worse in Italy. Basically, things tend to go better for people with confidence and a sense of humour. Some women operate best by ignoring rude and suggestive comments directed at them but aimed at boosting the caller's ego, avoiding anything which would aggravate the situation. Shout only *in extremis* (they can always shout louder).

One way of preventing hassle in towns is to dress smartly, look confident, busy, and as though you know where you are going. Depending on your age, this may make pesterers think twice – is this person with an official delegation, do they have a Tunisian husband? Observe what smart Tunisian women wear. Women from fairly traditional families may wear longish skirts, others opt for expensive sunglasses.

Another way to deal with the pestering male is to develop a schoolmarmish manner. Modestly dressed, you are interested in ancient ruins, architecture, birds, women's issues, economics, you are very serious person. This may put your pesterer off – or lead to some interesting conversation. Then you can lighten up if you get on with the person. And then they might show you areas of their town which you would otherwise miss.

Role playing can be tedious, however. In the final analysis, the twin concepts of *hishma* (shame) and *ihtiram* (respect) go a long way. You may get rid of a consistent pesterer by saying *haram alayk* ('shame on you') or *ma tehshemsh* ('have you no shame'). A Tunisian woman might have to give you lessons in saying these phrases with appropriate disdain. And finally, remember that you only have to deal with the hassle for part of your holiday. Some have to deal with macho attitudes all their lives.

Working in Tunisia

Working opportunities for foreigners are few and far between

Tunisia has a severe youth employment problem, with unemployment said to be running at around 15%. Hence numerous young Tunisians are tempted to take major risks and try to cross the Mediterranean by (almost) any means available for what they perceive to be a better life in Europe. All of which means no work opportunities for unskilled foreigners and few for those with skills. One possibility might be working as a holiday rep for a major company like **Panorama**. Contacts would have to be made via the UK, however, and the work is not well paid.

Another possible source of work is with the **British Council**, teaching English in one of their language teaching centres (downtown Tunis and La Marsa). Contact the main centre (second floor, above the *Banque de l'Habitat* on Avenue Habib Bourguiba, Tunis), on T71353568, F71353985, also see **www.britishcouncil.org.tn** The centre runs a one-month course for those wishing to learn to teach English (cost 1500 Dt), leading to the CELTA qualification.

If you have an MA degree in English, linguistics or foreign languages, it may be possible to get a post as an *assistant* (junior lecturer) in a university arts faculty. In practice, though initial contact with the university may be good, the paper work may take ages to process and you will not be paid until the academic year is nearly over. If you have some sort of special technical skill and wish to work in Tunisia, the best way is to get yourself recruited by a company from your country with business interests in North Africa.

Before you travel

Getting in

Visas
Have a photocopy of the key pages of your passport on you at all times when travelling outside Tunisia's main tourist areas

No visas are required for full passport holders of EU, USA, and Canada. Visitors from Australia and New Zealand/Aotearoa need visas which are best obtained in advance, but can, in principle, be given on arrival. On the aeroplane or boat, or at the border, travellers will be required to fill a form with standard personal and passport details, an exercise to be repeated in almost all hotels throughout the country. From the point of entry, EU travellers can stay in Tunisia for three months, while US visitors have four months.

Visa extensions are complicated to arrange and will require a visit to the local police station near your hotel in a larger town, as well as patience. An easier option is to leave Tunisia for a few days, either to Malta or Italy, both short flights away. Given the large number of foreigners resident in the upmarket Tunis suburbs of La Marsa and Carthage, it may be easiest to arrange visa extensions in these cities. The operation will probably entail a visit to the **Ministry of the Interior** on the Avenue Bourguiba in Tunis. It should be stressed, however, that the least time consuming procedure is to leave the country.

Tunisian embassies abroad

Australia See UK.

Algeria Rue Ammar Rahmani, El Biar, 16000 Algiers, T2-6920857

Austria 3-4 Ghaegastrasse, 1030 Vienna, T1-5815281/2

Belgium 278 Av de Tervueren, 1150 Brussels, T2-7717395

Canada 515 O'Connor St, Ottawa, Ontario, K1S 3P8, T613-2370330/2

Egypt 26 Rue el Jazirah, Zamalek, 11211 Cairo, T2-3404940

France 17-19 Rue de Lubeck, 75016 Paris, T1-45535094

Germany 110 Esplanade 12, 1100 Berlin, T30-4722064/7

Italy Via Asmara 5, 00199 Rome, T6-8604282

Libya Av Jehara, Sharia Bin Ashur, 3160 Tripoli, T21-607161

Morocco 6 Rue de Fès, Rabat, T7-730576

Netherlands Gentestraat 98, 2587 HX, The Hague, T70-3512251

Norway Haakon Vll'sgt 5B, 0161 Oslo, T22-831917

South Africa 850 Church St, Arcadia, 0007 Pretoria, T12-3426283

Sweden Drottningatan 73C, 11136 Stockholm, T8-6635370

Switzerland Kirchenfeldstrasse 63, 3005 Bern, T31-3528226

UK 29 Prince's Gate, London SW7 1QG, T020-7584 8117

USA 1515 Massachusetts Av NW, Washington DC 20005, T202-8621850

See the Tunis directory, page 117, for a list of foreign embassies and consulates in Tunis

Essentials

Residence permits

If you have come to Tunisia for work or to study Arabic, you will be able to obtain a residence permit (*carte de séjour*). You have to constitute a file (*dossier*) with all the necessary documents, photocopied and certified (*copie conforme*). Expect to waste much time going back and forth to your local police station because you have not been told the full list of documents necessary. The completed dossier goes to the Ministry of the Interior, and a *carte de séjour* may eventually be granted. Students of Arabic should note that there has been an unwillingness to grant residence permits in recent years.

Customs

Visitors may take in, free of duty, 400 g of tobacco, 200 cigarettes or 50 cigars and such personal items as a camera, binoculars, a portable radio receiver, computer or typewriter. You may also take your pet to Tunisia. It will need a health certificate and an anti-rabies certificate less than six months old.

Prohibited items

Narcotics Tunisia is not the Netherlands, and there are **extremely severe penalties** for possession of, or trade in, narcotic drugs: one to five years' imprisonment and/or fines. You do not want to be involved in a Tunisian remake of *Midnight Express*. Cannabis (*takrouri*) was part of everyday life in Tunisia until independence, after which it became illegal. The plant is still cultivated (in secret) in certain rural areas. If you want to have a quiet smoke, do not share with Tunisian friends, unless you know them really well. If caught, they will be in very serious trouble. Possession gives you a two year prison term. Be aware that wild **animal** skin and some other items openly on sale in Tunisia cannot be legally imported into the UK and EU. This includes products made from tortoise shell, snake skin, lizards and many fur products. It is too late to save these creatures but buying such products puts the death sentence on others. Visitors should certainly not purchase live animals for export from Tunisia and import into EU and USA as it is in most cases illegal and punishable by large fines and confiscation.

Travel insurance

Always take out travel insurance before you set off and read the small print carefully. Check that the policy covers the activities you intend or may end up doing. Also check exactly what your medical cover includes (for example, ambulance, helicopter rescue or emergency flights back home). Also check the payment protocol. You may have to cough up first (literally) before the insurance company reimburses you. It is always best to dig out all the receipts for expensive personal effects like jewellery or cameras. Take photos of these items and note down all serial numbers.. *STA Travel* and other reputable student travel organizations offer good value policies. Young travellers from North America can try the **International Student Insurance Service** (ISIS), which is available through *STA Travel*, T1-800-7770112, www.sta-travel.com The best policies for older travellers (UK) are offered by **Age Concern**, T01883-346964.

Vaccinations
See Health, page 59,
for further details

None required unless travelling from a country where yellow fever and/or cholera frequently occurs. You should be up to date with polio, tetanus, and typhoid protection. If you are going to be travelling in rural areas where hygiene is often a bit rough and ready, then having a hepatitis B shot is a good thing. You could also have a cholera shot, although there is no agreement among medics on how effective this is. There is no malaria in Tunisia.

What to take

Travellers tend to take too much. Most three-star Tunisian hotels, also some of the cheaper ones, will have a laundry service of some kind, and T-shirts and jeans are cheap anyway. A travel-pack will survive the holds of rural buses and sitting on the roof-rack of a louage. If you acquire a carpet, there is plenty of cheap luggage on sale – some Tunisians frequently travel down to Libya or the frontier at Ben Gardane to bring cheap merchandise back.

Regarding clothing, outside summer you will need woollens or a fleece for evenings. Longish cotton skirts are a good idea for women travelling in rural areas. Women visiting cities alone should have an item of smartish clothing. Tunisians like to dress well, and smartness is appreciated. (A generation ago, in many areas there was a lot of severe poverty.)

If you are hoping to travel out into the desert, you will need a warm sleeping bag. The penetrating cold of the desert at night is a well-known phenomenon, so bring your warm undergarments. The coastal towns can have a special damp cold in winter, so long johns are a good idea. Wear layers of clothing at these times. The following checklist might help you plan your packing:

Air-cushions for hard seating; cagoule (for wet Tunisian winter days); insect repellant/cream (essential); anti-mosquito plug-in device (very useful); neck pillow; driving licence; padlocks for luggage; photocopies of essential documents; plastic bags; short-wave radio; spare passport photographs, sun hat, sun protection cream, Swiss army knife; torch; umbrella; wet wipes; zip-lock bags. **Health kit** Anti-acid tablets; anti-diarrhoea tablets; anti-septic cream; condoms; contraceptive tablets; mini first-aid kit; sachets of rehydration salts; tampons; travel sickness pills; water sterilization tablets for desert travel.

Money

Currency
A list of banks can be
found in each town's
individual directory

The major unit of currency in Tunisia is the **dinar** (in this Handbook: Dt). 1 **dinar**=1,000 **millimes**. There are coins for 5 millimes (the aluminium *douro*), 50 and 100 millimes (yellow metal, confusingly similar), cupronickel 500 millimes, and the larger 1 dinar cupronickel coin. Early 2002 saw a new bi-metal 5 dinar coin come into circulation. There are notes for 5, 10, 20 and 30 **dinars**. Note that Tunisia uses international figures, not Arabic ones, so there is no confusion, although coins are labelled in Arabic only. Banknotes are labelled in Arabic and French. Most transactions are in cash.

The banknotes can be a little confusing, as there are two models in circulation for the lower denomination notes, as follows: for 5Dt, there is the old, now rare, reddish-pink note and the newer, smaller green Hannibal model, although even this is now being replaced by a coin; for 10Dt, there is the older brown and green note and the newer blue Ibn Khaldun. The 20Dt is pink and purple and shows 19th-century reformer Kheïreddine Pacha, while the 30Dt note showing national poet Abou Kacem Chabbi is green and yellow.

Note that Tunisians among themselves will count in older currency units. To the complete confusion of travellers, most Tunisians refer to **francs**, 1 franc being equal to 1 millime, although this is a unit existing only in speech. *Alf franc* (1,000 francs) is 1 dinar, *alfayn* is 2 dinars, *khams alaf* is 5 dinars, etc. Unless you are good at calculations, it's probably easiest to stick to dinars.

The rates of course fluctuate, and the dinar was held to be overvalued in some quarters in 2002. In August 2002, US $1 = 1.390Dt, UK £1 = 2.120DT and Euro 1 = 1.350DT. You can **on occasion** buy Tunisian dinars at bureaux de change at Gatwick and Heathrow airports. Dinars may not be taken out of Tunisia. If you have bought too many dinars, you can exchange them back into French francs at a bank on production of exchange receipts. However, as European cash and Visa cards function in Tunisian ATM/cashpoints (*guichets automatiques* or *DAB, distributeur automatique de billets*), in major towns it is possible to withdraw more or less exactly the amount one needs on a daily basis.

Arriving at Tunis-Carthage Airport, there are exchange facilities in the main concourse and several ATMs. There are also ATMs at Monastir and Djerba airports. Note, however, that at weekends the ATMs at the airports and in the cities can be temperamental, so have cash and travellers' cheques to exchange. The most reliable ATMs are those of the **BIAT** (*Banque internationale arabe de Tunisie*) identified by its Visa-like navy blue and orange colours. The Banque de l'Habitat ATMs are also generally reliable. Tunisia has a plethora of banks, and not all have kept up with ATM technology.

Cash on arrival

Banking hours are 0830-1130 and 1500-1630. In the summer and during the fasting month of Ramadan they are 0830-1400. The separate *bureaux de change* in the major cities – mainly *BIAT*, *STB* and *Banque de l'Habitat* – often open for longer hours (0800-1700), which in theory give the same rates of exchange but charge different amounts of commission. There are numerous banks in Tunisia, with *BIAT*, *Société tunisienne de banque* (STB – blue and white livery), *Banque de Tunisie* (blue and yellow) all widespread. In rural areas, the *Banque nationale agricole* (BNA) is the main bank. With several different desks for different purposes, banking in Tunisia can be a slow process. The easiest way to get hold of cash is to use your Visa or cash card at a cash dispenser – provided that this is in service. In smaller towns even quite close to Tunis or Sousse, the cashpoints can stay out of service for quite a while, so get your cash ready before you move out of the main centres.

Banking facilities

There is a fixed exchange rate for changing notes and no commission ought to be charged for this. A small commission will be charged for changing travellers' cheques.

Changing money

These are widely accepted at banks, top hotels, restaurants and shops, but it is wise to check first. *American Express* are represented by *Voyages Schwartz* in Tunisia, with limited services. Remember to keep all credit card receipts – and before you sign, check where the decimal marker (a comma in Tunisia, as in Europe, rather than a dot) has been placed and that there isn't a zero too many. You don't want to be paying thousands rather than tens of dinars.

Credit cards

Foreign currency may be imported freely. **Eurocheques** These are accepted in Tunisia, and can be a good way to make sure one will not run out of money. Try at banks

Currency regulations

with the *Eurocheque* sticker. **Travellers' cheques** These are usable in Tunisia, although the traveller may be sent from bank to bank before the appropriate one is found. Use travellers' cheques from a well known bank or company, and preferably with UK, US, or European currency, although this is not an absolute rule. Some hotels and shops will exchange travellers' cheques.

Cost of living As a **budget traveller**, it is possible to get by in Tunisia for US$25-30 a day. Accommodation, food and transport are all cheap, and there is a lot of atmosphere to take in for free. Cheap accommodation will cost around 8-12Dt a night. Anything less will be pretty rough, and probably unadvisable for women travelling alone. If your budget can stand it, then you can find nice rooms around the 20Dt price mark – although they may not necessarily be all that quiet.Out of season, there may be some latitude to negotiate in smaller hotels.

Prices for food and drink are non-negotiable, of course. In ordinary cafés, sample prices include: bottled water 700 mills, tea/coffee 300 to 500 mills, branded fizzy drink 400 mills. (A top tourist zone café will charge you considerably more.) You can have a very filling meal for 5Dt, a big, fat sandwich will cost you around 1.200Dt, seasonal fruit will be around 1Dt per kilo. Concerning transport, as a guideline, by shared taxi (*louage*), the nine hour trip from Tunis to Zarzis, in the far southeast of the country, costs 27Dt. Museum/site entrance tickets will be 2Dt (you have all the sites of Carthage for just 5.100Dt).

If you start buying imported goods, notably cosmetics, books and electrical goods, things can get expensive. The least central tourist areas (Djerba in particular, also Tabarka) are easily the most expensive places. If you are looking for small, kitsch presents, there are plenty of things to buy in Tunisia, and the prices, if you bargain, can be quite reasonable. Souk-sellers will often start with absurdly high prices for tourists, as the gullible (or those unfamiliar with the local currency) can be persuaded to part with large sums of money after much blarney. For 250Dt or more, you could go home with a nice bit of textile or carpet.

It you want to travel in a **moderate** degree of comfort, in summer you could expect to find a room for 40Dt in a simple resort hotel with a small pool. At this price, you would probably also have air-conditioning. Outside the high season (July and August), prices can be very reasonable indeed in some of the three-star hotels in Sousse and Hammamet. You could be eating out in the evening very well for 20Dt to 25Dt a head. Car hire might be your major expense, at around 200Dt a week for a small car, unlimited mileage.

The **upscale traveller** will find that in top quality hotels and nightclubs prices are similar to Europe. Hotel service may not always be what you are used to in this price bracket. Restaurants, however, are substantially cheaper than in Europe. A fine meal, without wine, can cost around 60Dt a head but upmarket restaurants bump their profits up by charging heavily for wine.

Getting there

Air

Most travellers fly to Tunisia, either from Europe, the Middle East or certain adjacent African countries. There are no direct flights from North America or Australasia. Sample flight times to Tunis: from Cairo is 4½ hours, from Paris 2 hours. *Tunisair* is the national flag carrier, and there are two main airports, Tunis-Carthage and Skanès-Monastir serving the Sahel region. Djerba is an important airport, and there are smaller airports at Sfax, Tozeur and Tabarka. There are regular internal flights to the first two, while

Tabarka handles only charter flights, there being insufficient internal demand. Handily, given the few flights into Tripoli, *Tunisair* operates a regular service from Tunis to the Libyan business capital.

While *Tunisair* has flights from most European capitals and numerous French and German cities, from the UK it only flies out of Heathrow (terminal 2), where *Air France* deals with check-in. Flight time from London to Tunis-Carthage is around 2½ hours. **British Airways/GB Airways** has at least four scheduled flights a week from London Gatwick to Tunis-Carthage, while regional UK airports have numerous charter flights to Tunis-Carthage, Skanès-Monastir and Djerba. Regarding flights from the UK, *Tunisair* seems unlikely to break the charter airlines hold on flights. A new Tunisian charter company, *Carthago Airlines*, was set up in 2002, however. NB *Tunisair* flights to and from London are often late.

From UK, Ireland & Europe
Tunisair reservations London, T020-7734 7644, F020-7734 6773

   Tunisair operates scheduled services from the French provinces to Tunisian regional airports, depending on the time of year. Demand is much greater in the summer, when French Tunisians return for the holidays. If leaving from Paris, note that *Tunisair* flights operate out of Orly-Sud, *Air France* flies from Roissy, terminal B.

Tunisair has numerous offices abroad including: **Egypt** 14 Talaat Harb, Cairo, T(202) 5753971, F5740677; **France** 17 Rue Daunou, 75002, Paris, T(33) 142961045, F140150115; **Germany** Kufurstendamm 171, 10707 Berlin, T(49) 30 8822047/48, F30 8816463; **Netherlands**, WTC Schipol, Tower D, 4th floor, Schipol Blvd 219, Amsterdam, T(31) 20 4057100, F20 405 7099; **Spain** Plaza de los Mostenses, 28015 Madrid, T(34) 915419490, F915423036, also Aeropuerto de Barajas, T913056358, F915874747.

See also www.tunisair.com

   If you buy your flight in Tunisia, note that most travel agents and airline offices apply two rates, *tarif résident* and *tarif non-résident*. If you are not resident in Tunisia, you will find yourself paying the latter rate, generally anything up to 50% more. Not all travel agents ask or apply this rate, however, and you should shop around. The same rules apply for ferry tickets bought by non-resident foreigners in Tunisia.

   On flights to Tunisia, the usual general airline restrictions apply with regard to luggage weight allowances before surcharge (*excédent de bagage*), normally 30 kg for first class and 20 kg for business and economy class. In principle, only one item of hand luggage is allowed, although given Tunisians' tendency to return from Europe with presents for all the family, the term 'one item' is subject to wide interpretation. If you have a small amount of luggage and are taking a regular *Tunisair* flight, other passengers in the check-in queue will no doubt ask you to check in something for them.

It is possible to obtain significantly cheaper tickets by avoiding school holiday times, by flying at night, by shopping around and by booking early to obtain one of the quota of discounted fares. **STA Travel**, 86 Old Brompton Rd, London, SW7 3LH, T020-7361 6100, www.statravel.co.uk   They have other branches in London, as well as in Brighton, Bristol, Cambridge, Leeds, Manchester, Newcastle-Upon-Tyne and Oxford and on many University campuses. Specialists in low-cost student/youth flights and tours, also good for student IDs and insurance. **Trailfinders**, 194 Kensington High St, London, W8 7RG, T020-7938 3939, www.trailfinders.com Useful websites include **www.cheap-flights.co.uk** and **www.dialaflight.com**

Discounts

Sea

Numerous ferries operate across the Mediterranean carrying both vehicles and foot passengers. Prices vary according to the season. Main points of departure are Marseille, Genoa, and Palermo, arrival is at Tunis port, La Goulette. In summer, certain ferries run from Toulon (occasionally) and Naples. Ferry is a far less convenient way to travel than

Ferries

aeroplane. Prices are not cheaper and even as a foot passenger you will have long waits at passport control and customs in the port at La Goulette. Expect to have considerable difficulty buying a ferry ticket at short notice in Tunis in the summer. The *CTN* has an office for this purpose on the Rue de Yougoslavie, behind the French Embassy.

The following companies do the Marseille/Genoa to La Goulette run: *CTN (Compagnie tunisienne de navigation)* and **SNCM** *(Société nationale maritime Corse-Méditerranée)* (61 Blvd des Dames, 13002 Marseille, T04-91563030). The *CTN* also has the following offices: in Paris, 12 Rue Godot-de-Mauroy, T(33) 0147421755, F0149242477, in Marseille 21 Rue Mazenod, (33) 0491915571, F0491914543; in Italy, Genoa, Nuovo Terminal Traghetti, Via Milano 51, 16126 Genoa T(010) 258041, F(010) 2698255; in the UK contact *Southern Ferries*, 179 Piccadilly, London, W1V 9DB, T020-7491 4968).

For completeness sake, **CTN offices in Tunisia** are as follows: Tunis, 122 Rue de Yougoslavie, T71322802, 71322775, 71335714, F71324855; La Goulette, Avenue Habib Bougatfa, T71735111; Sousse, Rue Abdallah Ibn Zoubeïr, T73229436, 73224861, F73224844; Sfax, 75 Rue Habib Maazoun, T74228022, F74298320. In spring 2002, there was no information whether a website would soon be created.

Road and rail

It is not possible to travel to Tunisia from Algeria at the present time, although on the election of President Bouteflika in 1999 there seemed to be a real chance of the situation improving. Access from Libya by land is by shared service taxi, although there are some buses which run from Tripoli into the Bab Alioua station in Tunis. Service taxis, mainly large Peugeot estate cars, leave from near the Bourguiba Mosque, close to the Dhat al Imad towers in downtown Tripoli. From here it is also possible to travel onward by bus to Egypt via Benghazi, Al Baydha and Tobrouk.

Touching down

Airport and port information

As mentioned above, the vast majority of tourists arrive by air in Tunisia at either Tunis, Monastir, or Djerba. Information on onward travel from point of arrival is given here by airport and, for La Goulette, by port. Note that yellow town taxis in Tunisia use meters – prices are 50% higher at night.

Tunis-Carthge Airport information, T71754000 or T71755000 **Aéroport international de Tunis-Carthage** Tunis' main airport is handily located midway between downtown Tunis and the upmarket coastal suburbs of La Marsa and Carthage. If you are staying in Tunis, taxi is the easiest way into town, under 10 minutes' ride away if the traffic is light, more during the day (cost around 4Dt). The coastal hotel strip at Raoued/Gammarth is slightly further, say 5Dt in a taxi. There is a taxi rank outside the airport terminal, and there is a bus for downtown as well. Car rental agencies are found on the ground floor of the terminus, along with bureaux de change.

If you are on a package to Hammamet, you will be met by a travel company representative, and will have a 50-minute bus ride down to your hotel. If you are travelling independently and arrive early enough in the day, you may want to move on from Tunis immediately. If you want to get the train, ask the taxi driver for *la gare, Barshelona*. If you want a louage for a southern destination, ask for *la station de louage, Moncef Bey*. Buses for the south go from the *gare routière*, Bab 'Alioua, buses and louages for the northwest, from the *gare routière*, Bab Saâdoun. Note that there is a second louage station at Bab 'Alioua, with cars for the Cap Bon and Hammamet.

Touching down

Business hours *Banks: 0830-1130 and 1500-1630. In the summer and during the fasting month of Ramadan they are 0830-1400. The separate bureaux de change in the major cities, mainly BIAT, STB and Banque de l'Habitat, often open for longer hours (0800-1700).* **Post office:** *0800-1230 and 1500-1800 and* **shops** *generally: 0800-1300 and 1500 to 1745, Monday-Thursday, with Friday-Saturday*

0800-1300, except in summer, when hours are 0730-1300. Hours during Ramadan are 0800-1400.
Emergency services *Police: 197, Fire: 198 (Protection civile), Ambulance: (SAMU): 190*
Directory enquiries: *(les renseignements), 120 for business, 121 for personal calls.*
Official time: *GMT +1 all year round.*
Weights and measures: *metric.*

Aéroport international de Skanès-Monastir This is the main airport for the Sahel region, ie Sousse, Monastir and Mahdia. Just outside the terminus building, you have a stop on the Sahel metro line, a train service which runs from Sousse to Mahdia. Buses for Sousse and Monastir are also available. Taxi drivers are well aware that tourists arriving are unfamiliar with the currency. A taxi into Monastir will be around 4Dt, into Sousse 7Dt 500. Shared taxis for Sousse and Monastir will stop on the main road beyond the railway line. There are car rental agencies on the main concourse.

Aéroport international de Djerba The airport on Djerba is near Mellita, in the northwest of the island, a short taxi ride (say 3Dt) from Houmt Souk, where most independent travellers stay. The main hotel strip (Sidi Mahares) starts some 12 km from the airport, and your taxi fare to your hotel will start at around 6Dt, depending on the distance. There are yellow and white service taxis for Libya outside the terminal building.

Port de La Goulette (Tunis) The boats from France and Italy and cruise ships come in to La Goulette. Formalities are often slow, especially in summer, when Tunisians resident abroad are returning with cars loaded to the gunnels with household items. There will be taxis waiting to do the 15-minute run from port to town centre (say 3Dt), across the causeway which crosses the Lac de Tunis. Otherwise, take the TGM (Tunis-Goulette-Marsa) light railway. Outside the port, you will see a big stone citadel. Leaving the fort on your left, go straight ahead, towards the petrol station (to the right of the road). Turn right after the petrol station and you will come to a TGM stop. Going into Tunis, you need to be on the far side of the line from the port.

Tourist information

In Tunisia, many of the main towns have **syndicats d'initiative** (town information offices) and branches of the national tourist office, the **ONTT**. On the whole, they are not much help, restricting their activities to giving out brochures about the different regions of the country. Hours are generally Monday-Thursday 0830-1300 and 1500-1745, Friday-Saturday 0830-1330.

For local tourist offices, see under Ins & outs for individual towns

Local customs and laws

Tunisians pay great attention to cleanliness and neatness. People are as smart as they can afford to be, and if you have to go to the police station or some other official building, shorts are not acceptable. Do not wander round towns and the souks in your skimpy top and brief shorts, unless you want to attract the full-on comments and the attention of the lads who work there. In a hot climate, it is probably better to cover up

Appearance

when away from the beach, anyway. Having said that, in the hottest weather, at home in their neighbourhood, Tunisian men will sit around in cafés playing cards with their shirts off. And many young Tunisian women keep up with the latest fashions – little linen numbers, *pantacourts* and navel-revealing tops were *de rigueur* in many quarters in summer 2001.

Bargaining Bargaining is expected in the tourist bazaars. Start lower than you would expect to pay, be polite and good humoured, enjoy the experience and if the final price doesn't suit walk away. The experience can be highly entertaining, and sometimes a little traumatic for the seller, who in extreme cases may resort to comments like 'you don't want to buy from me because you're a racist' (sic). In the end, the price you pay must be the price the item is worth to you. (How much would the same thing cost at home?) And then, think, 'do I really need this terracotta bowl/glittery scarf/furry camel?'. The answer to the question is generally NO. If you're a shopaholic, treat it all as a form of therapy: in Tunisia, shopping for inessentials is difficult because you have to bargain. As few shops take credit cards, you can give your plastic money a rest.

If you are really going to go in for tourist-style shopping with a vengeance, then the following tips might prove handy. Avoid actually buying trinkets in the first few days in Tunisia.Your pale (or red sunburnt) skin will say 'new arrival' to the salesmen in the souks. Salesmen (and you will generally be dealing with men) will want to find out your country of origin and your job, to get an idea of your purchasing power. Be inventive. Also they will enquire as to which hotel you're in. The counter tactic could be to pretend to be a student back-packer. In a tourist shop, get the salesman to give you the price he thinks the article is worth. Try to avoid giving a price yourself. Then think what the item costs at home. (Did you see a similar object at the back of the charity shop?). All in all, the souk experience requires you to be assertive without being rude. In the end, it's all a matter of tactics and wills.

Beggars Tunisia does not have the intense poverty of, say, Egypt and Morocco, and there are few beggars. It is unlikely that they will be too persistent. Have a few small coins ready. Arabic has polite phrases to refuse making a donation, namely *rebbi yenoub*, 'may God act for you', or *rebbi/Allah yusahel*, 'may God make things easier'.

Confidence The most common 'threat' to tourists is found where people are on the move, at ports and **tricksters** railway and bus stations. Strangers may offer extremely favourable currency exchange rates or spin 'hard luck' stories. Confidence tricksters are, by definition, extremely convincing and persuasive. Be warned if the offer seems too good to be true – that is probably what it is. Be distant, even a little bored by the whole thing. (Some of the methods are quite inventive: a few years ago, there was a young guy who would befriend attractive Nordic tourists in Houmt Souk, reading their palms with amazing accuracy – thanks to a briefing from his friend who worked at the frontier police post at the airport.)

Courtesy A certain amount of formality makes life run smoothly in Tunisia. You will see that there is much handshaking and kissing on the cheek. Entering an office or a meeting, or joining a group of friends, you should be sure to shake everyone's hand. With people you have come to know well, you kiss once on each cheek on meeting them, and probably on leaving them too. Even if there are 10 people or more in a room, greet everyone with a handshake.

Going into a shop or at a bank or PTT counter, say *bonjour* or *sabah el khir*. When leaving someone who is at work, say *Allah 'ayanek*, 'may God help you'. It may not be appropriate for men to shake hands with older headscarf-wearing 'religious' women. Use your common sense.

Saying thankyou, you have a barrage of terms at your disposal in Tunisian, including *merci alayk*, *inshallah merci*, *barakallaw fik*, and the more formal *shokran*. To a young

Bamboozling the visitor: whys and wherefores

At the weekly traditional market in Sousse, a man waves a crudely carved wooden camel under your nose: ' Only sixty dinars', but you move on, pressed forward by the crowd. There are at least another thousand people coming through, one of whom might be convinced into paying $60 (£30) for the small wooden dromedary in question. Getting off the tour bus at Nabeul, a man thrusts a reed pipe into your hand. 'C'est un cadeau', he declares warmly. Seconds later, this is followed by 'Give me dinars'. The tourist bubble has been pierced, we have malfunction in the brochure world of sky-blue swimming pools, palm trees and colourful bazaars.

As in any tourist destination, Tunisia's resorts have salesmen ready to benefit from visitors' unfamiliarity with local prices. The myth that bargaining is the basis for transactions in Tunisia, carefully maintained in the holiday literature, keeps the tourist souks going. Thus a pair of silverish metal bracelets can start out at 35Dt , only to descend, after 15 minutes' discussion, to 8Dt. (The profit margin will still be at least 50%.)

The truth of the matter is that for the character selling the souvenir beast, 60Dt is a real killing. Compare with this sum local salaries. A factory worker on a short term contract will be getting around 180Dt a month; someone more skilled, say in garment manufacture, will be on 250Dt. Neither have any job security. A tour rep will earn 450Dt, plus lots of good commissions for tours sold – though this is seasonal work. An experienced university lecturer might earn 800Dt. Tunisia's new rich BMW-wielding classes, in managerial positions in the private sector or banking, could be on 1500Dt or more a month, with an extra month's pay and access to various loans at preferential rates. Although many basic food products are subsidized, life for those at the bottom of the salary scale has got more difficult over the last five years. A visit to the doctor costs 12Dt and medicines have become expensive. Rents in the capital start at around 120Dt. A single minimum salary is clearly inadequate for even a small family. Thus those with the gift of the gab are tempted to make a fast buck in the tourist resorts. They are few in number – but can create a very unfavourable impression. Beware the bearers of free wooden flutes and other trinkets. Smile blandly and ignore – easier said than done.

person serving in a shop or restaurant, you might say *inshallah farhatik*, 'may you have a joyful wedding'.

Two final points: first, when it comes to getting onto public transport, politeness tends to go out of the window, and you have to be ready to push; second, be very careful never to criticize the régime because officials, waiters and taxi drivers may understand more English than you think.

Mosques

Visitors to mosques (where permitted) and other religious buildings will normally be expected to remove their shoes and cover-all garments will be available for hire to enable the required standard of dress to be met. Only a few mosques are visitable in Tunisia, including the Great Mosque and the Barber's Mosque in Kairouan, and the colonnade of the Zitouna Mosque in Tunis. On no account go into a mosque uninvited. You will be ejected unceremoniously.

Prohibitions

Ignore all offers of drugs. Narcotics traffic is a very serious offence in Tunisia, and you will be in real trouble if caught. Leave your desire for a quiet joint behind or go to Morocco. Penalties basically amount to a year's lock-up for every gram of dope found on you. Don't even think of providing hash to Tunisian friends, the sentences are too severe to make it worthwhile.

Essentials

Essentials

How big is your footprint?

The point of a holiday is, of course, to have a good time, but if it's relatively guilt-free as well, that's even better. Perfect ecotourism would ensure a good living for local inhabitants while not detracting from their traditional lifestyles, encroaching on their customs or spoiling their environment. Perfect ecotourism probably doesn't exist, but everyone can play their part. Here are a few points worth bearing in mind:

• *Think about where your money goes, and be fair and realistic about how cheaply you travel. Try and put money into local people's hands; drink local beer or fruit juice rather than imported brands and stay in locally-owned accommodation wherever possible*

• *Haggle with humour and not aggressively. Remember that you are likely to be much wealthier than the person you're buying from*

• *Think about what happens to your rubbish. Take biodegradable products and a water bottle filter. Be sensitive to limited resources like water, fuel and electricity*

• *Help preserve local wildlife and habitats by respecting rules and regulations, such as sticking to footpaths, not standing on coral and not buying products made from endangered plants or animals*

• *Don't treat people as part of the landscape, they may not want their picture taken. Ask first and respect their wishes*

• *Learn the local language and be mindful of local customs and norms. It can enhance your travel experience and you'll earn respect and be more readily welcomed by local people*

• *And finally, use your guidebook as a starting point, not the only source of information. Talk to local people, then discover your own adventure*

Timekeeping Tunisians in both private and public sectors are generally punctual, give or take 5 or 10 minutes. Meetings are best held Monday to Thursday. During Ramadan, especially the last two weeks, timekeeping tends to fall apart as Tunisians strive to combine work, fasting, big family meals and late night socializing. The latter two categories tend to win.

Tipping Tipping in Tunisia is important for waiters and others on low service sector wages. (A waiter might expect to take home 250Dt a month, and will be working extremely long hours.) Tips are thus very important. In hotels and restaurants the service has probably been included so a tip to the waiter is an optional extra. It does no harm to round up the taxi fare or the café bill. 500 mills is a generous tip in a café. If this is a café you go to frequently, being 'a tipper' definitely improves the service.

Safety

Personal security Travellers in Tunisia are unlikely to experience threats to personal security. Muslims are expected to honour the stranger in their midst. However basic common sense is needed for the protection of personal property, money and papers. Use hotel safes for valuable items as hotel rooms cannot be regarded as secure. When travelling, carry valuables as close to the body as possible, and where convenient, in more than one place. External pockets on bags and clothing should never be used for carrying valuables. Bag snatching and pick pocketing is more common in crowded tourist areas. It is obviously unwise to lay temptation in the way of a man whose annual income is less than the cost of your return airfare. It is wise to keep photocopies of important documents, a record of your passport number, travellers' cheque numbers and air ticket number somewhere separate from the actual items.

Police Report any incident which involves you or your possessions. An insurance claim for theft of any size will require the backing of a police report – which will be laboriously typed out for you (in Arabic) at the police station in whose area the incident took place. If involvement with the police is more serious, for instance a driving accident, remain calm, and contact the nearest consular office without delay.

The Tunisian police come in four types: the city police (grey blue uniforms), who do traffic duty and urban checkpoints; the Garde Nationale (Arabic: *el haras*), green and khaki uniforms, for rural areas; the *unités d'intervention*, black 'ninja' uniforms, help in crowd control at sporting events, and, of course, plain clothes police. As hire cars are easily identifiable by their blue licence plates, police will often flag them down for spot checks, as they do for cars with foreign licence plates. Show your papers and smile.

In the rural areas, the Garde Nationale has checkpoints on main routes and as you arrive in certain small towns. Drivers travelling frequently in these areas know when to slow down for these checkpoints. The Garde Nationale are polite and professional, and can be helpful on the state of roads, particularly after heavy rain. In remote country areas, they seem to get bored manning their checkpoints, and like to have a chat. They are especially hot on speeding offences: drive at 50 kph or less through small settlements.

Essentials

Where to stay

There is a very wide range of accommodation in Tunisia. In the major cities and the popular tourist resorts, the top quality hotel chains are represented. The best offer top class accommodation with the full range of personal and business facilities while the cheapest are spartan and on rare occasions, somewhat sordid. But even the cheapest hotels now seem to have proper mattresses instead of the foam ones, so hot and sweaty in summer.

Places to sleep are marked with a ■ *on maps*

Tunisia has a good spread of hotels. At the top end of the range, prices are on a par with Europe, though the service is often poor. There are no really classy hotels, though many of the new hotels in the 5-star category are truly glitzy. There are a lot of standard 3-star and 4-star beachside hotels, all offering more or less the same facilities. In comparison with Europe, prices for these medium range hotels are very reasonable if bought as part of a package. In almost every case, the advertised room price, that charged to the individual traveller, is higher than that paid by the package tourist and it may be worth bargaining. Out of season, prices in this category are very reasonable indeed. The disadvantage for the budget traveller is that they are often in *zones touristiques*, a long way from bus and louage stations.

Hotels
Credit cards are not in widespread use and may be used to pay bills ONLY in expensive hotels

At the cheaper end of the scale, standards are variable. For around 30Dt a night, you can find a very reasonable room indeed, with en suite bath in a city centre. At the 20Dt a night mark, accommodation will be of a perfectly reasonable standard too. Around 10Dt a night, there will be variations in standards. The problem for budget travellers visiting the cities is finding a room at the right place which is quiet and cool in summer.

The Tunisian hotel industry is undergoing some major changes. The big German tour operators are now building and running hotels whereas before they would just buy a certain percentage of beds for a season. A disagreeable side in these newer beach hotels under direct foreign rule is that you will have to wear a plastic bracelet – and pay a 5Dt fine if you take it off!

But basically, the vast majority of beach hotels, though efficient, are large and impersonal, and facilities (gym, pool, etc) are often on the small side. Service is not very accommodating, on the whole, although there are exceptions. Changes in legislation will allow small upmarket hotels and family-run guest houses to open, satisfying a definite demand in the market. In places like Mahdia and Tozeur, this is now beginning to happen.

Hotel categories

The present handbook uses seven categories of hotel based on prices in Tunisian dinars. In early 2002 a dinar was roughly equivalent to 1 euro or 1US$. Prices vary widely in some areas according to season. The classification here is for a double room, generally with breakfast.
AL 100Dt + An international class luxury hotel as found in the capital, large cities and major tourist centres. Good management ensures that all facilities for business and leisure travellers are of the highest international standard. In Tunis, hotels in this category include the Abou Nawas.
A 80Dt to 100Dt. A hotel with choice of restaurants, coffee shop, shops, bank, travel agent, swimming pool, some business facilities, some sports facilities, air-conditioned rooms with WC, bath/shower, TV, phone, mini-bar, daily clean linen.
B 40Dt to 80Dt. Offers most of the facilities

in **A** but without the luxury, reduced number of restaurants, smaller rooms, limited range of shops and sport. Offers pool and air-conditioned rooms with WC, shower/bath.
C 20Dt to 40Dt. Best medium range hotels found in the smaller towns and older central areas of larger towns. Usually comfortable, bank, shop, pool. Best rooms have air-conditioning, own bath/shower and WC.
D 10Dt to 20DT. Might be the best you can find in a small town. Best rooms should have own WC and bath/shower. Depending on management, will have room service and small restaurant.
E 5Dt to 10Dt. Simple provision. Perhaps fan cooler. May not have restaurant. Shared WC and showers with hot water (when available).
F under 5Dt. Very basic, shared toilet facilities, just about clean, insalubrious locations. Used by poorer locals.

The Ministry of Tourism makes great efforts to ensure that all hotels provide the facilities and services they are charging for. Nevertheless, there are some regional variations to note. In the **Aïn Draham**, (northwestern Tunisia), the winters are cold and the smaller hotels may not have any heating. **Djerba** and **Tabarka** have some very smart new beach hotels. **Hammamet-Sud**, aka **Hammamet Yasmine**, has some new hotels of truly megalomaniac proportions on the new beach front road. Prefer the older hotels nearer the town. All in all, unless you want nightlife, **Mahdia** is preferable to **Sousse** for a Mediterranean beach holiday with young kids. In the new Raoued/Gammarth area, **Tunis** now has some large, international standard beach hotels, perfect for a spring or autumn city break. **Sidi Bou Saïd** now has a Marrakech-style upmarket address in a converted palace (see box, Five stylish small hotels, page 39). An *hotel de charme* will be opening in the **Médina of Tunis** in 2003.

Many resort tourists spend very little time outside the hotel. To compensate selling off vast numbers of bed nights at cheap rates, hotels tend to charge heavily for drinks and extras. So don't forget your bottle of duty-free gin.

Camping Campsites are not widespread in Tunisia. At the remoter beaches, poorer Tunisians from inland areas will set up small tents to camp for a few days in summer. Hygiene in such places is rudimentary, however. On main beaches, there will be a Garde Nationale or police post who will move campers on. Camping is only really an option in remote locations – and you will have to watch your documents, which may be stolen from under your sleeping head. Basically, you are better to go for the security of staying in a cheap hotel. If you do opt to camp, assess the security of any site you choose and where possible ask permission from the local farm to avoid any unpleasantness.

Out of summer, it may be possible to set up a camping trip with a nomad and a couple of camels into the desert from Douz or Zaâfrane. Ask around at travel agents in Douz or at the all-purpose grocers in Zaâfrane. Bring a good warm sleeping bag, if possible, although trip organizers will probably have plenty of blankets.

Five stylish small hotels

Following the huge amount of coverage of Marrakech on European television, the Tunisian authorities are just beginning to wake up to the fact that there might be something more to tourism than vast, seaside developments. There is now a small number of small, stylish hotels, and more are planned for the future. All the following have strong chic factors and prices to match. Investigate.

- *Dar Saïd*, Rue Toumi, 2026 Sidi Bou Saïd, T71729666, F71729599, darsaid@gnet.tn, www.darsaid.com.tn   Pricey but worth it.
- *Dar Hayet*, Hammamet. T72260824, F72283399. A much expanded beachside villa. Though it has 52 rooms, retains much class and character. Reserve sea-facing rooms well in advance.
- *Dar Sidi*, Route de la Corniche, Rejich, Mahdia. T73687001, F73687003. Ten well decorated bungalows, small pool, restaurant.
- *Dar Dhiafa*, Er Riadh, Djerba, T75671166, F75670793, dar.dhiafa@gnet.tn   14 rooms and two small pools. Basic double starts at 170Dt.
- *Tamerza Palace*, Tamerza, nr Tozeur and Metlaoui, T76485322, tamerza.palace@planet.tn   Views of arid valley and ruined village from room terraces. A big but attractive hotel which merges into the landscape.

These are found in Tunisia as part of the International Youth Hostel Federation. They differ according to location and size, provide a common room, sleeping provision in dormitories, a self-catering kitchen and often budget meals. There is no maximum age limit, persons under 15 should be accompanied by an adult and in some hostels only male guests are accepted. Permission is necessary to stay more than three days in one hostel. Most hostels are open 1000-1200 and 1700-2200. Note that only a handful of hostels are actually run by the Tunisian Youth Hostels Association (médina of Tunis hostel on Rue Saïda Ajoula, Houmt Souk, Rmel south of Bizerte). The catch is of course that the hostels are closed during the day, and in summer you may very well want to siesta in the afternoon. Thus a cheap hotel may be a better option for part of your trip. Many of the hostels are no cheaper than hotels.

Youth hostels (Auberges de Jeunesse)

Getting around

Tunisia is a small country, well served by public transport. Links between all major towns are good, and the longest distance, Tunis to Djerba, can be done by air as well as by road. The amount of road improvement works in recent years has been impressive, and continues apace. For those without a hire car, visiting the archaeological sites can be time consuming, as they are not generally located close to major towns. Much time can be wasted in waiting for appropriate connecting transport.

Archaeology buffs should try to hire a car to reach remote sites

Air

Tunisair flights link Tunis with Djerba, Sfax, and Tozeur, and run to published but infinitely variable schedules. Early 2002 sample flight prices: Tunis to Djerba 60Dt one way, 95Dt return.

Road

Conditions vary from excellent dual carriageways to rural roads (unnervingly one-vehicle wide) and far-flung rough, unsurfaced *piste*. Problems can include very occasional blockage by snow in winter in the northwest, flash floods in spring, especially in the central regions, and sand at any time in the far south.

Bus Buses, the main and cheapest means of transport, link nearly all the towns. Air-conditioned coaches connect the biggest cities and keep more strictly to the timetable. The main operating company is the **SNTRI** (*Société nationale de transport inter-urbain*). Vehicles run by smaller, regional companies require greater patience and often work on the 'leave when fairly full' principle. Book as early as possible. Orderly queues become a jostling mass when the bus arrives. Town buses are usually crowded and getting off can be more difficult than getting on. Sorting out the routes and the fares makes taking a louage taxi a better option between towns. Tunis is the only town of any real size where you will need transport to get between sightseeing areas – use line 4 of the metro or a taxi for getting out to the Bardo Museum rather than the bus.

There are overnight buses from Tunis–Bab Alioua station for distant southern destinations, information on T71399391 or T71247368. Sample long-distance prices in early 2002, single tickets, were Tunis to Djerba 22Dt, Tunis to Tozeur 18Dt 500. (**NB** Bab Alioua is also referred to as Bab El Fella.) The schedule can also be found on the general information page at the back of *La Presse* newspaper. Look for the box marked **SNTRI** – *lignes nocturnes*.

Louage The larger, long distance taxis are good value, sometimes following routes not covered
(inter-city by service buses and almost always more frequent. They run on the 'leave when full'
taxis) principle and for more space or a quicker departure the unoccupied seats can be purchased. In general, these taxis are 25% more expensive than the bus.

Louages leave from special stations, often near the main bus stations. These range from the organized (the big Moncef Bey converted warehouse station in Tunis) to just a stretch of open ground near a village centre. Inter-city louages are white with a red stripe, while local louages are white with blue stripe. The range of vehicles is wide, including Renault and Peugeot estate cars and various forms of mini-van. In the country areas, the louage vans are referred to as *el nakl el rifi*, 'rural transport'. The trend at the moment is for the older, seven-seater 504 Peugeots to be replaced with Renault Espace type vehicles.

The disadvantage of louages is their suicidal speed. Drivers obviously try to fit in as many runs a day as possible, and drive like the clappers to do this. You may prefer to travel more sedately by train or bus. The best seat in a 504 is obviously up front, where you can wear a safety belt. The worst options, unless you are short, are the places in the third row, right at the back, and in the middle of the second row.

City taxis City taxis are bilious yellow in colour and always have a working meter. If the driver 'forgets' to put the meter on, seeing that you are unfamiliar with the country, insist politely that they do. Note that yellow taxis cannot be shared and that seat belts are compulsory for front-seat passengers. Certain taxi drivers in resorts like Hammamet and Nabeul do a roaring trade in taking tourists up to Tunis and Carthage for the day. They wait while you visit and pick you up at an agreed place. Make sure you agree the price beforehand, and only pay when you have been returned safely to your starting point. This is far from being the cheapest way to travel – rail and louage are safe and just as efficient.

Car hire A number of car hire companies have offices at the main airports, and cars can gener-
Car hire in Tunisia is ally be picked up on arrival. They are not cheap and the condition of the vehicles often
expensive. Better deals leaves much to be desired. Cheapest vehicles are Fiat Uno, Opel Corsa or Peugeot 205.
may be obtained by With a reliable company, cheapest quoted prices for a week in 2002 were between
booking from abroad 560Dt and 680Dt, the daily rate varying between 90Dt and 115Dt. A small company might quote as little as 280Dt a week for a week, unlimited kilometrage, insurance included. When you take a car, make sure that you check the tyres – the front tyres

must not be too worn. Check also that there is a spare tyre. This should be kept preferably in the boot, or padlocked under the car, as it may well be stolen if left unpadlocked. Seat belts are compulsory in the front.

The following car hire companies all have reasonable reputations. Budget, Central Office T71708000, F71707420, kaffel.brac@planet.tn plus offices at Tunis-Carthage Airport, T71842670; Hammamet, T72280670, F72280789; Sousse, T73227614, F73222377; Monastir Airport, T7352000, ext 7237; Houmt Souk, Djerba, T75653444, F75653438. *Hertz*, Rue des Entrepreneurs, Charguia II, T71702099, plus offices at Tunis-Carthage Airport, T71231822; Av Bourguiba, Tunis, T71256451; Av des Hotels, Hammamet, T72280187; Av H Bourguiba, Sousse, T73225428, F73226827; Mahdia, T73695255; Djerba, T75650196, F75650039; and Tozeur, T76460214, F76454468.

Drivers from northern Europe generally take a while to get used to the driving style and road conditions in Tunisia. Bearing the following points in mind will help avoid potential accidents. UK drivers should note that driving is on the right.

Driving conditions

Autoroute The oldest stretch of motorway (tolls payable) runs from Tunis to M'saken, just south of Sousse. The northern section is dual carriageway, the southern section three lane. (The Tunis to Bizerte autoroute was scheduled to open on 1 July 2002, charges were to be introduced after the initial summer period). Driving on the autoroute is often dangerous due to the mix of vehicles. Problems arise when overpowered saloon car driven fast by some wide boy meets slow moving pick-up truck. Look out also for louage taxis coming up behind you at high speed, flashing their headlights. Particularly dangerous times are Sunday evening when Tunis residents head back northwards after their weekend in Sousse or elsewhere. The Hammamet to Tunis stretch gets very crowded at the start of the weekend as well. Keep your temper at all costs.

Country roads Across Tunisia, country roads have been improved enormously since the early 1990s. Nevertheless, many roads are narrow and in places you may be forced onto the hard shoulder (such as it is) by a speeding oncoming lorry. There may well be a tyre-splitting drop from tarmac to hard shoulder. Moped riders are also dangerous in country areas and may swerve, brake or take unexpected turns without warning. Overtake or keep your distance. Driving in the early evening is also fraught with danger. Slow-moving agricultural vehicles, tractors with loaded trailers – and no lights – pull out onto the narrow roads without warning. Mopeds and bicycles generally seem to have no lights, so have your front seat passenger keep an eye out, too. There are practially no catseyes, and other car drivers tend not to dip their headlights until the last minute, if at all.

Particular stretches of road on which to take extra care are as follows: on the way to Djerba, the Arram to Ajim road, with drivers rushing to make the Djerba ferry; the Djerba causeway, a narrow road which winds slightly and can be dangerous at night due to the headlights of oncoming lorries; the rolling GP1 south of Gabès, and the winding first few kilometres out of Metlaoui on the way to Tozeur.

Urban driving This is problematic, too, even though speeds are not high. Traffic jostles for position at the lights (always respected), and procedure on roundabouts, if there are no lights, is different from the UK. You drive straight onto the roundabout, and then slow, allowing traffic coming from the right to come on. When all is clear, you move on round.

In urban areas the speed limit is 50 kph and is to be observed. There are speed patrols at key points. You may well be able to talk your way out of a fine. Stop signs are also to be respected. When at a stop sign, make sure you stop, or the police officer waiting behind a nearby eucalyptus tree will have reason to ask for your papers.

Essentials

Essentials

 Transport and common sense in the desert

The key to safe travel in desert regions is reliable and well equipped transport. Most travellers will simply use local bus and taxi services. For the motorist, motorcyclist or pedal cyclist there are ground rules which, if followed, will help to reduce risks. In normal circumstances travellers will remain on black-top roads and for this need only a well prepared two-wheel drive vehicle. Choose a machine which is known for its reliability and for which spares can be easily obtained. Across the whole of North Africa only Peugeot and Mercedes are found with adequate spares and servicing facilities. If you have a different type of car/truck, make sure that you take spares with you or have the means of getting spares sent out. Bear in mind that transport of spares to and from the desert areas might be tediously long. Petrol/benzene/gas is everywhere available though diesel is equally well distributed except in the smallest of southern settlements. Four-wheel drive transport is useful even for the traveller who normally remains on the black-top highway. Emergencies, diversions and unscheduled visits to off-road sites become less of a problem with all-terrain vehicles. Off the road, four-wheel drive is essential, normally with two vehicles travelling together.

Basic equipment

- Full tool kit, vehicle maintenance handbook and supplementary tools such as clamps, files, wire, spare parts kit supplied by car manufacturer, jump leads.
- Spare tyre/s, battery driven tyre pump, tyre levers, tyre repair kit, hydraulic jack, jack handle extension, base plate for jack.
- Spare fuel can/s, spare water container/s, cool bags.

Extra equipment for for those going off the black top roads

- Foot tyre pump, heavy duty hydraulic or air jack, power winch, sand channels, safety rockets, comprehensive first aid kit, radio-telephone where permitted.
- Emergency rations kit/s, matches, Benghazi burner
- Maps, compasses, latest road information, long term weather forecast, guides to navigation by sun and stars.

Basic but crucial driving rules

- If you can get a local guide who perhaps wants a lift to your precise destination, use him.
- Set out early in the morning after first light, rest during the heat of the day and use the cool of the evening for further travel.
- Never attempt to travel at night or when there is a sandstorm brewing or in progress.
- Always travel with at least two vehicles which should remain in close visual-contact.

Other general hints include not speeding across open flat desert in case the going changes without warning and your vehicle beds deeply into soft sand or a gully. Well maintained corrugated road surfaces can be taken at modest pace but rocky surfaces should be treated with great care to prevent undue wear on tyres. Sand seas are a challenge for drivers but need a cautious approach – ensure that your navigation lines are clear so that weaving between dunes does not disorientate the navigator. Especially in windy conditions, sight lines can vanish, leaving crews with little knowledge of where they are. Cresting dunes from dip slope to scarp needs care that the vehicle does not either bog down or overturn. Keep off salt flats after rain and floods especially in the winter and spring when water tables can rise and make the going hazardous in soft mud. Even when on marked and maintained tracks beware of approaching traffic.

In practice, pedestrians in most urban areas have a calming effect on traffic. People walk in the road, pavement or no pavement, and mothers seem to use their prams to test oncoming traffic's willingness to slow down. (One Tunis wag proposed that pedestrians pay road tax, too.) For the foreign driver, drive more carefully than you would normally, paying great attention to bicycles, mopeds and pedestrians.

In Tunisia, the visitor will find maps of the country on sale in kiosks and bookshops. The **Maps** better maps include the GeoCenter 1:800,000 map to Tunisia, with plans of Kairouan, Sousse and Tunis. Travellers will find certain inaccuaracies, especially in showing minor roads in rural areas. In the UK, try *Stanfords*, 12-14 Long Acre, WC2E 9LP, T020-7730 1314, near Covent Garden for maps. One of the best maps, not always available in Tunisia, is the Michelin sheet 958, Algérie Tunisie, 1:1,000,000. The tourist offices may provide free maps which are perfectly adequate for navigating between main towns, but not much more.

This is really only a consideration in outlying places not served by the very cheap public **Hitchhiking** transport. Here, eventually, a place on a truck or lorry will be available, for which a charge is made. Women should only hitch in an emergency.

Train

The *SNCFT* (*Société Nationale des Chemins de Fer Tunisiens*) is the national rail company. The information line at Tunis's main station is T71345511, T71254440. You may get directly through to information, or have to press 13 after the recorded message in French and Arabic. There is an information window in Tunis main station, over on the left as you walk into the main concourse. Trains have three classes: *confort*, 1st and 2nd. *Confort* has air-conditioning and big armchairs. Cheaper carriages can be crowded, especially on the day before and after public holidays. The trains have a buffet trolley selling drinks, biscuits and sandwiches. For air-conditioned trains, try to get your ticket in advance. Extra trains are laid on for Ramadan and public holidays.

Local rail transport includes the TGM (Tunis-Goulette-La Marsa) light railway (see map in Tunis transport section), the Tunis to Borj Cedria suburban line (*ligne de banlieue*) via Hammam Lif, and the Sahel light railway running from Sousse to Mahdia via Monastir. For long distance travel, there are two lines with plenty of passenger trains, the Tunis to Bizerte line, via Mateur, and the Tunis to Metlaoui line, via Sousse, Sfax and Gabès. (Some trains take a slightly different route avoiding Gabès.) Sadly, the line to Tabarka has been pulled up. There is a rare direct Tunis to Nabeul service, via Bir Bou Regba and Hammamet, although there are only one or two trains a day in either direction. For those wishing to head west, there is one passenger train a day to Kalaâ Khasba at 0600, and a Tunis to Ghardimaou service five times a day via Béja. Rail travel to Algeria is not an option at the moment.

Sample single fares in spring 2002 were as follows: Tunis to Bizerte, 2nd class 3Dt; Tunis to Sousse, 5Dt 700 2nd class, 8Dt 100 *confort*; Tunis to Metlaoui, 2nd class 14Dt, *confort* 20Dt; Tunis to Ghardimaou, 7Dt 2nd class; Tunis to Kalaâ Khasba, 8Dt 300. Sample journey times: Tunis to Bizerte, 1 hour 40 minutes; Tunis to Ghardimaou, 2 hours 50 minutes; Tunis to Sousse, 2 hours 20 minutes; Tunis to El Jem, 3 hours; Tunis to Gabès, 4 hours 50 minutes; Tunis to Kalaâ Khasba, 5 hours. The night train from Tunis to Metlaoui takes 8 hours 20 minutes. The SNCFT's special 'rail and museums' pass scheme, launched in 1999, was subsequently disbanded.

A word of warning regarding the main southern line. The names of the smaller stations are only given on the actual station building, and not on the platform. To be quite sure you know when you reach your destination, keep an eye out and sit near the front of the train – or ask. The public address system is only used for major stations, Arabic announcement first, French following.

Keeping in touch

Communications

Internet Internet access is expanding rapidly in Tunisia and even quite out of the way places now have their *publinets* where you can get on line. In downtown Tunis, the two most central *publinets* are on the corner of Rue de Grèce/Place Barcelone (first floor of decaying colonial building), and in the street parallel to the Avenue H Bourguiba behind *Chez Max*, just off Rue de Marseille. If all else fails you could just try the British Council library at Porte de France (old town end of Av H Bourguiba), where they have been known to let non-members get on line for 3Dt an hour. **NB** In the near future the British Council is scheduled to move to a new location out of town centre.

Do not be surprised if it proves very difficult to open your freemail boxes. Hotmail, Caramail and Yahoo are temperamental in Tunisia. Creative cybercafé owners should be able to help you locate your freemail box. All cybercafés show notices stressing that there are *sites interdits* (forbidden sites) which you should not access, although they do not tell you what they are.

Post
Local post offices are listed in the directory under individual towns
Stamps are available from post offices (PTT) and from certain news-stands and hotel shops. A letter to the Maghreb states costs 350 millimes, other Arab states 450 millimes, Africa 550 millimes, Europe 500 millimes, and to the rest of the world 600 millimes. There is no printed paper rate.

There is a Rapide Poste service, with offices at the airport, the central PTT and El Manar neighbourhood of Tunis. Rapide Poste has links with *DHL* and other international express mail services. Unfortunately, it is not much quicker than ordinary mail, and not always terribly reliable. The El Manar office stays open late.

Post office **opening hours** tend to be complex, varying between winter, summer (July and August) and Ramadan, which in 2003 will fall in November/December.

Telephone The international dialling code for Tunisia is 216. For the moment, *Tunisie Télécom* is the sole national service provider. Telephone numbers in Tunisia are 8 digits, and are expressed as whole numbers either in a block of 2 (regional 'code') and two blocks of 3, or three blocks of 2. Say 0 as *zéro*. Regional dialling codes begin 7 plus digit, eg 71, *soixante et onze*, for Tunis region. **You must dial all eight digits**, even within the region concerned. (Prior to 2001, numbers were six digit with regional codes beginning zero plus digit). 8 digit mobile phone numbers begin 98. The present guide gives six digit numbers with the regional two digit prefix in the margin. For full list of regional prefixes see box, page 45.

For international access, dial 00 plus country code. Directory enquiries is *les renseignements*, dial 1200 for business numbers, 1210 for personal numbers. The telephone directory is *l'annuaire*, yellow pages, *les pages jaunes*.

The best way to make an international call is from one of the ubiquitous *taxiphones*, as the public call centres are called. Calling from your hotel will be expensive. Taxiphones can be found in the centre of all major towns. Take plenty of 1Dt coins if it is an international call. There may be certain cabins or phones reserved for international calls, *appels internationaux*. The international operator is on 17, the *service des dérangements* is 11. If you want to reverse the charges, this is *un appel en PCV*, currently not possible with the USA.

Phoning a business, you will probably start by getting through to their switchboard (*le standard*). If you want a given extension number, you ask (for example) for *poste numéro xx*. Make sure you can say the numbers in French.

If you want to send a fax, many taxiphones have fax machines where you can receive and send faxes. Note that they are obliged to make a note of your passport/identity card details before they send your fax.

Regional dialling codes

All Tunisian phone numbers have eight digits, the first two digits being the regional prefix. Always dial all eight digits.

Regional dialling codes
71 *Tunis and around*
72 *Northeast, including Bizerte, Hammamet and Nabeul (Cap Bon)*
73 *Central coast, including Sousse, Mahdia, Monastir*
74 *Sfax*
75 *Gabès, Djerba, Kebili, Tataouine, Zarzis*
76 *Gafsa, Tozeur, Nefta*
77 *Kairouan, Kasserine*

78 *Le Kef, Tabarak and the Northwest*
98 *Mobile numbers*

Useful numbers
1200 *Directory enquiries (private numbers)*
1210 *Directory enquiries (business/services)*
1717 *Reversed charge calls*
198 *Fire*
197 *Police*
190 *Ambulance*

To dial Tunisia from abroad, 216 is the international access code followed by the eight-digit number.

Essentials

Media

Newspapers

Among the main newspapers are *Le Temps*, *Le Renouveau* and *La Presse*, all of which have sister papers in Arabic. *Le Renouveau* is the official organ of the ruling RCD, and thus can, on occasion, be quite critical in tone. *La Presse* carries a lot of advertising and calls to tender, a reflection of Tunisia's current consumer boom. It is good for sports coverage, and has back pages which carry lots of useful information (plane arrival and departure times for Tunis-Carthage airport, late night bus times, ads for Tunis restaurants). On Mondays, *La Presse* has a *page littéraire*, occasionally quite interesting. The arts coverage is hopeless, there are rarely previews of concerts and exhibitions, and no listings to speak of. In English, there is the weekly *Tunisia News*, a dull if worthy publication. For those who read Arabic, *Ech Chorouk* will keep you up to date with the doings of Tunisia's footballers and singers.

Television

If they haven't got a satellite dish, Tunisians have the choice of the main Tunis Channel 7 (in Arabic), which broadcasts news, Egyptian films and soap operas, sporting events and documentaries dubbed into Arabic. Locally produced material is limited to a Saturday night variety show, *Mindhar* (a current affairs programme), and the Ramadan soap opera. Tunisians also have Rai Uno, the main Italian channel, and France 2, much watched for news and current affairs, which is rebroadcast in Tunisia. For a couple of hours in the early evening, France 2 broadcasts are replaced by the local youth channel, which does quiz shows, a pop programme and news in English.

Tunisians' desire for entertainment has meant that satellite TV is considered essential by most households. Even in poor neighbourhoods, satellite dishes can be seen everywhere. Popular channels include the Egyptian and French channels along with *Al Jazeera*, a Qatari-based news and current affairs channel which started up when the BBC Arabic TV service closed. *Arte*, the Franco-German arts channel, has a loyal following.

Radio

There is a daily hour of English-language radio on RTCI (Radio Tunis Chaine Internationale), the local FM station, which also broadcasts in French, German, Italian and Spanish. There are no independent radio stations and none would seem to be planned.

Food and drink

Outside the hotels, Tunisian restaurant food is generally good, quite varied and by Western European standards, very reasonable in price. (Meals in the 3-star hotels tend to have a canteen-like quality.) Most local products are fresh and good quality. Food is well spiced but rarely *piquant*.

Types of restaurant
In most main towns you will find some very good restaurants indeed, offering a mixed Tuniso-Franco-Italian cuisine. Among the top restaurants in this category you have *L'Astragale* in the Cité Jardin, Tunis, and *Le Golfe*, at La Marsa. Somewhat cheaper, but very good value, is *Le Tchevap* at Carthage and *Le Bon Vieux Temps* in Sidi Bou Saïd. A fairly recent trend in the Tunisian restaurant industry is the 'old Tunis' style restaurant, of which the best example is *Dar Jeld*, at the Kasbah, Tunis. You might also try a cabaret restaurant – for example *El Mawel*, in Cité Jardin, Tunis – where there will be a loud oriental band and a dancer. Be warned, these places, on account of the *spectacle*, are not cheap. Try to avoid hotel à la carte restaurants. These seem to start out with high hopes, but because so much of the clientèle is on a budget, are rarely able to maintain standards. Outside Tunis, the towns will have just a scattering of good restaurants, formal evening dining out not really being a tradition among locals.

Along the coast and on the islands, there are some good fish restaurants. Fish in these eateries is generally sold by the 100 gram. The fish is weighed for you – there is no embarrassment about asking how much it will cost. If it's too pricey, then have *complet poisson*, a fish steak or small fish with chips and a fried vegetable and egg *tastira*. Among the better restaurants with fish on the menu are *Les Ombrelles* in Gammarth and *Le Daurade* at Haouaria.

The small restaurants without alcohol are cheaper. Restaurants with alcohol are more expensive, even though the quality of the food and service is not necessarily better. You will also find some reasonably priced restaurants with alcohol (*Le Carthage* and *Tantonville* in downtown Tunis or *El Farik* at Monastir). Prices are almost always indicated on the menu. As anywhere, be sure to check before you order. Few but the most upmarket restaurants take international credit cards. Few restaurants cater for vegetarians. Quality of service varies enormously, verging on the pompous in the 'heritage restaurants', unpredictable elsewhere. The best service is often in the small places, and can improve if you become a regular.

If you want a quick meal, Tunisia's cities have plenty of snack-restaurants where you can get a sandwich (*cassecroute*), a slice of pizza or a savoury doughnut (*ftira*). Sandwiches may be made in half a baguette or in *khubz tabouna*, round flat bread. Tuna and cheese is a popular combination, and *escalope de dinde* (turkey escalope) or *salami de dinde* are often on offer. Sandwiches are garnished with spoonfuls of various salads, and olives – mind your teeth on the stones.

Tunisian starters
If you are a vegetarian, you will probably be eating lots from this section. Without meat is *sans viande/bilesh leham*. *Chorba* – highly flavoured soup, tomato and oil base. *Brik* – deep-fried pastry containing egg and generally tuna, possibly potato and parsley, or even cheese. If you want your brik without tuna, say *sans thon/bilesh tun*. *Salade d'aubergines/Salata bitenjal* – grilled aubergines, finely chopped to a near paste-like consistency, served chilled with olive oil, lemon juice, and capers. Rare in restaurants. *Salade méchouia* – finely chopped, mixed grilled vegetables, decorated with tuna and egg, can be very *piquant*, served cold. *Salade tunisienne* – a variant of the *salade niçoise* with tomatoes, onions, green peppers, sometimes cucumber, and the usual tuna and egg garnish. *Ummek Houriya* – carrots boiled with some peeled garlic, mashed to a

Five choice seaside restaurants

Summer in Tunisia should mean time for leisurely lunches by the sea. As a change from the hotel beachside restaurants and snackeries, try some of the following, starting with the northernmost and working southwards:

- *Le Sport nautique*, Bizerte. The northern port city's choicest address, Quai Tarik-ibn-Ziad, T72432262.
- *La Daurade*, Haouaria. Just above the Roman quarries. View of the Zembra archipelago but no booze (bring your own, they turn a blind eye), T72269080.
- *El Mansoura*, Kélibia. Dining area with big glass windows overlooking the rocks. In summer, tables under parasols out among the rocks. Gets very busy, T72295169, F72273206.
- *El Farik*, Monastir. On the Corniche road on the Mahdia (south) side of town. Not a chic address but magnificent squid in cumin and tomato sauce (kammounia bil-karnit), T73468555.
- *Da Mario*, Djerba, T75757822. Right on the beach next to the Hotel Palm Beach. Relaxed Italian eatery.

All are reasonably priced. Those with plenty of cash can push the boat out and go for *Le Golfe* or *Les Ombrelles* at Gammarth in Tunis's chic northern suburbs.

Essentials

---

paste and seasoned with olive oil, a little vinegar, *harissa* and black pepper, served chilled and garnished with capers. Rare in restaurants.

These are generally found in working men's eateries or in souk areas. *Hergma* – a strong soup made from sheep or goats' feet, chopped and boiled at great length. *Lablabi* – a hearty soup of chick peas, served at any time of the day. Originally a dish of the poor, it is especially popular in winter.

Snack foods

Egg dishes *Chakchouka* – ratatouille with tomatoes, peppers, garlic and onions, egg is added at the end of the process. *Keftaji* – fried onions, pumpkin, tomatoes, peppers and eggs, served all chopped up with either meat balls (*ka'abir*) or maybe fried liver. *Tajine* – a form of quiche, with meat and vegetables, cooked in the oven. Varieties include *tajine ma'kouda*, which contains broad-leaved parsley, potato and peas and is sometimes flavoured with smoked herring (*renga*), and *tajine malsouka*, which is egg and chicken between layers of filo pastry. **Meat dishes** *Couscous* – steamed coarse semolina or millet served with vegetables and meat or fish. Typical dish eaten throughout the Maghreb. The Tunisian version has a tomato sauce, unlike the Algerian and Moroccan versions, where the sauce is served separately. The buttermilk now sold in cartons to accompany a good couscous is called *leben*. Other popular staples include *kamounia* (a slowly cooked meat, octopus or squid stew, strongly flavoured with cumin); *koucha* (roast lamb with potatoes and peppers cooked in the oven); and *loubiya* (stewed mutton with white beans). *Marcassin* (meat of the wild boar piglet, the only pork you are likely to find in this Muslim country) has a strong flavour and is served with a rich gravy. (**NB** It was banned from restaurants in 2001-02 for unknown reasons.) Pork is called *hallouf*, which is also slang for a 'tricky' person. At roadside restaurants, you will find *mechoui*, grilled meat (usually lamb) served with a small dish of harissa and olive oil. Look out too for *merguez*, small spicy mutton or beef sausages, generally grilled – the red colour gives an indication of the amount of chilli used in their preparation and is a guide to how fiery they will be.)

Typical main dishes

The best are the *rouget* (red mullet), *mulet* (mullet), *mérou* (cod), *loup de mer* (perch) and sole. You can have your fish *grillé/mechoui* (barbecued) or *frit/mukli* (fried).

Fish

Crevettes royales, *cigale de mer* and *homard* (lobster) are best eaten in places like Tabarka on the rocky northern coast and at Haouaria. *Kabkabou* is oven-baked fish with saffron, preserved lemons and vegetables. In places like Hergla, fish farming is a fast growing business, catering to the needs of tourist establishments. Connoisseurs claim they can tell the difference between farmed and 'natural' fish.

Ingredients The cooks of Tunisia have a wonderful selection of field-fresh ingredients to choose from. Vegetables and fruit are of a quality rarely equalled in northern Europe and North America. There are a number of typical pickles and ingredients used in Tunisian dishes: *akhchef* – preserved quince slices; *bnadak* – meat balls, spiced with dried mint, boiled in oil to preserve them; *filfil barr l'abid* – tiny red peppers used to decorate food and eaten to stimulate the appetite; *filfil m'sayer* – large green peppers, pickled whole; *harissa* – a thick piquant paste, used to give flavour to all sorts of dishes, and given as a dip at restaurants before the starters arrive (best *harissa 'arbi*, 'home-made harissa', comes from Nabeul, too much is best countered by eating bread rather than drinking water); *harous* – similar to *salade méchouia*, but contains green pepper only; *imalah* – crinkle-cut carrots, cauliflower and turnips preserved in brine, also given as a salty opener to a meal along with harissa; *limoun* – preserved lemons, used in fish dishes and occasionally salads; *turshi* – thin slices of pickled turnip, given as an appetizer.

Desserts Like all Mediterranean countries, Tunisia has many varieties of dessert, all very sweet and sticky. The Ottoman influence is clear. If you go to a Tunisian wedding, then you will almost certainly get the chance to try some of the many varieties of *helw*, small sweet cakes: *baklawa* – puff pastry with lots of honey and nuts; *bjaouia* – sort of cake combining almonds, pistachio nuts and puffed; *loukoum* – Turkish delight; *makroudh* – semolina cake with crushed dates, baked in oil and dipped in honey; *masfouf* – a dessert made from fine semolina flour served with dates, raisins, pistachio nuts and pine nuts, a meal in itself and particularly appreciated for the *suhour*, the early morning Ramadan meal taken before fasting begins; *m'lebbes* or *calissons de Sfax* – round sweets made of sweetened ground almonds covered in white icing sugar.

Fruit With its sunny Mediterranean climate, Tunisia produces fruit full of flavour. The most 'typical' fruit are dates (Arabic: *tmer*), and the season for fresh dates begins in October. There are over 100 types but the best, the *deglet nour*, come from the desert oases, particularly Tozeur and Nefta. *Pastèque* – watermelon, *della'* in Arabic – is particularly refreshing in summer. In early autumn, restaurants add bowls of ruby-red pomegranate seeds (Arabic: *rumène*) to their dessert menus. Served with sugary, rose-flavoured water, pomegranate is said to be good for the *transit intestinal*.

In recent years, plasticulture has increased the periods during which certain types of fresh fruit – notably strawberries and melons – are available. In the markets, depending on season, there are some local varieties of fruit to look out for. In spring, the soft, apricot-coloured *bousa'a*, as the medlar is called in Arabic, are ready in May (French term: *nèfles*). Easily bruised, quick to soften, they are rarely seen in northern European markets. In late June, a special variety of peach can be found, the flat, mole-skinned *boutabguia*, called *pêche de vigne* in French. When ripe, the *boutabguia* has wonderfully juicy white flesh. In July, crunchy little pears appear, known as *inzas bouguidma*, literally, 'bite-sized'. Still in high summer, there are numerous varieties of melons and grapes, the most evocatively named being the long, translucent green *bazoula* (breast-shaped) grapes. Autumn finds the markets full of citrus fruit: look out for lemon-like bergamotes or *lime* (the taste approximates to soapy Earl Grey) and tiny green *lime beldi*.

Drink The national drink is **tea**, which comes as *tay akhdhar/thé vert* (green tea) and *tay ahmar/thé rouge*, a dark sugar-saturated brew. In tourist-oriented places, it is often

Zgougou and Zrir

*Like any country, Tunisia has its fair share of desserts to celebrate festive occasions, the best known being a sort of pine-seed custard called **assida bi-zgougou** made specially for the Mouled, the annual celebration of the prophet Mohamed's birthday.*

Zgougou are the tiny black seeds found in pine cones. As a kilo of zgougou is expensive and the preparation of assida custard is difficult, expert cooking skills are called for. After washing, the pine seeds are put in the oven on a low heat until they begin to release their oil. The next step involves grinding up the seed and heating the result in a pan of water. After sieving, the resulting 'zgougou liquid' is mixed with sugar, flour and water and put on a low heat. Constant stirring is necessary to avoid lumps and sticking. When ready, the dark, almost mauve cream is poured into glass dishes. When it has cooled, a layer of ordinary custard is poured on top, which, when cool, is decorated with nuts.

*Zgougou being difficult to prepare, there are variations, the quickest and most common being **assida bou frioua** (hazelnut). For this version, the nuts are baked and then simply put through the*

blender. But as large quantities of assida have to be prepared and bowls to be sent out to all members of the family, preparation is quite a business. There is much competition between women to see who gets the family vote for the best assida bi-zgougou. And the taste? Unusual. For the uneducated European palate, the hazelnut version is easier to eat.

*Other desserts for special occasions include madmouja (for circumcisions), **sherbet** (for the sdeq, the proclaiming of the marriage bans at the mosque), and **zrir** (to celebrate a newborn child). Rich chewy madmouja is basically fried, sweetened pastry broken up and mixed with dates. Guests attending a circumcision may receive little packets of it wrapped in cellophane. Sherbet is sugary, flavoured water, a little like rosata, the sweet almond milk still popular in some circles during Ramadan. Zrir is a very thick, strongly flavoured nutty paste, served in tiny glasses to those visiting a mother and her newborn child. The idea is that it puts the mother back on her feet. And finally, **kunfid** are sugared almonds, delicately wrapped in voile and distributed to guests at weddings.*

served with tiny, white flavoursome pine-nuts floating in it, which makes it both more delicious and more expensive. **Coffee** is also widely drunk, and is as cheap as tea, between 300 and 800 millimes, for an *express*, depending on the type of café. The most common and cheapest **beer** is Celtia (a Tunisian make) but Tunisian-made Tuborg and Stella, as well as imported beers, can be found. Celtia *pression* (keg) can be found in some bars.

The Tunisians have been making wine for over 2,000 years. Today, the vast majority of wines are made by the **UCCV** (*Union centrale des coopératives vinicoles*), ie under the strict control of the state. Quality was somewhat irregular, given the departure of the Italian winegrowers in the early 1960s and the subsequent loss of savoir-faire. There were some major improvements in the late 1990s, however, with new equipment being introduced to control the vinification process and the arrival of new grape varieties. (Until recently, all the wine was fermented in the same six *cuves*, new oak barrels being too expensive). There are practically no imported wines available.

Wine
Especially recommended are the Tardi and Chais Valenza wines

On your way round a Tunisian supermarket's wine shelves or a restaurant menu, go for **red wines** as these are generally more reliable than the whites, although this is changing. Note however that the reds are probably more acidic than most palates are used to and vary in quality. It is difficult to recommend any particular wine. Among the most palatable of the red wines are those from Tebourba (try *Vieux Magon*) and the reds from Mornag (*Haut Mornag*). *Sidi Saâd* is the red in the trendy amphora shaped bottle. Of the lighter red wines, the *Clairet de Bizerte* has a loyal following. **Rosés** include *Haut Mornag, Sidi Rais* and *Château Mornag*. Lighter than the rosés are Tunisia's **vins gris**, including *Gris de Tunisie* and *Gris de Bizerte*. The **white wines**, generally dry, are more problematic, and the choice is generally limited to *Ugni Blanc* (dry) or the fuller *Muscat Sec de Kélibia* from the Cap Bon peninsula. Try also *Sidi Rais* and *Blanc de Blanc*. Of the **rough cheapies**, the rosé *Chateau Mornag* is an old favourite, real 'builders' wine' (*shreb bennay*), in local parlance. 2001 saw a new range of pricey wines launched under the grand sounding *Saint Augustin* (red) and *Elissa* (white) labels. The *Terrale* wines are best avoided, the bright labels being persuasive but no guarantee of quality. As elsewhere, there are worries about the herbicides used to clear the soil between the rows of vines. There are, however, a couple of old, family-owned concerns producing wine under more ecologically friendly conditions.

Other alcohol Tunisia also produces three types of very strong alcohol. *Boukha* is made from distilled figs, while *Thibarine* is a strong, sweet liqueur dreamed up by the White Fathers at their model farm at Thibar, near Dougga (hence the name). Both are available in special packaging at the airport duty-free. *Laghmi* is palm tree sap left to ferment for a while immediately after it is collected. Most imported alcohols are available generally in hotel bars, more rarely in city bars, and they are very expensive.

Bars & Outside restaurants, stores in the *Monoprix, Touta* and *Magasin Général* **supermarket**
buying alcohol **chains** all have alcohol sections, often separated from the main part of the supermarket. Thus buying wine can be quite an occasion and on a Saturday afternoon, the supermarket wine section attracts an interesting cross-section of society, some of whom will have come from a long way off to make their weekly purchase. The atmosphere is hearty. The bottles have no need of stylish labelling, customers know the limited selection by heart. Note that wine sales will be off-limits to all but foreigners during the month of Ramadan. The best selection of wines is probably at the *Carrefour* hypermarket, just off the Tunis to La Marsa autoroute.

In older neighbourhoods there are **débits d'alcohol** (off licences), which tend to be unmarked hole-in-the-wall type affairs. Bars tend to be very crowded and blokey. More upmarket bars are in very short supply, although there are one or two, including a pub with wooden panelling in a Sousse shopping mall (the *Rose and Crown* near the *Maracana* discothèque and the *Hotel Taj Marhaba*) and a German *brauhaus* in Hammamet on the main square. There is generally no pool or *flipper* (pinball) in bars. These can be found in *salles de jeux*, a separate affair altogether.

Soft drinks Both local and international soft drinks (*gazouz*) are widely available. Bottled water is very good and is available with all meals. There are now numerous brands of still water (*eau plate*), including *Safia* (the best known), *Sabrine, Hayet* and *Melliti*. In shops, the larger 1½ litre plastic bottles costs around 600 millimes. The smaller, resealable plastic bottles are just right for taking on short journeys. If you want fizzy (*eau gazeuse*) bottled water, the brand is *Garci*. *Boga* is the local lemonade, although *7-Up* is also available. *Boga Cidra* is a black fizzy drink made from carob beans. *Apla* and *Fruité* are fizzy fruit drinks, and in summer you could try *citronade*, freshly made from the huge lemons that Tunisia produces. (Note that citronade is not to be taken on hot bus journeys, as it goes off very quickly.) *Coca Cola* was subject to something of an informal, local boycott in early 2002, due to the firm's perceived financial support for the State of Israel, then in full repressive action against the Palestinian people.

Cafés are an interesting experience. Essentially an all-male affair, they range from the sedate city centre café, used in the day by men for sorting out business, tiny stand-up swallow-your-coffee type places and large *cafés populaires*, busy all day, packed and

Five quality shopping opportunities

- *El Hanout*, Carthage. Two shops with stylish products (ceramics, bits for the bathroom and kitchen), one at 4 Ave JF Kennedy, T71227086, the other on the main avenue, opposite the Mobil station.
- *Phénicia*, Le Kram, on your left, next to the pharmacy, just before the Salammbô stadium as you head for Carthage. Good selection of crafts.
- *El Makhzen*, 35 Rue Sidi Ben Arous, Médina of Tunis. Small atmospheric shop down from the intersection with the Rue de la Kasbah, almost opposite the main entrance to **Dar Hammouda Bacha**, recently restored palace with some nice glass, ceramics ant textiles.
- *Fella*, Médina of Hammamet, T72280426, just opposite the main entrance to the fort. Old fabrics used for modern creations.
- *Espace Kène*, Bouficha, on the GP1 between Hammamet and Sousse, T73252110, craft village best known for its furniture.

intensely smokey and noisy in the evenings. Upmarket residential areas now have trendy cafés, bright with neon lighting (see the Berges du Lac, Tunis and El Manar), where women can be seen. The bijou-tiled waterpipe café is an innovation of the early 1990s and smokers will want to try a *chicha* (hubbly-bubbly pipe). Stronger than cigarettes (but not the local Crystal cigarettes), the chicha is nevertheless a good way to start up a conversation. You will be asked what sort of tobacco you want: *mu'assal* (stickey-sweet, literally 'honeyed') or *tufah* (apple flavoured). Some cafés tend to focus on dominoes and cards. Both are played with huge gusto and there's much noise to be made slamming dominoes down on tables. Others are more sport-TV focused. Note that although the clientèle is the same, there is very rarely any overlap in activities between card-playing café and the boozers' den type bar.

Shopping

Tunisia has some interesting craftwork, although not of the variety and quality to be found in somewhere like Morocco. (Your stay in Tunisia could be the time you give your plastic cards a rest.) Unfortunately, a lot of the more interesting, good value items are difficult to transport, (ie rush mats, wrought iron) or are very expensive – silk traditional garments, for example. There is lots of pottery to be bought, and the same items, mostly made in Nabeul, can be found in resorts right across the country. If you are looking for cheap presents, then there is a wealth of things to choose from. The tourist souks are now full of junk from as far afield as Egypt, India, Pakistan and West Africa – just take your pick.

Recommended local shops and bargains are listed under Shopping in each town's Essentials section

In Tunisia the main types of handmade carpet are **kilims** (flat-weave carpets), **mergoums** and **knotted carpets** usually made of wool on a cotton base. The **classic knotted carpets** come from the vertical looms of Kairouan's homes and workshops. The patterns are geometrical, usually based on a central medallion in the form of single and double diamond shapes. Their weave is of hand knots of the *ghordes* type, with long tufts looped around the warp. **Mergoum**, the other popular weave, is different, having short tufts emerging on the underside of the warps. Of the two, it is the mergoum which are fairly cheap and made for the tourist trade. The classic Kairouan carpet, on the other hand, tends to appeal more to locals. Bold and colourful **kelims** are made in Djerba and Sbeïtla. Other southern towns, including Gabès, produce **flat-weave tapestries** with stylized camels and the like. Perhaps the easiest piece to take home is a **bakhnoug** or a

Carpets

ketifa, a tightly woven woolen shawl with cotton embroidery. Some of the more interesting ketifa pieces will have tie-dye and pompoms. Unfortunately, high quality bakhnoug are a rarity now. In 2002, carpet prices were low due to the fall in tourist numbers due to the conflict in Afghanistan – but not always so low as to be competitive with prices for Indian and Anatolian rugs in Europe. Remember, don't be pushed into buying a carpet. Make sure that you pick a rug that you like and can live with.

Good buys Finding something really original to take home will take time. Basketwork is a good, cheap find, and you might see some fine **rush matwork** in Nabeul. Some of the finer *nattes* with geometric designs make good wall-hangings. Old-fashioned hammered metal **kitchen articles** in copper or silvery zinc-plating (*maillechort/mqezder*) are also a good buy – try Souk Ennahas in Tunis or the main street in Kairouan. Then there is simple, rural **hand-shaped pottery** from the north, sometimes painted up with geometric designs. At Hergla, you can find traditional mats made from plaited **alfa grass** while in the Médina of Tunis you can find rather fine **traditional men's tunics** (the *jebba*) in silk and linen. Given that Tunisia is a major centre for garment manufacture, another option is to pick up a nice pair of jeans or a shirt in a modern shopping mall.

On the whole, however, the best things to buy in Tunisia are foodstuffs. The markets are full of spices, dried herbs and various condiments which cost a small fortune in European supermarkets. Try for olive oil, olives, capers, real harissa, bayleaves, garlic, dried mint and various spices. Dates are also a splendid present, and can be bought on the branch in kilo-size boxes. And you have various flower waters, especially orange and geranium, much used in traditional patisserie, and almond syrup (*sirop d'orgeat*) which makes a refreshing summer drink. Then there is green henna powder – best bought in Gabès. All in all, the 'consumables' side of souk shopping makes up for the lack of high quality handicrafts.

Holidays and festivals

Religious Religious holidays are scheduled according to the Hejira calendar, a lunar based calen-
holidays dar. (Given the clear night skies of Arabia, it is easily comprehensible that the Muslims should have adopted a year based upon the cycles of the moon.) The lunar year is shorter than the solar year, so the Muslim year moves forward by 11 days every Christian year. Thus in 10 years' time, Ramadan, currently in the winter, will be at the height of summer. Note that the start of Ramadan can vary by a day, depending on the *ru'ya*, whether the crescent moon has been observed or not by the religious authorities whose job it is to declare Ramadan. The AD year 2002 corresponds to the Muslim year 1421-1422; 2003 is 1422-1423. The main religious holidays are as follows:

Muharram First day of the Muslim year.

Mouloud Celebration of the Prophet Mohamed's birthday.

Ramadan A month of fasting and sexual abstinence during daylight hours.

Aïd es Seghir (the Lesser Aïd) A two-day holiday ending the month of Ramadan.

Aïd el Kebir (the Great Aïd) One-day holiday which comes 70 days after Aïd es Seghir. Commemorates how God rewarded Ibrahim's faith by sending down a lamb for him to sacrifice instead of his son. When possible, every family sacrifices a sheep on this day.

During Ramadan, the whole country switches to a different rhythm. Public offices go onto half time, and the general pace slows down during the daytime. Tunisians in general do not eat in public during the day, and the vast majority of cafés and restaurants, except those frequented by resident Europeans and tourists, are closed. The cities are quite lively at night however, with shops opening, especially in the second half of the month. Ramadan is an interesting time to visit Tunisia as a tourist, but to be avoided if possible when you need to do business.

Tunisia's main religious holidays

	2002	2003	2004	2005
Start of Ramadan	6 Nov	27 Oct	16 Oct	5 Oct
Aïd es Seghir (end of Ramadan)	6 Dec	25 Nov	14 Nov	4 Nov
Aïd el Kebir	23 Feb	12 Feb	31 Jan	21 Jan
1st Muharram (Rass el Am)	15 Mar	4 Mar	22 Feb	10 Feb
Mouloud	25 May	14 May	2 May	21 Apr

Friday is the Muslim holy day and services in the mosques on this day are better attended as there is a *khutba* or sermon in addition to prayers. On Friday mornings office hours are as usual, with the afternoon off for the civil service. The private sector works Friday afternoons, but takes Saturday mornings off. The public sector works Saturday mornings. The 'day of rest' is Sunday. Major football matches are on Sunday afternoons, and most shops, except those in tourist areas, are closed on that day.

Weekends & public holidays

The main public holidays in Tunisia are as follows:
1 January New Year's Day in the Gregorian calendar.
20 March Anniversary of independence.
21 March Youth Day (*Fête de la Jeunesse*).
9 April Anniversary of the 1938 Tunis riots during which a number of demonstrators died when French troops fired on the crowd.
1 May International labour day (*Fête du Travail*).
25 July Anniversary of the declaration of the Tunisian Republic in 1957.
13 August Women's Day (*Fête de la Femme*).
15 October Anniversary of the departure of French troops from Bizerte.
7 November Anniversary of President Ben Ali's coming to power in 1987. Start of 'the Era of the Change'.

Since the 1960s, the authorities have developed a number of festivals, of varying degrees of interest, listed here by time of year. Some are arts orientated (the July and October music festivals), others are more regional affairs which have grown out of local products and traditions. Still others are pure products of the expanding tourist industry.

Festivals *For details of local festivals, see the Essentials sections of individual towns*

March, Festival des ksour Tourist Office's effort to put the far south on the map. Parades, concerts and sporting events in Tataouine. None too exciting.
June, Festival de l'épervier Falconry festival in Haouaria, Cap Bon. Recently revived festival focusing on displays of hawking. Some local music, too.
July, Festival d'El Jem International symphony orchestras play in the splendid surroundings of the Roman colosseum in El Jem.
July, Festival de jazz, Tabarka The streets of the quiet northwestern port of Tabarka come alive with jazz for a week. Another festival which is on the up.
July, Festival du malouf, Testour Provincial town in northern Tunisia remembers its Andalusian musical heritage. Sleepy – like malouf.
July/August, Festival international de Carthage Roman theatre in the Tunis suburbs hosts concerts ranging from the mediocre to the magnificent. No quality theatre.
July/August, Festival international de Hammamet Small theatre in the grounds of the Villa Sebastien is the setting for the élite version of the Festival de Carthage.
August, Kharja de Sidi Bou Saïd Religious brotherhoods of Tunis gather to process up to the shrine of Sidi Bou Saïd.
November 2003, Festival de la Médina Annual Ramadan festival in the old city of Tunis. Restored historic buildings host early music and singers performing classic Arab and Tunisian repertoire. A handful of memorable concerts likely.

Essentials

December, Festival des oasis, Tozeur Popular festival in main southwestern oasis town. Parade, camel fights, concerts, all to pull in the tourists and celebrate the date harvest.

December, Festival du désert, Douz Another big desert festival. Displays of horsemanship, slougui (desert greyhound) and camel races, parades, etc. A jolly occasion.

Sport and special interest travel

Local sports facilities and events are listed in each town's Essentials section

With its pleasant Mediterranean weather conditions, Tunisia offers a variety of sports. Some of the hotel complexes have good tennis facilities, the number of golf courses (eight in 1999) is being expanded. And there are off-beat sports on offer too such as hot-air ballooning over the desert at Tozeur and sand yachting on the Chott El Djerid.

Cycling Quiet flat islands like Kerkennah and Djerba have lots of cycle hire places and bikes are a good way to explore. Elsewhere, the roads both urban and rural are pretty dangerous for cyclists. Pick-up trucks and four-wheel drive vehicles storm along quiet rural roads, paying little attention to anything two-wheeled. This said, serious cyclists may consider bringing in their own machine. Repairs are no problem, every small town has moped/cycle repair shops.

Hunting & shooting The shooting of wild boar and various game birds has long been popular with French and Italian parties. It is necessary to be part of an organized party for firearm permits during official hunting seasons. Certain hotels, including notably the *Hotel Morjane* in Tabarka and *Les Chênes* in Aïn Draham have in the past been much used by hunting parties from abroad. Contact **Club de Chasse** in Radès, (south Tunis suburbs) T71297011 for details.

Falconry Enthusiasts will find El Haouaria on Cap Bon the place to be in May and June. Contact the **Club to Fauconniers** at Haouaria. Locals have a tradition of domesticating migrating sparrowhawks to hunt quail for a couple of months. Some have permits to hunt with peregrine falcons.

Fishing **Inland fishing** There is no river fishing but there are some lakes on the Cap Bon where fishing is possible, although a permit must be obtained from the Ministry of Agriculture in Nabeul on Avenue Mongi Bali.

Sea fishing Tunisia offers lots of sea fishing with no permit required. The Kerkennah Islands are particularly suitable. The marinas of Tabarka, Monastir and Sousse all have boats which will take you out fishing.

Undersea fishing Any person wishing to undertake undersea fishing must file a request to the Director of Fisheries. The formula is the following: "I, the undersigned, family name, first name, date and place of birth, profession, address of residence, declare that I intend to take part in undersea fishing during this present year on the coastline of Tunisia. I certify that I am aware of the current regulations concerning this activity and I agree to exercise this activity in accordance with their provisions. Date and signature". This request should be accompanied by a medical certificate stating aptitude for undersea diving, by personal insurance and insurance for bodily injury to third parties. In practice, no one on a remote coast is likely to stop you to check whether you have a permit or not.

Football This is the national sport and Sunday afternoon is the time to watch.

Golf is an established sport in Tunisia albeit principally for foreign residents and visitors. There are eight first class golf courses across the country at Tabarka, La Soukra (Tunis northern suburbs), El Kantaoui (Sousse) and Djerba and two at each of Hammamet and Monastir. All bar La Soukra are on the coast and a further Tunis course is planned for the coast out at Raoued. Golfing is best from October to May. From June to September the sun and heat can be too much for many. Djerba, particularly agreeable in the winter, is a long way from other courses for a change of play. Best base for a golfing holiday would be Sousse, as other courses are in easy driving distance to the north (Hammamet and Tunis) and south (Monastir). With only one course and no internal flights, Tabarka is too isolated for a golf-only holiday.

For a golfing break in Tunisia, take golf and accommodation as a package. *Panorama Golf*, for example (UK) T01273-746877, F01273-205338, offer golf resort holidays at Hammamet and Port El Kantaoui. Most courses offer facilities for experienced players and for beginners on a long weekend or weekly plus basis. When pre-booking golf course starting times and discount rates can be negotiated. It is important that golfers take with them their *handicap certificates* since clubs in Tunisia demand sight of them before play is permitted. Tariffs for an 18-hole round run at approximately 33Dt in high season and 30Dt in low season, depending on the course, and 190Dt (high season) to 170Dt (low season) for a (6-day) week.

Tabarka course is set in more than 100 ha of pine and oak forest between the sea and the coastal hills. Designed by the Ronald Fream Group, it comprises an 18-hole layout (6,306 m off medal tees and a 9-hole golf school course of 1,400m. The course, adjacent to the new Tabarka Montazah Tourist complex with reasonable hotels, is managed by *Golf Montazah Tabarka*, Route Touristique, El Morjane, 8110 Tabarka, T78644028-38, F78644026.

Carthage (La Soukra) Course is situated close to the Tunis international airport at La Soukra. The par-66 18-hole course ranges from 4,432 m to 3,682 m according to choice of tee. There is a practice course and club house, and the club runs amateur competitions throughout the year. Course is only 10 km from downtown Tunis and 3 km from the beach hotels at Raoued and Gammarth. Contact *Golf de Carthage*, Chotrana 2, 2036 La Soukra, T71765919, F71765915.

El Kantaoui Golf Course is another Ronald Fream course, opened in 1979, set in 100 ha of slightly undulating olive groves which a drop right down to the sea front at El Kantaoui. The 27 holes (9,576 m off championship tees) are arranged in three 9-hole loops with a further 9 holes planned. Practice and driving range areas attached to the club, modern clubhouse. Plenty of large beach hotels nearby. Contact *Golf El Kantaoui*, Station Touristique d'El Kantaoui, 4089 Kantaoui, Hammam Sousse, T73241500, F73241755.

Djerba Golf Club is set by the sea shore as an 18-hole links championship complex, designed by Martin Hawtree (UK). It works in combination with an adjacent 9-hole intermediate course. The par-73 course (6,310 m) begins in a 9-hole loop through palms close to the sea, in which the 500 m par-5 7th hole runs through dunes. A second loop, with three par-5s, passes through a desert environment of palms and rocky outcrops. The clubhouse has a restaurant, bar and golf shop. The club is in Zone Touristique 4116 Midoun, Djerba, T75659055, F75659051.

Golf Citrus, northwest of Hammamet, is a large course (160 ha) in flat country covered in olive and citrus groves and with six small lakes. Built in the early 1990s, it comprises two Fream-designed 18-hole courses, the more challenging *La Forêt* (par 72, 6,175m) and the moderately testing *Les Oliviers* (par 72, 6,178 m), classified as moderately testing. There is also a 9-hole, par-28 executive course. All the usual facilties. Handicap requirement is 36. Management at *Citrus Golf*, BP 132, 8050 Hammamet, T72226500, F72226400.

Golf

Essentials

Tunisian golf courses

Essentials

★ Five top swimming spots

Long stretches of beach in Sousse and Hammamet, Monastir and Djerba are lined with tourist hotels. Finding somewhere that bit more interesting to swim requires an effort. The increasing numbers of Tunisians with cars means that beaches which were once used by locals get full in summer. Try the following:

- **Cap Serrat, north coast.** Track leads down to pleasant beach backed by eucalyptus trees. Quite busy in summer, however. Beware undertow.
- **Aïn Damous, Bizerte.** Long sandy beach on a north-facing coast outside Bizerte. Access is by a long track through the forest. Rarely crowded, even in summer. Between Tunis and Bizerte, try also the beaches at Sounine (rocky), near Ras Djebel and at Kalaât el Andalous (long and windy).
- **Haouaria.** Two fine options. Swimming in deep water off the rocks below the Roman quarries (north-west facing) or from sandy beach near the new port (south-east facing).
- **Tazerka.** Long sandy beach north of Nabeul.
- **Monastir.** In addition to the narrow sandy beach at Skanès, there is some interesting swimming off the small rocky peninsula just beyond the Marina.

Yasmine Golf Course, Hammamet, is located just to the north of the Citrus course. This is another Ronald Fream design, on a lightly wooded 80 ha site with two lakes. It has a full 18-hole course and 9 training holes tucked into the centre of the complex together with a practice tee. The 18-hole championship course (par 72, 6,115 m) has five separate teeing areas. Notably difficult holes are the par-5 10th (540 m), with its adjacent lake and bunkers, and the angled 15th (490 m). Contact *Golf Yasmine* Course, BP 61, Hammamet 8050, T72227665, F72226722.

Palm Links Monastir are located on the dunes between Sousse and Monastir, roughly half an hour's drive south of Port El Kantaoui. Less well-known than its neighbours to the north and south, the par-72, 18-hole course (6,140 m) is nonetheless worth a visit. There is a golf school on a 9-hole course and a 360 degree driving range and practice area are available. Contact: T73521910, F73521913.

Monastir Golf Course is among scattered olive groves on the coast outside Monastir in slightly broken country. The course is 6,140 m in length (18 holes, par 72) with a choice of five tees per hole. There is a 3-hole training course, practice area and driving range. Popular for golf holidays with a number of beginners and advanced courses running for 3-6 days. Location convenient for hotels at Port El Kantaoui, Sousse and Monastir. Contact *Golf de Monastir*, Route de Ouardanine, BP 168 – 5000 Monastir, T73500283, F73500285.

Hang-gliding Activities used to be based at Jebel Ressas, southeast of Tunis. Following an accident, the club was abandoned. Hang-gliders continue to fly off the mountain, however.

Horse riding & camel trekking Beach resorts may have horses for hire for a trot along the beach. Most will be open from March to September only. Resort with the best reputation for horse riding is probably Mahdia. There are also a couple of stables in the *zone touristique*, Tabarka. Try *Equitation Golf Beach*, T78671816. On Djerba, there is a small private riding club opposite the entrance to the *Hotel Dar Djerba*. There are projects under discussion to get long-distance pony trekking under way in the northwest (Tabarka) region. The *Belvédère Park*, Tunis, has a small pony club with ring (signposted). More advanced riders can try the *Club Hippique* at La Soukra in the vicinity of Tunis, although this is more for jumping than anything else. Also in the Tunis area, try the stables near the *Hotel Molka* at Raoued. For horse racing, head for the hippodrome at Ksar Saïd, in the northwest Tunis suburbs.

Camel trekking is an up-and-coming activity. Douz, close to the dunes of the Grand Erg Oriental, is the best base. It is possible to set up one-night trips into the desert. To really slow down, you need rather longer. Four nights of bivouac gives you the feel. Try Douz Voyages, T75470178 or ask around in the little grocers shops in nearby Zaâfrane. There are lots of new travel agencies in Douz offering treks of varying lengths, so shop around. The principle is that you walk alongside the camel for a lot of the time. You get up early to start walking. There is a short halt for lunch. On the whole, camp is pitched early, too. In the evenings, your guides will prepare a meal around an open fire and probably some desert-bread, baked in hot embers. Note that it gets very cold in the desert in winter, so bring a good sleeping bag. At New Year, the desert is popular with the German and Italian off-road brigade, so don't be surprised if the peace of your desert is shattered by the roar of all-terrain vehicles and bikes.

Sand yachting/ land yachting On the dunes and on Chott el Djerid organized in Tozeur. Best season November-May. Ask at hotels in Tozeur for details. May also be possible on Djerba, ask at the Syndicat d'initiative in Houmt Souk.

Tennis Large tourist complexes will have courts of varying quality. Some complexes have a large number of courts. *Cap Carthage* in Tunis has 30, *Club Mediterranée* on Djerba has 20. In Tunis, try the Club de Tennis on Rue Alain Savary, near the Belvédère, also the Club de Tennis de Carthage, near the Hannibal TGM station, which also has a popular restaurant, *Le Tie-Break*.

Watersports All the beach resorts will have windsurfing (*planche à voile*) and parascending. Sailing is less popular, though the marina at Sidi Bou Saïd has a small club. Best windsurfing is probably off the windier coasts of Bizerte and Tabarka.

Yachting There are 30 ports and anchorages varying from 5 to 380 berths. The main pleasure ports are Port el Kantaoui, Hammamet-Yasmine, Monastir, Sidi Bou Saïd and Tabarka. See map below.

Entry regulations and information Except in cases of *force majeure* which must be proved, any pleasure craft arriving by sea from a foreign point of departure may only berth in a harbour where there is a customs station and a police station.

Upon arrival at the port all persons on board must show their passports and complete individual registration cards. Moreover, with regard to personal safety of the persons on board, the harbour police may request that a list of equipment be completed and deposited at the harbour police office on each occasion that a pleasure craft puts to sea.

On entering any Tunisian port, any foreign vessel should be flying its national flag and the flag of Tunisia on the rear mast and at the brow, so that they are easily visible. Immediately upon entry the owner/user of the vessel must present himself at the customs office with all

Essentials

Yacht anchorages

necessary registration and identity papers. The other occupants must remain on board until entry formalities are complete and a certificate of free circulation has been granted. This certificate allows use of Tunisian territorial waters without further formalities until departure for another country at which time the certificate will be surrendered.

Cats and dogs must have a certificate of health and anti-rabies vaccination dated within the last six months.

Fishing is authorized by the regional offices of the Commissariat General à la Pêche located at all coastal ports.

Documents and charts which are highly recommended: French Hydrographic Service maps no 7014, 5017, 4314, 4315, 4316, 4244 and 4245.

Forecasts may be obtained from the marine weather centres at La Goulette, Sfax, Mahdia and Bizerte and from the harbour master's office at Sidi Bou Saïd, El Kantaoui and Monastir where marine weather reports, wind strength warnings, special weather reports (gale warnings) and daily marine weather forecasts are available. In addition all Tunisian national radio stations broadcast daily weather reports.

Weather notes for sailors During winter the Tunisian coast is in the depression track between the Azores and Siberian anticyclones. In summer the Azores high stretches east bringing good weather with steady breezes to an otherwise sheltered coast. In particular: the northeast coast as far as Bizerte commonly experiences winds from the northwest to west and occasionally from northeast to east. On all coasts the winds become very variable nearer to land. In summer the prevailing wind alternates from west to north with sea breezes blowing east to northeast.

On the eastern coast winds from the east prevail during the summer and are almost always moderate (forces 2 to 4). The occasional winds from the southeast can reach force 5 and cause heavy seas. Sirocco winds from the south may affect all sectors of the Tunisia coast. They are usually short-lived but can be strong and unpredictable. The southeast coastline is affected by major tides, with a difference between high and low water of approximately 1.8 m at Gabès and 1.4 m at Sfax.

Health

There are many well qualified doctors in Tunisia, all of whom speak French. The majority will understand basic English, and often speak it quite well. The availability of medical care does however diminish somewhat away from big cities. However, at least you can be reasonably sure that local practitioners have a lot of experience with the particular diseases of their region. A pharmacy or a large hotel should be able to provide you with names of recommended doctors (*médecins généralistes*). Hopefully, you will not need any more medical care than this. In cases of emergency, a large town will have an *SOS Médecins* or *SAMU* emergency service (call outs cost around 25Dt a call out). Note that the private *policliniques* generally offer far better (and more expensive) service than the public hospitals, which can be terribly overcrowded.

If you are a long way from medical help, a certain amount of self medication may be necessary and you will find that many of the drugs that are available have familiar names. However, always check the date stamping and buy from reputable pharmacists because the shelf life of some items, especially vaccines and antibiotics is markedly reduced in hot conditions.

With the following precautions and advice you should keep as healthy as usual. Make local enquiries about health risks if you are apprehensive. For completeness sake, the present section includes health risks for Libya.

Emergency medical numbers

Private doctor on call service (SAMU or
Médecins de garde)

Emergencies = les Urgences

Tunis Allô Docteur T71780000; Night calls
T71371802; Clinique St Augustin
T71783033, T71791093, T71785216
Bizerte Pharmacie de nuit T72439545
Le Kef Clinique Jugurtha T78204214,
T78202611
Tabarka SAMU T78673655/653;
Polyclinique Sidi Moussa
T78671200/78670312
Hammamet Emergencies, on Nabeul road
T72282333
Sousse Clinique Les Oliviers, on Route

touristique T73242711; Night calls
T73224444
Monastir T73241919
Kairouan Clinique Laouni T77230444
Sfax SAMU T74241894
Gabès Clinique Bon Secours T75271400,
Clinique Boulbaba T75280800
Gafsa Main hospital T76221200
Douz Regional hospital T75470323
Tozeur Regional hospital T76450400
Tataouine Regional hospital
T76860690/003
Djerba Clinique El Yasmine T75652032.
If stuck at night, get a taxi to take you to
the Pharmacie de nuit or a Clinique
privée. The Night Pharmacy should have
numbers of doctors and clinics.

Before you go

Take out medical insurance. You should have a dental check up, get spare glasses and,
if you suffer from a longstanding condition such as diabetes, high blood pressure,
heart/lung disease or a nervous disorder, arrange for a check up with your doctor who
can at the same time provide you with a letter explaining details of your disability (in
English and French). Check the current practice for malaria prevention.

Smallpox vaccination is no longer required. Neither is cholera vaccination, and there **Inoculations**
have been no outbreaks of the disease for years in Tunisia. Yellow fever vaccination is
not required for either Tunisia or Libya. Cholera vaccine is not effective which is the
main reason for not recommending it.

The following vaccinations are recommended:
Typhoid (monovalent): one dose followed by a booster in 1 month's time. Immunity
from this course lasts 2-3 years. Other injectable types are now becoming available as
are oral preparations marketed in some countries.
Poliomyelitis: this is a live vaccine, generally given orally and the full course consists
of 3 doses with a booster in tropical regions every 3-5 years.
Tetanus: 1 dose should be given with a booster at 6 weeks and another at 6 months
and 10 yearly boosters thereafter are recommended.
Children: should, in addition, be properly protected against diphtheria, whooping
cough, mumps and measles. Teenage girls, if they have not yet had the disease, should
be given rubella (German measles) vaccination. Consult your doctor for advice on BCG
inoculation against tuberculosis. The disease is still common in the region. North Africa
lies mainly outside the meningitis belt and the disease is probably no more common
than at home so vaccination is not indicated except during an epidemic.

Essentials

On the road

Infectious hepatitis (jaundice) This is common throughout North Africa, though less so in Tunisia and Libya. It seems to be frequently caught by travellers probably because, coming from countries with higher standards of hygiene, they have not contracted the disease in childhood and are therefore not immune like the majority of adults in developing countries. The main symptoms are stomach pains, lack of appetite, nausea, lassitude and yellowness of the eyes and skin. Medically speaking there are 2 types: the less serious, but more common, is hepatitis A for which the best protection is careful preparation of food, the avoidance of contaminated drinking water and scrupulous attention to toilet hygiene. Human normal immunoglobulin (gammaglobulin) confers considerable protection against the disease and is particularly useful in epidemics. It should be obtained from a reputable source and is certainly recommended for travellers who intend to live rough. The injection should be given as close as possible to your departure and, as the dose depends on the likely time you are to spend in potentially infected areas, the manufacturer's instructions should be followed. A new vaccination against hepatitis A is now generally available and probably provides much better immunity for 10 years but is more expensive, being 3 separate injections.

The other more serious version is hepatitis B which is acquired as a sexually transmitted disease, from a blood transfusion or injection with an unclean needle or possibly by insect bites. The symptoms are the same as hepatitis A but the incubation period is much longer.

You may have had jaundice before or you may have had hepatitis of either type before without becoming jaundiced, in which case it is possible that you could be immune to either hepatitis A or B. This immunity can be tested for before you travel. If you are not immune to hepatitis B already, a vaccine is available (3 shots over 6 months) and if you are not immune to hepatitis A already then you should consider vaccination (or gamma globulin if you are not going to be exposed for long).

Meningitis This is not a significant risk in Tunisia. Protection against meningococcal meningitis A and C is conferred by a vaccine which is freely available.

AIDS (Sida) In North Africa AIDS is probably less common than in most of Europe and North America but is presumably increasing in its incidence, though not as rapidly as in Sub-Saharan Africa, South America or Southeast Asia. Having said that, the spread of the disease has not been well documented in the North African region; the real picture is unclear. The disease is possibly still mainly confined to the well known high risk sections of the population i.e. gay men, intravenous drug abusers, prostitutes and children of infected mothers. Whether heterosexual transmission outside these groups is common or not, the main risk to travellers is from casual sex. The same precautions should be taken as when encountering any sexually transmitted disease.

The AIDS virus (HIV) can be passed via unsterile needles which have been previously used to inject an HIV positive patient but the risk of this is very small indeed. It would, however, be sensible to check that needles have been properly sterilized or disposable needles used. A private clinic in Tunisia will probably be using disposable needles anyway – but check. The chance of picking up hepatitis B in this way is much more of a danger. Be wary of carrying disposable needles yourself. Custom officials may find them suspicious. The risk of receiving a blood transfusion with blood infected with the HIV virus is greater than from dirty needles because of the amount of fluid exchanged. Supplies of blood for transfusion are now largely screened for HIV in all reputable hospitals so the risk must be very small indeed. Catching the AIDS virus does not necessarily produce an illness in itself; the only way to be sure if you feel you have been put at risk is to have a blood test for HIV antibodies on your return home.

Full acclimatization to high temperatures takes about 2 weeks and during this period it is normal to feel a degree of apathy, especially if the relative humidity is high. Drink plenty of water (up to 15 litres a day are required when working physically hard in hot, dry conditions), use salt on your food and avoid extreme exertion. Tepid showers are more cooling than hot or cold ones. Large hats do not cool you down but prevent sunburn. Remember that, especially in the mountains, there can be a large and sudden drop in temperature between sun and shade and between night and day so dress accordingly. Clear desert nights can prove astoundingly cold with a rapid drop in temperature as the sun goes down. Loose fitting cotton clothes are still the best for hot weather; warm jackets and woollens are essential after dark in some desert areas, and especially at high altitude.

Desert heat & cold

These can be a great nuisance. (In other parts of Africa, some are carriers of serious diseases such as malaria and yellow fever.) When camping out, the best way of keeping insects away at night is to sleep off the ground with a mosquito net and to burn mosquito coils containing Pyrethrum. Aerosol sprays or a 'flit' gun may be effective as are those little plug-in anti-mosquito devices. (Check that you have enough 'mats' for your stay, and note that Tunisia uses twin rounded pin plugs like those in France. Do you have an adaptor?)

Insects

You can use personal insect repellent, the best of which contain a high concentration of Diethyltoluamide. Liquid is best for arms and face (take care around eyes and make sure you do not dissolve the plastic of your spectacles). Aerosol spray on clothes and ankles deters mites and ticks. Liquid DET suspended in water can be used to impregnate cotton clothes and mosquito nets. Wide mesh mosquito nets are now available impregnated with an insecticide called Permethrin and are generally more effective, lighter to carry and more comfortable to sleep in. If you are bitten, itching may be relieved by cool baths and anti-histamine tablets (care with alcohol or driving) corticosteroid creams (great care – never use if any hint of sepsis) or by judicious scratching. Calamine lotion and cream have limited effectiveness and anti-histamine creams have a tendency to cause skin allergies and are therefore not generally recommended. Bites which become infected (commonly in dirty and dusty places) should be treated with a local antiseptic or antibiotic cream such as Cetrimide as should infected scratches. Skin infestations with body lice, crabs and scabies are unfortunately easy to pick up. Use Gamma benzene hexachloride for lice and Benzyl benzoate for scabies. Crotamiton cream (Eurax) alleviates itching and also kills a number of skin parasites. Malathion lotion 5 is good for lice but avoid the highly toxic full strength Malathion used as an agricultural insecticide.

Practically nobody escapes this one so be prepared for it. Some of these countries lead the world in their prevalence of diarrhoea. Most of the time intestinal upsets are due to the insanitary preparation of food. Do not eat uncooked fish or vegetables or meat (especially pork), fruit with the skin on (always peel your fruit yourself) or food that is exposed to flies. Eating large quantities of summer fruit such as grapes is not a good idea. Tap water is generally safe in large towns in Tunisia. Prefer bottled water, however – it is cheap and can save much misery. If your hotel has a central hot water supply this is safe to drink after cooling. Ice for drinks should be made from boiled water but rarely is, so stand your glass on the ice cubes, instead of putting them in the drink. Dirty water should first be strained through a filter bag (available from camping shops) and then boiled or treated. Bringing the water to a rolling boil at sea level is sufficient but at high altitude you have to boil the water for longer to ensure that all the microbes are killed. Various sterilising methods can be used and there are proprietary preparations containing chlorine or iodine compounds. Pasteurized or heat treated milk is now widely available as is icecream and yoghurt produced by the same methods.

Intestinal upsets

Essentials

Unpasteurized milk products including cheese and yoghurt are sources of tuberculosis, brucellosis, listeria and food poisoning germs. You can render fresh milk safe by heating it to 62°C for 30 mins followed by rapid cooling or by boiling it. Matured or processed cheeses are safer than fresh varieties.

Diarrhoea is usually the result of food poisoning, occasionally from contaminated water (including seawater when swimming near sewage outfalls). There are various causes – viruses, bacteria, protozoa (like amoeba) salmonella and cholera organisms. It may take one of several forms coming on suddenly, or rather slowly. It may be accompanied by vomiting or by severe abdominal pain and the passage of blood or mucus when it is called dysentery. Although your intestinal flora will adapt as you travel in Tunisia, you are at risk of getting diarrhoea when you eat poorly cooked food.

Diagnosis and treatment All kinds of diarrhoea, whether or not accompanied by vomiting, respond favourably to the replacement of water and salts taken as frequent small sips of some kind of rehydration solution. There are proprietary preparations consisting of sachets of powder which you dissolve in water or you can make your own by adding half a teaspoonful of salt (3.5 grams) and 4 tablespoonfuls of sugar (40 grams) to a litre of boiled water. If you can time the onset of diarrhoea to the minute, then it is probably viral or bacterial and/or the onset of dysentery. The treatment, in addition to rehydration, is Ciprofloxacin (widely available) 500 mgs every 12 hours.

If the diarrhoea has come on slowly or intermittently, then it is more likely to be protozoal i.e. caused by amoeba or giardia and antibiotics will have no effect. These cases are best treated by a doctor, as is any outbreak of diarrhoea continuing for more than 3 days. If there are severe stomach cramps, the following drugs may help: Loperamide (Imodium, Arret) and Diphenoxylate with Atropine (Lomotil).

Diarrhoea should be treated with lots of rest, fluid and salt replacement, antibiotics such as Ciprofloxacin for the bacterial types and special diagnostic tests and medical treatment for amoeba and giardia infections. Salmonella infections and cholera can be devastating diseases and it would be wise to get to a hospital as soon as possible if these were suspected. Note that fasting, peculiar diets and the consumption of large quantities of yoghurt have not been found useful in calming travellers' diarrhoea or in rehabilitating inflamed bowels. You should, however, avoid spicy foods and go for very plain couscous and/or rice.

Note that giving plenty of mineral water to drink plus rehydration salts has, especially in children, been a lifesaving technique. As there is some evidence that alcohol and milk might prolong diarrhoea, they should probably be avoided during and immediately after an attack. There are ways of preventing travellers' diarrhoea for short periods of time when visiting these countries by taking antibiotics but these are ineffective against viruses and, to some extent, against protozoa, so this technique should not be used other than in exceptional circumstances. Some preventives such as Enterovioform can have serious side effects if taken for long periods.

Diarrhoea can lead to you having a very sore and fragile-feeling stomach. In this case, powders taken mixed with mineral water ('stomach liners' or *pansement gastrique* in French) may be helpful. A pharmacy may sell you Actapulgite powder (Laboratoires Beaufour), which is effective in calming gastric pains and diarrhoea 'avec météorisme'.

Avoiding diarrhoea Always be careful what you drink – go for mineral water and fizzy drinks. Beware unwashed fruit. If you are going to be travelling in remote areas, carry Lomotil or Imodium, a powder to calm stomach pains (Actapulgite or equivalent) and an anti-bacterial drug like Intétrix, available at pharmacies throughout Tunisia. Self-medication is not a good thing, but sometimes needs must. If symptoms persist, see a doctor as quickly as possible when you get to a town.

First time exposure to countries where sections of the population live in extreme poverty can cause odd psychological reactions in visitors. Incessant pestering can be especially trying for women. You just have to be prepared for this and try not to over react. It is also oppressive for women to travel in towns where the local women have such a limited public presence. Travelling for a long period of time in a place where your first language is not spoken can also be a strain. Remember, they're not trying to be unhelpful, it may just be too difficult for them to make sense of your limited and approximate French or Arabic.

Mental pressures

If you are unlucky enough to be bitten by a venomous snake, spider, scorpion, lizard, centipede or sea creature try (within limits) to catch the animal for identification. The reactions to be expected are fright, swelling, pain and bruising around the bite, soreness of the regional lymph glands, nausea, vomiting and fever. If in addition any of the following symptoms supervene, get the victim to a doctor without delay: numbness, tingling of the face, muscular spasms, convulsions, shortness of breath or haemorrhage. Commercial snake bite or scorpion sting kits may be available but are only useful for the specific type of snake or scorpion for which they are designed. The serum has to be given intravenously, so is not much good unless you have had some practice in making injections into veins. If the bite is on a limb, immobilize it and apply a tight bandage between the bite and body, releasing it for 90 seconds every 15 minutes. Reassurance of the bitten person is very important because death by snake bite is in fact very rare. Do not slash the bite area and try to suck out the poison because this kind of heroism does more harm than good. Hospitals usually hold stocks of snake bite serum. Best precaution: do not walk in snake territory with bare feet, sandals or shorts and watch where you sit. Snakes on the whole are more frightened of large galumphing animals like humans, and will tend to disappear as they approach.

Snake bites & other stings

In cheap hotels, avoid spiders and scorpions by keeping your bed away from the wall and look under lavatory seats and inside your shoes in the morning. In the rare event of being bitten, consult a doctor.

If swimming in an area where there are poisonous fish such as stone or scorpion fish (also called by a variety of local names) or sea urchins (*retzi/oursins*) on rocky coasts, tread carefully or wear plimsolls or jellyshoes. The sting of such fish is intensely painful but can be helped by immersing the stung part in water as hot as you can bear for as long as it remains painful. This is not always very practical and you must take care not to scald yourself but it does work. Otherwise head for a GP to get a painkilling shot. In areas such as Hammamet where the weaver fish (*bilum* in Arabic, *vive* in French) hides in the sand in shallow water, with just its spine protruding for you to step on, local pharmacies stock the relevant painkillers.

Beach nasties

The burning power of the sun in Tunisia and Libya is phenomenal, especially in the desert. Strong sunlight may damage exposed skin. In the short term, burning can be severe, and even dangerous to children and some adults. There may also be a long term risk of skin cancer and certain individuals, if exposure is prolonged or repeated, are potentially at risk. Those with very fair skin, especially with blonde or red hair and those who hardly tan should be particularly careful about protecting themselves. Babies under 6 months should be kept out of the sun as much as possible. Try to avoid the beach between 2300 and 1500 when the burning power of the sun is at its height.

Sunburn & heat stroke

Normal temperate zone suntan lotions (protection factor up to 7) are not much good. You need to use the types designed specifically for the tropics or for mountaineers or skiers with an SPF, sun protection factor (against UVA) of between 7 and 15. Certain creams also protect against UVB and you should use these if you have a skin prone to burning. Glare from the sun can cause conjunctivitis so wear sunglasses, especially on the beach.

Protective clothing including a lightweight hat is a useful precaution and essential for children. The closely knitted fabric made from 80 percent polymide and 20 percent elastane will help protect a child's skin from damage. Be sure to apply sun lotion every 1 to 2 hours especially after swimming and towel drying. Sprays and roll-on sun screen products make putting lotion on more fun and are easier for children to use.

There are several varieties of heat stroke. The most common cause is severe dehydration. Avoid this by drinking lots of non-alcoholic fluid and adding some salt if you wish.

Other afflictions

Athletes foot and other fungal infections are best treated by exposure to sunshine and a proprietary preparation such as Tolnaftate. **Filariasis** causing such diseases as elephantiasis occurs in Mauritania and again is transmitted by mosquito. **Intestinal worms** do occur in insanitary areas and the more serious ones, such as hook-worm, can be contracted by walking bare foot on infested earth or beaches. **Leishmaniasis** causing a skin ulcer which will not heal is also present in most of the North African countries. It is transmitted by sand flies. **Prickly heat** is a common itchy rash avoided by frequent washing and by wearing loose clothing. It can be helped by the regular use of talcum powder to allow the skin to dry thoroughly after washing. **Rabies** is endemic throughout Tunisia. Remote rural communities invariably seem to have savage dogs in their vicinity. Their main role is to guard sheep and goats, however, they can go beserk as an outsider goes by on a bike. If you are bitten by a domestic animal, try to see a doctor at once. Treatment with human diploid vaccine is now extremely effective and worth seeking out if the likelihood of having contracted rabies is high. A course of anti-rabies vaccine might be a good idea before you go. In any case, steer clear of rough looking dogs.

When you get home

If you have had attacks of diarrhoea, it is worth having a stool specimen tested in case you have picked up amoebic dysentery. If you have been living rough, a blood test may be worthwhile to detect worms and other parasites.

Tunis and around

3

Tunis and around

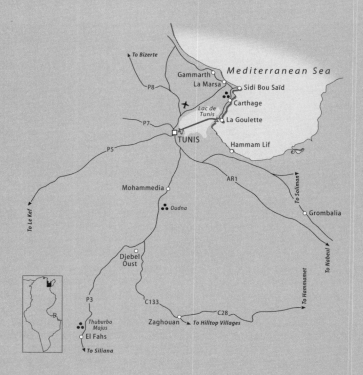

Tunis is the heart of modern Tunisia, the political capital and centre of economic life. Today's visitor comes to a Mediterranean city with sprawling suburbs – and some notable places to visit. Central Tunis has a dual core: the old town or **médina** is the original Muslim settlement, while next to it, on reclaimed land, is a fine city of boulevards and modern buildings. The **Bardo Museum** houses the world's finest collection of Roman mosaics. To the northeast of Tunis lies a string of beachside suburbs, including **Carthage** (also with a fine museum with objects from Punic and Roman times), and the whitewashed houses of **Sidi Bou Saïd**, everybody's favourite Mediterranean village. Going southwest from Tunis, the visitor keen on all things ancient may also want to visit the Roman sites of **Uthina** and **Thuburbo Majus** and view the grandiose remains of **Hadrian's Aqueduct**. Walkers and birdwatchers can climb twin-peaked **Boukornine** or the brooding **Djebel Ressas**. There are plenty of easy day excursions to small towns of Andalusian ancestry like **Zaghouan**, or one-time Berber villages like **Takrouna**, **Jeradou**, and **abandoned Zriba el Ulya**, also easily visited as day excursions from **Hammamet**.

Tunis تونس

Phone code: 71
Colour map 2, grid B3
Population: 1,200,000

Tunis is a major Mediterranean city. It is often visited by tourists on daytrips up from one of the resort towns. However, to cover the city and its main sites comfortably, you really need a couple of days: a morning could be spent at the Bardo Museum, with an afternoon strolling in the médina, including a visit to the Dar Ben Abdallah Museum; a second day, with lots of walking, would allow you to take in the numerous scattered sites of ancient Carthage, along with a visit to the bijou clifftop village of Sidi Bou Saïd.

Ins and outs

Getting there

See Transport, page 114, for further details and Airport information in Essentials, page 32

Arriving by air, you will come into the busy Aéroport de Tunis-Carthage, situated 7 km outside the city. (There are ATMs, also bureaux de change, in the baggage hall and in the main concourse. **NB** Late night arrivals will find the latter closed.) To reach the *centre ville (wust el-bled)*, where most hotels are located, the fastest option is to take a taxi from the stand just outside the airport exit. This should not cost more than 4Dt, although the driver may want more 'for baggage'. Beware of the unofficial taxis without meters. Another option is to take bus 35 that stops on Av Habib Bourguiba by *Tunisair*. The airport bus *normally* runs every 30 mins day and night, but from 2400 to 0600 there is only 1 every hr.

Coming in by train, there is only 1 main station, located on the Pl Barcelone (numerous cheap hotels nearby). By bus, you will come in at 1 of 2 stations: the Gare routière Sud at Bab Alioua (for all destinations south) is 15 mins walk from the city centre; to reach the city centre from the Gare routière Nord (coming from Bizerte and the northwest), you need to take either a green tram (for Station République), taxi or bus 3. Arriving by louage (shared taxi) from the south you will come in at the Moncef Bey louage station, 10 mins walk from the central avenue. Louages from the Cap Bon bring you into another station at Bab Alioua, again only 10-15 mins from the main areas of low-cost hotels at Bab Jedid and the city centre.

If you have hired a car, you will probably drive up the autoroute into Tunis from the south. Try not to arrive to coincide with the rush hour, when the traffic is hectic around Bab Alioua, the Blvd du 9-Avril and all roads heading northwards running to the west of the city centre.

Coming in by ship to the port at La Goulette, your cheapest option is to take the TGM light railway into the city (see La Goulette, page 119, for further details). Otherwise a taxi across the causeway is the fastest option.

Getting around

In terms of transport there are 3 options: overcrowded buses, the efficient light metro network, and yellow taxis. The Ville Nouvelle and the médina can be easily covered on foot. The Av H Bourguiba is the main street, leading up to the médina at its western end. It is crossed at right angles by the Av de Carthage/Av de Paris which leads up to République metro station. You will need to make use of public transport or taxi to get to the Bardo Museum and the northern coastal suburbs. The Bardo is easily reached by taxi (say 2.5Dt) or by green metro (line 4 from République station). Carthage and the coast are easily reached by the TGM (Tunis-Goulette-Marsa) light railway, whose terminus is at the eastern end of Av H Bourguiba. The train takes just over 30 mins to get to Carthage.

The yellow and white SNT buses are often crowded, but run to most destinations. There are private bus lines (green and white TGV and blue and yellow TUT) serving the more upmarket destinations like La Marsa, the Menzahs and El Manar.

24 hours in Tunis

With a hire car (or good luck with taxis) the very, very energetic traveller can cover the main cultural sites of Tunis and its northern suburbs in a packed 24 hours. In the summer, the damp heat would make 48 hours more realistic.

Get an early start at the national archaeological museum, the **Bardo**. Focus on the spectacular collection of Roman mosaics on the first floor, enjoy the architecture of a late-19th-century palace. Then head for the Kasbah for a rapid walking tour down into the souks of the **Médina** or old town. Lunch at one of the tiny restaurants near the Great Mosque. Cut down to the **Ville Nouvelle** (fine examples of early-20th-century architecture) and the **Avenue Habib Bourguiba**, heart of modern Tunis, probably crowded with office workers and school kids on their lunch break. Drink stop at a café terrace. Down the avenue to take the TGM light rail or a taxi to the northern suburbs. Ask for the *banlieue nord* (northern suburbs) and Musée de Carthage.

The sites of **Carthage** are scattered and much less spectacular than the excavated Roman cities of Tunisia's northern interior. Best view of the Carthage region is from esplanade of the Museum next to the former Basilica of St Louis. Museum visit optional if you've done the Bardo thoroughly. Then another taxi or the TGM to **Sidi Bou Saïd**, everyone's favourite bijou Mediterranean village. Stroll and view, take mint tea with pine nuts or almonds at the *Café Sidi Chabaâne*, then another stroll down to the port. Those with much cash will taxi to **La Marsa** for evening meal at *Le Cinquante Cinq* or further on to **Gammarth** for either *Le Golfe* or *Les Ombrelles*, both right on the seafront. Cheaper is *Arthé* at **La Marsa**. Also cheap and very cheerful is the *Café Tam-Tam* in Sidi Bou Saïd near the TGM station. Then back up the hill to the *Café des Nattes* for a final *thé bil-bunduk* (tea with pine nuts). An **evening promenade** near *Café Saf-Saf* at La Marsa is agreeable in summer.

Tunis and around

The tourist information offices are: *Tunisian National Tourist Office*, 1 Av Mohammed V (Pl de l'Afrique), T341077, F350997. Open 0730-1330 summer, 0830-1200 and 1500-1800 winter, closed Sun and public holidays. Not very helpful, but they may have a few illustrated brochures to hand out. **Tourist information**

Tunis is best visited in spring, autumn and early winter. The summer is oppressively hot and humid, and the city centre and its traffic best avoided at this time. Jan and Feb can be cold and damp and the days are short for sightseeing. **Best time to visit**

History

The history of Tunis, so close to Carthage, goes back to Punic times. In all likeliood there were Punic and later Roman settlements on the site of present-day Tunis. Roman and later architectural detailing recycled in the old town's buildings is just one indication of this. However, in ancient times, Tunis was a small settlement in the shadow of neighbouring Carthage, centre of the maritime Punic Empire in the western Mediterranean and later capital of the Roman province of Africa. For the whole of the 850-year period of Roman rule, Tunis was an unimportant satellite settlement, and the Latin sources make no mention of its even having made it to the status of *municipium*, a Roman town with some degree of self-rule.

Roman settlement However, the hinterland of Carthage, including the rich farmland of the Mornag plain to the south, was settled by Roman colonists, square blocks of land being allocated on the basis of careful surveying. Smaller settlements, like Tunis, were fitted into this grid, and some recent research sees that there is a correspondence between the street lines of the central médina of Tunis and those of a Roman *colonia*. Around the Zitouna Mosque, street intersections every 240 Roman feet can be identified.

A defensive site Thus the Muslim Arab invaders of the late seventh century took on a settlement which was already many hundreds of years old. They were no doubt seeking to establish a strong point in the central Mediterranean, but rather than settle in coastal Carthage, they opted for Tunis. The location, a low hill, several kilometres away from the Mediterranean, gave better protection from any marauding Byzantine fleets; from the western, land side, the site has protection in the form of a scarp slope overlooking a *sebkha* or salt lake, fed by winter rainfall. In addition, at Tunis the water table had the advantage of being close to the surface, making the construction of wells easy.

Subsequently, the médina was to grow in importance under a series of Islamic dynasties. As of the mid-19th century, the modern town of Tunis was

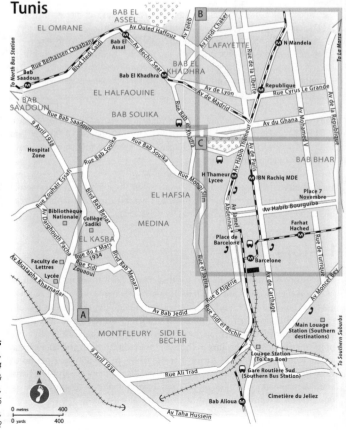

Tunis

Detail maps
A Tunis Médina,
page 74
B Belvédère &
Lafayette,
page 106
C Tunis centre,
page 102

laid out between the médina and the shallow Lac de Tunis, beginning the changes which were to lead to the central areas of the old town becoming a focus for the leisure and tourism industries. The Great Mosque Ezzitouna at the heart of the médina retained its role as the city's, and indeed the country's, religious centre.

The Aghlabids

The history of early Muslim dynasties and their struggles for power and influence – like that of Medieval dynasties in Europe, for that matter – is not easy to follow. In the eighth and ninth centuries, Islam had not yet assumed the definitive form it was to acquire under the Abbasids in 10th-century Baghdad. Fragile, warring Islamic dynasties in North Africa, though they had the advantages of the power vacuum left by the declining Byzantines and the fact that the Berber tribes were organized on an extremely localized basis, faced problems of communicating over huge distances and an eventual resurgence of Byzantine power. It was important for the new religion to stamp its presence on the region – hence the development of impressive mosques like the Ezzitouna in Tunis under the Aghlabids (794-905). The anarchy which had characterized the late eighth century was ended by the dynasty's founder, Ibrahim Ibn Al-Aghlab, and his successors were able to maintain the peace. There began a period of considerable artistic and architectural development, and it was under Abu Ibrahim Ahmad (856-863) that the Ezzitouna Mosque in Tunis was restored.

Hafsid Tunis (1230-1574)

It was under the rule of the Hafsid Dynasty (1230-1574) that Tunis blossomed, with more than 100,000 inhabitants within its walls. The geographer and philosopher Ibn Khaldoun (1232-1406) was born during this period in Tunis. During the 13th and 14th centuries, the central part of the old city reached its present size. The town grew important through trade with southern Europe, and as a centre of Malikite learning. The Hafsid sultans, originally vassals of the Almohads, had to establish their legitimacy to rule, and one way to do this was through the strengthening of Islamic orthodoxy. They founded a number of *medresas* or colleges where students of religion and law at the Zitouna Mosque were housed. By building a power base among a scholar class, the Hafsids thus hoped to counter the potentially dangerous leadership of soufi saints based in the countryside.

The 16th century, Ottoman & Habsburg conflict

Between 1534 and 1574 the town went through a period of turbulence. The Mediterranean was the theatre of fierce conflicts between the expansionist European powers and the Ottoman Turks, defenders of Islam. The city was first attacked by Kherredine Pasha, better known as the pirate Barbarossa, then captured by the Algerians and subsequently by Don Juan of Austria. It was only with the Turkish invasion, in 1574, that a period of calm returned. The influx of 80,000 Muslim refugees from Andalusia at the start of the 17th century gave a renewed vitality to the city and its surroundings. The Andalusians were skilled farmers, and gave a new impetus to the *chéchia* industry (the manufacture of the felt headgear that was exported throughout the Mediterranean for over three centuries).

Tunis was thus the capital of a minor Ottoman province. Links with Istanbul were always weak, however, and in the course of the 17th century, a local dynasty emerged in the form of the descendants of a corsair adventurer. By the early 18th century, the citizens of Tunis had had enough of dynastic infighting, and they called upon one Hussein Ben Ali to restore peace and order. By the end of the 18th century, his descendants had established dynastic rule.

Cosmopolitan Tunis: 1800-1950 In the early 19th century, the beys (as the rulers of Tunisia were called) did their best to keep up with the changes taking place on the northern side of the Mediterranean. The dangers facing the country became all the more apparent after the occupation of Algiers by France in 1830 and the increasing competition between the colonial powers. Despite the reforms initiated by Ahmed Bey (1837-55), and the efforts of reforming minister Kheïredine Pacha in the second half of the 19th century, pressure from the newly industrialiszing powers to the north grew. The city was to grow out of all recognition.

Epidemics in the early 19th century took a heavy toll among the local Muslim and Jewish populations. Even before the French declared their protectorate over Tunisia in 1881, there was an influx of Europeans. The Tunisian government granted concessions to Europeans in exchange for loans, and professional people moved in to manage the modern businesses. Poor Sicilian and Maltese immigrants provided the semi-skilled labour. A new neighbourhood began to take shape on reclaimed land to the east of the médina, the future *ville basse* or lower town. France built a fine new consulate (1860), and the foundations of the Cathedral of St Vincent de Paul were laid. A British company financed the construction of a railway to La Marsa between 1874-76.

Planning the Ville Nouvelle In the 1880s, the French hesitated as to whether they should continue to extend their *ville nouvelle* or new town to the east of the médina. After all, it had a reputation as an unsalubrious place, despite the sewage lines which had been put in by the Municipality founded in 1857. A new coastal location was felt to be suitable. Carthage was out of the question, given the proximity of a beylical palace. Radès, on the coast south of Tunis, would have been ideal. The strength of the Italian community made such a move impossible, however. The Italians had interests in a railway line linking Tunis to La Marsa and the La Goulette port. Italian interests, namely one Mme Fasciotti, also held the concession for rubble removal and dumping, an important operation given the amount of crumbling ramparts to be demolished and the value of the new infill land. Above all, the French had to placate Italian interests wherever possible, given the fact that the newly unified Kingdom of Italy had colonial designs too. Italian commercial interests had to be respected.

Thus the city centre of Tunis as we know it today was built on reclaimed land to the east of the old médina. Growth was rapid and one source mentions more than 800 new buildings going up between 1881 and 1894. As of 1860, the French had asserted economic authority in Tunisia. Between 1881 and 1900, they made their presence felt in physical terms. The old world of the médina, its people's lives codified by Muslim and Jewish law, was marginalized. The Europeans who had lived in the old town in the 1880s gradually moved out, eventually to be followed by the wealthier Muslim notables and the increasingly Europeanized Jews.

The main symbols of the new French protectorate were in place by the end of the 1890s: a new barracks at the Kasbah, completed 1898 (and today demolished), the cathedral, completely rebuilt by 1897, and, most importantly, the modern port, completed 1892.

In the first half of the 20th century, Tunis became a dual city. At its centre was the old town with its mosques and narrow streets. Around this old core spread the new town. Business was concentrated in the *ville basse*, new residential areas were created – leafy Montfleury, southwest of the médina, Lafayette, second home to the Jewish community with the large Art Déco Synagogue Daniel Osiris, the Cité Jardin and Mutuelleville.

By flying boat to Carthage

In 1922, the first regular air service between France and Tunisia was inaugurated with single-engined seaplanes carrying two passengers in an open cockpit. By 1932, the Air Union flying-boat company was running six flights a week from Marseilles to Tunis. The flight took six hours, carrying two pilots, a telegraphist, and six passengers at a top speed of 190 kph. There was a 45-minute pause for lunch and refuelling at Ajaccio. Also on the flights were baskets of carrier pigeons, just in case of radio problems. By 1932, the number of passengers carried annually had risen to 4,794 from a modest 140 intrepid travellers in 1922. Even the HE the Bey was to take a flight. Unfortunately however, the *hydravion* was felt to be uneconomic and its death knell was sounded by three-engined transport planes like the boneshaking Junkers 52. Nevertheless, right up to the Second World War flying boats continued to touch down on the lagoon at Kheïreddine. Passengers would disembark under the watchful eye of Air Union Tunis's commandant Monsieur Delavoye, a former naval officer turned *aéronaute* sporting a stylish Kitchener moustache. On the TGM light railway line linking Tunis to Carthage and La Marsa, there is still a station called 'Aéroport', a reminder of the days when air travel was something of an adventure, involving hours of sitting in wicker chairs, lulled by the drone of the aircraft engine.

Tunis was occupied by the Germans for six months during the Second World War. For both Axis and Allies, the city functioned as a staging post for supplies and troops. The port and parts of the city, notably Petite Sicile and the Kherba in the eastern médina, were bombarded. After the war, which wrought considerable damage in the Tunisian countryside, immigration from the rural areas increased dramatically. The population of the médina rose from 120,000 in 1936 to 230,000 in 1946. The Muslim bourgeoisie, increasingly westernized, sought homes in the new residential areas.

It was in the early 1950s that Tunis became a focus for an increasingly vocal nationalist movement. Happily, however, there was never any widespread violence. The independence movement was more of a pressure group formed by educated urban Tunisians, many of them from the Sahel. Independence was quickly conceded by France in 1956.

Since the mid-1950s, the population has risen from 400,000 to 1,200,000, resulting in vast expansion into the surrounding countryside, often at the expense of good farming land.

After independence, the Italian, Tunisian Jewish and French populations departed and the city's Muslim population acquired the property left behind at knock-down prices or by squatting. The movement of the old Tunisoise families out of the médina accelerated, and an influx of poor rural migrants brought about a huge change in the make-up of the oldest neighbourhoods. The great city residences were divided up as rooming houses or *oukalas*, in local parlance. **After Independence: demolition & expansion**

In the eyes of President Bourguiba, and indeed of many of the leading figures of the newly independent Tunisian Republic, the médina was a symbol of past oppressions, and as such was to be swept away. In the early 1960s, there were great schemes for opening up an avenue to extend the main Avenue Bourguiba as far as the Ezzitouna Mosque. In the event, nothing was done – the médina had far too many poor and potentially rebellious inhabitants, too costly to rehouse in one go. Numerous demolitions took place on the

Tunis and around

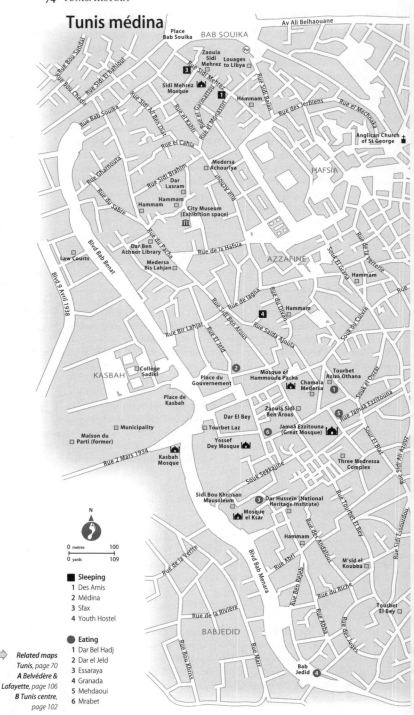

Tunis médina

Related maps
Tunis, page 70
A *Belvédère &*
Lafayette, page 106
B *Tunis centre*,
page 102

■ Sleeping
1 Des Amis
2 Médina
3 Sfax
4 Youth Hostel

● Eating
1 Dar Bel Hadj
2 Dar el Jeld
3 Essaraya
4 Granada
5 Mehdaoui
6 Mrabet

southern and western sides of the médina, however. The Kasbah barracks, most of the Sidi Abdallah gate and the walls from Bab el Assal at the northern end to the southern Bab el Fella were demolished and a modernist Maison du Parti constructed on the new Kasbah esplanade, while excavations of the site revealed traces of the original Hafsid fortress. (The finds were later replaced with a vast underground car park.)

The city centre also saw its share of new building. The 1950s saw the construction of the imposing Ministry of the Interior on the main avenue. Three large new hotels went up in the 1960s: the blue tower of the Hotel Africa, the distinctive inverted pyramid of the Hotel du Lac, and the bulky Hotel International, at the junction of the Avenue de Paris and the Avenue Bourguiba. The vast majority of old style apartment buildings survived, however. Meanwhile, vast new suburbs, often unplanned, were taking shape on the edge of the city.

Late 20th-century Tunis: the ever-expanding suburbs

Tunis in the late 20th century continued to grow. New residential areas appeared almost overnight. The most spectacular of the new neighbourhoods is the Berges du Lac, a new and rapidly expanding area built on land reclaimed from the lagoon which separates Tunis from its coastal suburbs. Tunis's first major shopping mall, the Lac Palace, is located here, and the business traveller may have call to visit clients in what is a neighbourhood. The Berges du Lac will more than double in size when the second phase of building is complete, linking up to Le Kram Ouest, home to the Foire Internationale de Tunis, the main trade fair complex. Despite its proximity to the noise and pollution of Tunis Carthage Airport, the Berges du Lac has attracted a lot of investment, and the area seems set to become the main business district, with banks remaining on the Avenue Mohamed V running from the old downtown area northwards towards the upmarket residential areas. Also relocating out to the Berges area are a number of embassies, including the USA embassy, now housed in bunker-like premises cleverly situated under the main flightpath into the airport. The British Embassy is apparently set to follow in 2004, abandoning its historic premises in the médina.

Like any other Mediterranean town, Tunis is increasingly segregated in socio-economic terms. The poorest social groups tend to opt for self-built housing west of the city centre. Beyond the Bardo area and the Cité Ibn Khaldoun lies the sprawling Tadhamen neighbourhood. An area of farmland until the early 1970s, land for housing was subdivided and put on the market illegally. The result is a vast, semi-planned low-income neighbourhood. To avoid social unrest, State agencies brought in the main utilities. Other areas of low-income unplanned housing include La Cagna and Ouardia south of the centre. There are other pockets elsewhere, too. It should be stressed, however, that Tunis does not have housing problems on anything like the scale of Casablanca's bidonvilles or the multi-occupancy of old cities like Fès.

Further major new neighbourhoods are under way, or on the planners' drawing boards, and the late 1990s buoyancy of the construction industry is probably a sign of the health of the Tunisian economy as a whole. North of the 1980s suburbs of El Manar, the new Cité Ennasr neighbourhood was taking shape. In the southern suburb of Radès, a new stadium and sports complex was built in 1999-2001 to host the Mediterranean Games. Plans were also well ahead for cleaning up the south Tunis industrial zone and creating new mixed-use neighbourhoods along the south side of the lagoon, a sort of mirror development to the Berges du Lac on the north side. Gammarth and the hotel strip at Raoued seemed set to expand as well. Some new developments are of high quality (Les Jardins de Carthage), others are of unmitigated tackiness (Le Palace), and others quite gargantuan in scale.

Preserving the Médina The development of new neighbourhoods has been accompanied by renewed interest in the oldest parts of the city centre, the historic médina and ville nouvelle areas, centring respectively on the souks and the Avenue Bourguiba. Upmarket restaurants have been successfully installed in the palatial surroundings of restored private residences in the upper Médina, and since the Municipal Theatre became a listed building, an awareness of the value of city centre buildings seems to have taken root. Major new exhibition space housing the Musée de la Ville de Tunis was created in a restored 19th-century building, the Palais Kheireddine, right at the heart of the old town. In 2002, Italian-funded work was proceeding apace on restoring the former Eglise de la Sainte-Croix on the Rue de la Zitouna, the aim being to create a new centre for the Mediterranean crafts. Heritage tourism, with buildings and galleries as a focus point, could well take off in old Tunis.

Revitalizing the Ville Nouvelle In the late 1990s, a long-mooted flagship project for revitalizing the Avenue Bourguiba, heart of the Bab Bhar neighbourhood of the Ville Nouvelle, was launched. In 2001, works proceeded apace to widen pavements, install new lighting and benches, restore façades and generally clean up the whole area. The crowning glory of the project? A gold-tipped clocktower with fountain on the main roundabout. The whole operation was complete in time for the opening ceremony of the autumn 2001 Mediterranean Games, and to judge by the number of people attracted into central Tunis, is a big success. The café terraces on the newly expanded pavements are certainly an improvement. Next on the drawing-boards is the revamping of the Avenue de France, the section of street which continues the Avenue Bourguiba up to the Porte de France.

The successful redevelopment of other areas of older property in central Tunis will depend on more than just government will and funding, however. Accessibility is a big issue, for example. Heavy vehicle traffic, on-street parking, narrow pavements and the general lack of places to sit and relax make Tunis in summer a difficult place for both visitor and locals. Tunis residents prefer the private car to public transport, and the result is growing vehicle pollution, although nothing as compared with Cairo and Istanbul.

Heritage at risk: traffic & demolition

The other major factor is pressure on property from redevelopers with little interest in heritage or neighbourhood character. While 2001 saw the restoration of many fine apartment buildings, there were also some major losses, including demolition of a fine art deco building on the Avenue Bourguiba and an early 20th-century villa on Rue d'Angleterre. The replacement buildings are generally mediocre in architectural terms and detrimental to the streetscape. How many further losses the city will have to sustain remains to be seen. This is sad, given that downtown Tunis has such potential as a place to visit, a pleasant Mediterranean destination with history, sites and quality of life. But then perhaps heritage trails and suchlike, the over-signposting of the city for tourists, would detract from the more subtle pleasures it offers to the stroller.

Sights

Tunis, while being an easy city to visit in terms of transport, does not have many obvious sites, apart from the two great museums at the Bardo and Carthage. It is more a matter of atmosphere. Lacking the density and human pressure of Fès or Marrakech, the médina or old town is a gentle introduction to the traditional Arab city: there are a number of restored buildings open to the visitor, and new museums are planned. Despite some recent redevelopment, the narrow streets and tree-lined avenues of the central areas of Tunis are still redolent of the mid-20th century, and the stroller will feel the presence of a recent cosmopolitan past – and indeed for a short time Tunis was a fashionable resort. The imaginative visitor may enjoy flashback moments to scenes from *Pépé le Moko* or *Casablanca*. The period 1850-1950 left behind it numerous handsome buildings, and the historic-building enthusiast will enjoy the architectural set pieces (the art nouveau Théâtre Municipal, the art deco Synagogue Daniel Osiris) and the numerous stylish apartment buildings which make the town such a catalogue of architectural styles.

When visiting Tunis, don't wear beachwear. You can walk around in brief shorts, shoulders uncovered, but expect to attract unwelcome attention/comments

Downtown Tunis: the médina and the Ville Nouvelle

The town is situated on the shores of a lake linked to the sea at La Goulette. The new city, with **Avenue Habib Bourguiba** as its centre, is laid out on a grid-iron plan. The médina, in contrast, is full of small, initially confusing, winding streets. The médina is no longer walled, as the French replaced the old walls with large boulevards all around the old city. However, cars cannot penetrate all the streets of the médina, making a welcome change from the overcrowded and noisy streets of the new town.

Children will like
the médina but watch
out for mopeds
hurtling down the
narrow streets

Visiting the médina can be a confusing business, especially if you are being rushed in and out on a whistlestop visit to the souks between the Bardo and Carthage. Old Tunis repays a more leisurely visit. Although the monuments are not spectacular, there is much of interest in the streets and boulevards of the central parts of the city. After some general background on the médina, there follows four short walking tours to help you get to know the town. The first two take in the most obvious sights, walks three and four are more for enthusiasts. The médina walks are followed by a fifth route to show you some of the better buildings in the Ville Nouvelle.

The médina:
background
& history

The médina of Tunis was founded some 13 centuries ago on a narrow strip of land lying between the Sebkhat Essedjoumi and the lagoon, separating the site of the future city from the sea. With a steep scarp slope falling down to the saltflats, and a number of outcrops, subsequently fortified, the site had good defensive potential. The water table being near the surface, every house was able to have its own well, an important factor in a land where the rain is often irregular. The Arab conquerors of the seventh and eighth centuries no doubt also chose this site for their settlement because of the availability of abundant building material in the declining city of Carthage. They preferred not to settle at Carthage to be out of reach of Byzantine naval raids. A nomad people, the Arabs had yet to gain mastery of the Mediterranean.

Architectural historians and specialists consider the médina of Tunis as an outstanding example of Arab-Muslim urban development. The dense web of narrow streets surrounding the main mosque is little changed since the Hafsid Dynasty (late Middle Ages). Much demolition and rebuilding has taken place since then, however, and there is little genuinely medieval building still left. There is, however, a huge variety of architectural styles, from the vernacular to modern-movement, to be seen in the streets of the médina and adjoining parts of the Ville Nouvelle.

The médina divides into three main areas: the central médina, the oldest core of the city; the *faubourg nord* or Bab Souika neighbourhood; and the *faubourg sud* or Bab Jazira neighbourhood, perhaps the least obvious of the three for the visitor. As elsewhere in Tunisia, mosques and monuments used as offices are not open to the public. Admission times of those which are accessible are given in the text. Note that ticket policy seems to vary. Some years, you can buy a ticket giving access to several monuments at the Dar Ben Abdallah (Museum of Traditional Arts). Other years, tickets are bought individually at the various monuments.

Walk 1
Faith & Trade:
the Zitouna
Mosque &
the souks

This walk takes you past the finest mosques of old Tunis, through the covered souks which were the commercial nerve centre of the city for centuries. The starting point is **Bab Bhar**, the old sea gate on Place de la Victoire, east side of the médina. The finishing point is the Kasbah esplanade on the west side of the médina. This is a short walk, where you will view buildings mainly from the outside. Still, allow at least 1¾ one hours.

Bab Bhar, restored in the 1980s, stands in isolation in front of the médina. Behind it stand the three-storey buildings of a neighbourhood once inhabited mainly by European merchants. With Bab Bhar behind you, the **British Embassy**, a whitewashed building in the Neo-Moorish style, is to your right. (On an insalubrious side street behind the Embassy is the old French merchants hostel, the **Fondouk des Francais**, currently being restored.) Ahead of you are the balconies of the **Palazzo Gneccho**, now a restaurant.

Head up the street to the left of the palazzo. This is Rue Jamaâ Ezzitouna, ex-Rue de l'Eglise, the main souk street in the médina and home to small shops selling all sorts of junk for the tourist. A few metres inside the médina on the left is the **Eglise de la Sainte Croix**, also currently being restored and scheduled to be turned into some sort of performance/gallery space.

Some 100 m up the Rue Jamaâ Ezzitouna, you could go left down Rue Sidi Ali Azouz for a few metres. With a little luck, you might be able to take a look into the **Zaouia of Sidi Ali Azouz** (on your right), and, on your left, down a narrow alley, at **Dar Bayram Turki**. This 17th-century building has a fine courtyard faced with stone. Now used as workshop space, it is a good example of the fate which has befallen many fine old homes in the old town. A few metres further on, the large building straight ahead of you was once a barracks. Double back to the Rue Jamaâ Ezzitouna. The street leads up past carpet and trinket sellers to a small open square in front of the **Great or Zitouna Mosque**, **Souk el Fekkia**, the former dried fruit market. To your left, there is a small neighbourhood plan in ceramic tiles on the wall. In front of you is the skifa or main portico of the Great Mosque. Before midday it is possible to go up onto the skifa to view the great courtyard.

Do not expect to be allowed up onto the porch of the Ezzitouna Mosque in skimpy attire

Jamaâ Ezzitouna is by far the most venerable mosque in Tunis, attributed to an early Arab conqueror, one Hassan Ibn Nu'man. Some reports date it back to the foundation of the Islamic city in 698. It was completely rebuilt by the Aghlabid Emir Ibrahim Ibn Ahmed in 856-63. The minaret was remodelled on a number of occasions, and the present version, with the interlinked lozenge design on the façades, dates from 1896. The same design is to be found on the nearby Kasbah Mosque. The courtyard gallery dates largely from the 17th century. The prayer hall dates back to the original foundation, and has columns 'quarried' from nearby Roman sites. It is spectacular but unfortunately, unless you are Muslim, off limits. This mosque has extensive cisterns under the main courtyard, which slopes so that a maximum of rainwater could be collected.

As you view Jamaâ Ezzitouna, note how it is surrounded on all sides by the souks. (There were originally stalls for rent under the skifa esplanade.) The Renaissance ideology of 'man as the measure of all things' never touched old Tunis. The médina lived closed in on itself, and there was never any need to create open spaces for fountains and statuary, as per the cities of Italy and Spain, post-Renaissance. Next go left in front of the mosque, to visit (if possible) the

Tunis and around

Walk 1: faith & trade

See Tunis médina map, page 74, for orientation

━━━ Walking Route

Not to scale

three **medresas** or colleges next to the mosque. These are on your right, and are the **Medresa Ennakhla**, **Medresa el Bachiya** and **Medresa Slimaniya**. Why are these important? The medresa was basically an institution providing accommodation for students following courses at a major mosque. The latter two were both established by 18th-century beys, and bear witness to the piety of their founders. The Slimaniya, built by Ali Pacha in memory of a favourite son, Suleiman, who died poisoned in a dynastic feud, is particularly fine (and is today occupied by medical NGOs). There are numerous other medresas in Tunis, and you can imagine the courtyards with students sitting against the columns, hard at work on some weighty religious text.

After the three medresas, double back to the square in front of Jamaâ Ezzitouna. You need to go left at the other end of Souk el Fekkia, up **Souk el Attarine**, the Perfumers' Souk. Here Tunis brides come to buy all their wedding paraphernalia: perfumes, candles, henna and silky cat baskets to put all the wedding presents in. There are things for tourists too, delicate gilt bottles and felt fishes covered in sequins to ward off the evil eye. Note that the souks closest to the Great Mosque are clean or noble trades, that is perfumers, sellers of once expensive dried fruit, booksellers and tailors.

Up Souk el Attarine you come to a junction, just below the minaret of the Ezzitouna, in fact. Here you can go straight ahead up **Souk Ettrouk**, once the street of the Turkish taylors. Halfway along is the *Café Mrabet*, an old saint's shrine now functioning as an attractive café, and probably one of the first cafés in the city. There is a slightly scruffy garden at the back with a good view of the minaret of the Ezzitouna. At the top of Souk Ettrouk, turn left into **Souk el Berka**, once the main slave market, now the centre of a flourishing jewellery arcade.

If you go right at the top of Souk Ettrouk, go straight ahead along a narrow street between the high walls of the **Dar el Bey**, today the Prime Minister's offices, on your left, and the outside wall of the chechia makers' souk, **Souk Echaouachia**, on your right. You should be able to cut through the souk and observe the *chaouachis* hard at work, felting and shaping the red felt caps or chechias once so characteristic of Tunis. Back in the 19th century, the cap makers were easily the wealthiest and most influential corporation in the city, masters of a pre-industrial manufacturing process. Your coffee stop could be here at the café in the souk, or, if you cut right through, at the street café on the Rue Sidi Ben Arous. Here you have a magnificent view of the Ezzitouna minaret. The same street also has a small well-stocked bookshop, *Le Diwan*, and an expensive craftshop, *Eddar*.

Going up this street, leaving the minaret behind you, you come to the **Hammouda Pacha mosque** on your right, a splendid 17th-century construction. The octagonal minaret is

Plan of Great Mosque Ez-Zitouna

(Only area 5 can be visited, before midday, by the non-muslim)

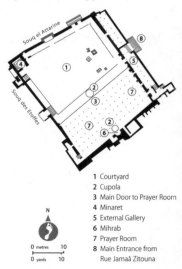

1 Courtyard
2 Cupola
3 Main Door to Prayer Room
4 Minaret
5 External Gallery
6 Mihrab
7 Prayer Room
8 Main Entrance from
  Rue Jamaâ Zitouna

N

0 metres   10
0 yards   10

characteristic of mosques following the Hanefite rite. (There are four main rites in mainstream Islam, the Malekite rite dominating in North Africa.) The Hanefite rite was brought by the Ottoman Turks, and the minaret would have been very much a political statement in its day, declaring the supremacy of Tunis' new masters.

At the junction at the top of the street, go straight ahead down the Rue Sidi Ben Arous. You will come to the **Place Romdhane Bey**, a small open area surrounded by small workshops. Go up a couple of steps on your left, and you will come to one of the covered streets or *sabats* so characteristic of the residential areas of Tunis. There is some magnificent architectural detail here, including a kitsch Tuniso-Roccoco double window feature. After the covered passage, turn left up the Rue El Jeld. Here you will come to some signs of incipient gentrification, including upmarket restaurant *Dar el Jeld*, and its annex, the Diwan Dar el Jeld. The **Galerie de la Médina** holds occasional exhibitions of contemporary Tunisian painters.

Rue el Jeld leads you to **Place du Gouvernement**, with its ficus trees, water feature and shiny granite paving. The Ministry of Finance, with its arcades, is a fine 19th-century building in a simple version of the Neo-Moorish style. At the top of Place du Gouvernement, you come to an area generally referred to as the **Kasbah**, after the long-vanished medieval fortifications. Cross the busy road and go up the steps, and from the main esplanade you will have a splendid view of some of the key historic buildings of Tunis. Be careful should you wish to take photographs – don't include men in uniforms in your photos.

Straight ahead of you are key government buildings, the Finance Ministry with its domes and crenellations and the Dar el Bey, entirely remodelled in the 19th century. This was the guest palace under the Husseinid beys. Moving clockwise, you come to the Aziz Othmana hospital complex, named after the medieval princess who was the hospital's original founder. The minaret to your right is that of the **Kasbah Mosque**, built 1231-35. The *darj wa ktef* lozenge motif on the façade recalls that this was a monument to the Almohad brand of Islam, a puritan movement that arose among the Masmouda Berbers of the High Atlas and spread eastwards across the Maghreb in the 12th century. The same motif, symbolizing loyalty to the Almohad cause, can be found on numerous minarets in North Africa. The galleries on the outside of the mosque are late 20th century, and the building should be imagined in context as the central point of a palace complex outside the médina. Still moving clockwise, there is the new Ministry of Culture and some remnant walls of the bastion of Sidi Abdallah. A large chunk of the remaining walls and a late 19th-century barracks were demolished after independence.

The largest building in the area, however, is the **Municipality of Tunis**, a vast construction facing directly onto the arcade, behind which is situated the **Maison du Parti**, a modernist building by Olivier Clément Cacoub, favourite architect of former president Habib Bourguiba. The Municipality, completed in 1999, features the *darj wa ktef* lozenge motif; the Almohad overtones have long since been forgotten. Try to get a look inside the Municipality: the overwrought decoration combines tiles, carved plasterwork and painted wood ceilings, all elements of 18th-century domestic decoration schemes, on a vast scale. The result is somewhat overwhelming.

The next key building is the mid-19th century **Collège Sadiki**. Founded by Kheireddine Pacha, under Sadok Bey (hence the name, Sadiki), the college was the first institution in Tunisia to dispense a modern secondary education. Architecturally, it is a typical Neo-Moorish building, with traditional features such as minaret and domes being used to 'dress' what is otherwise a typical school building, rather in the same way that Gothic features were used for 19th-century British public schools.

Finally, a number of other major buildings can be seen from the Kasbah esplanade. In the far distance, above a wooded hill, the mass of the Arab League headquarters can be seen, with next to it the box-like *Hilton Hotel*. Rather nearer, in the médina, and surrounded by houses, are the white egg-shell domes of **Sidi Mehrez**, a 17th-century mosque of Ottoman inspiration. Unlike the great mosques of Istanbul, it was never to have soaring, pointy topped minarets.

Walk 2
Beldis, beys
& a pirate
adventurer's
home

On this route through the médina you will discover some of the finest examples of Tunisoise domestic architecture, and you will be given an idea about life in one of the more residential areas of the city. The high point is Dar Ben Abdallah, palace home to the Museum of Traditional Life. Starting point: the Kasbah. Finish: Porte de France. Allow a good one hour 45 minutes.

From the Kasbah, make your way along the Boulevard Bab Menara. On your right are the Kasbah Mosque and then the late 19th-century block of the Ministry of Defence. Past a café, down a few steps, and you come to an open area where a small tomb marks the presence of a medieval saint from Majorca, commemorated because he converted to Islam. Go right of the tombs into the covered souk. In the middle of the street is another tomb, in the form of a red and green box, the last resting place of one **Sidi Bou Abdallah** who died here defending Tunis against the Spanish foe. Legend has it that Monty Python-like, he continued fighting even when his head had been chopped off.

At the first intersection, turn right into the Rue Ben Mahmoud. On your right, the first door is that of the **Musée Lapidaire Sidi Bou Khrissan**, a small museum of elaborate carved tombstones. Knock on the door, and a member of the family living inside will let you in (no tickets, make a donation). Ninth century Khorassanid emirs were once buried here. Today, the museum with its olive tree and ruined *koubba* is off the tourist circuit.

Walk 2: beldis, beys & a pirate adventurer

See Tunis médina map, page 74, for orientation

Not to scale

■ **Sleeping**
1 Maison Bleue Guest House

● **Eating**
1 Essaraya

— — Walking Route

After the museum, continue along the Rue Ben Mahmoud. You will pass the *Restaurant Essaraya*, a costly and kitsch 'restoration' of an old home (note plexiglas dome). Turning right after Essaraya, the street widens. On your right, down a narrow alley, Impasse Ettobjiya, is the recently restored **Dar Haddad**, which may eventually house some of the displays currently in Dar Ben Abdallah. At the end of this street, turn right, and the narrow covered passageway will bring you out onto Place du Château, a square currently used as a car park. On your right is one of Tunis' oldest mosques, **Jamaâ el Ksar**. The prayer hall, as usual closed to visitors, is below street level. The huge, irregular stone blocks of the lower walls suggest the mosque was built on a much older building. The minaret is 17th century.

The main building on this square (which could be quite pleasant, given a few trees) is **Dar Hussein**, currently home to the INP, the Tunisian National Heritage Institute. The building is 18th century, much added to in the 19th century, before being taken over by the French military authorities. The grumpy concierge may let you have a peek in at the rather fine main courtyard.

From Place du Château, head down the covered cobbled street to the right of the main door of Dar Hussein. This brings you to a small open space where there is a *hammam* or Turkish bath with the characteristic red and green door. Go left down the Rue Abri, and then right down the narrow **Rue des Andalous**, with its studded doors and vaulted sections, one of the finest streets in the médina. At the end, turn left down Rue du Riche. At the first junction, you come to the Rue Tourbet el Bey. (Going left here will allow you to have a look at the **Msid el Koubba**, a small domed structure where medieval sociologist Ibn Khaldoun is said to have prayed.) Turn right, and after about 75 m you will come to **Tourbet el Bey**, a mausoleum complex and last resting place of the Husseinid princes and princesses. Built by Ali Pasha II (1758-82), this monument is something of a curiosity. Most Islamic dynasties went in for splendid necropolises. It is somehow strange that the beys, who lived isolated from their subjects in palaces well outside the city, should have chosen to be buried in their midst. The first members of the dynasty had been buried in the Tourbet Sidi Kassem, Rue Sidi Kassem.

Abandoned to its fate after Tunisian independence, the Tourbet was recently restored. The term *tourbet* derives from the Turkish for tomb, and most of the great Tunisois families had family mausolea near their homes. The building is an odd stylistic mix. The outside features carved stonework with floral motifs, plus domes covered in the green, scale shaped tiles which mean 'burial place' or 'holy person's tomb' in the Tunis streetscape. Inside, the decoration is flamboyant. There are the characteristic 18th-century tiled panels (shiny replacement panels stand out a mile) and carved stucco work. In the Hall of the Reigning Princes, the lower walls have elaborate marble marquetry panels, a style imported from nearby Sicily. The princes' tombs are topped with their headgear, turbans and later fezzes of various sizes. ■ *The building can normally be visited 0930-1600 except Sun, entrance 3Dt. If it seems closed, knock hard, and someone may emerge to let you in (for an unofficial tip).*

After Tourbet el Bey, you may want to see a traditional Tunis family home. The restored **Dar Ben Abdallah**, today home to the **Museum of Traditional Arts**, is close by. Leaving the main door of Tourbet el Bey, go right, and right twice more, following the main outside wall of the Tourbet. On your left, you will come to the Rue Sidi Kassem. A few metres down this street, go right under an arch and you will come to the Dar Ben Abdallah, an 18th-century palace restored in the early 19th century by an officer of the Beylical army. He opted for the Italian touch (galleries, marble fountain with dolphin) very much in favour at the time. The museum divides into two parts. Off the main courtyard, are rooms with scenes from Tunisois family life in a fairly recent but idealized past. This is the world of the *beldia*, the old Muslim families of Tunis, proud of their traditions. Little did they know that their world was to be irrevocably destroyed by the changes of the 20th century. The museum also houses a small display of craft implements in a neighbouring stables area.

In the courtyard, the first room on your right deals with childhood. There are cases of small boys' embroidered circumcision costumes, and a scene with small girls learning embroidery from a *maâlema*. There are tiny couscous pots for small girls to play at cooking.

The next two rooms are devoted to women. There is a room showing a scene from upper-class daily life in the 19th century. Note the large, elaborate beds in the alcoves. In the next room along is the bride getting ready for her wedding. The scene is perhaps just before the bride's pre-wedding party. The *hannana* is there, no doubt ready to execute some henna designs on hands and feet, and the bride's friends in their best gear. The styles suggest the 1920s, maybe later. The display cabinets contain a range of silver and mother-of-pearl items. In a room to the left is a display devoted to the *hammam* in Tunis. (**NB**. Between these two rooms, through a small door, is an old fashioned Tunis kitchen.)

The final courtyard room is devoted to men. The scene shows the fiancé, accompanied by a religious scholar, asking for the hand of the daughter of the house. To the right of the main alcove is a room set up as an old-fashioned Tunis study. All the items necessary to a Tunis scholar, before the arrival of the printing press, are on display: inkwells, pencases, Koran-holders, and rosaries. There are some fine costumes as well.

After Dar Ben Abdallah, turn right out onto the Rue Sidi Kassem. The street leads you to onto the Rue des Teinturiers, and a large mosque, the early 18th-century **Jamaâ el Jedid**, will be on your right. Go down a covered street opposite the mosque, the Rue el Mbazaâ, which will take you to **Dar Othman**, 17th-century home of a corsair leader. The door has a strikingly modern black and white marble surround. The entrance hall or *driba* has impressive (mainly new) tile panels. Here, no doubt, Othman Dey, pirateer and governor of Tunis, would hold court. If you are allowed into the main courtyard, you will find a pleasant space planted with hibiscus, pomegranate and cypress trees. The building once housed the Department of Traditional Arts, managed by craft expert Jacques Revault. Trained in Morocco, Revault no doubt had a traditional Moroccan garden courtyard or *riyad* in mind when he had the courtyard at Dar Othman planted. Otherwise, Dar Othman follows the usual pattern for a Tunisois house, with narrow sleeping/reception rooms placed around a central courtyard. Today the building houses the offices of the Conservation de la Médina, one of two bodies working to preserve the old town and its monuments.

After viewing Dar Othman, double back up Rue Mbazaâ and turn right into Rue des Teinturiers. Going straight ahead, you will come to **Souk el Belat** and its numerous herborists stalls. (Traditional plant remedies for everything here.) The name of the souk derives from the Greek *palation*, doubtless after some former splendid palace in the area. Continue straight ahead, and you will come to the Rue Jamaâ Ezzitouna, the main tourist drag. Turn right, and head down towards the Porte de France, some five minutes' walk away, depending on the human traffic jams.

This route is more for médina enthusiasts. Although there are few monuments to visit, it takes you through areas of the old city with a vivid past. The Halfaouine area, in particular, is a lively part of the médina. You will see neighbourhoods which have been remodelled, two major mosques, and 19th-century palaces. Starting point is Porte de France, finishing point is the metro at Bab el Khadhra. Allow at least two hours. Café stops are at Bab Souika or on Place Halfaouine.

**Walk 3
From the
Hafsia to
Halfaouine:
urban re-
development
& 19th-century
palaces**

With Porte de France behind you, go right down the Rue des Glacières, the street leading off between the two cafés. Here you will discover lots of boutiques, bright with trendy clothes and footwear imported from Italy, France, Morocco and Turkey. Go straight ahead at the junction with the Rue Zarkoun. (If you want local music, there is a large cassette emporium here.) You are at the heart of the old **Quartier Franc**, home to the *fondouks* or foreign merchants' hostels. Most of the present buildings were built in the late 19th century, before the new Tunis, outside the médina walls, took shape. Walking along Rue des Glacières, between the crumbling walls, the Italian influence is clearly visible. Note that there is a good deal of demolition/rebuilding in the neighbourhood at present, which will no doubt alter its character.

At the end of Rue des Glacières, you come to a small open area, the entrance to the Hafsia neighbourhood. Until the mid-20th century, this was the Hara or Jewish quarter, an area of narrow streets and tiny courtyard houses. As of the mid-1970s, the neighbourhood was entirely rebuilt in a style that recalls the old médina. Along the main street through the neighbourhood, the Rue de la Hafsia, are two- and three-storey apartment buildings. Behind are small, modern courtyard houses.

Turn left up the Rue de la Hafsia. The garment trade is important in the area today. On your right, the fish souk is now home to the *friperie* (second-hand clothes stalls). There are several clothes wholesalers in the streets off to the left.

On your right, you will come across three large low-rise 1930s apartment buildings, the **immeubles du Dr Cassar**, named for a leading figure in the Tunis Jewish community. (Behind them a former synagogue can be identified by the menara candlestick motif on the metal doors.) The Jews of Tunis were

Tunis and around

Walk 3: from the Hafsia to Halfaouine

*See Tunis
médina map,
page 74,
for orientation*

Walking Route   Not to scale

Sidi Mehrez, patron saint of Tunis

Abou Mohamed Mahrez Ibn el Khalaf (d.1022), referred to as Sidi Mehrez, lived in the early 10th century, a turbulent and dangerous time for the inhabitants of Tunis. The northeastern Maghreb was ruled by a dynasty which owed allegiance to the Shi'ite Fatimids, based in Cairo. The population was taxed heavily to finance wars the Fatimids intended to fight against the Sunni caliph based in Baghdad. Eventually, in 943, an uprising led by one Abu Yazid developed into a general rebellion against Fatimid rule. Although Abu Yazid was eventually defeated by the Fatimids, it was only after

Tunis had been looted by his forces in 944. It was Sidi Mehrez who got the inhabitants of Tunis to work together to reconstruct their town. He reorganized the souks, and got permission for the Jews to settle within the walls. He was also involved in the theological debates pitting the Sunni Malikite scholars of Tunis against the Shi'ites. In the 10th century, Tunis was home to a number of defenders of Sunnni orthodoxy. Sidi Mehrez was cousin of one of the region's most famous scholars, Ibn Abi Zayid el Kayrawani (d.996), author of a synopsis of Malikite law which became famous far beyond the Maghreb.

quick to wake up to the possibilities of modern education, and soon adapted to the French protectorate. By the 1930s, a large part of the community had moved out to new residential areas like Lafayette, where they built a splendid art deco synagogue. The Hara was crumbling, and the poorest members of the community were rehoused in the Dr Cassar flats.

With the flats on your left, you have a splendid view to the white domes of **Sidi Mehrez**, today considered to be the patron saint of Tunis. Back in the 10th century, it was Sidi Mehrez who allowed the Jews to settle within the walls of Tunis. The story goes that he had a fine earring. He asked a Jewish jeweller to make him a copy, which the craftsman did. Sidi Mehrez granted the Jew's wish to live protected within the city walls. Criticized for his decision, Sidi Mehrez is said to have declared, "Why make such a fuss for a handful (*hara*) of Jews?" And so the Jewish neighbourhood came to be referred to as the Hara. Or so the story goes.

Continue up along Rue de la Hafsia, and turn right onto Rue du Tribunal. On this narrow street, the building on your right with the horseshoe arches is the early 20th-century Ecole Israelite. Rue du Tribunal opens up after 50 m into a pleasant square set with poplar trees. The fine white façades on your right belong to the new **Musée de la Ville de Tunis**, housed in the former **Palais Kheireddine**. Look out for temporary exhibitions here until such time as the museum is established.

Proceeding across the Place du Tribunal, the street narrows and turns sharp right and then left. On your left you will find the entrance to the **Club culturel Tahar Haddad**, housed in the undercroft of an early 19th-century palace, the Dar Lasram. Once a hotbed of the Tunis feminist movement, the club is a polite, artistic sort of place today. There is a small library. The club is closed at lunchtimes. Look out for evening concerts during Ramadan. Round the corner on your left is the entrance to **Dar Lasram**, restored in the early 1970s and today home to the Association de Sauvegarde de la Médina de Tunis (ASM). The palace today functions as design offices and meeting space for the ASM, which plays an important role in managing restoration and housing projects in the old neighbourhoods of Tunis. Ask nicely, express an interest in historic Tunis, and you will probably be allowed in to have a look around (no charge). The main patio is splendid, and there is a small display of the ASM's main projects.

After Dar Lasram, continue along the Rue du Tribunal. At the T-junction, go right. At the end, go left onto Rue el Mestiri, and follow the street until you reach the main souk. If you go right, you can view the entrance to the Zaouia or **shrine of Sidi Mehrez** (rebuilt 1862-63), opposite the mosque with the white domes which you saw from the Hafsia. The shrine is much frequented by women seeking the saint's blessing, and you will find many small stalls selling pilgrims' requisites (candles, little green and red flags, incenses). Going left, you will head up the crowded souk and come out though an arched gateway at **Bab Souika**. Go right to the fountain roundabout, and you will be able to view the results of the second urban redevelopment project on this walk.

The médina of Tunis sits at the heart of the Greater Tunis urban area. By the 1970s, there were severe traffic problems at Bab Souika, transit point for most of the east-west traffic. It was decided to redevelop the area. To resolve the traffic problem, tunnels were put under a new square. New building was to be 'in keeping' with the architecture of the médina. The result is a series of inoffensive, post-modern buildings with vaguely traditional detailing. (The apartment block facing you as you leave the souk has a distinct Rennie Mackintosh feel.) One of the more interesting buildings is the **Zaouia of Sidi Abdelkader** (the small domed building on your right, as you stand with the main square behind you), a shrine entirely rebuilt in a simple reworking of the 18th-century style.

Note that Bab Souika is something of a Tunis legend. It was home to the nationalist movement – and to bawdy night-time entertainments during Ramadan, the famous *cafés-chantants*. The area is also HQ for the Espérance sportive de Tunis, one of Tunis' two big football teams. Flags and banners in the club colours, red and yellow, will be draped round the square on big match days.

From Bab Souika, head down the **Rue Halfaouine**, the neighbourhood's main shopping street. (The only pedestrian street leading off the fountain roundabout, between a patisserie and an arcaded building.) There are piles of fresh fruit and vegetables, butchers and wholesale merchants of various kinds.

At the end of Rue Halfaouine, you come to the Place Halfaouine, a tree-shaded square overlooked by the elegant arcades and octagonal minaret of the **Jamaâ Sahib Ettabaâ** (**The Lord of the Seal's Mosque**). The mosque was completed in 1812, and is the focal point of a *kulliye*, a complex comprising medersa, souk, foundouk and hammam. (The imposing Zaouia of Sidi Chiha, behind the mosque, is a mid-19th-century foundation.) This complex was the first planned redevelopment of its kind in the médina, a clear reflection of the prestige of Youssef Sahib Ettabaâ, the super-minister under Hammouda Bey (1782-1814). The period was a prosperous one for Husseinid Tunisia, Europe being embroiled in the Napoleonic wars. Youssef Sahib Ettabaâ was to meet a violent end, leaving the minaret unfinished – and a legend grew up suggesting a similar fate for whomsoever attempted to complete it. It was only in 1970 that the legend was actually put to the test.

Zaouia of Sidi Abdelkader at Bab Souika

(Association Sanvegarde de la Médina de Tunis)

1 Entrance (stairs up)
2 Entrance passage
3 Patio
4 Stone bowl (scallop-edged)
5 Tiled basin
6 Limestone pavings
7 Room for visitors/ religious recitals
8 Ablutions
9 Mihrab
10 Prayer room (dome over)

N

0 metres 2
0 yards 2

Standing with the main façade of the mosque behind you, you have Youssef Sahib Ettabaâ's palace to your left, just to the right of the arched entrance of the covered Souk el Jedid. (On the street to the right of the mosque you also have the fine Hammam Sahib Ettabaâ, well worth a visit. Fans of Tunisian cinema will recognize it from scenes in the early 1990s 'coming of age in old Tunis' film, *Halfaouine, l'enfant des terrasses*.) Facing the trees, you have a pleasant covered café to your right, while on the lefthand side of the square is the **Palais du Théâtre**, yet another 19th-century palace, built by one Mustapha Khaznadar, state treasurer under Ahmed Bey (1837-55). Today the palace is used as rehearsal space by the Tunisian National Theatre. The building, a sort of Palladian villa behind high walls, is unique in the médina, and reflects the growing taste for all things Italian in 19th-century Tunis

After a coffee stop, head down the **Rue Souki Bil Khir** which leads off the end of the square. This is a street of carpenters' shops and private homes. There is a lot of new building, with workshops at street level and flats above. The simple whitewashed façades of the original vernacular architecture are disappearing, new homes have street-facing windows and tiled door surrounds. Eventually, after some 10 minutes' walking, you reach **Bab el Khadra**, formerly one of the most important gates into the northern part of the city. The twin gates are much restored, but there is a short stretch of 18th-century rampart. From outside Bab el Khadra, take the metro (or walk down Avenue de Madrid) back to République station (also referred to as Le Passage).

This walk will take you through the southern part of the médina of Tunis. You will discover the atmosphere of a residential part of the old town. Architecture buffs will come across a generous mix of styles, from a medieval gate to fine early 20th-century apartment buildings. Towards the end of the walk, you visit the National Ceramics Museum at Sidi Museum at Sidi Kacem Ezziligï. Starting point: Porte de France. Finish: the Kasbah esplanade. Allow around two hours, as there is a lot of walking to do.

With the Porte de France behind you, you have the two main entrances to the souk ahead of you: to your right, Rue de la Kasbah; on the left, Rue Jamaâ Ezzitouna. Don't take either of these. Instead, go sharp left down the **Rue de la Commission**, home to Tunis stationery and office supplies wholesalers. The street is lined with building which would not look out of place in Palermo or Naples, witness to the strong Italian presence in the city in the 19th century. Some 50 m down the street, on the right, is the pedimented façade of the **Maison Evangelisti**, home to one of the oldest Tuniso-Italian families. A marble wall plaque records that Italian liberation hero Garibaldi spent time here. Further along the street, the office supplies give way to cheap goods from the Far East. There are also great aromatic skeins of dried red chilli peppers, *filfil ahmar*, used to make the *harissa* paste which is an essential part of Tunisian cooking.

At the end of Rue de la Commission, turn right and you will come into a dusty car park which gives you a fine view of the minaret of the Great Mosque. This area, **La Kherba** ('the ruin') as it is called, resulted from Second World War bombardment. Today it provides essential loading space for vans and trucks bringing raw materials to the workshops of the médina and taking out finished goods. This is also the place to catch shared taxis to Libya and Algeria. Head up the narrow Rue Kuttab Louzir (keeping the Modern Movement primary school on your right), and you will come to **Souk el Blat**, an everyday covered shopping souk with lots of interesting-looking herborist stalls. Buy yourself a dried chameleon or some amber. From here you want to head straight down the **Rue des Teinturiers** to Bab Jazira. Be warned, as you come to the fresh fish and butchers' stalls, the street gets crowded with shoppers. But then this is local atmosphere.

Rue des Teinturiers ends on the **Place Bab Jazira**. There is a roundabout with a large marble fountain, and on the roundabout there is a mosque. The **Bab Jazira Mosque** was founded in medieval times and would have been the main mosque of the southern part of the city. The minaret, with its interlinked lozenge design, was remodelled in the late 19th century. There are some fine tiles at the base of the minaret. Beyond the minaret, there are apartment blocks dating from an extensive redevelopment of the neighbourhood in the 1960s. This was a time when the rural poor were migrating to Tunis, and the insensitive handling of the redevelopment operation led to urban rioting – and the creation of an association to study and preserve the médina (see Dar Lasram, walk 3).

Next, you want to head up the wide (but often traffic-choked) **Boulevard Bab Jedid**. The boulevard is lined with fine early 20th-century apartment buildings in a range of styles. Some have a very Haussman feel, others have plaster detailing with a hint of Rococco fantasy. The boulevard was laid out in place of the old ramparts, which were gradually dismantled in the late 19th century, the rubble being used for infill to create building land for the new Tunis growing up east of the médina.

Bab Jedid is home to the supporters of the Club Africain, one of the city centre's two big football teams. The club's red and white colours can be found adorning café awnings. Five minutes' brisk walk from Bab Jazira, you come to the actual **Bab Jedid**, the **New Gate**, the only fragment of mediaeval building surviving on this stretch of boulevard. Today home to the *Restaurant Granada*, this venerable gate dating from 1276 was built by the second Hafsid sovereign El Mustansir (1249-77), son of Abu Zakariya el Hafsi (1228-49), who consolidated the dynasty's hold of the eastern Maghreb. Behind the gate is a street where you can see blacksmiths hard at work, making the wrought iron for which Tunis is famous.

Walk 4: three gates & a tile-making saint

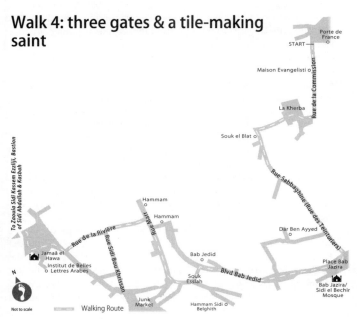

See Tunis médina map, page 74, for orientation

Opposite Bab Jedid is an open area still called Souk Esslah, Place des Armes, no doubt after some long-since vanished weaponry market. Today the area is home to eateries such as that of Ould Abba, famous for his *leblebi* (which may roughly be described as chickpea broth). Tunis night owls come here for a feed after the bars close.

From Place des Armes, turn right up a street which will lead you to Jamaâ el Hlak, its simple square minaret typical of the sobre mosques of the Malikite rite. After the mosque, head along a lively shopping street busy in the morning with numerous pavement stalls and students spilling out from the schools. This is the **Rue Marr** ('Street of the Passage'), along which the sultan would pass on high days and holidays on his way to the *mesalla*, the great open space on the Gorjani Heights, where he would lead the special prayers for the major festivals of the Muslim year, 'Id Esseghir' and 'Id el Adha'. About 150 m along the Rue Marr, almost opposite the red, white and green painted door of a *hammam*, turn left up **Rue de la Rivière** (Nahaj el Oued). This street will take you up through a quiet residential neighbourhood. (Halfway up, at a junction, you may want to go left to look at the fine, early 20th-century town-houses on the **Rue Sidi Bou Khrissan**.) At the end of this street, turn right, and you will come to a large well-shaded square, Place de Leader. Up at the top, on your left, you have another Hafsid mosque, **Jamaâ el Hawa** ('Mosque of the Air'), so named for its position at one of the highest points of the city, overlooking the brackish Lac Sejoumi. On the other side of the square, you have the new buildings of the University of Tunis theology school. And next to them, at the topmost point of the square, you have the final stop on this walk, the tomb of a pious tilemaker, the Zaouia of Sidi Kassem Ezzliji.

The shrine or **Zaouia Sidi Kassem Ezzliji** is the last resting place of a pious Andalusian craftsman who came to Tunis at the end of the 15th century. He won popularity for his good works and, more importantly, like the other Andalusian Muslim immigrants of the early 17th century, for bringing an important skill to the city: the Hispano-Moorish art of glazed tile-making. Sidi Kassem's tomb soon became an object of veneration and he had such prestige that some of the last Hafsid princes asked to be buried near it. In liturgical terms, Islam is not a complex religion. Thus the cult of saintly women and men, especially in the fringe areas of the Muslim world, served to relieve the austerity of everyday religious practice, providing a focus for people's need to identify with pious individuals, functioning as interecessors with the Divine. (Note that this is most definitely not part of mainstream Islamic practice.)

The neighbourhood and its *zaouia* became a focus for Moors expelled from Spain in 1607. One Abd el Ghayth el Qachach repaired the damage suffered by the *zaouia* during the 16th-century Hispano-Turkish wars, adding the current courtyard and the rooms around it. The inscription inside the actual burial chamber marking the location of Sidi Kassem's tomb and recounting his virtues dates from this time. In the 18th century, the building was completely renovated by Hussein Ben Ali, a mosque was built in the southeast of the site and the tomb was covered externally and internally with the decoration still visible today.

In the 20th century, the *zaouia* gradually fell into disrepair, the decoration deteriorated. In the early 1970s, a campaign sponsored by UNESCO and the Tunisian Ministry of Culture was launched to save the built heritage of the médina of Tunis. The Cultural Relations Department of the Spanish Ministry of Foreign Affairs put up the money to restore the *zaouia*. Restoration experts were sent over, and works were completed in 1979. The building today is much as it must have been in the 19th century.

Ibn Khaldoun, early sociologist and national symbol

Beturbanned Ibn Khaldoun, swathed in a great cloak, gazes down the Avenue Bourguiba, a large tome, no doubt his Muqadimma or Prolegomena under his arm. A man of extensive learning, whose merits as a thinker were only really recognized in the 20th century, Ibn Khaldoun (1322-1406) served various courts in North Africa and Andalusia. He wrote accounts of his travels, but is more widely known for his theory of North African society.

Ibn Khaldoun was the first thinker to have recognized that the Islamic ideal of the State had to be adapted to the political situation prevailing in tribal societies. His theory contends that new dynastic régimes emerge through the conquest of the lands of a decadent state by a rural warrior group, held together by traditional tribal solidarity or 'asabiya'. But after the hardy warriors had settled in the towns, their solidarity would weaken, destroyed by the easy living of the city. Hence they would resort to mercenaries

to maintain their authority, the costs of which implied heavy taxation. Thus the régime in turn was ripe for conquest by a tougher tribal group from the steppes or mountains. And so the cycle was repeated, unless the city-based rulers could replace tribal 'asabiya' with a stronger social glue, namely a government based on the prescriptions of Islamic law and practice.

Ibn Khaldoun's theory fitted nicely with the history of his day: the rise and fall of the Almoravid, Almohad, Merinid and Hafsid dynasties. Although it appears somewhat simplistic today, it is certainly based on the author's direct experience of political life in the Maghreb. More importantly, Ibn Khaldoun now appears as a national symbol, even figuring on the blue 10Dt banknote. For a small country with few intellectual figures, it is no doubt reassuring that a figure now considered as one of the leading mediaeval Muslim thinkers lived and wrote in Tunis.

Today, the rooms round the courtyard house a fine collection of Tunisian ceramics. On display are pieces ranging from modern rural ceramics, as well as medieval pieces. Greens, yellows and blues are the dominant colours. As elsewhere in the Mediterranean, red was not part of the ceramicists' palette, with the exception of 17th-century Iznik ware. The display is worthy homage to Sidi Kassem Ezzliji. Should you be interested, the potter's craft is maintained through evening courses held on the premises. And in the garden, there is a fine collection of Islamic tombstones, from various periods.

After visiting Sidi Kassem, head along the ring road, the Boulevard du 9 Avril 1938. On your right, you will come to the **Bastion of Sidi Abdallah**, the only section still surviving of the western walls of the city. Go down the street between bastion and some large recent buildings (the white concrete Maison du Parti and the new Municipalité de Tunis). The **Kasbah**, end point of this walk, is ahead of you on the left.

Of the modern neighbourhoods of Tunis, the *ville basse* or lower town, centring on the Avenue Bourguiba, goes back to the mid-19th century. (There is another area with some important colonial building up on Boulevard Bab Benat, leading north from the Kasbah.) This walk explores an interesting period of architectural and urban history, roughly 1850 to 1950. Starting point: the Statue of Ibn Khaldoun, Avenue Bourguiba. Finish: Le Passage. Allow a couple of hours, especially if you are going to take pictures. Never photograph any building with a uniformed presence outside.

Walk 5 Architectures 1850-1950, visiting the Ville Nouvelle

Next to the statue of a berobed, beturbanned **Ibn Khaldoun** (1979), you are at the epicentre of modern Tunis. Around you is a variety of buildings bearing witness to the huge changes that Tunis has seen since the 19th century. Facing the statue, on your left, you have the **French Embassy**, recently restored, a simple neo-classical, mid-19th-century building (1856-60) and the first significant construction outside the walls of the old city. In its day it must have been very significant, marking the supremacy of the French consuls over their counterparts. Opposite the embassy are the twin belltowers of the **Cathedral of St Vincent de Paul and St Olive** (1897, a pro-cathedral until 1964, when the Primatial Cathedral of St Louis at Carthage was downgraded). The cavernous, austere interior can be visited. (St Vincent de Paul, a saintly figure of the 17th century, was once thought to have worked among the Christians held as slaves in Tunis). Behind Ibn Khaldoun, to the left, built above the arcades at the start of the Avenue de France, is the **Immeuble National** (1950s?), in its day one of the most luxurious apartment buildings in the city.

The Avenue Bourguiba started life as the **Avenue de la Marine**, back in the 1850s, linking the médina to the customs building. On the site of the present cathedral, there would have been the small 17th-century Chapelle Saint-Antoine, no doubt built on or next to the ruined remains of the **Nova Arx**, a Spanish fort built in 1573. Later, under the French, this central street was renamed **Avenue Jules Ferry**, after one of the great figures of 19th-century French politics, the instigator of universal free primary education. After independence, the avenue, like so many other main streets in Tunisia's towns, was to take the name of the new Tunisian republic's first president, Habib Bourguiba.

Leaving Ibn Khaldoun behind you, head up the street towards the **Porte de France** or **Bab Bhar** (Sea Gate), once the main eastern gate into the city. (The Avenue Bourguiba here becomes Avenue de France.) The old city walls have disappeared; the gate, dating from the late 18th century when the walls were rebuilt under the supervision of a Dutch engineer, stands in isolation.

Here, on the eastern edge of the médina, you are looking at the buildings of the **Quartier Franc**, the Frankish or first European quarter. There is no real perceptible difference between the médina and the building on reclaimed land. Whereas in Algeria the French had often demolished large areas of building in the old Arab towns, in Tunisia they built alongside the old médinas. In Morocco, where the French presence started much later (1912), policy was to build new towns separate from the old cities. This was partly as a health measure. In the case of Tunis, the building of the new town next to the médina can be explained by a number of reasons. One of the main ones must have been the fact that it was impossible to expropriate Muslim-owned farmland and olive groves around the city. The only solution was to continue building on land reclaimed from the lagoon by the Italian Fasciotti family.

Leaving the Porte de France behind you, head down the **Rue Mustapha M'barek** (to your right, at 10 past the hour). The buildings on this street have some nice neo-Moorish touches in the shape of covered balconies with wooden fretwork, and some art nouveau mouldings. Next turn left onto Rue d'Allemagne, and right into the fish halls of the **Marché Central** (1891). The main fruit and vegetable area is housed under a fine wooden structure, and in its day must have represented an absolute revelation in Tunis. Enjoy the colour and smells of the fresh produce. (NB Closed Monday.) Cut through the market, and crossing after the butcher's alley, you come out onto the **Rue de Espagne** on the far side. Go left. On your right, on Rue Charles de Gaulle, is the imposing mass of the central **Post Office** (1893), a neoclassical building in the 19th-century *beaux-arts* tradition. It is surprising that such a significant building, symbolizing a communications revolution, should be so hemmed in.

Continue down the Rue Charles de Gaulle, and you come to a small tree-shaded square, once a place of considerable symbolic importance in colonial Tunis. Dominating the square, once known as Place Philippe Thomas, is the **Italian Embassy**, as impressive as the French Embassy on the main avenue. Until independence, the square had a statue to the memory of **Philippe Thomas**, a French army vet and amateur geologist who discovered phosphates in Tunisia in 1896 in the Metlaoui region. Soon after, Tunisia was exporting phosphates to France via a new railway built from Metlaoui to Sfax. Labour conditions in the phosphate mines were tough, and for obvious reasons the statue was removed after independence. On the far side of the square is the Place Barcelone and the **Gare de Tunis** or main railway station. The first railway terminus was built in 1878, the present building dates from 1979. The rail line to Le Kef was opened in 1876, and to Ghardimao on the Algerian frontier by 1880. Cross the Place Barcelone. On the far side, you will come to the main north-south axis of the city, here called the **Avenue de Carthage**, laid out in 1878. Fans of art nouveau architecture will want to head a few blocks south to photograph one of the few authentically art nouveau apartment buildings in Tunis. On the east side of the Avenue de Carthage, behind large trees, you can see the former **Municipality of Tunis**, a rather pompous, squat building. The Municipality has now moved to grandiose new premises up at the Kasbah. There are more fine apartment buildings behind the Municipality.

Head northwards up the Avenue de Carthage to the Avenue Bourguiba. At the intersection with the Rue de Yougoslave is the once elegant *Hotel Transatlantique*. (Fine Chemla tiles in reception.) Next along is the new **Palmarium** mall, a 1998 construction replacing a 1950s complex. This is now a popular place for young Tunisians to come and hang out, riding up and down the escalators. Back on the main drag, have a look at the white wedding cake of the **Théâtre Municipal**, the work of townhall architect Resplandy. Plaster sea-nymphs ride across the façade, inside all is gilt and cream woodwork and red velvet.

Cross the Avenue Bourguiba, following the metro line, and turn left up Rue Mokhtar Attia (ex-Rue Nahhas Pacha). This brings you out on Rue de Rome, at a junction with an interesting selection of buildings including: the recently restored former **Banque d'Algérie**, now the Tunis Governorate (*beaux-arts* style); the **Greek Orthodox Cathedral of St Andrew** and an eclectic apartment building with some fine mosaic detailing. (The archbishop is now based in Alexandria.) Head right, following the metro line, down the main Avenue Habib Thameur (ex-Avenue Roustan). On your right is the former **Lycée Carnot**, a vast 1930s construction, now one of Tunisia's top state lycées. On your left, you have the **Trésorerie Générale**, designed by Resplandy, with neo-Moorish decoration.

At this point, you may opt to head back to the Avenue Bourguiba for a citronade and a rest. Real architectural enthusiasts will want to continue up the Avenue Thameur to Le Passage, where there are some nice examples of Tunisian art deco, the angular *Hotel Ritza* for example. After Le Passage intersection, the Avenue de Paris becomes Avenue de la Liberté, and 10 minutes' walk further on you have the amazing art deco **Synagogue Daniel Osiris**, meeting point for the Jewish community in the Lafayette neighbourhood.

This walk gives an idea of the architecture to be found in Tunis's late-19th/early-20th-century neighbourhoods. Enthusiasts will find much to please them in areas both north and south of the central avenue. The area round the **Place Jeanne d'Arc** at the upper end of the Rue de Palestine also merits exploration, and close by on the **Place Pasteur** are a couple of interesting examples of the neo-Moorish style. Above all, Tunis is interesting for the mix of architecture. Under the French, the médina was left untouched, and a building boom took place. The result is a city with a catalogue of architectural styles dating from 1850 to 1950.

Tunis and around

Bardo Museum

Coach parties coming up from Hammamet arrive at around 1000, so try to arrive before then in summer. Small bookshop has souvenirs and guides in main European languages

The Bardo Museum is a must-visit, competing with museums at Leptis Magna and Tripoli for the title of most spectacular archaeological museum in the Maghreb. Founded in the late 19th century under Ali Bey (hence its original name, the Musée Alaouite), the museum is situated in a residential neighbourhood, some 5 km west of the town centre. This museum is one of the largest in North Africa. The great halls on the first floor contain an impressive collection of second- and third-century AD Roman mosaics. On display are the material remains of the main civilizations that flourished in what is now Tunisia. The Roman collections take pride of place, and the museum is famed for its vast collection of colourful mosaics depicting the daily life, pastimes and beliefs of the Roman populations in Africa. Unless it is on loan, you will also see a unique collection of Roman bronzes from a wreck discovered off Mahdia early last century. Some of the material dating from the Muslim medieval dynasties has gone to the Raqqada Museum, near Kairouan.

The museum is very crowded, especially mid-morning, as tour groups 'do' the Bardo before steaming off to Carthage and Sidi Bou Saïd. In the summer, the heat builds up and the upstairs rooms can be a little stuffy. The shop may have some material in English, notably a small, illustrated introduction to Tunisian mosaics published by Cérès Editions. Orientation in the actual building is confusing – as befits a rambling former royal palace. The collection can be easily done in a morning, although you may leave with a distinct feeling of archaeological indigestion.

■ *0900-1700 summer, 0930-1630 winter, closed Mon and main relgious holidays. 3Dt, extra charge for photography 1Dt. T513842. There are plenty of buses for the Bardo from the Parc Habib Thameur bus station, or take bus 3 from the TGM station or Av H Bourguiba and Av de Paris. There is also a green tram (metro line 4, destination Denden) from the central République station. A taxi from the town centre will cost around 3Dt. If coming by car, the museum is clearly signed once in the Bardo area of town but be warned that the entrance to the grounds is not clearly marked: if coming from central Tunis, at the 'fountain' junction keep fountains on your left (entrance to National Assembly and Bardo buildings behind railings and trees on your right). Take first right, and the entrance to the coach and car park is on your right after about 50 m. Just after the entrance is a low military bastion.*

History of the palace   Almost as impressive as the mosaics are the actual display rooms themselves. The first floor is composed of a series of great reception rooms and courts, some galleried, others with spectacular gilding – an indication of the style favoured by the 19th-century Husseinite princes. The Bardo Palace in fact dates back to the Middle Ages, when the Hafsid rulers built themselves pleasure palaces in the countryside and orchards around Tunis. The palace was extended under 17th-and 18th-century rulers, becoming the ideal setting for dynastic intrigue and the power-centre of the Husseinid Dynasty, suitably remote from the city of Tunis. By the mid-1800s, the Bardo had become a huge palace complex surrounded by walls and bastions. Parts of it were decaying. The French, keen to prove the 'Latinity' of North Africa, and in need of a place to display the impressive finds that their archaeologists kept discovering, converted part of the building into the Musée Alaouite (opened 1888), named for Ali Bey. Renamed the Musée National du Bardo, this is the museum you can visit today. The constant new discoveries meant that a further, second floor of mosaic display rooms had to be developed.

Visiting the Bardo in the 1830s

"Under the archway, and forming a rich and animated foreground, are seen groups of splendidly caparisoned horses, awaiting the return of their masters from the audience chamber: on the opposite side of the court, rises a wild flight of steps, almost covered by seated Arabs, wrapped in the graceful and classic folds of their sefsars and burnooses, patiently awaiting their turn to be ushered into the hall of justice. These steps lead to a covered gallery, supported by columns, where are seen walking about or forming little groups, many Moors, soldiers, officers and attendants in their gay attire."

Sir Grenville T. Temple, Excursions in the Mediterranean: Algiers and Tunis (London, 1835)

The plan shows the recommended route, with the main rooms and important features worth noting. It may be best just to wander, however, letting the museum draw you in, marvelling at skilled craftwork from 18 centuries ago, produced in one of the great centres of ancient Romanity.

Ground floor When in the **Entrance hall** and ticket office, there is a room of early Christian remains to your left. To the right, if open, is a room with the **Prehistory** exhibits – a collection of flint blades, bones, costume ornaments and engraved stones from the Acheulean, Mousterian, Ibero-Moorish, Capsian and Neolithic eras. This then leads into Punic and Libyic exhibits.

Visiting the Bardo

The Punic rooms have a first-century, small terracotta statue of the god Baal-Hammon (Thinissut, Cap Bon); a fourth-century group of three divinities, Pluto, Demeter and Kore (carrying a piglet); and a fourth-century stele of Priest and Child (Carthage). (Is the child being carried ready for sacrifice?) In the second room is a collection of masks made of glass paste or pottery generally placed in tombs with expressions designed to frighten evil spirits; personal decorations, necklaces et cetera; and a Punic tomb reconstruction in a smaller adjoining room with an arrangement of funeral objects (Cap Bon).

Punic rooms

Libyic exhibits include bas-reliefs showing gods; funeral monuments with bilingual inscriptions in Libyic/Punic or Libyic/Latin. The **Sarcophagus corridor** has two second-century marble sarcophagi, one representing the nine Muses (Porto Farina), the other the four seasons; a third-century Roman funeral effigy of a Romano/African citizen (Borj el Amri) and the Boglio stele, also third-century Roman, from a series dedicated to Saturn.

The **Thuburbo Majus** corridor and room have inscriptions, statues, marble wall panels, geometric and floral mosaics; a small bas-relief representing Maenads from first century – while the **Palaeo-Christian** corridor and room display a collection of tomb mosaics and church pavements. See particularly the fourth-century 'Ecclesia Mater' tomb mosaic (Tabarka) showing the section of a church with candles on the altar; tomb mosaic with two figures and seven crowns inscribed with the names of the seven martyrs; limestone font (Gightis) in centre of room; and tiles showing Biblical scenes.

Bulla Regia was one of the most important Roman settlements in Africa, a wealthy town at the heart of the wheat-growing region on the upper Medjerda. The Bulla Regia room (which follows on from the Palaeo-Christian room) displays items from northwest Tunisia's one time grain capital, close to present day Jendouba. From the Temple of Apollo, second century BC, comes a very languid god. A gallery of portraits of Roman emperors completes the ground-floor rooms.

Bulla Regia room

Tunis and around

On a staircase leading to the first floor is a series of mosaics (fourth-sixth centuries) from funeral monuments of the Christian era (Tabarka), some giving age and occupation of the deceased. There is also a statue of Apollo (Carthage).

First floor It is on the first floor that the Bardo is at its most impressive. Looking at the vast mosaics and the somewhat chipped statuary, you begin to feel the wealth and power of the Roman lords of ancient Africa, and how they sought to impress with displays of luxurious imagery, often mythological, sometimes

Bardo Museum

mundane. Though the Romans had huge estates, slavery and repression was the basis of the system. As an indication of just how the wealth was concentrated,the elder Pliny (writing in the first century AD) says that six men alone owned half the province of Africa. Senators came to own vast estates – and the Lord Julius mosaic in the Sousse room shows us a very pleasant country estate.

The **Ulysses** room is named after the famous Ulysses mosaic (Dougga) on display here. He is depicted bound to the ship's mast to prevent him following the sirens, on the right, playing musical instruments. Ulysses' companions have stopped their ears with wax (not visible) and are looking in the opposite direction to avoid the same fate. **Marine mosaics**

Other mosaics of a marine bent include the very large late-third/early-fourth-century (Utica) Neptune and Amphitrite in a chariot drawn by sea horses with two nereids seated on sea tigers, with three boats each with a bejewelled lady surrounded by cupids – the self crowning of a semi nude/bejewelled Venus, (fourth century, Carthage). There is also a mosaic of Marsyas the satyr and Apollo making music while Minerva looks on (judges?); the surrounds depict the four seasons (third century, El Djem). At one end of the room is a fountain (Thuburbo Majus), no doubt from the largest room of some sumptuous villa, with the head of Oceanus portrayed on the exterior and the interior decorated with nereids (sea nymphs) and sea monsters.

In the corridor is **Bacchus and Ariadne's** wedding mosaic from the fourth century (Thuburbo Majus).

El Djem is a Roman site north of Sfax in the Sahel region of modern Tunisia, chiefly famed for its vast amphitheatre, the third largest to have survived and the setting for large scale games and entertainments. El Djem was evidently a fun sort of place, as the surviving mosaics indicate. On display here are intricate *xenia* (still life) and other mosaics related to food and good times. There are men playing dice, animals (fish, duck) and musical instruments, all themes popular for decorating the dining rooms of wealthy villa owners in the third century. From the same period comes a hunting mosaic, complete with horses, hounds and a hiding hare. On the floor Bacchus rides his triumphal chariot drawn by tigers led by Pan. **El Djem room**

Dougga, a couple of hours' drive west of Tunis, is for many the country's most beautiful Roman site, set on a hillside looking out over fertile cornlands. In the Dougga room (don't miss the magnificent painted ceiling) are two ancient models of the city, one of the Square of the Capital and the other of the theatre. On the walls and floor are mosaics (La Chebba, Carthage and Thuburbo Majus). Neptune, placed centrally, is magnificent in his chariot with hunting and seasonal agricultural scenes around (second century, La Chebba, Sfax). Opposite are three dark-skinned giants working the forge of Vulcan, found in the Cyclops' baths (fourth century, Dougga); also Cup bearers serving guests (Dougga). **Dougga room**

The huge Sousse room houses a large collection of mosaics from Sousse, Carthage and Tabarka; the head and feet of a colossal statue of Jupiter (Thuburbo Majus); Punic, Greek and Roman lamps, ceramics (El Aouja near Kairouan); on the floor a third-century mosaic of Neptune surrounded by sea creatures (Sousse); the Lord Julius mosaic (early fifth century, Carthage) – depicting a central imposing villa and pictures of the cycle of the seasons and rural life; three big pavings from apses from private villas (Tabarka), probably **Sousse room**

Tunis and around

of the same age as the Carthage mosaic; and mosaics illustrating a circus (third century, Carthage) and chariot races (sixth century, Gafsa).

Sculpture Hall A great hall, complete with colonnade, gallery and high ornamented ceiling, houses sculpture, mainly from **Carthage**. In the centre is an altar dedicated to the 'Gens Augusta' with bas-reliefs on all four sides dated between the first century AD and first century BC; on the floor are two famous third-century mosaic pavements (Uthina/Oudna), the first of Bacchus surrounded by cupids among the vines and a second showing agricultural activities and hunting scenes. There are statues of Roman gods and an imposing statue of the Emperor Hadrian, creator of the great aqueduct which linked the springs of Mount Zaghouan to Carthage.

Althiburos room To the side in the Althiburos room are mosaics (Althiburos and Carthage); on the floor a fourth-century mosaic of Roman boats, all correctly titled; also a fourth-century banqueting scene with guests seated on benches rather than reclining on couches; and a mosaic of hunting scenes, a temple containing Apollo and Diana and a crane being sacrificed (fifth to seventh centuries, Carthage-Salammbo) indicating a survival of pagan practices into the Christian era. For the record, Althiburos, today an obscure site south of Le Kef close to the village of Medeina, was once a major stop on the Carthage to Tebessa road.

Virgil room The Virgil room is octagonal with a magnificent dome of carved plaster work. The third-century mosaic, showing a seated Virgil in meditation between the muses of history and tragedy (Sousse), is the only portrait of the poet. Whether Virgil ever visited Carthage is a matter of debate. Whatever, Aeneas, the hero of his epic, *The Aeneid*, fell in love with Carthage's Queen Dido, only to leave her heartbroken as he travelled on to Italy to found Rome. Dido committed suicide, and later in The Aeneid reappears to reproach her former love when he visits the Underworld. It is a serene epic poet, scroll in hand, who gazes at the visitor today. He is flanked by thoughtful muses, a wistful Melpomene (Tragedy), carrying a mask, and Clio (History), bearing another scroll.

In the centre of the floor the third-century mosaic has medallions with the signs of the zodiac surrounding godheads of the days of the week (Bir Chana near Zaghouan).

Jewellery room The ornamentation in the Jewellery room is mainly Punic, some from as long ago as the seventh century BC, mainly from Carthage but also Utica and Kerkouane. There are matching necklaces and earrings of tiny ceramic/ivory figures/objects, rings, seals et cetera, solid gold jewellery and gold plate on bronze.

Mahdia room The contents of a Roman ship was discovered off Mahdia by sponge divers early last century. The display (if not on loan) includes Hellenistic bronze and marble, furniture, pieces of the wrecked ship, and marble statues of Aphrodite (second to first century BC) which look only a little worse for wear after their immersion. The bronzes reflect the Romans taste for all things Greek. (A similarly fine selection, discovered at the Roman site of Volubilis near Meknès, is on display in the Musée Archaeologique in Rabat, Morocco.)

Marine mosaics At the back of the Mahdia room is a room of mosaics on marine themes. On display are sections of a huge mosaic of a seascape including dolphins, nereids and sea monsters (Carthage).

The Mausoleum room takes its name from a large Roman tomb displayed here. All four sides feature bas-reliefs with a strong symbolic charge: there is a proconsul's legate on horseback, fasces and funeral putti. On the walls are some important fourth-century mosaics from Thuburbo Majus, including a hunting scene, Venus doing her hair assisted by two putti, and Bacchus and Ariane, accompanied by a satyr and a bacchante.

Mausoleum room

The Uthina (Oudna) room has many mosaics of hunting or mythology. Of particular interest is the fine mosaic showing the remains of a meal. There is also a large pavement portraying Orpheus (unfortunately headless), with his lyre charming the wild beasts.

Uthina room

At this point it is necessary to go downstairs to see the **Folk art and traditions room** before ascending to view the **Islamic rooms** situated in the smaller, older (1831) building set around a patio. (With luck the displays will be open.) The hall displays artifacts from the 9th-13th centuries, including musical instruments, weapons, household objects; jewellery, in particular gold necklaces, bracelets and earrings; traditional costumes, furniture; parchments, manuscripts, verses of the Koran, most of the documents from the great mosque of Kairouan, in particular pages from the Blue Koran; *tiraz* fabrics with Koranic inscriptions; astralobes, sundials and compasses; and ceramics.

Tunisian folk art

The last room on this floor has a number of fourth-century mosaics, including one called Hunting the Wild Boar, showing three stages of the hunt; Venus being crowned by two female centaurs; and a splendid peacock with a spread tail.

The main staircase leads to the second floor, where the **gallery** overlooking the Carthage room contains terracotta statuettes of protective gods such as Venus and Mercury from temples and tombs. Here also are objects from necropoli of the first to third centuries, glasses, bowls, dishes from tombs, funeral urns and statuettes. Don't miss the surgeon's kit with lancets, scalpels and forceps.

Second floor

The corridors and rooms around the top of the stairs have yet more mosaics (fourth century), depicting Theseus slaying the Minotaur in a large maze of brown on cream, while the border depicts the walls and gates of a city (Thuburbo Majus); two mosaics on the theme of animal sports with a haloed Bacchus (El Djem) and a fourth-century example from Thelepte/Feriana; and a second-century paving (Thuburbo Majus), depicting a meditating poet seated on a column shaft, a mosaic in praise of intellect. In a separate room is a third-century Diana the Huntress on a deer, the medallions portraying animals of the hunt, boars, gazelle, et cetera (Thuburbo Majus); and Venus on a rock (third century, Utica).

The items in the Acholla room (a site north of Sfax) were collected from private houses. There is a splendid mosaic of Dionysus riding a tiger, guiding his mount with a thyrsus. The main piece in this room is the Triumph of Dionysus, showing the god standing in a chariot drawn by two sea-centaurs. Also shown are allegorical figures of Spring and Winter. Still on a marine theme, look out for the fountain mosaic portraying the head of the God Ocean, with two oversized lobster claws sticking out of his head. Another fine mosaic in this room depicts the Labours of Hercules. Each of 13 boxes shows a human, animal or monster symbolizing one of Hercules' labours.

Acholla room

If you are now looking for somewhere nearby to have a coffee or a meal while you digest what you have seen, there is not too much choice. There is a small pizzeria, almost opposite the entrance, crowded to the doors at lunchtime.

Leaving the Bardo

Tunis and around

Going left out of the entrance, across the main road junction, are two sandwich places. If you are on a short trip, it is probably best to head back to town (a taxi to the Kasbah, if rushed) to have lunch in the médina and take in something of the old city in the afternoon (if it is not too hot). To complete your dose of Tunisian heritage, you could aim for the **Dar Ben Abdallah Museum** in the Tourbet El Bey neighbourhood. ■ *Open until 1630, closed Mon.* (See Médina Walk 2, page 82.)

Other sights and attractions

Other museums **Numismatic Museum** Has an exhibition of Tunisian coins dating back to Carthaginian times. ■ *Free. T254000. Located in the entrance hall of the Central Bank, Rue Hedi Nouira.*

Postal Museum Clearly the most anorakish museum in Tunis, exhibits include Tunisian stamps and old telephones and post boxes, also a rather fine early postman's uniform. Clearly a must-do on your sixth visit to the city. ■ *Located in the main PTT building, entrance can go unnoticed on Rue d'Angleterre.*

Military Museum Set in a fine 19th-century palace, a short taxi ride from the Bardo, this museum has displays of Tunisian military history from the earliest times to the present. Little visited, but worth a look if you are in Tunis for some time. ■ *T520220. Palais de la Rose, Manouba.*

Museum of Husseinid Tunisia Even closer to the Bardo, this projected museum, set in a beylical palace used as a hospital until recently, will house portraits and memorabilia of the Husseinid beys. ■ *Turn right out of Bardo gate, cross road and 20 m on you will find the road leading to the entrance.*

Parc du Belvédère
Women are advised not to venture into the park unaccompanied

The city's green lung is the **Parc du Belvédère**, which occupies a large stretch of hillside separating upmarket residential neighbourhoods Mutuelleville and Notre Dame from El Omrane and quarters north of the médina. The lower areas near the main gates have some sizeable trees. From the upper reaches of the park, there are some splendid views over Tunis, the most interesting being to the southeast towards Korbous and Cap Bon and to Djebel Bou Kornine and Djebel Ressas. In the summer, the vegetation tends to dry out, leaving arid expanses between wilting trees. Two roads through the park are open to traffic and there are numerous narrow paths for pedestrians. The area is patrolled by mounted police, presumably on the look out for winos and courting couples. On the northern side of the park is a signposted jogging circuit, the *Parcours de santé*.

It's about a 30-minute walk to get to the top of the Belvédère hill, so you might take a taxi to the top and walk down, calling in at the **Koubba**, an orientalist domed pavilion, on the way. This is in an enclosed area with grass and trees, but a call might bring out the caretaker who, for a tip, will show you round. The view from the terrace is well worth the tip. The story goes that the building was constructed in Turkish style by the Bey of Tunis in 1789, as a retreat from his daughter. It consists of a large room surmounted by a magnificent dome decorated with exquisitely carved plaster work. In recent years, the Koubba has been used for filming Tunisian TV's Sunday morning breakfast show. ■ *To get to the park, take bus 5 from Pl de l'Indépendence and get off at Pl Pasteur; or Metro line 2 from Pl de Barcelona to Palestine station. It is then a short walk to the park.*

At the foot of the Belvédère hill, within the park, off Avenue Taieb Mehiri (ex-Albert I), is the entrance to the **Zoological Garden**. By the entrance is a café. Adjacent is a small lake complete with water fowl and three fountains. This is a well-established zoo, perhaps the only one that can be recommended in Tunisia. The zoo covers a large area and houses a full range of birds and animals but no indoor displays. The information is given in Arabic and French. ■ *0900-1800 (ticket office closes 1700), closed Mon. 3Dt, children under nine 1Dt, photographs 1Dt. Toilets 50 m to the left beyond entrance.*

Zoo
It's easy to get right up close to the cages, so keep an eye on children to avoid them being accidentally fed to the beasts

Tunis does not have a large amount of green space. In the city centre, the **Jardin Habib Thameur** is chiefly interesting for being on the site of the main Jewish cemetery. This was deconsecrated at the orders of ex-president Habib Bourguiba, leading to a massive loss of confidence in his government by members of the once numerous and influential Jewish community. The park does however provide a modicum of green in an otherwise noisy and traffic saturated city centre. Almost outside the urban area, north of Ariana on the Bizerte road, is the **Parc Ennahli**, a recent creation which provides somewhere for people to let their kids off the leash at weekends. In the new Berges du Lac neighbourhood is the **Dahdah** entertainment complex, with a full range of fairground rides, including a big wheel and dodgems. Not a cheap treat, but will certainly please most children. There is another funfair behind the swimming pool at the Bardo.

Other parks

The *Zone urbaine nord* has acquired a couple of new outdoor attractions, mainly of interest to those with a scientific bent. The vast new **Cité des Sciences**, heavily inspired by the Parisian institution of the same name, is set to open soon. There is a planetarium and within the building, a restored early waterwheel of the type once in use in parts of northern Tunisia. A reflecting pool and excavated pisé walls, the remains of late medieval Hafsid pleasure gardens, provide the focus of the inside area. A footbridge now takes visitors from the Cité des Sciences over the road to the **Arboretum**, originally part of the grounds of the INA, the National Agronomic Institute. Constituted for educational purposes, the collection of Tunisian trees and shrubs will please anyone in need of a spot of eye-soothing green in the Tunis summer. Opening date yet to be announced.

Cité des Sciences & arboretum

Essentials

Sleeping

Many of the cheaper hotels in the centre of Tunis have plenty of character (in the seedy sense of the term). There is little backpacker targeted accommodation. The cheapest hotels cater mainly for male Algerian visitors on shopping trips. In the mid-price range, there are several reasonable hotels close to the Pl Barcelone in the neighbourhood of the R de Grèce (hotels *de France, Salammbô, Transatlantique* and *Maison Dorée* in particular). Business travellers will find several acceptable hotels in the Belvédère district (*Les Ambassadeurs, El Mechtel, Le Belvédère*). These are generally better placed for meeting clients than the more pleasant (and expensive) coastal hotels in the Gammarth section of the Banlieue Nord (see below). The 5-star hotels are nothing special, and service can be just as effective in some of the smaller 4 and 3 stars. The best upmarket hotel today, popular with English-speaking clients, is probably *La Résidence* out at Raoued (see below page 136).

■ *on maps, pages 74, 102 and 106*
Price codes: see inside front cover

8-digit phone numbers begin: 71

For ease of reference, hotels are listed here according to area, starting with the areas with the cheaper accommodation and moving upwards (in price terms).

Médina

■ on map, page 74
Mainly cheap hotels
acceptable to hard
core travellers on
a budget. Not really
for women
travelling alone

E *Hotel de la Médina*, 1 Pl de la Victoire, T327497. Close to Bab Bhar and British Embassy, entrance on side street between 2 cafés, 25 rooms, clean, tidy and basic, shared toilets, the café/restaurant forms the front lower part of the hotel facing the square. (NB Beware overcharging in café). **E** *Hotel des Amis*, 7 R Mestiri, T565653. A short walk down Souq Sidi Mehrez, leading from Bab Souika, 24 rooms, shared bath and toilet, beds on iron frames, clean, basic but awkward to find on your first time. **E** *Hotel Sfax*, 5 R de l'Or, T260275. Short way down Souq Sidi Mehrez, leading from Bab Souika, 12 rooms, 4 doubles, communal toilet, no bathroom, use nearby hammam, iron bed frames, no breakfast, very basic.

The southern part of the Médina has some cheap accommodation, too. Try **E** *Hotel Souk*, 101 R des Teinturiers, T347398, 15 rooms, with 3 and 8 being the quietest, hot shower on each floor, clean and simple. Just off the Kherba in the south-central médina are 2 cheapies (coming from R Jazira, at the triangle where the Libyan louages are, go left up the alley). The **F** *Hotel des Alliés* (signed), T326595, opened 1936 and not much changed since then, is up a steep marble flight of stairs. The cheapest beds in Tunis, 12 rooms off a once-splendid patio, Turkish loos. High-ceilinged rooms with cream-painted metal beds, a bit hospital-like. Owner from Ghoumrassen. Only if really

Tunis centre

Related maps
Tunis, page 70
A Tunis Médina,
page 74
**B Belvédère &
Lafayette**, page 106

■ Sleeping	8 El Hana	15 Salammbo	3 Café de Paris
1 Africa (Méridien)	International	16 Tej	4 Chez Gaston
2 Carlton	9 El Omrane	17 Transatlantique	& Le Boléro
3 Commodore	10 Golf Royal		5 Chez Nous
4 De Bretagne	11 Maison Dorée	● Eating	6 Chez Slah
5 De France	12 Majestic	1 Abid	7 La Mama
6 De Suisse	13 Oriental Palace	2 Bouchoucha &	8 Les Margaritas
7 Du Lac	14 Ritza	Chez Noureddine	9 Le Regent

Tunis and around (side margin text)

stuck as basically works for a long established clientèle of small traders from south and Libya. The **F** *Hotel Mahouachi* T252518, entrance opposite *Les Alliés*, is another matter. No hot water, *consigne* (lock-up for bags), marble marquetry and sagging staircase hints of long-gone grandeur. Very last resort.

There are a good number of cheap hotels along the Blvd Bab Jedid, catering essentially for an Algerian/local clientele. The advantage over the médina hotels is that they are easier to find and, in the case of the Bab Jedid hotels, a little closer to the rail station. Close to the fountain, going up the slope, is the **E** *Hotel Jazira*, 23 Av Bab Djedid, T340225. All rooms with ceiling fan, some with shower, street-facing rooms very noisy. Still, a very good address at this price. About 150 m up the blvd, coming from the fountain roundabout, is a handy clutch of hotels mainly frequented by Algerian men over for a spot of intensive shopping (*le commerce de la valise*). On the left is **E** *Hotel El Quds*, 42 Av Bab Jedid but entrance on the side street, T241086, building converted from a clinic, some rooms with loo and bath, spartan and reception a bit niffy. On the right, is **E** *Hotel Bab Djedid*, aka *Chez el Hadi*, 51 Av Bab Dejdid, T/F336167. Building dates from 1992, 30 high-ceilinged rooms with basin, some with shower. Neon strip lights and metal bed frames complete the simple décor. Lots of rooms with 3 and 4 beds. NB roar of traffic from the street, chicha café on ground floor. Just behind on the tiny square is the **E** *Hotel Sahraoui*, T345341, 12 rooms, some with shower, another Algero-Moroccan address. A few metres further into the médina is the **E** *Hotel Sabra*, 86 R Tourbet el Bey, T340313, 24 rooms with up to 4 beds. Very basic, reception is the fine tiled entrance hall to an old house. Here the splendour stops. Rooms (metal bedsteads, foam mattresses) give onto a big white and blue courtyard. Simple, quiet but poor. Further up the blvd is **E** *Hotel Jasmin*, 56 Av Bab Djedid (opposite the UIB bank), T241240, 13 double, triple and quad rooms, 3rd floor rooms quietest. Last resort stuff. Closest to the Kasbah is **E** *Hotel de la Victoire*, 7 Blvd Bab Menara, 20 rooms (those on front are noisy), communal shower, clean.

Bab Djedid/ Bab Menara

Large number of hotels with a good sprinkling of reasonable, clean places, some 'with character', as they say. The area between Pl Barcelone and the Av H Bourguiba, around R de Grèce and R de Yougoslavie, has a good selection of mid-range places to stay.

South of Avenue Bourguiba
■ *on map, page 102*

B *Hotel Golf Royal*, R de Yougoslavie, T342422. Centrally located hotel in a street parallel to Av H Bourguiba. Expensive, poor value for money. Prefer the **B-C** *Hotel Commodor*, 17 R d'Allemagne opposite central market, T3243286, F324274. Immaculate, quiet hotel very handy for the médina, 48 rooms, most have bath, a/c, breakfast, refurbished 1999 – a good choice. Three floors but no lift. Slight disadvantage: most rooms are pretty dark as open onto narrow light shafts. But very quiet.

C *Hotel de Bretagne*, 7 R de Grèce, T252146. Good central location. 25 rooms, quite clean and quiet, some rooms now have a/c. Probably prefer the *Transatlantique* in this price bracket. Disadvantage: 1st-floor rooms directly over game 'arcade', so noisy. **C** *Hotel Maison Dorée*, 6 R de Hollande, just off Av de la Yougoslavie behind the French Embassy, T240631, F332401. Entrance down a side street. Must have been very swish in its day, good condition, spotlessly clean, good service, 1950s furniture adds charm, 54 rooms most with bath, some with a/c, breakfast included, restaurant *Les Margaritas* on R de Hollande has a good lunchtime menu at only 6dt. Good rooms include 115 and 215 (shower, wc, a/c), also the spacious 315, 403 (double), 405 (twin) and 410 (but without a/c and loo). Disadvantage? Tram noise in rooms overlooking R de Hollande. **C** *Hotel El Omrane*, 65 Av Farhat Hached, T345277, F354892, hotel.omrane@planet.tn Early 1990s, 89 rooms, 178 beds, one of the better hotels in this price bracket. Handy for the station, used by business travellers looking for something cheapish. TV and a/c in all rooms. **C** *Hotel El Oumara*, 42 bis R Ali Darghouth, T333122, F338030. Another lower end business hotel. Recommended. Location not as classy as (say) the *Carlton*, but very comfortable. **C** *Hotel de Russie*, 18 R de Russie, T328883, F321685. 23 rooms, some triple, best room 102. Clean, centrally located on a quiet street off R Jazira, very handy for southern bus and louage stations. Recommended.**C** *Hotel Tej*, 14 R Lt. Aziz Tej, T344899. Clean, overpriced, but has a/c. **C** *Hotel Transatlantique*, 106 Av de Yougoslavie, close to the intersection with Av de Carthage, T334319. Relatively quiet for a central hotel, most rooms with bath, breakfast included. Central heating in winter. A good central option, note the Chemla tiles in reception. Working lift. Disadvantage? Rooms overlooking Av de Carthage have noise of trams, ask for *côté cour*.

At the top of the cheap category is the **D** *Hotel Salammbô*, 6 R de Grèce, off Av H Bourguiba, T334252, F337498, hotel.salammbo@gnet.tn Clean hotel, 52 rooms on 4 floors, most with shower, otherwise 1Dt extra. Good reputation with budget travellers. Recommended. Disadavantage? Terrible flowery sheets and, as usual, street noise – light sleepers must ask for quiet room. Try rooms 28 or 29 (a triple with a/c and bath). **D** *Hotel de l'Agriculture*, 25 R Charles de Gaulle, T326394, F321685. Above lively café *Le Baccalauréat* and opposite *Hotel Cirta*. Women might get bothered here. Advantage is the a/c. But prefer by far the cheaper **D** *Hotel de France*, 8 R Mustapha M'Barek, T326244, F323314, hotelfrancetunis@yahoo.fr Very close to the médina. Must have been a very chic address in its day, spacious, pleasant rooms, enormous corridors, creaking lift, rooms 11 and 53 good or ask for rooms *côté jardin* (there's a tree out the back). Occasionally used by student groups, recommended. **D** *Hotel Dar Masmoudi*, 18 R du Maroc, off R d'Algerie, T322428, F327267. Close to main station and médina, most rooms with bath. Downside? Slightly seedy atmosphere, not recommended for women travelling alone, street-facing rooms noisy with kids from nearby school. Same management as *Hotel de l'Agriculture*. R de Suisse, a narrow link street between R de Holland and R Jamel Abd Ennasser, has a couple of cheapies, namely **D** *Hotel de Suisse*, 5 R de Suisse, T243821. 23 rooms, most with shower, clean, quiet. Will let you park your bike or motorbike in reception at night. A good second choice in the city centre cheapies. Rooms 207, 208, 305 and 308 are quiet. Top floor rooms very hot in summer. Nice management. Almost opposite is the **D** *Hotel Central*, T320422, clean, simple, metal-bedstead type place, most rooms with shower. Disadvantage? Noise from nearby metro line. Just creeping into the listings for this area is **D** *Hotel Sidi Behlassene*, 21 Av de la Gare, handy for the station, T344409. Turn left out of main station concourse, then left again, hotel is about 200 m on right just after bridge over rail line. Clientele brought in by taxi drivers. Not really recommended. Clean but noisy.

D-E *Hotel Cirta*, 42 Av Charles de Gaulle, T321584. Opposite the *Hotel de l'Agriculture*. Access to reception on 1st floor by marble staircase. Communal pay shower. All right but kind of sad. Room 18 quiet but gloomy. Just up the street from the *Hotel de France*, Porte de France direction, is **D** *Hotel Splendid*, R Mustapha M'barek, T322844, 36 rooms, from singles to triples. Lift and marble staircase are signs of former glory. Nice guy at reception. Cheap but prefer *Hotel de France* on this street.

E *Hotel d'Alger*, 5 R de Belgique, on Pl Barcelone, T326429, washbasin in most rooms, nice reception, go for courtyard-facing rooms, 4th-floor rooms are basically converted roof-terrace laundry rooms with splendid views over square but horribly hot in summer (and cold in winter). **E** *Hotel Bristol*, 30 R Mohamed Aziz Tej (starting at *Café de Paris*, head south down Av de Carthage and take first left), T254835, showers on landing, breakfast summer only. Simple, clean, old marble fireplaces, central heating in winter. An attractive eccentricity among Tunis's hotels: a non-profit making outfit, bought by members of Algerian freedom party, the FLN, in 1956, just after Tunisian independence. Fine for a couple of nights. **E** *Nouvel Hotel*, 3 Pl Mongi Bali, T243379. Avoid. Next to the station, not clean, communal showers, noisy, shady characters. Best cheapies here are **E** *Hotel Royal*, 19 R d'Espagne, T322780, near intersection with R Djazira, 30 rooms with sink, best rooms are 4 and 6. Minus points: rooms very small, inside-facing rooms stifling in summer. Good location, however. Also convenient for the station is **E** *Hotel Excelsior* R du Boucher, a narrow street off R d'Alger, T342917. 12 rooms with washbasin, shower on ground floor. Very cheap, receptionist does his best.

A couple of giants (*Africa* and *El Hana*). Best hotel on the north side is *Le Carlton*. **A** *Africa Méridien Hotel*, 50 Av H Bourguiba, old numbers were T347477, F347432. Large blue tower block in the middle of Tunis, total refurbishment 2001-2002, reopening date unknown. When part of the Méridien chain, it had 170 rooms, a/c, restaurants, bars, cinema, pool, conference facilities, etc. Expect much improved services. **A** *El Hana International*, 49 Av H Bourguiba, T331144. Informally known as the 'hôtel des deux avenues'. Large block at meeting point of Av H Bourguiba and Av de Paris. Pleasant rooftop bar open to all-comers with view over the city. Big new café terrace. **B** *Hotel Carlton*, 31 Av H Bourguiba, T330644, F338168, carlton@planet.tn Clean, 40 rooms with bath, a/c, slightly noisy position on main avenue. Minibus can meet you at the airport. Popular, so reservations a good idea. Recommended. **B** *Hotel Excel*, 35 Av H Bourguiba, T355088, F341929. Central position, TV, no breakfast, bar. A good choice if the *Carlton* is full.

Avenue Bourguiba
■ *on map, page 102*

Good selection of mid-price hotels in this area, plus a couple of decaying giants, the *Oriental Palace* and *Hotel du Lac*. **A** *Oriental Palace*, Av Jean Jaurès, T348846. Centrally located, just 5 mins from Av H Bourguiba, and often used for official party conferences. Characterized by large over-tiled lobby smelling of cheap disinfectant. Restaurant said to have a good floorshow with spectacular *danseuse orientale*. Not really worth it. **A-B** *Hotel du Lac*, Av H Bourguiba, central, T258322. Restaurant, 208 rooms all a/c. The 'upside-down pyramid' hotel near the east end of the Av H Bourguiba. Has seen better days. **B** *Hotel Oscar*, 12 R de Marseille, T344755, F354311. Opened late 1998, built after demolition of *El Quds* cinema, all 48 rooms with a/c and TV. Handy for eateries of the R de Marseille. **B-C** *Hotel Majestic*, Av de Paris, T332666, majestic@gnet.tn Old-fashioned, 100 rooms, all with a/c, large bar-terrace overlooking busy Av de Paris, restaurant. Newly weds get room 229 – 129 also good. Rooms overlooking the park on Av Habib Thameur sunny, agreeable in winter. Expect major renovation: hotel now belongs to Ben Yedder group, owners of *Dar Saïd* in Sidi Bou Saïd. Wide carpeted corridors and staircases show that this was once the city's premier address.

North of Avenue Bourguiba
■ *on map, page 102*

D *Hotel Ritza*, 35 Av Thameur, T245428, close to the Thameur park, 30 rooms, half with a/c, communal shower. Overlooks noisy junction (Pl République). Best rooms generally full as hotel used by dancers and artistes in the city-centre cabarets. Rooms 7, 16, 24, 32 have wc and shower. **D** *Hotel St Georges*, 16 R de Cologne, west of Av de la Liberté, T788664. 36 rooms, most with bath, a/c, restaurant, parking available. On the itinerary of has-beens' Tunis. Plus points: helpful reception, location close to interesting architecture and the blokey bar-restaurant which stays open late. Minus point: the noise from the bar in the small hours. **D** *Hotel Select House*, 2 Passage Paul Cambon, narrow side-street parallel to Av de Paris, close to the *Hotel Majestic* and *Medina Palace* shopping centre, T331336, 18 rooms, some recently revamped. Quiet. **D** *Hotel Ben Tili*, R Mohamed Ali, down a side-street near the *Banque de Tunisie*, almost opposite the Greek Cathedral, T335971. A converted clinic. The sort of place where young men from Tripoli meet their paramours. Disadvantage? Very noisy street-facing rooms. If all else full.

Tunis and around

Belvédère & Lafayette
■ *on map below*

AL *Hilton*, Av de la Ligue Arabe, T782100, F782208. Set high on a hill in upmarket residential area above the Belvédère, well outside the city centre, close to unfinished carcass of the Arab League building. Best placed hotel for the Menzah and Manar districts, handy for Mutuelleville and Lafayette as well. Conference rooms. Managed by the Marhaba Group today. Large, comfortable rooms, green and yellow, thick carpet. Soundproof rooms so no disturbance from current works programme, scheduled for completion 2004. Disadvantage? Uncontrollable a/c in the conference centre.

A *Abou Nawas*, Park Kennedy, Av Mohammed V, T350355, F352882, tunis@abounawas.com.tn Large hotel with all facilities close to the main banks. Well located for both city centre and Lafayette and Montplaisir, and a short taxi ride to the Menzahs, Berges du Lac and airport. In the early 1990s was the top hotel, now suffering from competition from new Banlieue Nord business-oriented hotels. Reception courteous, 2 restaurants (buffet, Italian) and Shéhérezade night club. Café in small mall next door, most shops closed. Conference centre (poor service). **A** *La Maison Blanche*, 45 Av Mohamed V, T849849, F793842, maison.blanche@planet.tn Perhaps the most

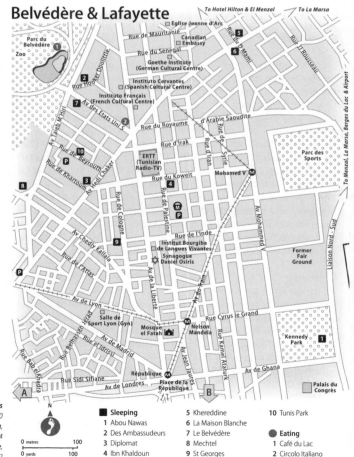

Belvédère & Lafayette

To Hotel Hilton & El Menzal — *To La Marsa*

To Menzah, La Marsa, Berges du Lac & Airport

Related maps
Tunis, page 70
A *Tunis médina,*
page 74
B *Tunis centre,*
page 102

0 metres 100
0 yards 100

■ Sleeping	
1 Abou Nawas	5 Khereddine
2 Des Ambassadeurs	6 La Maison Blanche
3 Diplomat	7 Le Belvédère
4 Ibn Khaldoun	8 Mechtel
	9 St Georges

10 Tunis Park

● Eating
1 Café du Lac
2 Circolo Italiano

interesting expensive address in the city. Suites only, all different in decoration, ranging from classic to kitsch. Good restaurant, popular brasserie.

B *Hotel des Ambassadeurs*, 75 Av Taïeb Mehiri, T788011, F780042, lesambassadeurs@ gnet.tn Small but nice rooms overlooking Belvédère Park, bathrooms better than *Mechtel*, magnetic key, a/c, acceptable restaurant, small bar. Good value, nice reception. **B** *Hotel Le Belvédère*, 10 Av des Etats-Unis, T783133, F782214, hotel.belvedere@ planet.tn Quiet, close to Belvédère Park, a/c, restaurant, one of the nicest of the business hotels (apart from plastic plants in reception). 2 categories of rooms, difference is in the bathroom, needs renovation in standard category, pleasant in superior category. Restaurant basic with willing service. Good value. **B** *Hotel Mechtel*, Av Taieb Mehiri, Belvédère, T780450, F782751, dir.marketing@abounawas.com.tn Basic business hotel with 450 rooms, often used for conferences, being upgraded in 2002. Minute pool, buffet restaurant has a good reputation, as does the Italian. Plus points: renovated rooms are very pleasant, hotel is well situated for getting to both city centre and Menzah and Manar districts, occasional cultural events in *El Teatro*, pocket theatre in same building. Disadvantage? Light sleepers should beware taking rooms on the upper floors when the nightclub reopens. **B** *Hotel Ibn Khaldoun*, 30 R du Koweït, just off R de Palestine, a block up from the Lafayette food market, T783211, F831689, hotelibn.khaldoun@planet.tn Prefer reservation by fax. A/c, agreeable restaurant in pastel tones, much improved by recent refurbishment. Pleasant, spacious rooms. Defect: damp smell in some corridors. **B** *Hotel National*, 14-16 R El Khartoum, T782955, F785707, hotel.national@planet.tn Willing reception, clean, large rooms (no balcony), bathrooms a headachey red-brick colour. Small restaurant for breakfast buffet, big dining room, everything blue, for other meals. Clean and good value. No car park.

B-C *Hotel Khereddine*, 2-4 Av Khereddine Pacha, T788211, F789418. Shifty atmosphere, odour of fried food in reception. Avoid. **C** *Tunis Park Hotel*, 7 R de Damas, obscure street off Av Taieb Mehiri by the Belvédère Park, T286696. 28 rooms, quiet and in need of refurbishment.

Tunisian Youth Hostel Association, 10 R Ali Bach Hamba, 1000 Tunis, T353227. 1) **Youth hostels**
Radès, 10 km southwest of Tunis, T483631. 120 beds, meals provided, take the train from the main station, a 10-minute walk from Radès station. 2) In the médina, 25 R Saïda Ajoula, T567850. 70 beds, 500 m from Place du Gouvernement (La Kasbah), 1.5 km from central station. 3) *Centre d'hébergement Jelili ez Zahra*, Oued Meliane Ezzahara, BP1140, T481547. 72 beds, kitchen, meals provided, take bus 26A from Pl Barcelone. 4) Possibility of staying in the Bardo University campus in the summer, contact T784241, R du Mali, Tunis.

Eating

Tunis has quite a range of restaurants, although exotic cuisine is more or less unrepresented. When Tunisians want something special, they go for a fish restaurant. Very basic French and Italian cooking is represented in some of the mid-range and expensive places. The real delights of Tunis cooking are to be found in the cheap places in odd corners of the Médina and the streets off Av H Bourguiba.

In the city centre, there is a good concentration of long-established places in the streets off Av H Bourguiba. The Lafayette district also has a few good places. Several upmarket 'old Tunis' type restaurants can be found in the Kasbah district of the Médina. There are some no-alcohol lunchtime haunts for business people in the Menzah area. The offspring of the middle class hang out at the pizzerias and cafés-glacier at the Arcades in El Manar.

In summer, people tend to head out of the city in the evening to eat at the Banlieue Nord restaurants. See recommendations on page 120 for further details

Tunis and around

Expensive *Bagdad*, Av H Bourguiba. Tunisian food accompanied by an '*awwada*' (small local band), belting out Arab and Tunisian favourite tunes. *Chez Gaston*, 73 R de Yougoslavie, T340417. Adequate, seafood specialities. *Chez Nous*, R de Marseille, T54043. French cooking with some Tunisian specialities, alcohol. Staff play party tricks. Has declined in recent years. Black and white photographs of stars of the 1960s and 1970s recall a once-glorious clientele. *Chez Slah*, 14 R Pierre de Coubertin, T258588. Perhaps the best restaurant in central Tunis, highly recommended but the bill will be large, essential to book, lunch 1215-1345, dinner 1915-2130. Good fish. To get there, locate *STB Bank* at clocktower end of Av H Bourguiba, take Av Pierre-de-Coubertin, cross over junction with *Mobil* garage, restaurant is in seemingly unlikely location about 20 m down street, on your left.

Mid-range *Le Boléro*, small restaurant hidden away in a side-street (passage El Guettar) off the R de Yougoslavie, almost opposite *Gaston's*. Alcohol and reasonable food. Has a slightly maverick air to it. Clients are Tunisian men seeking a low-key boozy lunch. *Le Cosmos*, R Ibn Khaldoun, opposite the cinemas. Unhappily closed in early 2002. Food was good, especially the fish, endearingly eccentric service. Especially popular during the Carthage Film Festival. *L'Etable*, Av H Bourguiba, near Pl d'Afrique, Tunisian specialities, alcohol. *La Mama*, R de Marseille, mixture of French, Italian and traditional Tunisian cooking, alcohol. Occasional live music. *Les Margaritas*, R de Hollande. This is the restaurant for the *Maison Dorée*. A very reasonably priced menu, and, some years and in season, tender *marcassin* (wild boar piglet). *Le Regent*, 16 R de Lieutenant Abdel Aziz Tej, behind the *Africa Hotel*, T341723. Popular with business people. On the unimaginative side, but more than adequate. At the top end of the mid-range price bracket. *Le Grill*, Av H Bourguiba, near the clocktower, opposite the Ministry of the Interior. Pavement terrace, alcohol, recently refurbished, a good little address for basics. The *Restaurant Bouchoucha* and *Chez Noureddine* are 2 fine eateries down on the R Farhat Hached, just by the metro stop (and before R de Turquie, on your right) as you head away from Pl Barcelone. Go at lunchtime, prefer *Bouchoucha*, which does excellent pasta (big portions) and specials like rabbit with mushrooms. Ambience: splendidly boozy, loud and cheerful. The clientele: dockworkers, traders from the central market, the occasional Italian tourist, etc. The boss and Abdessatar keep their cast of regulars in order. Also a feature are the street pedlars, who will sell you nuts, chickpeas, a fan or a mosque-shaped clock, or even a *sifsari* (traditional woman's cream wrap) – if you're feeling guilty about having lunch with lots of wine and the wife's at home.

Cheap *Restaurant Abid*, 98 R de Yougoslavie, near the intersection with R Ibn Khaldoun. Well-cooked filling food. Very reasonable prices. *Abdelaziz Elleuch*, 6 R de Caire, T257701. Couscous and fish. *Le Capitole*, 60 Av H Bourguiba. Cheap restaurant on 1st floor, almost above the *Café de Paris*. A well-established place with a very reasonably priced menu, attracts office workers to spend their tickets-restaurant. Highly recommended. *Le Carcassonne*, Av de Carthage, fine for a cheap fill-up. *Pizza Sprint*, small pizzeria next to the *Café de Paris* on the Av H Bourguiba, T343131. Generally perfectly acceptable but gets very crowded at lunchtime during the week. Good grilled green pepper salad. Alcohol. (The same people run *Pizza Sprint-Arthé* at La Marsa-Plage.) *Le Prince*, Pl de Barcelone, large self-service place 150 m across the square from the main train station, clean and cheap, some typical Tunisian food and the usual slices of pizza. Popular with young locals and office workers at lunchtime.

Expensive *L'Astragale*, 17 Av Charles Nicolle, Cité Jardin, T785080. A very fine restaurant in a converted villa, one of the most elegant eateries in Tunisia with prices to match. Its red and ochre décor and garden fountain would not look out of place in Marrakech. Not a huge choice on the menu – quality and refinement rather than quantity is the name of the game here. Altogether more ostentatious is *Le Baroque*, 32 R Félicien Challaye, T844220, F786512. Just off Av Charles Nicolle, which links Pl Pasteur with Menzah I. Entrance via a fine staircase through a terraced garden. French chef, excellent, varied menu, nouvelle cuisine. Very, very expensive. Meeting room and bar, chic and discrete. *Le Babylone*, 32 R El Moez, El Menzah I, T233999. A converted villa on a busy junction in the residential suburb of El Menzah. Plastic flowers hanging from the ceiling hard on the eye. Limited menu. Very last resort for entertaining clients.

Mid-range *Circolo Italiano* 102 Av de la Liberté, entrance opposite the French Cultural Centre, T288037. One of the best Italian addresses in Tunis, popular at both lunchtime (with business people and bank and embassy staff) and in the evenings (reservations a good idea). Officially, a private club for Tunis's Italian community. *La Romanesca*, 29 Av Ahmed Tlili, Menzah V, T753241. Excellent Italian food. No alcohol, as unfortunately the Ariana governorate has a dry policy. Otherwise a good address.

Suburban Tunis (Lafayette, Cité Jardin etc)
● *on map, page 106*

Expensive Several well established addresses here, and at least 2 new ones scheduled to open, a restaurant area in Dar Hammouda Pacha and a Moroccan restaurant nearby. For the moment, top address is *Dar el Jeld*, 5 R Dar el Jeld in the médina, off Pl du Gouvernement, T260916. Very good traditional Tunisian cooking provided in a home restored and converted to restaurant use by the Abdelkafi family. Upmarket dining to the tinkling sound of the lute. Try the *kabkabou* (fish with preserved lemons). Large portions, so go carefully if you want to have room for one of their really rather tempting desserts. Service formal. Closed Sun, booking recommended. Just down the street, the *Diwan Dar el Jeld*, in a similarly restored house, has banqueting and reception facilities and a giftshop with *Dar el Jeld* merchandise (Jasmine soap makes a good present). *Essaraya*, 6 R Ben Mahmoud, T560310. Also in a restored property, a 3 forks de luxe restaurant. The interior is (disappointingly?) kitsch. Unctuous welcome. You can eat Tunisian far more cheaply than this. Closed Sun. *Le Mrabet*, Souk Ettrouk, T563681. The original 'traditional cuisine' restaurant in the médina. On the 1st floor above the *Café Mrabet*. Floor show.

Médina
● *on map, page 74*

Mid-range *Dar Bel Hadj*, 17 R des Tamis, T336910 (just 5 mins from the Pl du Gouvernement, turn right onto R des Tamis as you go down R de la Kasbah). Private house, unauthentic restoration. No booze. If you think you might get lost, they have a noddy train to bring clients from the Kasbah esplanade. Go for *Dar el Jeld* or one of the cheap lunchtime places in the central médina for Tunisian food.

Cheap As elsewhere in Tunisia, the cheap eateries are generally the best, even if the seating conditions often leave a little to be desired. In this category, there are 2 sorts of restaurant in the médina, the lunchtime haunts of civil servants and students, mostly situated close to the Ezzitouna Mosque, and late-night places at Bab Jedid. Try *Mehdaoui*, under the covered passageway in front of the Great Mosque. Good nosh sitting at tables in the street. Fills up quickly at 1300, specials run out quickly. Lunch only. Nearby, *Am Chadli* (a no-name place) provides good lunchtime fare in cramped premises, too. (Facing the steps of the Great Mosque, go left, under the vaulted passageway, past a jeweller and a tailor on your left, and the eatery door is between nos 14 and 16). Menu changes daily, good choices include *hout muqli* (fried fish), *mirmiz* (beef stew with onion and tomato sauce), and *djedj mehchi* (chicken with an egg and parsley stuffing). *Grill Soltane* (chez Sidki), Blvd Bab Jedid, a few doors right of the old gate. For

Tunis and around

grilled fish and crevettes. Clean. *Ould Abba*. Late-night eatery on Pl des Armes at Bab Jedid. Stand at the zinc counter with the wide boys and assorted seedy characters and lap up a bowl of *lablabi* chick-pea soup. The mural décor changes regularly, but look out for the spangly Hand of Fatima set in the wall behind glass. (Is there a real hand in there?) Ould Abba himself presides over the proceedings. *Restaurant Granada*, Blvd Bab Jedid. Large dining room with TV actually in the former arms room of the old gate. Can work out expensive, but you can eat cheaply nevertheless.

Bars and cafés

Av H Bourguiba now has all the big café terraces you would expect of a Mediterranean city. The side-streets off the avenue, especially R de Marseille and around Pl Barcelone, have a selection of loud and boozy bars, not for the fainthearted. The revamped café of the *Café Africa*, by the *Africa Hotel*, should provide opportunity to watch the crowds. Best terraces open in spring 2002 were those of the *Hotel El Hana International* (fine rooftop bar-café, too) and that of the *Café de Paris*, corner of Av H Bourguiba and Av de Carthage. They took out the old, Parisian-style leatherette bench seating in the the late 1980s. Elegant once more after its facelift in 2001, urbane and a tad rakish, this is the place for a quiet mid-morning postcard session. Wakes up after siesta-hour, rendez-vous are made here if only those tables could talk. Attracts an odd but occasionally interesting mix of mainly male people. Serves alcohol. Capital bar of has-beens' Tunis must be the terrace of the *Hotel Majestic*, now mainly the haunt of Libyans over for a boozing spree. For a late drink in hearty male company try the bar of the *Hotel Saint-Georges*, up in Lafayette. The most tasteful (but still 100% blokeish) of the old bars must be the *Mario*, almost next to a pharmacy at the R d'Espagne end of Pl Barcelone. Politer male Tunisians tend to go for a meal with their booze. For the theatre set and courting couples, the café of the *Théâtre de l'Etoile du Nord* provides a faintly artsy-fartsy haven (no booze). The best sun-soaked terrace (cos traffic free) must be the one behind the Porte de France, the *Café Dinar*.

Chicha cafés The *chicha* or waterpipe café is a relatively recent feature on the Tunis street scene, compensating for the lack of brasseries and comfortable cafés. The most atmospheric chicha cafés are in the médina, with 1 or 2 good ones in Lafayette. Chichas can only be smoked inside the café. Try the following. *Café Ezzitouna*, on R Jamaâ Ezzitouna, on your left just before you get to the Great Mosque. Tiled walls, tiled benches, and a few seats in the street to watch the tourists come lumbering up through the souk. Good value on Ramadan evenings. *Café Mnouchi*, obscure doorway at the meeting of Souk el Leffa and Souk Kebabjia. Dark passageway set with ancient tile panels leads you into a courtyard full of cardplayers at lunchtimes, the souk sellers, apprentices and workmen of the médina letting off steam. *Chez Kamel*, on the sloping R Sidi Ben Arous, central médina, just below the minaret of the Zitouna Mosque. Tiny café where you sit cosily wedged in smoking your chicha. Good in winter. Late on summer nights it may be possible to smoke outside. Two more chicha cafés are on the small open area next to the entrance to Souk Essakagine, near Bab Menara, opposite the *Hotel de la Victoire*.

Patisseries Best central Tunis address is *Ben Yedder*, 7 R Charles-de-Gaulle, which as well as Tunisian sweetmeats does mean lunchtime sandwiches. In the Médina, best address is *Mourali*, near the top of R de la Kasbah, who do fruit juices as well as Tunisian sweets and sandwiches. Highly recommended. The city's topmost address must be *Les Galets*, 69 R Taïeb Mehiri, T796359, near the *Hotel Les Ambassadeurs*. Try their *mlebes boufrioua*, white sugar-coated hazelnut delight. A box of these will delight friends at home.

Entertainment

For nightlife of any kind, you will have to head out to the Banlieue Nord. There are a few other attractions in the form of art galleries and some good local theatre, in Tunisian Arabic. The French and Italian cultural centres occasionally bring over theatre, music and even the odd opera.

Art galleries

Club Tahar Haddad, 20 R du Tribunal, in the médina, T561275, occasional exhibitions; *Galerie Alyssa*, 3 Av Casablanca, Bardo, T223107; *Galerie Blel*, 70 Av d'Afrique, El Menzah, T231044.

Cinemas

The *Colisée*, dating from the 1930s, is the largest. The *Africa* cinema has probably been refitted, the *Oscar* on R de Marseille is cramped. Most of the other cinemas cater to macho tastes (kung-fu, Schwarzenegger and soft porn).

Hammams

Turkish baths are an institution in Tunisia. Many people go at least once a week. A visit to the hammam is a revitalizing experience and well worthwhile. Some hammams operate for men only, others for women only. Another pattern of opening reserves the morning for men and the afternoon for women (until 1800 after which the men can return). The oldest hammams are in the médina. Try any of the following: *Hammam Sahib Ettabaâ*, Halfaouine; *Hammam Sidi Belghayth*, R Hajjamine, Bab Jedid neighbourhood (men only). Sadly, a number of older hammams remain resolutely closed, including *Hammam Sabaghine* in the central médina and *Hammam Hafhouf*, R de la Rivière, near Pl du Leader. Could this be a sign of better bathrooms at home? Worse still, one of the best and oldest establishments, the *Hammam el Jeld* near the Kasbah, has been acquired by a property developer to be transformed into who knows what sort of tasteful tourist experience.

Music

The *Hotel Mechtel* has a nightclub on the top floor, scheduled to reopen in late 2002. There are occasional jazz evenings in the winter at *El Teatro*, a mini-theatre housed in the same complex. There are occasional concerts by foreign orchestras and ensembles at the Théâtre Municipal.

For Tunisian music, you will be best served during Ramadan, when there are concerts in restored buildings in the médina. At the conservative end of the range, you may find concerts of traditional choral music, *malouf*, by groups like the Rachidia. The crowd will be altogether more spontaneous at the café in the Souk Echaouachia off the R Sidi Ben Arous, where a small Tunisian band belts out favourites to an appreciative and sometimes rowdy crowd. If karaoke is your thing, you might try *La Brasserie*, the upmarket bar of the *Hotel La Maison Blanche* close to the intersection of the Av Mohamed V and Av Kheireddine Pacha.

Theatre

Municipal Theatre, Av H Bourguiba, T860888. Tunis's main theatre is a fine art nouveau wedding cake of a building on the city's main drag. Back before the Second World War, it must have seen opera and theatre productions with all the leading stars of the day. You could also look out for productions at *Le Quatrième Art* on Av de Paris, the city centre home to the Théâtre National Tunisien directed by the energetic Mohamed Driss. Almost opposite Le Quatrième Art is the *Maison de Culture Ibn Rachik*, which also occasionally hosts theatre and the odd art-house movie.

Shopping

Books

Tunisians are not great readers, and there are correspondingly few bookshops and libraries. There are a number of *papeteries*/bookshops on the Av de France, but most

Tunis and around

Perfume

The art of distilling perfume essences has all but disappeared (Announ has a small distillation unit off Souq en-Nahhas) and many of the essences on sale today are imported. Unromantically, they come in metal cans (stamped and sealed). The advantage is that the salesmen in Souq el-Attarine can make up your favourite eau de toilette to the strength you require

and at half the price. Maher in Souq el-Attarine (opposite the steps leading up to the 15th century ablutions building Midhat es-Soltane) does a fine imitation Kenzo for Men. More traditionally, various flower waters are on sale very cheaply (orange flower or geranium), and are excellent for perfuming fruit salads and Turkish coffee.

books are in Arabic or French. Paperbacks in English can be found in the souvenir shops in the larger hotels. If you read Arabic or French go to the *Librairie Clairefontaine*, 4 R d'Alger. The *Librairie Alif*, which used to be on the R de Hollande, is currently in search of new premises. Other bookshops in downtown Tunis which can occasionally turn up surprises include the much expanded *El Kitab* next to the *Colisée* cinema arcade on Av H Bourguiba and *Le Gai Savoir*, rather more academic, on Pl Barcelone. The bookshop in the Carlton shopping arcade, off Av H Bourguiba, has a good range of local books in French too. In El Menzah I, try the bookshop close to the mosque, opposite the *Touta* supermarket on the R Moez.

Handicrafts Tunisian craftsmanship can be excellent and it is possible (after a bit of bargaining) to get good deals, although ultimately the price you pay really depends on what the article is actually worth to you. Leather goods and brass objects are plentiful and of reasonable quality. There are some quite nice cheap ceramics, too. On the whole, however, the craftwork lacks the imagination and verve that characterizes the best Moroccan goods, without having the fine quality of European handmade items.

To get an idea of prices and the craft items produced, visit the *Office National de l'Artisanat*, (the *ONAT*), now housed in splendid premises at the intersection of Av H Bourguiba and the Av de Carthage. Their showroom displays crafts from around Tunisia. Prices are generally higher than elsewhere, but at least you can get an idea of what is available. The *ONAT* also has a list of the official prices for carpets according to the quality. You will find many of these, among lots of less interesting goods, in the médina in R Jemaa Zitouna. Be selective – there is an awful lot of imported junk in the souks these days. If you are looking for kitsch presents for people back at work, you will be spoilt for choice.

Upmarket gifts In the Lafayette district, on Av de la Liberté, try *Nakcha*, a small craft shop opposite the Centre culturel français. Good range of Tunisian and Moroccan craft items. Well off the tourist track is the *Galerie Morjana*, boutique No 219, on the 2nd floor of the *Lac Palace* mall, Berges du Lac. Expensive, but well worthwhile for its jewellery, frames, painted woodwork and various bits.

In the souks By the Great Mosque, the *Souq el Attarine* originally specialized in *perfumes*. The goods are more mixed these days, with modern perfumes and imitations outdistancing the traditionally made perfume essences. *Jewellery* can be found in the *Souq des Orfèvres*, and *Souq el Berka*. For *carpets and blankets* go to *Souq el Leffa*, but carpets are generally cheaper in Kairouan. If you get a carpet be sure you have the receipt and that there is a quality stamp on the back. *Leather* can be found in numerous touristy shops, including those on *Souq el Trouk*, an extension of Souk el Attarine. Quality is often mediocre, the styles on offer out of date. On *Souk el Belghadjia*, just off Souk el Attarine, you can find old style Tunis *footwear* among the modern styles.

If you are looking for cheap imported goods or household electrical goods, you could do worse than go to the covered market on the R Moncef Bey, visited by buses Nos 2 and 100 and next door to the main louage station for destinations south. If you are not looking for souvenirs, the best place to go is Av Charles de Gaulle in the new city where you will find supermarkets (*Monoprix*), chemists and camera shops. (Note that both the *Monoprix* and the *Magasin Général* on the Av de France sell alcohol.) There are many smart shops and boutiques in Tunis, especially in the area of Av Bourguiba, Av Habib Thameur and Av de France.

A sign of Tunisia's growing prosperity are the new shopping malls which sprung up in the second half of the 1990s. In downtown Tunis, there is the *Palmarium*, with plenty of shops selling expensive sports and leisure gear. Up in El Manar, you have the *Centre Makni*, complete with a Levi's boutique, and opposite it, the *Centre X*. Out on the La Marsa highway, the focal point of Les Berges du Lac is the *Lac Palace* mall. Fully a/c, it has 3 levels of shops around a central atrium where metal birds 'fly' and the retailers wait for the consumers. The setting may be wholly unecological, the concept is the same as the souks of the old médina. Here you will find *Galerie Morjana*, boutique No 219, on the 2nd floor. Expensive, but well worthwhile for its jewellery, frames, painted woodwork and various bits.

Mall shopping

Sport

For diving, it is best to contact the diving schools listed under Tabarka, home to most sub-aqua activity, in the Northern Tunisia chapter. Otherwise, try the Fédération des Activités Subaquatiques de Tunisie, Piscine olympique d'El Menzah, BP 486, 1082 Cité El Mahrajène, T234041, who have a small office which can provide information on diving events – most notably, underwater photography competitions. Tunisian kids, equipped with goggles, spend many happy hours fishing for sea-urchins (poor man's oysters) on the rockier sections of coastline.

Diving

The *Gliding Club* at Djebel Rassas south of Tunis was closed a few years ago after a particularly appalling accident. However, like the numerous birds of prey using the currents eddying round this strange mountain, hang-gliders continue to fly at weekends.

Gliding & flying

There is an 18-hole course at La Soukra (close to the airport) – see Golf, page 55, for further details – and a further course is planned on the salt-flats close to the Raoued beach hotels. Open 2004?

Golf

If you are looking for a gym, there are any number in central Tunis. The bigger hotels often have tiny 'fitness centres', which, given the high charges and limited equipment, have few takers. Of the gyms, one of the nicest is next to the metro line at 18 R de Lyon, T341454. The biggest is easily the *Panda Club*, on R du Train, close to Le Passage. Mon/Wed/Fri for women, Tue/Thu/Sat for men. Open early morning to 2100. There is a smaller Panda Club in a basement close to the R Jean Jaurès. Otherwise there are a number of gyms up in Menzah VI (*Gold's Gym* and others). Serious weightlifters might want to try the *Power Club* in the Ariana.

Gyms

Some of the hotels at Raoued can organize riding. Try also the *Club Hippique de la Soukra*, 15 km north of Tunis, T203054, and Ksar Saïd, 10 km from Tunis. Race meetings every Sun at Ksar Saïd, T223252.

Riding

At El Menzah (Cité Olympique) you take out a monthly membership, and times are limited to early morning and lunchtimes. Try also the pool at Menzah VI near the Cité

Swimming

Tunis and around

Jamil, open to the public at lunchtimes and in the evening. In summer, there is the municipal swimming pool on Pl Pasteur, although this is more for swimming lessons for local kids. The Gorjani Pool near the Faculté des Sciences Humaines is presently closed. The Bardo neighbourhood has a brand new pool, first right after main entrance to the Bardo Museum, open all day to those taking out membership. Wealthy Tunisians and residents take out summer memberships for the pools in the big hotels.

Tennis Try the Tennis Club on R Alain Savary, Cité Jardin (membership generally required). Out on the coast, the *Hotel Cap Carthage* has a large number of courts, or try to join the somewhat exclusive Carthage Tennis Club.

Tour operators

Abou Nawas Travel, 8 R Ibn Jazzar, 1002 Tunis, T781351, F782113. *Ariana Voyages*, 80 Av H Bourguiba, 2080 Ariana, T71516. *Atlas Voyages*, 6 R Saha Ibn Abbah, T286299. *Carthage Tours*, 59 Av H Bourguiba, T347015, F352740. *Tourafrica*, Av H Bourguiba, next to *Africa Hotel*. *Tunisian Travel Service*, 19 Av H Bourguiba, T348100, and 28 R Hassan Ibn Nomene, 1002 Tunis, T785855, F780682. *Ulysse Tours*, 31 Av de Paris, T344727 and 20 R 18 Janvier, T255082. *Voyages 2000*, 2 Av de France, T248554.

Transport

Local **Bus** You will probably only need to use a few routes during your stay in Tunis. For more information go to the bus station in front of the train station on Pl de Barcelone. Bus 3 leaves from Av H Bourguiba in front of *Tunisair*, or from Av de Paris in front of the *Hotel Majestic* and goes to the Bardo Museum and south bus station. Bus 5 leaves from Pl de l'Indépendence and goes to Pl Pasteur by Belvédère Park. Bus 35 leaves from Av H Bourguiba for a 30-min ride to the airport.

Car hire Many firms have an agent at the airport. *Avis*, Av H Bourguiba, in the *Africa Hotel* lobby, Av H Bourguiba, T341249; *Ben Jemaa*, Excelsior Garage, 53 Av de Paris, T240060; *Budget*, 14 Av de Carthage, T256806; *Carthage Tours*, 59 Av H Bourguiba, T254605; *Chartago Rent*, 3 Av H Bourguiba, T349168; *Europacar*, 17 Av H Bourguiba, T340303; *Garage selection*, 65 Av Hedi Chaker, T284698; *Hertz*, 29 Av H Bourguiba, T248559; *Topcar*, 23 Av H Bourguiba, T344121; *National Automobile Club of Tunisia (NACT)*, 29 Av H Bourguiba, T349837; *SOS Car recovery*, 6 R Ahmed Amine, T891000.

Car parking, central Tunis Parking in central Tunis is a nightmare during the day. You could try parking at the *Hotel Abou Nawas*. This is a convenient and safe place to park with a barrier and gatekeeper. Convenient for the metro, a short taxi ride or a 10-min walk to Pl de la République. Open every day, charges 0600-1300 0.35Dt, 1300-2100 0.35Dt, 2000-0600 2Dt. There is an underground car park at the *Palmarium* mall, behind the *Municipal Theatre*, and a small car park on R Kamal Ataturk. Note that Denver shoes or clamps are in use for illegal parking.

You often have to change metro trains at République if you are heading for the main station at Pl Barcelone. The two are 15-20 mins' apart on foot

Metro Tunis has a 5-line network of small green trams. All lines run into the city centre, severely adding to congestion as they are all above ground. Visitors may want to take the tram to get out to the Bardo Museum (take line 4, destination Den Den, at République, get off at Bardo). The central tram station is at the Pl Barcelone, along with the mainline train station and another large station is on Pl de la République. There is a ticket kiosk at each stop. Simply buy a ticket to the desired destination and board the next tram. The place names are clearly marked at each stop.

Taxis Tunis's bilious yellow taxis are quite cheap but generally difficult to find, particularly at rush hour. The maximum you should have to pay is 4-5Dt and that is for a long trip to La Marsa. All taxis have meters and use them, so make sure they have switched it on. Try also: *Allo Taxi*, T282211; *Telephone Taxi*, T492422.

Air Airline information *Air Algérie*, 28 Av de Paris, T341590. *Air France*, 1 R **Long distance** d'Athènes, T341577. *British Airways*, 17 Av H Bourguiba, T330046. *Egypt Air*, 49 Av H Bourguiba, T341182, in the *International Hotel*. *KLM*, 50 R Lucy Faure, T341309. *Lufthansa*, Av Ouled Haffouz, close to the Belvédère Park, in the *Mechtel Hotel*. *Tunisair*, 48 Av H Bourguiba, T259189, central office 133 Av de la Liberté, T288100. Reservations T700700, F700008. Prepaid tickets, T337169/330100. Freight office, T754000, 755000. **Internal flights**: *Tunisair* T336500, reservations on T700700, operates a number of internal flights. Sample prices: Tunis-Sfax 75.6Dt – daily; Tunis-Djerba 90.6Dt daily; Tunis-Tozeur 86Dt – daily except Tuesday and Wednesday (this may vary).

To get to the airport either take a taxi or bus 35 from Av H Bourguiba, opposite *Africa* **Transport** *Hotel*, 30 mins. **to airport**

Bus There are 2 bus stations in Tunis. The **Gare routière Nord**, for northern and **Road** northwestern destinations, is situated at Bab Saâdoun. To get there take bus 3 from Av H Bourguiba by *Hotel Africa Méridien*. Get off just after Bab Saâdoun, the bus station is on the right. For information about buses to the north, T562299/562532. Departures from here to Bizerte; Raf Raf and Ras el Djebel; Medjez el Bab and Béja, change here for Aïn Draham, Jendouba and Tabarka; Mateur and Tabarka; Medjez el Bab, Teboursouk and Le Kef, change here for Thala.

For southern destinations, the **Gare routière Sud** is at Bab El Fella and has buses to all other places including Algeria and Libya. To reach the station walk from the main

Tunis Metro & TGM

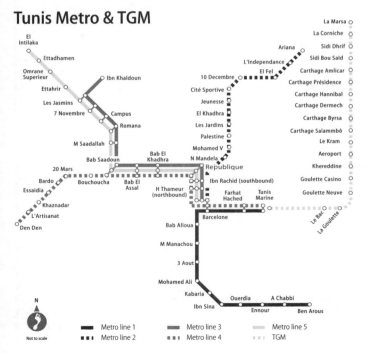

train station, a distance of 800 m. Take the R de La Gare on the right of the station, at the end of the street, go over a small road bridge, and you will see the station over on your right. For information about buses to the south, T495255/490440. Departures from here to Hammamet and Nabeul; to Kairouan via Enfida or El Fahs and on to Gafsa (change here for Tozeur and Nefta) or Kasserine; Sousse (change here for El Djem), Sfax and Gabès, change for Tataouine, Medenine, Ben Gardane, Zarzis and Matmata. **Buses to Algeria and Libya**: **Algeria** (Annaba) daily at 0700; **Libya** (Tripoli) Mon, Wed, Fri and Sun at 1700, cost 25Dt plus 2Dt/piece of luggage, takes 8-10 hrs. **NB** During the summer and the evening before public holidays, it can be difficult to get a seat on a bus. You may have to put up a bit of a fight at the ticket office. The best thing is to book. This service is available for most lines, but it is best to check.

Louages (inter-city taxis) Tunisia has a system of inter-city shared taxis. For destinations in the north of the country, you need the Bab Saâdoun bus station, for main southern destinations, the Moncef Bey louage station, and for the Cap Bon, the Bab Alioua louage station. The latter 2 are only 5 mins' walk from each other. Note that quite often destinations are indicated in Arabic only.

Sea **Ferry** T255239 for information, see page 31, *Compagnie Tunisienne de Navigation*, 5 Av Dag Hammarskjoeld, T242999. The *CTN* also has a major office on R de Yougoslavie, close to the intersection with R Jamel Abdel Nasser (ex-R Sadikia).

Train **TGM** The TGM (Tunis-La Goulette-La Marsa) is the train linking Tunis to the coastal resorts and suburbs. The station is at the end of Av H Bourguiba, T244696, beyond Pl de l'Afrique. It is open 24 hrs a day with trains every 10-15 mins during the day and every hr at night. The service goes to La Goulette, Carthage, Sidi Bou Saïd and La Marsa. The main train station is in the centre of the new city on Pl de Barcelone. Information: *SNCFT*, Av Farhat Hached, T244440/252225. **National departures** (times subject to seasonal variations): **Bizerte** 0550, 1130, 1600, 1830; **Bir Bou Regba** and **Sousse** 0710 (on to El Djem, Sfax, Mahares and Gabès); 0900, 1840 (on to Monastir); 1205, 1535 (on to Monastir and Mahdia); 1305, 1410, 1730 (on to El Djem and Sfax); 2120 (on to El Djem, Sfax, Gabès, Gafsa and Metlaoui); Nabeul 1420, 1805 to Hammamet and Nabeul. To **Algeria**: only 1 train goes on to Algiers, all others stop at the border. **Algiers** 1255; **Ghardimaou** (border with Algeria) 0635, 1200, 1425, 1620, 1750. All trains go via Béja and Jendouba (except the 1425). Sample fare: Tunis to Sfax 2nd class 8Dt, bicycle 6.5Dt; to Sousse 5Dt, to Gabès 12Dt, to Metlaoui 12Dt, to Gafsa 11Dt.

Directory

Banks *American Express*, c/o *Carthage Tour*, 59 Av H Bourguiba, T254820. Open 0800-1900, Sun 0900-1200. *BIAT*, Av H Bourguiba (American Express). *BT*; *STB*, Av H Bourguiba, by the *Africa Hotel*, open daily 0700-1900, has automatic cash dispenser for Visa and Mastercard holders. *UBCI*, Av H Bourguiba. Other banks with cash dispensers on the main avenue include the *BIAT* and the *Banque de l'Habitat*.

Communica- Internet cafés: An increasing presence in the city, with lots of new publinets in the
tions central area. Hourly charge is about 1Dt 400. Biggest publinet is at 35 R Mokhtar el Attia, T333893, behind the *Hotel Carlton* (25 computers). In the Médina, there is a tiny publinet near Bab Menara, not far from the *Restaurant Essaraya* on R Sidi Bou Khrissan. Publinets convenient for the central station include 1 in the building on the corner of Pl Barcelone at 14 R de Grèce, also the Design@surf at 10 R de Russie, T321173, www.publinet.da.ru, and 1 hidden away off R d'Algérie, *Publinet La Rencontre*, R Tijania, T352320, 2nd alley on left after the minaret as you come from Pl Barcelone,

clearly signposted. North of the Av H Bourguiba, you have: *Publinet Jean Jaurès*, 70 Av Jean Jaurès, near République/Le Passage central metro station, T350626, F253541, open 7 days a week from 0800, later on Sun; also 1 at 8 bis R de Madrid, near the intersection with R Borj Bourguiba and opposite *Air Algérie* on Av de Carthage, not far from the *Hotel Majestic*. The *British Council* at 5 Pl de la Victoire (the big white building behind the big stone gate at the city centre entrance to the médina) can provide visitors with internet access. They have 7 computers permanently on line. Open all week 1000-1700, Sat 0900-1200, closed Mon. Up in El Menzah I, there is a handy publinet on R Moez, not far from the junction with the main road to the Ariana. In Ariana there is a publinet next to the *Tunisie Telecom* building on the main street in Ariana. In north Tunis in El Manar, about 100 m before you reach the Centre Makni mall development, there is a small down-at-heel shopping centre on your right. Go into the central courtyard. The cybercentre is in small ground-floor premises. **Post Office**: main PTT R Charles de Gaulle, open Mon-Thur 0730-1230 and 1700-1900, Fri-Sat 0730-1330, Sun 0900-1100. **Telephone**: a 24-hr telephone centre is off R Gamal Abdul Nasser. The city also has numerous taxiphones (public call centres), some of which stay open late.

Algeria, 136 Av de la Liberté, T280082. **Belgium**, R du 1er-Juin, T781655, F792797. **Canada** (and Australian affairs), 3 R de Sénégal, T796557. **Egypt**, 16 R Essayouti, T230004. **France**, Pl de l'Indépendence, T358111, F253030. **Germany**, 18 Av Challaye, T281246. **Italy**, R de Russie, T361811 (open 0930-1130). **Ivory Coast**, 6 R Ibn Charaf, T283878. **Jordan**, 4 R Didon, T288401. **Libya**, 48 bis R du 1 juin, T283936. **Morocco**, 39 R du 1 Juin, T288063. **Netherlands**, 6 R Meycen, T287455. **New Zealand** (see UK). **Norway**, 7 Av H Bourguiba, T245933. **Senegal**, 122 Av de la Liberté, T282393, **Sweden**, 87 Av Taïeb Mehri, T283433. **Switzerland**, Immeuble Stramica, Berges du Lac, T962997, F965796. **UK**, 5 Pl de la Victoire, T245100, consulate on Av de la Liberté (both embassy and consulate will be moving to new premises in the Berges du Lac in 2004). **USA**, 144 Av de la Liberté, T282566 (a move is projected to a site off the Tunis-La Marsa highway near the American School).

Embassies & consulates

Men looking for a short-back-and-sides will have no problem in Tunis, a haircut costing around 3Dt. You can also be shaved with an old-fashioned cut-throat razor at the same time. Women seeking an unstructured natural look may have a little trouble finding a suitable hairdresser. Tunisian women like perms, blonde streaks and big hair. *Chantal* at Carthage (T275676), in the *Touta* supermarket complex, chic and expensive; *Donna* in La Soukra is the leading beauticians. Pay through the nose and then some. *Sofiène*, 22 R des Narcisses, Menzah V, T766362, is a reliable address in Carnoy/El Menzah V residential area. In Sidi Bou Saïd, *Enzo Martelli*, T747973, and *Crystal*, T741862, have a good name.

Hairdressers

Ambulance: T341250, T491286. **Chemists**: all night, 43 Av H Bourguiba, opposite *Africa Hotel*; 20 Av de la Liberté, by Av de Madrid; 44 Av Bab Djedid. On the door of any chemists you will find a list of those staying open at night (*pharmacies de garde*). **Doctor**: *SOS Médecins*, T341250 (to call out a general practitioner for a simple illness, cost of call 20Dt). Also try T346767, T780000 (SAMU). **Hospitals**: *Hôpital Principal Aziza Othmana*, Pl du Gouvernement, T633655. *Hôpital Ariana*, T713266. *Hôpital Charles Nicolle*, T663000. *Hôpital Habib Thameur*, T491600. *Hôpital Rabta*, T662276. *Institut Pasteur*, T680539. *SOS Ambulance*, T341250.

Medical services

Catholic: Cathedral on Av H Bourguiba, T247290. Services in French Sat 1830 and Sun 1100 and in Italian Sun 0900. Also St Jeanne d'Arc, 1 R de Jerusalem, T287213, Sat 1830 and Sun 1000. Foyer Familial, R du Parc, Radès, T245444. Sun 1000. 1 R des Vergers, 2000 Le Bardo, Khaznadar, T514850. Sun 0900.

Places of worship

Emergency services Fire: T198. Police: T197.

Useful numbers

Tunis and around

Tunis and around

Carthage and the Banlieue Nord

Northeast of Tunis is the Banlieue Nord, the northern suburbs, a coastal strip including the remains of Carthage, the most expensive residential areas and the nearest beaches. This growing suburban area extends for over 20 km along the coast, a succession of small settlements described as 'pearls on a necklace'. La Goulette is the first port of Tunis, very popular and very lively at night with the many restaurants along the bay. Carthage is most definitely a smart suburb and is famous for its Phoenician and Roman remains. Sidi Bou Saïd is the well known blue and white 'bird cage' village perched on the cliff top. Once elegant La Marsa has a beach which is pleasant out of season, while Gammarth has been rebranded as the Côtes de Carthage to fit its new role as an area of large expensive hotels. There are wide open sands, windsurfing and horseriding at Raoued.

Ins and outs

Getting there The Banlieue Nord is easily accessible on public transport, either by the TGM (Tunis-Goulette-Marsa) light railway or on the road that runs alongside it on the cause-way. The train has frequent stops. For those in search of Carthaginian remains, get off at Salammbô. For the amphitheatre and the museum up on the hill, get off at Carthage-Hannibal. Sidi Bou Saïd is also on the same line. You can also reach La Marsa by one of the green and white private line buses (TGV), downtown stop by the *Hotel Africa* in Tunis.

If you are travelling by car, there is a very practical, free ferry service between La Goulette and Radès, which enables travellers going south to bypass downtown Tunis. (A bridge is said to be planned for the near future.) The service runs 24 hrs a day.

Tunis region

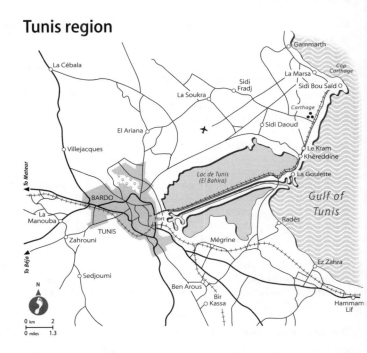

For short hops between the different areas of the northern suburbs, the visitor will find **Getting around** plenty of taxis available. Note that La Marsa Plage is the last stop on the light railway. For those without a car, taxi is the only real option for getting up to the hotels at Gammarth and Raoued. For visiting the ruins of Carthage, you may opt for a *calèche* (horse-drawn carriage) to drive round the leafy streets from sight to sight. Otherwise, be prepared for lots of pleasant walking. From the Tophet to the Carthage Museum on the hill is a walk of no more than 30 mins.

La Goulette   حلق الـوادى

La Goulette (The Gullet, Halk el Oued in Arabic) is at the narrow entrance to the Lac de Tunis and is the main port of Tunisia. Ferries leave here for Europe. It is dominated by a fortress built by Charles V of Spain in 1535, when he assisted the Hafsids in their fight against Barbarossa. It functions as a harbour, an important naval base, and a dormitory for Tunis. In summer evenings, the main street of La Goulette, with restaurants and bars everywhere, comes to life.

Phone code: 71
Colour map 2,
grid B3

Since the 19th century, La Goulette has been a summer resort. Gaston Loth, writing in the early 1900s, wrote that "There are five thousand people in La Goulette within the walls; in summer fifteen thousand are jammed into villas which neighbour the little town." Thanks to the railway line, it quickly developed as the centre of a cosmopolitan sort of coastal strip, where the families of French administrators and Italian entrepreneurs could enjoy the sea and sand alongside local Jewish residents. They were joined by such Muslim notables who did not have a *borj* at La Marsa or a summer residence at Sidi Bou Saïd. Court dignitaries built palaces further up the coast at Kheireddine. La Goulette remains popular as a summer resort even today, although the capital's wealthy have long since deserted it in favour of Hammamet and more remote elsewheres.

La Goulette has few sights. You might be able to have a look around the **Sights** **Karraka** and enjoy a splendid view over the harbour and the Gulf of Tunis. The fortress, which was built by the Habsburg forces in the 16th century, was a prison and no doubt has an appropriately gruesome history. In summer, concerts are held in the main courtyard. The Karraka is also, on occasion, the setting for ram fights (*béliomachie*), a 'sport' which has a small if devoted following. ■ *Entrance 1Dt, photography 3Dt.*

On your left as you come into La Goulette by car you may see an area dominated by the tall square tower of a church. This is **La Petite Sicile**, now largely demolished, once home to a considerable Italian, Tunisian Jewish and Maltese community. The one time multi-culturalism of the area is celebrated in Férid Boughedir's feel-good-movie, *Un été à la Goulette*. The film, set just before the outbreak of the Six Day War of 1967, tells the tale of adolescent loves in a community where three religions, Judaism, Islam and Catholicism, still managed to co-exist.

La Goulette now has the equestrian statue of former President Habib Bourguiba which originally stood in Place d'Afrique in Tunis. Astride a proud stallion, Tunisia's befezzed first president strikes the pose of a 19th-century South American liberation leader.

Travelling over the causeway from Tunis, you may note fishermen in small boats out on the lagoon, the **Lac de Tunis** (El Bahira). In many cases, they are not netting fish but dredging for shellfish. These are sent to Korbous, where they are suspended in sacks in the clean sea water there until the grime of their original surroundings has been washed from their systems. Each case sold from Korbous has a government controlled certificate. In the winter months, you can spot cormorants and flocks of flamingos out on the lagoon.

Eating La Goulette was once the place for a summer night out. Sadly, its restaurants, famed for their fresh fish, have declined in quality, and the charm of alfresco eating on the Av Franklin Roosevelt is marred by the quantity of traffic. The newer restaurants are gaudy (*Le Lucullus*) or bottom of the range *gargottes*, which can be fun in their way. Note that fish is sold by weight, with prices given per 100 g. Get the waiter to tell you what you will be paying, as the bill can be severe. Otherwise go for the fixed price *poisson complet* (grilled fish with chips and *tastira*, an egg and fried vegetable sauce). On the seaside promenade are lots of cafés, and you might find a stand making old-style *brik à l'oeuf* or barbecuing spicy merguez sausages.

Expensive *Le Café Vert*, 68 R Franklin Roosevelt, T736156. Expect to pay at least 30Dt a head with wine. Generally considered the most reliable address in La Goulette, business entertains its clients here. However, the food does not compensate for being wedged in on plastic chairs at tables right next to the exhaust fumes. In this price bracket, better go the whole hog and eat at a really upmarket place on the coast at Gammarth.

Mid-range Expect to pay around 25Dt a head in the following. *Le Chalet*, 42 Av Franklin Roosevelt, T735138. The one with the pleasant open courtyard with a palm tree. Choose your crustacean from the vivarium. Recommended. *Club Les Jasmins*, 6 R Bach Hamba, La Goulette, T736016. Discreet entrance to the left of the *Restaurant Vénus* on the main roundabout as you come into La Goulette from Tunis. Authentic kosher Jewish cuisine supervised by owner William Sebag. Good *kémia* (appetizers) and a splendid *poisson malin* in spicy tomato sauce. Quiet courtyard away from the traffic. *Mamie Lily*, 14 Av Pasteur, La Goulette-Casino, T737633. Traditional Tunisian Jewish cooking. Mixed reports. *Restaurant Vénus*, 2 Av H Bourguiba, La Goulette, T737541. Large restaurant with terraces overlooking the main drag. A bit of a factory. Adequate.

Sport **Yachting** Club de la Goulette, T276017.

Tour operators *Asfar el Hana*, 64 Av H Bourguiba, T736761.

Directory **Useful numbers** Port de la Goulette, T735300. Port de Radès, T449300.

La Goulette & Kheirreddine

● Eating
1 Club Les Jasmines
2 Le Café Vert
3 Le Chalet
4 Mamie Lily
5 Vénus

Not to scale

Carthage ﻗﺮﻃﺎﺝ

Carthage today is lush green suburb. On the slopes below the old basilica, old Tunis money resides next to ambassadors and assorted foreigners. There is a scattering of schools and municipal buildings and, here and there between the villas, small archaeological sites pop up. A stroll through Salammbô to Carthage can make a very pleasant afternoon. The microclimate is superb: everything seems to grow, and you can see why the Phoenicians chose to put their most important trading post here.

Although the Roman and Punic ruins are not spectacular, they are well worth seeing. Remember that Carthage had a long history, and was one of the most important cities in the Roman Empire. It was also a nerve-centre for early Christianity. The smaller sites are worth visiting too, including in particular the Tophet and the Palaeo-Christian Museum. The main museum on the hill is surprisingly dull for a site with so much history to tell.

Phone code: 71
Colour map 2,
grid B3

History

According to Roman epic poet Virgil, Carthage was founded in 814 BC by the Phoenician Princess Dido (Didon), who came there as a refugee after her husband had been killed by her brother, Pygmalion. According to Greek legends, she fled from Tyre in the eastern Mediterranean to North Africa where she bought land from local ruler Iarbas. The story of the sale is that Dido agreed to acquire land no more than could be covered by an ox hide. Cleverly, she cut the hide into narrow strips and so surrounded a much larger area than the locals had bargained on selling. It was certainly enough to build a new city, which the Phoenician settlers named *Kart Hadascht*, meaning New Town.

Legendary beginnings

Other largely apocryphal tales tell of Dido's courtship with Aeneas, the Trojan warrior and future founder of Rome, an affair celebrated in Purcell's 17th-century opera *Dido and Aeneas*, based on Book Four of Virgil's classic, the *Aeneid*. Dido reputedly died of a broken heart when Aeneas resumed his wanderings. In fact the two were not living at the same period – but why spoil a good yarn?

Another tale goes that local king Iarbas was the son of Jupiter and an African nymph. Iarbas wanted to marry Dido. She, however, was determined to remain faithful to the memory of her late husband. Thus she built a pyre as if preparing an offering to the gods, and then committed suicide by leaping into the flames. A more dramatic method of escaping a suitor's attentions could hardly be imagined.

Certainly the foundation of Carthage was an enormous success. It soon became a major power and trade centre, with as many as 500,000 residents, making it the third-largest city in the empire after Rome and Alexandria. It attempted to rival both the Greeks and the Romans by setting its sights, unsuccessfully, on Sicily. Everybody knows the extraordinary story of Hannibal who crossed the Alps with 40,000 men and 38 elephants to attack Rome. The Romans eventually took revenge and Scipio's armies won a decisive battle in Zama in 202 BC. Carthage was subjected to a siege lasting three years and was eventually seized and razed to the ground in 146 BC to the delight of Cato, who had had this in mind for some time.

Carthage, Mediterranean power

Tunis and around

Ancient Carthage: main dates

814 BC	*Founded by Tyrian princess Dido*	*44 BC*	*Carthage refounded as Colonia*
260 BC	*Beginning of the three Punic*		*Julia by Caesar Augustus*
	wars between Carthage and	*AD 14*	*The city much increased in*
	Rome		*prosperity*
146 BC	*Carthage destroyed after a three*	*AD 439*	*Carthage seized by Vandals for*
	year siege by the Romans		*one century*
122 BC	*Gracchus attempted to refound*	*AD 533*	*Reconquest by Byzantines*
	Carthage	*AD 698*	*Fall of Carthage*

Rome in African capital

However, this was not to be the end of Carthage as the Romans, under Caesar Augustus in 44 BC, returned to make it the capital of the Roman Province of Africa, the cultural and intellectual centre. At this time Carthage was known as Rome's bread basket due to its fertile hinterland. It collapsed as a significant power after the successive invasions of the Vandals, Byzantines and Arabs.

Excavating Carthage

After the Arab invasion of the late seventh century, Carthage was mainly used as a source of building material for Islamic monuments and the expanding city of Tunis. By the 19th century, there was little to see. The myth of ancient Carthage remained alive, however, nourished by the classical education dispensed in Europe's schools and universities. British traveller Sir Grenville Temple described his reaction after climbing Byrsa Hill: "... my heart sang within me, when, ascending one of its hills (from whose summit the eye embraces a view of the whole surrounding country to the edge of the sea) I beheld nothing more than a few scattered and shapeless masses of masonry." The beys granted permits to 'quarry' Carthage.

The first, rather amateur excavations were started in 1857 by Beulé. The situation was to improve shortly after the arrival of the French. Under the leadership of Cardinal Lavigerie, the Pères Blancs set to work, excavating Carthage's past with energy and enthusiasm. A major museum was established on Byrsa Hill. In the early 1970s, UNESCO and the Tunisian government sponsored a major campaign to save the ancient sites. Research teams from 14 countries participated, each working on a specific area. The British under Henry Hurst revealed the secrets of the Punic ports, while the French worked on a unique Punic residential quarter up on Byrsa Hill.

Today, the site of ancient Carthage – some 545 ha, including almost the whole area of the municipalities of Carthage and Sidi Bou Saïd, plus parts of La Marsa and La Goulette – is a national archaeological park. Much still remains to be excavated on this unique site, and every year teams of archaeologists return to continue the quest.

Visiting the sites of Carthage

A short visit to Carthage only gives an overview. Tours provided by hotels are usually only half-day affairs, hardly adequate to get from one end of Carthage to the other (3 km) and visit a few remains on some of the 12 main sites. Enthusiasts of all things ancient will want to allow at least a full day if possible. If you are not a ruins enthusiast, try to take in a selection of sites located close to each other. Starting early, you could start in the Salammbô area at the southernmost site, the Tophet, view the Punic Ports, the Palaeo-Christian Museum and the main museum on the hill. (You could also do the Oceanographic Museum at the same time.) Real enthusiasts would want to pack in the Antonine Baths and a look at the theatre before lunch. ■ *All sites here open 0800-1900 summer, 0830-1730 winter, closed Sun. Entrance 200Dt, photography 2Dt covers all sites and the museum, valid only for day of issue.*

Get off at the TGM station at Carthage Salammbo and walk down towards the sea. Take second left turn, and the Tophet, which simplifying broadly can be described as an ancient Punic crematorium, is on your right behind a tangly hedge. Further along the road you come to the Oceanographic Museum (in a large 19th-century building to your right) and the Punic Ports. It is then only a short walk up to the TGM station at Carthage Byrsa.

**The Tophet,
the Oceano-
graphic
Museum &
the Punic Ports**

The **Tophet** houses the remains of the sanctuary of the Carthaginian divinities Tanit and Baal-Hammon, the oldest Punic religious site in Carthage. There is not much left to see. According to legend, for seven centuries the noble Carthaginian families brought their children here to be ritually sacrificed, and urns containing ashes and remains of many children have in fact been found. This site was discovered in 1921 and is considered to be the largest of all known sacrificial compounds. The ashes of the victims, sometimes small children but more often birds and young animals, were placed in a stone-lined trench. Other offerings such as dishes and lucky charms were buried too. When the whole area was filled with covered trenches, a layer of earth was placed across and the whole process began again.

The **Oceanographic Museum** is of most interest to those who are keen on fish and fishing. Children will like the new aquaria in the basement. There is an extensive collection of stuffed birds upstairs, and some nice models of the different types of sailboat no longer found on Tunisia's coasts. You can also learn about the different islands and islets in Tunisian territorial waters.

The main **harbour** used to be the very heart of Carthaginian prosperity. The northern basin functioned as a naval base, boasting safe anchorage for 220 vessels. It was circular in shape and bordered by quays. The southern base, originally rectangular in shape, was for merchant ships. The ports, well protected from attack, must have been the keystone of Punic commerce, situated as they were right in the middle of the Mediterranean.

**The Punic Ports
& Admiralty
Island**

The small **island** in the middle of the northern port was the subject of research by a British archaeological mission in the 1970s, which revealed a fascinating Roman docking system. The island was built up as a circular space, with a spine carrying an upper service gantry, below which ships could be winched up into a covered dry dock. A bridge linked the island to the shore. This sophisticated dock was constructed to handle exports of wheat to Rome. Adjacent was the **Commercial Harbour** joined to the sea by a dredged channel. This harbour was a large circular basin surrounded by large warehouses.

Tunis and around

Carthage

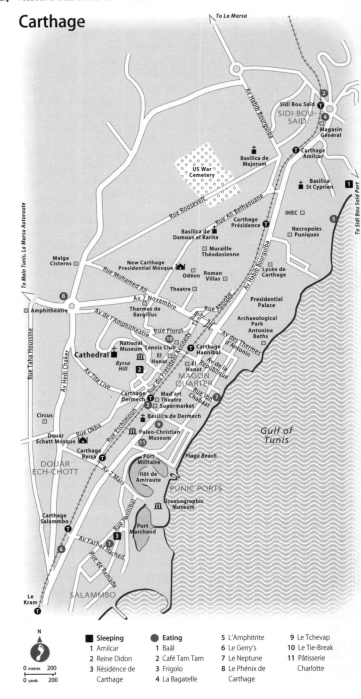

Tunis and around

To La Marsa

To Main Tunis, La Marsa Autoroute

To Sidi Bou Saïd Port

SIDI-BOU-SAÏD

Sidi Bou Saïd

Magasin Général

Carthage Amilcar

Basilica St Cyprien

Basilica de Majorum

US War Cemetery

Rue Roosevelt

Rue Ali Belhaouane

IHEC

Carthage Présidence

Necropoies Puniques

Basilica de Damous el Karita

Muraille Théodosienne

Malga Cisterns

New Carthage Presidential Mosque

Rue Mohamed Ali

Odéon

Roman Villas

Lycée de Carthage

Theatre

Av des Thermes d'Antonin

Amphitheatre

Av 7 Novembre

Thermes de Bargillus

Av de l'Amphitheatre

Rue Florus

Presidential Palace

Archaeological Park

Antonine Baths

Rue Taha Houssine

Rue Hedi Chaker

National Museum

Tennis Club

Cathedral

Byrsa Hill

El Hanat

Av Tite Live

Carthage Hannibal

El Hanat

Av de la République

Carthage Dermech

Mad'art Theatre

MAGON QUARTER

Rue Ibn Chabaat

Supermarket

Circus

Basilica de Dermech

Av Z Mars

Douar Echatt Mosque

Rue Okba

Paleo-Christian Museum

Gulf of Tunis

DOUAR ECH-CHOTT

Carthage Byrsa

Port Militaire

Plage Beach

Ilôt de Amiraute

PUNIC PORTS

Oceanographic Museum

Carthage Salammbo

Av Farhat Hached

Port Marchand

Rue Hannibal

Rue Remada

Le Kram

SALAMMBO

N

0 metres 200
0 yards 200

Sleeping
1 Amilcar
2 Reine Didon
3 Résidénce de Carthage

Eating
1 Baâl
2 Café Tam Tam
3 Frigolo
4 La Bagatelle

5 L'Amphitrite
6 Le Gerry's
7 Le Neptune
8 Le Phénix de Carthage

9 Le Tchevap
10 Le Tie-Break
11 Pâtisserie Charlotte

The Aeneid, founding myth of empire

Probably written between 29 and 19 BC, and still unfinished when Virgil died, The Aeneid tells the tale of a warrior hero, Aeneas, who was to found Rome. Though son of Venus and a Trojan mortal, Anchises, Aeneas is of very different stuff to the Greek heroes of Iliad and Odyssey. Though watched over by gods and goddesses, Aeneas is a human being, hesitant and weak. A Trojan, he leaves his hometown behind in ruins, and his journey across the Mediterranean to Italy is a hard one. In Book IV, he nearly loses all in Carthage, distracted by his love for a foreign queen.

For Virgil, Aeneas is the vehicle by which, as a writer, he can raise issues about Rome's destiny as an imperial power. The Romans of the first century BC were sought explanations for their city state's rise to Mediterranean dominance. The Aeneid, a 12 book epic poem, was one such explanation. Rome, like Aeneas, won through, but only after much lonely struggle. The imperial peace under Augustus was the logical conclusion of the fight which left Rome master in the lands of kingdoms destroyed, not the least of them Carthage.

Tunis and around

The **Antiquarium** situated alongside Avenue Habib Bourguiba has exhibits from excavations of the harbour and the surrounding area. There are numerous coins (over 9,000) and pieces of metal and marble. The best exhibit is the mosaic from the House of the Greek Charioteers.

Alight at TGM station Carthage Hannibal. Walk up Avenue de l'Amphithéatre to the summit of **Mount Byrsa**, the onetime Acropolis of Punic and Roman Carthage, an ideal viewpoint. The **Byrsa Quarter** (see below) recently discovered by French archaeologists, dates from the time of Hannibal and gives an idea of urban life in the early second century BC. We have to be grateful that when the Romans returned to rebuild Carthage they covered over the ruins of the 146 BC destruction on Byrsa Hill with thick layers of rubble and earth – a Roman landfill programme. Hence the whole segment of history was preserved for later examination.

Mount Byrsa & the Carthage Museum

The **Musée de Carthage**, T730036, situated by the former Basilica Saint-Louis at the top of Byrsa Hill, presents some of the finer finds from the Carthage excavations. The approach road winds round the shoulder of the hill with vestiges of ruins protruding from the hillside. The road terminates in a car park in front of the cathedral. Entrance kiosk to the museum and the second century BC Punic ruins is to the right of the Basilica.

Once inside the museum grounds, follow the path from the entrance kiosk (NB toilets). Either before or after the museum, it is worth making a short detour to wander among the partly restored walls of the Byrsa Quarter, on the southern slopes of the hill. Here you will find the remains of a Punic residential neighbourhood (second century BC), built in a regular rectangular grid, houses, water tanks, drains, plastered walls, tiled floors. The garden facing the museum entrance is also worth a look. This was the site of an ancient basilica and there are lots of pillars and carved stonework for examination. The walls of the garden are inlaid with small pieces found in the area.

Preceding seawards from the kiosk, you turn left to reach the front of the museum building and the main door, where there are some rather plain sarcophagi on display on either side. By contrast, just inside on the right are two fourth-century BC sarcophagi with recumbent statues on the lid. This is the room devoted to Punic stelae and sarcophagi. The Paleo-Christian room is on the left as you enter. It contains some important terracotta tiles and two sculptured panels known as *The Adoration of the Kings and The Annunciation*. Opposite the entrance is the room devoted to modern scientific methods relating to excavations and archaeology. Upstairs to the left is an amazing display of oil lamps, while the rest of the room is divided into the main periods of Carthaginian history. Items from Punic Carthage denoted with beige include items from graves: Roman Carthage (blue) has ceramics, glassware and sculpture in marble; Christian and Byzantine Carthage (pink) has figurines, ivory, terracotta tiles and glassware; Arab Carthage, mainly ceramics, is denoted in green. There is no leaflet to explain about the exhibits though most are named in Arabic, English and French. It is a worthwhile stop, but is overshadowed by the magnificent collection in the Bardo museum, and in terms of the intelligence of the display, by the mid-1990s museum at Chemtou.

Basilica of St Louis & further orientation The most spectacular building on the site, until recently, was clearly the large early 20th-century basilica, once dedicated to St Louis. (The adjoining seminary is now the museum). Now referred to as the **Acropolium**, it is maintained and regularly used for concerts. In recent years, it has been the setting for the Octobre musical de Carthage and a spring dance festival. Down the western side of the hill, near the roundabout with the *Phénix de Carthage* restaurant, are the **amphitheatre** (to the south side of the main road) and the **cisterns of La Malga**, on the north side, behind the *Phénix*. Returning towards the sea down Avenue du 7-Novembre, the **Odeon Hill** area is on the left (north) with the theatre behind which lie the Roman Villas. Real archaeology enthusiasts may want to visit the **Basilica of Damous el Karita** (on the road to Sidi Bou Saïd) and the **Basilica of St Cyprien** (hidden away north of the Lycée de Carthage and the IHEC), before backtracking to the **Baths of Antoninus**. After ticking these off, you will have visited all the major sites and be ready to head back to the Carthage-Hannibal TGM station.

Grande Mosquée de Carthage In 2001-2002, a new presidential mosque went up on the Carthage to Sidi Bou Saïd road, close to Damous el Karita. Handily close to the presidential palace, the **Grande Mosquée de Carthage**, built in the purest neo-traditional style, is no doubt scheduled for use during national prayers on major religious occasions. It replaces a couple of rather unsightly low-rise housing blocks, the Cité de l'Aviation, which housed military personnel working in the palace. It is unlikely that the mosque will be open to the non-Muslim public.

Odeon Hill: the theatre & Roman villas The **Odeon Quarter** is set to the west of the railway and Avenue Habib Bourguiba. The Roman theatre which could hold 10,000 spectators is located in the Odeon area, though most of what can be seen is a restoration. The original pieces exist only in fragmentary form (see diagram), but at least give an idea of what the entire seating area (*cavea*) of the monument was once like. The semicircular *orchestra* with some of its original marble flooring can still be seen too. Although not exactly true to the original, the theatre is spectacular, especially when heaving with a crowd on a hot summer night during the annual **Festival International de Carthage**.

Also on Odeon Hill, north of the theatre, are a series of excavations of fine Roman villas (on the whole badly restored) and similar buildings, reached via the entrance at the *nymphaion* with its water feature. The villas are of classical proportions, built around the peristyle or central pillared courtyard giving access to the main living rooms. This form can be seen clearly in the famous and now restored fifth-sixth century **House of the Aviary**, named after the subject of a mosaic found at the site bearing a well executed polychrome of a fowl and fruit, now in the Bardo Museum. This house has an octagonal garden in the middle of its courtyard. Many of the artefacts on show here in the house, including statues and a bust of Dionysus, are from other sites at Carthage. Other adjacent villas such as the **House of the Horse** and the Odeon itself are worth a visit. The Odeon was an indoor theatre but only its confused ruins remain – most of the material has long gone, used to construct new buildings.

In the **amphitheatre**, built during Hadrian's reign and capable of seating 35,000 spectators, early Christians were thrown to the lions and gladiators as entertainment for the audience. Unfortunately there is very little to see since only limited excavation work has been carried out. The cisterns at La Maalga, behind Le Phénix de Carthage entertainment complex, were the main reservoirs for the Carthage water supply. Their very size and complexity is a good indication of the population of the ancient city. They are currently being restored.

The **circus** was on the extreme west of the city. Only the outline can be made out. It would have been used for chariot racing as depicted in the mosaic exhibited in the antiquarium, the four teams wearing distinguishing colours. The site later became a cemetery.

Northwest of Byrsa hill: minor sights

The **Antonine Baths**, once the biggest baths in North Africa and the third largest in the Roman world, were truly enormous. They are in a splendid position between Avenue Habib Bourguiba and the sea and are one of the best preserved sites in Carthage. Even though there are only a few pieces of building still standing, they give, with a little imagination, a good idea of the grandeur that was.

On the seafront: the Antonine Baths

Their construction began under Hadrian and Antonius officiated at the opening ceremony in the middle of the second century. The finance for the project, donated by some rich inhabitant, gives an indication of the wealth at that time. The complex array of rooms in the baths is shown on the plan below. The layout is symmetrical around a central axis of the swimming pool, with the *frigidarium* and *calderium* running from the seashore frontage to the second façade facing west onto the archaeological gardens. The two wings each contained a *palaestra* or open pillared exercise yard, an indoor gymnasium, hot bath, *tepidarium* and *destrictarium* or warmed cleaning room. A *laconicum* or sweating room was included, while the main *frigidarium* was shared by both wings. Many of the minor rooms are hexagonal or octagonal in shape. Water for the baths came from the main city aqueduct. Being at sea level, the heating and service areas had to be built above ground, the boilers immediately below the heated rooms for efficiency and economy.

Antonine Baths

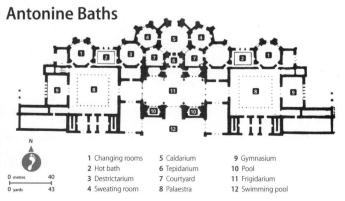

1 Changing rooms	5 Caldarium	9 Gymnasium
2 Hot bath	6 Tepidarium	10 Pool
3 Destrictarium	7 Courtyard	11 Frigidarium
4 Sweating room	8 Palaestra	12 Swimming pool

0 metres 40
0 yards 43

Tunis and around

Without visiting Carthage

Eleventh century Arab historian and geographer Al Bakri (died 1094) recounted the splendours of Carthage in his writings, even though he never visited the site. However, he had read widely, and learned much about the city from the oral traditions so important in the Arab intellectual circles of his day. Even though he knew neither its precise name and location, he described the amphitheatre with certain admiration:

"The most marvellous monument of Carthage is the house of entertainment which is also called thiater. *It is composed of a circle of arcades supported on columns and topped by other arcades similar to those of the ground floor. On the walls of this edifice, one can see images of all the animals and craftsmen. One can distinguish figures representing the winds: the east wind has a smiling face, the west wind wears a frown. Marble is so abundant in Carthage that if all the inhabitants of Ifrikiya were to assemble to remove blocks and transport them elsewhere, they would be unable to complete the task. In Carthage one can*

also see the Moallaca, *the 'hanging' castle of great height and grandeur. It is composed of round arched vaults, with several floors. Towards the west of this edifice is the castle known by the name of* thiater, *the very same which contains the house of entertainment which we have just mentioned. It has many doors and skylights, and several floors. Above each door one remarks the image of an animal in marble, and figures representing craftsmen of all classes."*

Al Bakri also tells of a castle "which too has several floors resting on marble columns of a enormous height and thickness. On the capital of one of these columns twelve men could sit cross-legged, with in their midst a table from which to eat and drink. They are fluted, these columns, white as snow and shining like crystal; some still stand, others have fallen." Few columns like these remain today. In the 19th century, Carthage was to become something of an open-cast mine for the European consuls seeking costly stone to export to their homelands.

To the south of the baths lie the present-day **archaeological gardens**, comprising two main northwest-southeast roads (Decumanus III to IV) of the original gridiron layout of roads and their crossroads (Cardo). Originally the road system was aligned along the summit of the acropolis of Byrsa (northwest-southeast) and defined all the blocks of property in the city. The residual area encompassed by the archaeological gardens is mainly in ruins, but the former esplanade of the baths can be identified together with its porticos and annexes, of which the most singular is the latrines, laid out in two great 35-m semicircles. There is a small basilica in this same corner featuring a main aisle and two side aisles, but the main church in the gardens is to the west – that of the late Byzantine Dermech Basilica (Douimès). Part of the Punic necropolis is the only sign of the older foundation in the gardens. The Schola House on Decumanus III has a peristyle and contained fine mosaics.

So many of the original stones of Carthage have been taken. Many originally here were used in the construction of Tunis. Others travelled much further and make-up parts of a number of monuments including Pisa cathedral.

On the seafront: the Magon Quarter The **Magon Quarter** dating from the fifth century BC is approached down Avenue de la République. It was destroyed in 146 BC and rebuilt under Caesar Augustus. Following the excavations by the German Archaeological Institute, the site was turned into a garden and it is possible to walk along the restored Roman road by the sea front. A small museum displays household items, found during excavations. Models and diagrams illustrate the development of the Punic settlement and the rebuilding a century after its destruction.

After leaving Carthage and before reaching Sidi Bou Saïd, take a left turn to the American Military Cemetery. There is a car park inside the entrance gates and a visitors' reception and restroom.

The American Military Cemetery

On a site covering over 10 ha are the graves of 2,841 American military men and women (240 unnamed), who died in the fighting which culminated in the liberation of Tunisia. Walk down the steps and along the tree-shaded avenue to the immaculate lawn marked with rows of white crosses. The tablets of the missing consist of a wall 120-m long, on which names and particulars of 3,724 persons are inscribed. Three modern wall mosaics show the movements of the Allied Forces in North Africa and the Mediterranean during the Second World War. This is a fine example, if a sad one, of a cemetery in a foreign land, carefully designed to blend with the surroundings. ■ *Summer (16 Apr-15 Sep) 0800-1800 Mon to Sat, Sun and holidays opens 1 hr later, in winter closes 1 hr earlier.*

Essentially an area of upmarket villas, Carthage has few hotels. Fingers crossed that the revamped *Reine Didon* will be a success. **A** *Hotel Reine Didon*, R Mendès France, on Byrsa Hill. Currently undergoing refurbishment, numbers were T733433, F732599. It is hoped that the current refurbishment, slow but no doubt careful, will turn the *Reine Didon* into one of Tunisia's top hotels. Certainly, the views will be superb. **A-B** *Hotel Résidence de Carthage*, 16 R Hannibal, Salammbô, T734918, F730125. 12 rooms with heating and shower, recently renovated, clean, hotel restaurant *Le Punique* has a good name (see below), 10 mins from beach, excellent position for visiting the Punic Ports but no other real advantage. High prices for what's on offer.

Sleeping
■ *on map, page 124*
Phone code: 71

Carthage, as you would expect of such an upscale area, has a nice choice of eateries. **Expensive** *Le Punique*, *Hotel-Résidence de Carthage*, 16 R Hannibal, Salammbô, T731072. **Mid-range** *Le Gerry's*, at Salammbô on the main drag, T73008. On the ground floor of the block of flats opposite the stadium. Good if unimaginative Italian food. Alcohol and reasonable prices make this restaurant popular with young locals. Good service. Pleasant outside dining area. Recommended. *Le Neptune*, 2 R Ibn Chabbat, T731456. Hidden away in the residential streets to the right of the main road as you leave Le Kram and Salammbô behind you. Right on the sea. Pleasant. Perhaps a little on the expensive side. Regulars get a good welcome. *Le Tchevap*, on main road, almost opposite Carthage main supermarket, T277089. At the expensive end of the mid-range price bracket, good pasta and filet de sole, very decent service, for once. Recommended. The Italian restaurant of the *Palm Hotel*, Le Kram, right on the beach, has had some good reports. (Look for signs at main roundabout in Le Kram.) A recent arrival, right on the beach at Salammbô, is *L'Odyssée*, T720911. Nice terrace overlooking a lively beach, starters around 3Dt, specialities around 12Dt, pasta 6Dt. Chef's pride is his *agneau berbère au four*, with lots of rosemary and garlic. **Cheap** *Frigolo*, next to the Le Passage supermarket at Carthage-Dermech, T275959. Does good ice-cream, cakes, fruit teas and snacks. The usual sloppy service lets the place down, however. For extremely good cakes, you need the *Pâtisserie Charlotte*, over the road from the supermarket, heading back towards Le Kram. *Le Vagabondo*, Av H Bourguiba, Le Kram. A no frills (and no alcohol) sort of place which does very reasonable pizzas and a mean spaghetti fruits de mer. Recommended. There are plenty of cheap sandwich places along the main drag on Le Kram.

Eating
● *on map, page 124*

Le Comptoir d'Amilcar, about 1 km from Sidi Bou Saïd, on your left on main road as you approach the Lycée de Carthage. Expensive furniture shop, but also has more portable

Shopping

Tunis and around

stuff in the form of lamps, wrought-iron items and household linen. *El Hanout* and *El Hanout - enfant*, R J.F. Kennedy, Carthage-Hannibal (1st left as you go uphill on Av de l'Amphithéâtre from Carthage-Hannibal station). Bijou emporium with lots of expensive itemlets. Nice handmade toys, lamps and fittings for children's rooms at *El Hanout - enfant*. Down where Le Kram turns into Salammbô, on the main drag, next to the bank just before the stadium, you have **Phénicia**, a personable little shop with an excellent range of contemporary ceramics, textiles, embroidery and jewellery. One of the few shops to stock really authentic Tunisian crafts. Definitely worth a visit.

Directory   **Banks** There is a handy *BIAT* and *Amen Bank* with cashpoints in Le Kram, also a *UBCI* with cashpoint almost opposite the Palaeo-Christian Museum. Otherwise, nip up the road/rail line to Sidi Bou Saïd to change cash. **Communications** Internet: If you can't get into town, there are some internet access places in the Carthage area. By the time of going to print, there should almost certainly be a publinet in one of the side-streets near the stadium in Salammbô. Otherwise try *Club Informatique de Carthage, CIC*, close to the Antonine Baths, almost opposite Carthage PTT (post office), and a couple of doors down from police station. Look for small plaque next to door. You have to become a member of the club. Access times are very irregular, according to the training sessions they are running. Bureaucratic, rude staff. Best bet between 1600 and 1800. *Cyberespace Sidi Daoud*, out of the way unless you have a car, as you leave Carthage for Sidi Daoud, about 200 m before the junction with the La Marsa highway, on your left in a converted garage. Again, irregular hrs, 6 computers. **Medical services** There are plenty of pharmacies, including a night chemists in Le Kram on the main street.

Sidi Bou Saïd   سيدي أبو سعيد

Phone code: 71
Colour map 2, grid B3

Hilltop Sidi Bou Saïd is everyone's favourite Mediterranean village, a jumble of whitewashed houses with blue-painted doors and windows on a hilltop overlooking the sea. Until a couple of decades ago it was quite an isolated place, a fact hard to remember these days when the village car park is full of tourist buses. Yet the back alleys of the village maintain their charm. Cats snooze on doorsteps, canaries trill behind lattice work windows, and elaborate studded doors pose for photographs. And from the heights of the village, there are some breathtaking views out across the Mediterranean and the Gulf of Tunis.

History   The original Sidi Bou Saïd was a mystic back in the 13th century. In 1207, Abou Saïd Khalaf Ben Yahia el Béji, returning to Tunis from a pilgrimage to Mecca, settled on the Djebel el Manar (Lighthouse Hill), all the better to commune with the divine. For some 20 years he resided out on the coast, arousing the admiration of the local fishing community for his ascetic ways. Abou Saïd's fame spread to Tunis, and on his death in 1236 he was practically the patron saint of the village. (The Tunisian Arabic term 'sidi' roughly corresponds to the Christian saint, although there is no practice of canonization in Islam.) The tomb of Sidi Bou Saïd gradually became a place of pilgrimage, and his disciples continued his ascetic ways. Other soufis settled on Djebel Manar.

In the 18th century, the Husseinid beys rebuilt the tomb and extended the mosque. In order to benefit from the saint's *baraka* (blessing), they made the village their summer resort, and despite the distance from Tunis, a number of old Tunisois families followed suit, building themselves pleasant summer residences in the clifftop village with its views over the Mediterranean, the Cap Bon and Carthage. Under Naceur Bey, in 1915, the village was given listed status to protect it from the ravages of potential developers. Sea bathing became fashionable, and the old families built themselves wooden bathing cabins on stilts over the sea down by the discreet village beach.

But it was a French baron who did a lot to put Sidi Bou Saïd on the map. The story goes that Baron Rodolphe d'Erlanger, scion of a Parisian banking house which had lent Tunisia large sums of money, fell in love with the village on a visit in 1908. He acquired a piece of prime land overlooking the Mediterranean, and with his Italian wife, the beautiful Bettina Amidei, had a palace constructed, the Dar Nejma Ezzahra, 'the House of the Star of Venus'. Works lasted from 1912 to 1921, but it was with a heavy heart that the baron completed his dream Tunisian residence, for he lost his son in the First World War.

The musical baron

During the Germans' brief occupation of Tunisia in the Second World War, Nejma Ezzahra was deemed a suitable billet for Italian aviators. War correspondent Alan Moorhead described meeting *la Baronne* after the Axis rout: she had emerged from a remote wing to find the champagne all drunk and the white peacocks eaten. To the south, the port of La Goulette was 'a festering mass of twisted steel'. In the late 1980s, the palace became property of the Tunisian State. It remains a building unique in Tunisia. Essentially it is an early 20th-century British country house dressed up in orientalist garb and as such it is definitely worth a visit (see below).

Something of a backwater, yet close to Tunis, Sidi Bou Saïd once attracted intellectuals and artists. André Gide passed through on one of his North African perambulations, painters Paul Klee and Macke are said to have been dazzled by its shapes and colours. In the late 1960s, philosopher Michel Foucault lived for a couple of years in Dar Patou in the upper village. For his habit of keeping a human skull as a decorative feature in his study, he gained a reputation as a necromancer. He taught at the University of Tunis, witnessing the intense student riots of March 1968. Foucault was impressed by the fervour of the Tunis students, by how their Marxism gave them the moral energy to run huge risks, including that of imprisonment. It all turned out to be something of a precursor for the Paris studentuprising of May 1968. And Foucault came to see politics as a limit-experience, like eroticism and art.

Artists & gentrification

In the 1980s, the lower village expanded with a new mini-mall and villa developments, while the upper village kept its mix of decaying gentry, fishermen and eccentric foreigners. But being picturesque and close to Tunis made gentrification inevitable in the 1990s. Local money began to be pumped into new property. Some of the seemingly oldest homes are in fact recent creations of top Tunisian traditionalist architect Tarak Ben Miled, one of whose earliest projects was the holiday village in a simple vernacular style down by the port. Latest major addition to Sidi Bou Saïd is the 2000 architecture school on the La Marsa road.

At Sidi Bou Saïd the walls are white, the woodwork is blue. The doors are set with patterns of black-painted nails, no doubt forming highly traditional patterns. Whitewashing the walls is certainly a long established practice. How traditional the blue of the doors is remains an unanswered question. Guides will tell you that blue is the Arab colour of happiness (that's a good one) or that it keeps the flies off (possibly). The modern lacquer paint must be a long way off the original blue stains which may have been used for woodwork in the past. Note that the *Café des Nattes* makes extensive use of red and green in its colour scheme, as befits a place that was once the ante-chamber to the tomb of the saint himself.

Colours, tastes & smells

The character of Sidi Bou lies in tiny details, in tastes and smells as well as colour. At the *Café des Nattes*, up a steep flight of steps leading off the cobbled square in the centre of the village, the drinks are Turkish coffee (*kahwa 'arbi'*), scented with geranium or orange flower water, and mint tea with pine nuts, or even fresh almonds, when in season. The tea is a rich butter toffee brown, and is pure liquid mint with almost the consistency of a liqueur. If this isn't sweet enough for you, just round the corner below the *Café des Nattes* is a hole-in-the-wall shop selling *bonbalone*, fried doughnuts dipped in sugar.

The most characteristic smell of Sidi Bou Saïd has to be jasmine. The flower sellers go by, with round baskets of jasmine bouquets balanced on their heads. "Smeen, smeen", they cry. For men, a *mechmoum*, a delicately made bouquet lodged behind the ear, is *de rigueur*. (Wearing it behind the left ear means you're single, and behind the right ear that you're married.) Women wear long necklaces of jasmine flowers. And note that there are two types of jasmine on sale: the strong smelling pinkish *yasmine* and the more delicate waxy cream blossoms of *fell* or *jasmin d'Arabie*.

Backstreets & panoramas Another place to have a drink, particularly at sunset, is the *Café Sidi Chabaane*, situated at the end of the village. The view from here over the sea is quite exceptional. There are two routes from the upper village down to the harbour: one following the road which leads to the promontory at the end of the village, the other a steep flight of steps to the right just before the *Hotel Dar Saïd*.

Being on every tourist's itinerary, Sidi Bou Saïd can get very crowded, especially in summer, but most people tend to congregate in the main streets and it is possible to find some peace in the small back streets. Look out for the lighthouse. At the very top of Sidi Bou Saïd, towards Sidi Dhrif, a presidential palace is being built to accommodate official guests.

The Kharja The Kharja (from the Arabic *kharaja*, to bring out), marks the high point of the Sidi Bou Saïd summer. This is the annual pilgrimage to the tomb of Sidi Bou Saïd, which generally takes place in August. In days gone by, with the beldi families and at least part of the court in residence for the summer, members of the different religious brotherhoods of Tunis would come to the village to pay homage to the saint. The banners of the saint would be brought out and paraded through the village, accompanied by chanting and a swaying line of members of the Aïssaoua brotherhood. There is no way you can miss the Kharja when it's on. The main street is packed, and the unmistakeable thud of drums and tambourines accompanies the procession as it moves slowly up through the crowded village. Non-Muslims will not, however, see the transe-dance ceremonies that take place in the main courtyard of the mosque.

Dar Nejma Ezzahra The Baron d'Erlanger's palace was constructed between 1912 and 1922 by Tunisian builders and decorated by Moroccan craftsmen. D'Erlanger had a marked artistic bent, being both a gifted amateur painter and a musician. He was instrumental in bringing together Arab musicians, and it was at his instigation that the First Congress of Arab Music was held in Cairo, under the patronage of the King of Egypt, in 1932. Rodolphe d'Erlanger also sponsored a five-volume history of Arab music in French, the first in any European language. It is thus highly appropriate that the palace on which he lavished so much attention, and which was such a magnet for artists and musicians, is now a historic monument, functioning as the *Centre for Arab and Mediterranean Music*. Here is housed the most complete collection of Tunisian musical instruments. ■ *Summer 0900-1200 and 1600-1900, winter 0900-1200 and 1400-1700. Entrance 3Dt*

As one of the capital's great picturesque property locations, Sidi Bou Saïd does not have a lot of accommodation. At the time of writing, the holiday village by the beach at the foot of the hill was (still) undergoing a refit. Happily for those with much cash, the *Dar Saïd* is now open, and most pleasant it is too. As you arrive at the village, there is a *simsar* (informal real-estate agent) who hangs out in a small kiosk on your left before you reach the spring. For a longer stay, he may be able to find you something.

AL *Hotel Dar Saïd*, R Toumi, upmarket *résidence de charme* in the upper village, T729666, F729599, www.darsaid.com, darsaid@gnet.tn Until recently a rather decrepit address, this is now one of the smoothest places to stay in Tunisia. 150-year-old building built round an attractive central courtyard, pool, hammam for private rental. Rooms either in new block up a marble staircase at the back or in the older part, many with views over the Gulf of Tunis. Rooms decorated in creams and beige with marble and traditional tiles, many with high ceilings and bath en suite. Rooms 12, 14 and 15 rented together have a private patio. New restaurant across the street will have seminar rooms. Efficient, professional management. Hotel now belongs to Ben Yedder family (Amen Banque) and Jackie Kennedy stayed here.

B *Hotel Amilcar*, at the foot of Sidi Bou Saïd cliff, T470788. 1970s cliff of a building down on the beach below *SBS*. All 250 rooms have a view over the Gulf looking towards the Cap Bon peninsula, private beach, pool. Situated next to a rather jolly beach which gets very crowded in summer, given its handiness for public transport. Good out of season, deals sometimes possible. **C** *Sidi Bou Saïd*, on a hill slightly out of the village, T740411. 34 rooms, good standard, pool, view looking out westwards towards Tunis. Restaurant has a good reputation. **D** *Hotel Bou Fares*, central, upper village, T740091. As you face the staircase of the *Café des Nattes*, go left. 8 rooms centred around a fig-tree shaded patio in a converted house, very clean and cheap, cold in winter, excellent breakfast, no restaurant, vital to book in the summer season. The manager and his mates can be found doing impromptu jam sessions on their lute and guitar in the courtyard. A popular address.

Self-catering Dar Lasram in the upper village, owned by the Turki family, used to have very upmarket accommodation for short lets in the grounds of their palatial dwelling, close to the main car park.

Very expensive *Dar Zarrouk*, not yet open in spring 2002, this is the restaurant across the street from the *Dar Saïd* (see above). It will have superb views and beautiful décor, if the restored hotel is anything to go by, and will seat 300. Before closing in the early 1990s, *Dar Zarrouk* catered to the Sousse day-trip trade. Info suggests that new clientele will be official and business. *Restaurant le Pirate*, T748266. By the harbour at the bottom of the cliff, specializes in fish and seafood, expensive but worth it as the food is excellent. Service variable.

Expensive *L'Amphitrite*, T747591, on the beach down at Amilcar, usual fish specialities. Good for a leisurely lunch, evenings less satisfactory. A popular address. *Le Bon Vieux Temps*, T744788, F728100. Try to reserve. Leaving the central *Café des Nattes* on your left, head straight ahead, the restaurant is on your left after 200 m. An offshoot of the restaurant of the same name in La Marsa, has had very good reports – although some say portions too small. Good view from terrace across Gulf of Tunis.

Mid-range *Restaurant La Bagatelle*, at the bottom of the hill before the village, good setting, good food, very popular. *Raïs Lebhar*, between the *Bagatelle* and the roundabout, acceptable but unexciting.

Sleeping
■ *on map, page 124*
Phone code: 71

Eating
● *on map, page 124*

Tunis and around

Cheap *Restaurant Chergui*, T740987, on the main street, on the right of *Café des Nattes*. Large terrace with a fantastic view, food is good value, if not very exciting. The sort of place to have a *brik à l'oeuf* and barbecued lamb. Popular. *Café Tam Tam*, T728535, on your left as you come up from the station. Good (but narrow) terrace above the street, so you can watch all the trendies coming up to parade round Sidi Bou. Excellent pizzas, but no booze, attentive, pleasant service, bright and cheerful décor. Recommended for an outing with the kids. (Adults might like the chicken tarragon.) Also does take-away meals. At the bottom of the village, there are any number of sandwich places which stay open late, plus the *Gelateria di Ricardo*. The place next to the orange-tree café on the roundabout (roast chicken) is clean and efficient.

Entertainment **Dance classes** Want to learn oriental dancing? Try the *Espace forme et beauté* at 17 Av de la République, Carthage-Amilcar, T741326. Classes by Mme Houda Maknassi Rouissi.

Galleries Sidi Bou Saïd has a reputation as a painter's paradise, a sort of Tunisian Montmartre, and a number of contemporary painters have (or have had) their ateliers here, including Jellal Ben Abdallah the miniaturist, Brahim Dhahhak, and Rachid Koreïchi, master of the calligraphed sign. In particular, try the *Galerie Chérif Fine Art*, 20 R de la République and *Galerie Ammar Farhat*, 3 R Sidi el Ghemrini. The *Musée de Sidi Bou Saïd*, on your right as you go up the hill, is not in fact a museum, but rather hosts exhibitions of varying quality.

Hammam Recommended is *Hammam Sidi Bou Saïd* in the street opposite the *Magasin Général* in the lower part of the town. Modern and tiled, it lacks the character of the older hammams in the médina.

Sport **Sailing** The ancient fishing port has been developed as a marina, with a sailing club and a windsurfing school. There are 360 berths (minimum-maximum draft 2-4 m) and all the necessary services are now in place including a 26 tonne travel lift.

Directory **Banks** For changing money, the *UIB* and the *Banque du Sud* are in the new part of town at the bottom of the hill. **Medical services** Chemist: all night pharmacy next to the *UIB* bank.

La Marsa and Gammarth

Phone code: 71
Colour map 2, grid B3

At the end of the TGM line is the once royal resort of La Marsa (lit. 'the port'). The town grew up around a beylical palace, and among the new constructions a scattering of early-20th-century villas still survives. After independence, the palace was almost completely demolished by vengeful minister Taïeb Mehiri. The town retains traces of the enervating atmosphere of an old-fashioned summer resort. There is a long beach (crowded in summer) and a promenade with palm trees. There is little to do apart from sit on the beach or contemplate the world from a café. Merging with La Marsa is upscale Gammarth with its villas and chic restaurants. And beyond the hill is Raoued, a long windy beach backed by a salt marsh, today lined with tourist hotels.

Sights La Marsa is a quiet sort of place during the day. In the early evening and at weekends, the area around the TGM station comes alive with families out to enjoy the air and an ice-cream. Enjoy the atmosphere, smoke a chicha at the *Café Safsaf*, or maybe take in an exhibition at the *Galerie Mille Feuilles*.

If you need some sights, then the remains of the beylical palace can be found down a side-street near the *Café Safsaf*. At the end of the street, you come to a junction where the elegant Municipalité de La Marsa sits opposite the French ambassador's residence. Cross the road, and a right turn after some 50 m will take you into Marsa-Cubes, a small area of villa housing next to the beach. This is a nice place to swim.

The Palais Abdillia

Turning left at the Municipality, you have a long tree-lined avenue which will take you to La Marsa-Ville and the main bus station. Cross over to Tunisie-Télécom and go right. Beyond a dusty open space popular with pétanque players in the early evening, you will see the restored 16th-century Hafsid Palais Abdillia. Rumour has it that a future Museum of Modern Art is to be housed in the premises. The palace, an unusual survival, is well worth a visit should there be a temporary exhibition on show. The story behind the palace runs that Hafsid ruler Abu Abdullah Mohammed had a sickly daughter for whom fresh sea air was recommended. Not to be found wanting, Abu Abdullah had three palaces constructed at La Marsa, of which only this, the third, remains. It follows the classic design with the main rooms arranged around an open central courtyard complete with fountain. The dominant feature, a high tower, offers superb views. (The palace entrance is in a side-street round the back.)

After a look at the Abdillia, you may want to go back to La Marsa Plage. Retrace your steps, cross opposite the bus station to the line of shops. Down a side-street to the right of the newsagents, there are a couple of very popular sandwich shops, one *Ould el Bey*, run by a descendant of the former ruling family, no less. In need of a beer? The options are limited, as the *Café-Restaurant el Hafsi*, a La Marsa institution, is shortly to be redeveloped. However, up Rue du Maroc on the Corniche you have the splendidly kitsch *Hotel Plaza*, for pizza and a quiet beer.

Sleeping

■ *on map, page 136*
Phone code: 71

Hotels are listed here under **La Marsa/Gammarth** (a selection of older establishments) and **Raoued**, aka **Côtes de Carthage**. Here the hotels are almost all recent, 3-star and above establishments, good value if you've bought your package in Europe. The Raoued stretch of coast is very crowded in Jul and Aug, and beach hygiene tends to suffer. There are some good hotels here, much used by business travellers and out-of-season-breakers.

La Marsa/Gammarth AL *Abou Nawas*, Blvd Taieb Méhiri, Lower Gammarth, T741444, F740400. 45 apartments, 127 rms with a/c, pool in summer, good beach, 6 restaurants/bars, excellent food. A toney establishment. **AL** *Le Palace*, up on the heights of Gammarth, opposite the presidential villas, T912000, F911971, lepalace@lepalace.com.tn Vast complex with conference centre. Comfortable rooms, large pool and semi-abandoned Egyptian-style casino. Far from being the best address in this price bracket, nevertheless. NB No beach. **B** *Mégara*, on Blvd Taieb Méhiri, Lower Gammarth T740366, F740916. A 1970s hotel built out of and around an old villa. 77 rooms, pool, mature gardens. Loyal clientele with memories of Tunisois summers past. Best features: the Chemla tiles in the older sections, the trees. Rooms clean but a bit tatty, could do with a refit. Never mind. **B** *Plaza Corniche*, 22 R du Maroc, La Marsa-Corniche, T743577, F742554, only hotel in La Marsa itself, in the residential Corniche area. Converted villa with 11 rooms on quiet street, close to sea but no beach. Bar and pizzeria, truly kitsch décor, small nightclub. **C** *La Tour Blanche* on the Av Mehiri, Gammarth, T271647. Overlooking the beach. Nice pool. Just after the *Mégara* on Blvd Taieb Méhiri is the *Tour Blanche*, T774788, F747247. Must have been splendid when new, still acceptable, rooms overlook narrow beach, crowded in summer. Plus point: handy for trendy restaurants.

Raoued AL *Golden Tulip*, Av de la Promenade, Côtes de Carthage, T913000, F913913, www.goldentuliphotels.nl/gtcarthage Up on the hill with views over the Mediterranean. High quality, spacious rooms with internet access. Ambitious features: 3 pools, 1 with fantasy ruins. Nice touch: reproduction ancient mosaics in public areas. 10-pin bowling nearby, La Marsa a short taxi ride away. Disadvantage: very pricey. Also has an à la carte Italian restaurant, *La Stalla*. Remains to be seen what sort of standard they can maintain. **AL** *La Résidence*, Raoued, T910101, F910444, residence.tun@gnet.tn Probably the nicest hotel on the Raoued strip, completed 1997, has Leading Hotels of the World label. A serious competitor for the Abou Nawas chain for the business end of the market. Well equipped, tastefully furnished rooms, all with balcony. Large thalassotherapy centre with traditional hammam – have a seaweed skin treatment. However, if on business with meetings in Tunis, bear in mind that you will have to brave the morning traffic on the La Marsa-Tunis highway. Basically, good for a mini-break spring or autumn, excellent if the company's paying. **A** *Hotel Renaissance*, T910900, 912020, new Sep 2002, 36th hotel in the Mariott chain, 223 rooms, 22 suites, an excellent business address right on the beach. Ambitious features: Tunis's first Thai restaurant, the *White Elephant*, and an open-air disco with dance floors on beach. Plus points: internet access in all rooms (check if in service), huge pool with scallop shell. Minor disadvantage: rooms on small side.

B *Dar Naouar*, T741000, 740309, open Apr-Oct, naouar.dar@gnet.tn Holiday village style, right on the beach, pleasant rooms with a/c, large pool, windsurfers, open-air theatre. Full in summer. Just opposite is the **B-C** *Acqua Viva*, T748567, F342411, 110 rooms. Club atmosphere, poolside entertainments. Best feature: pool with water slides. The older hotels of the zone are located at the forest end of the Raoued beach strip, including **B-C** *Cap Carthage*, T740064, F741980, 350 rooms. Mid-1980s hotel, oldest in the strip and looking a little dated, used by tour groups. Numerous tennis courts. Perfectly adequate. **B-C** *Karim*, T740700, F741200, 220 rooms. Nearby is the **B-C** *Molka*, T740242, F741646, 206 rooms. One of the older, mid-1990s beach hotels, all usual facilities, works with tour groups. Best feature: nearby riding stables.

Eating
● *on map below*

La Marsa and Gammarth have a large number of eateries in the top price bracket, as you might expect in a neighbourhood with some of the country's leading fortunes and diplomats' homes. Note however that service is very up and down. Regulars tend to get preferential treatment, for others the service can be indifferent.

Gammarth & Raoued

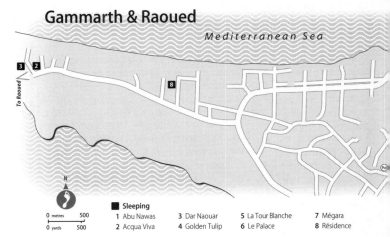

Mediterranean Sea

To Raoued

N

0 metres 500
0 yards 500

■ **Sleeping**
1 Abu Nawas
2 Acqua Viva
3 Dar Naouar
4 Golden Tulip
5 La Tour Blanche
6 Le Palace
7 Mégara
8 Résidence

Expensive *Au Bon Vieux Temps*, on the roundabout at La Marsa Plage, T774322. Some very good French cooking indeed. Portions on the small side. *Le Golfe*, overlooking the beach at 5 R Larbi Zarrouk, near the *Hotel Abou Nawas*, Gammarth, T748219. Generally held to be the best restaurant in this neck of the woods. Service steady. Try their filet de Saint Pierre or the paella. *La Falaise*, on your left as you begin the steep climb up to Sidi Bou Saïd coming from La Marsa, T747806. Try their couscous au poisson, expensive but reliable. Overlooking the sea, there is a clutch of trendy, pricey places to eat on the Lower Gammarth road, aka Av Taïeb Mehiri, beyond the *Hotel Megara*. *Les Dunes*, Lower Gammarth, T743379. Last on left before the road begins the climb up to the heights of Gammarth. Seafood a speciality, good food, best in winter (warmer atmosphere). Service on the smarmy side. *Le Grand Bleu*. Up on the clifftop with views looking out over the sea, T746900. Excellent service if you are with an official delegation, variable for occasional visitors. The next door piano-bar is popular. *Les Ombrelles*, T742964. Superb location right on the seafront in Lower Gammarth. Expensive drinks. Best in summer. *Le Sindbad*, T749876, seafront, Lower Gammarth. Pricey and popular with a young set, expensive wine list will bump the cost of a meal up considerably. Not rated as highly by locals as *Les Ombrelles*.

Mid-range Easily the best place in this price bracket is *Pizza-Sprint Arthé* at 5 R Ibn Abi Rabiaâ. Good starters (try the *involtini de crevettes*), pizzas, a good range of pasta and pleasant desserts including mousse au chocolat and fondant au chocolat, served in the pleasant garden of a villa. Children can be let off the leash safe from the traffic. Occasional exhibitions of local crafts in the villa. Easy to find: turn left out of the TGM and right at the end of the road. Downside: no alcohol, but they are working on this. Also try the *Hotel Plaza* , R du Maroc, La Marsa-Corniche, T743577. This must be one of the most overdecorated places in Tunisia, despite heavy competition from places in Sousse and Tozeur. On balmy summer nights, disco balls glitter between the palm trees. The kids will love the tack of it all, adults can have a quiet beer with their pizza (see also under Bars). A new address to watch will be the *Cinquante-Cinq (55)*, just opposite *Arthé*, at 55 R Omar Ibn Abi Rabiaâ, T776149. Opening soon, 140-seat restaurant with trendy bar (see below).

Cheap Have a tea at the *Café Safsaf*, and try some of their pastries or Tunisian food. Steaming hot *leblebi* in winter or *plat tunisien*, also *fricassées* and freshly made potato crisps. There are numerous *casse-crouteries* (stand-up sandwich bars) at La Marsa. Try *Chez Joseph* at La Marsa-Plage, or *Ould el Bey* at La Marsa-Ville.

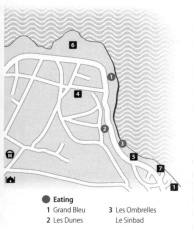

Eating
1 Grand Bleu
2 Les Dunes
3 Les Ombrelles
Le Sinbad

Bars & nightclubs The northern suburbs now have a choice selection of bars, including *Le Grand blue*, *Le Plaza*, *Koubbat el Haoua*, *La Closerie* and *Le Sindbad*. Attached to a small hotel, La Marsa has a well established bar and club, *La Plaza*, 22 R du Maroc, T743577, F742554. Though the clientele is eager to display its money, a drink by the pool can be pleasant in the early evening. Rumour has it that it is something of a 30s singletons' pick-up point. Busy most nights. Up on the heights of Gammarth, close to the *Hotel le Palace*, the *Le Grand bleu* functions as restaurant and piano-bar, complete with popular trilingual karaoke. Arrive about midnight, busy most nights. The fashionable place for a pre-club drink is at the snooty *Le Sindbad*

Tunis and around

Tunis and around

Koum echtah! Get up and dance!

A sticky July evening, 11pm, in the suburbs of a Tunisian city. The Salle des fêtes, the public hall used for weddings, is hot and packed. Family groups, or rather, women and children, sedately seated, for the moment, at round plastic tables, sip bright orange fizzy drink through straws. The men prop up the walls, waiters circulate with trays covered with mosaics of sticky helw. At the front, on twin thrones set against a wall of artificial flowers, sit bride and groom, he in smart Boss suit, she in a white extravaganza, features fixed under pancake make-up. Perspiring under the spotlights, they gaze out over the wedding scene. Somewhere to the side, a four-piece band is blaring out the wedding favourites. Drum between his knees, an enthusiastic darboukji pounds out the rhythm. In the narrow gap between bridal dais and tables, a group of svelte young women, jade-black hair cascading, scarves around their hips, dance. Arms sketch serpentine shapes in the air, fingers click, hips move with just the right hint of eroticism. 'Koum echtah' says a beheadscarved granny to her small granddaughters, 'Get up and dance'. And so they do, arms aloft, hips swaying, smiling wildly, diminutive versions of the women at the front.

Though they make it look so easy, it really isn't – as many a tourist has found out, dragged up on the floor by the belly-dancer at a folkloric evening in a hotel. The humiliation is all part of the entertainment, of course. Effortless-seeming Tunisian dancing requires as much technique as any dance form. In childhood, little girls watch their peers and imitate. And like kids everywhere, young Tunisians learn dance from the television. The great Egyptian films of the 1950s and 1960s were full of raqs sharqi numbers ('belly-dance', to use the English term), performed by the inimitable Tahia Carioca, Zizi Mustapha and others. In a recent Tunisian film, Satin rouge, a seedy cabaret is the setting for a sensual initiation: a roguish danseuse introduces a dried-up widow to the self-revelatory power of ech chttih, Oriental dancing.

Every Arab country has its variations, of course. Men from Upper Egypt dance tahtib, a leaping stick-clashing affair, while Lebanese and Palestinians have a lively line-dance, the debké. Moroccan men are more restrained, shaking their shoulders, while Kabyle women vibrate their buttocks to the music. In Tunisia, mizoued, the bagpipe music of the countryside, gets both sexes going. 'Dayri, dayri', 'turn, turn, . . .', and off they go. The men hold up their arms stiffly at 45 degrees to the floor. Scarves around their hips, they gyrate their hips like the women, imitating Hédi Hebouba, the great mizoued star of the 1970s who made it all right for Tunisian men to dance in public.

The documented history of dance in Tunis is short. No doubt the European Tunisois danced the tango and the foxtrot and other danses de salon at the Palmarium. But back in the 1930s, raucous audiences enjoyed the café-chantant, ancestor of today's Oriental cabarets like the Mawal and karaoke bars like Le Grand bleu. One Mme Kyriacopoulos had a dance academy and after independence Hamadi Laghbabi, energetic collector of traditional steps and rhythms, founded the National Dance Troop. Tunis has produced a handful of choreographers and dance artists with international recognition, including Imed Jemaâ and Nawal Skandrani.

And if you want to learn to dance? In the 1990s, expatriate Middle Eastern dancers set up classes for danse orientale in many a European capital. In Tunis, private dance-schools like the Espace Ikaâ now run such classes too. And very popular with local women they are too, surprisingly perhaps in a culture where the complex movements of oriental dancing are acquired within the family. The clientèle for the classes? Women who never managed to pick up dance by osmosis when they were small and yet who still want to acquire this most powerful implement of feminine seduction. For at any Tunisian wedding, the social poise of future spouses is up for sharp scrutiny by the massed potential mothers-in-law.

piano-bar – right on the beach at Gammarth, just along from the *Cyklone* and next to the restaurant *Les Ombrelles*. Karaoke and live music on Fri/Sat. In La Soukra, off the La Marsa-Tunis highway, the bar of *La Closerie* is a place for wealthy students and friends to be seen (summer only). Now emerging as the place for a drink and a dance is **Koubbat el Haoua**, in the domed art deco building built on stilts over the water at La Marsa-Plage. Managed by Hamdi, formerly of the **Sindbad**, this revamped bar with piste for a little bop has real potential.

Early 2002 saw three new addresses with potential, although whether they will hold the road is another matter. The **Cinquante-cinq (55)** is a new restaurant with bar in La Marsa-Plage, opposite the restaurant *Arthé*. Converted bijou villa, very trendy décor, yet to get an alcohol licence at time of writing. The **Le Chao-Bar**, a new bar attached to the **Restaurant L'Orient** on the heights of Gammarth, after *Le Palace* in the Raoued direction, may be little more than a trendy flash-in-the-pan. The **Zanzibar** at the **Touring Club** is in same area. Aiming to be *jeune et branché*, attracts an 18-35 crowd between 2300 and 0200.

Trendy clubbing in the northern suburbs is very much a winter affair. In summer *le Tout Tunis* moves on down to Hammamet and Sousse for its nocturnal pleasures. (In Hammamet, try *Manhattan*, *Le Guitoun* or the *Ranch Club*, in Sousse the big names are *Samara* and *La Maracana*, just 2 hrs down the motorway in the Taj Marhaba complex). Meanwhile, in Raoued, the best address if you're in a group is undoubtedly **Le Cotton Club**, just opposite the entrance to the *Hotel La Résidence*. Here you'll find the *jeunesse dorée* in bulk, but only at weekends, from around 0100 to 0400. Busy in the school year, except May-Jun, depending on timing of the baccalauréat exams. In the late 1990s, **Le Queen** at the *Hotel Karim* was popular. The other big address for a dance is *Le Boeuf sur le Toit* n La Soukra (see below).

In Gammarth, the *Hotel La Tour Blanche* has a club which changes its name every few years – the current appellation is **Cyklone**. And finally, an RIP: the nicest of the Banlieue Nord clubs, **La Barraka**, housed in a converted barn down a track on the La Marsa/Sidi Bou Saïd road, a long established Tunis institution, was demolished in 1999, much to the distress of numerous Tunis clubbers of all ages.

Shopping **Galleries** *Espace d'Art Mille Feuilles*, La Marsa-Plage, above the bookshop. Exhibitions of local and foreign artists' work in the spacious gallery, also hosts occasional poetry recitals, book launches and other events of a literary bent. Diminutive and dynamic manager Hayat Larnaout is something of a figure and can advise on books on Tunisia in French. Those interested in glass will want to take a look at the new **Espace Sadika**, a complex of traditional whitewashed buildings near the roundabout at the start of the Raoued hotel zone housing exhibition space and workshops devoted to glass blowing. You could pick up an opaque glass lampshade (350 Dt) or some chunky glasses (8Dt).

Transport **Car rental** *Hotel Cap Carthage*, T741596, and at *Hotel Molka*, T740118. *Tunisair*, La Marsa-Ville T775222, T740680, F746455.

Directory **Communications** Internet: *Le Net-Club*, 4 R du Cheikh Zarrouk, off Av H Bourguiba, T727128. **Post office:** R du 9-Avril-1938, near the main mosque in La Marsa-Plage. **Entertainment** Cinema: in the new Complexe Le Zephyr on the roundabout at La Marsa-Plage. Opening scheduled for summer 2002. **Hairdressers** Try Dalila Mathari, a Tunis legend, at the salon de coiffure of the *Hotel Abou Nawas*, Gammarth. Held to be a true artist, by some. (Does hair for fashion shows.) **Medical services** Chemist: all night pharmacy in the street between *UIB* and *ATB* banks in La Marsa-Ville, T775770. **Doctor:** 18 R Ezzine Ben Achour, T741206, 744215. **Places of worship** Catholic: Station TGM, Sidi Dhrif, T740854. Services Sat at 1930 and Sun at 1000. Also 1 R Scipion, T734228. Service in French Sat 1700, English Sun 0930.

La Soukra

Between the Banlieue Nord and the airport, north of the main Tunis-La Marsa highway, is the up-and-coming residential area of La Soukra. Once an area of *souani*, orchards surrounded by ranks of tall cypress trees, it is increasingly being built up with up-scale villas hidden in extensive grounds. Proximity to the highway, La Marsa and the new Lac development make it all the more desirable. For the tourist with a hire car, the antique shops and galleries on the main road, the eucalyptus-lined Avenue Fatouma Bourguiba, might be worth a look. The area also has Tunisia's oldest golf course (see Golf, page 55, for further details) and a sprinkling of trendy restaurants. For those starved of the pleasures of mall shopping, there is a large new Carrefour supermarket. To access the Avenue Fatouma Bourguiba, coming from La Marsa, fork right at the junction with the Carrefour hypermarket on your right. (Large building on your right after turn is main regional hospital, the CHU Mongi Slim)

Eating La Soukra now has several large restaurants with dance floors, in addition to a couple of more discrete places. As one would expect in such an area, restaurants are on the expensive side. The *Carrefour* complex has a mall-type restaurant area with varied eating experiences, including an overpriced Lebanese. Main plus is the a/c in summer.

Expensive *Le Boeuf sur le Toit* ('the cow on the roof'), a restaurant with a dance floor, has a relaxed atmosphere (Franco-Tunisian management). The food ordinary (say 20Dt a head for full wack), but a good mix of nationalities. The minstrel-type floorshow, performed by black Tunisians, may be offensive to some. To get there, take a taxi to La Soukra, the restaurant is near the *Boukhobza* distillery and the entrance to the golf course. Restaurant easily identified by expensive 4WD vehicles parked-up outside and large black-and-white cow over entrance.

Mid-range *La Closerie*, near the hospital and *Carrefour*, T765537, F765790. A trendy place serving mainly Italian food, open everyday except Mon, in summer open every day, evenings only. Pleasant lawn area round small pool, occasional exhibitions, bar is lively in summer with a young and *branché* crowd. At the top end of the mid-range category. Minus points: uncomfortable iron chairs and small portions (11 pieces of ravioli at 12Dt is *un peu cher*, it has to be said). Standards well maintained. New in 2001 was *Le Picasol*, 88 Av Fatouma Bourguiba, T864451, on the left shortly after the *Carrefour* turn-off. Large restaurant with *piste de danse* in converted industrial building. Local painters' works form part of decoration. Cuisine with a Spanish touch (paella, pulpo gallego, tapas), nice atmosphere, relaxed clients welcome. Thematic evenings twice a month, alcohol licence on the way. Also new in 2001 was *Le Soft*, 81 Av Fatouma Bourguiba, opposite entrance to future theme park, T863093. Salon de thé on 1st floor, tiny 16-seater restaurant on ground floor, small terrace. Varied menus: specialities gigot farci, bouillabaisse. French management. Again, no alcohol for the moment.

Tunis, Banlieue Sud (Southern Suburbs)

South of Tunis are the newly sprawling suburbs of Ben Arous, Radès, Ez Zahra, Hammam Lif and Borj Cedria. The energetic will want to climb twin-peaked Bou Kornine. (Birdwatchers may find some rare raptors, although the Bou Kornine has attracted a lot of visitors of late.) There are some pleasant beaches, particularly at Borj Cedria. Colonial architecture buffs will seek out interesting buildings at Hammam Lif, while strollers will enjoy the evening paseo along the pedestrian corniche here.

A coastal resort, once mainly for the bourgeois of Tunis, situated at the foot of **Hammam Lif**
Djebel Bou Kornine whose rocky outcrops slope to the edge of the road. There
are a couple of hammams here, not terribly well managed but functioning with
naturally hot springwater (2.80Dt per session). Spa enthusiasts will want to head
for the better establishments at Korbous, Hammam Zriba and Hammam Jdidi.

Borj Cedria, the last place on the southern suburbs rail line, has a quarry producing reddish marble of moderate quality stone. More importantly for the sun
seeker it also has a good beach used by people from Tunis at weekends and in
summer. Many of them come out by train. Borj Cedria, with its beach backed by
pine and eucalyptus forest, once felt quite remote. The amount of new housing in
the area has changed this, and further developments are planned for the future.

The Banlieue Sud has 2 main sorts of hotel. There are the tourist hotels and holiday **Sleeping**
clubs (*Dar*, *Médi-Sea*, *Selwa*) at Borj Cedria, and a large tourist hotel at Ez Zahra. Less
ambitiously, there are a few cheap places at Hammam Lif.

B *Médi-Sea*, Route touristique, 2055 Borj Cedria, T430261, F430013. Expensive in high
season. **C** *Dar*, 2055 Borj Cedria, T290188. 144 beach bungalows. **C** *Salwa*, T290764,
116 rooms, pool. **D** *Hotel du Bon Repos*, R Bel Hassen Chedli, Hammam Lif, T291458.
Short walking distance from the main road on slope of Djebel Bou Kornine, fairly basic,
18 rooms, some with separate bath and toilet, some have shared facilities, some rooms
have fine view over bay to Sidi Bou Saïd, no restaurant. **F** *Hotel Majed*, 1 R Salammbô
(the main road through Hammam Lif). 10 rooms, shared facilities, very basic. *Youth
hostel Banlieue Sud*, T483631, 10 km from Tunis, 10 mins from Radès station. 56 beds,
meals available, book as it takes groups and can get full.

Gulf Travel Agency, 70 Av de la République, Hammam Lif, T292100, F291954. **Tour operators**
Romulus Voyages, Km 12 Ezzahra, T450544, F450582. *Mondial Tours*, Place 9 Avril,
Hammam Lif, T293727.

Southern suburbs are served by regular (every ½ hr) trains from the main Tunis station **Transport**
on Pl Barcelone. Radès has a particularly useful feature, the passenger and car ferry to
La Goulette, which enables you to avoid driving through Tunis. It operates all day, carries 10 cars, takes 5 mins and costs nothing.

South of Tunis: Roman towns and hilltop villages

Southwest of Tunis is an area of fertile rolling countryside, a wealthy region
back in Roman times as the large number of Roman settlements demonstrates. An **aqueduct**, the longest in the Roman world, once transported the
spring water from forbidding Mount Zaghouan to Carthage. In a hire car, the
energetic visitor can easily take in the Roman sites of **Oudna**, **Thuburbo
Maius** and **Zaghouan** in a day, with possibly a stop at **Djebel Oust** (remains
of Roman baths) for lunch. Also worth a visit are the once isolated hill villages
of the region south of Zaghouan: **Takrouna**, now well on the tourist itinerar-
ies, abandoned **Zriba** and **Jeradou**. The Roman remains, although not as
spectacular as sites in the interior like Dougga, Sbeïtla and El Djem, are worth
a look, and a pleasant day out can be put together by combining them with a
trip up **Mount Zaghouan** or to one of the hilltop villages. Such excursions can
be done equally well from both Hammamet and Tunis.

Touring the region south of Tunis

For a 'south of Tunis circuit', exit Tunis along the motorway through Ouardia and Kabaria, suburbs of cheap housing, mixed small-scale industry and uncontrolled development. Turn right for Fouchana and Kairouan along the GP3. This will take you past car-breaking yards and urban sprawl to Fouchana and Mohamedia, site of the crumbling remains of Ahmed Bey's vast palace complex, once touted as the 'Tunisian Versailles'.

Hadrian's aqueduct Beyond Mohamedia, farming takes over and the wide corn lands open up with views of distant hills. And there is Hadrian's aqueduct which once took water to Carthage. It appears first on the west and then on the east, the road cutting through a breach south of Mohammedia. Where parts of the supporting structure have crumbled away the actual aqueduct has fallen and here it is possible to view a cross-section of the amazing structure. The channel carrying the water was oval, large enough for a man to walk along, lined with cement to prevent leakage and covered to prevent evaporation. The structure was brought back into use in the 19th century, when French engineer Colin restored it to bring water to the growing town of Tunis.

The accuracy of the Roman engineering is awesome considering the equipment available. To maintain the level the aqueduct required varying heights for the supporting pillars. As you follow the aqueduct note that the pillars get wider where the structure gets higher and needs more support to soar above the land. As the contours rise again the structure is less spectacular and runs at about one metre above the ground here, as it did when it cut through the centre of Mohammedia to the north.

South from Oudna At 23 km from Tunis is the left turn to Oudna, Roman Uthina. Here you may branch off for the Roman site on the C133. After visiting Oudna, one possibility is to continue along the GP3/C133 heading south to Zaghouan, which you approach via an attractive avenue of huge eucalyptus trees. Another option is to take the more direct C36 for Zaghouan. (One possible lunch stop is the small restaurant next to the Nymphaeum archaeological site, in the shadow of Mount Zaghouan.)

The other option at the Oudna turn-off is to continue along the GP3 in the direction of El Fahs. The other major Roman site in this region, Thuburbo Maius, is some 20 km further on, just 3 km before the sleepy agricultural town of El Fahs. From El Fahs, you have a direct run back eastwards into Zaghouan. Also in the region is a semi-forgotten spa town, Djebel Oust. Specialists looking for excavated provincial Roman bath houses will want to make the detour. Following the P3 south of Oudna, turn left on to the C133. The spa complex is clearly visible on your right after a couple of kilometres.

The hilltop villages lie south of Zaghouan. For **Zriba**, some 10 km south of Zaghouan, you will turn off the main road at the new village of Zriba, heading for Hammam Zriba. If you have a solid sort of hire car, then you turn off for Upper Zriba (Zriba el 'Ulya') before the cement works. Park the car on the side of the track in the shade of an olive tree when the going gets too rough. There is no one to pull you out. It will take you 30 minutes to walk to the village which lies hidden in a small col up in the hills.

Takrouna is altogether more obvious, 25 km south of Zaghouan on the Enfida road (and is dealt with in the next chapter as an excursion from Hammamet). For **Jeradou**, perhaps the least spectacular of the three villages, you need to turn off south as you head from Zaghouan to Hammamet.

Nestling on the north-facing foothills of the Djebel Mekrima, Uthina is **Uthina**
famous for the quantity and quality of its mosaics, most of which are now on
display in the Bardo Museum along with sculpture and inscriptions from the
site. Only certain areas have been excavated and it was from the upper-class
residential area to the north that many mosaics came. Among the remains discovered are a large public baths, some huge cisterns and a theatre. It is clear
that much still remains to be discovered on this site.

The capitol Perhaps the most spectacular feature is the large vaulted
chamber, topped by a French farmer's home, which occupies the site of the
former main temple. You will see a large square – the farmyard, which was
once the forum. The 'ramp' below the front door to the farmer's house was
once the temple steps, and at the bottom, there are some huge stone drums,
140 cm across, which means that the main temple here would have had columns around 14.5 m high! There are piles of marble fragments, an indication
of the wealth of the temple. Below, in the large vaulted chamber, there are six
stone piers which would have supported the columns' weight. The foundations of the much smaller, flanking temples have been partly excavated. At the
back, you can see the semicircular back wall of the cella, the temple sanctuary,
partly masked by later Byzantine masonry.

The baths As you leave the forum, you can see Uthina's vast cisterns on
your right, just behind some farm buildings. Head for the baths, large
mounds of rubble clearly visible about 200 m east. Kids will love this bit.
Underground vaulted rooms – for storing fuel? – have been excavated (use
your pocket torch). Looking back towards the capitol/farmer's house, you
can see the remains of the aqueduct close to the cisterns.

The amphitheatre The other main area of recent archaeology is the
amphitheatre, just next to the car park. It is partly carved out of the hillside,
rather than being a free-standing structure as at El Djem. A number of blocks
have been replaced. The large blocks all have small 'grip-holes' in them, to
enable the Roman cranes to lift and swing them into place. You will also see
that the blocks often have rough sides, to enable plaster rendering or mortar to
adhere to the surface. There is a lot of work to do, however, if ever the amphitheatre is to be home to entertainments again, like the theatre at Carthage.

Marine mosaics from Uthina One of the largest houses uncovered at
Uthina, known today as the House of the Laberii, was a splendid dwelling with
numerous rooms and even more numerous outbuildings. All the rooms and
the atrium were paved with rich mosaics. You will have to go to the Bardo (see
page 94) to see the fine mosaic of Venus seated on a rock while three cupids play
with her veil, or the huge 'oceanic' picture with Neptune, Amphrite, sea-horse
drawn chariots around three boats carrying three ladies and a cluster of cupids.

Djebel Oust, 30 km southwest from Tunis, is one of Tunisia's three main **Detour to**
health spas (the others being Hammam Bourguiba in the Northwest and **the spa at**
Korbous, now privately managed, on the northwest side of the Cap Bon). **Djebel Oust**
After a long period of uncertainty about the thermal treatment centre's future,
the Ministry of Health has taken the complex over. Considerable investment
will be necessary. The spa has the atmosphere of a backwater East European
bathing establishment of the 1960s. The concrete carcass of an unfinished
swimming pool stands below the hotel, close to the excavations of a Roman
bathing establishment.

After your peek at the remains of ancient bathing arrangements, drivers
may want to head on to Zaghouan. Turn right out of the 'hotel zone', and head
along the resurfaced, recently widened road. Keep straight on where Bir

Mcherga is signposted right. Djebel Zaghouan soon looms up ahead. You pass a STEG electricity station and the turn-off right for another route to El Fahs. Approaching the urban area, slow down. The Garde nationale is lying in wait near the large hospital to the left of the road to catch unruly motorists.

Sleeping C *Les Thermes*, T604477, F640074, 98 beds, bungalows available. Cheap lunchtime menu. **D** *Cheylus*, T677240, F677074, 90 beds.

Zaghouan ﺯﻏﻮﺍﻥ

Phone code: 72
Colour map 2,
grid C3

Zaghouan, Roman Ziqua, was the starting point of the complex system of second century AD cisterns and aqueducts which carried fresh water over 132 km to Carthage. Today's Zaghouan is dominated by the towering 1,300 m high Djebel Zaghouan. The spring and the beginning of the aqueduct can be visited, about 2 km out of town. The real interest, however, is the beauty of the site.

Ins & outs Lying 60 km south of Tunis, 22 km from El Fahs, Zaghouan has a regular bus service from Tunis and louages from Tunis and Hammamet. It makes a good day trip, which can become strenuous if you want to walk up the mountain. Nearest point to Zaghouan on the autoroute is Bouficha, 31 km away.

Orientation Although it is really quite small, Zaghouan is a little confusing, especially if you are driving. Coming from the Jebel Oust direction, the wide road leads you past the big hospital (on your left). Follow through at the first 'fountain' roundabout, and you will find banks and pharmacies are on your right. A little further on, uphill, a louage parking area is on your left. (NB A useful bank with a cashpoint, the *BNA*, is next to the louages.) Just after the louages, veer right uphill and wind up through old Zaghouan. Follow the sign for the Temple des eaux at the square with the police station. Going uphill on a narrow one-way road, old whitewashed buildings on either side, you pass the Zaouia of Sidi Ali Azouz on your right (see below), and then after about 200 m, you reach the 'strange cactus roundabout'. From here the Temple des eaux is again signposted, also a recent restaurant on the same route, *L'Aigle Royal*.

Sights Zaghouan is built on the lower slopes of Djebel Zaghouan. Close to the centre of the village, opposite the municipal food market, is a second-century honorific **arch**, dating from the time when Zaghouan was Roman Ziqua. Climb up the steps to the arch, noting the bull's head on the keystone. Continue along a street lined with cheap eateries and shops, turn sharp right uphill, and you come to a small square with a café and the police station. Close to the square is a former church, now used as a private school, and the more recent Jamaâ Errahma, with its octagonal minaret. There is a wall fountain with a decorative tile surround. Take the narrow street uphill, and you will come to the **Zaouia of Sidi Ali Azouz**, on your right, now a centre for Koran studies. (Take a peek through the door.) After the zaouia, on your right, is a small shop selling honey and the *nisri* rose-water (at 18Dt a litre!) for which the town is famous.

Small children should not be allowed to roam unattended as there are some sharp drops into the empty stone basins

The narrow street widens, and you can continue upwards to the **Temple des Nymphes** some 2 km distant. The dignity of the ancient site has been impaired by the addition of a new arch and some 'environmental awareness' statuary, including a fat blue water drop and the usual fennec fox (or is it a bat-eared rat?) in a tight blue jumpsuit. There is a small café-restaurant (slow service, basic food) here, with views towards the temple and across the plain. The temple, which dates from the reign of Hadrian (early second century) is built into the hillside with steps leading up to a semicircular wall. The 12 alcoves in the wall once held life-size statues (of nymphs?), but unfortunately all have now gone. The pool in the centre has been restored and again (occasionally) holds water. Contemplate the panoramic view, north and east over the plain towards the sea. The Romans must have done just the same. Rising steeply behind you is Djebel Zaghouan. The temple steps down have been renewed making access much safer.

There is no entry charge to the Nymphaeum. New concrete villas have appeared on the wooded hillside between the town and the temple. It is now possible to drive practically the whole way to the top of Djebel Zaghouan.

Rose-water production

Andalusian immigrants introduced rose cultivation here in 1795 and from this has developed the rose essence production for which this region is justly famous. The rose essence is very popular in cakes and pastries. A project to increase the area of the already considerable rose gardens has just been finished, and a wild rose nursery is to be developed. The wild rose festival is held here each May.

Sleeping

C *Les Nymphes*, 1.5 km out of town on road leading to Roman site – currently closed, refurbishment said to be planned (this was a quiet place with 80 beds, in wooded surroundings). The youth hostel or *Maison des Jeunes* was said to be simple and practical (85 beds, meals available, T675265). Visited in May 2002, it was firmly closed. Open in summer only?

Tour operators

Gulf Travel Agency, 70 Av de la République, Hammam Lif, T292100, F291954. *Romulus Voyages*, Km 12 Ezzahra, T450544, F450582. *Mondial Tours*, Place 9 Avril, Hammam Lif, T293727.

Directory

Medical services   A new regional hospital opened here in 1996.

West of Zaghouan to Hammamet

The C28 road east from Zaghouan leads to Hammamet. It leads down through the prairie-like cereal fields to the *oued* and the almond and olive groves. The road skirts a small lake with a spectacular rocky ridge as a backdrop and crosses the plain. It comes to the villages of **Hammam Jedidi** and **Sidi Jedidi**, the latter to be avoided at all costs on a Tuesday when coaches deposit their passengers to view an 'authentic market'. Despite the neighbouring quarry, Hamman Jedidi is interesting on account of the hot springs, and Tunis residents rent little houses here to enjoy the waters *en famille*. The intensive cultivation continues to the motorway and the outskirts of Hammamet.

South of Zaghouan: the hillcrest villages

The C133 road south from Zaghouan, leading eventually to **Enfida**, has plenty of interesting detours in the form of old hillcrest settlements, best covered in your own transport. Those without can easily reach **Hammam Zriba** by louage, and if energetic enough can take the hour's walk up to **Zriba el Ulya** ('Upper Zriba'), the old village. For those with plenty of time and probably doing their MA in Tunisian Studies, **Djeradou** is certainly worth a look. Otherwise, belt on to **Takrouna** (see chapter 4, covered as an excursion from Hammamet).

On the C133, the first crossroads, a few kilometres out of Zaghouan, is signed left for Hammamet and right for Souaf and Ansarine. Head straight on. The right turn-off for **Zriba Jedida** (Nouvelle Zriba), some 10 km from Zaghouan, is just after the *Agil* petrol station with the white dome and is easily overshot. Head along the wide avenue with its recently planted trees. There are pharmacies, also a mosque on the left. At the clock junction, go left and follow through. Eventually, you approach an old quarry area where sits Hammam Zriba. For the old village, 5 km away, turn off over the bridge over the Oued el Hammam, just on your left as you reach the village.

The route up to old village of **Zriba el Ulya**, some 7 km, is practicable in a standard car, provided it hasn't rained. After crossing the bridge, go for the right-hand track which, if it seems rough at first, improves after a few hundred metres, running through pleasant olive groves set with vaulted buildings emitting whiffs of guano. Here be battery chickens. Then the road dips down to a ford, generally waterless, set with a concrete slab to facilitate crossing. If the weather has been wet, you may have to leave the car here. The village is still out of sight behind a rocky spur in the hillside, ahead and on the left. Follow the track across the fields, and after about 1.5 km, you begin to climb up a regravelled section. A small dam is visible on your right. The track becomes seriously stony as you reach the first houses. You can either risk your tyres and continue for a bit, or pull over and leave the car here.

Up in the village, you can sit among the ruins and watch the birds of prey circle overhead. This old Berber village sits in a col below a rocky outcrop. There are views northwards across to **Djebel Zaghouan** (1,295 m). The village has a fortified granary or *kalaâ*, a small mosque with a much decayed oblong crenellated tower and a *zaouia*, to Sidi Abdelkader el Jilani complete with cupola. Under the French protectorate, the village was an important rural centre, and the main streets paved with blocks of stone. Just below the village proper, the large building on your left, today used as a stables, is a school from the reconstruction period, 1943-48. Designed by architect Kyriacopoulos, model schools, built according to local techniques with stone and brick vaulting, were constructed across Tunisia.

After the two old Zribas, the modern version near the road, seems a dull affair, especially on hot summer afternoons. In fact, it is a post-independence settlement, established on the main road as part of a policy to end local particularities and bring isolated communities into contact with the modernizing Tunisian Republic. No doubt there were financial considerations, it being cheaper to build a new settlement on the plain rather than to take modern services and infrastructure up to the old village.

The Berber village of **Djeradou** can also be reached from this road, though easier access, avoiding a very rough road, is from the C35. The villagers work with esparto, plaiting long bands of this tough grass which is then turned into a variety of bags and baskets, olive mats and panniers. The same technique is much in evidence at the coastal village of **Hergla**. From the ruined fort can be seen the square white mosque and the domed *zaouia*.

Thuburbo Majus

Ins & outs
Colour map 2, grid C2

This is 60 km south along the P3 from Tunis. Access by bus or louage from Tunis. Get off at El Fahs and walk (3 km) or get a taxi. If coming from Tunis, ask the driver to stop at Thuburbo Majus (before you get to El Fahs) from which it is a short walk to the site. It is better not to follow the signposts, but to cut across between the two hills, just behind the signpost. There is a car park at the entrance, a small café and a clean toilet. Open 0800-1200 and 1500-1900 in summer and 0930-1630 in winter, closed Mon, entrance 2Dt, photography 1Dt.

History
Thuburbo Majus was originally a Punic city, but when the Romans conquered Carthage they agreed to pay dues to Rome and so survived. In 27 BC the Emperor Augustus founded a colony of veterans in order to control the strategic situation of the city. Thuburbo Majus was placed in a strategic position, encircled by hills except to the west, permitting a close watch on movement of people and trade between the plain and the coast along the route of

the Oued el Kebir. The hinterland, a fertile land producing cereals in abundance, provided a further boost to the economy, added to that of toll/tax collection. The Punic heritage mixed well with the Roman presence and it was at this time that most of the major monuments were repaired or reconstructed, such as the Capitol and the Baths. The town declined as the Romans' authority slackened. With the Vandals in power the town reverted to a village.

Thuburbo Majus is a large site on the hill slopes, overlooking a fertile agricultural plain and the Oued Kebir which provided the water. It was at an important crossing of trade routes which permitted collection of tolls. The production of cereals, olives and wine were important factors in the city's prosperity.

Exploring the site

This large city covered over 40 ha. The **Forum** and the **Capitol** dominate the ruins. The forum is well preserved. It was built between AD 161-192 and restored with some changes in layout around AD 376. It stands 49 m square, surrounded by a portico on three sides. The fourth side leads, by means of a broad flight of stairs, to the Capitol built in AD 168. This is the best place to visit first as it enables one to view the whole site. Great efforts were made to raise the level of this building to give it the height it needed for its imposing position overlooking the town. Six fluted Corinthian columns, each 8½ m high, continue to dominate the site. Dedications were made to Emperor Marcus Aurelius and to Commodius. The temple is also dedicated to the triad of Jupiter, Juno and Minerva. The head and foot, all that remains of the statue of Jupiter, once an impossible 8 m high, are in the Bardo Museum.

To the northeast of the Forum are the remains of the **Curia** (town hall/meeting place of the council). The **Temple of Peace** adjacent to/part of Curia has a marble-paved courtyard with a peristyle leading on to a large hall paved with marble. It is thought a statue to Peace stood here.

Thuburbo Majus

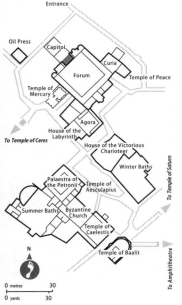

Entrance
Oil Press
Capitol
Curia
Forum
Temple of Peace
Temple of Mercury
Agora
House of the Labyrinth
To Temple of Ceres
House of the Victorious Charioteer
Winter Baths
To Temple of Saturn
Palaestra of the Petronii
Temple of Aesculapius
Summer Baths
Byzantine Church
Temple of Caelestis
Temple of Baalit
To Amphitheatre
N
0 metres 30
0 yards 30

The **Temple of Mercury**, built in AD 211, has an unusual circular courtyard though the outer walls are straight. The eight column bases remain. He was the god of Merchants and overlooked the market area.

The **Agora**, the paved market place, stood opposite the Capitol and beyond the south corner of the Forum. There are two smaller annexes. This was used for retail of produce but also as a gathering place. The arcades on three sides were divided into 21 small shop spaces.

The **Winter Baths**, covering 1,600 sq m, were completely rebuilt between AD 395 and 408. They were very luxurious. There were more than 20 rooms here decorated with elegant mosaics, square pools, round pools, fountains, latrines and urinals. The entrance from the small square was a four-column portico. The **Summer Baths** were larger, covering 2,400 sq m. These were restored in AD 361. Here there were cold, warm

Tunis and around

and hot rooms, all with lavish decoration – much marble, many mosaics and fountains. These were fed from three large cisterns.

The **Palaestra of the Petronii** was built in AD 225 and named after the family who endowed the construction – Petronius Felix. This, a rectangular area surrounded by a portico (supported by grey/black marble columns which still stand), was for games and gymnastic activities (wrestling, boxing) before bathing. The mosaic from here, depicting these activities, is in the Bardo Museum. In the south corner there are alphabetic signs carved into the pavement, explained as a Roman game rather like Lexicon.

The large, very overgrown area to the southeast of Palaestra was a shrine to the god of healing, the **Temple of Aesculapius**.

Further east is the **Temple of Caelestis** (Tanit) who required the periodic sacrifice of young children (see Carthage).

On the other side of the track is the **Temple of Baalit**. She was a Punic goddess who slipped into the Roman mythology. The building has three straight sides while the short northeast side is semicircular and has a door opening on to a small square, smaller than but similar to the square before the Winter baths.

The **Temple of Saturn** (not much left here), to the west of the site and at the highest point in town, later became a church. Again there is evidence of 'building up the land' before constructing the temple.

The ruins of the **Amphitheatre**, hollowed out of the hillside, can be found to the very edge of the site. Nearby is one of the cisterns for water supply. This cistern to the south of the site is huge – large enough to have an inner gallery constructed on the inside rim.

The **oil factories** behind and to the west of the Capitol are a reminder of the activities which helped to make this town so prosperous.

In the residential area around the Forum were homes of wealthy Roman inhabitants. They are named after the mosaics found there – for example Neptune, Theseus. Another residential has been excavated in the southwest area by the summer and winter baths. The **House of the Victorious Charioteer** by the Winter Baths had rich mosaics and painted stucco. The **House of the Labyrinth** is by the market. From here was retrieved the well known fourth-century mosaic which covered the floor of the *frigidarium* in the baths of this private house. The mosaic, in the form of a maze (labyrinth) has at the centre Theseus cutting off the head of the Minator. The ground surrounding the two figures is littered with bits of humans, the remains of the monster's victims. The mosaic is bordered with walls and gates, depicting the city. This mosaic is in the Bardo Museum.

The **Temple of Cérès**, to the west of the site, on sloping ground, had a courtyard 30 m by 30 m, the centre decorated with mosaics and a portico with three gateways. Later this was turned into a church, using half of the courtyard. A number of tombs were found in the church, one containing jewels.

Sleeping   There is no accommodation at or near the site. Thuburbo Majus makes a good day trip from Tunis, returning via Zaghouan. The nearest youth hostel is in Zaghouan, convenient for travellers going southwards to Enfida and Sousse. This may be closed outside the summer season.

El Fahs   El Fahs, a busy agricultural centre, larger than Zaghouan, holds an important cattle market each Saturday. Expensive harvesting equipment is for sale. There are several engineering establishments here, more advanced than the casual car/van repair merchants on the outskirts of every town.

Cap Bon Peninsula

4

Cap Bon Peninsula

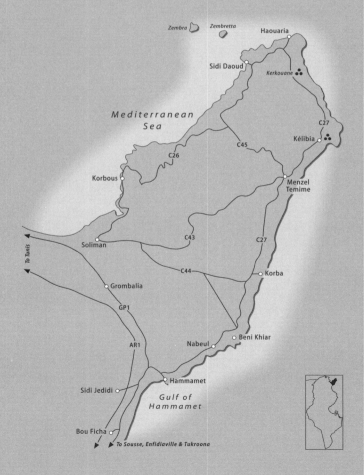

The Cap Bon, protruding like a thumb into the Mediterranean, is one of the most fertile regions in Tunisia. From Tunis, across the sea, the steep and rocky coast of the peninsula's northwest coast is clearly visible. On the sheltered southeast coast, there are fine sand beaches and small towns all the way down to the tourist resort of **Nabeul,** and half-an-hour's drive from here is the burgeoning resort of **Hammamet**. Once a quiet fishing port, the village has become a sprawling town with a vast new beach resort, Hammamet-Sud, also known as Hammamet-Yasmine. There is much of interest in the region, however. Inland lies the hill-crest village of **Takrouna**, while at the tip of the Cap Bon lie the remains of a remote Punic settlement, **Kerkouane,** and quiet stretches of coast can still be found. Birdwatchers will find much to delight them on **coastal lagoons** and above all at **Haouaria** during the twice yearly migrations across the Mediterranean.

Cap Bon Peninsula

Background

With an area of 2,837 sq km, much of it fertile agricultural land with abundant water, the Cap Bon has long been an important farming region. Roman writers noted the fertility of the area. Wrote Diodorus of Sicily, describing a fourth-century invasion: "Agathocles led his army towards the big city [Carthage?]. All the lands he crossed were set with gardens and orchards watered by numerous springs and canals. Along the route were well-constructed country houses, built with lime, a sign of widespread wealth. The houses were filled with all the things which make life pleasant, stored up by the inhabitants thanks to a long peace. The land was planted with vines, olive trees and a whole host of fruit trees."

Today the southwestern part of the Cap Bon is still an important fruit producing region, with the majority of Tunisia's citrus fruit coming from the region around Menzel Bouzelfa and important vineyards around Grombalia. Inland, cultivation turns to dry farming. Running down the centre of the peninsula is a line of hills which culminate in the west at Djebel Sidi Abderrahman (421 m) and in the east at Djebel Ben Oulid (637 m), virtually separating the north coast from the southeasterly region.

Along the southeastern coast market gardening is important. Korba is famed for strawberry production, and Nabeul for its *harissa*, the spicy chilli paste which is such an essential part of Tunisian cooking.

The administrative centre of the region is Nabeul, also important as an industrial town, with pottery, stonecarving and manufacturing important. The other main economic factor in the region is the development of the all-year holiday hotels to serve the package-holiday market. Fortunately, the main *zones touristiques* are located in the Hammamet area, accessible from the main motorway by fast link roads. Kélibia, Korba and other towns of the southeastern Cap Bon have seen considerable expansion too, with new suburbs of Tunisian-owned holiday homes growing up. Today the Cap Bon has a population of over 500,000, concentrated along the southeast coast.

Northwest coast

The northwestern coast of the Cap Bon makes a pleasant excursion from Tunis or Hammamet. Coming from Tunis, the first town of interest is **Soliman**, founded by 17th-century Andalusian immigrants. There are sandy beaches nearby. Then, on a rocky stretch of coast, you have the tiny spa of **Korbous**. After the cliffs, you have more beach – **Port aux Princes** is one possible bathing spot, frequented almost exclusively by locals. Then after kilometres of farmland, you are at the tip of the Cap Bon. There is the fishing port of **Sidi Daoud** and **Haouaria**, ancient Aquilaria, famed for its falconry festival and ancient underground quarries. For those looking for unusual if unspectacular ancient remains, **Kerkouane**, a unique Punic site a few kilometres round the Cape, is an essential stop. If you need to stay overnight, there are small hotels in Korbous, Haouaria and Kélibia. If travelling with your own car from Tunis, then driving on to Nabeul or Hammamet is perfectly feasible.

Getting there   Visiting the towns and beaches of the northwest coast of the Cap Bon with a hire car from Tunis or Hammamet-Nabeul is no problem at all, although it can make quite a long day out with children. The country roads are being improved all the time, and there are small restaurants in the little towns.

Cap Bon Peninsula

Things to do

- Swim at **Sidi El Mehrezi** between Hammamet and Nabeul.
- Visit the ruins of the **Punic** round town of Kerkouane, followed by a swim at **Kélibia**.
- Take a look at the ancient underground quarries of **Haouaria**, followed by lunch at the *Daurade* and a swim off the rocks.
- Visit the hill crest village of **Takrouna**, followed by a visit to the **Kène craft village** near Bouficha.
- A taste for obscure spa villages might take you to **Korbous** on the coast (fangotherapy or mudbaths) and **Hammam Zriba** (to mix with the country people on a day out).

By public transport, things are considerably slower. By bus or louage, you can easily travel up to Haouaria and do the Roman grottoes and Kerkouane in a day. You would really be pushing it if you wanted to see Soliman and Korbous as well. Soliman plus beach could make a nice day-trip from Tunis, although unless you are Muslim, you won't see the inside of the mosque. For getting to Kerkouane from Haouaria, there are buses that can drop you at the top of the minor road leading down to the site.

From Tunis to Soliman

Taking the main dual carriageway out of Tunis, turn off left for Hammam Lif, as for the Olympic Stadium, Radès. A fast road takes you to Hammam Lif, which is followed by a slow and busy stretch of road (numerous traffic lights) running alongside the railway track to Borj Cedria. There is usually a Garde nationale presence at the junction at the end of the railway line (where you can hang a right to visit the German War Cemetery, signposted). Go left, after the junction, across the rail tracks, and a fast new road (completed 2001) takes you past new villa developments and chicken houses to Soliman. It is now possible for drivers to avoid the town completely on the new bypass, signposted Korbous, and you can go round the town coming out near Menzel Bouzelfa.

Soliman   سليمان

The market town of Soliman goes back to the 17th century, and like many other small towns in Tunisia, takes great pride in its Andalusian heritage. The town is named after its patron, a rich Turkish farmer who came to this area around 1600 and began the construction of a new town. The subsequent influx of immigrants from Andalucía left their mark in the form of building style, irrigation methods and even culinary preferences. The town was severly hit by the plague in the 19th century, and only really recovered in the 20th century.

Phone code: 72
Colour map 2, grid B4

The town centre with its trees, arcades and cafés is a pleasant sort of place. Soliman's most outstanding architectural feature is its **Malikite Mosque**, whose solid square minaret dominates the town centre. Parts of the building are roofed with Spanish-style rounded tiles recalling that the building was founded in the early 17th century by Andalusian refugees. (The main mosque in Testour has a similarly strong Andalusian identity.)

Otherwise, things Andalusian are rather elusive in Soliman today. Taking a walk through the town, you will be struck by the amount of new buildings. In many other modern Tunisian towns, this is often very jarring. Here at least the style is quite harmonious. Old features, stone-framed doorways and the like,

Cap Bon Peninsula

are fast disappearing. In a few years' time, the whole character of the town will have been radically altered, with two- and three-storey building and façades with large windows taking the place of the original vernacular houses. But such is the price of progress …

Soliman Plage Across the flat marsh land northwest of the town lies the beach area of Soliman
& Sidi Raïs Plage, where locals and migrant workers have built themselves summer homes. There is a good stretch of fine sand and two hotels. In summer, there may be a 'Noddy train' doing the 4-km journey between town and beach, otherwise you share a taxi, 300 millimes a place. Note that the beach closest to the vague square which functions as taxi and bus terminus gets very crowded in summer.

Moving northeast of Soliman, Sidi Raïs is 3 km from the C26 across flat marshland. There are a few seaside holiday homes built on stilts over the water's edge on a beach of fine sand. This is where the Tunisian families from the surrounding areas come each weekend or for their longer holidays. There is a small jetty where a few local fishing boats tie up and from which they sell their daily catch of fresh fish.

Sleeping **B** *Solymar*, T71290105, F71290155. Right on beach of fine white sand, 200 rooms (400 beds) with bath and toilet, restaurant, pool, nightly disco entertainment. Other hotels on this beach strip are covered in the previous chapter under Tunis, Banlieue Sud, as they are close to the south Tunis suburb of Borj Cedria.

Tour operators *Mek Tours*, 9 bis Av de la République, T290177, F291600. *Soly Holiday*, 8 R Hedi Chaker, T291649, F291753.

From Soliman to the southeast coast: cutting across the Cap Bon

The main road from Soliman through the flat marshlands to the west connects with the GP1 near Bordj Cedria. This will take you down to Hammamet. Otherwise, take the C43, direction Menzel Bou Zelfa. No need to go into Menzel Bou Zelfa if you are headed for Korba, the C44 road runs across the Cap Bon.

If you are going from Soliman to Kélibia, you must go through Menzel Bou Zelfa. The town has a small tree-planted square, the attractive older building is disappearing. Then, after Menzel Bou Zelfa, the urban sprawl disappears, and the road (C43) will take you up to Menzel Temime across heath and open farmland until finally, 12 km further on, you reach Kélibia.

From Soliman to Bir Meroua

From Soliman, the C26 runs northeastwards up to El Haouaria, a distance of some 60 km. Leaving Soliman, the road runs straight through flat farmland, past cypress windbreaks protecting the citrus trees, new factories and roadside *mechoui* stalls, active mainly in summer. In winter and spring, there are stalls selling great piles of oranges, in summer, melons and grapes are on offer. After the Sidi Rais turn-off, the Djebel Korbous rises on the left to cut out any views of the sea. At the small village of Bir Meroua, there is a complicated junction where you can turn off left for the beach at Port aux Princes, some 8 km away, about half of which is down a country track. In summer, this gets busy with pick-up trucks packed with extended families heading for a day at the beach.

From Soliman to Korbous via Sidi Rais

Until 2000, it was possible to continue along the coast road to **Korbous** via Sidi Rais, a short stretch of road with drops down to the sea and views of rugged, unspoilt splendour. Unfortunately, rock falls made the road unsafe, and it is now off-limits to vehicle traffic. When the road reopens, this detour is recommended even if you have no intention of stopping in Korbous. (**NB** Though scenic, the road is not for nervous drivers, although it may be widened.) The view towards La Goulette and Sidi Bou Saïd is very impressive.

Soliman to Korbous via Brij

After the Sidi Rais turn-off, continue to a junction with confusing signs which indicate you turn right for Bir Meroua, left (straight on really, but you have to stop) for Korbous. The road winds through pleasant countryside, between eucalyptus trees and cactus hedges, olive groves and the odd bit of plasticulture. Just before Brij, there is a biological farm signposted on the left (*miel*, honey). After Brij, continue on to Douala, a sort of rural ribbon-settlement, after which begins the climb up to the cliffs above Korbous. Drivers need to take care and ensure their hire cars have good brakes as they begin the descent. There are views down to the cove of Aïn Kala Sira on the right. Passing a sprinkling of parked cars and ramshackle seaside restaurants at the sulphurous springs of Aïn Atrous, Korbous is reached. In a taxi, the whole trip from Soliman to Korbous via Brij should take 30 minutes.

Korbous   الهـوارية

A small spa resort, said to have seven springs, Korbous would be a splendid setting for an Agatha Christie novel. Poirot would be twirling his moustache, gazing out over the glittering sea as the sun goes down. ('The Crime of the Moorish Baths' would be the title.) On a wild, rocky coast, in a tiny narrow valley, Korbous is an unlikely place. There are a couple of large hotels, and a villa looking down from a rock. The main spa building has a minaret. Once, perhaps, taking the waters here was chic. You could take a stroll along the cliff road to **Aïn Oktor** and its curious concrete wigwam, once a trendy bar à eau. There are groups of daytripping Tunisian students, the tour buses stop off and thunder on. Yet, in the evenings, Korbous in its rocky setting has an outpost feel, almost as though it were on the edge of some great ocean.

Phone code: 72
Colour map 2, grid B4

There are no banks in Korbous, so come armed with cash

Getting there Korbous is fairly easily accessible by public transport from Tunis and Soliman. If you are driving from Tunis, allow at least 1 hr 40 mins, as you may be held up in traffic leaving Tunis. By public transport can seem complex, however. There are a few direct buses, but if you take a louage you will need to change at Soliman. Following a major accident, buses now no longer go down the steep road to the town, but stop at a car park (with superb views) at the top of the cliff.

Ins & outs

Getting around No particular problems here – apart from getting back up to the bus-stop at the top of the cliff, a 3-km walk from the village. Enterprising locals with a car will run you up for 500 millimes, sometimes there is a minibus service, although the vehicle is often out of order.

The Romans, a people in love with bathing establishments if ever there was one, were first in at *Aquae Calidae Carpitanae*. No doubt they had the usual

Cap Bon Peninsula

well-appointed pleasure baths, no traces of which have survived, however. In the early 19th century, reforming ruler Ahmed Bey had a pavilion here for enjoying the thermal springs. In the 1950s, Korbous was home to one Charles Carpentier, known as Sidi Karbanti to the locals. His tomb was in the village, but the Main Rouge, the irredentist settler terrorist group, unburied him, refusing to admit that a Frenchman could have been integrated into local society to the point of being considered a holy man by the people of the region.

Tunisia's first president, Habib Bourguiba, had palaces and residences in all the right places, and Korbous was no exception. The villa on the hilltop was one of his summer homes. (His second wife, Wassila Ben Ammar, had her summer pavilion along the coast at Port aux Princes.) Korbous's other claim to fame is the **Zerziha Stone**, on your left through an arch as you head up the street for the *Hotel des Sources*. Adopting the correct position, women in search of a cure for sterility may slide down it. All Korbous children have played on this 'slide' at one time or another in their childhood.

The springs The waters of Korbous are the real cure here, it has to be said, and are used for treating arthritis and rheumatism, obesity, cellulite and hypertension. They are faintly radioactive, contain calcium, sodium and sulphur, and sometimes smell of rotten eggs. They come boiling out of the earth at a hefty 60°C. Moving northeastwards along the coast, the springs have splendid names like Aïn Oktor and Aïn Chifa, Aïn El Atrous and Aïn Kala Sirra.

Aïn Oktor is the first spring you reach, approaching Korbous from the Soliman direction. The isolated hotel complex, overlooking the sea, dates from 1966, and was designed, like so many other public buildings of the period, by President Bourguiba's then-favourite architect, Olivier Clément Cacoub. The spring water emerges slowly, its name meaning 'the spring which emerges drop by drop', and contains a high proportion of chlorine and soda used in the treatment of kidney disorders and urinary problems.

Aïn Chifa is the main spring in the village. For those in need of a cure, there is the thermal institute where you can enjoy such delights as *fangiothérapie* (mud baths) and other treatments which will leave you feeling squeaky clean. ■ *0800-1600, every day of the year, T284520*. The main, everyday baths is called the **Arraka** (from the Arabic *arak*, sweat), and in the underground grotto you really will get a sweat going. A new baths has been built above the old Arraka, and men and women's hours alternate between the two. Disappointingly, there are no great quantities of water in the Arraka. (In terms of water flow, the hot springs at Hammam Zriba are far better.) Behind the Arraka, overlooking the sea, is a much neglected (and probably closed) café, built next to the **Aïn Sbia** (Spring of the Young Girl).

Rather more exciting is **Aïn Atrous** (Billy Goat Spring), 1 km north of the village on the main road. The spring gushes out of a duct in the hillside at 50°C and runs across the rocks for a few metres before tumbling down about 3 m over a few rocks into the sea. The smell of hydrogen sulphide is difficult to avoid. You can sit with your feet in a small concrete basin while wisps of steam and whiffs of rotten eggs rise from the nearly scalding water. Even in winter it is possible – though not really pleasant – to bathe in the sea here. There is a car park and a few small cafés and restaurants close by (the *Restaurant Nouri*, first on your right as you come in from outside, is said to be the best.) Aïn Atrous is a favourite spot for locals, so Saturday and Sunday are very busy.

Beyond Aïn Atrous, the main road swings up right, eventually giving you some superb views across the sea to Tunis. Walking along a narrow path along the hillside above the sea, you can eventually drop down to a small bay with a pebbly beach after a couple of kilometres walk. (Four-wheel drive vehicles could also get some way down, access from the main road much higher up than Aïn Atrous.) This is **Aïn Kala Sirra** (*kala* being an inlet, *sirra* a sort of fish), where there is a tiny grotto with a trickle of water used by local people for mud baths. Off the coast here there is a hot spring bubbling up into the sea – find it if you can. You might do some snorkelling here, and the area is quite popular for underwater fishing.

Sleeping
Phone code: 72

Most of the hotels are fairly expensive and used by the people 'taking the waters'. Sadly, the recently privatized hotel *Aïn Oktor* – 4 km along the road to Soliman, overlooking the sea, now owned by the president of one of the leading football clubs – was closed in 2002, although works were scheduled to start soon. Hopefully the buildings will be returned to their original minimalist splendour.

C *Résidence des Thermes*, T284755, F284755, at top of main street, 5-min walk from spa baths, clean, tidy rooms with balcony on 2 floors, 18 twin-bedded rooms, all with bath and toilet, heating, a/c, meals if required are provided in newly built restaurant across the road. This is the smart option, but a refit is definitely in order. The next 2 addresses are accessed, as you come up from the coast and old spa centre, by turning left, just after the colonial building with the stone-built ground floor, on to a steep road. *Les Sources* is on your right, the brown-painted block with white balconies. For *El Kabira*, continue on road which goes round to left, reception is on right in apartment building under arcades, poorly signed. **C** *Les Sources*, T284540, F284601.Terrace above and around pool, 103 beds, thermal cures, pool. Competing for the best hotel in Korbous spot is **C** *Résidence El Kabira*, T/F284822, a time-share place (of a sort), with a series of (poorly equipped) self-catering flats, with special rates for more than 3 days. Standard of maintenance is low, but reception are helpful. Not actually in Korbous, but listed here for convenience, the **C** *Chiraz* is at Sidi Rais on the old coast route de Korbous, T293230. 16 beds, pool, small personal hotel, popular restaurant and bar, reserve in summer.

Eating

The *Résidence des Thermes* has a pizzeria, operational summer only. The *Restaurant Dhib* in town centre, on left as you go down hill, next to police station, serves good cheap meals. Why is the café at Aïn Sbia, behind the Arraka, left so badly maintained? Sad. There is a bar, *La Brise* at Sidi Rais, possibly still operational.

Spa baths

If you have the time, you could try the spa in the building with the minaret. Although they are very obliging at reception, the place has a rather lacklustre feel to it. (Is the spa water pool *still* out of order?) The spa is open 0800-2000, there is no need to reserve (they say), 5Dt will buy you time in a *bain de barbotage*, a sort of jacuzzi, while a *bain de boue* (mud bath) is 10Dt, which seems pretty reasonable.

Transport

Road Bus: there are 4 buses a day from Tunis to Korbous from Bab Alioua, return buses to Tunis are at 0615, 0930, 1400 and 1600. Returning buses may not leave on time. **Louage**: from Tunis, taking a louage is somewhat faster. Coming from both Tunis and Haouaria, you will have to change at Soliman. At the bus station/louage stop, you pick up a yellow taxi which does the run to Korbous via the villages of Brij and Douala (1Dt500). Sometimes the taxi stops at Douala and the driver will leave you in the hands of an unofficial cab which will take you into Korbous for 500 millimes.

From Bir Meroua to El Haouaria

Bir Meroua is on the C26 and is reached directly from Soliman or recognized as the sharp left turn towards El Haouaria when approached from the coast.

Cap Bon Peninsula

Cap Bon Peninsula

 Festivals on the Cap Bon

The towns and villages of the Cap Bon all seem to have an annual festival of some kind, some centred on the local agricultural speciality, others with a traditional or cultural content. Sponsored by the local authorities, these are generally occasions which allow otherwise rural backwaters to get a bit of the limelight in the sleepy Tunisian press. They include:

March /April
Orange Flower Festival at Menzel Bou Zelfa

Late April/early May
Spring Festival at Nabeul

Late June
Falconry Festival at Haouaria

July and August
International Festival of Hammamet (theatre and music)

August *(every other year)*
Amateur Theatre Festival at Korba

September
Festival of the Vine at Grombalia

After **Sidi Aïssa**, you drive through rolling countryside, with occasional views of the sea glinting in the distance off to the left. Vines, cereals and vegetables (lots of tomatoes) are cultivated.

There are stands of cane and on occasion the road is lined with eucalyptus. After Tozghrane and Zaouiet el Magaïez, the land gets drier and the views open up. **Zaouiet el Mgaïez**, a one horse sort of town whose chief claims to fame are an elaborately tiled modern minaret and the production of baskets and beach parasols from local cane, holds a busy market in the main street each Wednesday. But as in many other localities like it across the Cap Bon, signs of development are everywhere. There are new school buildings and lots of powerlines, and wherever you go the children look well dressed and well fed.

Detour to Sidi Daoud Driving up to Haouaria, you can make a quick detour to Sidi Daoud, a small fishing port just off the coast road to Korbous. On the way to nowhere, with views looking out to the steep cliffs of the islands of Zembra and Zembretta, Sidi Daoud feels a remote place. The strangeness is enhanced by a large fish-canning plant. In late May to early June each year, the fishermen of the area take part in the *matanza*, the high point of the fishing season when shoals of large tuna fish (at times weighing more than 200 kg), innocently migrating from the Atlantic Ocean via the Straits of Gibraltar, are caught in carefully positioned nets, only to be dragged towards the shore and then harpooned between the boats. The panicking tuna thrash the nets, and the sea foams with blood. Enthusiasts may be able to get permission to go on the *matanza*. The event is more talked about in the tourist brochures than actually viewed by camcorders, however.

Sidi Daoud has factories which deal with the tuna fish and then export it to other Mediterranean countries. Tunisian red-meat tuna, canned with olive oil, is very good, and the top brand is El Manar. Note that the Romans caught on to this: Sidi Daoud occupies the site of ancient Missua, whose shipowners' corporation was represented at Ostia. No doubt salt fish was being shipped to Rome.

There are moorings at Sidi Daoud for pleasure boats – between 1.8 m and 3 m in depth – with all the expected facilities, security and comfort. Near here is the tiny beach of **Bir Jeddi**, about 2 km down a wooded track from the village. The beach is fine sand, but has lots of pebbles too. There are some huts for hire and a cool freshwater spring near the remains of an old cemetery.

Back on the main road, you continue northeastwards the short distance towards El Haouaria, Ghar el Kebir and Cap Bon. On your left, a line of giant windmills comes into view, Tunisia's first wind farm. In French, such huge, silent structures are called *éoliennes*, a reference to Aeolus, god of the winds.

El Haouaria   الهوارية

Approaching from the Korbous direction, El Haouaria appears in the bare land-scape as an expanse of low, flat-roofed houses below the gently rising mass of the djebel. There is the usual tall, onion-domed Cap Bon minaret. The town is a sleepy sort of place. For the tourist, attractions include the bizarre underground Roman quarries, the off-chance of seeing someone flying a falcon, and the low-key beach at Rass Eddreck. The scenery is rugged, and birdwatchers will have much to look at during the annual trans-Mediterranean migrations.

Phone code: 72
Colour map 2, grid A6

Getting there El Haouaria is easily accessible by public transport from Tunis, Nabeul and Kélibia. If you are driving from Tunis, allow at least 1hr 40mins, as you may be held up in traffic leaving Tunis. The louages and buses come into the station on Av Habib Bourguiba in the town centre.

Ins & outs

Getting around No particular problems here. The Roman quarries and the falconry centre are some 30 mins' walk out of the town centre. If you want to get down to the Ras Eddreck beach, then either hitch or, in season, take the local bus from the main square. For Kerkouane, you would need to take a local bus or louage to Kélibia, and get off at Kerdouane, signposted some 3 km after the one-horse settlement of Dar Allouche. Getting back, you might have to hitch or try to flag down the bus.

Cap Bon Peninsula

Sights

In Roman times, El Haouaria was referred to as Aquilaria, 'the place of eagles'. The capture and rearing of falcons, still part of local life today, was no doubt an important activity in ancient times. The present-day **Falconry Festival** goes back to 1967 when the tourist board decided to do something to cash in on this 'feature' of an out of the way corner of the Cap Bon. The festival rather died a death in the 1980s, but re-emerged as a three-day event in 1995. Modern Haouaria has erected a large concrete hawk as a monument to its birds and their handlers, smack in the town centre.

The festival (*Le Festival de l'Epervier*) is held each May or June. The country people bring their hawks to put them through their paces in front of other bird handlers. Live prey are used for these flying displays, and the falconers operate their birds with no mean skill.

Two sorts of birds are used at El Haouaria for falconry: the sparrowhawk (*épervier* in French, *essaf* in Tunisian Arabic) and the peregrine falcon (*faucon pélérin* or *el burni*). Sparrowhawk are captured up on the mountain during the April migration from Africa, and after around three weeks' training are ready to hunt in time for the festival. Quail is the favourite prey. Generally, after the festival, most of the sparrowhawks are released. Takes of the much rarer peregrine falcons are very closely controlled. Only one or two nestlings may be taken each year, and the young birds are reared in capacity. Permits are issued to bona fide falconers only.

Today El Haouaria has a gleaming white new **falconry centre** (*Nadi el Bayazara*) up on the hill on the road to the Roman quarries (up on your right before you get to the crenellated *Restaurant Les Grottes*). There is a carnival atmosphere about the town during the festival, which coincides with the start of the hunting season. If you miss the festival, then you might be lucky at the *Restaurant La Daurade* and see the owner put his resident falcon through its paces.

The Roman quarries (Les Grottes)

Children should not be let too far off the leash in the vicinity of the caves, as not all have had iron bars placed over their 'access hatches'. Also tread heavily so the snakes can hear (or rather feel) you coming

Three km from the village on the shore near the extremity of the Cap are the **Ghar el Kebir Caves**. It is thought that the rock quarried from here was used to build parts of Carthage. There are said to be 97 caves in total. There is a car park and a restaurant (*La Daurade*) by the car park next to the new entrance building. It is a short easy walk to the main caves which are interlinked and have small openings in the roof, originally for the exit of the quarried stone, so daylight can now enter. Caper plants grow in the sandy stone, hanging down through the openings. If you are accompanied by a guide, they will point out the 'camel' of stone in the big hall, a female we are told. The mountains along the coast and behind the villages offer interesting walks. ■ *0800-1900 summer, 0900-1700 winter. 1Dt 100, free access for international student card holders.*

Ancient quarrying technique

The question is, why did the Romans opt for quarrying on this remote stretch of coast? One major factor must have been the accessibility of such a large amount of easily worked soft sandstone right on the coast. The stone could be easily shipped to Carthage and other settlements across the Bay of Tunis. One wonders whether Aquilaria sandstone was used for the great amphitheatre at El Djem, speculating about the difficulties of transporting stone blocks to an inland site. And then there is the matter of how they worked the stone. As they cut down from above, the quarry workers created pyramid-shaped underground chambers. The operation was a skilled one, especially when it came to hoisting the blocks out through the 'skylights'. No room for cutting the blocks to the wrong size. Getting the blocks on the fragile ancient ships would have been another skilled manoeuvre using simple cranes. Depending on the demand for the stone, there must have been a sizeable population living out at ancient Haouaria.

Just down from the caves, below *Le Daurade* and another café-type place (no beers, hideous piped music), there is a good spot for swimming. Although the rocks are sharp, you can dive straight into several metres of clear water. Bring your mask, there are shoals of small fish. The local children fish for *retzy* (sea urchins).

Zembra & Zembretta

Zembra and Zembretta are small, steep-cliffed islands about 8 nautical miles northwest from the coast by Sidi Daoud. Zembra is clearly visible from the Roman quarries at Haouaria, and the view at sunset is magnificent. The sea for 1½ nautical miles beyond low tide is designated a *nature reserve* with no fishing – professional or sports – allowed. Grey puffins nest here. There used to be a hotel and a diving centre. For their names alone the islands would be worth visiting, but they are now occupied by the military. Access is only given to authorized research teams, so their unique biotopes look set to go undisturbed for some time yet.

Zembra rises straight out of the sea to its summit of 435 m. Evidence shows that it was colonized from the time of the Phoenicians. The Romans called the islands the *Aégimures*. Zembra's special feature? A special type of rabbit, thought to descend from animals introduced by Phoenician sailors, perhaps to ensure a source of meat if forced to spend time on the island. Zembretta, the smaller of the two islands as its name suggests, has a lighthouse.

Ras Eddrak

Towards the end of the Cap Bon peninsula there is a beautiful little beach, Ras Eddrak, which is quite secluded and still relatively unknown. A number of holiday homes have gone up and it is possible to find month-long summer lets, though at a price. (Starting at 800Dt a month in summer, fully furnished.) It is 4 km from the village along a road leading to the end of the peninsula. The view from the end of Cap Bon is superb. It is said that on a clear night the lights of Sicily, 140 km away, can be seen. In the late 1990s, as part of Tunisia's effort to improve conditions for small-scale fishing operations, a small port was built under the cliff at the end of Ras Eddrak beach. Fishermen can usually be persuaded to part with part of their succulent catch here. A rough but manageable track now leads along the cliff, past the port. Following the goat track round, you will reach some small, pebbly beaches, quite a rarity in Tunisia. (There is another right up in the northwest, at Melloula, a few kilometres west of Tabarka.)The pebbles gurgle away in the ebb and flow of the clear water. But note that though the water is often calm, winds can blow up and make the sea turbulent and dangerous, particularly if you are swimming close to the rocks.

Essentials

C-D *Hotel de l'Epervier*, Av H Bourguiba, T297017, F297258. 28 beds in 10 a/c rooms, bath, local TV, some rooms giving on to a courtyard, others on to street. Pretty solid restaurant famed for fish and seafood. **E** *Dar Toubib*, T297163.

Sleeping
Phone code: 72

Mid-range *Restaurant de l'Epervier* (English spoken). Recommended. If you can stand the sub-Disney castle décor, then try the *Restaurant les Grottes*, T297296, easily recognized at the top of the rise on the way to the *grottes romaines*. As home to most of El Haouaria's hard drinkers, this can get quite busy, although coach parties also fetch up here during the day. The sunset views over the sea to Zembretta are stunning from the terraces at the back. Much better, and far less offensive on the eye, is *La Daurade*, T269080, F269090, next to the car park for the Roman quarries. Here you can eat fairly cheaply, or even pretty expensively if you go for some clawed sea-beast (*langouste*, *cigale de mer* or whatever) fresh from the depths and beautifully prepared. You might see the resident falcon, Antar, pulling a sparrow to pieces for its lunch.

Eating

Boat trips Ask M. Hamadi at his *La Daurade*, T98249866, for details of trips out to see on his glass-bottomed boat. Points of departure are from the sea down the hill below the restaurant or from the new port at Ras Eddrak. From early May to late Oct groups of up to 30 can enjoy a trip round Cap Bon with a barbecued lunch of freshly caught fish and sea urchins. Stops for diving and swimming in places inaccessible by land. Prices (2002) 30Dt adult, 15Dt child. Timings approx. 0900-1500.

Sport

Falconry *Club des Fauconniers*, Aquilaria, on road to quarries, open 1000-1600 daily. Said to do occasional displays of falconry during the season (Jun-Jul).

Road Bus: irregular bus service, either via the north coast from Tunis (slow because the bus stops everywhere) or via Kélibia. **Louage**: taking a louage is much faster.

Transport

Banks On Av Habib Bourguiba near the Post Office. **Communications** Post Office: at the start of Av Habib Bourguiba, by the louages and bus station.

Directory

Cap Bon Peninsula

Southeast coast

From Haouaria to Kélibia via Kerkouane

Kélibia is just a 20-minute drive from Haouaria along the much improved C27 road, Kerkouane being the main stop-off en route. You pass through some small, strung-out settlements, including **Dar Allouche** (two petrol stations). After Kerkouane (a left turn after the long concrete wall of a private estate), the road runs through a small forest and then the farming villages of Ezzahra and **Hammam el Ghezez** (splendid beaches, no concrete monster hotels) and the sandy spit of Ras Mellah. One way to reach the beach is across the fields, but don't get the car bogged down in the sandy tracks. Another option, for archaeology buffs in need of a swim, is as follows: after Kerkouane, and roughtly 2 km before the Ezzahra roundabout, there is a turning left into the forest marked Centre national de la jeunesse (scout camp). Where the track ends and meets the sea, turn left and you will find recent excavations where the archaeologists have brought to light the remains of a Coptic church, grain stores, and a water system. The diggings continue ... Outside the main compound, scattered bits of ruins can be found in the sea, echoing Kerkouane, and proving once more that the ancients knew how to pick a site for a settlement.

After this historical sidetrack, continue on the C27 to Kélibia (two approaches, via new *zone touristique*/Mansoura or into the town). As you approach Kélibia, the mass of the town's fortress can be distinguished, high up on its hill.

Kerkouane   كركوان

Phone code: 72
Colour map 2, grid B6

Set in a Brittany-like corner of Tunisia, the ruins of Kerkouane, although not as spectacular as the great inland Numidian and Roman towns, have a charm of their own. Perhaps it is the site's location, on the edge of a low cliff overlooking the Mediterranean, backed by a hinterland of dark, windswept pines and heath. Certainly it must have something to do with the fact that Kerkouane, unlike so many other ancient sites, was never built upon by subsequent peoples. The old Punic town decayed into a jungle of briars, gorse and tamarisk, waiting for some archaeologist prince-charming. Today the visitor has a labyrinth of low intersecting walls and courtyards to contemplate, relieved here and there by a truncated column or two. Kerkouane does not deliver up its secrets readily.

■ *0800-1900 summer, 0930-1600 winter. 1Dt, photography 1Dt, T294033.* If you are lucky, the small site museum, inaugurated June 1987, may be open. Here are displayed some of the finest discoveries at Kerkouane, including the sole example of a carved wooden Punic coffin. Enthusiasts of things pre-Roman might want to go in search of the Punic necropolis of Sidi Salem near Menzel Temime, further down the coast.

History Kerkouane is thought to have been built in the sixth-century BC and probably abandoned following the fall of Carthage to the Romans in 146. It may, however, have been abandoned earlier. The settlement had a small port, and it is likely that its people made their living both from the sea and the farming. The murex, a shellfish well known in ancient times, was harvested and processed at Kerkouane for its purple dye, and may have been one of the town's main sources of wealth. The ruins of Kerkouane were discovered in 1952 by Charles

Cap Bon Peninsula

What did the Punics do for lunch?

The ancient Mediterranean world had neither the tomato nor the potato, and even the vegetation in ancient Tunisia must have been very different to today. There were no eucalyptus trees (a 19th-century introduction), no prickly pear hedges nor giant yuccas, both of which were introduced from the New World. What might have been the mainstays of the Punic diet? One thing is certain, the Punic peoples were noted farmers, and the Greeks considered Mago, fourth-century author of a treatise on agriculture, now lost, as the father of farming.

Echoes of what the Punic peoples were eating come down to us in the ancient texts. Another, more visual remnant, are terracotta models discovered in tombs. One such model, from fifth-century Carthage, shows a beheadscarved woman making bread in a round cylindrical pisé oven of the type still used to make flat tabouna bread in rural Tunisia today. Terracotta model fruit of various kinds has also been discovered in tombs.

The Cap Bon was a verdant region where Carthaginian nobles had estates. They grew fruit almonds, grapes, figs and pomegranates, mala punica or 'Punic apples' to the Romans, but not citrus fruits, which did not arrive until modern times. They were good at bee-keeping, honey being the only available sweetener. The Greek and Latin historians tell us that cabbages and 'Carthage thistles' or artichokes featured in the market gardens. The Carthaginians are also said to have had an inordinate love of garlic, and the chick pea is referred to by one author as the punicum cicer. With bread, chick peas and eggs, plus a few spices, the Carthaginians had all the ingredients to conjure up something very like the modern Tunisian leblebi, a hot broth popular on winter mornings.

To complete the picture, the Carthaginians were also a dab hand at wine-making, and Latin writer Columella quoutes Mago's vinification methods at some length. The consumption of wine was severely controlled, however, and Plato describes how in Carthage wine was off limits for soldiers on campaign, ship's pilots, slaves (male and female), magistrates and men and women intending to procreate. The very existence of such a list of proscriptions suggests that things had been getting a little out of hand with a few boozy lunches too many taking their toll of Carthaginian business acumen.

Cap Bon Peninsula

Saumagne and Pierre Cintas, and there have been excavations on and off ever since, as funds and enthusiasm permitted. What the actual Punic name of Kerkouane was, we do not know, as surviving Punic written records, mainly inscriptions, are rare to say the least.

Several decades before the discovery of the actual town of Kerkouane, archaeologists became aware of an ancient presence in the area. Some 500 m northwest of the ancient town lies a burial area, with vaults carved into a hillside looking out over the sea. This necropolis was discovered completely by chance by a local notable, a *meddeb* or Koran schoolteacher, in 1929. On discovering that the tombs contained scarabs, jewellery, and black-figure ceramics, he was to mine his discovery for all it was worth, selling off the most valuable finds to treasure hunters. Other funerary objects and pottery were too cumbersome, and were broken up to fill in already ransacked tombs.

The necropolis of Arg el Ghazouani

The 'official' discovery of the necropolis had to wait until one J. Combre, an officer appointed to conduct a local murder enquiry, met the *meddeb*. He noted that our teacher's wife was wearing a superb pair of gold earrings, obviously of great age. The teacher eventually told the tale of the tomb robberies, but official awareness does not seem to have put an end to the pillage. In the

Our lady Tanit

At Carthage, Tanit, goddess of Phoenician origin, was referred to as 'lady'. Mother goddess, symbol of fertility, her name often precedes that of Baal-Hammon on the stelae of Carthage. In all probability, Tanit and Baal-Hammon formed a sort of divine couple.

The Tanit sign is to be found on stelae and is formed by a triangle topped by a horizontal line on which rests a circle. The general theory is that it is a stylized representation of a female figure, shown in long, flowing robes. At Kerkouane, a famous example of the Tanit sign is to be found in a proto-mosaic pavement, picked out in white against a dull-red ground. It has also be found decorating funerary chambers, stamped on the handles of amphorae and on terracotta medallions.

What was the function of the Tanit sign? It may be that the Tanit is derived from the Egyptian ankh, symbol of life. Thus when it is placed on the doorstep of a home, it has a great protective force. In funerary chambers, the Tanit would seem to promote the forces of life over death. It is one of the earliest sacred signs known in North Africa. Today Tunisians use the fish (hout) and the khomsa, the so-called Hand of Fatima. But some see the Tanit still very much present in contemporary Tunisia. Feminist film-maker Nadia El Fani created a dream-like short feature film, Tanitez-moi (1992), emphasizing the Carthaginian side in the identity of today's Tunisian women.

light of the finds at Arg el Ghazouani, archaeologist Cintas began to research tombs elsewhere in the region. Despite all the pillaging, there were tombs which survived unopened into the 1960s and later. In July 1970, a tomb at Arg el Ghazouani was found to contain a wooden sarcophagus, its lid carved with the bas-relief image of a woman, thought by some to be Ashtart, protector goddess of the dead. This piece can be viewed today in the site museum.

The discovery of Kerkouane

Kerkouane was discovered almost by accident. It was the sort of scoop that archaeologists dream of. In fact, the area could all too easily have gone the way of so many other sites, the land subdivided for villa development, with building too far advanced for anything to be done. One version of the story goes that Charles Saumagne was a great amateur fisherman. One afternoon in 1952, sitting on the cliffs of Kerkouane, he noticed some black-glaze pot shards and fragments of stucco in the soil. As an archaeologist, he immediately gave this loose surface material a closer inspection, realizing that it was probably pre-Roman. The Department of Antiquities was informed, and test-trenches were dug. The results were conclusive, for with almost the first shovelful, a Punic mask was brought to light.

A unique survival

Looking out across the low expanse of sunbaked ruins, you may find yourself thinking: so why is this place so important? Quite simply, Kerkouane is practically unique. Unless archaeology in the Levant or possibly Sardinia comes up trumps, then Kerkouane is the only example of a Punic settlement to have survived untouched until the present day. Other sites were practically all built upon by later settlers, foremost among which were the Romans. Given that their boats had to be drawn up on the shore at night, the Phoenicians and Punics tended to pick good safe places to establish their settlements. Carthage is a case in point. And the Romans were not likely to miss out on such good places when they took over the Punic lands.

Why the Romans did not establish a settlement at Kerkouane is another question. It may be that they preferred Hammam Ghezaz further down the coast. Or perhaps the quarrying activities at Haouaria took all their energies.

Further reading on Kerkouane

Those interested in all things Punic will want to find out more. M'hamed Hassine Fantar is the acknowledged Tunisian expert on Kerkouane, to the point that the site is nicknamed 'Fantarville'. Look out for his scholarly works, or the generalist Kerkouane, a Punic town in the Berber region of Tamezrat *(Alif: Tunis, 1998). Other names to have published on the site include Cintas and Mahjoubi.*

Hassine Fantar, today the leading authority on Kerkouane, sees the town as being a sort of ethno-cultural melting pot, with Libyic, Punic and Greek influences all present. The rock tombs in the area attest to a strong Libyic presence, while a Greek black-figure wine jug from the site can be dated to the sixth century BC. Excavations of the houses have not brought to light any material later than the third century BC, which would suggest that the town was pillaged and abandoned at the time of Roman consul M. Atilius Regulus's invasion of Africa in 256 BC. The town was never to rise again. **Dating Kerkouane**

From an aerial photograph, you get a very clear idea of the town's layout. There were long streets, some open public areas and blocks of building which on closer inspection turn out to be carefully planned town houses. The main streets are wide, often about 4 m, and the houses tend to follow a courtyard plan. **Streets & town-houses**

Looking over the ruins of the houses, the untrained eye begins to pick out clues to what was actually here in Punic days. The people of Kerkouane were a clean lot, and you can see stone guttering and some very modern hip-baths, carefully finished in stone-chip rendering. The walls were mainly built with rubble-stone, strengthened here and there by big rectangular upright stones or orthostats (to use the technical term). This building technique is referred to as *opus africanum* ('African work') by the archeologists. Interior walls might be built using an earth, lime and gravel mix packed down between wooden formwork.

Here and there, you may come across some rough hewn steps, an indication that there was a first floor, perhaps a light wood-built structure. The buildings probably had flat, terrace roofs, and there were stone waterspouts to ensure that water did not accumulate on the roofs. No doubt the roofing technology was not so very different from that used until the mid-20th century in many urban Tunisian homes: the room was covered with a bed of juniper or pine trunks, subsequently covered with rammed earth and gravel; the whole roof was then sealed with lime wash. Sometimes a stone pillar in the middle of a large room would be used to hold the roof up, and Ionic column capitals have been discovered. Another solution was to place a pine trunk in an amphora, and use it as a central pillar, the amphora protecting the wood from any ground damp. Kerkouane does not seem to have had any elaborate arches or vaulting.

The Kerkouanese liked to have their homes well-finished. A form of stucco was in use, and here and there you can see layers of stucco flaking on the clay-and-gravel walls. (So don't go jumping up and down on the walls.) There may well have been wall paintings like the simple elegant designs discovered in certain Punic burial chambers. Floors had the most elegant finish, however. The preferred paving technique, referred to by archaeologists as *opus signinum*, involved setting white marble chips in a hard mix of old pottery and primitive cementing. The resulting overall colour is terracotta pink flecked with white.

The site museum If it is open, the site museum is definitely worth a look, giving a bit more of an insight into the everyday goings-on in ancient Kerkouane. There are a few items from Carthage and other sites (the column capitals from Gammarth). Under the porticoes are amphorae and bits of masonry, inside are sundry items related to both work and worship. There are weights and obsidian objects, murex shells and basalt grindstones, pottery, both local and imported, stelae and altars. There are amulets, toilet requisites, scarabs and glass-paste decorative items. The jewellery, if on display, has an interesting story to tell. The vast majority was discovered in the burial grounds near Kerkouane. Many of the finest tomb finds, discovered before Punic archaeology really got going in the 1950s, found their way abroad. The Fragonard museum at Grasse, for example, has a fine collection of perfume flasks.

The Lady of Kerkouane The most unusual item in the museum has to be the wooden sarcophagus carved with the image of the goddess Ashtart, protector of the dead. The robed goddess is almost complete, with only the feet missing. The find is unique, no other example of Punic wood-carving has survived. After the discovery, wood-conservation experts were flown in from Switzerland, and in the event, the statue had to be flown off to Zurich for treatment.

The survival of Kerkouane In many ways, the survival of Kerkouane is as miraculous as that of Ashtart on the sarcophagus lid. Once exposed to the elements, however, to sea winds and mist, the walls are really rather vulnerable. Visiting the site, avoid walking on the walls and roped off areas (a cross warden might well come racing up anyway to warn you off). A photograph in a genuine Punic bathtub is a tempting proposition, but if everyone clambered in and out, the pink rendering would become fragile. Save the ancient heritage photo-call for the headless statues at the Bardo Museum.

Kélibia   قليبية

Phone code: 72
Colour map 2, grid B6
Population: 35,000

Kélibia is one of those attractive backwater sort of places. Too far from Hammamet to have attracted the developers' interest, it has neither baleful, calculating souks nor stretches of lumpish hotels (yet). There are some entirely beautiful beaches, a busy fishing port, and a hilltop fort, no doubt home to the odd Ottoman ghost. Kélibia is a working town: farming, furniture making and serving the needs of the local rural communities keep people busy, so tourism is just a sideline. There is nothing swish here, but everything for a siesta-like stay.

Ins and outs

Getting there Kélibia is easily accessed on public transport. There are buses and louages from Bab Alioua (Tunis) and Nabeul. Unfortunately, the hydrofoil link from Trapani in Italy has been discontinued. This is, however, the sort of service which could be resumed in the near future.

Getting around Buses and louages come into the central Av Ali Belhaouane. From here, it is a short walk to the *Pension Anis*. Other hotels are really a taxi ride away. (The Youth Hostel is nearly 2 km away, below the fort.) To get to the ruins at Kerkouane, you could take the local Haouaria bus, or a louage and ask to be let off at the turn off for the site.

History

Kélibia is one of the more pleasant small towns on the southeastern coast of the Cap Bon. Settlement goes back to Punic times. Phoenician traders no doubt appreciated the defensive value of the site: Kélibia holds the key to the straits separating Africa from Sicily. Greek historians referred to the town as Aspis, the Greek for 'shield'. The Romans adopted the same term, and redubbed Aspis as Clupea, 'shield' in Latin. Today, the town is dominated by an impressive fortress, symbol of the 18th/19th-century Husseinid Dynasty's authority over the Cap Bon. There has been a fortress on the site since Punic times. From the outside, at the base of one of the recent square towers, the base of a Punic fortification is clearly visible. The remains of a large Punic necropolis has been discovered near the *Hotel Mansoura*.

Kélibia is home to an important fishing fleet with a commercial fish market on the quayside. The main catch is 'blue' fish. The quiet port was modernized to become the main fishing port of Cap Bon and is at times a haven for the whole Cap Bon fleet comprising well over 350 coastal fishing boats, around 50 trawlers and a few boats for game fish. Unfortunately, Tunisian fishing fleets suffer from heavy competition from better equipped, more powerful Italian vessels.

There is also a thriving shipbuilding and ship repair section at the port. Until recently, there was also a hydrofoil ferry link to Trapani in Italy. In the late afternoon, the fishing fleet can be seen chugging up the coast for night fishing. (Some lamparo fishing still goes on.) On summer nights, all Kélibia seems to come out for a paseo in the port area. Families, gaggles of local kids, scooters and sundry strollers parade along the quay and up to the *Café Sidi el Bahri*.

Note also that the best lettuces in Tunisia are grown in the Kélibia region. The town is an important furniture-making centre and many workshops can be seen in and around the town. A pleasant white wine, the *Muscat sec de Kélibia*, is a legacy of early-20th-century Italian settlement. Unfortunately, the grape juice is sent up to the main UCCV production unit in Tunis for fermenting, so boringly there are no jolly *dégustations* in the local winery.

Sights

Kélibia fortress sits on top of a 150-m-high rocky hill. The present structure would seem to go back to the Byzantine sixth century, but has been changed and rebuilt many times since. The crenellated walls, almost complete, are made of huge blocks of stone and are reinforced with square towers at the corners. The fortress surrounds the remains of a much more ancient fort and some deep wells. Inside the fortress there are several vaulted rooms, one of which, with three naves, was probably a chapel. The fortress is accessible up a steep road leading off the road north of the port. Excavations in the vicinity of the fort are of Roman **Clupea**. Alternate years, generally in July, a minor international amateur film festival is held here. ■ *0800-1900 summer, 0830-1700 winter. 2 Dt or free for students*

Beaches North of Kélibia, **Mansoura** with its graceful beaches is a pleasant little corner of Tunisia, despite the growing number of mediocre concrete bunker-villas. The water is green-glass clear, the sand fine and white, and there is a very 1970s restaurant where the chairs and tables are set on little platforms around the rock pools: too pleasant to be true in the early summer. Further up the coast is **Hammam el Ghezaz** and the sandly headland of Ras el Melah.

For many years, rumour went that there would be an 'integrated touristic development' in the Mansoura area, but it seemed that Hammamet had

Cap Bon Peninsula

sucked in all the investment – given the easy motorway access, the economies of scale linked to vast infrastructure development and the Hammamet label. So far only one large hotel has been completed and given investors' worries about the dip in tourism in the autumn of 2001, further constructions to ruin this wonderfully unspoiled stretch of coast were thankfully postponed.

Essentials

Sleeping Accommodation is limited, most in the **C** category. In summer, try to reserve. Most tourists here are Tunisians, in rented villas or staying with family or in second homes.

A *Kélibia Beach* Brand new hotel which has partly ruined the beach at Kélibia. Was to be a hotel-club and so off-limits to all except those reserving from abroad at time of going to press. Policy may change.

C *Pension Anis*, centrally located in Kélibia town, T295777, F273128. 12 rooms, only 2 with ensuite bathrooms and TV. Pleasant staff, highly recommended restaurant. **C** *Belle Etoile*, T274374, F275302, on main road to fort and port. New hotel with 24 spacious rooms, ensuite shower or bath, satellite TV, a/c. Small pool. Terraces but no garden or seafront. Good bet for an overnight if you are touring. **C** *Palmarina* (ex-*Hotel Ennasim*) T274062, F274055. 36 rooms, a/c, satellite TV, pleasant views of the port from seaward-facing rooms but unpleasant seaweedy beach, but then this is the beach nearest the port, pool (clean?). **C-D** *Florida* Long established small hotel, by the sea, T296248. Now rather overshadowed by the neighbouring *Palmarina*. Home to most of Kélibia's hard drinkers and only to be used as a last resort. 25 beds, most rooms with sea view, shaded terrace. Choice of rooms or bungalow accommodation (ie room with small veranda). **C-D** *Mamounia Holiday Village*, 208 beds, T296088, F286858. Close to the new sports hall. Accommodation in simple, whitewashed vaulted buildings with verandas. Small pool. Might suit families. A quiet sort of place which no doubt had its heyday back in the 1970s. **NB** Jungle gel and other mosquito repellants essential. Beach seaweedy, prices negotiable out of season.

Youth hostel: T296105, 80 beds, on the road to Mansoura, by the sea, below the fort. Reservations essential in summer.

Eating **Mid-range** *El Mansoura*, T296321. Right on the sea. A very popular address for a long, slow lunch. Gets very crowded at weekends. Not cheap, but not expensive either given the level of service. *Hotel Palmarina* (see above) has a very reasonably priced set menu. *Restaurant Anis*, Av Erriadh, Kélibia's most upmarket place. Not far from the main market. Specialities include elaborate fish dishes like *Lotte au poivre vert* and *St Pierre à la crème*. Highly recommended.

Cheap *Café Sidi el Bahri*, by the port. Kélibia's happening place in the evening. Chairs among the rocks and on the sand. Limited menu. More of a café than a restaurant. *Café el Borj*. Just below the fortress, next to a saint's tomb among the pine trees. with fine views looking northwards over Mansoura towards Kerkouane. Plastic chairs and overamplified music spoil what is really a rather wonderful place. No food but good *café turc*. *Clupea*, T296296. A bar more than a restaurant. *Dina*, on R Ibn Khaldoun in the town centre. Does the usual pizzas. Fine for a cheap fill-up.

Sport Some watersports are available but the resort is not really set up for this. Harbour has berths for 20 yachts, min-max draught 2-5 m, with all the expected facilities. For a trip out to sea, try the *Bateau Carthage*, a mock Spanish galleon owned by M. Jemaâ Ben

Hassen, T98287781, available for rent for day or half-day group tours along the coast, boarding at either Kélibia or Beni Khiar harbour (on board barbecue, coastal sightseeing, maybe snorkelling). Book well in advance in summer season.

Kerkouane Voyages, Pl Sidi Abdessalem, T295370, F296836. Can also arrange car hire **Tour operators** for a small number of vehicles. *Select Voyages*, R Ibn Khaldoun, T273118 may also arrange car hire.

Road Buses leave every hr in the morning to El Haouaria and there are frequent **Transport** departures to Nabeul. Bus and louages from Tunis leave from Bab Alioua. **Sea** The 4-hr hydrofoil link with Trapani in Sicily has been discontinued. To be resumed?

Banks *Banque nationale agricole* in the centre is said to have the most reliable **Directory** ATM. (There are 2 others, including 1 near the roundabout on the south side of town). Best to bring cash for weekend rather than being subject to vagaries of poorly maintained technology.

South to Nabeul via Menzel Temime and Korba

Some 12 km south of Kélibia is the busy agricultural town of Menzel Temime **Menzel** with an Ariane rocket of a minaret, no doubt built with donations from pros- **Temime** perous local farmers. Groundnuts (or peanuts) are grown in the area north of *Phone code: 72* the town towards El Haouaria. For those who want to see how salted peanuts *Colour map 2, grid B6* start off life, then this is the place to visit. The plants actually push the seed *Population: 30,000* pods down into the ground, hence the name. Peppers are another major crop here, and the house fronts are hung with strings of pimentos, big, bunchy garlands the colour of drying blood.

Human settlement in the Menzel Temime area goes back to at least the fourth century BC. Ruins have been found out in the farmland. There are some ancient caves, perhaps first century BC, badly signposted, dug in the rocks overlooking the beach. As per usual, the various invaders/settlers left their mark, there being Roman cisterns, fortresses, mosques and mausoleums.

Sleeping D *Temime*, 88 beds, T298262-266, F298291. **Youth hostel**, 40 beds, T298116.

A good straight road lined with eucalyptus runs from Menzel Temime to **Menzel** Korba. Agriculture enthusiasts will note extensive cultivation and some **Temime to** beef-cattle rearing. The level of mechanization ranges from camel and **Korba** horse-powered ploughs to sophisticated, heavy machinery. Approaching Korba the salt lakes and marshes to the southeast become more extensive. There are fields devoted to tomatoes and pimentos, processed/concentrated in local factories, and battery chicken farms.

Korba is a small town on the coast road just 20 km north of Nabeul. It stands **Korba** on the Oued Bou Eddine. Once upon a time, there was a *Club Méditerranée* *Phone code: 72* here. A rough road leads inland up to a barrage on the *oued*. Korba's claim to *Colour map 2, grid C5* fame today is strawberry production. Extensive areas next to the sea have been developed with moderately ugly suburbs of holiday homes.

There aren't too many sights in Korba. Almost nothing of the ancient city of *Julia Curubis* remains, although you might seek out the traces of the aqueduct. Curubis is thought to have been the seat of an archbishop associated with the presence of St Cyprien here in AD 275. From the Islamic period there are remains of the mausoleum of Sidi Moaouia and a mini *ribat* to protect the

Cap Bon Peninsula

settlement from attacks by pirates. Every other year, in August, there is a week-long national festival of amateur theatre. Market day is Sunday.

Sleeping   Former *Club Méditerranée*, T226400, is currently being renovated but is due to open in 2000. *Youth hostel*, T298116. 100 beds, meals provided, family run.

Nabeul   نـابـل

Phone code: 72
Colour map 2, grid C5
Population: 50,000

One of the first places to attract tourist development on the Cap Bon, Nabeul has long featured in the holiday brochures. It has a long clean beach, with some large hotels, and swathes of new estates of second homes. Nabeul also makes the best harissa (red chilli pepper) paste in Tunisia. It would be nice if the town had some sort of real attraction. While there are few nice bits of early 20th century official architecture, most of the local vernacular and Italian-style building is being altered out of all recognition. Nabeul has a roundabout with a big araucaria tree in a giant ceramic pot, shops of pottery for visitors, and lots of industry on the northwestern outskirts. The people are a friendly lot, and tourism is not the mainstay as it is in Hammamet: no one seems very bothered about history, culture and projecting a tourist image in Nabeul.

Ins and outs

Getting there
See also Transport, page 177, for further details

Easily accessible by public transport, Nabeul is reached by buses and louages from Tunis, Kélibia and Hammamet. The main bus and louage station is on Av Habib Thameur. There is a second bus and louage station for Cap Bon destinations on Av Farhat Hached, near the weekly market. You can also come into Nabeul by train from Tunis, the station being in the middle of town on the Av H Bourguiba, just where this turns into the main avenue leading to the sea.

Getting around

Nabeul can easily be done on foot. The main concentration of small hotels is 15-20 mins' walk south of the town centre (left out of bus station). If you want to get out to the beaches at, say, Maâmoura to the north, get a local bus from Av Habib Thameur.

Tourist information

The **Regional Tourism Bureau** is set back from the road on Av Taieb Mehiri, T286737, towards the beach, heading from town centre. Bus and train times are normally posted outside the office. Closed in winter. The **Nabeul Tourist Office** is at Pl 7 Novembre, T223006.

History

The modern town of Nabeul, 65 km southeast of Tunis, has become a place of some importance: it is the capital of the Governorate of the Cap Bon, and so there are various regional government buildings and colleges. The name Nabeul is a corruption of the ancient Neapolis ('new town'). A Roman area has been excavated, and can be seen beside the *Hotel Aquarius*, not far from the beach, 1 km to the southeast of the central area. The original Phoenician town was occupied by Roman troops during the third Punic war in 148 BC.

Sights

Colonia Julia Neapolis   Colonia Julia Neapolis was apparently developed by Julius Caesar on an earlier Punic site. Under Caesar Augustus it grew in importance, developing quickly, and by 258 had obtained the status of a full blown Roman city or *colonia*. Note the Romans had a hierarchy of cities in their provinces: first came the *colonia*, whose inhabitants were Roman citizens; the *municipium* had fewer rights, and elected two representatives a year; at the bottom of the scale were the *civitates* or native towns and villages. Nabeul was thus well up on the Romanity index.

The ruins are rather unspectacular, but you can see the 'House of Nymphs', from which the seven beautiful mosaics now exhibited in the town's museum (closed) were removed. It is also said to be the place where Artemonis, a superb horse, doted on by his Roman master, was buried. Just beside it there is a 'factory' where fish entrails were processed to make the famous highly flavoured *garum* seasoning. This condiment was used in many Roman dishes.

The Roman excavations

The entrance to the site off the Route Touristique is a gate (where there may still be a sign reading 'This is closed'). Continue about 50 m further east and take the track which leads to the sea. About 200 m down the track on the left is a small gate, the entrance. The site, which is privately owned, extends to about 8 ha and it is now you wish you had memorized the map from the entrance of the museum in Nabeul. ■ *0900-1200 daily. Dt1, photos Dt1.*

Nabeul's small museum is in a small park at 44 Avenue Habib Bourguiba, just opposite the railway station and the famous ceramic *jarre* roundabout. There are displays, the best of the local remains from nearby Neapolis and a few from the excavations at Kerkouane and Kélibia. It is built round the traditional square courtyard with a gallery to the left exhibiting Punic pottery and statuettes and an extensive display of pottery and oil lamps through to the third century AD.

Museum
Should by now be open. The information here describes the collection as it was; once reopened the collections should be broadly similar

Opposite the entrance is a fine display of mosaics. The best by far is a life-size mosaic showing the vanquished Priam (?) kneeling before a seated Agamemnon, with Mercury and Achilles (?) standing behind them, and another showing Mars standing behind a reclining Neptune. There are rather touching terracotta statuettes from the Punic necropolis and shrine of Thinissut, near Bir Bou Regba (Hammamet). One represents the goddess-mother breast-feeding her baby, while another is of a sinister lion-headed goddess. The figurines were probably made as grave-furniture.

The museum, unfortunately, does not provide a descriptive leaflet, and while the pottery has labels in Arabic and French, for the mosaics it is necessary to use the services of a guide who will require a tip. There is a map of the site of Neapolis on display at the entrance to the museum. ■ *Likely opening times: 0930-1630 winter, 0800-1200 and 1500-1900 summer, closed Mon. 1Dt plus 1Dt for photography. The adjacent park provides benches and shade.*

Nabeul's speciality is pottery, its largest industry after tourism. The art of polychrome ceramics was introduced in the 15th century by the Andalusians. All along the Avenue Farhat Hached you will see stalls of pottery: there is blue and white standard Mediterranean tourist ware, and slightly more upmarket stuff with simple floral or fish motifs with a faint Habitat feel. Production covers the whole span, from the simplest earthen water jar to the white and gilded pot pineapple. The quantities of pottery are such that Jean Genet, visiting Tunisia back in the 1970s, worried that Tunisia would be quarried away to nothing for its clay.

The pottery industry

Little actual pot-making can be observed today, as the potteries are now industrial concerns located on the outskirts (much of the clay is in fact

Cap Bon Peninsula

imported today!). The following factories might be of some interest: *Maison de l'Artisanat* on Avenue Habib Bourguiba, well down towards the beach, T285438, no showroom; *Ceramics Kedidi* on Route de Tunis, T287576, about 1½ km from the town centre, extensive showroom, mainly tiles; *Poterie Artistique Gasteli*, Zone Industrielle, Route de Tunis, T222247, about 1½ km from the town centre, employs about 100 people and will allow visitors to view the manufacturing process (no need for individuals to book, parties must contact M Hedi Hichaeri or M Maghrebi). Showroom at 190 Avenue Habib Thameur, shop at 117 Avenue Farhat Hached.

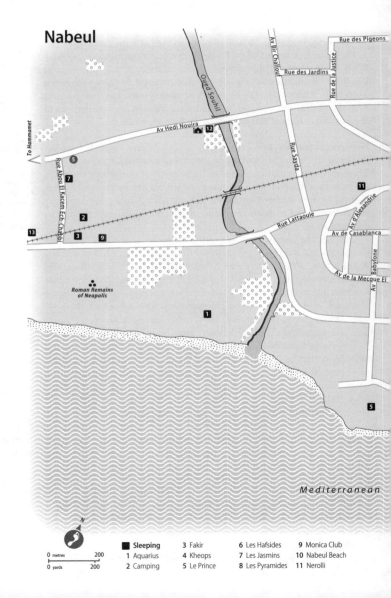

Nabeul

Cap Bon Peninsula

■ **Sleeping**	3 Fakir	6 Les Hafsides	9 Monica Club
1 Aquarius	4 Kheops	7 Les Jasmins	10 Nabeul Beach
2 Camping	5 Le Prince	8 Les Pyramides	11 Nerolli

The recent history of pot-making in Nabeul is interesting, although there is very little written on the subject. Under the French protectorate, a special department encouraged the revival of different crafts. The Chemla brothers developed the art of tile-making, and their fine tile panels, generally signed, can be seen even today on various façades in Tunis (*Restaurant Baghdad* on Avenue Bourguiba, base of the mosque at Bab Jazira). Spanish models were copied too, possibly thanks to immigrants fleeing the political turmoil in Spain in the late 1930s. With the ready availability of high quality clay, the pottery industry at Nabeul has never looked back.

Cap Bon Peninsula

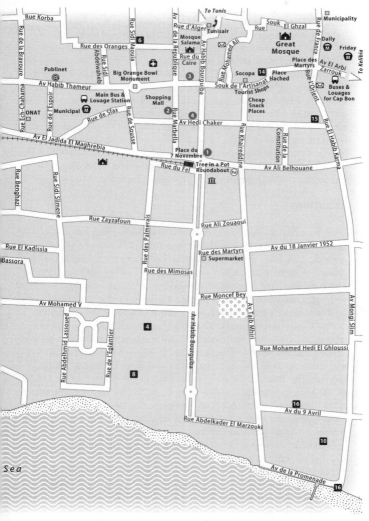

12 Pension El Habib	15 Pension Mustapha	● **Eating**	3 Café Er Rachidia
13 Pension les Oliviers	16 Youth Hostel	1 Les Arcades	4 L'Olivier
14 Pension les Roses		2 Le Bon Kif	5 Slovenia

Other crafts: survivals & revivals   Nabeul is noted for mats woven from rushes and esparto grass, silver and silk embroidery, and the distillation of jasmine, wild orange flowers and roses. These fragrant essences called *zhar* are prized by the locals for their soothing qualities. (Be assured a few drops in the milk will make a fretful baby sleep soundly.)

A craft industry that has taken off in a big way since the mid-1980s is **stone-carving** at the neighbouring town of Dar Chaâbane el Fehri, a few kilometres to the northeast but now effectively part of the greater Nabeul area. The Tunisian construction industry boomed in the 1990s, and new home owners were in need of signs of distinction for their façades. What could be easier than sandstone columns and facing, cut to measure at Dar Chaâbane? These stone features, once limited to the immediate area, can now be found on hotels (generally in the *café maure*) and villas all across Tunisia.

More threatened by technology is the craft of **rush-mat making**. Until the 1970s, no self-respecting mosque would be without its rush mats or *hassira* (pl. *Hsur*). The large areas to be covered, plus the need to renew the mats regularly, meant that generations of Nabeulians were kept busy at their horizontal floor looms. After independence, a number of trendy tourist products, including small floor mats, trays, baskets, lampshades and seating, were created. Traditionally styled cafés had to have rush mats too, essentially the narrow strips decorated with green and mauve arches to put round the walls behind stone benches. In the 1990s, however, the industry was dealt a severe blow in the form of large, cheap plastic floor mats imported from China via Libya. Now only a few workshops remain. The careful and ecological art of creating expanses of fragrant golden-yellow matting may soon be lost forever.

Excursions

Beni Khiar   If you have time on your hands, and enthusiasm for weaving, you might go to Beni Khiar, a small town a few kilometres north of Nabeul. The Hilalians, a nomadic tribe from Upper Egypt, established a settlement here in the 11th century. A century later, a *ksar* was established, carefully set back from the pirate-infested coast. The nomads settled here and supported themselves by weaving, a handicraft for which they are still famous today. The mosque was built later, outside the main *ksar*, and is all that remains of this settlement.

Beni Khiar still specializes in the spinning and weaving of wool, using natural dyes. It produces the traditional stripped blankets, the *kachabia*, a hooded cape and the fine weave and black stitched needlework carpets in small workshops or individual homes. Some of the workshops were built half underground. The finished material is also used in the making of traditional clothing like the *burnous* as well as tents. These, like the reed mats, produced in the same small-scale fashion, are part of the Cap Bon tradition. There are many *kouttab* and *zaouia*, indicating the importance of Beni Khiar as a long established centre of Koranic learning.

Four kilometres from the town is a small attractive lake. It is long and narrow, but the water is clear and deep.

Natural gas has been located in the area of **Es Somaa**, 8 km north of Nabeul and at **Belli**, some 20 km west of Nabeul. A gas flare amidst the fields indicates production is underway.

Farming the Cap Bon

For those who like their figures, there are over 180,000 ha of arable land on the Cap Bon peninsula. The annual rainfall varies between 360 mm and 670 mm. Irrigation water used to be raised from wells by camels or donkeys, but today the few wells that remain are backed by eight dams and many hill lakes which provide a storage capacity of over 200 million cubic m.

In terms of national fruit and vegetable production, the Cap Bon in the 1990s was a major player, with the Korba region producing 90% of strawberries and the triangle formed by Menzel Bou Zelfa, Soliman and Beni Khalled accounting for 70% of citrus fruit, including the unique Maltaise juice oranges and the rare leem or bergamote. Grombalia, Bir Bou Regba and Bou Argoub account for 80% of table and wine grapes.

The Cap Bon also produces olives, almonds and market garden produce (early potatoes, fennel, carrots and broad beans) in vast quantities, making maximum use of its position between the capital and the tourist centres. Local markets as well as national markets play an important part. Cereals are also grown and there is some pasture for beef rearing.

Essentials

Nabeul does not have a vast range of hotels. Its big plus are the small, family-run pensions, situated for the most part down towards the Neapolis excavations and the Hammamet end of town. Some of these places have been going for years, building up a clientele by word of mouth rather than by working with tour companies. If you are really stuck for accommodation here, continue on to the Mrezga *zone touristique* between Nabeul and Hammamet, although none of the accommodation here will be very cheap.

Sleeping
■ *on map,*
page 172
Phone code: 72

B *Hotel Kheops*, Av Mohamed V, T286555, F286024, hotel.kheops@planet.tn Good restaurant, Olympic size pool, indoor pool, 300 rooms, a/c, bath, TV, phone, terrace, watersports, tennis, disco. Soundproofing in rooms none too good. **B** *Hotel Les Pyramides*, Av H Bourguiba, T285444, F287461. Large hotel with accommodation in 176 individual units, also 74 rooms, beach, pool, organized activities. Right on beach, an extension of the Kheops complex (you have access to its facilities). **B** *Nabeul Beach*, R du 9-Avril 1938, T286111, F286429, nabeul.beach@planet.tn 181 rooms, 96 individual accommodation units. Recently renovated.

B-C *Hotel Les Jasmins*, R Abou Kacem Chabbi, T285343, F285073. 53 rooms,188 beds, pool, restaurant, about 1 km in direction of Hammamet, a discrete, older hotel, comfortable, although needing a refit has a certain charm. Pleasant shaded terrace next to bar. Reservations essential in summer. **C** *Pension Les Oliviers*, R de Havana, off R Abou Kacem Chabbi, opposite *Hotel Les Jasmins*, T286865, pensionlesoliviers@yahoo.fr One of the oldest established family-run hotels. Highly recommended. People come back year after year. Reservations essential for summer. **C** *Hotel Fakir*, opposite the Roman remains of Neapolis, T285477, F287616. Late-1990s hotel, small, pleasant 2-5 bedded rooms off a large spiral staircase. 500m from beach, very welcoming owner prefers individual travellers to groups.

D *Les Hafsides*, 4 R Sidi Maaouia, T285823. Just off Av Habib Thameur near the 'orange monument'. 16 beds, toilet in rooms, shared bath, small Tunisian style hotel close to town centre. **D** *Pension Mustapha*, Av Habib el Karma on corner with Av Ali Belhouane, T222262, 286729. 5 rooms with wash-basin, shared toilet and bath, no restaurant, clean Tunisian style hotel close to the souk. Street-facing rooms

Cap Bon Peninsula

noisy.**F** *Pension el Habib*, Av Habib Thameur, T287190. On the outskirts of Nabeul coming from Hammamet, beach, very clean, communal bath/toilets, all rooms with handbasin, roof terrace, main road slightly noisy. **E** *Pension Les Roses*, R Farhat Hached, T285570. Clean, well kept, central (the main plus point), toilets and showers (extra) on landing. A bit gloomy but very reasonable for the price.

Camping *Hotel les Jasmins*, T285343. On the road to Hammamet, 1 km out of town, hot/cold water, shop, restaurant, in orange grove, 1 ha under shade, prices 1.9Dt per person (under 18 1.3Dt), tent 1.3Dt, caravan 1.5Dt, car 1.1Dt, electricity 1.7Dt, shower 2Dt. Access to pool of neighbouring hotel.

Youth hostels *Auberge de jeunesse*, 2 km from town centre at the end of Av Mongi Slim, by the beach, T285547. 56 beds, (closed Feb?), around 5dt per night. Often full in summer, small dormitory rooms sleeping 8 in bunk beds, no hot showers. Also *Maison des Jeunes*, Av Taieb Mehiri, T286689, F221401, 80 beds, clean, meals available, don't expect hot water.

Eating
● *on map, page 173*

Nothing very special in the way of restaurants here, apart from the pricey *Slovenia* (see below), which has nevertheless had mixed reports.

Expensive *L'Olivier*, Av Hédi Chaker, close to the intersection with Av H Bourguiba, T286613. Décor and food delightful, excellent service. *Slovenia*, T285343, perhaps the best address, south of the town centre on the main rd to Hammamet just before the turn-off to the *Hotel les Jasmins*. Chef Rafik Tlatli is one of Tunisia's most innovative chefs, author of a fine coffee-table book of recipes entitled *Saveurs de Tunisie* (Tunis: Geste Editions, 1998). The hotel behind the restaurant has a pleasant shaded terrace bar where the locals come for a drink.

Mid-range *Au Bon Kif*, Av Habib Thameur, T222783. One of the better eateries, specialiszing in seafood. Can work out expensive. *Le Corail*, Av H Bourguiba, T223342. *La Rodinella*, 116 Av H Bourguiba on corner of Av Farhat Hached, pleasant, central. *La Rotonde*, T285782, Av Taieb Mehiri, another seafood place.

Cheap *Les Arcades*, opposite the *Galerie Gasteli*, on Av H Bourguiba, near the main *jarre* roundabout. Slow service, small dry pizzas – avoid. *Karim* snack bar in central square. For snacks in summer, there are places along the beach.

Cafés and ice-cream The main 'traditional' café in central Nabeul, the place for meeting people, is *Er Rachidia*, Av Habib Thameur on corner of Av H Bourguiba, the place for people-watching, being located several steps above street level, tables on covered area overlooking busy street. Stop here after your pottery-shopping spree. *Gelateria Coky*, next to the restaurant *Les Trois Etoiles* on Av Hédi Chaker. Italian-run, nice service. **NB** their *nocciola* (hazelnut ice-cream) is particularly good. Another possibility is *Le Malouf*, Av H Bourguiba, close to post office. Small Tunisian style café.

Festivals **Nabeul International Fair**, Av H Bourguiba (early Apr each year), details from T285374, F223242.

Shopping You might visit the rather sleepy *ONAT/SOCOPA* shop on Av Thameur to see the usual range of Tunisian products and check the prices – no pressure, just wander. The traditional green/yellow pottery is a good buy. There is a modern shopping centre, opposite the hospital on Av Habib Thameur, where you'll find camera film, clothes and suncreams. There is no médina in Nabeul, the shopping areas along Av Farhat Hached and through to Av Habib el Karma taking its place. Good selection of pots at *Céramiqe Slama*, 190 Av Farhat Hached. Look out for the big decorative plates, a very good buy. Also on Av Farhat Hached, try *Boutique 101* for a good selection of traditional slippers and spangly oriental costumes. The better quality shops and restaurants are found on Av Habib Bourguiba between Av Farhat Hached and Pl du 7 Novembre, where a full grown Norfolk Island pine tree sprouts out of a decorative ceramic pot forming the middle of the roundabout.

Sport

Adjacent to Nabeul the port of Béni Khiyar has moorings for 15 pleasure boats, with a depth of 1-3 m. All facilities are available.

Transport

Local Car hire: *Avis*, *Hotel Kheops*, T286555. *Hertz*, Av Thameur, T285327. *Europacar*, Av Farhat Hached, T287085. *Express Car*, Av Habib Thameur, T287014. *Méditerranée Car*, Nabeul Centre, T224835, and Av Farhat Hached, T221073. *Next Car*, Av H Bourguiba, T272355. *Nova Rent*, Av H Bourguiba, T222072. *Rent a Car*, Av Thameur, T286679. *Royal Car*, R Sidi Maaouia, T287333. **Taxi**: *Allô Taxi*, 222444.

Long distance Train: There is 1 train a day to Tunis 0545, otherwise the nearest trains are at Bir Bou Regba reached by bus or louage. Information T285054. **Bus**: the bus station is on Av Thameur (information T285261). Times given here change according to season and demand. There are frequent buses to **Hammamet** starting at 0530, **Tunis** (every hr, sometimes 2 an hr), **Zaghouan**, **Sousse** starting at 0645, **Mahdia** starting at 0730 and **Kairouan** (direct at 0600, 0800 and 1215, but check). Buses frequent from Nabeul to **Kélibia** and **El Haouaria** with final departure from Kélibia 1830. **Louages**: Av Farhat Hached, T286081. **Taxi**: *Allô Taxi Express*, T222444.

Tour operators

Delta Travel, 156 Av H Bourguiba, T271077, F271177. *Eagle International Travel*, 58 Av H Bourguiba, T223355, F223263. *Leader Tours*, Nabeul Centre, T271626, F271166. *Salama Voyages*, 18 Av H Bourguiba, T285804, F287043. *Sept Voyages*, 10 R de l'Oranger, T286998, F286998.

Directory

Airline offices *Tunisair* 178 Av H Bourguiba, T286200/775. **Banks** Most banks are on Av H Bourguiba and Av Farhat Hached, in the town centre. The *STB* has 24-hr ATM. **Communications** Internet: *Publinet* on Av Habib Thameur, opposite R de l'Espoir, T230032, almost opposite the *Socopa* artisanat centre. Open till 2100. Also on 53 R des Palmiers, large rooftop sign clearly visible from train station, T232936. **Post:** main office, Av H Bourguiba, open Mon-Sat 0800-1800, also Av Mongi Slim. **Medical services Regional Hospital**, Av Mohammed Tahar Mâamouri, T285633. *Clinique Les Violettes*, Route d'Hammamet, T286668, F286240. *Clinique Ibn Rochd*, R Mongi Slim, T286668, F286240. **Night pharmacy**, Av Habib Thameur, opposite hospital, T287542. **Useful addresses Police:** Av Bourguiba, T285474; **Garde nationale**, Av Taieb Mehri, T286153.

Cap Bon Peninsula

Hammamet الحمامات

Phone code: 72
Colour map 2, grid C5
Population: 100,000

Tourism in Tunisia would not be where it is today without Hammamet. In the first half of the 20th century, visitors discovered a tiny médina, the Mediterranean lapping its honey-coloured walls. Fishermen pulled their boats up on fine white sand, every local family had a shady orchard. The microclimate of Hammamet was discovered by European aesthetes in the 1930s. They indulged themselves with homes of cool vaulted rooms and gardens of cypresses, orange trees and plunge pools. The first tourist hotels were built in this spirit, their silhouettes carefully concealed behind the tree line. The 1990s saw new construction on an unprecedented scale. Bed capacity will be more than doubled in the new southern hotel zone. Hammamet is now a sprawling town. The microclimate and the beach are still the same, however. In odd corners, traces of the delicate simplicity of old Hammamet have survived the convulsion of mass property development.

Ins and outs

Getting there
See Transport, page 187, for further details

Hammamet, located 65 km from Tunis, is easily accessible by public transport, there being buses, louages and trains. If you arrive on a package, there will be a fairly quick transfer (say 75 mins maximum) from Tunis-Carthage airport. Buses come into the new bus station at Baraket Sahel, 5 km from Hammamet, while some louages come into a station centrally located at R Mongi Slim. The nearest train station is at Bir Bou Regba, a 4 km taxi ride from the centre.

Getting around
There are 5 main tourist areas in Hammamet: the M'rezga Zone Touristique Nord, north of the town; the town centre proper centering on the médina (hotels here include the *Alya*, the *Bel Azur*, the *Bellevue*, the *Yasmina* and the *Résidence Hammamet*); another *zone touristique* southwest of the médina with the oldest hotels (*Les Orangers, Le Miramar* etc); the Zone Touristique Sud (*Hotel Sheraton* etc); and finally the new Hammamet-Sud development, aka Hammamet Yasmine (including the marina). Taxis are the way to get from zone to zone. Children will probably like the 'Noddy train'.

Hammamet overview

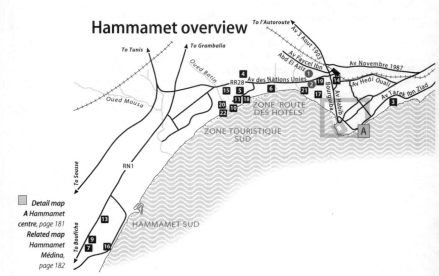

Detail map
A Hammamet
centre, page 181
Related map
Hammamet
Médina,
page 182

Cap Bon Peninsula

The tourist information office is at 32 Av H Bourguiba, by the new shopping complex in the town centre, T280423. **Tourist information**

History

Hammamet was known as **Pupput** to the Romans. It was a stopping point on the Roman road which linked Carthage to Hadrumetum. The city developed as a result of the expansion of agriculture and maritime trade and also thanks to the generous sponsorship of a wealthy patron, Salvius Julianus. Subsequent 'visitors' included the Sicilians, the Spaniards and the Ottoman Turks. **Orientation: central Hammamet**

Today Hammamet is one of the leading tourist resorts in Tunisia, along with Sousse and Djerba. In the 1950s, there was little more than a sleepy village adjoining a beautiful beach. There were two hotels. The locals prospered quietly on agriculture, fishing, crafts including weaving and embroidery and the production of orange flower essence. Elegant Italians and others of taste acquired discreet homes in the ramparts of the médina or in the citrus groves.

Tourism took off in the 1970s. One of Hammamet's first hotels, the *Phénicia*, was designed by presidential architect Cacoub. A first batch of hotels, including *Les Orangers*, *Le Miramar* and *Le Fourati*, adopted the garden-hotel concept, with the buildings concealed in extensive grounds. In the 1980s, a second major tourist zone was launched at M'rezga, north of Hammamet. The latest phase, Hammamet Sud, constructed on a salt marsh, is on an entirely new scale. A four-lane boulevard separates the beach from the first line of hotels, all 5-star. Glitz is the order of the day, the lobbies are decorated in styles ranging from the Louis-Farouk to an indeterminate marble opulence. The centrepiece of the zone will be an artificial mini-médina. The long term results of this development remain to be seen – notably on the beach. One effect may be to create a demand for the simpler and more central older hotels, which, suitably upgraded, may be tempted to move upmarket.

Hammamet now welcomes tourists in their thousands. On a bedrock of conservative Cap Bon rural life, a Euro-structure of mass tourism has grown up. The days of the peaceful fishing village are long gone. There is a German brewery across the car park from the minaret, and on summer evenings,

Cap Bon Peninsula

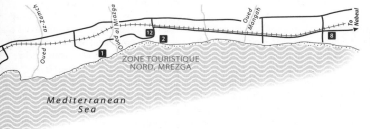

Mediterranean Sea

ZONE TOURISTIQUE NORD, MREZGA

N

0 metres 200
0 yards 200

■ **Sleeping**
1 Abou Nawas
2 Al Manar
3 Bel Azur
4 Bennila
5 Citronniers
6 Continental
7 Dar Zakarya
8 Fekir
9 Flora Park
10 Fourati
11 Hammamet
12 Hammamet Club
13 Hostellerie L'Ecrin
14 Kacem Centre
15 Les Orangers
16 Mehari
17 Milano
18 Miramar
19 Olympia
20 Phénicia
21 Résidence de la Paix
22 Sheraton

● **Eating**
1 Dar Lella
2 Sidi Slim

central Hammamet is as gridlocked as downtown Tunis. The town now stretches over 2 km north inland and some 7 km along the coast.

Sights

The Villa Sébastian & the International Culture Centre

Driving through Hammamet, here and there you will see studded doors set in whitewashed walls over which the greenery spills, indications that here is an upscale home enshaded by giant eucalyptus and gnarly fig trees. You can, however, visit the former villa of millionaire aesthete **Georges Sebastian**. In 1959, the property was bought by the state and made into an International Cultural Centre (see below). The caretaker will show you round. The lounge is worth seeing with its long table and simple wrought-iron chairs and the walls hung with contemporary Tunisian paintings. The novel four-seater sunken bath is the shape of a cross (presumably mixed bathing – all very avant-garde) rather like four hip baths. The caretaker will operate the water system. (A similar style of bath can be seen at Kerkouane.) The rather small guest bedroom can be viewed. Here Von Arnim, Rommel, Montgomery and Churchill were accommodated according to the fluctuations of the Second World War, no doubt making maximum use of the beach in between bouts of moving counters around on a large map of North Africa. ■ *0830-1800 daily except Mon. 1Dt, photography 1Dt.*

In summer, you might also try to get to a show at the open-air theatre built in the grounds. The annual **International Festival**, held here in July/August, had ambitions to be a summer showcase for the performing arts, with dance, theatre and music all on view. The theatre was the brainchild of Cecyl Hourani, one of President Bourguiba's advisors, and Ali Ben Ayed, the country's leading actor and descendant of a noble family. Bourguiba, who had enjoyed amateur dramatics in his youth, approved the project, and the theatre, Greek and open-air in design, went up in the 1960s. In its heyday, the festival attracted North African dramatists like Saddiki and Kaki, and productions by Peter Brook, Littlewood and Béjart. Ali Ben Ayed staged *Othello* there in Arabic, playing the title-role. Unfortunately, Ben Ayed died before his time, and the festival rather lost direction. Today, you might catch summer performances by raï singers like Faudel. Other recent performers have included Césaria Evora, the barefoot diva of Cap Vert, and the odd jazz band.

Central Hammamet

The modern town has kept a little of its charm, even though changes are going ahead apace. The most recent victim was the one time Hotel de France, a fine 1920s building with a history. Handily opposite the médina there is a commercial centre (you will find the banks with ATMs (the BIAT) and a supermarket here). The médina, surrounded by its walls and lying adjacent to the sea, manages to maintain a certain mystique. The **beach** continues to be an attraction; to the east, from the cemetery up towards the hotel region it is of fine white sand, some 30 m wide with safe bathing. Escape from the tourist shops and walk around the small back streets. On the beach, there might be some fishermen picturesquely mending their nets, but fishing no longer has the importance of earlier days and some of the boats on the beach are more attractive than they are seaworthy.

Stepping off the main street, Avenue de la République, for a glimpse of the real Hammamet will reveal a host of small workshops and food shops, selling everything you could need from soap to live chickens. On the main streets, there are eclectically styled low-rise buildings; new villas are set among the older run-down dwellings off the main roads. Black-painted studs are used to make geometric designs on the doors; some of the motifs resemble old-fashioned country women's tattoos and symbols found on flat-weave textiles.

The médina

The small (but perfectly shaped) médina is the main landmark in Hammamet, built right on the beach. Originally constructed in 904, frequently damaged and restored, the walls protect the Great Mosque and narrow, winding streets. Near the kasbah these contain numerous stalls intent on attracting the tourists. The rest of the médina is made up of private dwellings; the impressive doors set into the otherwise blank walls are an attraction in their own right. The most exclusive homes tend to be on the sea-facing side of the médina – no longer do waves lap the walls as a walkway has been constructed.

The médina contains many reminders of the holy men who spent time in Hammamet. Among them is **Sidi Bou Hadid** (12th century) who may have come from Morocco, perhaps Sakiet el Hamra. It is said that shortly before he died he instructed his family to put his corpse into a coffin and throw it into the sea. He wanted the waves and currents to decide on his final resting place. His tomb was to be built where his coffin was washed ashore. Legend has it that the sea spirits built his tomb by the town walls, from where he can keep watch over the Gulf of Hammamet. For this reason he has become the particular saint of the fishermen who make offerings to him and in times of real danger call on his assistance. He is said to be buried in the médina in the shrine which bears his name, right under the ramparts. Like the former entrance to the shrine of Sidi Bou Saïd in Tunis, this today functions as a very popular café, the romantic place to watch the sun go down over the sea.

The Dar Hammamet in the médina is a **Museum of Traditional Dress**. Not really a museum, more of a half-converted house. The three rooms have an interesting collection of traditional female clothing and wedding garments.

Dar Hammamet

Cap Bon Peninsula

Hammamet centre

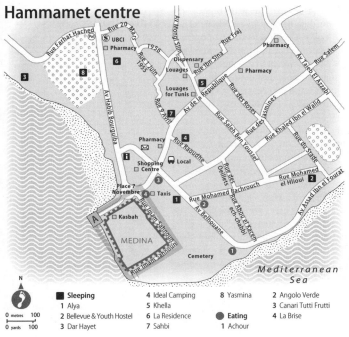

Detail map
A Hammamet Médina,
page 182

Related map Hammamet overview,
page 178

N

0 metres 100
0 yards 100

■ **Sleeping**
1 Alya
2 Bellevue & Youth Hostel
3 Dar Hayet
4 Ideal Camping
5 Khella
6 La Residence
7 Sahbi
8 Yasmina

● **Eating**
1 Achour
2 Angolo Verde
3 Canari Tutti Frutti
4 La Brise

One room is set out as a bedroom. There are additional costumes in the cabinets. This is another place recommended for watching the sunset from the roof. ■ *0900-1700 daily. 1.5Dt adults, 0.5Dt children under 10. T281206. Enter from the square by the cemetery or follow the signs by the sea front.*

Great Mosque The Great Mosque is most easily reached through the gate from the market place from where the minaret can be seen. It is not outstanding, but is obvious by its white square tower where the upper part and just below the crenellations are covered with yellow tiles patterned in black. At ground level in the white wall there are several light-brown wooden doors set in a stone surround. On each is a clear message in four European languages to keep out.

Kasbah The Kasbah has ancient origins, as you might expect. It was first constructed between 893 and 904 under the Aghlabite Dynasty. The walls were recently restored, with lots of new pointing. The building you see today, filling the western corner of the médina, dates back to between 1463 and 1474 and was built while the Hafsids were in power. Its restored walls rise over the surrounding souvenir shops. There are some splendid views to the northwest over the the Gulf of Hammamet and the beach (and the garish shopping centre with its oversized signs) and to the southwest over the Mediterranean. The médina's walls practically rise out of the water. To the west you might pick out the Djebel Zaghouan (1,295 m). These views from the walkway and the battlements are certainly worth the 1Dt entrance fee (photography free). In the north corner of the kasbah is a squat tower on which there is a small café (there are many pleasanter places), while the inner courtyard is bare apart from a few trees which provide welcome shade in the summer. There are three cannon and several horse-drawn ploughs on display but no museum.

War memorial Next to the car park outside the médina, the tall white modern memorial, sweeping skywards, commemorates the dead of the Second World War. Adjacent to it, on the wall forming the boundary between the market place and the cemetery, is a high relief frieze depicting the horrors of war.

Ancient Pupput The ancient town of Pupput, a staging post on the road from Carthage to Hadrumetum (modern Sousse), has become a small archaeological site next to the *Hotel Samira Beach*. The remains are slight, but of importance. There are some fine late Roman mosaics here, and a good deal has been written about their hidden symbolism. ■ *Summer 0800-1300, 1500-1900 daily, winter 0830-1730, daily. 1dt.*

Related maps
Hammamet overview, page 178
Hammamet centre, page 181

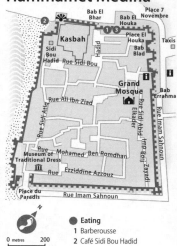

Hammamet Médina

Eating
1 Barberousse
2 Café Sidi Bou Hadid
3 La Médina

Cap Bon Peninsula

Essentials

Hammamet has few independent travellers, and there are few rock-bottom cheap places to stay. Having said that, the package market is fickle, and outside the high season it may be possible to pick up some very good deals indeed. It may be that with the doubling of its bed capacity, Hammamet has overreached itself, in which case there should be reasonable rates in some of the older hotels in need of a little refurbishment. Note however that by booking a package, you get a few days on a clean beach and a good base from which to explore Tunisia. Given the huge number of hotels at Hammamet, the following is just a selection.

Sleeping

Town centre **B** *Hotel Bel Azur*, Av Assad Ibn el Fourat, BP13 - 8050 Hammamet, T280544, F280275, www.orangers.com.tu About 2½ km north of town centre. 620 beds, located on the water's edge in extensive (12 ha) landscaped grounds, very high standard, all sports facilities available. **B** *Hotel Kacem Centre*, Av Habib Bourguiba, near train station, T279580, F279588. 67 rooms with 2-ring hob and fridge, crockery and utensils, 2 pools, roof terrace with BBQ, a/c, 800 m to private beach shared with *Yasmina*, restaurant, fitness centre. **B** *Hotel la Résidence*, 72 Av Habib Bourguiba, T280406, F280396. Slightly Moorish style, 184 rooms with 2-ring hob, fridge, and a few utensils and crockery, rooftop pool heated in winter, full a/c, restaurant, 10 mins from beach. Very central. **B** *Hotel Yasmina*, Av Bourguiba, T280022, F280593. Attractive early 1970s hotel. Small buildings in pleasant grounds with mature shade trees. Nice pool. Fine view over beach to the old town. Pleasant, slightly faded style. Central but peaceful location. Recommended.

■ *on map, page 181*
Budget travellers may have a hard time finding accommodation

C *Hotel Alya*, R Ali Belhaouane, T280218, F282365. Central, on street leading from *Canari Tutti Frutti* towards sea. Very clean, half the rooms look over the médina, the others over a street, roof terrace, bar, 300 m from beach. Very good option in low season, but bring your long johns as the heating isn't too reliable. **C** *Hotel Khella*, Av de la République, T283900. 10 mins walk from médina, hence quiet, 71 rooms with bath, a/c, heating, good, clean, modern hotel. **C** *Milano*, T280768, R des Fontaines beds. A small pension type place not too far from the beach west of the centre. **C** *Hotel Olympia*, Av des Nations Unies, T280622, F283142. 36 rooms with shower and heating, no restaurant but many in vicinity, a clean, tidy hotel, close to station on the busy main rd leading to the main southern hotel zones. Avoid street-facing rooms. **C** *Hotel Bellevue*, Blvd Ibn el Fourat, T281121, F283156. Not the most attractive of buildings but close to beach and médina, clean rooms, most with view. **D** *Hotel Sahbi*, town centre, T280807. 200 m from beach, pleasant large rooms, some with views.

Close to the centre (Hammamet Plage/R de Nevers) **AL** *Dar Hayet*, 10 mins' walk along beach from Kasbah, T282856, F283399. Décor outstanding, comfort superb. Pool small, no garden, but you are right on the beach. For the moment, perhaps the only establishment in Hammamet that can justifiably be termed a *hôtel de charme*. Expensive though, with prices ranging from 120Dt to 230Dt according to season. **A** *Hotel Miramar*, R de Nevers, T280344, F280586, 3 km west of town centre. Gardens lead on to beach, all facilities expected, this is one of the original tourist hotels that has recently been extended: make sure to get a room in the newer part as those in the older part are showing their age (this part only **B** standard) and the a/c is noisy.

■ *on map, page 178*

B *Hotel Continental*, T280220, F280409. Right on the beach, a/c, with bath, terrace, restaurant, bar, covered pool, TV, shop, boutiques, sauna, fitness room, tennis, watersports, shares with adjacent *Hotel Parc Plage*, all facilities. Good bargains available out of season. **B** *Hotel Fourati*, R de Nevers, T280388, F280508, 3 km west of town centre. Enter through

Cap Bon Peninsula

gardens to reception, gardens lead down to beach, 772 beds, all facilities, 1 heated indoor pool, 2 outdoor pools. **B** *Hotel Hammamet*, R de Nevers, T280366, F282105, 3 km west of town centre. Of high standard but does not front the beach which is a 5-min walk, 674 rooms, all services include a/c and heating, 1 heated indoor pool, 1 outdoor pool. Too little garden on this overbuilt site. **B** *Hotel Les Orangers/Hotel Les Orangers Beach Resort*, R de Nevers, T280144, F281077, www.orangers.com.tu 766 beds in typical tourist hotel including indoor and outdoor pools. **B** *Bennila*, T280356. Simple pension not far from Centre culturel international – coming from Hammamet, turn left after the CCI and bank, *Bennila* is on your right. Small, clean, popular place with a swimming pool. Short walk to beach. **B** *Résidence de la Paix*, off the Corniche Rd, T283400, F2828710. Self-catering – apartment for 2 in summer, 75Dt a night. Unattractive lawn area at the back, minute 1st-floor pool. Play area for kids. 50 m from beach. **C** *Les Citronniers*, R de Nevers, Route des Hotels, by *Bennila*, T281650, F282601, hotel.lescitronniers@planet.tn Started off as a tiny place and has expanded over the years, now has 60 rooms. Modern, very close to beach, barbecue, drinks, food on the beach. Disadvantage? No views, often full with groups in season, tiny pool.

■ on map, page 178 **Zone Touristique Nord (M'rezga)** **A** *Hotel Abou Nawas*, T281344, F281089. The usual good hotel product from the local Abou Nawas. Indoor pool, gardens etc. All a bit lacking in soul. On the beach. **A** *Hotel Al Manar*, T281333, F280772. 200 rooms, 6 floors, a/c, 2 pools, 5 tennis courts, banks, shops, restaurants. **A-B** *Hotel Hammamet-Club*, T281882, F281670. 337 rooms on 2 floors, a/c, splendid beach, indoor pool complex, outdoor Olympic-size pool, many activities, good food, large rooms facing the sea.

■ on map, page 178 **Zone Touristique Sud** **A** *Hotel Phénicia*, Av Moncef Bey, T226331, F280337. Closed for refurbishment in early 2002, will no doubt reopen as a very luxurious place. Originally designed by former presidential architect Cacoub in the late 1960s, and once somewhat isolated, 7 km west of Hammamet. 14 ha of garden fronting on to the beach, 370 rooms including suites, all facilities plus indoor heated pool which connects to outside pool, also separate outside pool, luxurious reception lounge. Very highly recommended in its price range. **A** *Sheraton*, T225555, F227301, Av Moncef Bey. Has a very good name with expatriates. Large, simply furnished rooms in grounds next to the beach. Usual water-based activities on offer.

■ on map, page 178
Note that many of the
hotels here are a long
way from the beach
and you will have at
least one main road to
cross, if not two **Hammamet-Sud** (Hammamet-Yasmine, a new zone of truly gigantesque proportions) This is the latest addition to Hammamet's hotel zones. Be warned: construction works on the marina and further hotels mean that building will be in progress until at least 2003. The area is too new for the hotels to have mature grounds. To get to the centre you will need to take taxis. Prefer the older hotels in Hammamet-Plage. **AL** *Hasdrubal Thalassa*, T248800. A very big hotel. If you have the money to pay their prices, then you probably rent Caribbean islands for your holidays anyway. Prefer one of the less pretentious places nearer to Hammamet. **A** *Hotel Flora Park*, Hammamet Sud, T227727 F226601, hotel.florapark@planet.tn Decorated by the same team as the *Dar Hayet*. Elegant, part of the Spanish *Tryp Hotels* chain. One of the best if you are going to stay in this part of Hammamet, but you have 2 main roads to cross to get to the beach. **A** *Hotel Mehari*, T249155. Large 5-star hotel on the seafront rd which feels like a multi-storey city-centre hotel. Too formal to be a relaxing beach hotel, though might be good for small conferences. All the usual facilities. Tiny indoor pool and small curvy rooftop pool. Kids' play area but not much garden. **B** *Hostellerie L'Ecrin*, T248465, F227375, a/c. Despite being some way from the beach, this is one of the most attractive hotels in Hammamet-Sud. The reception is elegant and if you are on a winter break, you'll find a log fire in the main bar. The rooms are on the small side, but nicely decorated, a/c. Recommended. **B** *Hotel Dar Zakarya*, T248500, F248551, 46 rooms. Pleasant small hotel next

Cap Bon Peninsula

to the *Hotel Flora Park*. Has a fair-sized pool and nice bar. The restaurant *Le Clos du Safran* had a good name when it opened. Disadvantage: 2 main roads to cross to get to the beach.

Next to the autoroute C *Hotel Samaris*, 6 km from town on the P1 road to Tunis, T226353. Family-run hotel and campsite to the west of town but convenient after coming off the motorway. Don't be put off by the approach for once inside there is a warm welcome from the owner. Traditional décor in reception. To the right is the comfortable small restaurant while straight ahead is the terrace (meals served). The centrepiece is an ancient olive press found on the site. The 20 rooms off courtyard, near main building, are simply furnished with twin beds, a/c, heating, shower and wc. There are 3 studios which sleep 4 people and have cooking facilities at 50Dt per day. The thick stone walls make this a rarity: a quiet hotel. **Camping** Adjacent to *Samaris* in 2 ha enclosed site, electricity, toilets and showers, shares the pool. Fees 3Dt per person; 1.5Dt per car and per tent; 2.5Dt per caravan. Beach is 5 mins by car.

Apartments for rent Try the villa opposite the *Hotel Alya* (see above). Also, look out for signs *appartement/studios à louer* on the R de la Corniche.

Camping *Ideal Camping*, 34 Av de la République, T280302. Adequate, restaurant, electric hook-ups, shaded area, book in summer, tent 2.5Dt, car 2.5Dt, person 1.5Dt per night. **Youth hostel** T280440. 100 beds, meals, central location, beside *Hotel Bellevue*.

Hammamet has but a handful of really classy places to eat, the sort where you start with a large gin and tonic on a wonderful terrace overlooking the sea. There are plenty of pizzerias, however, and a reasonable meal with wine can be had in the restaurants in the Centre Commercial across the roundabout from the médina.

Eating
■ *on maps, pages 178, 181 and 182*

Expensive *Restaurant Achour*, T280140. Central, R Ali Belhouane, once upon a time, the best restaurant in Hammamet, a reputation which has slipped in recent years. Still, the garden area is attractive, and upmarket foreigners summering in Hammamet will eat here at least once a week. *Aquarium*, Av des Nations Unies, opposite *Hotel des Charmes*, T282449. Recently renovated. *La Cupola*, Av du Koweit, T281138. *Dar Lella*, R Patrice Lumumba, T280871. Speciality *musli allouche*, oven-baked lamb. A stylish place once upon a time. Small garden area – a little overpriced. *Dar Sidi*, Centre Khayem, T289985. *La Pergola*, upstairs at the back of the busy shopping centre opposite the médina. Perhaps the best in this central area, T280993. *Le Pomodoro*, T281254, downtown Hammamet, near the palm-tree esplanade. Vastly overrated, small portions. *La Scala*, T280768, the Italian restaurant of the *Pension Milano*. Candlelit dining, excellent pasta. Recommended.

Mid-range *Angolo Verde*, on R Ali Belhaouane, near *Hotel Alya*, T262641. Good *plats du jour*, excellent pasta, good service. Nice terrace and fine ice-cream from the gelateria next door. Highly recommended. Same owners as the new *Buenavista* bar. *Restaurant Barberousse*, T282037, in the médina, great terrace with views and therefore very popular which means that service is not what it should be. *Le Grand Bleu*, downtown Hammamet, tables on beach under parasols. Access off main palm-tree esplanade next to *Syndicat d'initiative*. Lunchtime menu 10Dt. *La Médina*, in square near kasbah, T281728. Popular, large, get a table on the terrace if possible for a fine view over the médina, beach and esplanade, especially interesting on market day, use the entrance from the sea front – seafood salad 12Dt, royal couscous 7Dt. *Restaurant de la Poste*, central square, opposite the médina, T280023, has a nice terrace and views across to the fort. Can get very busy. *La Sirène*, Av Assad Ibn el Fourat, right on beach opposite sports stadium, 10-15 mins walk from town so quieter.

Cap Bon Peninsula

Cheap You could eat pretty cheaply, say 6Dt a head, by having just a simple main course at one of the restaurants in the shopping centre diagonally across the round-about from the médina. In same area, especially on Av de la République, there are various cheap eateries. In particular, try *La Brise*, T280073, on your right as you head up Av de la République away from médina. Cheerful, colourful tiled décor, stays open till about 2100. Next door is *Le Palmier Café Bar* (rough and ready). Coming in by train, you'll find cheap eateries close to the station on the av leading into the town centre.

Cafés & patisseries
■ *on maps, pages 181 and 182*

At some time during your stay in Hammamet, you will wind up sitting on the terrace of the *Canari Tutti Frutti* juice bar, at the junction of Av de la République and Av Ali Belhaouane. Look out for the patisserie next door. Try the *m'lebbes*, round mini-almond cakes with white icing. Just below the walls of the kasbah, next to the beach, is the *Café Sidi Bou Hadid*. Facing the square-faced central clock is the blokey *Café Hechiri*, its terrace shaded by mulberry trees. For ice-cream, you have *Le Tiramisù*, next to the *Restaurant Angolo Verde* on Av Ali Belhaouane. A very good address. As yet there are no small personable places in Hammamet-Sud. However, expect to find some attractive places round the brand-new marina.

Bars & nightclubs

Most of the larger hotels have nightclubs, none of which have much spirit to them. The happening bars and clubs are located mainly to the south of Hammamet, on the road to Sousse, in the direction of the Route des Hotels. Unless you have a hire car, you'll be taking a taxi to get there. Both *Le Ranch Club*, Av Moncef Bey, and the *Manhattan* attract a young crowd. Nearby is the *Buenavista Social Club*, complete, as its name suggests, with posters of Che Guevara and other Cuban features. Popular – same management as the *Angolo Verde*. *Le Guitoun*, although a little grotty, is another happening address. The place to be seen for the *jeunesse dorée* in summer is *Le Calypso*, also Av Moncef Bey. Still close to Hammamet Sud, but moving heavily downmarket, try the *Garsa* (bar) on the main GP1 (Route de Sousse), which attracts a mixed clientele of long-distance lorry drivers and the odd Italian tourist.

Entertainment

Cinema In shopping centre, performances at 1500 and 2100. Prices 2Dt and 1.5Dt. **Hammam** Turkish bath (Bain Maure) near the Great Mosque in the médina. **Theatre** *Centre Culturel International*, T280656, summer only, concerts and very occasionally plays in the open-air theatre during the annual arts festival.

Shopping
Market day: Thu

Apart from the obvious trinket places in the médina, there are not a whole lot of things to buy in Hammamet, so your credit cards can sleep easy. The following may be of some use:

In the médina *Fella*, a fashion boutique in a rather 1970s sense of the term. Easily found on the main square in the médina, part of a converted house. *Fella* (Arabian 'jasmine') was Madame Couture-Caftan back in the heady days of Hammamet's take-off as a tourist destination. Look out for the black-and-white enlargements of old fashion shows. Pick up something pricey to waft around the hotel in. There are a few bits of local embroidered clothing on display. Shop also has nice cotton beach towels. (There is a second *Fella* outlet on the Pl Pasteur, Tunis-Belvédère, currently closed for renovation).

Elsewhere *Khamsa*, small eclectic junk-cum-postcard shop on Av Bourguiba, almost opposite the primary school as you walk towards the *Hotel Résidence*. Can turn up some interesting things. *Er Rayhane*, Av des Nations-Unies, T261914. Not far from the **Centre culturel international**. Specializes in wrought iron (not easy to get on the plane). Also stocks large cotton throws and some ceramics.

Books There is a reasonable bookshop in the shopping centre, the *Librairie Boudhina*, diagonally across from the médina, selling informative books in many European languages. Handy newsagents here too.

All watersports available, also horse- and camel-riding, golf, tennis, and go-karting. **Sports** Ask at any hotel. *Yasmine Golf Course*, T227001, F226722, 18 holes. *Citrus Golf Course*, T226500, F226400, 2 18-hole courses, par 72, 28-30Dt per day. See Golf, page 55, for further details.

Carthage Tours, R Dag Hammarskjold, T281926, F281166. *Hammamet Travel Service*, R **Tour operators** Dag Hammarskjold, T280193, F281936. *Tourafrica*, R Dag Hammarskjold, T280446, F278225. *Tunisia Explorer*, Av des Nations Unies, T283275, F282766. *Tunisian Travel Service*, Av des Nations Unies, T280040. *Visit Tunisia*, 48 Av du Koweit, T287427, F283120.

Local Car hire: *Avis*, Route de la Gare, T280164. *Europacar*, Av des Nations Unies, **Transport** T280146. *Hertz*, Av des Hotels, opposite *Hotel Miramar*, T280187. *Intercar*, Av des Nations Unies, T280423. *Topcar*, Av des Nations Unies, T281247. *Tri Car*, Av Habib Bourguiba, T283580, F283576. **Cycle hire**: 2Dt per hr or 10Dt per day from *Hotel Kacem* Centre. **Taxi**: yellow taxi rank in front of the médina. Also note reliable *Allô Taxi* service, T222444.

Long distance Train: The direct service from Tunis has been reduced in recent years *See Footnotes,* to a couple of trains each day from Tunis. Otherwise get off at nearest station on main *page 491, for* line, **Bir Bou Regba**, for services north to Tunis and south to Sousse, Sfax and Gabès, *train timetables* and pick up a shuttle train to Hammamet. By bus or louage, Bir Bou Regba is a 4-km ride from central Hammamet. Information T280174. The usual dumb 'Noddy train' provides a shuttle service from the hotels to the town centre on a leave-when-full basis. (Hold on to the kids.) At slack times it waits by the médina for customers. If you get off at Bir Bou Regba, you continue by bus or taxi (taxi fare to Hammamet about 4Dt). The 2nd class train ticket to Tunis is 4.6Dt. Take care at Bir Bou Regba as the name is marked on the station building but not on the platform – and cannot therefore be seen by passengers on the train.(This may have been rectified.)

Bus: The main *gare routière* (bus and louage station) used to be close to the médina, on Av de la République, a few metres up from *Tutti Frutti* on the same side of the street. It has recently been moved out to Baraket Sahel, T227711, 5 km away, so you'll probably need to take a taxi there – taxi from bus station to Hammamet-Centre, slightly under 4Dt. Frequent bus departures for **Tunis, Sousse** and **Nabeul**. Fewer departures (1 a day) **Kélibia** and **Haouaria**. All journeys to **Korbous** are via Soliman; to Monastir and Mahdia. 4 buses a day for **Zaghouan** (and El Fahs). The **louage** station is on Av Mongi Slim, a left off Av de la République as you head away from the centre.

Banks Money can be changed in the big hotels or the banks in the centre of town. **Directory** There are banks with ATMs on Av H Bourguiba, also a *BIAT*, on Av de la République not far from the post office. There is a bank in the médina, in the square by the kasbah, which is generally open Sun when all other banks are closed. **Communications Internet**: near the railway station on Av Bourguiba, also on Av de la République, about 200 m after the *Hotel Mirage* heading away from the centre. **Post Office**: Av de la République, T250598. Mon-Sat 0730-1230 and 1700-1900 in summer, winter 0800-1200 and 1500-1800. **Hairdresser** Short back and sides at *Bahles*, near *Hotel Alya*, on R du Stade, close to *Angolo Verde* restaurant. **Medical services Emergencies:** opposite the Casino on the road to Nabeul, T282333. **Chemist**: Av de la République. The night pharmacy is on same street, opposite *Hotel Mirage*, T280876/257. **Hospital**: in the town-centre, T280136. **Places of worship Catholic**: 13 R du Lycée, off R du Stade, adjacent to college, marked Eglise

Catholique in ceramic tiles. The church, built in traditional Arab style, is only open for service Sat 1700 and Sun 1100, but the tree-shaded garden and bench seats are available at all times. Contact the priest at Grombalia, T255232, in winter and Hammamet, T280865, in summer. Protestant services are also held here. **Useful Addresses** Police: Av Habib Bourguiba, T280027. **Toilets:**If in the médina at Hammamet, useful loos at the *Café Sidi Bou Hdid*, also *Canari Tutti Frutti*.

Around Hammamet

Inland from Hammamet, to the west and south, are a number of easily reached villages and Roman sites which are definitely worthwhile if you have your own transport. **Zaghouan** *(see previous chapter) is a short bus ride away, while you could easily take in the villages of* **Hammam Jedidi**, **Jéradou** *and* **Zriba** *(see also previous chapter), or, more ambitiously, the* **Kène** *craft village (good textile collection), north of Bou Ficha, the pleasant Roman site of* **Phéradi Maius**, *and, most spectacularly,* **Takrouna** *on its rocky outcrop.* **Enfida** *has a museum with a few finds from the region.*

The white villages: Bou Ficha, Takrouna, Sidi Khélifa and Sidi Jedidi

For Le Corbusier, whitewash was as old as human buildings. Right from the earliest times, people used lime-wash for their homes, creating a clean environment and a pleasing aesthetic effect. In the villages of the Tunisian coast, lime was used to good effect on the barrel vaults used to roof the little rectangular houses. In villages south of Hammamet, you can see some good examples of Tunisian rural building, not all (as yet) disfigured by imported reinforced-concrete post and slab technology.

Getting to the 'white villages' of the hinterland of Hammamet is slow without your own transport. Perhaps **Takrouna** is the best, although **Zriba** (see previous chapter) is well worthwhile, and there is a possibility of overnighting at the springs of Hammam Zriba.

Kène craft village If you are driving, take the GP1 south of Hammamet towards **Bou Ficha**. Without going into the town, you will come to the white buildings of the Kène craft village on your right, behind a line of eucalyptus trees. The word *kène* means 'was' in Arabic. Here the reference is *kène min zaman*, 'once upon a time', and the village, the brainchild of civil engineer Slah Smaoui, a man deeply attached to the region, houses craft workshops, museum displays and a restaurant-café (food nothing special). There is plenty of parking, and it will take you close on 45 minutes to look around thoroughly. On summer evenings, displays of local folklore with dinner under a tent are organized in an open area adjacent to the village. There may even be an authentic local lady under the tent to give you a *harkous* (henna-dot) pattern on your hand. ■ *T73252110, F73252112. 2Dt, under 15s free.*

Along with watching the various craftspeople, including weavers, if they are at work, the best part of the village is probably the textile collection, well displayed and representative of most regions of Tunisia. Here, without badgering, you can get a feel for what the country's flat-weave or *kelim* carpets are like. There are *mergoums*, too, and a fine collection of women's costumes, including tunics with elaborate silk appliqué work and lace and velvet waistcoats from Hammamet and Sousse. Appliqué sequin designs were another feature, appreciated in more 'modern' urban areas.

The Kène craft village is an almost unique example of private money going into a carefully put together heritage project. The old forms of the region's traditional architecture have been put to new use to good effect.

A 20-minute drive from Kène, and you are at **Sidi Khélifa**, where there are some pleasant Roman ruins and a model village, constructed by the Ministry of Public Works to plans by Smaoui. Start, however, with the Roman site, the former Phéradi Maius, where major excavations were first undertaken back in 1966. In 1972, the baths were brought to light. There is a triumphal arch and up on the hill the ruins of what might have been a temple, later transformed into a small fort. The stone-flagged forum, with what must have been tiny lock-up shops around it, is particularly atmospheric. There is also a nymphaeum, 'a temple of the waters'. Given the quality of the spring water, this is entirely understandable. Bring a plastic bottle so you can fill up at the spring of Aïn Khélifa, close to the site, which you should be able to spot by the concrete well-head and the presence of someone filling up a container of some kind. The spring water has a beautiful, soft feel in the mouth. After the ruins, have a look at the new model village north of the original settlement. The aim was to show what could be done with traditional technology and, you have to admit, the project is rather successful. The proof, however, of such operations, is in the subsequent building. Can people still be persuaded to use the original, local technologies? Or would they really rather have houses with big balconies and individualized decorative features?

Sidi Khélifa & Phéradi Maius

After Sidi Khélifa, head back to the GP1 and down to **Enfida** (ex-Enfidaville), famous in the 19th century for various financial scandals surrounding the ownership of the great Enfida estate. In the mid-20th century, Enfida, and the neighbouring hill-crest village of Takrouna, were the scenes of some fierce fighting during the Second World War. You could take a quick look at the town museum, housed in the former French church, which has a collection of stelae and mosaics.

Takrouna
Colour map 1, grid B5

The main aim of being here, however, is to get to **Takrouna**, a village of vaulted houses perched in the region's best defensive position high above the plain. (To get there, take the Zaghouan turn-off; there may be a *nakl reefee* local minibus running up to the village.) Takrouna is now on the tourist trail, as it should be, given its beautiful location. The road climbs steeply up the rocky hill, past olive trees and prickly pears. From the top is a breathtaking view towards Djebel Zaghouan and the surrounding lands. As at Zriba and Jeradou, the main building of the village besides the mosque is the Zaouia of Sidi Abdel Kader, witness to the influence of the Kadiriya *tarika* or brotherhood last century.

The people of Takrouna make a living from agriculture and making the alfa mats used in the oil presses. As in other rural areas, the men may migrate to the building sites of the growing tourist towns, or work as seasonal labour in the hotels. At Takrouna, you may notice a number of blond children, as is the case in quite a number of Tunisia's remoter hill villages, once peopled almost exclusively by Berber stock.

From Takrouna, head north along the C133 to **Aïn Mdeker**, the extensive remains of ancient Mediccera (for enthusiasts only, to be honest), including remains of a Byzantine wall. For yet more (unspectacular) ruins, there is **Aïn Batria**, site of ancient Biia, 20 km north of Takrouna along the same road. The

North from Takrouna

Cap Bon Peninsula

best plan, however, is to head on up to **Zriba** (**Ezzriba**), described in the previous chapter. (Turn left for **Hammam Zriba**, have a look around, and then have a shot at getting some way to the old village of Zriba (Zriba El Alya, unsignposted), some 5 km up in the hills along the piste which turns left before the quarry as you come into Hammam Zriba.)

To return to Hammamet, you can continue on to **Zaghouan** (see previous chapter), about 40 km in all from Takrouna, and then head back coastwards along the C28 which will take you across farmland via Hammam Jedidi and Sidi Jedidi. (Zaghouan to Hammamet 35 km.) **Hammam Jedidi** is another place which has sprung up thanks to the hot springs. It is popular with Tunisian families, and if you are interested in doing a tour of minor spa towns it probably should be on your itinerary. Families rent or own small vaulted houses supplied with spring water.

Sidi Jedidi
Colour map 2,
grid C4

Sidi Jedidi, about 12 km west of Hammamet, is named after Cheikh Mohammed Jedidi, a holy man of Moroccan birth who lived in the region. He was favoured by Mohammed Ben Hassan, a Hafsid prince, who gave him 18,000 ha on which this hamlet stands. Looking round for something to fill out their day-excursions, tour operators began to offer a visit to 'a typical country market' at Sidi Jedidi. But with the presence of tourism, the nature of the market has changed. The rural communities have become increasingly prosperous, and no longer have to do so much self-provisioning. There is plenty of plastic and ordinary mass-produced clothing on offer.

Hammamet to Tunis: rolling countryside and Mussolini's villa

Heading northwest to Tunis from Hammamet there are two parallel roads, the A1 autoroute and the P1 trunk road. The A1 is a toll road, and the first *péage* is south of Tunis near Mornag (1Dt for an ordinary car). At Hammamet, there are two access points for the autoroute, one from the main road south, close to the GP1, the other from the Hammamet Nord zone. The A1 takes you through rolling countryside with views towards the distant mountains. Nearer peaks include **Djebel Bou Kornine** (Two Horns, 576 m) to the east, part of a national park, and **Djebel Ressas** (Mountain of Lead, 795 m), about halfway to Tunis. Do not relax your concentration as sheep still graze the verges. The GP1 provides a slower journey through small towns like Grombalia. Another option is to take the train, which runs beside the GP1 most of the way. As the carriages are high up, you have quite a good view of the vineyards near Grombalia.

Should you want to visit a 'natural' local market, then the Wednesday market at **Bou Argoub**, on the GP1, 17 km north of Hammamet, might do. There are no trinkets or souvenirs for tourists here. There are (as yet) no tourists. Many of the dwellings in this region and on towards Grombalia are Italian in style, with pitched roofs and clay tiles. The railway station buildings at Fondouk Djedid, Grombalia and Bou Argoub are typical country-town Italian, especially the latter with its two storeys surmounted by a sloping roof and its shuttered windows. The whitewashed walls and blue-painted woodwork give a local touch to a sleepy piece of Italian provincial building.

The unusual feature of this journey back up to Tunis is the presence of the **Villa du Zodiaque**, built for Benito **Mussolini** on a low rise to the west of the GP1, a few kilometres south of Grombalia. (Look out for signs to the Cité Hached, a small self-built housing area left of the GP1 as you go north. Head up the unsurfaced track past the new houses.) The building, with its domed tower, is easily visible across the fields from the A1 as well.

Back in the 1930s, it would seem that some wealthy Italian farmer had the idea of constructing the villa for the Duce. Tunisia, with its large Italian population, was a theatre for Franco-Italian rivalry in the years leading up to the Second World War. With Mussolini in power, the Italian consul-general began to wield an influence as great as that of the French resident-général. No doubt the Italian thought the Duce might take up residence there when he conquered Tunisia. The French, in reaction to the growing Italian threat, decided to give French nationality to any non-Muslim born on Tunisian soil.

The villa today survives in a sort of half-life. The structure is intact, although the finishing was extensively damaged when the building was used as a professional training school in the 1970s. Today, a caretaker lives in part of the ground floor, and he'll very kindly show you round for a small tip.

The Villa du Zodiaque is a fine example of the Italian modernist style. It is built to a perfectly round floor plan: the curve is queen here. A splendid circular galleried hall (used for receptions?) is topped by a simple dome set with tiny skylights as in an old-style Turkish bath. Access to the first-floor rooms (which have magnificent views over the countryside) is via a staircase housed in a cylinder topped with a green-tiled dome. Inside, the most interesting feature is the mosaics. On the ground floor are animals (a giraffe, a wounded gazelle, an eagle) and people (a Roman soldier, an archer, a dancing woman, a bedouin woman, a Corsican head). Are these symbols of Italy's longed-for African empire? On the first floor are mosaic star signs – hence the name Villa du Zodiaque. Is this a reference to some Roman mosaic – or just a whimsical gesture to the owner's taste for astrology ? Whatever, it is a shame that such a unique structure, as fine as Le Corbusier's Villa Savoye or Mallet-Steven's Villa Noailles at Hyères, be abandoned to its fate. A UFO of a building out in the fertile farmland of the Cap Bon, its finely crafted forms have a simple, plastic elegance, refreshing after the para-Moorish social-housing style of the 1990s hotels.

In need of sustenance after meditating on the decline of minimalist architecture, call in at the much-transformed terracotta villa on the rising ground to the north. This is now the grandly dubbed *Château Bacchus*, T72259825, F72259255, manager's mobile T98309812. Downstairs is a café with chicha, bar billiards, pizza and snacks, just next to the enormous salle des mariages. The villa also caters to the Hammamet holiday-group trade with special soirées touristiques. Small children might like the slides and running around on the lawn. Depressingly, for parents, the restaurant has no alcohol licence, despite being set in the heart of wine-making country.

Grombalia

With around 20,000 inhabitants, Grombalia – Roman Colombaria – is an important route centre and focus point for the surrounding agricultural region. Nothing remains of Roman days, and today the oldest remains here date from the 16th century, the time of the evacuation of Andalucia by the Moors. The oldest mosque here, built by one Mustapha Cardenas, dates from that time. He also found time to have a a public fountain and hammam built, as well as a beautiful dwelling for himself. The olive presses found here, which date from that time, indicate the quick growth in prosperity of the region.

It is in September that Grombalia has its annual moment of glory. A **Festival of the Grape** is held to celebrate the town's central position in wine and table grape production, for since protectoral times the main vineyards in the Cap Bon peninsula have been centred around the town. Until the 1960s,

Colour map 2, grid C4

See Essentials, page 49, for further details about Tunisian wine

Cap Bon Peninsula

much of the wine was exported to France for blending and the vineyards covered a greater area than they do today. While the vine still plays an important part in the agricultural scene here there is less evidence of future development, few young vines being brought on for replacement or new vineyards. The vine produces a good crop for up to 50 years and then in reducing quantities for up to 100 years, so although it may look old and gnarled in the winter it will burst forth in the spring. Unlike the terraced fields of France and Germany the vineyards here are planted on flat ground.

Back in the late 19th century, the spread of phylloxera on vines in mainland Europe encouraged grape-growing in Tunisia, though in the inter-war years phylloxera took its toll of Tunisian vineyards too. New grafted stocks were subsequently introduced. Today, wine production runs at 200,000-400,000 hectolitres per year, two-thirds of which is consumed in Tunisia. The industry looks set to expand in the coming years as domestic demand grows, due to Tunisia's growing prosperity and the tourist industry. New grape varieties have been introduced thanks to some German joint ventures, and the quality of wines is said to be improving.

As Grombalia is the centre of a vine-growing region, there are many roadside stalls in the season and much activity when the grapes are ready for wine production. There is a large market for clothes and shoes each Monday in the street by the railway station. The goods are piled high on trestle tables, a lively affair. Unhindered by visitors, wine-growing Grombalia goes about its business. Note that there is a lively lorry drivers' restaurant (good Tunisian nosh in huge quantities) on the main drag, on the west (left-hand) side of the road, opposite the building with the arcades as you head north.

Transport **Train** Trains from Grombalia to **Tunis** (via Hammam Lif) 0639, 0716, 0813, 1432, 1614, 1953; Grombalia to **Sousse** with onward travel to Mahdia, Sfax, Gabès and Gafsa 0701, 1558, 1748, and 1922.

A short trip: Grombalia to Aïn Tébournok For a quick dip into the Tunisian hinterland, and if you have a hire car, you might want to make a side trip to Aïn Tébournok from Grombalia. Take the road from Grombalia towards the Tunis-Sousse motorway, but continue straight across the motorway bridge heading for Aïn Tebournouk (Tebournoug), a further 5½ km westwards. The road runs gently upwards. Pay great attention, as lorries thunder down from the brickworks and quarries up in the hills. (This is where the building materials for Hammamet's new monster hotels are coming from.) About halfway to Aïn Tebournouk, you will see a splendid, early-20th-century farmer's residence up on your right. Overlooking vineyards and orchards, it signals the prosperity of the French and their farming methods in the region. Now abandoned, the house is worth a photo as a rare example of a 'neo-Moorish meets early 1900s French suburban' style. As colonial farmhouses go, it also looks pretty haunted.

At Aïn Tebournouk are the remains of an ancient Roman town, down on your left, just past the café. The site has been partly walled, to prevent further encroachments from new building. Clearly visible are the main temples – three rooms off a small esplanade, and a narrow paved street with a small honorific (?) arch. There are massive foundations of dressed stone, and plenty of rubble, indicating that this was yet another prosperous ancient settlement.

Once at Aïn Tébournok, you could continue south to the **Barrage Masri** which shelters under Djebel el Behelil (556 m), or on the return take the left turn to a smaller, and rather more attractive barrage (depending on the rainfall) which shelters under Djebel Makki (641 m).

Northern Tunisia

5

Northern Tunisia

Inland, northern Tunisia has rolling landscapes reminiscent of Andalusia and impressive Roman sites, each with a unique character. **Dougga** stands with imperial confidence on a hillside overlooking a wide valley, while **Bulla Regia** has villas hidden underground to avoid the crushing summer heat. **Chemtou** was the quarry colony which exported fine golden marble to the temples of ancient Rome. Here and there are miscellaneous ancient bridges and Byzantine fortifications.

The coast between Bizerte and the Algerian border offers steep cliffs, small bays and secluded beaches, most well off the main routes. In the lee of the Khroumirie Mountains sits **Tabarka**, its fishing harbour built close to a fine Genoese fort. This is a town half-awaiting a mass tourist influx. Happily the region's short summer season (and infrastructure costs) has kept development to a minimum. In summer the temperature, although high, is far more bearable than in the south, thanks to the thickly wooded hills inland from the coast. Further east, under a couple of hours from Tunis, the **Bizerte** region has coastlines both rocky and sandy and the **Djebel Ichkeul National Park**. There are also some fine east-facing beaches at places with evocative names like **Raf Raf**, **Sounine** and **Cap Zbib**.

Background

The northern regions of Tunisia have a lot to offer the visitor. The distances are not great, the roads constantly being improved, and you can easily include the region on a circular tour of the country. The region has two main port-towns: Bizerte, with tree-lined avenues, petrol refineries, ship-repair and naval base; and Tabarka, important as the only major town in northwest Tunisia and being developed for tourism in a low-key sort of way. The coast divides into two main areas: the east-facing coast south of Bizerte, with several fine beaches; and the longer north-facing seaboard, where many of the beaches are accessible only by four-wheel drive. Prevailing winds make the waters of the north-facing shores rougher. The coast here is often rocky, and this, coupled with the hills of the hinterland, has meant little development.

The coast running from Kalaât el Andalus to Bizerte has escaped mainstream tourist development as well. Most summer visitors are Tunisian residents abroad, as the region once exported large numbers of guest workers. Many have built holiday homes in once sleepy villages such as Raf Raf. Agriculture and fishing are still important but various light industries, including garment manufacture at Ras Djebel, have contributed to the massive expansion of Bizerte's satellite towns such as Menzel Jamil.

It remains to be seen whether anything more than standard three-star beach tourism can be developed for northern Tunisia. Diving is gaining popularity, and the Tabarka dive schools maintain a fair standard. In contrast to the mountain regions of Morocco, there is little local initiative to develop hill-walking, and no tradition of cheap local accommodation. There are also no signs of a network of long-distance footpaths being established. Summer 1999 saw a project to develop horse-trekking in the Tabarka area, but for the moment, more independent forms of tourism remain underdeveloped. The subsidy system does not work in their favour. For the local tourism companies, they lack the obvious investment potential of the beach hotel.

Numidian & Roman antiquity The inland areas of northern Tunisia have some fine ancient sites, easily covered with a hire car. The three outstanding sites are Dougga, Bulla Regia and Chemtou, and there are some more obscure destinations like Thuburnica near Ghardimaou, Trajan's bridge south of Béja and Mustis. In the spring, these sites are a botanist's delight, smothered as they are in wild flowers.

If you are travelling by public transport, then Dougga is easily visited from Tunis in a day (bus or louage from Bab Saâdoun, taxi or walk from Téboursouk). Without own transport, Bulla Regia and Chemtou have to be visited from Jendouba, there being *nakl reefee* minibuses to the latter. With a car, if you got a very early start from Tunis, you could, with plenty of energy and preferably two drivers, do all three main sites. The best place to stay overnight would be in Kef or Aïn Draham. This might be an overdose of ruins, however, and it would be better to take time, and do Testour, Dougga and Le Kef in one day, followed by Bulla Regia, Chemtou and Aïn Draham the next, especially as there is now a very good site museum at Chemtou.

Also in the region is **Béja**, a very pleasant town to wander round with an attractive médina and fine protectoral buildings. **Testour** is a reminder that large numbers of Andalusian Muslims were settled in Tunisia in the 17th century. (The village's Iberian feel has notbeen totally masked by concrete constructions.) And finally, on the hills above Medjez el Bab, are two obscure villages: Chaouach and Toukabeur, commanding views of the Medjerda plain.

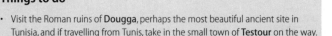

Things to do

- Visit the Roman ruins of **Dougga**, perhaps the most beautiful ancient site in Tunisia, and if travelling from Tunis, take in the small town of **Testour** on the way.
- Explore the hilltop town of **Le Kef**.
- In Bizerte, lunch at the *Sport Nautique* and swim at the remote(ish) beach of **Aïn Damous**.
- Visit the Roman marble quarry site of **Chemtou** and one of Tunisia's best small museums.
- In Tabarka, eat in one of the marina restaurants (good for lobster) and have Turkish coffee at the *Café Andalous*.

Tunis to Bizerte

South of Bizerte (or north from Tunis) are a number of villages, some like El Alia, founded by Andalusian immigrants in the 17th century. Closest to Tunis is the wide and windy beach of Kalaât El Andalus. Further north, still on the same stretch of coast, is Ghar el Melh, formerly Porto Farina, and the beach of Sidi Ali el Mekki. Round the headland of Cap Farina, and more sheltered, is Raf Raf with its beautiful sand beach, while at nearby Sounine, the coast gets rockier. This is an area increasingly favoured by Tunis families for their summer homes. Finally, after Ras Djebel, comes the rocky headland of Cap Zbib. Some 5 km south of Bizerte, you have the beach of Rmel, wide sands backed by dunes and forest. With a car, a summer day trip from Tunis or Bizerte could easily take in the Roman site of Utica and one of the beaches. The Tunis to Bizerte autoroute was scheduled to come into operation in July 2002. Tolls were to begin in the autumn. This new road will speed up driving times between the two cities and almost certainly make the old main road, the GP8, a whole lot safer.

Driving northwards from Tunis up the P8 road, the first major settlement, 28 km out of Tunis, to the right of the road, is **Pont-de-Bizerte** (ex-Protville), where you turn off for **Kalaât el Andalous**. As its name, meaning 'Citadel of the Andalusians', suggests, the village was originally founded by Andalusian refugees. It is situated on what was once a headland before the sea retreated leaving a wide fertile plain, today an agricultural area. Some houses were put up as part of the Medjerda development project sponsored by the World Bank. Market day is Wednesday. Beside the main mosque are post office, bank, petrol and the Haj Ali café. Little remains of the Andalusian past, however. The beach is some five minutes drive across the plain. In summer there are lifeguards and numerous local families enjoying the sands and sea. If you want to escape the crowded beaches around Tunis, and have your own transport, this is probably your best bet.

Kalaât el Andalous

Northern Tunisia

Utica

Colour map 2, grid B2 At **Zana**, 35 km out of Tunis, you come to the turn-off for the Roman site of Utica, a once-major settlement of which very little remains today.

Getting there & around Best visited as a short stop on the way to Bizerte or one of the beaches. The site is clearly signposted 2½ km east from the new town of Zana, on the main road. The museum is on the left, with shade for parking and picnics, with the actual ruins another 500 m down the road. For enthusiasts only if travelling by public transport.

History Like many ancient cities in Tunisia, Utica was first a Punic city founded in 1101 BC, and later taken over by the Romans. It was the first capital of the Roman province of Africa and, as such, rich in public monuments. Utica was a port, exporting agricultural produce from its rich hinterland. The Oued Medjerda has silted up the bay on which Utica stood, leaving it 15 km from the shore. Once though, Utica's superb strategic location was second only to that of Carthage.

With the fall of Carthage in 146 BC, Utica became the capital of the province, and the settlement prospered as a garrison for Roman troops and the residence of many rich and powerful Roman citizens. The reinstatement of Carthage returned Utica to second place. Utica's collapse, like that of other Roman cities, came with the invasions by the Vandals and the Byzantines. The final fall came after the Arab conquest.

The site The Roman site is not extensive and has only been partially excavated. There is evidence of the replacement of smaller buildings by something much larger and grander (due to a more important role as capital perhaps) and in some cases a duplication (two theatres). One of the theatres is centrally placed, the other cut into the hillside. The residential area contains houses, built in the classical style, and often named for the mosaic decorations discovered there, ie House of the Hunt. ■ *0830-1730 winter, 0800-1900 summer, closed Mon and public holidays. 2Dt and 1Dt photography charge.*

The houses The **House of the Cascades** is a large dwelling centred round a patio, on to which opened the imposing *triclinium* as well as smaller chambers, many with basins and fountains. The adjacent **House of the Hunt** had a large garden surrounded by a patio and numerous rooms, one of which contained the famous mosaic. The **House of the Capitals** had capitals representing human figures. The **House of the Treasure** produced a hoard of coins. Some mosaics remain, preserved under wooden covers which the guide will lift for you. The scenes are mainly

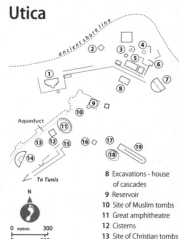

Utica

1 Great baths
2 Cisterns
3 Temple (republican period)
4 Palace
5 New forum
6 Great baths
7 Theatre (imperial period)
8 Excavations - house of cascades
9 Reservoir
10 Site of Muslim tombs
11 Great amphitheatre
12 Cisterns
13 Site of Christian tombs
14 Old theatre (republican period)
15 Museum
16 Roman mausoleum
17 Site of Roman tombs
18 Little amphitheatre
19 Circus (republican period)

fishing. The huge Utica mosaic with Neptune and Aphrodite in a sea-horse drawn chariot, Nereids on sea tigers and all overlooked by Oceanus, can be seen in the Ulysses Room at the Bardo Museum. Look out for the use of yellow Chemtou marble as well as the white and green marble from Greece. At the foot of the hill are the great baths, great in size, covering over 26,000 sq m. The cisterns and conduits to service this were fed from an aqueduct and water tower which came in at the highest point where the remains of the water tower, sometimes referred to as the citadel, can be found.

The small **Museum** has two main rooms. The Punic room has some gold brooches and earrings from the fourth to the third century BC, oil lamps from the seventh to the first century BC, vases from Greece and Italy, indicating trade and small sarcophagi for the bones and ashes of children who, according to legend, were sacrificed here. The Roman room has statues, an inscription from the first to second century AD, a mosaic of a hunting scene and an interesting diagram of the excavations of the House of Cascades. There is no accommodation at Utica.

House of the Cascades

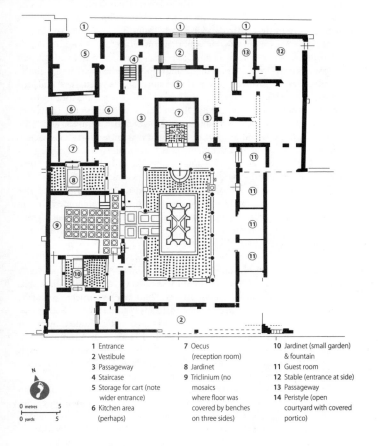

1 Entrance	**7** Oecus	**10** Jardinet (small garden)
2 Vestibule	(reception room)	& fountain
3 Passageway	**8** Jardinet	**11** Guest room
4 Staircase	**9** Triclinium (no	**12** Stable (entrance at side)
5 Storage for cart (note	mosaics	**13** Passageway
wider entrance)	where floor was	**14** Peristyle (open
6 Kitchen area	covered by benches	courtyard with covered
(perhaps)	on three sides)	portico)

N

0 metres 5
0 yards 5

Southeast of Bizerte

From Utica, you can either return to the main P8 to travel on to Bizerte, or follow the narrow country roads to coastal settlements like **Ghar El Melh** (ex-Porto Farina) and the beaches at **Ras Sidi Ali el Mekki**, **Raf Raf**, **Sounine** and **Cap Zbib**. There is a beautiful selection of swimming places to choose from, popular with locals but undiscovered by package tourism – although there were rumours of a marina development project at Sidi Ali el Mekki in the late 1980s.

Ghar el Melh (Porto Farina)

Phone code: 72
Colour map 2, grid A3

Until the early 19th century, Ghar el Melh, in its earlier incarnation as Porto Farina, was quite a happening place as the Beylik of Tunis' main naval base. The coast silted up, however, and the same fate befell this port as had already overcome Utica. Today, Ghar el Melh lives to the rhythm of the farming year and the large numbers of day-trippers passing through in summer.

History The lagoon at Ghar el Melh emerges from the mists of history in the 16th century. In 1535, Charles V's fleet sheltered in the lagoon one night on the way to besiege La Goulette. Although the Spaniards noted its potential, it wasn't until 1638 that the Kabudan of the Tunis fleet, Usta Murad Ibn Abdallah, a convert of Italian origin, decided to develop a port. Round-keeled vessels, and in particular galleons, were of growing importance in his fleet, as opposed to the galleys, and it was essential to have safe anchorage for them and prevent Christian pirates from taking refuge in the lagoon. Under Usta Murad, a fortified dock was constructed, complete with stores and slave quarters, and protected by a fort, today called the Borj el Wustani, the middle fort. In 1653, English admiral Blake was sent by Oliver Cromwell to punish the Tunis corsairs and damaged the new fortifications. However, between 1653 and 1665, Mustapha Laz Dey had the port restored and two further forts constructed, the Borj el Loutani to the east and the Borj Tunis to the west. A shipyard was added later in the century, and a full wall in the early 18th century. Porto Farina thus became the main naval port for the Regency of Tunis.

The approaches to the port gradually silted up, however. Ahmed Bey (1837-55) decided to build a modern port, and works were undertaken, at huge cost, with a palace being constructed to house the beylical suite. There was no solution to the silting, however, and Porto Farina became headquarters for a new infantry regiment instead.

Sights Surprisingly perhaps, the building undertaken under Ahmed Bey has largely disappeared, while the three 17th-century bastions and the port are still visible. The shipyard and gallery are a mass of ruins. The octagonal corner towers of the Borj el Wustani and the Burj el Loutani are clearly visible. In their day, they represented a considerable innovation, and were no doubt introduced by master builders of Andalusian Muslim origin. The **Borj Tunis**, with its rounded front made up of vaulted chambers, represents the biggest innovation, however. Such a system meant that the fort could absorb more bombardment than a classic rampart, and could have more than one range of cannons.

Today, the lagoon at Ghar el Melh is a peaceful place, its depth of barely 1 m making any military activity unlikely. There is a fair amount of fishing, with the main fish caught being red mullet, bream, perch, sole and eel. After the village, the road goes on 6 km to the splendid beach of **Ras Sidi Ali el Mekki** with a small café/shop and straw cubicles for camping, rented at 5Dt per day. At the

Ancient mosaics of Tunisia

The Romans made a fine art of 'decorating a surface with designs made up of closely set, usually variously coloured, small pieces of material such as stone, pottery, glass, tile or shell': mosaics.

These first mosaics were constructed from pebbles and small stones set in clay, and usually the colours were black or white. The inclusion of other coloured stones, glass, and even broken pottery and shells, was introduced at a later date. The production of small, natural clay and polychrome tiles known as tesserae developed even later as designs for mosaics became more complicated and regular shaped pieces were required.

Although Africa was one of Rome's first overseas provinces, the actual process of Romanization was very slow and there were certainly no major developments before the late second century AD. Despite this late development, the mosaics of North Africa are more numerous and much better preserved than those remaining anywhere else from the empire, due to a combination of climatic conditions and less population pressure. The area we know as Tunisia is richer in mosaics than any other country and provides an enormous number of examples, mainly from the fourth century.

The earliest mosaics in North Africa were very simple, and it is assumed that early examples of more elaborate designs were produced by imported labour or constructed in Italy.

The wealthy Romans decorated both their private and public buildings with mosaics. They were a luxury and though primarily decorative, their size and sophistication would certainly advertise the wealth of the patron. Generally, the finer specimens were in the better, more visited parts of the house, and ornamental/geometric rather than pictorial designs were found in less important areas.

There are clear indications that the central part of the mosaics were constructed by 'master' craftsmen, while the geometric designs and borders were done by workers who were less well trained, and often produced a lower standard of work. Subject matter of the mosaics is frequently repeated and similar examples can be found on many different sites. Examples of the pattern being drawn in the underlying clay have been found but are not common. The workmen must have followed some pattern, especially where the work was more complicated. The recurrence of identical motifs across a wide area shows that designs were probably chosen from a common stock and not drawn for each building.

The common themes to look out for are: hunting scenes and scenes showing rural life; seasons and seasonal activities; scenes from literature; scenes from mythology. The all-important central medallion was set in a circle, square, oval or polygon and the whole mosaic was surrounded with a border usually exhibiting a geometric design. Most common were the three strand rope and Greek key borders.

Northern Tunisia

---

end of the peninsula, built partially into the cliff, is the *marabout* of Sidi Ali el Mekki, a place of pilgrimage. Outside the summer season, this is an attractive and secluded spot.

If you are using public transport, take buses 5 and 3A, via Aousdja, from Tunis and **Transport** Bizerte. There are no buses east to Sidi Ali el-Mekki.

Raf Raf   رفراف

Phone code: 72
Colour map 2, grid A2
Population 10,000

The little town of Raf Raf divides into two parts: the town proper at the top of the hill; and the beach-side suburb where many wealthy Tunisois and migrant workers have pleasant second homes. A steep road dips down from Raf Raf Ville to Raf Raf Plage. The setting is superb, with white sand, clear water, and the fortress-like mass of the Ile Pilau posing strategically for a photograph. Walk along the beach until the crowds thin out. You could also try to walk up the headland, via the track to the watchtower.

Sights

For the moment, there is little accommodation at Raf Raf. Despite some fairly hideous new building, the place does, however, make a pleasant day excursion from either Tunis or Bizerte, especially at the beginning and the end of the summer season. In July and August, on **Friday market** and especially at weekends, Raf Raf gets very crowded with trippers and the approach roads become jammed with cars. (Raf Raf produces the best table grapes in Tunisia, on sale, in season, all along the road.)

Fishing enthusiasts will want to observe the local beach **fishing** technique. During the seasonal migrations of mackerel, the fisherman attaches a female fish to a line and allows her to swim out parallel to the coast. Then, hawkeyed, he watches the water for the approach of a male fish, and waits for the appropriate moment to cast his net. The technique is clearly one that can only be mastered with patience and observation. (In the spring and early summer, similar techniques are used for trapping male goldfinches which, as the visitor will soon notice, are much appreciated as songbirds for homes and shops.)

Sleeping & eating

If you really want to spend time in Raf Raf, there are a fair number of holiday homes which stay empty for much of the year. There may also be cane beach *cabanes* available for rent. **C** *Hotel Dalia*, T447668. Small, only 22 rooms, about half with sea view, very clean, close to beach, open all year, expensive due to location. The restaurant in the *Hotel Dalia* is good, clean and cheap. You can eat outside and watch the sea and the visitors. There are a few other restaurants along the beach, try *Restaurant Andalous*. These eateries tend to be overpriced for what they are.

Transport

Road Bus: reachable by bus from Ras Djebel and Tunis (No 1B, 2-hr ride, 1 bus a day from Bab Saâdoun). Departures for Bizerte and Ras Djebel. 1 bus a day to Tunis. **Louages**: also available, but in summer towards the end of the day it can be quite crowded as everybody is leaving. Hitching may take time as most cars are already full.

Sounine

Further north, Sounine has a rocky beach, some large and not very tasteful weekend homes, a few huts for rent on beach, *Café Budan* on corner, also *Café l'Escale* for snacks. In spring every electricity pylon has a storks' nest. In autumn the fields are full of tall white squills.

Ras Djebel, Metline and Cap Zbib

Phone code: 72
Colour map 2, grid A2

Ras Djebel is a large modern settlement on the coast, east of Bizerte on the road to the beaches of Raf Raf. In recent years, the town has grown quite prosperous thanks to the presence of a large garment factory, working mainly for Lee Cooper and owned by an industrial group headed by Hédi Jilani, president of the Tunisian Federation of Industry or UTICA. The town has a café, a patisserie and the *Hotel Okba* but not much else of interest. By contrast the surrounding area is very beautiful. The beach at Ras Djebel is very crowded in the summer and as most people prefer to camp near the town, anywhere further west is better. To the northwest, **Metline** is a small town built into the hillside, while rocky **Cap Zbib** offers magnificent views and the road from Bizerte to Ras Djebel is very scenic with a panoramic view over the coast by Bizerte. On the beach is a tiny marina with fishing boats. Drive with care as the road stops dead 1 m from the cliff edge. Those in the know turn left.

Leaving Ras Djebel, you might head inland towards the P8, and the village of **El Alia**, built at a crossroads. In its day, this would have been a splendid example of the settlements built by immigrants from Andalucía. Thistles were traditionally grown in the region for the felting of *chechias*, the small red fez-like caps on which so much of the wealth of the Andalusian communities of Tunis was built.

Menzel Bourguiba (ex-Ferryville)

Situated some 20 km southwest of Bizerte, at the westernmost point of the Lac de Bizerte, Ferryville was purpose-built in the 1880s at the same time as the naval base at Bizerte, and named after Jules Ferry who was then in charge of colonial affairs. Renamed Menzel Bourguiba after independent Tunisia's first president, the town's military installations were to prove useful to Tunisia. In the 1960s, when self-sufficiency was the watchword for the newly independent nation states of Africa, Tunisia had to have a steelworks. Menzel Bourguiba, located close to the shipyards and petrol refineries of Bizerte, was ideally placed for the new installations, named *El Fouladh* (Arabic for steel). In the late 1990s, as the Tunisian State sought to withdraw from industrial activity, El Fouladh was ripe for privatization. Whether this diminutive steelworks can survive remains to be seen. Success or failure will have huge effects on the town. There is now a second industry in the form of garment factories, however. This requires very different sort of skills and labour to the steel mill.

Phone code: 72
Colour map 2,
grid A1

Menzel Bourguiba has some nice pieces of period architecture, including a bandstand and characteristic detached houses with pitched red-tiled roofs, presumably built to house personnel working for the naval yards.

D *Hotel Ichkeul*, a fair way out of Menzel Bourguiba at Guengla, on Lac Bizerte. Owner also runs Tardi vintners. Good reports of the restaurant. **E** *Hotel Moderne*, small and downmarket, in the centre of Menzel Bourguiba, T460551. Bar.

Sleeping

Via Bizerte, R du 18 Janvier, T460756.

Tour operators

Lac Ichkeul (Garaet Ichkeul)

Lying west of the Lac de Bizerte and Menzel Bourguiba, **Lac Ichkeul** was a unique biotope, created by the shifting seasonal balance of salt and fresh water in a large and shallow inland lake. The area is dominated by **Djebel Ichkeul**, where a small écomusée is located. Bring your binoculars. Apart from various resident waterfowl and the lead-grey water buffalo out on the water meadows, you may be lucky enough to see large flocks of overwintering migrant grey-lag geese in winter. The best time to visit is November to February.

Phone code: 72
Colour map 2, grid A1

Lac Ichkeul is awkward to get to without your own transport, and your birdwatching will be improved if you can drive round the lake. You could get the Bizerte–Mateur bus or louage, and ask to get off at the turn-off for the Parc National, a few kms after Tinja on the main P11. Otherwise, you could get a taxi from Menzel Bourguiba to this point,

Ins & outs

Northern Tunisia

Northern Tunisia

Buffaloes and Madame Butterfly

One of the most surprising sights at Ichkeul are the small herds of water buffaloes grazing on the plain below the djebel. The origins of these animals are obscure. One story goes that they descend from a pair given to the bey of Tunis by the king of Sicily in 1729. Another version runs that they were imported by Ahmed Bey (1837-55), a modernizing monarch, who felt they would be the ideal solution to towing his field artillery around. When the buffaloes proved unequal to the task, they were released at Ichkeul. When the French took over in 1881, there were over 1,000 of these beasts at Ichkeul, who presumably found the seasonal marshes like the rice-paddies of their homeland. The buffaloes were the personal property of HH the Bey, who would grant the occasional buffalo-hunting licence. In the Second World War, American troops stationed in the area nearly wiped out the herd in search of fresh meat.

Finally, still on an Asian theme, in the mid-1990s Lac Ichkeul was considered sufficiently similar to Japan to be used as the setting for a film version of Madame Butterfly. A mock-up Japanese village was constructed on the edge of the lake, with Oriental accessories and extras being flown in from Paris's China Town.

or maybe into the park to the main gate. From the railway-crossing to the park gate is 5½ km, from main gate to ecomuseum a further 3½ km. The minor road beyond the museum is closed to traffic, but walkers are welcome on the circular route round Djebel Ichkeul. The minor road marked south of the lake on Michelin 172 to the C51 does not exist.

Background
Note that the Tourist Office in Bizerte can on occasion arrange visits

The Lac Ichkeul area is a conservation area of 12,600 ha, with a mixed habitat comprising shallow lake (1-3 m deep), marshy pasture and maquis-covered mountain. The area was designated by UNESCO in 1977 as a biosphere reserve. (The only other such site acknowledged by UNESCO is the Everglades in Florida.) The lake was unique in that while it had fresh water in winter, in summer its waters turned saline. In summer, high evaporation levels meant that the water level fell to 1½ m or less, leading to inflow from the saline Lac de Bizerte via the 5-km-long Oued Tindja. Salinity rose to 20 g per litre. In winter, with the seasonal rains, the balance shifted, with the rivers supplying fresh water; the depth rose to 3 m and salinity fell to 5 g per litre. Thanks to the warm winter, large seasonal beds of waterplants could grow, thus providing food for huge flocks of migrant birds.

For birdlilfe, Ichkeul is arguably the most interesting of Tunisia's six national parks. Water birds and waders are among the thousands of over-wintering migrants (over-wintering greylag geese can number 15,000) found here. Among the animal species are water buffalo, wild boar, porcupine, otter and jackal. There are numerous reptiles and amphibians, too.

Birdwatchers may see the purple gallinule (French: *talève sultane*), the retiring marbled teal (*sarcelle marbrée*) and maybe even the white-headed duck. The coot (*foulque macroule*) feeds on water weed. Of the waders, the easiest to spot are the black-and-white avocets and the white storks, which can be seen nesting in various places in northern Tunisia.

The greylag goose (*oie cendrée*) was the park's most famous migrant visitor, feeding on club rush. The highest number recorded was 20,500, while 15,000 was a more regular figure. The numbers are down considerably, however, with figures around 4,500 in the late 1990s. The fresh water from the rivers which used to flow into the lake in winter is now being put to other uses. As part of the 'mobilization of the waters of the North', a large new dam on the

Oued Sejnène, west of Ichkeul, was built, sharply reducing fresh-water inflow. The effect of reduced fresh-water input can be seen in the area round the lake. The once extensive reed-beds have receded, and there is far less cane than there used to be. In the local vernacular tradition, houses were roofed with reeds. The preferred option today is plastic sheeting. Given the changes in the ecosystem, the question remains as to whether it will continue to merit its UNESCO classification. The authorities are said to be keen to maintain the water balance in the lake by artificial methods.

There is a small ecological museum high above the car park, overlooking the lake. This has information of interest to birdwatchers and ecologists. There is a display of stuffed birds and information on the workings of the lake's special ecosystem. ■ *0700-1800. Free.*

Ecological museum

Bizerte   بنزرت

Tunisia's fourth largest city, and the biggest town in the north of the country, Bizerte is an atmospheric sort of place. There is a small médina, and a picturesque port area, with angular 18th-century bastions and streets of white walls and blue doors and shutters. The town feels quintessentially early 20th century cosmopolitan Mediterranean, even though the population is wholly Muslim today. There are apartment buildings like those in any French provincial town. There are squares, a fine church, plane trees and promenades of palm trees, and a club nautique. When the French departed, jetties, breakwaters and port installations stayed, giving the town a brisk, naval air.

Phone code: 72
Colour map 2,
grid A1

Northern Tunisia

   Bizerte's streets have all the usual variety of Tunisian provincial life: shiny new shops with consumer goods, workshops spilling out onto the pavement, repairing motorcycles, varnishing furniture. In the spring, you will see merchants with piles of fragrant geraniums for making flower essence. At the fish market, you will find the harvest of the local fishing fleet. Bizerte is a pleasant place for a stopover. And nearby, at Rmel and Ras Angela, are some splendid beaches. Note also that Cap Blanc is the northernmost point of Africa.

Ins and outs

Bizerte is 64 km from Tunis, bus Nos 44 and 62, 1¼ hrs by louage, a pleasant, slightly hilly, journey along the P8 through fertile farmland with large areas of olives and vines. The road crosses the wide flood plain of the Oued Medjerda, Tunisia's only permanently flowing river. Travelling by car, you may want to stop off at the Roman site of Utica, a few km off the road, or you could spend a couple of hrs at 1 of the small beach resorts like Ghar el Melh, Raf Raf or Sounine.

Getting there
See Transport,
page 210,
for further details

The main sites of Bizerte can easily be covered on foot. You may want to go to the Corniche and its beaches and to Cap Blanc, a short taxi ride out of the town centre, north of the town. The beaches northwest of Bizerte, notably Ras Angela, require your own transport. The beach at Remel, south of the town, is easily reached by local bus.

Getting around

National Tourist Office (ONTT), 1 R d'Istambul, T432703/432897. Hard to find, situated by the canal, about 100 m before the bridge, towards the sea.

Information

History

Bizerte goes back to Punic times when the natural harbour attracted the Phoenician sailors. The town was destroyed with the fall of Carthage, but later rebuilt by Caesar, and known as **Hippo Diarrythus**. Conquered by the Arabs in 661, Bizerte expanded during the Hafsid dynasty. The arrival of the Moors from Spain in the 17th century, as in other cities in Tunisia, gave it a new lease of life and guaranteed its fortune. The opening of the Suez Canal in 1869, and the arrival, in 1882, of the French who appreciated its strategically important position and turned the town into a naval arsenal, were other important factors in Bizerte's development.

The arsenal had a key strategic role, controlling the Straits of Sicily. The naval base was the second largest in North Africa, after Mers el Kébir, and was thus a major objective of the Axis armies. The Germans occupied Bizerte in 1942, the Allies took it back again in 1943. At Tunisia's independence, France kept

Northern Tunisia

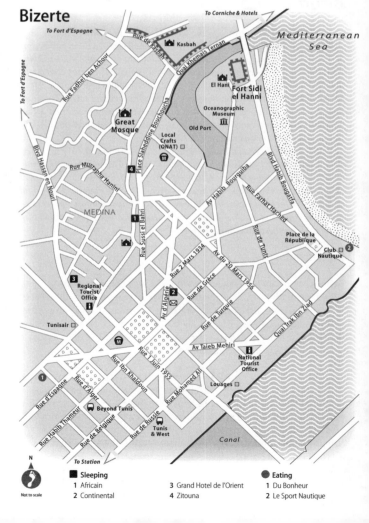

Bizerte

N Not to scale

Sleeping	Eating
1 Africain	1 Du Bonheur
2 Continental	2 Le Sport Nautique
3 Grand Hotel de l'Orient	
4 Zitouna	

control of the military installations. In the late 1950s, relations between France and Tunisia deteriorated, with the latter angered at the French attack on Algerian nationalists in the Tunisian village of Sakiet Sidi Youssef. France devalued the franc (to which the dinar was linked) without consulting Tunisia. Populist pressure called for France to evacuate the Bizerte base, which it eventually did on 15 October 1964. Open hostility had broken out in July 1961, with Tunisian civilian lives being lost senselessly in a doomed attack on the base.

Since independence the industrial sector has expanded. There is an oil refinery. A large steelmill, El Fouladh, was set up at Menzel Bourguiba (ex-Ferryville), a few kilometres southwest of the town. Bizerte lies north of the swing bridge over the 8-km-long canal which joins the inland Lake of Bizerte (111 sq km) to the open sea. Here some commercial fishing takes place, mullet, bream and sole being the main catch. The road from the bridge leads into the regular grid pattern of streets, laid out in the late 19th century, beyond which lies the médina and the old port. The late 1990s saw much new building on the northern and western outskirts of the town, mainly low-cost housing to the west, and villas along the Corniche. Bizerte now also has a special development zone, and it is hoped this will bring in further industrial investment. At the moment many businesses are linked to the port and refineries.

Sights

The old harbour is charming with its blue and white houses overlooking the fishing boats, and in the evening it has a different but equally pleasant atmosphere. From there you can penetrate into the **Kasbah**, the old fortified médina. (Over the modern bridge is another old neighbourhood, the **Ksiba**, or 'little kasbah'.) The labyrinth of little streets is fascinating to walk through. It is the sort of place where you should wander through the narrow alleys, 'peeping into doorways where craftsmen can be seen at work using techniques centuries old'. The octagonal minaret of the Grand Mosque was recently over-restored.

Above and behind the town is the **Fort d'Espagne**, built between 1570 and 1573 by the Pacha of Algiers to plans by Gabriel Serbelloni. The fort was completed under the Spaniard. It has been sufficiently repaired to be used, once in a while, as an open-air auditorium.

The new city is pleasant with its squares and cafés. Close to the port is the covered market. In the area are one or two small shops with some desultory craft work. In the **Fort de Sidi el Hani**, in the Ksiba district, Bizerte has a sleepy **Oceanographic Museum**, which sounds most impressive. The 11-storey blue tower block provides an interesting note in the old harbour district, and was originally built as officers' flats.

Bizerte suffered severe damage during the Second World War, and was thus the object of a number of redevelopment schemes during the reconstruction period 1943-48. A whole new town was planned for **Zarzouna**, south of Bizerte. The architecture of this time was firmly based on local models and techniques, given the shortages of steel and concrete. Architecture enthusiasts may want to look out for a couple of interesting buildings from the period, the **Ecole des Jeunes Filles** (architect J Lecouteur) close to the old harbour on Place Salaheddine Bouchoucha, and the **Contrôle civil de Zarzouna** (architect J Marmey) high on a hill, overlooking the town, to the south. The **Church of Notre Dame** (architect R Guy) dates from the same period.

Perhaps the most striking feature on the Bizerte skyline is the great bridge. The channel separating the two halves of the town is 240 m wide and 12 m deep, allowing ships of up to 80,000 tonnes into port. Until 1904 there was a swing bridge, subsequently replaced by two ferries. The present bridge, Bizerte's answer to Sydney Harbour, climbing 15 m above the channel, came into service in 1980. A middle section opens up to allow large boats into the port.

Beaches   There are some good **beaches** on either side of the town, but the most popular one is at **Remel** ('sands') over the bridge to the south (try the No 8 bus from the Menzel Jamil stop at the bus station). The beach is backed by pine forest, and there are a couple of large wrecked vessels, dating from the Second World War, rusting away in the water just off the beach.

Some 10 km out of Bizerte, there is the headland of **Cap Angela**. North of town, the Corniche runs between coast and a smart neighbourhood with hotels, restaurants and smart residential areas climbing up the hillside (look out for the villa built to look like a ship). Then the road winds upwards and pine forest appears. Turn right down a track through the forest, leave the car at the small village, and make the 20-minute walk up **Cap Blanc**, one of the northernmost points in Africa. There is a radio station and superb views over the sea, and, to the west, over forest to the beaches at Cap Angela. After coming down from Cap Blanc, the really energetic can head down through the forest, following the driveable track, to the long sandy beach of **Aïn Damous**. Cars can get most of the way down, but the going is tricky, especially if there are a lot of vehicles. The final descent to the beach is a steep and winding 100 m or so. Bring provisions if you are going to make a day of it.

Essentials

Sleeping   There is entirely adequate accommodation in Bizerte to suit all budgets. The hotels are
■ *on map, page 206*   either out on the Corniche, starting about 1 km out of the town, or in the town centre. Note that street names in the médina are in Arabic script only.

Corniche hotels   **B** *Bizerta Resort*, Rte de la Corniche, very close to the town, T436966, F422955, hbizerta@gnet.tn Opened 2001, Bizerte's premier address, right on the beach. 100 rooms, including 24 communicating, well equipped, with direct phone, satellite TV, a/c, etc. Roomy suites, many rooms with sea view. Indoor and outdoor pools, conference facilities. Café-jardin with a vaguely Caribbean feel. Credit cards accepted. **B** *Petit Mousse*, Rte de la Corniche, T432185, F437595, 6 km out of Bizerte on the Corniche. A rarity in Tunisia, a small pleasant hotel (12 rooms), good atmosphere, beach across the road, one of Bizerte's better restaurants, eat outside in garden or on terrace in summer. The downside? Street-facing rooms noisy. Expensive for what it is. **C** *Apart'hotel Résidence Aïn Meriyem*, T422615, F433459. A popular choice for beach holidays. 296 beds in bungalow-type accommodation. Outdoor pool, fair service, restaurant has a good name. **C** *Corniche*, Rte de la Corniche, T431831, F431830, 4 km out of town. Low season prices acceptable, beach, 87 rooms with sea view, fly screens, no a/c, pool, nightclub. Prime location but poor management. **C** *Jalta*, Rte de la Corniche, T431169, F434277. Next to the *Nador*, a package sort of place. **C** *Nador*, T431848, F433817. Next to *Corniche*, simpler and much more pleasant, 105 rooms, beach, pool, no disco, tennis, fully booked in summer with package tours. **C** *El Khayem*, Rte de la Corniche, 5 km from town. The most remote (and cheapest) of the hotels on the coast, T4321220. Nothing special.

Town centre hotels   **C** *Hotel de la Plage*, Av Mohamed Rejiba, T444792. 20 nice rooms, some with showers, a/c to be added partially. Handy for the Blvd Habib Bougatfa, the sea-front road near the port. **C-D** *Hotel El Feth*, Av Bourguiba, T/F430596, near the mosque in the heart of town, 20 clean rooms, most with shower, otherwise minimum comfort, entirely acceptable, wc on landing. Out of season very cheap. Room rate includes bread and jam breakfast. Close to bus stations but nearly a km to the beach. **D** *Grand Hotel de l'Orient*, Blvd Hassan Ennouri, some 50 m off Av Bourguiba, T421499. **E** *Hotel Africain*, on a busy street leading from new town to médina, opposite food market, T434412. A dozen rooms with varying numbers of beds. Good cheap option, but loos and showers are on ground floor. Nearby is the **E** *Zitouna*, Pl Slaheddine Bouchoucha, T431447. Some rooms round patio, some (noisy) overlooking street, also some without windows. No showers. Last resort stuff, really. **E** *Hotel Continental*, R d'Istambul, T431436. Probably one of the best deals if you want a cold shower and a clean, cheap bed, but don't expect much else.

Camping   Permitted at *Remel Plage* hostel (see below).

Youth hostels   1 km north of city centre up Blvd Hassan en Nouri, a street that runs away from Av Habib Bourguiba near *Tunisair*. Kitchen but meals provided, 100 beds, T431608. Use if the town centre cheapies are full. Downside: none too clean and nearly a 1 km uphill trek from bus station. Very inconvenient for both beach and sites. Also *Centre de la Jeunesse à Remel Plage*, T440819. 3 km from city centre close to beach in a pine wood, any bus going south of the canal will stop at the turn off, if driving there are signs. Two options: pitch your tent (2Dt) or stay in one of the buildings, family or double rooms 5Dt a head. 50 beds only, reservations essential in summer, closed Feb. A good option but can get mucky and crowded in summer.

Expensive   *Le Sport Nautique*, Port de Plaisance, T433262. Should really be listed under mid-range, but given here as you can eat very expensively. Fills up at Sun lunchtimes with provincial bourgeoisie and families. Probably the best address in Bizerte, with view over a bit of harbour. Can run up a fish couscous (order in advance).

Eating
● *on map, page 206*

Mid-range   *Belle Plage*, Corniche, T431817. Location overlooking the beach is perfect but service can be off-hand. *Restaurant du Bonheur*, R Thaalbi, T431047, town centre location, closed Sun evening and Ramadan. New section has a/c! Alcohol served with the fish dishes. Not as reasonably priced as it used to be. *L'Eden*, 4 km from town on Corniche, T439023. Alfresco dining in summer, cosy-ish dining room for winter, good wine list for Tunisia. Sat evening to be avoided if you dislike loud musical entertainments by local musicians. *Le Petit Mousse*, in hotel of same name, does good fish and cuisine française. But is it worth the price? Just about, given the lack of choice in Bizerte. The place is really trading on its reputation from 30 years ago – if there was competition, it would have had to look to its laurels long ago. Note also you can eat in the garden Jun-Sep (pizzas, barbecue, alcohol served).

Cheap   *La Mamina*, T433695, R d'Espagne. Pizzas and lasagne. There are some good sandwich-type places near the *Monoprix* and the market in the ville nouvelle.

Of a summer's evening, take time for a citronade and a *chicha* at the *Café Le Pacha*, with terrace overlooking the old port. On hot afternoons or in winter, take refuge in the vaulted interior. Best cakes and icecreams are at *Pâtisserie Djemili Le Chantilly*, 20 Av Taïeb Mehiri, just round the corner from the Monoprix. No seats, but all of trendy young Bizerte hangs out here between about 1730 to 2000 of a summer evening.

Cafés & patisseries

Nothing very exciting in this department. The Festival of Bizerte is held in Jul/Aug, with much the same stars doing the summer festival circuit elsewhere in Tunisia. Note that Bizerte is the birthplace of Khemaïs Ternane, one of early 20th century Tunisia's most popular songwriters.

Festivals

Northern Tunisia

Shopping   *National Handicrafts Centre (ONAT)*, next to *Café Le Pacha* on Quai Khemais Ternane, overlooking old harbour, T431091. Usual selection of handicrafts. It can't really be said that Bizerte has any specific craftwork. Tunisian residents might want to try to contact *Fouchali* for high quality wrought-ironwork (small showroom on R Sassi el Bahri). Otherwise the nearest this part of the world gets to craftwork is the rough pottery made by rural women out in the Sejnène area west of Bizerte (best bought from roadside stalls).

Sport   *Club Nautique*, T432262, on the right of the main beach in town, hires out surfboards and does various other watersports. Sub-aqua fishing is quite popular in the region. The *Corniche* hotel organizes water-skiing and rents surfboards. Horse riding is offered at some of the hotels. Some of the big hotels and small enterprises hire out bicycles, which is a cheap way of getting to the beach. Municipal swimming pool (heated) on Blvd Hassan en Nouri. Marina for 100 boats.

Tour operators   *International Voyages*, 35 Av Habib Bourguiba, T432885, F433547. *Tourafrica*, Av Habib Bourguiba, T432315.

Transport   **Local   Car hire**: *ABC*, 33 Av Habib Bourguiba, T434624, F436350. *Avis*, 7 R d'Alger, T433076. *Budget*, 7 R d'Alger, T432174. *Europcar*, 52 Av d'Algérie, T439018, also at 19 R Med Rejiba, Pl des Martyrs, T431455. *Hertz*, Pl des Martyrs, T433679. *Inter Rent*, 19 R Mohammed Rejiba, T431455. *Mattei*, R d'Alger, T431508. *Next Car*, 80 Blvd Hassan en Nouri, T433668.

Long distance   Air: nearest airport is Tunis, information from *Tunisair*, 76 Av Habib Bourguiba, T432201. **Train**: station is approximately 15 mins walk southwest along canal out of town, T431070. To Tunis 0540, 0810, 1350, 1835. **Bus**: main bus station is by the bridge over the canal. Information from *Société Régionale de Transport*, Quai Tarak Ibn Ziad, T431371/736. A short walk north up Av d'Algérie to the town centre. Information from *Société Nationale de Transport* on T431222/431317. Bus station for places west, as far as Tabarka, is on R d'Alger. Frequent buses to **Tunis** and **Ras Djebel**; change at Ras Djebel for **Raf Raf** and **Ghar el Melh; Aïn Draham** (via Tabarka) leaves early morning. **Louages**: leave by the canal under the bridge to all destinations, but some are harder to obtain if the demand is low. Louages terminate on the Quai Tarak Ibn Ziad under the bridge or at the north end of Av d'Algérie. Sometimes available at the station. **Sea**: *Navitour*, 29 Av d'Algérie, T431440. **Port – Harbour Master's Office**, T431688.

Directory   **Banks** The banks arrange a rota so one always stays open later. Plenty of banks around the main Pl du 7-Novembre (the square with the Municipality). *BNT*, R 1er Juin. *STB*, R Farhat Hached, there is also another branch behind the ONAT, by the old harbour. *Amen Bank*, Av Bourguiba takes Eurocheques and Visa. **Communications** Internet: *Publinet*, R Habib Tameur, T423600, not far from bus stations. **Post**: main office, 6 Av d'Algérie. Takes parcels as well. Around the back of main building is the telecoms office, also on R el Médina and Pl Pasteur. **Medical services** Chemist: all night, *Sparfi*, 28 R Ali Belhaouane, T439545. **Hospital**: R du 3 Août, T431422. **Places of worship** Catholic: 120 Av Habib Bourguiba, T432386. Service Sun 1030. **Useful addresses** Police: R du 20 Mars 1956, T431200/1.

Bizerte to Tabarka

West of Bizerte, the coastline is wild and remote all the way to Tabarka. The *Colour map1,* sea is hidden by thick forests noted as a refuge for the last lion (killed 1925) *grid A2-4* and the last panther (1932) known in Tunisia. The coastline is worth trying to reach, especially if you like deserted beaches, although access is difficult. By car from Bizerte to Tabarka take the road west towards Menzel Bourguiba and turn right 5 km after Bizerte on the C51, in the direction of Sejnène. This road joins the C57, skirting Lac Ichkeul, before joining up with the main P7 for **Sejnène** (pottery), **Nefza** (storks) and **Tabarka** (red coral).

Closest to Bizerte is the beach at **Ras Angela**. (Note that GeoCenter world **Sejnène &** map labels Rass Ben Sekka and Rass el Koran with little precision.) Going **the northern** west of Bizerte, follow signs for **Bechateur**. There is only one route down to **beaches** the beach at Ras Angela. If you are tempted to camp out or sleep rough, keep your passport etc close to the body. Valuables can be stolen from under your sleeping head.

During the North African campaigns of the Second World War, the Allied drive eastwards to Mateur and Bizerte passed by Sejnène, then just a wayside hamlet. Here the so-called Bald Hill and Green Hill where of key strategic importance. In the winter of 1942-43, in bitter cold and rain, the Argylls and the Germans fought it out, shelling each other until the hillsides were pocked with craters of red mud. Later the British parachutists were brought in, one of the places where they were used as ordinary infantry. According to Alan Moorhead's account, they were feared by the Axis troops as "the most terrible animals". As he put it in *The End in Africa*, the last part of his published chronicles of the African campaigns, the parachutists " ...had become so well acquainted with death they had no fear of it any longer ... It was not that pity or grief had gone out of them, but that they were living in a well of danger ... it was all very largely a technical matter – whether you got you machine-gun burst in first and in the right direction." The destruction of war seems very remote in the smiling countryside of northern Tunisia today. But sinister rumour says that USA forces make use of Tunisia's remote northern beaches for landing exercises.

Moving westwards, the next easily accessible beach is at **Cap Serrat**, some 25 km from **Sejnène**. From Sejnène, the C66, which eventually turns into gravelly/sandy track, takes you down to pale sands backed by meadows green even in summer. A tiny river, banks lined with oleander and cane, flows into the sea. There are showers and a couple of seasonal restaurants.

Sejnène is one of those rural one-street villages which expanded rapidly in the 1990s, becoming the local centre, giving vastly improved access to health and education to a once isolated rural population. Sejnène gets packed with Peugeot trucks, the odd mule and women in their colourful best on **Thursday market day**. The area is known for its **hand-modelled pottery**, animals and statuettes, generally sold as 'Berber style' pottery in tourist areas, and you will find small displays of the pottery along the roadside. The most attractive items are the tiny animals, the *kanouns* (braseros) and the wide flat dishes. Note that this pottery is generally fired at quite low temperatures, given that the women have to collect the brushwood for the kiln by hand. This means that the final product is often quite breakable.

After Sejnène, the next easily accessible beach is at **Sidi Mechrig**. Turn right at Tamera, 10 km before Nefza, and follow the narrow metalled road which leads up over the Jbel el Hamar, through great stands of eucalyptus before

Northern Tunisia

1741, the fall of the comptoir of Cap Negro

An 18th-century historian recounts the fall of Tamkart (Cap Negro) to Younes, son of Ali Pacha. "Before leaving Tabarka, Younes had the message sent from Bizerte to the French community in Tamkart that he wanted to see them on the aforementioned date, to confirm the peace existing between them and the Muslims. I am not certain when the peninsula of Tamkart was occupied by the king of France, but he had a fort and the stores necessary to the trade in wheat, barley, oil, wax and wool built there, for this trade took place there with the whole of Ifrikia. The king established a captain, an interpreter, secretaries and guards, none of whom was allowed to have a woman with him. When Younes arrived at Tamkart with his horsemen, after leaving Tabarka, the French understood that they were in no position to resist, and surrendered. Ships were sent up from Bizerte, and Younes had the Christians embarked and sent to the French consul in Tunis. He set up camp on the peninsula, gathered together everything which could be found, including the canons, and sent everything to Tunis on small boats. The sheikhs of the neighbouring Nefza and Mogods came to him with provisions, horses and presents. Then he left, leaving the Caid Brahim Ben Sassi to represent him, with orders to have all the buildings in this place demolished."

Mohamed Seghir Ben Youssef, Tarikh el mashra' el malaki *(1764).*

reaching a wide heathland with views over the sea towards La Galite. Sidi Mechrig has a narrow beach and the ruins of what might be a Roman baths. (The surf and depth of the water as you go in make unsupervised bathing unsuitable for very small children.) Local people set up camp here for the summer. There is a small, unclassified hotel.

Cap Negro (once known as Tamkart) is one of the most inaccessible of the northern beaches. You will definitely need a good four-wheel-drive vehicle. Coming from Bizerte, a couple of kilometres before Nefza, there is a badly signposted turn-off right, near the viaduct, for Cap Negro. The drive takes you along earth tracks through cork oak forest, where there are a few isolated farms. After some 10 km, the track gets increasingly stony. Ordinary cars give up on the climb towards the coast after the *maison forestière*. At the top of an arid, stony mountain, you come to a steep drop down to Cap Negro. There are a few visitors, and the police post will be delighted to be able to check your passport and car documents. Back in the 1970s, there was a small seasonal hotel. Now there are just the remains of a few 18th-century port buildings.

Closer to Tabarka is the **Zouara** beach, only 20 km before the town. Turn right off the Bizerte road before Aïn Sebna (a sign indicates the way) and follow a fairly easy track for 5 km. This is a beautiful beach with fine sand, but again there is no infrastructure whatsoever, just the odd seasonal shack. (Bathers should note that the currents can be strong.) This is the 'local beach' for inland Béja. The construction of the Sidi el Barrak dam on the Oued Zouara, which brought large amounts of silt down from the mountains to form the beach, may change the area somewhat.

Tabarka طبرقة

Tabarka, ancient Thabraca, is a pleasant low-key resort in the far northwestern corner of Tunisia. It is a sleepy sort of place, and the appearance of a zone touristique has not disturbed the pace of life. With its port and fishing boats, rocky island set with pines and topped with fort and lighthouse and sand beaches stretching eastwards along the coast, Tabarka would be an ideal setting for a 1950s Italian movie. The town centre is as yet largely unspoiled by new development and many of the new constructions have the red-tiled roofs of the older buildings. Looking inland, there are green forested hills, a welcome relief in the summer after the burnt landscapes of the interior.

Phone code: 78
Colour map 1, grid A2

Ins and outs

Tabarka is about 4 hrs' drive from Tunis. There are several routes, all scenic. The winding GP17 from Jendouba via Aïn Draham is the most spectacular. The GP7 coming in from Nefza to the east has been improved, as has the MC52 north from Béja to Nefza. So take your pick. Tabarka is also easily accessible by bus and louage. From Tunis, buses and louages run from the Gare routière at Bab Saâdoun. Arriving in Tabarka, the louage station is on the main street, Av Habib Bourguiba. From the long distance bus station on R du Peuple, turn left down the hill to the central square. The local bus station is about 50 m up the hill from the main square.

In season, charter flights from various European destinations arrive at the airport 9 km east of town at Ras Rajel.

Getting there
See Transport, page 218, for further details

You may need to take a taxi from the town centre to *zone touristique* and vice versa. The Musée du Liège (Cork Museum) is also a 25-min walk out of the town centre, so you might take a taxi for that. Aïn Draham is an easy day-trip by louage.

Getting around

Tourist offices on the beach-front promenade, after the main square on the right, T673555, F673428. Open 0900-1200 and 1600-1900. Only basic information.

Information

History

The origins of the town can be traced back to Haron (fifth century BC) who is said to have established a trading post here. The Phoenician town was called *Thabraca*, meaning 'place in the shade'. As a third-century Roman town it was noted for the export of wild beasts, wood for building, lead and iron from its mines and yellow marble from the quarries of Chemtou.

Thabraca played an important role in developments associated with luxurious buildings – painters, decorators, sculptors and ceramic artists made it the town of 'arts'. Mosaic artists founded a school here whose prestige won wide renown abroad for three centuries. The walls of the staircase in the Bardo Museum which leads from the ground floor to the galleries above are covered with tomb mosaics from Tabarka dating from the fourth and sixth centuries.

The town prospered with the spread of Christianity in the fifth century and especially during the reign of the Fatmids in the 10th century. In the 16th century it regained its status as a strategic harbour for merchant shipping, with the Genoese Lomellini family taking control of the island in 1542. The Genoese were in the Habsburg camp, and throughout the 17th century, the French made no secret of their designs on the island of Tabarka. They already had an important trading post, Bastion de France, near La Calle, some 30 km to the west, and another at Cap Negro.

Northern Tunisia

The result of much intrigue was an expeditionary force led by Younes, son of Ali Pacha in 1741. Both Tabarka and Cap Negro were taken by the beylical forces. Younes had the town of Tabarka destroyed, although he left the fort intact. The Tabarquins were taken prisoner and transported to Tunis, where they were housed at Bab Souika. Wrote 18th century Tunisian historian Mohamed Seghir Ben Yousef: "Among these prisoners, all the young girls who seemed attractive were taken by the pacha or his sons. The boys were also taken by the pacha to be brought up with the mamlouks; those who showed themselves intelligent were invited to convert to Islam, which they did in general out of fear, after which the pacha had them circumcised, named them Mustapha or Ismail and gave them employment." The other Tabarquins, given their skills, easily settled into life in the city. The destruction of the Genoese settlement and the *comptoir* at Cap Negro had unfortunate side-effects for the region, leading to the decline of Béja.

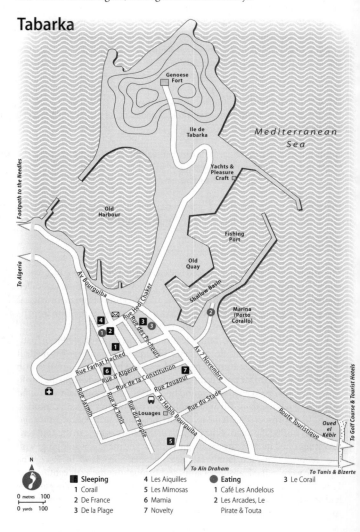

Tabarka

■ Sleeping		● Eating	
1 Corail	4 Les Aiguilles	1 Café Les Andelous	3 Le Corail
2 De France	5 Les Mimosas	2 Les Arcades, Le	
3 De la Plage	6 Mamia	Pirate & Touta	
	7 Novelty		

Northern Tunisia *(side margin)*

France became important at Tabarka in 1781 when the Compagnie royale d'Afrique succeeded in gaining exclusive coral-harvesting rights in the waters from Tabarka to Tripoli. A consulate was set up in 1804. The fortress was gradually abandoned. In the Second World War, the fortress was a centre for the Free French, and would have been in the line of fire of Axis forces attempting to enter the Constantinois over the frontier.

Tabarka is known today for its fishing: lobsters, shrimps, prawns and crayfish form an important part of the catch. For those who wish to look at the fish, the local dive schools organize excursions to the *Grotte des Mérous*, where you can make friends with large cod and other denizens of the deep.

Sights

Tabarka's two main sights are the Genoese fort and a weird, eroded rock formation, Les Aiguilles. The latter is just west of town – walk along the promenade, which follows the bay across which you can see the old fort built by the Genoese. The **Aiguilles** ('The Needles'), some 20 m high, are moderately impressive, carved out of the rock by sea and wind. The view from the top of the old fort is impressive and it is worth the effort of walking up the hill. Probably best not to photograph close to, as the military appear to be in residence for the moment. The fort once dominated an island ruled as a trading strong point by the Lomellini family. The causeway is a 20th-century addition.

Tabarka is the centre for **diving** on the north coast and the diving centre in the Yachting Club on the sea front is open all year. The club also organizes other watersport activities including underwater photography. In the autumn, **wild boar hunting** attracts a following of mainly Italian visitors and a few locals. There is now an 18-hole golf course on the *route touristique*. The course, part of which overlooks the sea – see Golf, page 55, for further details.

The **Musée Archéologique** was once in the 'basilica'. The collections of Roman mosaics, votive stelae etc, may be transferred to the Genoese Citadel. The basilica, where jazz evenings and other summer concerts are held, is in fact a Roman cistern (capacity 2,700 cubic m) which must have kept the public fountains of the ancient town supplied. The Pères Blancs transformed the cistern into a church. ■ *0830-1730 winter, 0900-1300 and 1500-1900 summer, closed Mon, entrance 1Dt*. You might also walk up to the **Borj Messaoud**, a small restored Husseinid fortress dating from the 18th century.

There is a **military cemetery** with 500 Second World War graves 15 km east of town on the P7. ■ *0730-1430, Sat-Thu*.

Jazz festival In the summer, a minor jazz festival, lasting about a week, brings together an interesting mix of jazz fans from the capital, tourists from the hotels and bemused locals (almost exclusively male). Back in the 1970s, Tabarka's slogan, invented by energetic young promoter Lotfi Belhassine, was 'Ne bronzez pas idiot' ('You don't have to tan like an idiot', rough translation). The original jazz festival was part of this strategy. In recent years, the festival has varied between the end of the summer, and, more recently, late June/early July. The events range from rather stiff concerts held in the hotels in the presence of local bigwigs to the more entertaining soirées in the open air, in the street outside the *Café Andalous* and the *Hotel Les Aiguilles*. Smoke a *chicha* at a café terrace and listen to jazz. What more could you ask for?

Local beaches There is a fine stretch of sand east of the town, running from the port to the new *zone touristique*, where the golf course directly overlooks some small coves. If

On the origins of an Italian enclave

"In 1530, or thereabouts, Jean Doria, commander of four galleys belonging to his uncle and adoptive father, André Doria, having heard that Dragut, the famous pirate of Algiers, was at the island of Corsica with six galleys, set out on the attack and captured him. Doria mocked Dragut about how such a famous pirate had let himself be taken. Dragut, a proud man, replied that the thing which made him most angry was that he had been captured by a ragassou, a mere young man. Doria, angered by this answer, had him clapped in irons, and Dragut was transferred to the galleys of one M Lomellini, of Genoa, who dealt with his ransom. Among a number of things, Dragut promised to give him the island of Tabarka for its coral fishing. He kept his promise, and

the gift was confirmed by the firmans of Soliman II, Ottoman emperor who had conquered the kingdom of Tunis. Later Lomellini reached an agreement with Charles V, who agreed to have a citadel built there and maintain a garrison to defend the island, on the condition that the Genoese who traded there pay him five percent on all their trade. The agreement was kept for some time, and Charles V had the castle, which I have just described, constructed. He took stones from ancient Tabraca, and a number of stones with epitaphs can be found in the castle."

Jean-André Peyssonel, Voyage dans les régences de Tunis et d'Alger *(extract from the tenth letter, Cap Nègre, 28 November 1724)*.

you fancy a change, there is the beach at **Melloula**, 7 km west of Tabarka on the road to Algeria. Leave the car at the top, and you have a 20-minute walk down the hillside to the pebbly beach, one of the few in Tunisia. East of Tabarka, there are beaches at **Barkoukech** (near the airport), Jebbara and Aïn Sobh.

The archipelago of La Galite
These islands are basically an off-limits nature reserve

Out in the Mediterranean, about 60 km from Tabarka, lies an archipelago of seven small islands (**La Galite**, *Jalta* in Arabic, is the largest; the others have names like Le Gallo, Pollastro and La Gallina). La Galite is clearly visible from Cap Serrat on a clear day. Once the islands were inhabited by a few fishermen and their families. La Galite, about 5 by 2 km, was a stopping-off point for Phoenician mariners, and was peopled in Roman times. There are abandoned quarries, caves, remains of Roman tombs and Punic relics. La Garde mountain (361 m) is the highest point. Generally the islands are off-limits, partly in order to preserve the peace and quiet of the rare monk seals living on Galiton. There is occasional talk in the Tunisian press of developing day-trips to the islands, but 60 km is a trek and requires a fairly powerful boat (which could all to easily be used for more illicit purposes, like shipping migrants across to Italy). You could ask at the diving schools in the port area about the possibility of a visit.

Essentials

Sleeping
■ *on map, page 214*
Price codes:
see inside front cover

Tabarka has a good range of hotels, although demand tends to exceed supply in the summer months. Although new A/B grade hotels along the route touristique have increased the number of beds available, in summer booking is essential. Hotels are listed here according to area: town centre or *zone touristique*. Note that there is less very cheap accommodation here than in the larger tourist resorts. Good out-of-season bargains are available. If staying in cheaper accommodation in the town centre, check if they have heating in winter – or bring your longjohns.

Zone touristique A *Abou Nawas Montazah*, T673532, F673530. 306 rooms with balcony, phone, heating, no a/c, no fly screens, superb Olympic size pool, beach site, tennis, windsurfing, scuba-diving tuition, exercise room and sauna, minimal carpeting so noise echoes through hotel at every step. **A** *Iberotel Méhari*, T670001/3, F673943. 200 rooms, much quieter than *Montazah*, good restaurant, pool, beach site, tennis. Just across the road is the **B** *Résidence Iberotel Méhari*, T671444/5, F673943. Self-catering units set in a small pine wood. Safe play area for children, some units with view over golf course. Minimal kitchenware supplied. Residents have use of indoor and outdoor pools in main hotel. Also in this zone, look out for a new top class hotel, opening planned for summer 2002, the **A?** *Dar Ismaïl*. **B** *Morjane*, on the road behind the sand-dunes, T644453, F673888. 160 rooms, the first hotel built on the beach, very convenient. Attractively simple. Staff at reception range from the very unpleasant to the very accommodating. **B** *Golf Beach Hotel*, T673002, F673918. Spacious rooms, a bit overdecorated. Small gym, pool, sauna, tennis. **B** *Royal Golf Marhaba*, T644002, F673838. More of the same.

Town centre B-C *Les Mimosas*, on the left as you enter the town, T673018, F673276. On top of a hill overlooking the bay, rather nice round pool, 60 rooms with sea view, 10 in main building, others (many poorly soundproofed) in independent wing with balconies. Good breakfast. Reasonable restaurant. First impression: a charming place. Second impression: needs more careful management. **C** *Hotel Corail*, 76 Av Habib Bourguiba, on corner with R Tazerka, T673082, 50 beds, cheap, but only recommended if funds are low or everything else is full. No ensuite rooms. **C** *Hotel de la Plage*, R des Pecheurs, T670039. 14 beds. Clean but spartan, no heating in winter. **C** *Hotel Novelty*, Av Habib Bourguiba, T670176 F673008. Mid-1990s hotel, 26 rooms, central, very clean. Streetside rooms a little noisy. Terrace café downstairs. **C** *Hotel de France*, Av Habib Bourguiba, T644577. 38 beds, restaurant, old-fashioned charm, probably the best of the cheap hotels, recently revamped. **D** *Pension de famille Mamia*, 11 R de Tunis, T671058, F670638, basic sort of place, 20 2/3-bed rooms on 2 floors, no heating in winter, showers extra – but close to a hammam, also to a mosque for your early morning call. Tunisian clientele.

Expensive *Le Pirate*, Porto Corallo, T670061. For some this is the best address in Tabarka. Compare with the *Restaurant Touta*, also in Porto Corallo, T671018, closes during Ramadan. Another good marina eatery. Terrace with view of port and fort. The full wack for around 20Dt, possibly more, depending on your choice of fish. **Mid-range** *Hotel Les Aiguilles* has an entirely acceptable restaurant with outside terrace. 3-course menu 10Dt. Bill can be steep if you go for à la carte. Alcohol. *Hotel de France*, Av Habib Bourguiba, reasonable food at very decent prices. *Les Arcades*, Porto Corallo, T670069. *Le Pescadou*, close to Porto Corallo, T671580. Tunisian food – has had some good reports. **Cheap** *Le Corail*, Av Bourguiba, 2 blocks after the *Hotel Novelty* as you head eastwards. Reasonably priced, filling Tunisian food. *Novelty 66*, Av Habib Bourguiba, T670367.

Eating
● *on map, page 214*

The *Café Les Andalous* is the great Tabarka classic, where demon card players work out surrounded by walls covered in antique junk and painted tiles. On the same street, try the shaded café terrace of the *Hotel Les Aiguilles*. Otherwise, you could walk up to the *Hotel Les Mimosas* for a drink. In the port area there are plenty of café terraces.

Cafés

Diving *Club de plongée du Yachting Club*, Port de Tabarka, T/F671478, the first sub-aqua sports centre in Tunisia, recommended by the Tunisian National Tourist Office, open all year, best season Apr-Oct. Dive sites only 15 mins by boat. Only those with club membership may participate in diving – in other words you have to join – but the club premises are of a very high standard and the changing facilities excellent. Competent monitors, rescue equipment available. Try also *Loisirs de Tabarka*, T670664, F794226,

Sport

Northern Tunisia

diving.tunisie@planet.tn On the north quay of the port, works with the UCPA, a French sports tourism organization. They might also do you a trip out to La Galite. Snorkels can be rented from *Magasin Sinbad d'Equipment Marin*, at the port. In the *zone touristique*, diving is available at the *Mehari Diving Centre*, 'Le Crab', T673136, F673868, PADI affiliated, has a range of courses available; also *Aquamarin*, T673508. **Golf** *Tabarka Golf*, T671031, F671026, 18-hole course, 6,400 m, par 72, fees 30-35Dt per day. One of the few courses in the world to have 7 holes right on the sea. See Golf, page 55, for further details. **Horse riding** Can be arranged at the hotels. There may be some horse-trekking available in the near future. Try *Golf Beach Equitation*, T671816, near the *Golf Beach Hotel*, open mid-Mar to late Sep, around 20Dt for 2 hrs. **Sailing** The marina has 50 moorings with planned extension to 280 berths. **Tennis** At the hotels. **Walking** The region's forested, hilly scenery would seem ideal for walkers. For the moment, there are no hiking marked footpaths and no detailed maps available. Try *Tabarka Voyages*, T673740, F673726, on the Aïn Draham rd for further information.

Shopping
Market day: Friday

Handicrafts Little of interest apart from Tabarka briar pipes (although the shop that did these on Av Bourguiba, near the *Hotel Novelty*, has closed) and the ubiquitous coral. In fact, Mediterranean red coral is now severely endangered, having been collected for jewellery for centuries. Prices reflect the rarity and difficulty of collecting the coral. **Other souvenirs** You will also find lots of crude arbutus wood carvings of eagles, snakes, stags etc. In the soft toy range, the *Select Shop* in the port had some rather nice furry wild boars (*hallouf*) along with the more usual camels.

Tour operators

Tabarka Voyages, Av Ennasr (Route d'Aïn Draham), T673740, F673726. *Tunisie Voyages* in *Hotel Mehari*, T673136, F673868. *Ulysse Tour*, Blvd du 7-Novembre, T673582, F673622. *Vaga Tours*, Cité des Arts, T644416, F654803.

Transport

Local *Allô Taxi*, T673636. **Car hire** *Hertz*, Port Corallo, T/F670670. *Europcar*, Blvd du 7-Novembre, T67083; at airport, T640005, F640133.

Long distance Air: T680113, 680005, internal flights to Tunis taking 40 mins have been discontinued. Most of the air traffic is now charter flights. *Tunisair* at the airport are on T680082/092, F680111. **Road**: there are 2 bus stations, long distance (SNTRI) and local (SRTJ and SRT du Kef). The long distance **bus** station is on R du Peuple (1st street on the right going uphill from the central square). Information from SNTRI, R de Peuple, on T444048. Departures **Tunis** (via Mateur) 0400, 0500, 0730, 0900, 1545; **Tunis** (via Béja) 0600, 1000, 1300. The buses for towns in the region depart from the station 50 m uphill from the central square. Frequent departures to **Aïn Draham** and **Jendouba**. 2 buses a day to **Bizerte**. Information from SRT de Jendouba, Av Habib Bourguiba, on T644097. **Louages**: the station is at the beginning of Av Habib Bourguiba. Departures for **Jendouba, Aïn Draham, Le Kef** and sometimes **Tunis**. **'Noddy train'**: from tourist hotels to marina/old harbour along tourist road. Leaves on the hour from old harbour. **Sea**: Port – Harbour Master's Office, T670599, F673595.

Directory

Banks *BNT* and *UIB*, Av Habib Bourguiba. *BNA* on R de Peuple. **Medical services** Hospital:, R de Calle, T670023; *Clinque Sidi Moussa* 1 Av Bourguiba, opposite *Hotel Les Aiguilles*, T671200, 670312; *SAMU* (emergency call out), T673665/653; **Night Pharmacy**, 5 R Ali Zouaoui. **Communications** Internet: *Publinet*, on the beach-front promenade, close to tourist office. **Post office**: Av Hédi Chaker, T644417, Mon-Fri 0830-1230 and 1500-1800, Sat 0830-1330. **Useful addresses** Police station: R du Peuple, T644021. **Maritime police**, Port de Tabarka. **Border police**: Melloula, T632889/860. **Police-Babouche-Algerian border**: T655150.

Southwards from Tabarka

Heading southwards from Tabarka, the road, flanked by tall eucalyptus, runs across flat meadowland. After crossing the Oued Rannagha, you begin the winding climb up towards Aïn Draham. (There are wonderful views back towards the coast.) The vegetation changes, the cork oak replaces the maquis and the oleander. At Babouch (21 km from Tabarka), there is a turning west to **Hammam Bourguiba**, 17 km, a thermal spa greatly prized by the Romans. There are two springs, the lower emerging at 38.5°C and the higher at 50°C. The spa facilities are still managed by the Office National du Thermalisme and the ONTT, the Tunisian Tourist Board. The high sulphur levels in the water are good for treating respiratory problems. In the vaporium, the treatment is to inhale vapour from nose cups, the aim being to 'coat' the nasal mucus and sinuses.

Sleeping C *Hotel Hammam Bourguiba*, T78632517, F78632497. Open all year, has 40 rooms and 20 bungalows and is used by Tunisians taking treatment.

This road also leads to the Algerian border but the crossing in this area has about 10 km between control posts, a walk not to be undertaken lightly. Border post control at Babouch, T78647150. | **Tunisio-Algerian border**

Aïn Draham عين دراهم

Aïn Draham is located up in the Khroumirie Mountains. Surrounded by wooded hills, it is a one-street sort of place, focusing on a main road lined with big old trees and whitewashed buildings. The cafés are torpid, the people look poorer than in east-coast Tunisia, on the main 'square' stalls sell local craftwork. Happily, there are signs that prosperity is on its way: newly built housing, all roofed in local red tiles, spreads out on the surrounding slopes, upmarket hotels have appeared in the region. Coming up from the inland plains in summer, the cool air of Aïn Draham is a welcome change. The town is popular as a base for hunters in winter, the wild boar that go rootling through the cork oak forest being the main target. In chilly years, city Tunisians come up to Aïn Draham to see the snow. In summer, you will find some pleasant walks in the surrounding hills, maybe even some horse riding. A short drive south, off the Jendouba road, the Lutyens-style village of Beni M'tir feels like some half-forgotten 1930s hill station.

Phone code: 78
Colour map 1, grid A2

Getting there Aïn Draham can be reached by public transport from Tabarka and Jendouba. Journey time by louage from Tabarka is about 45 mins, from Jendouba 80 mins. **Getting around** The town is easily visited on foot. Getting up to Beni M'tir is awkward, although it may be possible to find a louage. **Information** Tourist office: *Syndicat D'Initiative*, Av Habib Bourguiba, towards the top, T647115. | **Ins & outs**
See Transport, page 221, for further details

To start with some etymology, Aïn Draham means 'spring of the dirhams', the dirham being a long-established currency unit in the Middle East (and official currency in Morocco and the UAE today) that derives from the Greek drachma. | **History**

Aïn Draham lies 175 km west of Tunis and 26 km south of Tabarka. The present settlement, stretched out along the main Jendouba–Tabarka road, dates from protectoral times. The steep red-tiled roofs – an indication of snowy winters – make the town feel like some Basque country settlement that fetched up in North Africa. Thick cork-oak forests surround the town, running up to 1,000 m into the mountains. Aïn Draham is the sort of place where French army officers' wives might have escaped the sticky summer heat of Tunis. In winter, temperatures can get down to freezing, and some years, snow is common. Aïn Draham is also the heart of the wild boar hunting region and it can be difficult to find places in hotels during the season from October to March.

Sights On the main drag, the *Association du Patrimoine Populaire et Historique d'Aïn Draham* (welcoming staff) has a small office with a display of local handicrafts. Just north of Aïn Draham, to the west of the road, is **Col des Ruines**. This small detour has splendid views as does the terrace of *Hotel Nour el Aïn*. Also popular for an afternoon's walk is Djebel Bir, the other 'summit' in the area.

The local craftwork, although enthusiastically executed, is often of poor quality. You may find some nice large ash-wood bowls. On the roads into Aïn Draham, small children make whooping noises from the side of the road to attract the driver's attention. On sale, according to the season, may be ferns and red-berried *subhan el khallak* in cork-bark pots, shell necklaces, arbutus-wood model wild boar and gazelles with a very East African flavour.

Beni M'Tir Beni M'Tir is a spectacular detour off the main road south of Aïn Draham. The reservoir, built in 1955 on the Oued el Lil, a tributary of the Oued Medjerda, is one of Tunisia's largest. The village of Beni M'tir, built high up among the cork-oak woods, is a curious place. The buildings have a 1920s Lutyens feel. There is a church and a mosque, and a large square overlooked by a small café with a fireplace which must have been a pleasant, snug place in its day. Shutters and doors have been given a rather tasteless red-and-black paint job. Beni M'Tir feels like it was built for a population of wealthy weekenders who have not been around for many a year.

Sleeping **B** *La Forêt*, on the Jendouba road, T655302, F655335. The Aïn Draham area's most
Winter travellers: expensive hotel, opened late 1990s. Expensive for what's on offer (rooms a little
check that your hotel cramped) but they have good heating. Indoor pool being built. **B-C** *Hotel Nour el Aïn*,
has good heating T655600, F655185. 60 rooms, open all year, covered heated pool, health club, interna-
when you book tional menu, busiest in hunting season. Views north over the town, south towards
Tabarka. Tracks run off into the woods if you fancy a stroll. **B** *Hotel Rihana* T655391,
F655578. 3-star place, best in central Aïn Draham, 74 rooms, good services. Same management as **C** *Les Chênes*, 7 km out of town in the Jendouba direction, up in the
woods, T655211, F655315. Looking very worn, 32 rooms, make sure you have a look at
the rooms before deciding whether to stay. Open fireplaces in rooms can fill your room
with smoke … Could be wonderful. Is this the hotel once called *Transatlantique* that
Second World War correspondent Alan Moorhead stayed in? Said to organize
wild-boar hunting. Also has a riding centre. **C** *Résidence Les Pins*, on the main street,
T656200, F656182, recent building, 40 rooms, loo and shower, TV, also serves food.
Clean and simple. **C-D** *Beau Séjour*, Av Habib Bourguiba, T647005. Central, 50 rooms,
most with loo and shower, a place once used by the French hunting fraternity. Book in
summer. Restaurant. Most rooms are in main accommodation block (glacial in winter),
separate from the reception. Expensive for what's on offer, but certainly atmospheric:
stuffed animals and staff like something out of the Adams Family. Have a nice stay.

Youth hostel At the top of the hill, off road to Jendouba, T/F655087. 150 beds,
7Dt/px with breakfast, rooms with 2/4 beds, some with shower, those in new block
slightly better.

Mid-range and cheap Not much choice, unless you want to try one of the big hotels **Eating** for an expensive feed. There are the usual cheap eateries on the main drag. Try, for example, the *Café de la Republique*, the restaurant of *Le Beau Séjour* (do they still do *marcassin*, wild boar piglet, or has the Ministry of Health banned this?), or *Le Khemir* very cheap and cheerful.

Wild-boar hunting Oct-Feb, see *Hotel Les Chênes*. They can also do riding, around **Sport** 10Dt/hour, 40Dt/day. For wild-boar hunting, see also *Ulysse Tours* in Tabarka, T78673582. The recent sports complex 6 km south of town is used mainly by Tunisian football teams training in the summer.

Road Bus: the station is at the bottom of Av Habib Bourguiba, on the right, by the ceme- **Transport** tery. Frequent buses to **Tunis**, **Jendouba** and **Tabarka**. **Louages**: the station is situated at the top of Av Habib Bourguiba, on the square. Main routes are to **Jendouba** and **Tabarka**.

Banks All on Av Habib Bourguiba. *BNT, STB* are opposite *Association du Patrimoine*, **Directory** and *BNA* is beyond the Tourist Office. **Communications** Post Office: Av Habib Bourguiba, T647118. Further up the road after the *Association du Patrimoine*. **Medical services** Hospital: on Route de l'Hôpital, T647047. **Useful addresses** Police: Av Habib Bourguiba, T647150.

South from Aïn Draham

Moving south from Aïn Draham, the road continues to twist up through the woods, with here and there some superb views across hills and plains. You pass the *Hotel La Forêt* with its view looking back up to Aïn Draham and then, more isolated, the *Hotel Les Chênes*, shortly after which is the turn-off for the hill-village of **Beni M'tir**.

At 45 km from Aïn Draham you reach **Fernana**, interesting for an anecdote about how the tribes decided to pay their taxes to the bey. At Fernana (which means 'oak'), the tribal leaders would assemble under a great oak tree and await the tree's decision on whether they should pay or not. The movement of the branches meant 'no', and it was a rare year that the branches did not move. The importance of the story is that it demonstrates that the tribes were practically independent from central authority, right up until the development of the Tunisian nation state in the mid-20th century.

After Fernana, it is another 15 km before you come to a crossroads, just north of **Jendouba**, where you can opt to go left to **Bulla Regia** (3 km) or right to **Chemtou**, ancient Simitthu, some 17 km away.

Bulla Regia ﺑﻼﺭﻳﺠﻴﺔ

Under the Djebel Rebia, situated on a flat plain, Bulla Regia is one of the most Colour map 1, grid B2 *unusual sites in northern Tunisia. This was a town whose wealth was built on cereal farming, for the plains of northern Tunisia came to provide Rome with large quantities of grain. Bulla Regia's wealthy farmers and merchants saw no reason to deprive themselves of pleasant surroundings, and their underground homes, almost unique in the ancient world, were opulent and refined. Some of the building work is still impressive: stone for the Romans seems to have been like butter, they sliced through it to make the most complicated joints and vaults. It is doubtful whether today's concrete and brick homes down the road in Jendouba achieve the same degree of comfort as the trogolodyte villas of Bulla Regia.*

Northern Tunisia

Ins & outs   **Getting there** Bulla Regia lies 3 km east of the Aïn Draham–Jendouba road. Take a bus from Jendouba and ask to get off at Bulla Regia. The intersection is 6 km north of Jendouba and is signed to Bulla Regia and Bou Salem. You will have to walk or hitch the remaining 3 km. **Getting around** As you drive up from the crossroads, the Antiquarium (museum) and guichet iis on your right, along with the South Baths and the Church of Alexander. The vast majority of the site is on your left. An hr is the minimum time to allow for exploring the site. Do not miss the House of the Hunt (Maison de la Chasse). There is no accommodation at the site. Visit the museum first (café and toilets), where you may be able to buy a guide book.

History   In 2 BC, Bulla Regia was the capital of one of the three small kingdoms set up by the Romans in Numidia after the death of Masinissa. Prosperity was to come under the rule of Hadrian, when the town was raised to the status of *colonia* (AD 117). The economic development of the town was based on its strategic position on trade routes and the fertility of the surrounding plain which produced grain in abundance. The finest houses date from the third century AD. There are the remains of two basilicas dating from Byzantine times.

It is probable that Bulla Regia grew up to serve the needs of the grain trade in the upper Medjerda valley. Italian agriculture was devastated by the Second Punic War and the social uprisings of the last years of the Republic. It was under Numidian ruler Masinissa that the region's potential was revealed. Masinissa, tribal chief of the Massyli, built himself a North African Kingdom. Seizing Carthage's grain lands, he began to export to Rome.

Eventually, the Numidian lands were to come into the imperial system in the mid-first century BC. By the second century BC, Rome had developed a voracious appetite for grain. It is estimated that the empire's capital required 400,000 tonnes per annum, with the army requiring a further 100,000 tonnes. Africa was better placed than Egypt to satsify the demand, being only three to five sailing days from Rome's main port, Ostia, as opposed to 17 to 22 days from Alexandria to Ostia. Risks of shipwreck and transport costs were thus lower. Africa also had climatic advantages: fairly reliable winter rains, mild frost-free springs and good summer sun. The Roman peace did the rest, creating conditions in which irrigation works could be built and towns like Bulla Regia could grow and flourish.

The site   The ruins are laid out on terraces below the steep slopes of Djebel Rebia (647 m) overlooking a large plain, which is particularly hot in summer and cold in winter. The Roman builders' solution to this climatic problem was to build houses partly underground, a system which can be seen still in use today at Matmata in south-central Tunisia.

These **underground villas** are the main attraction in Bulla Regia. Despite earthquake damage to the surface features, many of the villas are well preserved due to their unusual architecture. Like normal, aboveground villas, the general style was to have the eating and sleeping rooms centred around a large underground courtyard, thus giving the owners – wealthy people, judging from the luxurious decoration – the chance to

Bulla Regia

escape the winter cold and the glare and heat of the summers. Despite being underground, these homes were carefully orientated to benefit from the sunlight at different times of day. The villas were no doubt the first really comfortable houses in the region.

The decision to develop underground homes required the right sort of technical solution. In the **Maison de la Chasse**, note that the ceilings are arched. To build these vaults, the inventive Roman builders came up with the hollow terracotta tube. Bottomless bottle-shaped tubes, the neck generally facing upwards, were slotted together to form arches and then sealed with cement. No doubt the inside of the vault was plastered and decorated. Given the materials available perhaps this was the best solution for creating strong but light roofing. Originally, the system was used only for simple barrel vaults. Later it was applied to domes and more complicated forms of vaulting.

Most of the better mosaics have been taken to the Bardo Museum (see Tunis page 94), but in the **House of Fishing** and the **House of Amphitrite** some magnificent mosaics are still in place. Above-ground structures which are still visible include the **Theatre** complete with stage, the **Memmian Baths**, the **Forum**, the **Temple of Apollo**, and a Christian Basilica. The **Forum** is a rectangular area with religious and public buildings on all four sides. To the west is the Capitol of which little remains, to the north stands the Temple of Apollo, more ancient than the Forum on to which it opens by means of a small courtyard. A quite remarkable group of statues found here are on display in the Bardo Museum, in particular that of Apollo which gave its name to the temple. A hall with double apse and paved geometric mosaics in very poor condition stands to the east.

The Memmian Baths (some of the walls of the *frigidarium* still standing) are by the entrance to the site. Beneath are basement rooms with groin vaults. In 1942, a hoard of 70 seventh-century Byzantine pieces of gold was discovered in an underground villa north of the Memmian Baths, now renamed the Treasure House, indicating occupancy up to that late period. Here an examination of the mosaic pattern shows the arrangement of the dining room. ■ *0800-1900 in summer, 0830-1730 in winter, closed Mon. 2Dt, photography fee 1Dt.*

Chemtou   شمتو

The ancient Simittus, modern Chemtou, is yet another unusual Roman site. Here   Colour map 1, grid B1
you can see the impressive results of ancient industrial archaeology, intelligently displayed and interpreted in a superb museum. Simittuss was one of the most important quarries of the Roman world, supplying a unique golden marble to decorate opulent building schemes: imperial propaganda through overblown architecture. Spreading out below a rocky, half-quarried hill, the site of Simittuss, once home to a slave army and Roman overlords, is an unassuming place today. Sheep graze over the lumpy terrain which still conceals a whole town. Children splash in the water by the titanic blocks of the ruined bridge. There are skylarks and redstarts and the occasional hovering bird of prey. To the west, the grey hills rise up towards the Algerian frontier. Do not miss the view from the top of the quarry hill.

Getting there The C59 is now fully metalled the whole way to Chemtou from the   **Ins & outs**
turn-off on the main P17 Aïn Draham to Jendouba road (distance 17 km). If you don't have your own transport, you should be able to get a rural minibus up from Jendouba in the morning, although the minibus may stop at the settlement a few kms short of the site. As you come into Chemtou by car, take a left turn and the road will bring you up and over between 2 parts of the hill. You then come down to the car park and museum.

History The original Numidian settlement of Simittus became a Roman colony under Augustus (27 BC to AD 14), taking on the name Colonia Iulia Augusta Numidica Simmithensium. It was also known by the snappier acronym CIANS.

The colony quickly won fame for its **yellow marble**, *il giallo antico*, which continued to be quarried until Byzantine times. This city was situated at the junction of two important routes: west from Carthage through Bulla Regia and south from Tabarka (*Thabraca*). It covered a large area (about 80 ha), both on the hilltop by the quarries where there are huge masonry blocks belonging to a ruined Roman temple (perhaps dedicated to Saturn), and below where there are large baths (ruins) and the complicated water system that supplied and connected them to the aqueduct. Here too was a theatre, parts of which have been excavated, a forum, a basilica and a building thought to be a *schola*.

Il giallo antico Yellow marble from Chemtou was to become the height of fashion in Rome. Pliny the Elder tells of elegant Emilius Lepidus ordering a table in thuya wood from the Atlas and having his doorsteps done in yellow Chemtou marble. In 46 BC, the quarries became part of the ruling Iulii family's property. Later they became part of the imperial domains. In 44 BC, when Julius Caesar was assassinated, the Roman plebs erected a column of Chemtou marble to his memory.

In an imperial system where the succession went through periods of turbulence, the ruling caste was ever seeking for new ways to impress its power on the people. Splendid building was one way to do this, fine stone, and in particular marble, helped. From Greece came green Thessalian marble and green porphyry, while Phrygia produced a prized veiny marble. Egypt was the source of pink and grey granite and red porphyry. Africa produced 'the golden rock of the Numidians'. In large pieces, this stone was rather fragile, and so it tended to be used for veneering and occasional columns. The Pantheon, built from 118 to 124 under Hadrian, made use of it. The colour of Chemtou marble eventually became a poetic commonplace: Martial describes an amphitheatre lion as having 'a mane similar in colour to Numidian marble'. In fact, the colour of the marble quarried at Chemtou varied considerably, from white through veiny yellows to greys and greenish-ochres, as a display of samples in the site museum shows.

The museum Situated between the craggy hill dominating the site and the River Medjerda, the site museum is all that you could ask for. Although the finds are not obviously spectacular, they do tell a story. The displays are excellent, and the place is not too big for children to get bored in. For the English-speaking visitor, there is the slight drawback of displays being labelled in French, German and Arabic only. However, the displays are sufficiently well thought out for school French and imagination to get you a long way.

There is a good display of the evolution of the **Libyic script**, the first writing system in the region. The geometric forms are well known, and bilingual Libyic and Latin inscriptions have been discovered. Like later Semitic alphabets, ancient Libyic was a consonant-based system, the vowels being left unmarked. Most of the texts known today are from Dougga and Makthar and are funerary inscriptions.

There is a telling panel about the analysis of 337 skeletons from a **Numidian necropolis** discovered under the later Roman forum. Basically, the bone analysis revealed different stages in the local people's development. Prior to 3000 BC, 80% of children never got beyond the age of six, and life expectancy was only 50. From 300 to 100 BC, the bones are more resistant, the skeletons better preserved. The men have more distorted skeletons (bow-legged, distorted femurs), possibly as they spent much time as mounted warriors? Finally, in the third period, post-100 BC, the skeletons are in an even better condition, with no fractures due to violence, indicating more settled times.

Despite the limited archaeological discoveries, the museum is interesting on the Numidian Kingdoms, which basically flourished in the second century BC, during the long reigns of Masinissa (202-148 BC) and Micipsisa (148-118 BC.) This was a time of prosperity for the local Massyli tribe, and agriculture developed considerably on the Medjerda plains. (Numidia's independent status later unravelled with dynastic infighting in the first century BC.) The museum has a mock up of the **Numidian monument**, thought to have been built under Micipsa around 130 BC to the glory of Masinissa. This would make the building contemporary to the Dougga monument to Masinissa. The monument, as restituted here, is endearingly eclectic, hung with stone shields and breast plates, the roof defined by an Egyptian cornice-line and supported by Doric pilasters. Later the building became a temple to Saturn, before being switched over to the incense-heavy rites of Byzantine Christianity. (Think of Roman Catholicism grafting itself on to animist rites in contemporary Africa.)

Other interesting items in the museum include ancient tools and explanations of the slave barracks. There is a display of small ornamental statues of Venus at different stages in their production, and a copy of the unique Baal Saturn plate, of which the original is in the Louvre. All things Hellenic indicated taste in the wealthy Roman household. One might decorate one's villa with copies of fifth century Greek statuary, and the sophisticates of Chemtou were no exception: there is a copy of the Dresden Youth (**Le jeune de Dresde**), from an original by Polycleitus, which no doubt adorned some atrium. In a niche, the results of patient archaeological work are on show in the shape of the partly restored terra-cotta statue of the emperor Commodus as Hercules (recognizable by the skin of the Nemean lion). And there is the inevitable mosaic, a representation of *Dionysos cosmocrator*, Dionysus lord of the universe, a popular theme in African mosaics.

Perhaps the most spectacular discovery at Chemtou was the **hoard** of coins uncovered in May 1993 when the museum was being constructed. An earthenware pot was brought to light containing 1,648 gold pieces, weighing over 7 kg. A careful study of the emperors on these coins indicated that the hoard was buried a few years before the Vandal invasion, towards AD 420. ■ *1000-1700 Oct-Mar, 0900-1800 Apr-Sep.*

Ancient Simittus was explored in the 19th century in a limited sort of way. How- **The site**
ever, it wasn't until 1970 that serious excavations got going, with the Institut National du Patrimoine working with the German archaeological school in Rome, led by F Rakob. The main buildings explored were the workers barracks ('camp des ouvriers') and the Numidian monument at the summit of the hill.

Outside the museum, there is an interesting stretch of Roman road which has been unearthed, and no doubt great plaques of marble were transported along it and down to the river. Leaving the museum, if you turn left down a rough track, you will come to the forum, with remains of its nympheum, basilica, and some Numidian tombs. The theatre is straight ahead, and were you to follow the track straight on, and turn right, you come to the remains of the baths.

More impressive, however, are the remaining arches of a huge **bridge**, built by the III Legion in 112 in Trajan's reign, over the Oued Medjerda, then known as the Bagrada. Apparently, the bridge was washed away in serious flooding in the fourth century. The system set up for a **water-driven cornmill** either by or on the bridge (locks, sluices and water channels) can be discerned. This is an unusual feature, the only one of its kind known in Africa, and represents the height of Roman mechanical technology.

The quarries The overgrown terrain of Chemtou today is still dominated by the craggy hill site of the quarries. Perhaps the most impressive thing is the transport of the marble. Great columns, carved from a single block, were transported over the Khroumirie Mountains and down to Tabarka. The first recorded road, 60 km long, was built under Hadrian in 129. Perhaps prior to then the stone was shipped out down the river. The whole quarrying process was highly organized, with blocks of marble cut to various standard sizes and marked with the name of the reigning Emperor, the proconsul for Africa and the quarry manager. In fact, large numbers of blocks from the first and second centuries AD were discovered stored ready for use in the Marmorata neighbourhood of Rome when it was cleared in the 19th century. But it was not just in the imperial capital where the state was building to impress. Across the provinces of the empire, cities conducted extensive building programmes that demanded costly stone.

Thuburnica: If you wish to carry on south from Chemtou, note that the track across the **another minor** river bed leading to the P6 requires a four-wheel-drive vehicle. For real enthu-**Roman site** siasts, the track directly west from Chemtou leads to **Thuburnica**, a visit for *Colour map 1, grid B1* the really dedicated, but not without interest. (There is a well-preserved Roman bridge.) Thuburnica can also be reached by a right turn just after Ghardimaou, signposted 'Tubournic 13 km'. The ruins are in a red stone, and there is a post-Second World War mock Roman villa (architect Paul Herbé), built for a wealthy French farmer.

South from Chemtou to Jendouba

Jendouba Jendouba is an important crossroads and administrative centre 44 km south *Phone code: 78* of Tabarka and 154 km west of Tunis, providing easy access to Bulla Regia, Chemtou and the Algerian border. All the main banks have branches here.

Sleeping D *Simithu*, on the right, by the roundabout when arriving from Bulla Regia, T631695, F631743. New hotel, 26 rooms, restaurant, on the main road, not very appealing. **D** *Hotel Atlas*, R du 1er Juin 1955, T603217, F603113. Behind the police station, probably the only decent hotel in town, last resort stuff.

Transport Train The train station is off the main square, by the police station. Departures **Tunis** 0554, 1033, 1240, 1515, 1653. **Bus** The bus station is to west of town, past the railway lines. Information on T630411. Frequent local buses to **Tunis**, **Le Kef**, **Tabarka** and **Aïn Draham**, also buses to the border at Ghardimaou. They do not cross the border so you will have to cross on foot. **Louages**: for **Ghardimaou** they leave from the station on Blvd Sakiet Sidi Sousse. For Tunis they leave from R 1 Juin 1955.

West from Jendouba : Parc National de Feidja

Ghardimaou, 34 km west of Jendouba, is on the way out towards Algeria. It is not worth a visit on its own account. There is the **E** Hotel *Thubernic*, T78660043, if you wish to stay on the way to Feidja national park.

Feidja is one of Tunisia's six national parks, 17 km up in the hills near the Algerian frontier, set up to protect the Barbary deer. To get there, take the P6 out of Jendouba and turn north just before the frontier post. You may well be flagged down by border police in any case and asked to show papers. There is a winding metalled road right up to the tiny settlement of **Aïn Soltane**, and then on to the end of the road, where there is a forest nursery, a semi-abandoned summer youth hostel and a national guard post. Should you wish to continue up into the national park, they will want to take your passport. A four-wheel drive will be necessary if you wish to drive, otherwise you will have to walk from here. No information on the national park was available in the area. Although a wish to develop 'eco-tourism' has been expressed in the Tunisian press, Feidja's location on the frontier with Algeria, where the security situation is delicate, to say the least, would seem to have put the brakes on public investment in park infrastructure, despite the efforts of the GDZ (German International Cooperation).

Parc National de Feidja
Border at Ghardimaou, T78645004

The Barbary deer was brought back from near extinction by the creation of the reserve in the 1960s, with 420 ha set aside especially for it. The deer can be heard braying in the rutting period in the late summer. Other features of the park include numerous woodpeckers, a plantation of cedars, that most emblematic tree of the Atlas Mountains, and traces of Libyic and Numidian settlement. If you are very lucky, you might catch a glimpse of the secretive and spotted cerval.

East from Jendouba to Béja

Before proceeding south to Le Kef (below), visitors are recommended to find time to make a journey northeast to **Béja**, either by road or railway. For the first 22 km to Bou Salem, both are alongside the **Oued Medjerda**, the only river in Tunisia which flows all year round. The road crosses the two main tributaries, the Oued Mellègue and Oued Tessa, which can be spectacular in flood and very disappointing at other times, while the railway line from Jendouba to Béja runs along the far side of the main valley.

Bou Salem is a large successful market town dealing with the agricultural produce, mainly cereals but some grapes and livestock, of this fertile valley. You can see why the Romans referred to this area as their 'bread basket'. From Bou Salem the road climbs up wooded slopes to Béja, while the railway crosses and recrosses the main river before turning north to Béja.

Béja   باجة

Ancient Vaga (modern Béja) has had an eventful history. Today it is a quietly prosperous market town, overlooked by the usual Husseinid fortifications. It has a pleasant médina with mosques and zaouias, and some very fine early 20th-century building. Béja makes a relaxing short halt on the way to the Roman sites of the northwest. It's a shame that there's not more of it to visit.

Phone code: 78
Colour map 1, grid B2

The town has had a lively history, marked by various unfriendly visitors, including Genseric's Vandals in the mid-fifth century and the Fatimid hordes in the 10th century. Today, fortunately for the residents, there is less excitement, but it is worth a wander round the médina and up towards the keep in the kasbah area for a fine view of the town. Béja has a good location, surrounded by excellent agricultural land and hills to the northwest. It is possible to see from the expanses of cereals why this town was the largest grain market of the Roman Africa. Today, it is still a very busy junction of six important roads.

Sights

Ancient intrigue: Sophonisbe, Masinissa, Syphax and the Romans

By 204 BC, Hannibal, despite the elephants and the strategy, had lost all hope of defeating Rome. Tough-nut Roman general Scipio decided to defeat the Carthaginians on their home ground in Africa. He came to a semi-alliance with Syphax, leader of the Masaesyli, a most powerful African clan who ruled over vast expanses of western Numidia. Carthage was threatened but then, inconveniently for Scipio, love intervened.

The ageing Syphax fell for Sophonisbe, daughter of Hasdrubal, the general responsible for Carthage's defence. Hasdrubal gave his daughter's hand in marriage, Syphax changed sides. Scipio was left with the rather more problematic support of Masinissa, young ruler of the other major tribe, the Massyli of eastern Numidia.

The situation was not an easy one. But then things took a surprising turn. Though Masinissa's forces were nearly exterminated by Syphax, Masinissa himself survived. There was a resurgence in support for him, and he headed south to await the arrival of Scipio's armies. Landing near Utica in 204 BC with 30,000 men, Scipio had a slow start. Then he managed to set fire to the Punic-Numidian camp, and defeated Hasdrubal in battle near Carthage. He also took Syphax. Masinissa seized his chance, and invaded Cirta, Syphax' capital.

Masinissa was met by the ravishing Sophonisbe. She begged Masinissa not to hand her over to the Romans. So moving were her appeals, that he fell in love with her, marrying her the same day. Syphax was furious, Scipio worried about the potential loss of an ally. He demanded that Masinissa hand over Sophonisbe, wife of the captive Syphax. But Masinissa remembered his promise that she would never pass into Roman hands. He sent her a cup of poison, which she drank as the only way out.

Masinissa went on to do well, of course: he was given the official title of king by Rome and awarded a triumph. Sophonisbe continued into history as another Punic tragedy queen. With her name attached to the Espace Sophonisbe, an élitist women's club in the modern suburb of Carthage, she is unlikely to be forgotten.

The old town has the usual mosques and zaouias. From the town centre, leaving the Maison de la Culture (the former church) on your left, head down the bustling Rue Kheïreddine with its market stalls and shops. At Bab el Aïn, there is a pleasant small square with an old public fountain. An effort seems to have been made in this part of Béja to avoid jarring modern building. The shop-fronts have old-style wooden awnings painted caper-green. Walking around these old neighbourhoods, you can get a feel for life in a Tunisian provincial town. The **Grand Mosque** has a striking red minaret, with Almohad motifs. Look out for the green-domed Zaouia of Sidi Abdel Kader, which today functions as a crêche.

Overlooking the médina area, the Byzantine **Kasbah** was named Theodoriana after the emperor Justinian's wife. It is now used by the army. Though the fortress was remodelled on numerous occasions, it bears witness to the re-establishment of Byzantine authority in Africa in the early sixth century AD.

Sleeping C *Hotel Vaga*, T450818, F465902, 36 beds. Has recently moved upmarket. E *Hotel Hiba*, 5 Av de la République, a few doors down from the Municipality, T457244, F456299. Not as good as the nearby E *Hotel Phénix*, Av de la République, almost opposite the Municipality, T450188, F450679. 30 beds. E *Hotel Bou Tefaha*, R Farhat Hached, street parallel to R Kheïreddine, opposite the Zaouia de Sidi Bou Tefaha. Basic. **Youth hostel** Opposite the bus station, T450621. 80 beds, meals available.

The bus and train stations are at the bottom of the main street with frequent connections to/from Tunis and Jendouba. **Transport**

Medical emergencies Hospital on Av Bourguiba. Pharmacie de nuit opposite the cinema behind the former church. **Travel agents** *Vaga Tours*, Av 18 Janvier, T451805. **Directory**

Around Béja

A monument to tough Roman engineering, Trajan's Bridge – once part of the Roman east-west road network – lies not far from the minor road C76 about 13 km southwest of Béja. To get there locate the Béja bypass, which runs south of the town. If coming from the Tunis direction (east), turn left on to the Boulevard de l'Environnement (large sign in central reservation). To your right is the new self-built housing area, Maâgoula. Follow the paved road for around 7½ km. You come to a point where eucalyptus trees line the road. Go right down a track, lined with eucalyptus. After rainy weather, small cars risk getting bogged down here. On your left is farmland, much of which can be under water; on your right, on high ground, you may see a train go by. After about 4 km, you come to the old railway track, abandoned because of the rising waters of the **Sidi Salem dam lake**. Trajan's bridge is on your left, almost opposite a small obelisk war memorial surrounded by tamarisk trees. **Trajan's Bridge**

This three-arched Roman bridge, which seemingly has nothing to do with Trajan at all, is still probably in splendid condition. However, thanks to the dam, the bridge now resembles Trajan's hump-backed whale for much of the year – when it is visible at all. If you want to see the top of the bridge, visit late summer/early autumn, when the dam waters are low. With its 70-m span, the bridge dates from the time of Tiberius.

Even if the bridge is practically invisible, this is a good excursion for birdwatchers. The flooded woodland plus narrow mudflats along the lake shores are good terrain for all sorts of birds, notably waders. About 1 km after Trajan's Bridge, you will come to the old railway bridge (views across the lake), still used by isolated rural communities on the south side.

There are two Second World War cemeteries in the Béja area. One, with 396 graves, is just outside the northern limits of Béja. A smaller one is at **Thibar**, 11 km south of Béja, convenient if Dougga is on your itinerary. Leaving Béja on the road to Jendouha, turn left about 100 m after the roadside village of Hammam Siyala, at the sign marked 'Sehili'. (Coming from the west, you could take the better C75, south of **Bou Salem**.) The road winds up to Thibar, and the cemetery, with some 60 graves, is about 800 m north of the village, adjacent to the agricultural college. ■ *Both open 0730-1430 Sat-Thu.* **Second World War cemeteries**

The college at Thibar was founded by the White Fathers in 1895 and was developed as a model farm. Though fertile, the area was unhealthy and malaria-infested (*Dherbet el bounyar, wa la cherbet min Thibar* - 'Better to be stabbed than drink Thibar water' went the local adage), and the region was infested with panthers and hyenas. The Fathers set about developing a model farm, including vineyards – and rather typically of French monks, set about inventing a local speciality, coming up with the tawny **Thibarine liqueur**, available at Carthage airport in exotically shaped bottles. The White Fathers also developed a strain of sheep, and zebu/cow crosses adapted to the local climate. After independence, the Fathers remained at Thibar until 1975. The Domaine St Joseph still functions as an agricultural college. **Domaine St Joseph**

Northern Tunisia

Djebba North of Thibar, follow the signs for Montazah Jebba or Parc Jebba and head for the **Djebba National Park**, a hilly area with a seasonal waterfall and some caves. The road crosses the plain and climbs up through fig and apple orchards to Djebba village. Eventually you come to a car park under the over-hanging cliff, and an area fitted out with Tahiti-style parasols.

Djebba was the site of a statue to **Notre Dame de Goraâ**. In 1902, the White Fathers had the idea of setting up a statue to the Virgin. Perhaps they had dreams of creating a sort of African Lourdes, although there doesn't seem to have been any miracles performed. The necessary 450 francs was collected, and in May 1903, the Fathers, equipped with a ladder 16 m long, placed the statue high up on a ledge, next to a curious wall set with arrow slits perched up in the cliff face. A local legend runs that this is where the Seven Sleepers slept. The small statue, a standard catholic representation of the Virgin Mary – referred to by the locals as Sitt Miriyem – survived until 1998, when someone had the bright idea of stealing it. Surprised by the warden, the thieves dropped the statue, breaking its arm. It is now under lock and key in a concrete bunker under the cliff face.

If you have time, climb up to the top of **Djebel Goraâ** (900 m) which will give you a magnificent view over the region. Steps have been built into the cliff face, so you can get to the stoney plateau above Djebba very easily. From the top there are superb views over the Béja plain. Djebba (and indeed Thibar) are well protected from hot summer south winds by the Djebel Goraâ. The village's tiny houses are set among orchards. In the middle distance, Thibar can be seen, its fields defined by tall dark cypresses, below an Aleppo pine forest.

From Thibar, the C75 winds up and across barren hills to **Teboursouk**. Heading south, there is a left turn off for **Aïn Melliti** (3½ km), which pro-duces mineral water and is home to the ruins of Roman Henchir Mastria. After this turn-off, Teboursouk is 19 km further south.

Southwest from Jendouba to Le Kef From Jendouba, head south on the P17 for Le Kef, some 60 km away. You can either head for the main east-west P5 Tunis to Le Kef road, or turn off right for Nebeur, a small town on the Oued Mellegue dam. A minor road will bring you into the northern approaches of Kef.

Le Kef الكاف

Phone code: 78
Colour map 1, grid B2

Le Kef (from 'el kef', Arabic for 'the crag'), 58 km south of Jendouba, is perched 750 m up on a rocky hill. It is an attractive place with a long history, mainly mili-tary in nature due to its important strategic position. It was settled by the Romans and various Muslim dynasties. In the 18th and 19th centuries, it was the third largest town in Tunisia. Le Kef was taken by France in 1881, and its military role was reinforced. During the Second World War it became the provisional capital of the still-free Tunisia. Today the town is an important regional centre, untouched by tourism, but with some interesting sights to visit.

Ins and outs

Getting there Le Kef can be reached by louage from Tunis, Jendouba, Kalaâ el Khasbah, Kalaât Senam
See Transport, page 232, for further details and Tajerouine. There are a couple of daily buses from Kairouan (3½ hrs), Sakiet Sidi Youssef, Sfax (4½ hrs), and Sousse, nearly 4 hrs away. There are more frequent buses from Béja (2 hrs), Makthar, Téboursouk and Testour.

The main sights in Le Kef can all easily be done on foot in a couple of hrs. If you are **Getting around**
thinking of day-trips, Kalaât Senam is a good 1¾ hrs drive. By public transport, it might
be possible to do this as a day-trip with a very early start. (For Kalaât Senam and Haïdra
see chapter 6, Central Tunisia.) Another possible trip from Le Kef is out to the tiny hot
spring (50°C) at Hammam Mellegue, some 10 km west of the town.

History

Le Kef has a long history and in classical times was a major town, known to the
Romans as Sicca Veneria. The epithet 'Veneria' was added by the Romans,
probably because there was a Carthaginian temple on the site, dedicated to the
Phoenician goddess Astarte, identified by the Romans with Venus. Sacred
prostitution may have been part of the Punic cult of Astarte. Sicca Veneria had
a brief moment centre stage after the First Punic War, when Carthage made
the error of sending her mercenaries, called back from Sicily, there. A large
number of discontented soldiers assembled in an isolated town inevitably led
to rebellion, and the War of the Mercenaries was fought from 240 to 237 BC.
Sicca Veneria flourished in the second and third centuries BC. It became the
seat of a bishopric, and was the site of a number of monasteries.

Le Kef became an important regional centre once more in the 17th and 18th
centuries, due to its strategic location in the marchlands dividing the territories
of the Beylik of Tunis and the Beylik of Constantine. Certain Husseinid beys
lived in fear that some of their male relatives would try to overthrow them with
the support of the Beylik of Algiers. (In conclusion to a complicated episode of
dynastic politics, the Bey of Constantine's army conquered Tunis from Ali Bey I
in 1756.) Le Kef thus occupied a key geopolitical position. Under the French,
the town, although home to a garrison, began to lose ground to the farming
towns of the Medjerda plain and the port cities of eastern Tunisia.

Sights

With its steep streets, Le Kef is an atmospheric sort of place. Views open up over
the surrounding region. The Roman presence is very real, right in the heart of
the town, with the spring and half-excavated ancient baths. The people at the
Association de Sauvegarde de la Médina's little office, located on Place de
l'Indépendance, can be very helpful. All in all, it's a place for wandering. There is
a Mediterranean feel without the crowds of fatally picturesque Sidi Bou Saïd.

Starting your walking tour of Le Kef, you might have a look at **Dar el Kous**
behind Avenue Habib Bourguiba. This is a fourth-century Christian basilica
dedicated to St Peter. If closed, the warden can normally be contacted through
the ASM office. **Ras el Aïn** was/is the spring in the middle of Le Kef which supported the town in Roman times. Evidence of channels and a cistern remain.

The **Kasbah** occupies the highest part of Le Kef. The present fortifications
go back to the early 17th century, and were much altered under the
Husseinids and the French. Much ancient building material was recycled during the building of the earliest parts. The view is impressive. In summer the
Bou Makhlouf Festival takes place in the courtyard. ■ *1Dt. Sometimes closed
if a film crew is in the middle of making some epic.* The **Mosque of Sidi Bou
Makhlouf,** a reminder of a half-forgotten saint of Fassi origin, is just below the
kasbah. This is a very beautiful mosque with interesting domes and an octago-
nal minaret. The inside is highly decorated with ceramics and stucco. The
Regional Museum of Popular Arts and Traditions is located on the place Sidi
Ali Aïssa in the former Zaouia of Sidi Ali Ben Aïssa, of the Rahmaniya *tarika*

Northern Tunisia

(order). There are four rooms, the most interesting presents elements of the everyday nomadic life, including a large tent of the type seen occasionally today in the southern regions. There is also some interesting information on the soufi orders. ■ *0930-1630 winter, 0900-1300 and 1500-1900 summer, closed Mon. 2Dt.*

Excursions

A minor road, the C72, climbs north to the side of the 1,500 ha lake held back by the **Nebeur Dam**. The lake is an impressive 18 km long. A better view is obtained from the dam on the Oued Mellègue by turning off the road to Jendouba after the steep winding road passes Nebeur. You could also head for **Hammam Mellègue**, a primitive spa of Roman origins some 10 km down a piste leading off the P5 road for Sakiet Sidi Youssef west of Le Kef. The bus for Sakiet could drop you at the beginning of the piste; unless you get lucky with a lift in a Peugeot truck, you'll walk the rest. The spring waters are popular with locals, women having the mornings for bathing, men the afternoons – but there are better places in Tunisia to sample the delights of hot springs, such as Hammam Zriba, Kébili, Steftimia, El Hamma de Gabès and El Hamma du Djérid.

Northeast of Le Kef, some 9 km down a piste opposite the entrance to the Presidential Palace, are the remains of a monastery on the **Djebel Dyr** (*dyr* means 'monastery' in Arabic). The site is now partly occupied by a farm.

Essentials

Sleeping

There is reasonable accommodation in Le Kef to suit all budgets

C *Hotel Les Pins*, on Blvd de l'Environnement outside town on the northern side, T204300, F202411. 27 rooms giving on to a central courtyard, all with loo, hot water and heating. Good value. **C** *Hotel Sicca Veneria*, Pl de l'Indépendence, T/F202389. Ugly but central, 34 rooms, relatively cheap, restaurant. Coming up for renovation. **C** *Hotel Résidence Venus*, R Mouldi Khamessi, but no street name to be seen, T/F204695. 20 rooms, most with bath, good value, helpful owner, organizes wild-boar hunting. To get there, head up R de la Source, turn right on to R Ali Belhaouane, then take 2nd left. With a name like *Résidence Vénus*, this has to be a reasonable address. **C-D** *Hotel Ramzi*, a newish address on R Hédi Chaker, near the post office, about 100 m down from the central square and the *Sicca Veneria*, T230079. No breakfast but ensuite shower and loo. Not bad at all. **D** *Hotel Les Remparts*, R des Remparts, T202100, F224766. In town centre opposite the *PTT*. **E** *El Médina*, 18 R Farhat Hached, T204183. Simple, fairly clean and welcoming. Rooms with 2-4 beds, loos and showers not too clean. **E** *La Source*, Pl de la Source, T204397. 9 rooms, central, set around a patio next to the muezzin's loudspeaker, not very clean, shabby.

Eating

Not too much choice here, but nothing to break your budget either. **Mid-range** *Restaurant Chez Venus*, Av Habib Bourguiba. Very pleasant atmosphere, probably the best food in town, a bit more expensive than the others. This is the restaurant related to the hotel of the same name. **Cheap** *Restaurant el Andalous*, on R Hédi Chaker opposite the *PTT*. Perfectly adequate for a fill-up. On same street, try also *Restaurant Ramzi*, which has a good name. Other options include: *Restaurant Chez Nous*, on R de la Source, next to the *Hotel de l'Auberge*; *Restaurant Ed Dyr*, Av Hédi Chaker, near the Esso station (good value); and *Restaurant Les Ruines*, up a side-street near the ASM du Kef's offices, open every day, midday and evening, specials of the day, etc.

Tour operators

Nord Ouest Voyages, R Essour, T221839.

Transport

Road Bus: the bus station is a 20-min walk downhill from Pl de l'Indépendence. Information: T226025 for SNTRI services (Tunis), T223168 for SRT du Kef services. Frequent buses to **Tunis** and **Jendouba**, connections also to **Sfax, Kairouan, Nabeul, Gafsa, Sousse** and **Bizerte. Louages**: the louage station is by the bus station. Last louage out is about 1800, but occasionally 1 leaves later, depending on the driver. **Train**: an awkward and slow journey from Tunis on the Kalaâ el Khasba train, getting off at Le Sers, just a 20-min louage ride southeast of Le Kef.

Banks *STB*, Pl de l'Indépendence; *BT*, Av Hédi Chaker. Try also the *BNA* behind the **Directory**
Hotel Sicca Veneria. **Communications** Internet: *Publinet* opposite *Hotel Sicca Veneria*, T200479, stays open late. **Post Office**: Av Hédi Chaker. **Medical services Hospital**: on the Sakiet Sidi Youssef rd, T420900. Private clinic: *Clinque Jugurtha*, R du Dr Salah Majed, T204214, 202611. **Chemist**: all-night pharmacy on R Souk Ahras, turn right just before *PTT*.

East from Le Kef to Dougga (Teboursouk) and Testour

The P5 from Le Kef runs roughly northeastwards towards Tunis, passing through an interesting mixture of small Tunisian towns and ancient remains of Roman and Byzantine origin. This is a rich agricultural area of pasture, cereals and wooded hills. Dougga and Testour are the two must-sees on this route.

Roman **Mustis** is just north of the present-day town of Krib, on the left at Km 119. Here are the ruins of a triumphal arch and a paved Roman street, among other things ancient. The site is entered through a green gate and the visit will not take long. The best of the ruins is the Byzantine citadel, the walls of which are clearly defined. This is constructed of pieces removed from the older buildings. Parts of the Christian basilica with three naves, to the west, are less obvious. There are temples to Apollo, Cérès and Pluto, and to the southeast of the site is the *zaouia* of Sidi Abd Rebba. There is a triumphal arch at each end of the town, the better preserved being along the road towards Teboursouk 300 m east of the main group of ruins. The original construction date is not known.

A couple of kilometres after Krib, there is a relais-restaurant to the right of the road where you can lunch (with wine) for around 15Dt a head.

A further 10 km along the P5, ancient-world enthusiasts will want to note the remains of a Byzantine fort on a hill to the north of the road. This is the site of the ancient settlement of **Agbia**. There is no sign, just take the track across a field. Immediately beyond, on the left, is a turn to **Dougga**. This is a very rough route and a long walk. The best approach is from Teboursouk.

On towards Tunis the older part of **Teboursouk**, on a hillside, overlooks the P5, while the modern part of town lies along the main road. Some 10 km before you reach Testour at **Aïn Tounga** are more ancient ruins, immediately to the east of the road. There is an imposing Byzantine fortress (along with the one at remote Ksar Lamsa near Siliana, one of the best preserved in Tunisia), and the remains of Roman Thignica. Next stop is **Testour**, the ancient town of Tichila, home of the Moors driven from Spain in the 17th century.

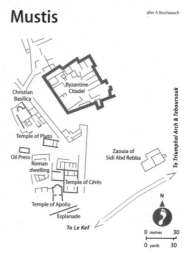

Mustis

after A Beschaouch

Christian Basilica

Byzantine Citadel

Temple of Pluto

Oil Press

Roman dwelling

Temple of Cérès

Zaouia of Sidi Abd Rebba

Temple of Apollo

Esplanade

To Le Kef

To Triumphal Arch & Teboursouk

N

0 metres 30
0 yards 30

Northern Tunisia

Dougga دقة

Colour map 1, grid B2 With an exhilarating view of plain and distant hills, Dougga has the best location of any of Tunisia's ancient cities. It is an alluring place; the grand imperial monuments are improbably intact. The classic views of the site – the theatre, the capitol – are postcard famous. But despite all the columns and pediments, there is plenty of higgledy-piggledy masonry, and children will have a splendid time fighting imaginary battles among the passages and overgrown walls. In fact, the Romans built on an earlier town, and proud Masinissa must surely have held court here. The streets are still Romanly well-paved, and you half expect to look up and find some Numidian beauty and her suite processing to the Licinian Baths. Dougga feels like a confident, healthy place, and complements the picture of the Roman good life inspired by the great mosaics of the Bardo Museum.

Dougga

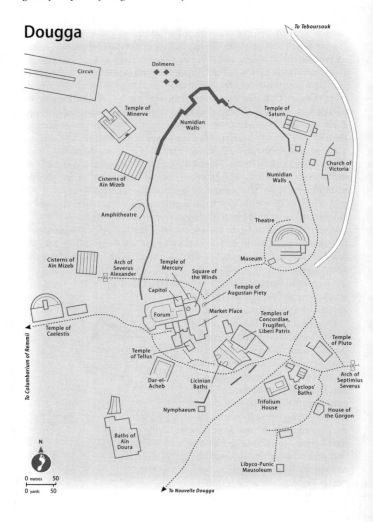

Ins and outs

The Roman ruins of Dougga are 100 km west of Tunis, 7 km south of the town of Teboursouk, and very clearly signed. Dougga is an easy day-trip from the capital by both private and public transport. There are frequent buses from Le Kef and Tunis to Teboursouk. From there, you may find a taxi to take you up to the site.

Getting there *See Transport, page 242, for further details*

Once at Teboursouk, another option is to take a bus or louage to the new settlement of Dougga (built to house the folk who were living on the site until the 1960s) and walk up a track behind the village. The ruins start 3 km further on along the track.

The ruins cover a considerable area. For a short visit, start with the Theatre (near the car park), move on to the central forum area (Temple of Mercury, Capitol), then take a look at the Arch of Alexander Severus and the Temple of Caelestis before heading back to the central area, where you could then do the Licinian Baths and the residential area below them, including the Trifolium House and the House of the Gorgon. The visit would finish at the Libico-Punic Mausoleum below the central part of the town.

Getting around

With more time, a good circuit would take you from the Theatre over the back of the site to the dolmens, Temple of Minerva, Circus and Cisterns of Aïn Mizeb. Then you would come back to the centre of the town, passing via the Arch of Alexander Severus and the Temple of Caelestis. The central forum area is next on this route, to be followed, as for the previous circuit, by Licinian Baths and lower residential area.

History

The Roman ruins known as **Thugga** are spread out across a plateau and on to the steep side of the *djebel* overlooking the Oued Khaled. It was originally a Numidian town allied with Rome against Carthage. As a consequence, after the downfall of Carthage, the town was granted a certain degree of independence. Romanization only started towards AD 150, after two centuries of coexistence. By the time Carthage had been rebuilt by the Romans, Dougga had become the economic and administrative centre of a very rich agricultural area. It also controlled the route to the coast, and enjoyed great prosperity. Having become a Roman colony by the end of the second century, the town reached the height of its wealth under the rule of Septimius Severus. It was awarded an imposing name – Colonia Licinia Septima Aurelia Alexandriana Thuggenses – to match its importance. Its downfall in the fourth century was caused by the heavy dues paid to the Romans and religious quarrels. When the Vandals invaded, most of the population had moved to Teboursouk.

The ruins

Dougga, at 25 ha, is one of the largest of the Roman sites in Tunisia and certainly one of the most dramatic. The ruins are on a sloping site, and it is possible to do a superficial visit in an hour or so, although it is really worthwhile spending a great deal more time. On arrival, one of the 'guides' hanging round the entrance will no doubt want to show you around. Most of these guides are unofficial and do not hold a card issued by the Tourist Office. If you are in a hurry, it can be a good idea to take one, but be careful to agree on the price beforehand. Otherwise, there is a lot to see at Dougga, and to make things more digestible, the city is divided here into seven manageable chunks, plus notes on some miscellaneous buildings.

So what makes Dougga really special? Basically, it is the sheer concentration of well-preserved or well-restored Roman buildings. You have the whole

Northern Tunisia

range, buildings for worship, work and leisure, all within a few minutes walk of each other. This, coupled with the panoramic views, must have made Dougga a splendid place to live in. ■ *0830-1730 winter, 0700-1900 summer, closed Mon. 2Dt, photography 1Dt. Café and reasonable toilets at entrance.*

Theatre   Close to the car park, the first major monument is the much restored **Theatre,** originally built in AD 168-9, and a typical example of a Roman theatre. It is quite modest in size, but could nevertheless seat 3,500 people on its 19 semi-circular tiers, in three stages, cut into the hill slope. This ensured the stability of the structure and simplified construction. The seating was closed off at the top by a portico, since destroyed, and it is suggested that a temporary screen or blind was erected over the seating to protect the spectators from the sun. Some of the columns have been re-erected on the stage, but now that the back wall of the stage has disappeared a person seated in the *cavea* (seating) obtains a splendid panoramic view of the plain below.

Central area   At the heart of ancient Thugga was the Capitol, with the Temples of Augustan Piety and Mercury adjoining. The Forum and the Market were close by. These were the public buildings and places where the men who ran the city would have been able to meet, arranging to discuss matters at the Forum or participating at the various rituals held in the temples.

The **Temple of Augustan Piety** was a small raised sanctuary with a smaller vestibule entered from the west by a stair. The engraving on the architrave supported by columns with Corinthian capitols indicated its name and use.

Approaching the forum and the great mass of the main temple, the visitor comes to the **Square of the Winds** (French: *Rose des Vents*), which is named after a compass-based inscription naming 12 winds cut into the paving. This square has in fact a semicircular wall at its east end, behind which stand the Temple of Fortune and Temple of Augustan Piety. This section contains the **Temple of Mercury**, constructed in AD 180-92 and composed of three chapels, the rectangular central one being larger; the lateral chapels, much smaller, almost hemispherical in plan. All three are dedicated to the same god, Mercury. As god of, among other things, trade, it is significant that the Temple of Mercury faces towards the market (see also Thuburbo Majus where a similar arrangement exists).

The **Market** is bordered on its two longer sides by a series of small shops which were built under the portico – now vanished. Each shop was exactly the same size. In the centre stood a fountain. The south end held a large alcove which probably held a statue of Mercury. To the right and the left of this alcove, a doorway leads out to separate stairways which descended to rooms below.

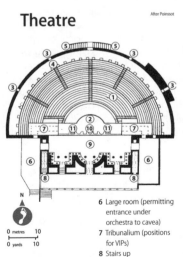

Theatre

After Poinssot

N
0 metres 10
0 yards 10

1 Cavea (19 semicircular tiers of seating)
2 Orchestra
3 Doorway/entrance
4 Staircase (interior)
5 Staircase (exterior)
6 Large room (permitting entrance under orchestra to cavea)
7 Tribunalium (positions for VIPs)
8 Stairs up
9 Proscaenium (stage)
10 Pulpitum (about 1m high with rectangular & semi-circular niches)
11 Stairs from orchestra to stage

On temple building and Roman piety

The classic Roman temple as we think of it today owed much to Greek and Etruscan models. Looking at the Capitol at Dougga, you can see Greek columns used on the main entrance but not on all sides of the building, as would have been the case in a Greek temple. Temple buildings like the Capitol were designed to impress, dominating the central area of a town from their raised platforms. They had elegant flights of steps leading to their entrances, ideal to set off the pomp of ritual processions. Note however that these temples were not built like churches to accommodate large congregations: they were places where priests and senior people would officiate at the cults.

Temples were an essential part of the process of Romanization, places symbolizing the power of the Empire where rites in Latin were celebrated. In North Africa, where the cities were new and there was no long tradition of great building, the temples often had a triple dedication to Jupiter, Juno and Minerva. Roman gods were grafted on to local deities, the cult of Saturn taking over that of Punic Baal-Hammon for instance. Temples could also be dedicated to abstract deities, and emperors would show their munificence by building temples. Eventually, temples began to be dedicated to deified emperors. There was a fine temple to Septimius Severus at Djemila in present-day Algeria, for example.

You cannot miss the **Capitol**, with its impressive set of steps and six huge, fluted monolithic columns over 8 m high on the edge of the portico. It is considered by some to be the most beautiful Roman monument in the whole of North Africa. It was built between 166 and 169 and dedicated to Jupiter, Juno and Minerva. The Corinthian capitols on these huge columns support an architraved frieze, bearing a dedication to the Triad for the salvation of the emperors Marcus Aurelius and Lucius Verus. The pediment features a bas-relief of an eagle making off with a human figure. Behind the portico is a *cella*, 13 m by 14 m, entered by a central doorway and divided into three parts, each with a niche in the end wall. The central, largest, niche once held a white marble statue of Jupiter and the smaller side niches statues of the other two deities. Beneath the podium constructed to lift this capitol to its elevated position is a crypt, in three compartments, used at one time as a fort and at another perhaps as a church. A model of the Capitol area is on display in the Dougga Room at the Bardo Museum.

The open piazza in front of the Capitol (24 m by 38 m) at the base of the staircase opens on the west side into an open space which is the **Forum**, also dating from the end of the second century. It was the centre of public life and administration. Few of the original 35 columns (red-veined marble from Chemtou with white capitals) and base remain. The floor beneath the porticos which once surrounded three sides of the building was mosaic tiles.

When times became less secure in Byzantine times, the centre of

Temple of Mercury & Square of the Winds

After Poinssot

Portico

Names of 12 winds engraved here

Part of Byzantine wall

Esplanade of white limestone

N

3 steps

Not to scale

Dougga was extensively remodelled for defensive reasons. At the Forum, traces of the Byzantine fortifications can be seen to the north (a rectangular tower) and south (a rectangular support) of the Forum. The fort, covering some 2,800 sq m, in fact enclosed both the Forum and the Capitol and the gateways to the north and south. Much of the stone used to construct this fort was taken from older buildings on this site.

Also close to the central area is the small **Temple of Tellus**, the goddess of crop fertility. Nearby are the remains of a building referred to today as the **Dar el Acheb** (entry via a grand doorway with two Corinthian columns). It was probably a temple originally. The four rectangular basins enclosed in the larger rectangular building were accessed from a door to the north. Perhaps these basins were for the storage of oil or even for ritual washing.

Arch of Severus Alexander & around Close to the central area, two pleasant ruins not to be missed are the Arch of Severus Alexander and the Temple of Caelestis. Latin sources tell us little about Severus Alexander, emperor during 222-35, but no doubt he took an interest in African affairs, his arch, tastefully placed among the olive trees, presumably commemorating some munificence or other. The arch, 4-m wide, spanned a road, paved in a herring-bone pattern, which would have been one of the main access points to the city.

Nearby, look out for the **Temple of Caelestis**, also constructed during the reign of Alexander Severus, a few years before Christianity began to gain a hold in this part of North Africa. The rectangular sanctuary, once entirely enclosed by columns, is approached by an elegant flight of steps. There is a large, closed semicircular courtyard with a portico on the curved side.

Licinian Baths & around This third-century gift to the city by the Licinii family is a very large and complicated building. The furnace room, the hot room with the pipes visible in the walls, the cold room and the *palaestra* or exercise room remain.

The **Temples of Concordia**, **Frugifer** and **Bacchus (Liber Pater)** were constructed between 128-38 AD. The Temple of Bacchus is the largest and has a large square central area flanked by porticos, while at the northwest side are five rooms, the largest in the centre, while in the opposite direction was a small theatre, seats still present.

Below the Licinian baths, heading away from the Forum, is a complex area of ruined housing where you can also see sections of the ancient **Numidian walls**, part of the same fortifications running north of the Theatre and west of the Temple of Saturn. In this neighbourhood, look out for the well-preserved **House of Dionysus and Ulysses**, where part of the first floor still survives. Now in the Bardo Museum, the great mosaic of Ulysses, tied to the mast of his ship as he sailed past the Sirens, comes from this house.

Lower residential area Below the Licinian Baths is an area where city homes and a further, smaller, bath complex have been excavated. **The House of the Trifolium** (traditionally presented by guides as Dougga's brothel) dates

Temple of Caelestis

After Poinssot

0 metres 10
0 yards 10

1 Rectangular sanctuary
2 Columns surrounding sanctuary
3 Flight of 11 stairs
4 Semi-circular courtyard
5 Side entrance
6 Remaining columns which supported semi-circular portico
7 Chambers below courtyard
8 Ablutions area

Public Baths – Roman style

Although the larger private houses had their own bathing facilities, most Roman citizens made use of the public baths – for which a charge was made. The men and women were strictly segregated, using separate facilities or using the baths at different times of the day. Associated with the public baths was the palaestra or exercise room, small shops and sometimes even a library. Visitors to the public hammam in Tunis will find this account very familiar.

The first room in the bathing part was for the removal of outdoor garments – there were niches in the wall for storing the clothes. The body was smoothed with oil, generally olive oil, and then the would-be

bather went into the exercise room to get his circulation moving and to raise his body temperature. From there he went to the hot room and steam room, where attendants removed the oil and perspiration with a strigil. Next came the warm room, then the cold room which was normally large enough to contain a swimming pool. Fresh oil was smoothed on the body at the end of the operation.

Obviously this smooth operation only worked because of the ingenious and complicated engineering of the building, the organization of water supply and the numerous servants and attendants stoking fires.

---

from the third century and is the best conserved and largest house discovered on the site. It is built on two levels with the entrance at street level and the rooms a floor below. The stairs on the north side of the house lead to a rectangular central garden or *viridium*. There was a small semicircular pool at one end, surrounded by a portico with a mosaic floor. The private quarters to the southwest have the vaulted, trefoil-shaped room from which the house was given its present name.

Next to the House of the Trifolium, the **Cyclops' Baths** are named after the magnificent mosaic taken from the floor of the cold room here and now on display at the Bardo Museum (see page 94). The baths are not in a very good state, except for the communal latrine (good photo opportunity). The extremely realistic mosaic, dated as fourth century, shows the three giants, the Cyclops, working at the forge in the cavern belonging to Vulcan, the god of Hell. It is unusual to find figures of such gigantic proportions (well, they were giants) or with such dark skins depicted on Roman mosaics. Further down towards the Libyco-Punic Mausoleum, the visitor comes to the **House of the Gorgon**, named after the mosaic discovered here showing the Gorgon's head held in the hand of Perseus.

Licinian Baths

<small>After Poinssot</small>

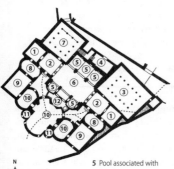

N

0 metres 20
0 yards 20

1 Apodyteria (undressing room)
2 Vestibule
3 Palaestra (exercise room)
4 Ante-room
5 Pool associated with Frigidarium
6 Frigidarium (cold room)
7 Entrance hall
8 Sudatorium (sweating room)
9 Laconicum (hot room - dry)
10 Calidarium (hot room)
11 Boiler room
12 Tepidarium (warm room)

In the lower part of the city, looking for all the world like a lost piece from a giant's chess game, the **Numido-Punic Mausoleum** is perhaps Tunisia's most famous pre-Roman ruin. In its day, it no

Numido-Punic Monument

Who were the Severans?

*The names of emperors **Septimius Severus** (193-211) and **Severus Alexander** (222-35) pop up regularly at Roman sites throughout Tunisia. At Dougga, there are triumphal arches to both these rulers. What was special about them? Fast rewind to the late second century AD, when Rome went through a particularly difficult patch under emperor Commodus. From 180-93, Commodus lived a life of debauchery in Rome, renaming the city Commodiana and spending his time showing off his brute force fighting with wild beasts in the colosseum. Eventually, he was strangled by a wrestling partner. In the power struggle that ensued among the military, one Septimius Severus, an aristocrat from Leptis Magna (in present day Libya), came out on top after four years of civil war.*

Septimius Severus was the right strong man at the right time. He realized that the Empire faced some formidable enemies, notably on the eastern frontier, and hence was to rule from the frontier provinces. He added Mesopotamia to Rome's dominions, expanded the army, and opened up the career structure to soldiers from the ranks. His dying words to his sons are said to have been "Do not quarrel with each other, pay the troops, and despise the rest."

Septimius Severus did not forget his African origins. In 202-203, he overwintered in Africa. He had huge works undertaken at Leptis Magna, and Leptis, Carthage and Utica were given immunity from provincial taxes. The emperor had acquired huge

properties in Africa Proconsularis, the lands of senators executed for their support of his rival Clodius Albinus. This no doubt gave him the resources for his considerable largesse towards Africa's cities, recognized by the construction of triumphal arches.

*Unfortunately, Septimius Severus' sons **Caracalla** and **Geta** were not of the same stuff as their father. Dynastic infighting followed, with Caracalla murdering Geta, only to be murdered by his own troops. **Elagabalus** (218-22) was also murdered after a short reign decadent by even Rome's standards, and his cousin, the young **Severus Alexander**, was to succeed in 222. He too was eventually murdered by the army. The Severan Dynasty disappeared, and 26 emperors followed in 50 years. But though the mid-third century proved to be a time of chaos in Rome, the provinces of Africa prospered. Septimius Severus had broken the power of the warlike desert tribes, Numidia had been made a separate province and the defences reorganized.*

Despite the vast sums spent on building programmes and the army, the Severan period saw a development which was to have long-lasting effects for Europe. Septimius Severus named Papinian praetorian prefect. Along with jurists Ulpian and Julius Paulus, he laid the bases of the Roman law which was eventually codified by the emperor Justinian in the sixth century. And under Caracalla, an edict was issued granting Roman citizenship to virtually all free men in the Empire.

doubt belonged to a series of similar monuments being put up in the nascent towns of the Numidian tribal monarchy. Dating from the third-second century BC, drawing stylistic inspiration from archaic Greece and ancient Egypt, the monument hints at a faint influence of Hellenistic models. (The third and second centuries BC were a time when massive building works were undertaken in the Hellenistic Kingdoms of Asia Minor.) The mausoleum is dedicated to the Numidian Prince Ateban, son of Iepmatath, son of Pallu, according to the bilingual Libyic and Punic inscription, which also gives the name of the architect as Abarish. It is thought Ateban was a contemporary of Massinissa. The three-storey tower rises from a plinth of five steps and culminates in a pyramid. The central section is reminiscent of a Greek temple. Originally, the pyramidal roof would have been flanked by birds with female faces, all set to guide the deceased's soul through the labyrinths of the afterlife.

Take a minute to place this in context: it was a historic building when the Romans were building Dougga.

Having survived over 2,000 years, the 21-m high building was virtually destroyed by the British Consul in Tunis in the 1840s, who took the stones bearing the bilingual inscriptions back to the British Museum. Happily, Poinssot and his team in 1908-10 were able to reconstruct the mausoleum. With its simple silhouette, today it is one of the most calm and elegant monuments at Dougga. (For mausoleum enthusiasts, a similar building, deassembled by Italian archaeologists, can be seen at Sabratha in Libya.)

Retracing your steps up towards the House of the Trefoil, and turning right, you come to the **Arch of Septimius Severus** (AD 193-211), put up in this emperor's honour in AD 205 after Thugga was made a *municipium* at his command, giving the community at Thugga partial rights of Roman citizenship. The arch marked the eastern entrance to the city, sitting astride a road some 5 m in width made of large limestone pieces set in a herring-bone pattern. This was the main road to Carthage.

If you have time, then you could go up to the back of the theatre's seating area, and explore the plateau beyond, tracing a circle to come out close to the Arch of Severus Alexander. The remains here are not spectacular, but give an idea of the extent of the city.

Round the back of the Theatre to the Temple of Caelestis

Northern Tunisia

Moving away from the theatre, there are views on your right towards Teboursouk and the ground drops away in a steep cliff. You will come to the **Sanctuary of Neptune**, a small rectangular sanctuary down off the plateau built near the now non-existent road that led to the Temple of Saturn. (Entrance via a door in the east wall and a niche in the west wall opposite.)

Further on is the **Temple of Saturn** (AD 195), its dominant position overlooking the valley, signalling the importance of the cult. Apparently it was built over the site of an earlier Baal-Hammon-Saturn sanctuary. It is aligned almost east-west. The outer vestibule (some of the original Corinthian columns still stand) leads into the rectangular central courtyard which originally had a gallery on three sides. At the west end are three equal-sized chapels. The central chapel once contained a marble statue of Saturn and that to the left a statue of a man dressed in a toga, the benefactor. Changes in the construction have made the entrance arrangements a little complicated.

Temple of Saturn

After Poinsot

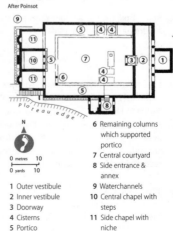

Approaching the Sanctuary of Neptune from the Theatre, to your right you have a small Christian cemetery in which stands the **Christian basilica** (fourth-fifth century AD). Many stones taken from the Theatre and the Temple of Saturn were used in its construction. There are three aisles separated by two rows of columns. The central aisle is wider and longer ending in an altar. Two sets of stairs lead down to the crypt.

From the church return to the top of the plateau and follow the line of the Numidian walls. There is one small section, only 130 m in length, of

1 Outer vestibule	6 Remaining columns which supported portico
2 Inner vestibule	7 Central courtyard
3 Doorway	8 Side entrance & annex
4 Cisterns	9 Waterchannels
5 Portico	10 Central chapel with steps
	11 Side chapel with niche

very ancient walls with parts of two towers on the outer side. You may also be able to pick out some **dolmens**, stones set up as funerary monuments in some distant pre-Libyic past. Little remains of the **Circus**. This is a very large rectangular area aligned east-west on the edge of the plateau. It is dated at AD 214 with additions some 10 years later. Down the centre is the *spina*, a raised area 190 m long which ends in semicircles. Did the spectators sit on the rocks to watch the charioteers race round this central strip?

The **Temple of Minerva** (AD 138-61) remains only in outline. Enter by a central door into a large rectangular courtyard with a line of columns at each side. The sanctuary (outer and inner) at the northwest was reached up stairs.

The **Cisterns of Aïn Mizeb** were a vital part of the town's survival. They are made up of seven long reservoirs (each 35 x 5 m) set 1 m apart, which stored water from the spring to the west. The method of construction and the lining to prevent leakage can still be examined where these cisterns are exposed. Having separate compartments prevented total loss if one part was damaged and permitted cleaning and repairs without cutting off the supply. The **Cisterns of Aïn el Hammam** are similar to those further north. There are five parallel reservoirs (each 34 x 3 m) and one short one across the end all fed from a spring a distance to the southwest.

After the cisterns, the **Arch of Severus Alexander** is clearly visible. The **Temple of Caelestis** is on your right, and turning left, you head back towards the central part of the city.

Miscellaneous buildings Down below the Dar el Acheb, there are a number of minor ruins to look out for, including a **private chapel to Juno** (the Exhedra of Juno Regina), the **Columbarium of the Remmii**, a large funerary monument containing the tombs of the Remmii family, and the **Baths of Aïn Doura and cistern**. From these baths, heading towards the House of the Trifolium, you will come to a small **nymphaeum** or fountain on your left. The water for this also came from Aïn el Hammam.

Sleeping It is possible to stay overnight in **Teboursouk**, although there is only one hotel there.
Phone code: 78 **D** *Hotel Thugga*, on main rd to Tunis, T465713. 66 beds, has obviously seen better days, rather poor quality, used by tour groups for a lunch stop. **Youth hostel**: in Teboursouk, 40 beds, T465095.

Transport **Road Bus**: there is an hourly bus to **Le Kef** and **Tunis** and many links to **Béja** and **Jendouba**. Information, T465016.

Testour تستور

Phone code: 78 Like nearby Slouguia and Medjez el Bab, Testour is a 17th-century
Colour map 1, grid B3 Andalusian foundation, a pleasant place for a short stop on the way from Tunis to Dougga. The Great Mosque has an unusual minaret, while the main street lined with one-storey shops with tiled roofs manages to maintain the faintest of Spanish flavours. But for how long? Modern building fashions have arrived, and the remainder of Testour's Andalusian heritage may well be replaced by the usual concrete homes.

History The town of Testour, built on the south bank of the Oued Medjerda, lies halfway between Teboursouk and Medjez el Bab. It stands on the site of Roman Tichilla and small pieces of this are found incorporated into the more modern fabric of the town and apparently into the Great Mosque. The modern town

The flames of passion

The Hara, the Jewish quarter of Tunis, gave the demi-monde of 1920s Tunis a tragic figure in the form of minor diva Habiba Msika (1895-1930), chiefly remembered today for such classics as Ala sarir en-nawm dallani *('On the bed of sleep he spoiled me, he gave me beer and champagne'). Her fan-club, the* asakir el-lil, *'soldiers of the night', followed her from concert to concert. She was dubbed* habibat el kul, *'beloved of all'.*

Habiba also conquered the heart of an elderly Jewish merchant from Testour, one Elyaou Mimouni. The bargain was the usual one: beauty for monied attentions. But Habiba was cruel, and Mimouni found himself rejected by family and home-town. The besotted merchant eventually went wild with jealousy at his diva's varied loves. He burned down Msika's townhouse on the Rue de Bône with the expensive songstress inside.

Such a tragedy could not go unfilmed, and in the late 1990s, Tunisian film producer Selma Baccar turned the fiery tale of the diva's life and loves into a film, Habiba Msika ou la danse du feu. *The house built by Msika's lover for her in Testour is now the Maison de la Culture, down a side-street on the right as you head away from the Great Mosque.*

But Habiba Msika was also touched by the political currents of the time. At La Marsa's Café Saf-Saf, at a famous concert in 1925, she struck a blow for liberty, turning the final song baladi, oh baladi *('my homeland') into* baladi tounis ou fiha el hurria *('my homeland is Tunisia, where there is freedom').*

dates from the flight of the Moors from Andalucía. The Spanish influence is very muted now. There are few women out and about, and with the men chatting of weather and farm-produce at the market stalls, swathed in earth-brown *kachabia* cloaks in winter, the feel is very much of a working agricultural town.

The eastern approach to Testour is dominated by the high-flown minaret of the town's **Great Mosque**, built in a style faintly reminiscent of the Italo-Spanish renaissance. The square tower is topped with two octagonal blocks. The expert opinion is that the little pinnacles decorating the square tower and the sundial hark back to the mosques of Aragon. Perhaps the sundial was used for getting prayer times right. The other key feature of the mosque is the tiled roof of the prayer hall, set with an unusual dome feature placed over the *mihrab* or prayer niche. In fact, this was not the first mosque on the site, as a ruined square tower in the back streets behind the mosque shows.

The other aspect that makes Testour so 'Andalusian' is its regular layout. A long, central street runs into the main square, off which the mosque is located. The square, surrounded by small shops, would have been the commercial hub of the new settlement back in the 17th century. Perhaps the immigrants sought to recreate the feel of the *plaza mayor* of the towns they had left behind. One early-18th-century visitor, F Ximenez, noted that at Testour "the square is in the middle of the village where the Moors who founded it held festivities with bulls in the Spanish manner." Such traditions are long gone.

The travellers of the 18th century often showed a certain approval of the Morisco villages. After a long period during which the northern part of Tunisia had been dominated by nomad tribes, the Andalusians managed to create new towns, benefiting from the more powerful rule of law established by the Ottoman deys. Wrote traveller Peyssonel in the early 1720s, "the towns and villages were rare in this kingdom before the arrival of the Andalusians. Most of the towns to be seen today owe their foundation or at least their

The importance of the Andalusians

re-foundation to them, because before them the natural or bedouin Moors preferred to live under tents in the countryside, as is still the case."

Other sights   With time, the Andalusians were absorbed into the rest of the population, and later building lacks the Iberian touch. The other main monument in Testour, the **Zaouia of Sidi Nasser el Baraouachi**, built in 1733, is a standard 18th-century building for religious gatherings. It is down a side-street to the left at the far end of the village from the main square. Here you can have a peek at the quiet colonnaded courtyard with its orange tree, and look in at the prayer hall with the saint's catafalque. Local women are said to come here seeking a cure for sterility. The other minor sight at Testour, if still in operation, is the traditional tile and **brick works** above the river bank in the area below the Great Mosque.

Malouf festival   An annual Festival of Malouf is generally held at the end of June. *Malouf* is a form of Hispano-Arabic choral music brought from Andalucía by the escaping Moors. (If this is your thing, try to catch a concert by the Rachidia in Tunis, possibly during the Ramadan Festival de la Médina.)

Sleeping   As yet, there are no hotels in Testour. For eating, there are 1 or 2 *gargottes* doing fry-ups
& eating   on the main street. Market day is Fri.

Transport   Testour is about 90 mins' drive from Tunis. There are buses and louages from Tunis, Béja, Medjez el Bab, and Teboursouk.

Medjez El Bab

Phone code: 78   A market town and an important crossing point of the Oued Medjerda, Medjez
Colour map 1, grid B3   el Bab was built on the site of the ancient Membressa. The present town is a creation of the Andalusian immigrants who settled here in 1611. The Great Mosque had a number of Andalusian features but has suffered at the hands of the restorers in recent years. The old bridge over the Medjerda was built in 1675-77 under Mourad II. A new bypass and bridge were constructed in the 1990s. With the improved roads, Medjez is only one hour from Tunis and 40 minutes from Béja by car. (Buses and louages arrive in the central square.)

Up in the hills, some 13 km to the northwest of Medjez el Bab, are the villages of **Toukaber** (ancient Thuccabor), **Chaouach** and **Heïdous**, the first two being most easily accessible along narrow climbing roads. Chaouach looks out over the remains of ancient Sua, a settlement which was no doubt prosperous back in the second century AD. Look out for the rock tombs, or *haouanet*,as they are known, at both sites. The modern world is catching up with these settlements. Olive trees, wheat and barley are cultivated as of old, but as elsewhere in Tunisia's villages, electricity has arrived.

The British First and Eighth armies suffered losses here in the Second World War, and there are two **military cemeteries** in the area. One is three kilometres southwest of town on the P5 with 2,900 graves and a memorial to soldiers who died in Tunisia and Algeria and have no known grave. The other has 240 graves and is 17 km west of town on the P6 beside the church in the town of Oued Zarga. ■ *Both 0730-1430 Sat-Thu.*

Sleeping   E *Hotel Membressa*, small, 14 rooms, communal shower, T460121. Not much of a place. Loud and beery bar.

Central Tunisia

6

Central Tunisia

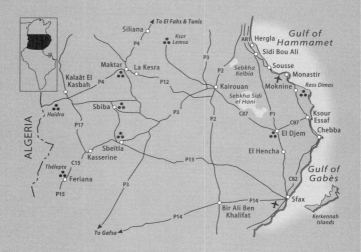

The central regions of Tunisia stretch across steppelands from the rolling grainlands of the north to the pre-Saharan areas. In the east is the Sahel (lit : 'the coast'), a flat region planted with thousands upon thousands of regularly spaced olive trees and home to Tunisia's textile industry. Here are the tourist towns of **Sousse** *and* **Monastir**, *picturesque* **Mahdia**, *and industrious* **Sfax**. *Off the coast, there are the soporific* **Islands of Kerkennah**. *Inland from Sousse lies the holy city of* **Kairouan**, *centred on its honey-coloured mosque, and the Roman city of* **Sbeïtla**, *perhaps the best preserved in the country. The great colosseum of* **El Djem**, *north of Sfax, the third largest in the Roman world, is a spectacular sight. But away from the coast the landscapes open up, and enthusiastic drivers will want to head inland to ancient* **Makthar** *and hillcrest* **La Kessera**, *mysterious* **Jugurtha's Table** *and* **Haïdra**, *legionary base on a remote Roman frontier.*

Background

The *Sahel*, or shoreland, is the low-lying eastern coastal plain of Tunisia extending from the Gulf of Hammamet to the Gulf of Gabès, and inland some 50 km, reaching a maximum altitude of around 275 m. Because of its good beaches and pleasant climate, tempered in summer by cool sea breezes, the northern Sahel has seen considerable tourist development. North of **Sousse**, the development now extends some 20 km right up to Chott Myriam. South of Sousse, **Skanès** and **Monastir**, hometown of Tunisia's first president, were especially favoured in the 1960s and 1970s. The southern Sahel, focusing on **Sfax**, has had a rather different destiny. Sfax is the main port for southern Tunisia, a thriving industrial town, with little to hold the visitor. But just off the coast are the **Kerkennah Islands**, sleepy and curiously self-contained.

The Sahel region has a long history, going back to the Carthaginians and the Romans, with the amphitheatre in **El Djem** (Thysdrus) being one of the most important ancient sites in North Africa. The médinas in most of the coastal towns have been preserved and there are some very digestible museums. A few hours' drive west from the coast are some superb Roman cities and some wonderful landscapes.

A large number of visitors to the Sahel come in on packages, staying in either **Sousse** or **Monastir**, although **Mahdia**, south of Monastir, now has some large hotels. If you are based in Sousse or Monastir, you are well placed to see a lot of Tunisia, whether you are travelling by public transport or in a car. Sousse, being larger, has the better onward connections, and **Kairouan**, **Hammamet** and **El Djem** are all within easy travelling distance. It would be a bit difficult to see the sites of Tunis and area in a day-trip, so you might consider an overnight stay. With a few days' car-hire, you can do some splendid circuits into the steppelands of the interior, with overnights at **Kasserine** or **Sbeïtla**. There are some fine landscapes northwest of Kairouan, around **La Kessera**, a hillcrest village, and **Makthar**, another Roman site. Archaeology buffs will find some excellent **obscure ancient sites** to explore in this area.

Based in Sousse or Monastir, you are not too far from the **Djerid**, the southwestern oasis area of Tunisia. You could take an organized trip, the so-called 'desert safari', or travel down by public transport (it is about six hours to **Tozeur**). This region requires a couple of overnight stays to make it worthwhile.

Sousse سوسة

Phone code: 73
Colour map 1, grid C5

With its beaches of fine sand, turquoise sea and great white hotels, Sousse, Pearl of the Sahel, is everybody's image of a 20th-century beach resort. Sousse does not have that faint tinge of decadence that characterizes Hammamet, nor does it have that total slowdown you feel on sleepy Djerba. Sousse is the safe, Mediterranean holiday town par excellence. It would suit young families looking for a quiet all-inclusive type of holiday, or perhaps third-age people looking for an off-season base from which to explore historic médinas and Roman sites. For budget travellers, it can make a relaxing stop over for a couple of nights on an all-Tunisia tour.

Things to do

★

- Tour the historic city of **Kairouan**. Pick up a kilo of honey-sticky makroudh (date cakes) or some beaten copper, zinc-plated traditional kitchenware.
- En route for the Roman site of Makthar, visit the hill-crest village of **La Kessera** up in the pine woods.
- Take at stroll in the Médina of Sousse, visiting a restored traditional house, **Dar Essid** and its belvedere café.
- Out towards the Algerian frontier, take in the remote Roman site of **Haidra** and the flat topped mountain of **Kelaat Senam** (Jugurtha's Table).
- Feed in one of the fish restaurants of Monastir, *El Farik* or the one in the fishing port (*Le Pirate*).

Ins and outs

Buses come here from all the major cities to 1 of the 4 bus stations, either on **1** Bab el Djedid (from all points south) or **2** by Pl Farhat Hached, the main square (from the north). Buses from beach areas north of Sousse arrive at **3** Place Sidi Yahia, on the north side of the médina. Finally, coming in from Le Kef and the northwest, you will arrive at **4** the *gare routière* on Pl Léopold Senghor.

> **Getting there**
> *See Transport, page 259, for further details*

The train station is very convenient, right in the middle of the town on Blvd Hassouna Ayachi. Louages arrive at a station 2 km southwest of the town centre (on the opposite side of town to the hotel strip). If you are arriving from the nearest airport, Skanès/Monastir International, 20 km away, take the regional railway ('metro') into town (20-min ride). A taxi from the airport should cost no more than 8Dt.

Most of the package hotels are located on the Corniche or on the coast north of the town, there being a first concentration immediately north of the centre, and a second concentration around Port el Kantaoui. Taxi is the quickest means of moving between the two. During the day, there is a 'Noddy train' as well as there are buses, too. For a change of scene, Monastir and Mahdia, both beach resorts south of Sousse with historic old quarters, are easily accessible by metro leaving from the station on Av Mohamed V, south of the main Pl F Hached in the town centre. Buses for Hergla go from Pl Sidi Yahia, on the north side of the médina.

> **Getting around**

The heart of Sousse is a busy, large junction-cum-square, the Pl Farhat Hached, located where médina, new town and port zone meet. The entrance to the médina is a pedestrian area, key landmark the *Soula Shopping Centre* on the corner on your right as you head into the old town. There are a number of useful things here, including cheap eateries and téléboutiques. Back on Pl Farhat Hached, Av Hassen Ayyachi takes you up to the train station, about 100 m away. Main artery of the new town, Av Habib Bourguiba, has ATMs, more cheap eateries, and pharmacies. After the Abou Nawas Bou Jaâfar, it divides into two, Blvd Hédi Chaker along the sea-front promenade, and the busy Rte de la Corniche, parallel to it (lots of eateries and first-generation package hotels here). The two eventually merge where the Hana chain hotels begin, and the Av du 7-Novembre runs on north all the way to Port el Kantaoui.

> **Orientation**

The tourist information offices are at **Regional ONTT**, 1 Av Habib Bourguiba, by Pl Farhat Hached, T225157, open 0730-1930 most days. The local office is opposite, T220431. At Port el Kantaoui, the tourist office (T241799) is on the left as you enter through the archway into the marina – the manager is very helpful.

> **Information**

Central Tunisia

History

With a population of over 300,000, Sousse is the now the third largest city in Tunisia after Tunis and Sfax. Situated at the southern end of the long curve in Tunisia's east coastline known as the Gulf of Hammamet, it is a growing town with an important service sector. The history of Sousse goes back to the ninth century BC when it was founded as a Phoenician trading post, a fact which makes Sousse one of the oldest ports in the Mediterranean. In the fourth century BC, when Carthage became the leading city in the area, Sousse entered its sphere of influence. During the second Punic-Roman war, Hannibal used Sousse as his base, but was beaten in 202 BC. During the third Punic-Roman war, Sousse switched allegiance to Rome, thereby avoiding destruction and gaining the status of free town, acquiring the Latin name of **Hadrumetum**. Unfortunately, with the victory of Caesar over the armies of Pompeii in Thapsus (46 BC), just down the coast, Sousse found itself on the wrong side, and Caesar imposed heavy taxation on the town. Nevertheless under the rule of Trajan (AD 98-117) the city became an important commercial centre.

Under Diocletian (284-305), Sousse became capital of the new province of Byzacium, and was the home of a flourishing Christian community – witness the catacombs. Under later invasions, Sousse had a few name changes. Under the Vandals, it was renamed **Hunericopolis**; retaken by the Byzantines, it was redubbed **Justinianopolis**. With the Arab invasions of the seventh century, it was destroyed.

In the ninth century, with the coming of the Aghlabid dynasty to Kairouan, it again prospered, as that inland city's port. It was from Sousse that the Muslim armies heading for Sicily would have embarked. Sousse was taken in the 12th century by the Sicily-based Normans, mid-Mediterranean regional power of the day, and in the 16th century by Spain. With its port installations, the city was a target in the Second World War, and was seriously damaged in 1942-43.

Since the 1960s, Sousse has become a major town, with service industries and tourism important in the local economy. The main north-south autoroute has put Sousse within 100 minutes of the capital, new university buildings and hospitals have been built west of the city. But perhaps the most striking change is in the area north of Sousse: an almost unbroken strip of hotels runs the whole way up to Chott Meriem and Akouda. The area immediately north of the town centre, all traffic and low-rise blocks topped with oversized neon lights, is singlularly unattractive. Further north, Port el Kantaoui, Tunisia's first purpose-built marina with self-catering accomodation, has been a great success, still popular nearly 20 years after it was opened.

Sights

The centre of Sousse, despite the proximity of the port and much industry south of the town, is pleasant. The walled médina, looking down towards the sea, contains narrow, winding streets and some interesting sights, at least enough to keep you busy for a day.

Médina Sousse's prime sight is clearly its fine old médina, still surrounded (unlike Tunis) by long stretches of the original walls, first built in 859 and restored in 1205. The way to enter the médina is either via Bab el Djedid, or through the Place des Martyrs beside the central square which leads to the Great Mosque. The breach in the walls was the result of bombardments during 1943. There are a number of buildings to aim for in the médina to give some direction to your wanderings. Close to the central Place Hached, the most obvious are the **Ribat** (visitable) and the **Grand Mosque**. There are other fine religious buildings viewable from the outside, and a private home restored as a museum. Up at the highest point is the **Kasbah**, its museum housing a small but worthwhile collection of mosaics. Sousse will give you in condensed form what you will be missing if you don't have time to make the trek up to Tunis on a day-trip.

The **Great Mosque** dominates an esplanade leading towards the Ribat. Built in the ninth century by the Aghlabid Emir Abou Abbas Mohammed, it was probably a conversion of a kasbah built a few years earlier. Further renovations and restorations have taken place. On two corners, large, round towers dominate the marble floored courtyard and make it look like the fortress it may originally have been. Overall the monument is very simple, the courtyard being decorated solely by inscriptions around its sides. Only the courtyard can be visited. ■ *0800-1300, closed Fri. Entrance tickets 2Dt can be bought opposite the mosque and at the local ONTT.*

Perhaps the most venerable buildings in Sousse, the **Ribat** was part of a series of nineth century coastal strongpoints built to defend the coast of Ifrikiya from the marauding Christians. It is generally described as 'a sort of fortified monastery', although there is no monastic movement in Islam. Constructed under Aghlabid ruler Ziyedet Allah I, it was completed in 820. No doubt it functioned as a centre for mustering the embryonic Muslim community against outside attacks. Like most other early Islamic buildings in Ifrikiya, the Ribat at Sousse was built using materials from older sites, as can be seen at

Central Tunisia

Sousse

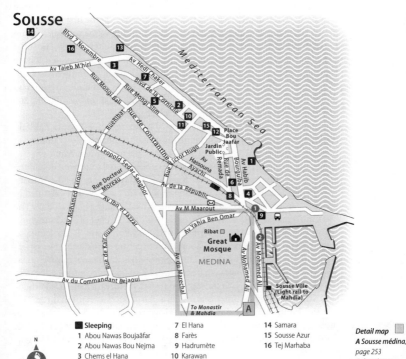

Sleeping		
1 Abou Nawas Boujaâfar	7 El Hana	14 Samara
2 Abou Nawas Bou Nejma	8 Farès	15 Sousse Azur
3 Chems el Hana	9 Hadrumète	16 Tej Marhaba
4 Claridge	10 Karawan	
5 Corniche Plaza	11 Le Printemps	● Eating
6 Du Parc	12 Nour Justina	1 Le Bouheur
	13 Riadh Palms	2 Le Lido

N
0 metres 200
0 yards 200

Detail map ■
A Sousse médina,
page 253
Related map
Port El Kantaoui,
page 258

Kidnapped by an eagle

One of the finest mosaics at Sousse Archaeological Museum portrays Jupiter and his cupbearer, Ganymede. The latter is shown wearing a Phrygian cap and a minimal cape in royal purple, as is appropriate for a favourite of the King of the Gods. He doesn't seem to be offering much resistance to his kidnapping. The central panel is surrounded with 8 medallions featuring springing wild animals. Elsewhere in the museum, (opposite the entrance), Ganymede appears in marble, doing his best to escape the talons of the eagle-god. The theme of Jupiter and the beautiful Ganymede was a popular one for wall-paintings, mosaics and statuary in Roman antiquity. The story goes that Jupiter transformed himself into an eagle and bore Ganymede up to heaven, there to be his cupbearer. (Jupiter had done a similar trick before, changing himself into a swan, all the better to carry off the nymph Leda). Another fine representation of Ganymede and the eagle can be found in the form of a fine ivory statuette, painstakingly reassembled, at the Palaeo-Christian Museum in Carthage.

Still on the theme of eagles, in the Roman Empire, they were the symbol of imperial strength and war. On an emperor's death, he would be cremated, and an eagle would bear his soul to heaven. Monuments might be decorated with an image of such imperial apotheosis. The capitol at Dougga had one such bas-relief, symbolising the apotheosis of Antoninus Pius.

the entrance where antique columns are placed on either side of the door. There is nothing elaborate about the Ribat: it is 38 m square with towers at all four corners, the main one being the lookout tower. On the first floor a large prayer room takes up all the south side. Go to the top of the watch tower, up the narrow stairway, whence there is a good view over city and sea. The Ribat has been much restored, and the buildings which once surrounded it have been cleared away so you can see the Ribat as an urban monument, isolated from context, much as it must have been when it was first built, although no doubt the sea came right up to the walls. ■ *0800-1900 summer, 0930-1200 and 1400-1800 winter, closed Mon. 1Dt, photography fee 1Dt.*

In the médina, one of the more unusual buildings is the **Zaouia Zakkak**, distinguished by its rather bijou Hanefite octagonal minaret. You cannot visit the inside, and it is extremely unusual for a zaouia to have a minaret.

The highest point of the historic centre of Sousse, the southwest end of the médina, is dominated by the **Kasbah**, today home to the **Musée Archéologique**. The Kasbah was built in the 11th century, and extended in the 16th, around an old signal tower (the Khalef) dating back to 859. The Museum's main exhibits are collections from the Tophet of Hadrumetum, votive and funerary stones, sacrificial urns and Punic jars. It also contains many well preserved **mosaics**. Though the collection is smaller and less spectacular than that at the Bardo in Tunis, Sousse has its share of masterpieces. The majority of the mosaics are from the third and fourth centuries, the central theme being the sea (Neptune in his chariot, pictures of fish, etc). Particularly worth seeing is the third-century *Triumph of Bacchus* in room three. This mosaic, found in Sousse, illustrates the victory of a young god over the forces of evil. Another mosaic nearby portrays *Jupiter and Ganymede.* ■ *0800-1200, 1600-1900 summer, 0930-1200, 1400-1800 winter, closed Mon. 2Dt, photography fee 1Dt, T233695. Entrance via Blvd du Maréchal Tito.*

Back in the médina, the **Souks** are mainly situated around the north end of the Rue d'Angleterre. On the west is Souk el Reba, specializing in fabrics and perfume. Again on the right is the Khalaout el Koubba, a building whose original function is unknown but which was probably built in the 19th century. Continue up the Souk el Reba and go out by Bab el Gharbi and turn left along the walls to come to the kasbah and the museum. After visiting the museum re-enter the médina by following the walls to the Bab el Khabli. Following the Rue el Hadjira will bring you back to the Rue d'Angleterre. Prices in the tourist shops on Rue d'Angleterre can be expensive. Do you really want to spend precious swimming time on bargaining for a furry camel or a tooled leather pouf? Either drive a hard bargain or find another activity.

Finally, a note on a couple of minor attractions in the médina of Sousse. Starting at Place Farhat Hached, follow the Rue du Rempart-Nord round and up until you come to **Dar Essid**, a restored 20th-century house. The owners take great pride in their restored home. The living rooms off the courtyard

Other sights

Central Tunisia (side tab)

Sousse mèdina

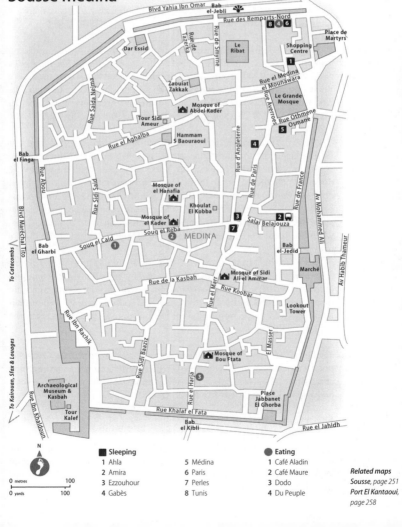

Sleeping		**Eating**
1 Ahla	5 Médina	1 Café Aladin
2 Amira	6 Paris	2 Café Maure
3 Ezzouhour	7 Perles	3 Dodo
4 Gabès	8 Tunis	4 Du Peuple

Related maps
Sousse, page 251
Port El Kantaoui, page 258

0 metres 100
0 yards 100

have their original furnishings, and you can get an idea of how comfortably-off Muslims would have lived in Sousse last century. ■ *1000-1900 May-Sep, 1000-1800 Oct-Apr.*

The other heritage museum is **Khalouat el Koubba**, just off Souk el Rba in the heart of the médina. The original function of the building is unknown, although *khaloua* is the term used for a saint's retreat or cell (*khalouat el koubba*, 'the domed retreat'). The building is believed to date from 11th/12th centuries. Today it houses a museum of traditional Tunisian marriage customs. The dome, with its zigzag ribbing, is probably unique in North Africa.

On the south side of the médina, the **House of the Tragic Poet** will be worth a visit for people collecting minor Roman sites. (Turn left out of Kasbah, head down Avenue Ibn Khaldoun, fork right after 200 m).

Back on the north side of the town centre, close to the Place Sidi Boujaâfar, at the start of the Corniche, the **Jardin Zoologique**, has several shaded walkways between the aviaries with birds which range from budgerigars to ostriches. It provides a shaded resting area for entrance 0.25Dt and there is a café and a toilet by the gate.

Catacombs of the Good Shepherd Visiting catacombs seems a promise of much excitement, and Sousse has 5 km of them, almost all off-limits. The Catacombs of the Good Shepherd are a good 20 minutes' walk from the western end of the médina. To get there, take Rue Commandant Béjaoui west from the Kasbah, then go first left on Rue Abdou Hamed el Ghazali. The catacombs are on a street on your left after 10 minutes' walk. ■ *Tue-Sun 0800-1200, 1500-1900 summer, 0900-1200, 1400-1800 winter.*

Unlike the Romans, the early Christian communities did not practise cremation. Generally, the Christians were too poor to buy land for burial. For the communities in Rome, Naples, and North Africa, the solution was to dig down into the rock, creating tunnels were shrouded bodies could be placed on ledges (*loculi*) or in niches. In the days of anti-Christian persecution, catacombs provided a gathering place for Christians where they might gather at some martyr's grave. The catacombs might also be attacked by mobs. Later, when Christianity was accepted, basilicas were built above ground on the site of catacombs.

At Sousse, there are more than 250 galleries containing up to 15,000 tombs, testimony to the importance of early Christianity in North Africa. They were built and used between the second and fourth centuries. The catacombs were discovered in 1888, and in the recently restored section, there are few hundred metres open for inspection, and some tombs fronted with glass to reveal the contents within.

Beach The beach of fine sand, cleaned every morning, starts in front of the Corniche, but it is much nicer, and less crowded further north. Surfboards can be rented at certain hotels and on the beach. In the evenings, Soussis and tourists enjoy a *paseo* up and down the sea-front promenade.

Excursions north of Sousse

If you hire a car, there are some excellent day-trips to do from Sousse. One such circuit, north of Sousse, could take you to **Enfida** (museum and Second World War graves), the hilltop village of **Takrouna** and the Kène Craft Centre (see pages 188 and 189). You could finish up at Hergla.

Hergla, the Roman Horrea Coelia, is a former fishing village located on a low **Hergla**
rise overlooking the sea with some narrow fine-sand beaches to the north.
Hergla is clearly signed off the autoroute (there is a péage), or can be reached by
driving north from **Kantaoui** on the main road running via **Chott Miriem** (lots
of unmarked 'sleeping policemen'). There are some beautiful beaches at Chott
Miriem, popular with Tunisian migrant workers many of whom have summer
homes in self-built housing areas close to the beach. Just before Hergla is a
lagoon (prime birdwatching territory?) with a small fish farm. Look out for the
remains of an old stone bridge to the east of the road. (If you wish to avoid
Hergla, a new road from the roundabout to the south of the village takes you
directly across the plain to the autoroute for Tunis and the north.)

Hergla's most important building is a mausoleum in honour of Sidi Bou
Mendil ('the saint with the handkerchief'), who was said to be able to transform any piece of cloth into a magic flying carpet to whisk him off to the Holy
Land of Arabia. Hergla also has a go-kart rink. The local craft is esparto grass
weaving, as at nearby Takrouna and Jeradou. Originally, woven and plaited
esparto grass was the raw material for a whole series of utilitarian products,
including donkey bags and *scourtins*, round mats used in the olive oil presses
to filter the oil. Today, you can also find decorative fish and table mats in the
small shops around the main square, plus a couple of small restaurants catering to the tourist trade. Hergla's beaches have not escaped the attention of the
planners in the Ministry of Tourism. A *zone touristique* is scheduled for the
region, plus a brand new airport, Tunisia's third most important after
Tunis-Carthage and Skanès-Monastir, to be constructed on the plain to the
north. Located close to the main north-south autoroute, this will be ideally
located for supplying tourists to both Sousse and Hammamet.

The 'big citadel', an undistinguished sort of place on the northern outskirts of **Kalaâ Kebira**
Sousse, has lost most of its agricultural charm. The Olive Festival in December
might be worth a visit if you are an oil fan.

Essentials

Most hotels are fully booked in summer. Budget travellers should note that there are **Sleeping**
some good places to stay in the médina and that there can be some real out-of-season ■ *on maps,*
bargains in the beach-side hotels. In the upmarket category, the best rooms are said to *pages 251 and 253*
be in the *Orient Palace*, *Diar el Andalus*, and *Mouradi Palace*. *Phone code: 73*

Some of the hotels here can be a little awkward to find. To locate the hotels *Paris* and **Médina**
Sarra, facing the *Soula Shopping Centre*, go right, locate Neptune mosaic at end of
rempart, go straight up hill, keeping city wall on right. **D** *Hotel Amira*, 52 R de France,
near Bab Djedid in the médina, T/F226325. 25 rooms, half with bath, some with view,
panoramic roof terrace. Popular, try to reserve. **D** *Hotel Aya*, odd little new hotel above
jewellers' workshops in an un-named alley near the Musée El Kobba, T/F228589. 11
rooms with TV, shower, a/c. Best rooms 1 and 2. Rooms 7 and 8 noisy as close to café.
D *Hotel Médina*, behind the Great Mosque on R de Paris, 15 R Othman Osman,
T221722, F221794. At the top of this price bracket. 55 rooms at present, 20 to be added
in new block, very clean, some rooms with bath, also some 4-bed mini-suites, some
rooms a bit cramped, roof terrace, restaurant/bar, no phone bookings, so arrive early in
summer. Takes tour groups, will change money. **D** *Hotel de Paris*, 15 R du Rempart
Nord, by the walls close to Pl Farhat Hached, T220564. Very clean, rooms open on to
courtyard galleries or spacious roof terrace. All rooms with basin without hot water.
Best rooms? B22, B27 (triple), B28 double). Drawback? Modern construction, therefore

Central Tunisia

top-floor rooms could be stifling in summer. **D** *Hotel Sarra*, still on R du Rempart Nord, a bit further up than *Hotel de Paris*. 11 room family-run establishment, lots of blue and white paint and tiles. Few clients in winter. Drawbacks? No washbasins in rooms, gas-heated hot water. Plus points? Clean and quiet. Best room C1.

E *Hotel Ahla*, Pl de la Grande Mosquée, T200570. Clean and cheap, central location near the Great Mosque. Underwent a major refit in early 2002. 16 rooms, 5 individual, 1 double, 2 triples. Best rooms overlooking Ribat are 6, 7, 14 and 15. Handy for pizzeria downstairs. **E** *Hotel de Gabès*, 12 R de Paris, T226977. A little complicated to find: from the *Hotel Médina*, go right at fork and look for door on your right, head up a steep marble staircase. Definitely best of the very cheap hotels, clean but basic, no breakfast, some rooms on roof, good views from terrace, only 14 rooms so book in summer, room for bicycles. Drawbacks: only 2 showers. **E** *Hotel Ezzouhour*, 48 R de Paris, T228729. Very simple, some rooms with bath, otherwise communal shower, very cheap, pleasant manager. **E** *Hotel Perles*, 71 R de Paris, T224609. In the médina, very small, could be cleaner, communal shower, cheapest hotel in Sousse. **E** *Hotel de Tunis*, near the Ribat on R de l'Eglise. Sagging marble staircase leads up to covered patio of once fine house. Decay everywhere – only for the very hardy. Windowless, cell-like rooms.

Av Bourguiba & around **A** *Abou Nawas Boujaâfar*, 474 beds, on the main drag, T226030, F226595, boujaafar@ abounawas.com.tn Has one of the first thalassotherapy centres in Tunisia. Small gym and sauna. Good choice for the city centre, off-season prices very reasonable. **C** *Hotel Farès*, Blvd Hassouna Ayachi, just off Pl Farhat Hached, T227800. 180 beds, central, private beach 200 m away, a/c, high rooms with view. **C** *Le Claridge*, Av Habib Bourguiba, T224759. 60 beds, centre of new town. A bit of a Sousse institution in its day. Noisy street-side rooms, but clean. rooms have a rather dated feel. **C** *Hotel Hadrumète*, Pl Assed Ibn el Fourat, T226291/2. by port, all 35 rooms with bath, heating, clean, good restaurant, pool, UFO-type building houses outside bar. In the 1970s, this must have been a very chic address indeed. Remnants of the original décor survive – see the spiral marble staircase. East-facing rooms best in summer. Recommended apart from the occasional cockroach. Good value for money. **C** *Sousse Azur*, 5 R Amilcar, off Av Habib Bourguiba, T226960, 227760, F228145. 20 rooms, some with balcony, restaurant, coffee lounge, 10 mins from town centre. German clientele. Drawback? Street-facing rooms are noisy. Plus? Small bar with alcohol.

Corniche **A** *Hotel Chems el Hana*, T226900, F226076. Elegant, 243 rooms with bath, a/c, phone, TV, terrace, 2 restaurants, 2 pools, fitness centre, tennis, near the sea and quite near the médina, conference room for 150, wheelchair access. Part of the El Hana complex designed by Clément Cacoub. Very 1970s. **B** *Nour Justinia*, on Corniche, T226382. 422 beds, sea front, food and service is reputedly not quite up to scratch. **B** *Riadh Palms*, Blvd du 7-Novembre, T225700, F228347. Vast package place, marble lobby furnished with pseudo-antiques. **B** *Samara*, Blvd Abdelhamid Kadhi, T226699, F226879. Another large hotel, very handy for the disco of the same name. **B** *Tej Marhaba*, Av Taïeb Mehiri, T229800, F229815. Large recent hotel next to busy shopping complex (which has a popular upmarket bar, the *Rose and Crown*). Indoor pool and all usual facilities. Busy road to cross to get to beach. **B-C** *Résidence el Faracha*, R du Papillon (Faracha in Arabic), T227279, F227270, in a quiet street not far from Blvd de la Corniche. (Turn into R Naceur Bey at the *Hotel Printemps*, then go right after *Restaurant La Mamma*). 15 rooms, decorated with tiles, has a good name. **C** *Hotel Karawan*, Av Hédi Chaker, T226139 F225307. Package hotel on main drag, close to Nour Justinia. Noted for its lively bar. **C** *Corniche Plaza*, on Blvd de la Corniche, T226763. Small, well-run hotel. **C** *Le Printemps*, Blvd de la Corniche, T229335, F224055. 69 rooms for 2-4 persons, with hob, fridge and utensils, bar, tea room, hairdresser, commercial centre, restaurant,

5-min walk from town centre. **C** *Résidence Jeunesse 21*, R Monji Slim, T213373. Small pension-type place with 20 rooms in a new building. No heating but a good reception. Well located down a street opposite the *Abou Nawas Nejma* complex.

Youth hostel   T227548. 3 km out along Tunis road, at Plage Boujaâfar, 2 km from station, kitchen, meals available, 90 beds.

A *Orient Palace*, 558 beds, T24288, F243345. Access just after *Médina City* shopping centre, on your right as you come up from Sousse. **A-B** *Tour Khalaf*, T241844, F243868. Vast beachside hotel between the *Marhaba Club* and *Hotel El Ksar*. **B** *Marhaba* T242180, F243867. Yet another large beachfront hotel, part of the vast Marhaba complex. **B** *Shéhérazade* T241412, F241531. Entirely acceptable beach hotel.

Route touristique on the way to Kantaoui
Large package hotels

There are some very large and posh hotels here, especially handy if you're playing golf. **A** *Diar el Andalous* T246200, F246348, diarelandalous@abounawas.com.tn Luxurious in its day, built around a network of garden patios. (Won an Agha Khan architecture prize for design.) 300 rooms, beach, a/c, indoor and outdoor pools, lots of tennis courts, disco, watersports. Justifiably popular. **A** *Hannibal Palace* Port el Kantaoui, T241577, F242341. Another oversized '5-star' hotel. Let down by the service. Needs reclassifying. **A** *Hotel Hasdrubal* Port el Kantaoui, T241944, F241969. Better than the *Hannibal Palace*. **A** *Marhaba Palace* T243633. Just like a palace, 250 splendid rooms, indoor and outdoor pools, tennis, garden. Just north of the marina area. **B** *Les Maisons de la Mer* T241799, F241961. Pleasant self-catering accomodation at Port el Kantaoui, ranging from studios for 2 to small flats sleeping 6. Good value out of season. Office is to left of the mock-fortified gate, the main entrance to Kantaoui. Minus point? Kitchens poorly equipped. Plus? Freedom from food and constraints of hotel restaurants. **B** *Hotel El Kanta* T348666, F348656. Nice accommodation, handy for golf course and marina. Restaurant *La Fontaine* has quite a good name.

Hammam Sousse/ Kantaoui area
■ *on map, page 258*
Don't look for cheap hotels in this area

B *Hotel Soviva*, Rte de Hergla, north of Kantaoui, T246145. Lots of fun to be had on the water slides in the pool complex here. **C** *Tennis Méditerranée*, Rte de Hergla, Chott Meriem T248055, F248060.

Chott Meriem

Given that the people of Sousse are great ones for eating out, and that most hard-up package tourists prefer to eat in, there are not many top-notch restaurants in town. There are plenty of cheap and mid-range places, however, displaying menus in many languages. Small restaurants in the old town may have menus in Arabic only.

Eating
● *on maps, pages 251 and 253*

Expensive   The prime address in down-town Sousse is held to be Le Lido, T225329. Head south from Pl Farhat Hached down the road which takes you to the Sahel Metro train station. Restaurant is on your left. Has a mixed clientèle of Tunisian men who like their food and booze and tourist regulars. A little overpriced but still a good address. *Le Bonheur*, T225742, Pl Farhat Hached, good grilled meat and fish, large terrace on the street. *Restaurant des Remparts*, T226326, R de l'Eglise, by médina walls close to Pl Farhat Hached, more expensive because it serves alcohol.

Médina & Centre-Ville

Mid-range   *Le Gourmet*, Av Habib Bourguiba, T224751, is one possibility. On Pl Farhat Hached, *Le Cristal*, T225294, may be suitable. Has a good reputation and alcohol. Have a look too at the places on the R de Remada, which runs parallel to Av Bourguiba, on the west side. Something may attract your eye. A bit out of the way in the médina is *Restaurant Dodo*, T212326, a successful little place on R el Hajra, the continuation of the R de Paris.

Central Tunisia

Cheap *Restaurant du Peuple*, on R du Rempart Nord, in the médina, simple but tasty food, has a very good name. Also in the médina, there is the pizzeria-restaurant of the the *Hotel Ahla*, near the Ribat and the Great Mosque, and a couple of fine sandwich places on the pedestrian street near the *Soula Shopping Centre*. Otherwise, there are plenty of cheap eateries on the Corniche, rather fewer on Av Bourguiba.

Port el   There are no cheap eats at Kantaoui. Hotel restaurants also provide (pricey) meals.
Kantaoui   **Expensive** A fair selection of pricier places here, including *La Daurade*, T244893, good, but very pricey. *L'Escale*, T241791, was at one time held to be a top address. **Mid-range** *Neptune VI*, floating restaurant, T241799, giant prawns special. *Les Emirs*, T240865, and *Le Restaurant Méditerranée*, T240788.

Bars, cafés   In Sousse centre, try *Chérif* located on Av Bourguiba between the *Restaurant Les*
& clubs   *Jasmins* and *Sousse Palace*. There are a number of cafés on Pl Farhat Hached. In the Médina, there is a small traditional café near the Musée de la Kobba in R Souk el Reba. Try also the *Café Aladinon*, R Souk el Caïd, on your left as you go uphill. (Has terrace with view of the old town).The best view, however, is from the roof-top café at the *Musée Dar Essid*, on the north side of the médina on R du Rempart Nord.

A short taxi-ride out of the centre is the *Casa del Gelato*, Blvd du 7-Novembre, near the *Hotel Hill Diar*. Las Vegas kitsch block of mirror glass and marble on the main drag up to Port el Kantaoui. Large amounts of ice-cream should please the kids.

Nightclubs   Most of the hotels have small, uninteresting nightclubs. Sousse has 2 large clubs, both at the north end of the town centre, *Maracana* and *Samarra*. Fashions come and go, and as *Maracana* is more recent, it is trendier. When it opened, *Samarra* billed itself as the biggest discotheque in Africa.

Sport   **Diving** *Port el Kantoui International Diving Centre*, Port de Plaisance, T241799, recognized by the watersport federation and open all year. Prices at Diving Centre: 1st dive 20Dt; exploration 22Dt; night dive 25Dt; 6 dives 110Dt; open-water training 250Dt. However, if you really want to dive, you should go to Tabarka. **Golf** *Golf El Kantaoui*, T231755, has a 27-hole tournament golf course, 9,576 m, green fees 30-40Dt per round, lessons available. *Palm Links Golf Course* and *Monastir Golf Course*, shaded by olive trees, are both 18 hole, par 72, 6,140 m. See Golf, page 55, for further details. **Gym** Beach club near swimming pool at north end of Kantaoui, T241799, 4Dt per session, has weights and organizes aerobics etc. **Sailing and fishing** Yachts and catamarans can be hired from the yacht basin or you can take a trip in an ancient sailing boat. *Aquascope* trips are available to view underwater life. The harbour has berths for 340 yachts, minimum-maximum draft 2-4 m. See Yachting, page 57, for further details. Also on offer at quayside are fishing and sailing trips. Unfortunately for the *Aquascope*, which can view 25 m down into the sea, the sea bed off Sousse is featureless and the

Port El Kantaoui

To Diar el Andalous, GP1 & Hergla

Mediterranean Sea

R Jerba

Imp Kanta

Rue du Pinson
Rue du Canard

Rue des Aigles

Rue de la Tourterelle

Main Quay

Quay des Sirènes

Entrance to Marina

Shops

Harbour Master's Office

President Bourguiba

Les Alouettes

Quay Amilcar

Quay Jugurtha

Arrival Quay

Port de Plaisance - El Kantaoui

To Sousse

Not to scale

■ **Sleeping**
1 Hannibal Palace
2 Hasdrubal

3 Les Maisons de la Mer
4 Marhaba Palace

water rather murky. Try a camel ride, instead or some natural sea-water healing. **Thalassotherapy** *Abou Nawas Bou Jaâfar* offers a range of treatments 'for total well-being' including indoor heated sea-water pool, 2 saunas, Turkish baths, gym, solarium and relaxation room.

Casino *El Hana Palace Hotel*, T243000. **Concerts** Sousse International Festival in **Entertainment** Jul/Aug, various venues, including open-air theatre. **Football** The local team is the Etoile du Sahel, red and white kit, which has done quite well in recent years in African and Arab competitions.

Fixed price articles, the usual selection at *Socopa* in *Hotel Abou Nawas Bou Jaâfar* and **Shopping** the larger Soula Centre off Pl Farhat Hached. *Monoprix*, Pl Farhat Hached; *Magasin Général*, R Khaled Ibn Walid; Blvd de la Corniche, Complex Nejma; Port el Kantaoui.

Local Car hire: Avis, Rte de la Corniche, T225901; **Ben Jemma Rent a Car**, R 2 Mars, La **Transport** Corniche, T224002; **Budget**, 63 Av Habib Bourguiba, T224041; **Europcar**, Rte de la Corniche, T226252; **Hertz**, Av Habib Bourguiba, T225428; **Inter Rent**, Rte de la Corniche, T227562. Take a look at the agencies on the Corniche road and compare prices.

Long distance Air: Tunisair, Av Habib Bourguiba, T227955, for details of flights from Skanes/Monastir airport, T260300. **Train**: Sahel Metro goes all the way to **Mahdia** along the coast stopping at all the resorts, small towns and Monastir international airport (0.6Dt single). Hourly from 0600-2000. The trip **Sousse-Mahdia** takes just under 1 hr (3.75Dt return). First train from Mahdia 0500, last train out of Mahdia 1855. Station is at south end of Av Mohammed V, 100 m down from the Bab Djedid towards the harbour, T225321. **For Tunis**: the station is on Blvd Hassouna Ayachi, up the road from Pl Farhat Hached. Information on T224955, 225280. Departures to **Tunis**, **Gabès El Djem/Sfax**, **Gafsa/Metlaoui**. For **Hammamet** and **Nabeul** get off at **Sidi Bou Regba** and continue journey by bus or louage. 'Noddy trains' between Sousse and Port el Kantaoui leave Pl Boujaâfar in Sousse on the hour 0900-1800 in winter, 0900-2300 in summer, returning at half past the hour. There's a blue train and a yellow train, tickets can't be transferred. Adults 3Dt return, children under 8 years 2Dt. **Bus**: there are 4 bus stations. Information on T224202. Departures from **Place Sidi Yahia**, north wall of the médina, a sort of extension of the Pl Farhat Hached, for Port el Kantaoui and Hergla, and Monastir and Mahdia (but metro best for the latter 2). Departures from **Bab el Djedid**, on east side of médina, to all points south, including **Kairouan** (1½ hrs, 2.39Dt); **Gabès** (5 hrs, 9.27Dt) and **Sfax** (2½ hrs, 4.96Dt); **Djerba** (via Zarzis); **Kebili** (7¼ hrs, 12.96Dt); **Douz** (7¼ hrs, 13.9Dt); **Medenine**; **Matmata** (7 hrs, 10.74Dt); **Tataouine** (9 hrs, 13Dt). Departures from **Pl du Port** to **Tunis** (including night departures) and **Bizerte**. Departures from the **gare routière** for points northwest, including Enfida, Le Kef and El Fahs. **Louages**: the louage station has moved from Bab el Djedid, on R Mohammed Ali, to Souk el Ahad, near camel market on Rte de Sfax, 2 km out of town centre. Take a taxi as it's a 30-min walk. **Taxi**: yellow taxis have meters. **Sea** *Compagnie Tunisienne de Navigation (CTN)*, R Abdallah Ibn Zoubeir, T224861, F224844.

Banks Banks with ATMs can be found on Av Bourguiba. Money can also be changed **Directory** in any of the large hotels. **Communications** Internet: *Publinet* clearly signed on 1st floor of a building in R de Remada. **Post Office**: Av de la République, just off Pl Farhat Hached, T224750. **Parcel Post**: R Ali Bey, T225492. **Medical services** Chemist: open nights, 38 Av de la République, T224795. 45 Rte de la Corniche. Av H Thameur. Chemists display names of those open late. **General practitioners**: *Hotel Abou Nawas Bou Jaâfar* recommends Dr Jaballah, T242522, 98400104. Hospital: *Clinique Les Oliviers*, Blvd du 7-Novembre, T242711, 242753. Probably the first option. *Hôpital universitaire*

Central Tunisia

Farhat Hached, Av Farhat Hached, R Ibn el Jazzar, T221411. *CHU*, Sahloul, Hammam-Sousse, T241411. Dialysis Centre, Blvd du 7 Novembre, Rte Touristique, T242711. **Places of Worship** Catholic: Eglise St Felix, 1 R de Constantine, T224596. Service in French, Sat 1815 and Sun 0930. **Evangelical Church**: 16 R de Malte, T224073. **Synagogue**: in R Amilcar. **Useful addresses** Customs Authority: Pl de l'Indépendance, T227700. **National Guard**: Av Leopold Sedar Sanghor, T225588. **Police**: R Pasteur, T225566.

Skanès and Monastir المنستير

Phone code: 73
Colour map 1, grid C6
Arabic script is
for Monastir

Monastir could have been just another sleepy Sahel coastal town. Being the birthplace of independence leader Habib Bourguiba, however, meant that things turned out rather differently. Like leaders elsewhere in Africa who built themselves concrete capitals in the bush, Tunisia's first president wanted a city to mark his country's accession to nation-state status. So sleepy, walled Monastir, a quiet coastal place, had to be extensively remodelled. But this being Tunisia, the results of the building programme are homely rather than grandiose. The town acquired a gold-domed mausoleum, some impressive modernist public buildings and an esplanade. Along the sandy coastline west of Monastir, some of the first hotels devoted to mass tourism went up, including the Skanès Palace, Tunisia's first five star hotel.

Ins and outs

Getting there
See Transport, page 266, for further details

A lot of north European visitors fly into the *Aéroport international de Skanès-Monastir*. The airport is 9 km from Monastir. If you are not being met by a tour-company bus, then you can get into Monastir by rail (the airport has a rail station outside), or by bus or taxi. Taxi drivers are ready to profit from new arrivals' disorientation, so study your banknotes carefully. The ride into Monastir should cost 5-6 Dt maximum. Local shared taxis also do the same run and are considerably cheaper. There are also car-rental companies at the airport, although cheap cars are in demand during high season, so book in advance.

Getting around
The region is served by rail, with the Sahel Metro running from Mahdia to Sousse via the airport and Monastir. The bus, train and louage stations are on Av des Martyrs, next to the R Mahmoud Bourguiba, the main street leading through the town and just 5 mins' walk from the Ribat.

Tourist information
The tourist office is at *ONTT*, Quartier Chraga, in front of the Habib Bourguiba Mosque, T461960. Also in front of the airport, T461205.

History

Situated on a headland some 25 km south of Sousse, Monastir is an attractive fishing port with an elegant promenade along the bay. The journey from Sousse improves as you leave the industrial area of Sousse behind. The huge factory on the outskirts makes couscous. The salt pans at Sahline Sebkha are extensive, an unusual sight for visitors from northern Europe but common in these warm Mediterranean areas. The dried salt is collected, purified and exported.

Sponge fishing is carried on here as well as the catching of most indigenous fish and shellfish.

Ancient origins
Back in Roman times, Monastir was called **Ruspina**, a corruption of the Punic name Rous Penna, and it served as Julius Caesar's operations base for his

The education of Monastir's most famous son

Monastir's most famous son is undoubtedly Habib Bourguiba, founder of Tunisia's nationalist movement and first president of the Tunisian Republic (declared 1957). Born on 3 August 1903, he was to leave an indelible mark on Tunisian life, propelling the country from the rank of sleepy Mediterreanean statelet under French protection to that of a pragmatic, modernizing nation with Arab nationalist credentials.

Bourguiba was the product of a particular environment. While Tunis, with its cosmopolitan population, had no difficulty coping with French rule, which in any case brought new business opportunities and improvements in the city, the small farmers of the Sahel had different attitudes. They quickly seized the importance of modern education, and in the early 1900s, began to have their children educated in bilingual private schools – 70 out of the 90 écoles franco-arabes existing before independence were in the Sahel region. By the 1930s, sons of ordinary families like the Bourguibas were competing with Tunis notables' children for jobs open to Muslims in the administration. Many, like Habib Bourguiba, were going to France for a university education.

In his memoirs, Habib Bourguiba tended to present himself as belonging to a deprived family. In fact his father, retiring from the Beylical army in 1893, was a notable on the Monastir town council, and held various local posts. The family was wealthy enough to send Habib's two elder brothers to the prestigious Sadiki College in Tunis. Habib almost followed the same track, but was forced to drop out of the Sadiki through illness. He returned to schooling at the Lycée Carnot, switching from the establishment that trained members of the Muslim élite to the one dominated by French students. This was a practical move. Through professions like law, accessible to those with a French education, social mobility was possible. In 1924, after completing his baccalauréat, Habib Bourguiba headed for Paris and a law degree. He returned in 1927, marked by French culture, and bringing with him a French wife.

Despite all this education, he was to remain an outsider in all the circles that counted in 1930s Tunis – French administration, traditional Muslim, and cosmopolitan middle-class. The difficulties were both social and professional, and Bourguiba was to move from being a young lawyer trying to build a career to the unstable status of nationalist activist.

African campaign. Part of the triple ramparts from this time still survive. During the 11th century, when nearby Mahdia was the Fatmid capital and Kairouan was out of favour, Monastir was an important regional centre with a fortress built to defend the Muslim coastal settlements against incursions from the Christian north. The Ribat or fortress was held to have special virtues. It was said that spending three days as part of the garrison in Monastir opened the gates to paradise. After the departure of the Fatimids from Mahdia for Egypt, the town lost its regional importance, although the fortifications were improved in Ottoman times.

Sights

Monastir's most famous monument is the **Ribat of Harthouma**, whose walls and turrets will be familiar to all who have seen Monty Python's *The Life of Brian*. The much restored fortifications of the Ribat were built in 796 by Harthouma Ibn el Ayoune, as part of the coastal look-out system. One of the oldest and largest of the military structures built by the Arabs in North Africa, it was later refortified and surrounded by an additional wall during the ninth and

11th centuries, which gives the whole edifice an interesting mixture of contrasting styles and shapes, but the initial plan remains – a courtyard surrounded by accommodation (primitive) for the defenders and a prayer hall now beautifully set out as the **Islamic Museum**. It is very interesting actually to see the inside of one of these forts. Small children should be watched closely as there are no safety barriers and some of the steps and walks by the walls are unprotected. Note that the building may be off-limits if filming is in progress. The Ribat also featured in the 13-episode serial *Jesus of Nazareth* and *Raiders of the Lost Ark*.

The entrance is at the foot of one of the towers, where a corridor flanked by former guard rooms and now used as a ticket office leads into the central courtyard. There is a good view over the sea from the top of the Nador (lookout tower). The museum is well laid out, with good details about the exhibits: gravestones, glass, pages of Koran, pieces of pottery found here at the Ribat, small pipes, pots and oil lamps, leather covers, exquisite old fabrics, a display of coins and a unique wooden Arab astrolabe (for measuring altitude), made in Cordoba and dating back to the 10th century.

There are, in the courtyard, more engraved stelae and tombstones dating back from the 11th and 12th centuries. ■ *0800-1900 summer, 0900-1200 and 1400-1800 winter. Closed Mon. 2Dt, photography 1Dt, no flash or tripods. T461276. Allow at least 1 hr to potter about and get the feel of the place.*

Close to the main Ribat is the smaller **Ribat of Sidi Dhouib**. Also ruins of a similar construction are to be found at the entrance to *Hotel Esplanade*. Plans are to preserve these ruins as they now stand. Another ruined fort stands at the end of Cap Monastir. Also in in the neighbourhood of the Ribat, the **Great Mosque** was built in the ninth century and extended in the 11th century.

The **Habib Bourguiba Mausoleum** at the north end of the cemetery is an imposing affair, a huge square building with a huge golden cupola flanked by two splendid matching minarets. It is approached via a vast paved concourse which cuts through the Sidi el Mazari cemetery at the southern end of which are two new ornate tombs. As one approaches the ornate iron gates (with decorative script on each gate) a man with a key may appear and let you get even nearer – for a tip.

In the cemetery near the Habib Bourguiba Mausoleum is the **Koubba of Sidi el Mazari** built in AD 1149. This can be visited, if respectfully dressed. The Mausoleum was built in 1963 at the same time as the **Habib Bourguiba Mosque**. The mosque (off-limits to non-Muslims) is on Rue de l'Indépend- ence in the old town and was built following the richly decorated 'traditional' style of architecture. The entrance to the prayer hall is through 19 intricately carved teak doors, made by the craftsmen of Kairouan. Once inside, the huge vaulted prayer hall is supported by 86 pink marble columns. There is a large dome before the *mihrab* which is inlaid with golden mosaics and decorated with small onyx columns.

Ribat of Harthouma

N

Not to scale

1 Courtyard
2 Accommodation for defenders
3 Steps up
4 Circular look out tower
5 Small prayer hall
6 Women's Ribat
7 Prayer hall now used as museum
8 Entrance
9 Small polygonal tower

8th Century
9th Century
11th Century
16 & 17th Century
18 & 19th Century

The **médina** has a few suitably picturesque bits and pieces: balconies etc. It was extensively remodelled in the 1960s, and the walls have been restored. It is an interesting area of Monastir with small retail outlets but none of the associated small-scale manufacturing often found in other médinas. There is a small tower on the corner of the médina opposite the post office which seems to have no function now.

Near the mosque and Tourist Office, a **Museum of Traditional Costume** on Rue de l'Indépendence has some nice displays of clothing. ■ *Mon-Sat 0900-1200 and 1400-1730, closed Sun. 1Dt*. For local life, there is the weekly **Saturday market** with the usual goods in Souk Essebt on Place Guedir El Foul and the Rue Salem B'Chir near the bus station.

There are a few very minor sights to seek out on the coast, including the **birth place of Habib Bourguiba** on Place 3 August, on the Route de la Corniche overlooking the old fishing port. It has a blue door and tile work around door and windows. A faded plaque to the right hand side of the door indicates its importance. There are some quite interesting **caves** cut into the sandstone rock which protects the south side of the old fishing harbour as a breakwater. These were used as stores and some still have doors. The shore of the harbour here is covered with many rusty anchors.

On the coast

From the marina, you can walk out to the **Ile Ghedamsi**. Follow the track at the end of the marina area which leads out to the point and to the small (inaccessible on foot) island beyond. It is a pleasant walk (30 minutes) round the koubba and, surprisingly, three tennis courts. There are good views, close down to the tiny natural harbour with the El Kahlia caves cut into the promontory, where the fishermen pull up their boats and wash their nets and beyond over Monastir or north to Skanès. At the very end of the promontory are the remains of a fort which is being excavated and renovated. The path goes round the edge of this fort and in places there is very limited foot room over a very steep drop.

Day trips can be arranged to the **Kuriat Islands** which lie about 15 km east. For more information, go to the office at end of port. These islands are used by the Cap Monastir diving centre.

Essentials

The number of places to stay in Monastir is quite limited. The hotels are expensive but not of high quality. Out of season many are closed or are undergoing redecoration. Try Skanès or Mahdia for 4-star comfort or Sousse for a wider choice.

Sleeping

The hotels in Monastir are close to the town centre, on the Corniche. The *Sidi Mansour*, one of the oldest hotels, awaits redevelopment.

Monastir
■ *on map, page 264*

A *Hotel-Club L'Esplanade*, T461146, F460050, on the Corniche, opposite the Marina, close to the Ribat. Renovated 1996, pleasant. Works with German tour-groups. **B** *Apart-Hotel Cap Monastir*, reception on the left before you go into the marina, T462305, 464999, www.caesium.fr/capmonastir Clean and pleasant self-catering accommodation right on the marina. Attracts lots of Tunisian families in summer. (Flat sleeping 4, 125Dt per night in high season, discounts out of season). The *Apart-Hotel* gives you freedom to do your own thing in a way impossible in the usual 4-star palaces. Kitchen equipment very limited. Recommended. Note that reception will want a 100Dt cash deposit, returned when apartment has been checked after departure. *Hotel Résidence Corniche*, near intersection of Av Bourguiba and Rte de la Corniche, T461451, small 15-room hotel, comfortable. **B** *El Habib*, T462944. Has both rooms and small flats.

Central Tunisia

C *Hotel Kahla*, Av Taïeb Mehiri, southeast of town centre, T464570, F467881. Self-catering accomodation as well as rooms in 4-storey building (no lift). All rooms with tiny shower and loo room. Alcohol available. **B** *Hotel Monastir Beach*, Rte de la Corniche, on beach just down from the *Ribat*, T464766/7, F463594. Large rooms, not always well cleaned, some a/c. Ground floor rooms right on beach, quite noisy. Bar, restaurant, reservations essential in high season. **C** *Hotel Mourabou*, Rte de Khniss to southeast of centre, T460111. Rooms with bathroom, heating, fan in summer, not always too clean. Reasonably priced. **C** *Hotel Yasmine*, Rte de la Falaise, T462511. Pleasant small hotel with the most kitsch façade on the Falaise (whitewashed with lots of blue decorative twiddly bits). 23 beds in 16 rooms (heated in winter, electric fan in summer); have they done up the bathrooms? Welcoming, beach across the road and down the cliff and a good restaurant frequented by locals. Pricey in summer. Main disadvantage: a bit out of the way.

Youth hostel R de Libye, town centre, near the railway station in the Maison des jeunes, T461216, open all year, 60 beds, 5Dt per person in 8-bed dormitory rooms, no double or family room. Said to be on the noisy side.

West of Monastir/ Skanès A good number of hotels are situated in the Skanès zone, strung out all along the Dkhila beach strip west of Monastir. There is little to fault them, they are all big, concrete and harmless. The beach, however, is narrow in places and a bit disappointing.

A *Hotel Kuriat Palace*, T521200, F520049, kuriat.palace@gnet.tn The most expensive of the hotels in this area. Has all the usual facilities. **A** *Sidi Mansour*, T460023. **A** *Skanès El Hana*, T462256. Another big package hotel, part of the El Hana chain. **A** *Skanès Palace*, T520350, F520294, skanes.palace@planet.tn 228 well fitted out rooms, nice grounds, must have been very swish in its day. Unfortunately, the

Central Monastir

Sleeping	5 Youth Hostel	3 King's	◯ Central Streets
1 El Habib		4 Orient	1 Rue Mohammed Shim
2 Esplanade	● **Eating**	5 Panorama	2 Rue des Tripolitains
3 Monastir Beach	1 El Médina		3 Rue du L'Independence
4 Sidi Mansour	2 Hannibal		

refurbishment brought lots of 'traditional' decorative touches which have destroyed the simplicity of the original design. **A-B** *Abou Nawas Sunrise*, T521644, F521282, abounawas.sunrise@abounawas.com 314 rooms in neo-Moorish holiday village type accommodation. Pool, tennis courts, watersports and children's club. Closed mid-Nov to mid-Mar. Good value out of high summer. **A-B** *Hotel Thalassa*, T520520, F520500. New in 1999. Works mainly with tour-groups. Ill-proportioned entry in a vaguely neo-classical style, vast lobby, etc. All the usual facilities. Good value out of season. **B** *Hotel Les Palmiers*, T520636, F502149, own beach, 65 simple rooms, comfortable. **C** *Hotel Chems*, T466290, F466106, huge and impersonal.

Expensive *Cap Grill*, T460923. On left as you enter the marina, attracts a more upmarket sort of clientele and is used for local business people entertaining. Expect to pay about 30Dt a head. *Le King's*, T463394, in the *Complexe El Habib* on the Corniche. Good service, has a good reputation. Around 35Dt a head for the full wack. *Marina The Captain*, T461449, F473820. Bar-restaurant and top address in the marina at Monastir (turn left through main entrance, *The Captain* is on your left at the far end of the quay). Around 30Dt a head. *Le Pirate*, T468126, in an odd wooden building in the new fishing port 1½ km south of town centre – take a taxi. High level of service, business takes its clients here. Recommended, try to reserve. Closed Mon and at midday, except Sun in summer. Good menu at 16Dt a head, no alcohol because in port zone.

Eating
● *on map, page 264*

Mid-range *El Farik*, about 500 m south of the main town beach, right on the coast. The restaurant, which dates back to 1966, is housed in a sort of concrete UFO built on a rocky bit of coast. Basically a boozers' den, with the good seafood and chilled wine that you can find in this sort of eatery in Tunisia. (Excellent mussels and *kamounia bil-karnit*, octopus stew in a rich cumin-flavoured sauce.) If you sit outside on summer afternoons, the local kids will keep you entertained by diving off the parapet. In its day, *El Farik* must have been the happening place in Monastir. About 15Dt a head for a really good feed, but you could pay much less. *El Médina*, Pl de l'Independence, corner of Av de l'Independence, opposite médina wall, small, clean, pavement tables, friendly staff, menu in English, 0900-1800. *Restaurant Hannibal*, in médina behind Office National de l'Artisanant, T461097. Also on Rte de la Corniche are *Orient* and *Panorama*. *Restaurant Le Chandelier*, T462232/462305. At the heart of the marina, on your right as you come in. Fairly recommendable. Pleasant service, good food. *Restaurant de Tunisie*, Av Ali Belhouane, behind *Hotel Hadrumete*, Dutch owned, Tunisian and Indian food.

Cheap *La Pizzeria*, T460923, in marina. Try also *Snack-Quick*, behind the Ribat near the Governorate. Clients include both tourists and locals. *Snax-Kebab Bab Brichka*, on the left after the entrance to the médina, opposite the *Monoprix*.

For a place to smoke a *chicha*, try the *Café Abbès*, at the start of the street with the trees, on the corner opposite the gardens of the Governorate. Near the train station, try *Le Pacha* for ice-cream and cakes.

Cafés & ice cream

Cinemas There are a number of cinemas in the town, including one in the marina. **Hammam** In the médina, R de Tunis.

Entertainment

Office National de l'Artisanat, 0900-1900 daily, except Sun 1100-1700, usual selection of craft items. On outer edge of médina facing east towards *Hotel Esplanade*. *Magasin Général*, Pl de l'Independence, in town centre. *Monoprix*, R de Tunis, opposite médina wall.

Shopping

Central Tunisia

Sport **Golf** *Palm Links* golf course, T466910/2, F466913, 10 km out of town, on road beyond Skanès towards Sousse, 6,140 m, 18 holes, par 72, green fees 30-40Dt. See Golf, page 55, for further details. **Fishing** Excursions from Monastir – weekly mini-cruises to the Kuriat islands. Trip on El Kahlia for amateur anglers, provision of rods, lines and trolls. Details, T461156. **Watersports** Including scuba-diving and sailing, at the Cap Monastir. Underwater diving school, T461156. Monastir Yacht club has 386 berths. Marina T462305. For further details see Essentials: Sport.

Tour operators *ATAC Tour* in *Hotel Rivage*, T230955. *Atlas Voyages* in *Hotel Chems*, T233350. *B'Chire Voyages*, Av Habib Bourguiba, T261066. *Carthage Tours*, in *Hotel Habib* on Corniche, T461847. *Skanes Travel Service* in *Hotel Sahara Beach*, R de 2 Mars 1934, T261088. *Tourafrica*, Av Habib Bourguiba, T461381.

Transport **Local Car hire**: *Avis*, airport, T463031. *Europcar*, airport, T461314. *Hertz*, Av Habib Bourguiba, T461404, and at airport, T461314. *Inter rent*, airport, T461314. *Nova Rent*, Av Habib Bourguiba, T467826.

Long distance Air: *Tunisair* at airport, T460300, and in Monastir close to *Hotel Ribat*, T462550. Flight information Skanes/Monastir airport, T461314. **Train**: Opposite the bus station. Information, T460755. **Tunis** (via Sousse) 0610, 1238, 1758 (5Dt). **'Sahel Metro'** has a stop outside the airport and continues on to **Sousse** and **Mahdia** along the coast every hr, 0600-2000. **Bus**: the bus station is at the south end of Av de la République. Information, T461059. Departures to **Tunis** 0445; **Sfax** 0500, 0600, 1100. There are also frequent buses to **Sousse** (6Dt). **Louages**: leave from in front of the bus station. **Taxi**: some taxi drivers take advantage of tourists – check there is a meter or agree a price.

Directory **Banks** *STB*, Av Habib Bourguiba, T261383. *UIB*, Av Habib Bourguiba, T261400. *BNT*, Pl de l'Indépendence, T261057. *BNT*, Pl de l'Indépendence, T261495. Money can also be changed in large hotels. **Communications** Post Office: Av Habib Bourguiba, by the Palais des Congrès (conference centre), T260176, also at railway station and airport. **Medical Services** Chemist: *Charhine*, Av Habib Bourguiba, and *Karoui*, Av de la République. **Hospital**: *Hôpital Fattouma Bourguiba*, Av Fattouma Bourguiba, T461141. **Places of worship** Catholic: *Chez les Soeurs*, Zone du Stade, T431931, services Sat 1800 and Sun 0900. **Useful addresses** Customs: at port, T462305. **Fire**: R de Libye, T197. **Garage**: 3 garages on Av Habib Bourguiba. **Petrol**: Agil, Mobil or Ruspina, all on Av Habib Bourguiba. **Police**: R Chedli Kallala, T461432.

South from Monastir to Mahdia

Going south from Monastir to Mahdia you cross one of the most populated areas in the country, after the capital region. The small settlements seem to run one into another, and the building continues to expand into the olive groves and market gardens. Total driving time between the two major towns is about an hour, the slowing factors being traffic in the narrow streets of the ribbon settlements and poor road signs at Teboulba.

For those using public transport, this route is best done on the railway known as the Sahel Metro. There are stations at Khnis, Ksar Hellal and Teboulba in addition to those on the published timetable. Travelling by bus will require changes at Moknine or Ksar Hellal.

If you are driving, the corniche to the south of the old fishing port at Monastir soon loses its attraction. You pass between shallow sea (on your left) and a new villa zone (on your right). For Mahdia, you go left at the first main junction (round stadium on your left) and pass through a ribbon settlement before reaching **Khnis** a few minutes later. Here, at the second roundabout, you take the coast road for **Moknine**. On this route, **Lamta**, five minutes further on, has more sprawl and a minor archaeological site on the left (seaward) side of the road. **Teboulba**, a surprisingly large centre, some fifteen minutes from Lamta, is the next possible stop. (There is the *Café Restaurant Venisia*, all false stone facing, as you arrive.) Teboulba's current prosperity is in part built on agriculture. Fruit trees have more or less replaced the olives here, along with potatoes and tomatoes under plastic cover. The drive through the town to continue on the Mahdia road is confusing, to say the least.

A few minutes after Teboulba is the small port of **Bekalta**, situated near the Byzantine ruins of **Rass Dimass** which, as the name suggests (*Ra* is Arabic for head), stand on the headland. The C82 road now runs through olive groves next to the metro line. At the first major junction, you can turn off left for Mahdia's *zone touristique*. The direct road runs through an area of fig trees, olives and plasticulture.

Note too that 15 km south of Monastir is **Uzitta** (today called Henchir Makhreba) which was closely associated with Caesar's campaign in Africa. Its ruins are on a slightly elevated position overlooking the plain. During excavations a residential district was uncovered with a number of villas. Many were very luxurious with private baths and mosaic tiled floors.

Mahdia ٱلمهدية

Situated on the headland of Cap d'Afrique, the old town is surrounded by sea on three sides. An ancient Punic port, Mahdia followed Carthage and Kairouan as the capital of Tunisia in the 10th century. The city of the Mahdi, 'the rightly guided imam' has fine mosques and homes, chunks of wall crumbling next to the medieval Fatimid port, and a small but busy fishing habour. (One colonial writer, a little grandly perhaps, described Mahdia as the 'African Monaco'.) In recent years the dignity and repose of Mahdia has been disturbed by mushrooming beach hotels. The old Mahdois families are deeply attached to their town, however, and it is a pleasant place to visit. The médina has a medieval toy town feel: the Spanish fort is neat, not mean and brooding, the Great Mosque feels proudly restored, not the heart of an empire flaring with a crusading mission.

Phone code: 73
Colour map 3,
grid C6

Mahdia is easily accessible by public transport, the best way to get there being the Sahel light railway (Monastir is 1 hr away by train, Sousse 1½ hrs). Otherwise there are louages in from Sousse, Sfax, Ksar Hellal and El Djem. From Monastir, you have to change louage at Ksar Hellal or Moknine. By road, Mahdia is 100 km from Sfax, 62 km from Sousse and 40 km from El Djem.

Getting there
See Transport,
page 273, for
further details

The train station is conveniently central. The bus and louage station is 3 km west of town on Av Belhaouane. Unless you're a good walker, you'll be getting bus or taxi into the town centre. Note that all hotels, bar one, are in the *zone touristique*, say 1Dt taxi ride from the town centre. There are couple of metro stations for the zone touristique, Sidi Messaoud (for the *Hotel Mahdia*) and Mahdia Zone Touristique.

Getting around

The tourist office is inside the médina's main gate, Skifa el Kahla, on the right in R el Moez, T680000. Friendly but uninformative.

Information

The Av Farhat Hached takes you into town from the bus and train stations. Just before you reach the port and the Médina, there are a handful of restaurants on your left (sea

Orientation

Central Tunisia

on your right). There is a clean loo in the very central *Café Malibu* opposite the *Shell* station. For ATMs, head for the *BIAT*, just opposite the Skifa Kahla, or the *Banque de Tunisie* branch in the fish market buildings. Pharmacies, inlcuding a pharmacie de nuit, can be found on the small tree-lined pedestrian zone, just on from the *Café Malibu*. For post office, wander into the Médina and locate the Pl du Caire.

History

Mahdia, Tunisia's second-largest fishing port, 60 km south of Sousse, and 50 km from the airport, is a charming little town which has (to some extent) escaped the tourist mania of the rest of the coast. The town goes back to the early 10th century, and was founded by the Shi'ite Fatimid dynasty as a jumping-off point for their conquest of Egypt. In 969 they successfully conquered the lower Nile valley, and founded Cairo. Mahdia, the town of the Mahdi, as the Shi'ite caliph was called, reverted to a peaceful provincial existence spiced up by a bit of piracy and the occasional invasion. The town, situated on a peninsula, had a fine defensive position, and the Fatimids left behind a small harbour.

The history of Mahdia is closely linked with the Shi'ite branch of Islam. The Shi'ites believe that the Caliph must descend from Ali and Fatima (the Prophet's daughter). After a seven-year war with the Aghlabids, Ubaydallah, known as El Mehdi ('the rightly guided one'), the founder of the Fatimid Dynasty (followers of Fatima), finally secured victory and sought to establish his own capital. Mahdia was founded in 912 on an easily defended site and El Mehdi settled in the still unfinished town in 921 in order to reinforce his power and protect himself. However, his cruelty and his enemies' hatred made peace short-lived. In 944 the city was besieged (unsuccessfully) for eight months by the army of one Abou Yazid. Eventually, the third Fatimid caliph moved the capital to a palace complex closer to Kairouan, Sabra el Mansouriya. The inhabitants of the abandoned capital turned to the sea for their livelihood: fishing, commerce and piracy brought prosperous times.

In the medieval Mediterranean world, with its ever-shifting frontiers, reprisals were not slow in coming, with first an unsuccessful Christian

Mahdia

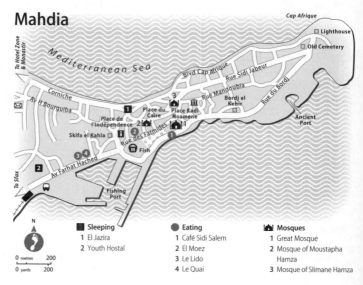

Sleeping
1 El Jazira
2 Youth Hostal

Eating
1 Café Sidi Salem
2 El Moez
3 Le Lido
4 Le Quai

Mosques
1 Great Mosque
2 Mosque of Moustapha Hamza
3 Mosque of Slimane Hamza

expedition to dislodge the pirates in 1088, then the occupation by Roger of Sicily from 1148 to 1160. (The Normans of Sicily also took Djerba, Gabès, Sfax and Tripoli.) Later various other attempts were made to rid the town of the pirates, by a joint French-Genoese force in 1390 and in 1550 by Charles V of Spain. The Spanish were finally successful in 1550, but when forced to evacuate in 1554 resorted to blowing up the ramparts.

Eventually, the inhabitants had to revert to more traditional ways of life, such as olive cultivation and the production and weaving of silk. Under the Husseinid beys, the town became home to a cosmopolitan population, with Albanians, Anatolians and Greeks, Italians and French. In the late 19th century, the Sicilians began to come over to Mahdia for the fishing, introducing the *lamparo* night-fishing technique. They nicknamed Mahdia 'the sardine city', and built a new neighbourhood north of the port. Today, Mahdia is one of the largest fishing ports in Tunisia, mackerel and sardines forming a major part of the catch.

The traditional olive cultivation around the town and especially north of Mahdia has declined to be replaced by market gardening. Vegetables such as tomatoes, pepper, melons, and fennel are the crops grown in the plastic covered, tunnel shaped, head-high greenhouses. Tourism is now an important employer, too.

Sights

Start your visit to Mahdia by walking right round the edge of the promontory, beginning on the north side, along the Boulevard du Cap Afrique up to the lighthouse and back down on the south side. At the tip, you will come to a large **cemetery**, where – on the most exposed part of the peninsula where nothing grows – the Mahdois have buried their dead for centuries. As local poet Moncef Ghachem wrote, "Nowhere else creates a feeling of peace, a spiritual unwinding like this cemetery beside the sea." On the south side of the peninsula, you will also come across the remains of the **Fatimid port** from which the 11th-century invasion of Egypt was launched. It seems that the entrance was defended by two towers, linked by an arch. The port fell to Christian ships in 1088. After passing Mahdia's fortress, the Bordj el Kebir, on your right, you will pass an area of excavations of the Fatimid palace. Before reaching the Great Mosque, call in on the *Café Sidi Salem* to admire the view and perhaps swim off the rocks.

Begin your walk around the médina at the **Skifa el Kahla** ('The Black Passage'), the monumental gateway to the old town. At the time of El Mehdi only troops and a few privileged people lived within the walls in order to minimize the risk of rebellion. The people lived outside, but within the walls were their shops and workshops. This meant that starting a rebellion during the day could jeopardize the life of their families outside, while to do so during the night would lead to the loss of their livelihood. The present gate was built in 1554, after El Mehdi's time, following the departure of the Spanish.

Outside the gate, the new **Museum of Mahdia**, housed in a superb early-20th-century building, is just to the right. The collections are not spectacular or particularly well displayed, but it is nice to see a building of this sort recycled. Eventually some of the finds from the famous Mahdia wreck, a Roman ship loaded with statuary and bronzes discovered off the town in 1907, may be displayed here. For the moment, they can be seen in the Bardo Museum in Tunis when not on international loan. ■ *0930-1600 winter, 0900-1300 and 1500-1900 summer (1 Apr to 15 Sep), closed Mon.*

Médina

Central Tunisia

The Mahdia wreck

Archaeologists Merlin and Poinssot describe the wreck spotted by sponge divers nearly 5 km off the coast of Mahdia in 1907.

"Thirty-nine metres down we noted some 60 columns of different sizes, lying on top of each other, in 7 rows running from north to south for 24 m ... These were the main item of freight in the ship which sank at this place. They were not, however, the sole or most sensational item ... digging into the muddy sand which partially covered the columns, after cutting through a 20 cm thick layer of wood, which was the bridge of the lost ship, items of far greater value were discovered, the objects which filled the hold: noble effigies, fine statuettes and reliefs in bronze and marble, fragments of containers or utensils with delicate fittings, fragments of luxury decorative marble pieces, a whole set of items indicative of skilled craft techniques, thanks to which we have a reflection of high Hellenic art."

A Merlin and L Poinssot, Cratères et candélabres de marbre trouvés en mer près de Mahdia (1930)

The **médina** is beautiful even though there are not many specific things to see. Until recently, it had not suffered too much from unsympathetic redevelopment – until someone decided to build something modern on the pretty Place du Caire, the main square in the médina. Heading towards the citadel on the main tourist street, you will find a partly restored dwelling on your right, the *Maison pilote*, partially renovated by students from the University of Nantes as part of a summer project. Mahdia courtyard houses have a characteristic look. In practical terms, the problem of water was solved by all homes having both a well and a cistern. Taking the street leading away from the Place du Caire towards the *Hotel Jazira*, a couple of other minor sites to look out for are an abandoned medresa (on the left) and the former church (on the right).

In the médina, you will be able to see **cloth-weavers** in action. Looking through a doorway of one of the numerous weaving workshops, you may see someone involved in the elaborate foot-dance required to operate the typical weaver's loom. The products are high quality striped silks for wedding costumes and cotton *foutas* (towels). Curiously, when it comes to looms, there is a gender divide in Tunisia's cities: men operate horizontal cloth looms, while women work at vertical carpet looms. In the evening, you could spend time at one of the cafés on Place du Caire.

The honey-coloured walls of the Fatimid **Great Mosque** (founded 921 by Ubaydallah el Mahdi) dominate the Place Kadi Nomen, to your right at the top of the main street. There is something a bit too perfect about the walls, and indeed the mosque was totally rebuilt in 1963 following the original 10th-century plans. This was the first Fatimid mosque ever built and its reconstruction must have had important symbolic value for the recently independent Tunisian state. In architectural terms, there are several interesting things that can be spotted by the non-Muslim visitor, even if the interior is off-limits. Note the splendid arched main entrance – possibly inspired by Roman triumphal arches? This was the grand ceremonial entrance for the Fatimid imam. The spirit is very different to that of earlier mosques. In most of Tunisia's towns, the souks and houses come right up to the walls of the oldest, central mosques; there is no perspective looking across an esplanade as here. (Maybe housing was demolished in the early 1960s during the restoration.) The area separating the Mosque from the new port, dating from the beginning of the century, is landfill created when the port was dredged.

This impressive fortress, built on the highest point of the headland, was built around the same period as the Skifa el Kahla. The Bordj overlooks the sea. The corner bastions were added in the 18th century. The view from the top is good, the architectural interest a bit limited. ■ *0930-1630 winter, 0900-1200 and 1400-1800 summer, closed Mon. 1Dt.* **Bordj el Kebir**

Around the town, the coast is rocky and the water clear. The best beaches are north of the town, out towards the new hotels. The zone touristique is 5 km north, served by local bus 36B, or take a taxi. **Beaches**

Some 14 km south of Mahdia, just beyond the small town of **Ksour Essaf**, are the remains of Roman Sullecthum at the coastal village of **Salakta**. The **Salakta Museum,** situated on the site of Sullectum, next to the ancient cemetery, has some interesting items. There is a splendid mosaic showing a lion, the emblem of a rich shipowner of the city at that time, and a funerary breastplate of a Carthaginian general. As English archaeologists did a lot of work on Roman pottery here, there are English captions in the museum. Nevertheless, this is a site of rather specialist interest. ■ *0930-1630 winter, 0900-1200 and 1400-1800 summer, closed Mon. To get to Salakta, take a louage from Ksour Essaf.* **Excursion south of Mahdia**

Essentials

The *zone touristique* has expanded considerably with many large expensive hotels. For the budget traveller, some of these might be just about accessible for a night of comfort off-season. (NB there are big variations in prices here between low and high season.) Budget accommodation in the old town is limited to the hotels *Médina* and *Jazira*. Old favourites the *Rand* and the *Sables d'Or* are closed, scheduled for redevelopment. Those looking for more the more personal touch might try the *Dar Sidi*. **Sleeping**
All hotels have direct beach access

Route Touristique L *Mahdia Palace Tryp*, along Rte Touristique, T696777, F696810. 5-star hotel, opened 1995, built on a truly palatial scale. 333 attractive rooms with wood detailing. In low season, 2 people might get away with 90Dt with breakfast. In high season, the same room goes for 256Dt. A very dear do, but good outdoor pool with little islands and nice indoor pool for winter use. On one of the best sections of beach in Mahdia with beautiful fine sand. Largely German clientele feels no need to leave the complex. **A** *Abou Nawas Bordj (club luxe)*, Rte de la Corniche, T694602, F696632. Extensive grounds, the usual effectively managed Abou Nawas hotel. **A** *Mansour*, T696696, F696669, 225 rooms. Nice rooms, many sea-facing. Service said to be good. **B** *Abou Nawas Cap Mahdia*, Rte Touristique, T680300, F680405. Attractive cream-painted buildings. Horse riding and water sports, closed winter, good value. In season, generally full with package groups. **B** *Cap Sérail*, along Rte Touristique, T695011. Smaller than your average *palace touristik*. **B** *El Mehdi*, Rte de la Corniche, T671287, F671309. 295 a/c rooms with bath, telephone and balcony, some family rooms, restaurants with local and international dishes, bar, Moorish café, TV room, indoor and outdoor pools. **B-C** *Dar Sidi*, 3 km out of Mahdia at Rejiche, phone T687001/2 for directions. Small upmarket guest-house type accommodation in traditional buildings. Has had some good reports.

Old town and nearby C-D *Corniche*, Av 7 Novembre, T694201, F692196. On the corniche, a good 20 mins' walk from the town. Quite noisy in summer because of location on busy sea-front road. 16 rooms with bath, small, cheap, good restaurant, not on beach side of road. Prices vary from 12Dt low season to double for high season. **D** *Hotel el Jazira*, R Ibn el Fourat, not far from Skifa el Kahla, on north side of médina, ■ *on map, page 268*

T681629, F680274. 7 simple rooms, all with washbasin and electric radiators, clean, renovated in 2001. Student groups can sleep out on terrace in summer for 5Dt/px. Rooms 9, 11, and 12 have sea view, twin rooms 9 and 12 are the best. Plastic flowers excepted, a good little address. Can be noisy at night. **D** *Hotel La Médina*, in the old town, signed from the tree-planted pedestrian esplanade, up an alley on your left (street name in Arabic only). At top end (in price terms) of this category, an extended family house, converted to a hotel in 1999. Much tiling, spotlessly clean, palm-wood furniture in rooftop rooms. 4 rooms on courtyard, 4 on first floor, 2 on terrace. Evening meal 5Dt. Rent-a-bike 15Dt 1 bike, 25Dt 2 bikes.

Youth hostel In the new part of Mahdia, T681559. 60 beds, meals available, family rooms, very clean, good view from roof, signposted from train station, about 5 mins' walk down the street running to the right of the *Esso* station, in 2nd street on left. 5Dt/px. Rooms with 2-5 beds. Hot showers.

Eating
● *on map, page 268*

Mahdia has a good selection of mid-range restaurants, with a line of restaurants along Av Farhat Hached (most with alcohol, catering to tourists and local men and their friends) and a couple of pleasant places in the old town and along the Corniche, too.

Expensive/Mid-range *Dar Ech Chat*, Rte Touristique, T695210, beach restaurant open May-Oct. Try their pasta aux fruits de mer. *Restaurant Le Lido*, Av Farhat Hached, T681339, has a local clientele that likes its food. Salads 3.5Dt, octopus salad 7D, good selection of wines – quite pricey for this type of restaurant, check the bill. May take credit cards.

Mid-range *L' Espadon*, near *Hotel Corniche*, T681476. Small, boozy place right on the beach. Occasionally does fish couscous and other sea food dishes. Stays open late in summer. Steak 4Dt, sandwich 1Dt500, Celtia beer 2Dt high season, 1Dt600 low season. *Restaurant Pizzeria Italia*, on Av Tahar Sfar, Rte de la Corniche, T695296. *Neptune*, Av 7 Novembre, start of Corniche, beside the Mahdia Centre tower block, T681927. Clean, fish dishes sold by weight before cooking. Alcohol, has a 1st floor terrace with view over the sea. On Av Farhat Hached, try *Restaurant Le Quai* (the one with the children's castle façade), T681867. Grilled fish, alcohol. More reasonable than the neighbouring *Lido*. Fish couscous 12Dt, starters around 4Dt, poisson du jour 8Dt, bottle of wine around 9Dt.

Cheap *Restaurant Errais*, Av Farhat Hached, fairly cheap eatery (3Dt – 5Dt) but unlike the others on this street has no booze. *Restaurant de la Médina*, in the market building roughly behind the *Banque de Tunisie* and the arcades, excellent for fish, stuffed calamar, kamounia. *Restaurant el Moez*, as you stand facing the museum, take street on your right, entrance is about 20 m along on right after *Mahdia Voyages* travel agency. Cheap and handy local restaurant, no alcohol. All along the side of the **harbour** there are small cafés, fish appearing frequently on the menu. The **market** on the east side of port sells fish daily and other fresh produce and general goods on Friday.

Cafés & bars The most obvious café in the old town is the *Sidi Salem* (same management as the *Hotel Jazira*), which with its seaside, south-facing position is splendid for winter sunning and summer evenings. Does food in season. The beautiful location just about compensates for the plastic chairs and the attempted decoration. In the heart of the old town, try the *Café Gamra* under the arcades on Pl du Caire. Like the nearby café with the birdcages, the choice of drinks is limited. Atmosphere is all. Still in the médina, the trendy address, which also does food, is the *Café Amicco/La Koucha*, an Italian-run establishment in a converted old bakery near the *Hotel Jazira*. Also does pizzas, pastry and ice-cream. Glass-fronted terrace. Snug inside in winter, lively in summer. Convenient on arriving is the *Café Malibu*, popular with locals. Serious male drinkers may want to look in on *Le Corsaire* on the Av Farhat Hached or *L'Espadon* (see Eating). The main off-licence, the *Magasin du Quai*, is just next door to the *Restaurant Le Lido* (see Eating).

The Samba in the *Hotel Mahdi* is set to be the best nightclub during the high season. **Nightclub**

Riding Try the *Abou Nawas Hotel-Club Cap Mahdia* for information, T680300. **Sport** **Watersports** In season, all the usual watersports are available in the *zone touristique* hotels.

Abou Nawas Travel, Av Tahar Sfar, La Corniche, T696222, F696224. *Cap Voyages*, 196 **Tour operators** Av Habib Bourguiba, T680355, F680629. *Fatimides Voyages*, 191 Av Habib Bourguiba, T680763, F694590.

Local Taxis: *Abou Nawas*, T695900. **Long distance Train**: Sahel metro train every **Transport** hr 0500-1800 to **Monastir**, **Skanes/Monastir airport** and **Sousse**. Train station, T680177, is down the street from the bus station, by the harbour. **Tunis** (via Sousse) 1135, 1645. Takes 4 hrs. **Bus**: the bus station, T680372, is by the harbour on Pl 1st May. Frequent buses to **Sousse** and **Monastir**. Less frequent buses to **Tunis**, Sfax, **Gabès** and **Kairouan**. **Louages**: a long, hot 3-km walk from the town centre, take a taxi. Louages run to **El Djem**, **Kairouan**, **Monastir**, **Sfax** and **Sousse**.

Banks *BNT* on Pl de l'Indépendence. *BT* and *STB* on Av Habib Bourguiba. **Car** **Directory** **hire** *Avis*, Av Habib Bourguiba, T696342; *Hertz*, Av Bourguiba, T695255; *Jet Car Loisirs*, Av Bourguiba, T681796; *Self Drive*, Av Bourguiba, T/F696863. **Communications** Post Office: in the new part of town on Av Habib Bourguiba. **Useful addresses** Police: Av Habib Bourguiba, near supermarket. Port: Harbour Master's Office, T681595.

Southwest from Mahdia to El Djem

South of Mahdia are a few small coastal settlements, Er Zgana and Rejiche being the main ones. **Ksour Essaf**, 7 km inland and 10 km from Mahdia, is larger, its prosperity built on agriculture. From Ksour Essaf, the C87 takes you on to El Djem, an essential stop for all those interested in imperial Rome's taste for violent sports.

El Djem ﺍﻟﺠﻢ

A small town in the middle of a plain of olive trees, El Djem would be of little interest if it were not for its imposing Roman amphitheatre, one of the most surprising sights in Tunisia. The sheer bulk of the building, largest of all Roman monuments in Africa, is breathtaking. The sheer size of the ochre stone walls and arches and a thought for the simple technology in use in Roman times to build them makes this a breathtaking monument. But it was also a setting for mass entertainment of the cruellest kind: watching men fight each other to the death, or the slaughter of wild beasts, was the ancient equivalent of a Hollywood spectacular.

Phone code: 73
Colour map 3, grid A5
Population: 10,000

Ins and outs

The train station on main Tunis-Sousse-Sfax line is 10 mins' east of the amphitheatre **Getting there** and SRT bus station is by the museum, 500 m from the amphitheatre. In summer the buses are full and it is difficult to find a place. The louages and SNTRI buses terminate in

Central Tunisia

the street by the station. Tunis is a 3-hr train ride from El Djem, and there are frequent louages from Sousse and Mehdia.

Getting around The entrance to El Djem from the east is graced by three columns, part of the town's great heritage and on the other side of the road is a workshop which produces mosaics. Does nothing change?

History

The ancient town of Thysdrus was probably founded in Punic times, but it was only under the Romans, in particular the rule of Hadrian (117-138), that the town prospered. Hadrian encouraged the continued cultivation of olive trees and the town became an important centre for the manufacture and export of olive oil. By the third century the town reached its peak, as the ruins of luxurious villas testify. The population was over 30,000. In addition to the owners of the villas there was a large rural population. But, due to political rivalries within the Empire, El Djem's fortunes gradually decreased, and were finally brought to an end during the Arab invasion, when the olive groves were set on fire, definitively ending El Djem's commercial prosperity.

Sights

Main amphitheatre Thysdrus covered an area of 150-200 ha, the size of the remaining monuments giving a clear indication of the scale of the original city. The huge **Amphitheatre**, 148 m long by 122 m wide, has a perimeter of over 425 m. The long axis of the arena is 65 m and the shorter axis 39 m. The tiers rose to more than 35 m providing seating for a capacity of 45,000 spectators. It was the third-largest amphitheatre in the Roman Empire and the most famous and best preserved in Africa. Lack of inscriptions prevents accurate dating but construction, which is attributed to Emperor Gordien I who owned land and property in the area, began in the second century AD between 230 and 238. When one considers that the nearest quarries were over 30 km away, the task must have been enormous. The building was never completed due to lack of funds and political instability. The stone was too soft for fine sculpture, hence the simplicity of the decoration. The theatre was used for some of the spectacular shows so dear to the heart of Emperor Gordien – wild beasts fighting to the death, martyrs or prisoners being thrown to the wild animals, good family viewing. Some of the scenes were recorded in the mosaics found here.

In later years, the amphitheatre was used as a rebel stronghold. The legend of the underground tunnels leading from El Djem to the sea refers back to

El Djem

To Sousse, GP1
Av Farhat Hached
Rue de Libye
Roman Villas
Rue Golam Kacem
Office National de l'Artisanat
Av Mongi Slim
Amphitheatre
Rue Khaldoun
Rue Habib Thameu
Chemist
To Mahdia
Rue Ali Belhareth
Rue de la Grande Mosquée
Av Habib Bourguiba
Rue H Habaleih
Chemist
Av Hedi Chaker
Bus
Av Taïeb Mehiri
Av Mohammed V
To Souassi & Kairouan
Archaeological Institute
Rue Nicenne
To Fadhel Bachour
Rue Fadhel Bachour
Small Amphitheatres
N
To Sfax
Not to scale

■ **Sleeping**
1 Relais Julius

Carnage under the sun – thumbs up for the great amphitheatre of El Djem

A good guide to the level of the 'Romanity' of a city was the presence of an amphitheatre. These great buildings for public entertainment existed right across the Roman Empire. The amphitheatre of Thysdrus in the sleepy modern town of El Djem was, after the Colosseum in Rome and the amphitheatre in Capua, the largest in the Empire.

It is difficult to see where the Roman practice of public slaughter came from. The Greeks were certainly too refined for such practices. Yet the populace of the Empire developed a taste for the munera, *the bloody spectacles provided as bounty by the magistrates or as a tribute to the deceased. Pliny in his* Natural History *tells the tale of the origin of the amphitheatre. In 53 BC, in Italy, a candidate for the tribune's office in search of votes devised a new electioneering technique. Two semicircular wooden theatres were set up back to back, mounted on a swivel. Thus two plays could be put on at the same time. But the gimmick was revealed in the afternoon, when the two theatres were swung round on their pivots to form a circle where a* munus *or gladiatorial show was held.*

Under Augustus the munus *became an important (and sinister) way for rulers to interact with those they ruled. The primitive wooden structures gave way to magnificent stone buildings and the word* amphitheatrum *was coined to describe these settings for various brutish 'sports' depicted in gory graphic detail in the mosaic floors of the ancient Thysdritan home. In addition to the* hoplomachia *or*

gladiatorial fights there were re-enactments of various myths (Pasiphae and the bull, among others) and in the later Empire, the followers of Christianity, then viewed as a dangerous sect with secret ceremonies, were a particular target. Blood spilling on to the ground and disguising of Christian martyrs as initiates of Caelestis would transform torture into sacrifice. Damnatio ad bestias *(being condemned to the beasts), however, was reserved for common criminals and certain prisoners of war. The huge resources devoted to the shipping of rare beasts to Rome for slaughter is testimony to the importance of the amphitheatre shows and also evidence of the wealth of the Empire and the extent to which this wealth could be squandered.*

The inhabitants of the province of Africa, to go by the evidence of the mosaics, preferred venationes *or the exhibition and 'hunting' of big cats and other wild beasts. (See the* Tiger attacking two wild asses *in the El Djem museum.) For a long time it was thought that mock sea battles were a feature of Thysdritan entertainment but unfortunately archaeology has laid this particular myth firmly to rest.*

Today's visitor to Thysdrus can clamber up into the highest parts of the seating and look down into the arena just as the Roman spectator would have done. Mercifully the slaughter of people and beasts is no longer considered great entertainment and little disturbs the quiet of the great building apart from the clicking of camera shutters and cooing of pigeons nesting in the crumbling stonework.

Central Tunisia

Kahena, a Berber princess who rebelled against Islam and used the amphitheatre as a fortress. She is said to have waved wriggling fish at the troops surrounding her stronghold, taunting them with her freedom of movement. In 1695, Mohammed Bey ordered a hole to be made in the amphitheatre's walls to prevent its use during any further uprisings by the local population who protested about his heavy taxation. The breach in the walls was further enlarged in 1850 during another tax revolt. The theatre was thereafter used as a convenient source of building stones by the inhabitants of the town. Nevertheless the bulk of the original building remains and it is a truly impressive sight. ■ *Open daily from dawn till dusk. 2Dt, photography permit 1Dt. Includes entry to museum.*

Smaller amphitheatres & other excavations El Djem has two smaller amphitheatres, one built on top of the other. These are just a short distance to the south of the main amphitheatre and can be found on the other side of the road to Sfax. The older, more primitive one, dating from the first century, was simply cut into the rock and the second one, which was to last until the building of the large amphitheatre, was erected against the hillside on top of the remains of the first. Behind the museum, about 250 m to the west of the small amphitheatre, there is a group of villas bounded by a Roman **necropolis** to the south and a well preserved, paved street to the east. The houses are of the classic Roman style with a garden surrounded by a peristyle with richly decorated rooms.

The large number of fine **Roman villas** excavated at El Djem are indicative of the considerable wealth of the town. The dwellings, built around an inner courtyard and surrounded by a colonnaded gallery, were paved with colourful mosaics depicting mythological themes. **Mosaics** from the earlier excavations of these villas are now displayed in the Bardo Museum in Tunis, in Sousse and in the local museum in El Djem. In the more recently discovered villas the mosaics have been left in situ. The baths, covering a surface area of over 2,000 sq m, revealed some fine mosaics too.

The **Archaeological Museum**, clearly signed, is 500 m from the amphitheatre on the road to Sfax, set in a replica of a Roman villa. Here are yet more magnificent mosaics. In the main room is a famous mosaic showing Orpheus charming the beasts with his music, while in the end room are two lively mosaic scenes, *Lions devouring a wild boar* and next to it *Tiger attacking two wild asses*. These were found in a villa which once stood beside the museum. ■ *0700-1900 summer, 0730-1730 winter, entrance included with ticket to amphitheatre. Clean toilets.*

Wealthy Romans liked to display their taste and status, and one way to do this was with **wall-paintings** (which do not seem to have been widespread in ancient Africa) and **mosaic pavings**. Certain themes were more popular than others. The inhabitants of El Djem seem to have been good-time people, and liked scenes with the muses, to remind them of the arts, of animals and of boozy romps, liberally decorated with vine leaves and cupids. There is Minerva judging the musical contest between Apollo and Marsyas, for example. The careful detail of the mosaics is impressive: for example, in one Dionysian mosaic, you have a border full of lurking grasshoppers, frogs, rats, snails and lizards. The entire pavement is trellised with vines and set with tiny birds, animals and cupids. There is a ladder-carrying cupid, off to the grape harvest. In the central medallion, three chubby *putti*, urged on by a naked woman, are tying up a bald, bearded and pot-bellied Silenus (Bacchus's father) with floral garlands.

Another theme dear to villa owners was the four seasons. The countryside was close by, and the wealth of the city depended on farming. A small mosaic with a central medallion containing the bust of a bearded old man is a good example of this concern. Six circles contain the Sun (Apollo), the Moon (Artemis) and the four seasons – Spring in green, Summer in red, bare breasted and vine-draped Autumn and darkly cloaked Winter.

Music in the ampitheatre First held in 1986, El Djem's small-scale annual **International Music Festival** takes place in late July/early August in the amphitheatre. The festival tends to feature European symphony and chamber orchestras, although there have been concerts of lyric music and the occasional opera too. Thousands of candles light the building. The nightime noises of El Djem (the last call to prayer, amplified music from a distant marriage, the braying of a donkey) are the exotic backdrop for concerts which can range from Mozart to jazz.

Ancient foodies and the unswept room

From looking at the mosaics in museums across Tunisia, it is clear that inhabitants of Roman Africa liked a good meal. Food was a very popular theme, and the Greek term xenia *is used to designate food mosaics, veritable illustrated menus on the floor. The* xenia, *one of the ancestors of the painted still life, was developed by African mosaic artists to decorate the floors of the* triclinium *(the dining room) in private homes. Vitruvius describes* xenia *as being just like food, ready to be eaten. Dating mainly from the late second/early third century, these mosaics show us that Roman Africa was a place of plenty. Its people enjoyed eating goat, antelope, gazelle, wild boar, hare, and various farmyard birds. Animals are portrayed alive, sometimes tied-up, and also as dead game, straight from the larder. There are mosaics showing seafood – fish, crustaceans and shellfish, as well as fruit and vegetables, baskets of flowers, bowls and flasks. One of the*

famous El Djem xenia *mosaics shows a wine bottle in a basketwork container and an elegant stemmed glass. No doubt these mosaics were the essential finishing touch for an upper-crust home, clear proof of the wealth and generosity of their proud owners.*

An unusual variation on the xenia *theme was the* asaroton, *'the unswept room'. In these mosaics, crumbs and bits of leftovers from a meal are portrayed scattered on the floor. So why have pictures of half-eaten food on your* triclinium *floor? Was there an obscure aesthetic taste for 'disorder', or did these mosaics have a magic force, ensuring continuity in the daily life of a home? We cannot know for certain. In the* triclinium *of the House of the Months at Thysdrus (El Jecu), there was an 'unswept' mosaic strip surrounding a central panel. Remains of chicken and fish, shellfish and crustaceans, eggshells, fruit peelings and wilted flowers are clearly visible.*

Central Tunisia

Essentials

C *Hotel Club el Ksar*, T632800, 632864, 5 km north of El Djem on Rte de Sousse, 35 a/c rooms, TV possible, bar, restaurant, pool. **C** *Relais Julius*, off the main square by train station and near bus stop, T630044, F630523. Simple, clean, cheap, 15 double rooms with bath around the courtyard, fan in summer, restaurant, ask for a room with a view of the amphitheatre. Noisy, as railway line nearby.

Sleeping
■ *on map, page 274*

Mid-range *Relais Julius* is quite good value and the only place in El Djem where you're going to get a beer. Next door is *Restaurant du Bonheur*, T690306, with a/c. **Cheap** More cheaply, the cafés in front of the amphitheatre offer menus generally comprising *mechoui* (barbecued lamb) and salad of some kind. Check prices when you order. Café Bacchus (no alcohol despite name) opposite site, distinctive blue and white décor, shaded terrace, coffee and mint tea, basic toilet. Try also the *Restaurant La Kahina*, a/c and Tunisian favourites. If you are driving and heading south for Sfax, you may want to eat at the barbecue restaurants a few km out of town on the roadside.

Eating

Surprisingly, El Djem has some quite interesting shopping opportunities. Look out for the chunky puppet-type wooden animals with the articulated joints. You can also find replicas of ancient carvings or metal statuettes, old agricultural implements and cooking pots which no one wants in the age of plastic and stainless steel. **Supermarket** On Av Habib Bourguiba. Market day Monday, opposite train station. Also visit the mosaic workshop on the by-pass where you can order your reproduction mosaic of the four-seasons table top for the patio.

Shopping

Transport **Train** 4 or 5 departures a day north for **Tunis** (via Sousse) and south for **Sfax**, **Gabès** (via Sfax); **Gafsa** and **Metlaoui**. **Bus** The SNTRI bus station and the louage stop is opposite the train station. SRT buses go from near the museum. Frequent buses to **Sfax**, **Sousse**, **Gabès** and **Tunis**. **Louages** depart from near the Relais Julius.

Kairouan القيروان

Phone code: 77
Colour map 3, grid A4

Isolated on featureless steppe and founded in the seventh century by nomad Arab conquerors, Kairouan is a tough, puritan place. Winter is bitter and summer turns the region into a frying pan. Blonde and brazen beaches, kidney-shaped hotel pools, discos and casinos are a world away. See the Great Mosque of Okba Ibn Nafi, built of tawny brick and pillaged ancient masonry, appreciate the much restored Aghlabid reservoirs and wander the sculptural streets of the médina, explore the sleepy souks, observe the industrious girl carpet-weavers, buy some sticky date cakes and meditate on vanished dynasties at the museum of Rakkada. But there is little else that will draw the visitor in: the town has neither pleasant oasis nor restaurants for the chattering classes. Half-forgotten capital, Kairouan and its threadbare splendours are now just a place on the way to somewhere.

Ins and outs

Getting there
See Transport,
page 289, for
further details

Drivers approaching Kairouan will find that traffic is now taken round the town on a wide new bypass. Coming from Tunis, at the first roundabout (carpet monument) take the first exit for Tozeur if you want to carry on southwest; the second exit takes you into Kairouan past the *Hotel Amina*. Buses and louages from Le Kef, Makthar, and El Fahs, Tunis, Sousse, Sfax and Gabès, arrive at the main bus and louage station located a good 20-min walk northwest of the médina. To get to the main area of budget accommodation, you need to get to the Bab ech Chouhada (Pl des Martyrs) area, on the south side of the médina, and the adjacent modern town. The easy option is to take a taxi (ask for *Hotel Sabra*) for no more than 1Dt – see Transport on page 289 for directions if you wish to walk.

Getting around Central Kairouan is small enough to be visited on foot but note that the Museum of Islamic Art at Rakkada is a few km southwest of town (see page 287 for directions).

Orientation Outside the médina, modern Kairouan sprawls west and south. Orientation is complicated by the fact that plaques with street names are in short supply. Av Dr Hamda Laâouani is a useful street taking you directly away from Bab ech Chouhada (starts with tourist office on your left) towards a junction with Av de la République. It has banks with ATMs and pharmacies. Turning first right on Av de la République you find the *Hotel Tunisia* on your left. Second right off Av du Dr Laâouani, just after the *UBCI*, takes you to the *Restauran Karawan*, one of the restaurants in the area which stay open in the evening. Some 50 m further on is Post Office roundabout.

Information &
site tickets

The main tourist office is opposite *Hotel Continental*, near the Aghlabid Pools, open 0800-1730 daily except Sun 0800-1200, T230452. This is where you should equip yourself with a **multi-site ticket** costing 4.2Dt, valid for a day, for entry to (French names in brackets): 1. The Great Mosque (*Mosquée Okba ibn Nafi*); 2.The (so-called) Barber's Mosque (*Zaouia Sidi Sahab*); 3. The Aghlabid Pools (*Bassins aghlabites*); 4. Zaouia of Sidi Amor Abbada (*Mausolée de Sidi Abbada*); 5. Zaouia of Sidi Abid el Ghariani (*Mausolée de Sidi Abid*); 6. National Museum of Islamic Art (*Musée de Rakkada*); 7. Bir Barouta. Note that the Great Mosque is closed from 1400 every day, and from 1200 on Fri. The Museum of Islamic Art (closed Mon), opens 0900-1600. There is a supplementary photo fee of 1Dt for the Great Mosque and the Sidi Sahab Mosque. Official guides can also be recruited at the tourist office, and at 15Dt (maximum) for a good 2 hrs this option might be worth it if you have a small group. Note that of these sights, the Aghlabid Pools, the Barber's Mosque, and the museum at Rakkada are some way from the centre. Try to check whether the Rakkada Museum is actually open if you call in at the tourist office.

Background

The spiritual and religious capital of Tunisia, the city was the first base for the conquering Arab Muslim armies from the east, back in the seventh century. Still surrounded by its historic walls, the town has a strong character. Kairouan is also the capital of traditional carpet manufacture and the market town for Tunisia's main fruit growing area. It stands at the junction of roads to Tunis, Sousse and Gafsa.

Kairouan is the city where the visitor can get a feel for the evolution of Islam in North Africa. Getting a hold on names of places and rulers, you begin to understand how the Muslim religion took root, developing with the dynasties into the religion as it is lived today. The city is also a lesson in just how small and fragile the medieval Muslim state was in North Africa. For a leading city, it was actually very small but totally dominated by its vast mosque, rather as English wool towns developed in the shadow of huge churches. Piety was everywhere. Around the top of the austere sandy-coloured minarets run friezes with the wording "There is no god but Allah and Mohamed is his prophet" picked out in brick. Here and there, green doors indicate the presence of tiny neighbourhood prayer rooms or *msejed*.

History

The Romans, who knew a thing or two about city building, never considered the plain at Kairouan as a location. (There was a Roman city some 25 km to the northwest at Aïn Jelloula.) Siting a city in such an inhospitable place takes some explanation, and fortunately there is a founding legend for just this purpose. Back in 671, a few decades after the Muslim Arabs had conquered the Middle East and Egypt, Okba ibn Nafi, companion of the prophet Mohamed and warrior leader, was leading an army into Byzantine Africa. He halted his troops at the edge of an arid, wild-beast infested valley (which no longer seems to exist), and called out "Inhabitants of the valley, depart, for we are stopping here." At which, all the various snakes, scorpions and creepy-crawlies emerged from their hiding places and headed out of the valley where Okba's troops were able to camp in complete safety.

Founding Kairouan

Extra reassurance was provided for the Muslim forces when Okba's horse stumbled across a goblet which had been lost in Mecca. Water flowed from this miraculous cup, directly from the sacred spring of Zemzem in Mecca. The site was clearly ripe for a holy city, and Kairouan was founded. In fact, there were other more pressing reasons for the choice of location. The early Arab armies were rapid light cavalry, well able to harry slower infantry forces, but worried about attacks from troops which could be landed by the Byzantine fleet. The interior and its strategic water points was dominated by Christian towns with strong forts, while up in the mountains the tiny Berber communities had no reason to accept a marauding army from Arabia. Any major base camp for the eastern Maghreb had to take these potential threats into account.

Early medicine in Kairouan : the Jewish contribution

One of the high points of Aghlabid rule in Kairouan was the development of medical knowledge. The early Aghlabid princes built hospitals in the main towns. Medicine in these far off times was above all a family affair. In the troubled years of the late 10th century, Ziyadet Allah III had Jewish physicians brought over from Egypt, among them Ishak ben Imran al-Israili and Abou Yacoub Ishak ben Suleyman (later known as Isaac Judaeus in Europe). Both studied in Baghdad, and won fame in Kairouan, teaching medicine and treating the Aghlabid princes.

Ishak ben Imran earned the nickname 'the prince of physicians'. He is said to have written 13 works, the most famous of which is his Anatomy of Melancholy, which refers to ancient Greek sources. Wrote Ishak ben Imran: "I have not read a single satisfactory book by an Ancient writer on the subject of melancholy ...

Rufus of Ephesus limits his study to a single type, the hypochondriac form ... Hypochondria originates at the mouth of the stomach; other forms are born in the brain itself." Ben Imran also wrote treatises on fevers and urines. His work, while drawing on the Greeks, is also filled with a wealth of personal observation.

Kairouan's greatest Muslim physician of the 10th century was Ahmad ibn al Jazzar (died 980). His father and uncle were doctors, and he studied under Ishak ben Suleyman. He was also a pharmacologist, developing an advanced selection of plant remedies. His most famous work, Zad el Mousafir (Provision for the Traveller), is a 156 chapter work describing all the illnesses known to Al Jazzar, giving their names in Persian, Greek, Syriac and spoken Arabic. He proposes three types of treatment: minor surgery, phytotherapy and minerals.

In the event, the Berbers counter-attacked, winning two significant victories, the more important in 688. Hostilities did not last long, however, with the Berbers gradually converting to Islam.

Aghlabid prosperity During the ninth century, Kairouan prospered as home to the local Aghlabid Dynasty, achieving independence from the Caliphate of Baghdad. The city saw much building activity under the Aghlabid emirs, notably Ziyadet Allah I. (They also undertook extensive building works elsewhere, notably at Tunis where the Zitouna Mosque was extended.) Two major issues dominated politics in Aghlabid Kairouan: the relationship with the military (a well-established Arab army or *jund*), and matters theological. Kairouan also developed into something of a medical research centre, with Jews and Muslims working to develop a heritage of medical knowledge passed down from ancient Greece.

Malikite Islam How did Kairouan come to be such a centre of Islamic learning under the Aghlabid princes? The prophet Mohamed had left behind him a scattered body of teachings, which had to be codified. This was the work of religious scholars, sponsored by the caliphs, rulers of the Middle Eastern Islamic state, to whom all other Muslim rulers owed allegiance. And then the codified teachings had to be disseminated across the Islamic lands – hence the importance of regional centres like Kairouan in fringe areas of the Islamic world.

One of the leading scholars of the eighth century was Malik ibn Anas (died 795). Many Ifrikiyans travelled to the East to attend his seminars. With Islam laying down so many rules for life, it was inevitable that a major body of legal knowledge should emerge to interpret the grey areas. At Kairouan, the Malikite school emerged, winning the support of the people through its rigorous approach: only Koranic prescriptions and the traditions of the Prophet could be valid bases for law. The scholarly Imam Sahnoun produced a comprehensive digest of Malikite law, *Al Mudawwana*.

There was a social point to all this legal activity. The Aghlabid princes, who followed the more intellectual Hanafite school of Islam, were seen by the people as a decadent, oppressive lot. Criticism started with their tax policy, and then went on to their lifestyle, which included lots of carousing and singing-girls. (They obviously tolerated wine production.) On the whole, however, they were able to avoid major friction with the people and the Malikite scholars. After all, they spent generously on new religious buildings, and built new fortifications to protect the coasts from marauding Christians (the Ribat at Sousse in particular).

A royal capital

Things all went horribly wrong, however, in the late eighth century. Mohamed II (864-75) who came to the throne aged 13, quickly developed a taste for dissipation and frivolity and died prematurely. His governor in Kairouan (the future Ibrahim II, emir from 875-902) won a reputation for fairness. But he later turned into a tyrant, massacring members of the Arab military caste and crucifying an Arab aristocrat. In 876, he began building a vast royal residence at Rakkada, near Kairouan, recruiting a corps of black slave troops. The military aristocracy saw its influence declining, and this, combined with various exactions, explains the success of the Shi'ite Fatimids in overthrowing the last Aghlabids in 910. Aghlabid rule had lasted little more than a century.

The Fatimid interlude

Without going into the obscure intricacies of Shi'ite politics in early 10th century North Africa, the Aghlabid rulers had made themselves sufficiently detested to be easily overthrown. Shi'ite preacher Abu Abdallah created a movement which won popular support, and in 909 Shi'ite leader Ubaydallah Saïd made his triumphant entry into Rakkada. He claimed to be the *mahdi*, claiming descent from the Prophet's daughter Fatima, hence the name of his dynasty, the Fatimids. But establishing a state in Ifrikiya was just a stepping stone to conquests further east, and in 915 he began building a new capital at Mahdiya on the coast.

Fatimid rule was to weigh heavily on the Sunni Muslims of Ifrikiya. The Malikites were persecuted, and although the Fatimids were not a decadent lot, nor did they spend on religious buildings. Tax revenues went into campaigns against the Sunni caliphate in Egypt. Rebellion was inevitable, and came in the form of Kharijite leader Abou Yazid, who easily won control of Kairouan with Sunni support. All of Ifrikiya – bar Mahdiya – was lost in 944. Abu Yazid failed to take the Fatimid capital, and the revolt failed, with a new Fatimid caliph, El-Mansour ('the victorious') defeating Abu Yazid at Kairouan in 947. In 953, he began the construction of a new capital, Sabra el-Mansouriya, just 2 km away from Kairouan. This meant the older settlement was bypassed commercially, most trade being done in the new city.

The curse of the Fatimids

The real decline of Kairouan came with the invasion from Egypt in the 1050s, when the city changed its allegiance from the Fatimids in Cairo to the Sunni Abbasids in Baghdad. By way of vengeance, the Shi'ite Fatimids allotted Ifrikiya as booty to the warlike Banu Hilal, who had been stirring up trouble in southern Egypt for some time. Opinions are divided as to the actual extent of the devastation caused by the **Hilalian invasion**: Ibn Khaldoun, for one, who was writing in the following century, attributes a severe economic decline in Ifrikiya to the havoc caused by the Banu Hilal. One result of the arrival of large

Central Tunisia

numbers of Arab-speaking nomads was the arabisation of the countryside, which had no doubt continued to be home to Berber and Latin-speaking communities. Berber communities were to remain intact further west, and in isolated inland pockets in Ifrikiya.

Kairouan in Hafsid & Husseinid times

Under the Hafsids, the centre of power shifted in Ifrikiya. Relations changed with Europe, trade with the Italian merchant cities developed, it was important for the capital to be on the coast. Kairouan was thus left by the Hafsid court in favour of Tunis, which after all had a far more agreeable climate. The development of the coastal cities continued in the 17th and 18th centuries, as first Ottoman deys and beys, and subsequently Husseinid beys became involved in profitable piracy. Kairouan thus became a backwater, albeit an important one. It maintained a holy aura, and the tradition (spurious?) went that seven visits to Kairouan were equivalent to the hajj, the pilgrimage to Mecca which every Muslim is supposed to perform once in their lifetime. Wrote traveller Peyssonel in 1724, "The Arabs' veneration for Cairouan is so great that the beys of Tunis have always exempted the inhabitants of this city from all taxes and have granted them so many privileges Jews and Christians are not allowed to live there lest they pollute their sanctuary." When French troops arrived in 1881, however, the town surrendered without a shot being fired. No doubt rumours of what the French had done in Algeria's cities were fresh in the minds of Kairouan's notables.

Kairouan the pious?

Based on its bygone theological glories, Kairouan today has some claims to be an important **religious centre**, the leading holy city in the Maghreb region, preceded in status only by Mecca, Médina and Jerusalem. Islamic intellectual debate is probably more alive in Morocco, however, where the great Karaouiyine University at Fès (originally founded by migrants from Kairouan) is a focus for a certain modernist brand of Muslim thought.

Restoring Kairouan

Today, Kairouan is a rapidly expanding town, with a major university at Rakkada, carpet manufacture, some light industry and food processing. The large amounts of new building around the town are testimony to present-day economic buoyancy. There is also considerable interest on the part of the authorities in the city's built heritage. International Islamic organizations, mainly funded by the oil states, are impressed by the amount of ancient Muslim building, while the Tunisian authorities are keen to be seen conserving anything that will reinforce their Islamic credentials. Restoration proceeds apace, the architectural highspots are now labelled and visitable. In the

The invasion of the Arab tribes C10 and C12 AD

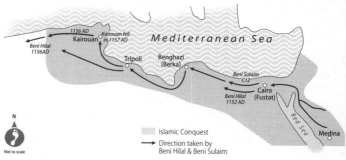

Ifrikiya, Kairouan and turbulent dynasties: a name check

The term **Ifrikiya**, an Arabization of the Latin 'Africa', came to be used for what is now eastern Algeria and Tunisia under the **Aghlabid** dynasty (founded by one **Ibrahim el Aghlab**), who ruled from **Kairouan** from 800 to 909. Simplifying grossly, the Aghlabids were eventually replaced in Ifrikiya by the **Fatimids**, a Shi'ite dyanasty who ruled from **Mahdiya** before moving on to conquer Egypt in 970. The new city of Cairo became the Fatimid capital in 973. To rule Ifrikiya, they left behind them viceroys, who established an independent Sunni dynasty, the **Zirids**, who finally broke with the Fatimids in

1044. By way of vengeance, the latter unleashed the **Hilalian tribes** on Ifrikiya in the 1050s. In the 12th century, Sicily flourished under a **Norman dynasty**, and a number of Ifrikiyan coastal towns came under Norman rule. In the late 1100s, the Berber **Almohad** dynasty conquered Andalusia and the Maghreb. The Almohads' hold over Ifrikiya declined in the early 1200s. They appointed one Abdul Wahid, son of Abu Hafs Umar, a leading Almohad figure, as viceroy. The cycle repeated itself as a new dynasty, the **Hafsids**, established itself at Tunis, ruling until the early 16th century.

médina, the repaved main street is animated in a pleasant, provincial way. There is even a heritage trail, easy to follow with yellow hexagonal paving and brown ceramic tiles indicating monuments. Ultimately, however, all the religious heritage means the town has a ponderous atmosphere, and it is nice to get back to the Mediterranean pleasures of the coastal towns.

Sights

If time is short, you might consider a guided tour of the town. These can be booked at the Great Mosque. However, the sights are actually quite limited, and for many people, a look at the Great Mosque, a wander down the main street to take in the atmosphere and Bir Barouta, and a peek in at the zaouia house which today houses the Association Sauvegarde de la Médina de Kairouan will be sufficient. You probably need two hours to take in something of Kairouan, adding a further 1½ hours for a trip out to the Museum of Islamic Art at Rakkada.

See Information on page 278 for details about multi-site tickets

There can be some confusion with street names in Kairouan, some have two names and the locals you ask will recognize neither unless you get the pronunciation spot on. Accept this as a challenge which adds to the charm of the place. Also, there is a problem with street signs, which in many places are inexistent.

A large part of the médina's walls have survived, notably the section near the Great Mosque. In fact, compared with Tunis or Sousse, the médina is small, so it is fairly difficult to get totally lost. There is a main street which leads from Bab ech Chouhada to Bab Tunis, on which you will find stalls selling *makroud*, (sticky date cakes), various everyday shops, carpet emporia, and Bir Barouta, after which, on the right, there is a small covered souk. Further up, again on the right following the signs for the *Hotel Marhala*, is a small busy market. If you have time, there are a number of minor sights worth visiting in the médina.

The médina

If you enter the médina at Bab ech Chouhada, you might start your culture hunt with a look in at the **Zaouia of Sidi Abid el Ghariani** (second street on the right after the main gate, look for fine doorway on your right). This burial place of Sidi Abid, a 13th-century saint, was constructed in the 14th century. Of particular interest is the room with the mausoleum. The ceiling is

Central Tunisia

extremely finely worked wood, with fine plasterwork all around. The building is a good example of the courtyard style of building which dominated in Kairouan, used for both religious buildings and homes. Today the zaouia houses the office of the Association Sauveguarde de la Médina, an organization dedicated to helping to preserve the médina, and the regional office of the National Art and Archaeology Institute. ■ *Open for a quick look around during office hours.*

Continuing up the main drag, turn right just before Bir Barouta, up the Rue de la Mosquée des Trois Portes, and you will eventually come to the **Mosque of the Three Doors** (Jamaâ Thelethe Bibene) on your right. Founded by an immigrant from Córdoba in 866, the mosque has an interesting façade with carved inscriptions. If you look at the column capitals, recycled from Byzantine monuments, you will see some much eroded birds, their beaks broken or heads removed, testimony to the fact that Islamic art prefers to avoid the representation of living beings. Nearby, you may hear goldfinches tweeting in the weavers' workshops.

At the end of Rue de la Mosquée des Trois Portes, turn left down a narrow street and you will come to Rue Tahar Zarrouk. Turn right here, then left at the end of it on to the wide Boulevard Ibrahim ibn Aghlab, which will bring you to the imposing buttressed ochre walls of the Great Mosque. (Another way to reach this monument is to head through an area of workshops, then down the Rue Khadraouine with its restored façades.)

The Great Mosque of Okba ibn Nafi

The **Great Mosque** was founded with the city by Okba ibn Nafi in 671. The building includes much ancient masonry, recycled from earlier Roman and Byzantine buildings. It is the oldest mosque in western Islam. It was severely damaged during the rebellion of 688, was virtually rebuilt in the ninth century and later enlarged in the same severe style. The age of the minaret is open to debate, although the bottom section is thought to date from 730. The main dome is of ribbed brick in a herring-bone design.

Although it is not obvious to the visitor, both prayer hall and sloping courtyard are trapezoid in shape. Here there are pillared cloisters with easily missed wooden ceilings. Both the east and west porticoes have two aisles supported by three lines of arches. The **vast courtyard**, one of the largest in any mosque in Tunisia, is half-paved in white marble, the remainder paved with limestone blocks in which there is a differentiated path, not quite central, which leads to the minaret. Towards one corner is a sundial indicating the

Great Mosque of Okba ibn Nafi

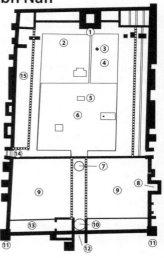

1 Three-tiered Minaret
2 Courtyard paved with limestone
3 Sun dial
4 Marble path to minaret
5 Cistern
6 Courtyard paved with marble
7 Cupola
8 Lalla Rihana Gate
9 Prayer Hall
10 Cupola with ribbed dome
11 Small tower with dome
12 Mihrab
13 Maksoura
14 Entrance
15 Pillared cloisters

times of the five daily prayers. Close to the sundial the rain water was collected in a cistern for use in ritual ablutions.

Thought to date from 836, the **square minaret** (31.5 m high), rises in three sections diminishing in size towards the top where there is a ribbed dome. (Ask if it is possible to climb up the 128 steps for a superb view.) One theory goes that the minaret was inspired by the pharos of Alexandria.

The **prayer hall** is filled with numerous imposing red granite and white and green marble columns brought from vanquished Roman cities. Unfortunately non-Muslims are unable to view the internal wooden ceilings, the lavishly decorated and carved doors, woodcarving on the pulpit, nor the ninth-century tiles from Baghdad in the niche which faces Mecca. You can, however, see that red *mergoum* Kairouan carpets cover the woven reed mats (*hsur*) used to cover the floor. Further reed mats wrapped around the columns stop worshippers from getting a cold back.

So why is the the Great Mosque laid out like it is? Compared with the Byzantine basilicas which the Arab conquerors would have found when they took towns like Sbeïtla, the mosque marks a sharp break. Gone are the high vaulted ceilings of the basilicas as the Roman building technology got lost in the conquest. Rather the new occupiers needed a large, ritually pure space. Islamic worship is based on the principle of facing Mecca. The worshippers face the *mihrab*, the niche indicating the direction of Islam's holiest city. The 70-m width of the mosque allows long lines of worshippers to form parallel to the *mihrab* wall. If the number of worshippers grew, the covered area could easily be extended by adding further colonnades across the courtyard and roofing them. There was no need for a prayer hall much larger than the one in existence as medieval Kairouan was a small place. When large numbers of people gathered for the prayers on great occasions, the overspill could be easily contained in the courtyard. And then on any major religious holiday, the city would use its *musalla* or open prayer ground.

Still in the médina, have a look in at **Bir Barouta** (Barouta's well), a domed building just to the right of the main street as you head away from Bab ech Chouhada. Up the steep stairs are a small café and a large piece of functioning medieval technology in the form of a water-wheel activated by a blinkered camel. The story goes that a dog called Barouta came across the spring, an answer to his pious master's prayers some time back in the 13th century.

Other sights

Unfortunately for the early inhabitants of Kairouan, there were no useful bits of Roman aqueduct to be brought back into service. The solution to the water supply problem was found by sultan Abou Ibrahim Ahmed who had large *fesquiyet* or reservoirs constructed. Originally, there were 14 pools. Of these **Aghlabid Pools**, built in the ninth century, two survive today, to the north of the town. The pools were seemingly part of a much more elaborate water system. The Cherichera aqueduct was constructed to carry water from over 36 km away to the west. The smaller pool was used to settle the silt carried in the water. The clear water was stored in the big pool (diameter 128 m, depth 5 m). Although the pools may have resolved Kairouan's recurring water supply problem, they also added a health risk. They proved to be a superb breeding ground for mosquitoes. ■ *0830-1730 winter, 0800-1200 and 1500-1900 summer.*

Zaouia Sidi Sahbi is the burial place of one of the Prophet's companions, Abou Djama el Balaoui. It is known as the **Barber's Mosque** because Abou el Balaoui carried about with him three hairs from the Prophet's beard, from which he would never be parted. The present building with its elegant minaret dates back to the 17th century. It is beautifully decorated with the usual

Central Tunisia

ceramic tile-work. To get to the mausoleum, you first pass through a small room and continue along an open air corridor. The next small room, with a finely worked plaster ceiling, opens on to the delightful main courtyard (square in shape and bordered on three sides by colonnades), with the mausoleum which houses the tomb. A small room off to one side houses the tomb of **Sidi Cherif ibn Hindu**, master-builder of the Great Mosque. Access to the mausoleum is reserved to Muslims. Notice the painted wooden ceilings under the arcade surrounding the courtyard. On Friday when circumcision ceremonies take place and during the Mouled (the Prophet's birthday), there are numerous pilgrims.

Another fairly peripheral monument is the **Zaouia of Sidi Amor Abbada**, a 19th-century blacksmith who had a penchant for designing large Tolkienesque metal objects, including huge anchors (to hold Tunisia to the land?) and immense swords fit for a dragon slayer. A number of these items are on display in his seven-domed tomb, although some seem to have been stolen. It's all rather curious, and there is little to tell you about how and why such an obviously expensive building was put up by a blacksmith around 1860. The lack of information tells you something about Tunisian attitudes to saints' shrines in the post-independence period. In the 19th century, the beys and their ministers frequently sponsored the construction of new zaouias. In the 1960s, with Tunisia becoming a modern nation state, the practice of visiting saints to seek blessing was severely stigmatized.

National Museum of Islamic Art & Culture

The **Palace of Rakkada**, 11 km southwest of Kairouan on the GP2, was ex-president Habib Bourguiba's official Kairouan residence and today houses Tunisia's most important collections of Islamic Art. The palace was designed by architect Jacques Marmey, proponent of a style of architecture derived from the simplest of traditional forms. Why Bourguiba chose to have a palace on this site is open to debate. As Rakkada was the second royal town of the Aghlabid Dynasty, perhaps he was seeking to confirm his place in the pantheon of Tunisian rulers. As a former royal complex, the site has archaeological importance in its own right.

The collections are not as spectacular, however, as those at the Bardo. Islamic culture rejects representations of the living form, so there is neither sculpture nor painting. There are some fine 10th-century manuscripts, leather bindings, coins, and some pieces of minor ceramics and glassware. There is a display of fine glass flasks from Mansouriya. The walls are hung with old views of the ribats in Monastir and Sousse. All of this requires a certain amount of imagination to put it in context, however. Displays are labelled in Arabic only, and there is no guidebook on sale.

The entrance hall used to have a wooden model of the great mosque of Kairouan on a scale of 1:50. It is quite superb. The interior of the minaret and central nave are exposed and allow the observer a better grasp of the layout of this magnificent building. On the other side is a copy of the mosque's *mihrab* where the sculpted plaster work of floral and geometrical designs has been faithfully reproduced. There are 28 panels of stucco arranged seven by four.

The fact that the displays of the Rakkada Museum are so limited tells us much about the poverty of material culture in this part of North Africa in the Middle Ages. The great irrigation works of the Roman period had been abandoned, the towns were small and situated essentially on the coast, where they were heavily fortified against outside attack. It was not until the 17th century that Tunisia's cities were to receive more lasting, quality building. Ottoman protection and the development of trade with Europe provided the conditions for urban development. ■ *0900-1600 daily, Fri 0900-1300, closed Mon. 1.5Dt. For drivers, museum is signed, along with Gabès and Bouhajla, at the Post Office roundabout (see map). Walkers should continue straight ahead for about 5 mins until they reach an untidy junction (cheap eateries on way). Here look out for the yellow-striped minibuses parked next to a pharmacy on the left. Ask for 'Reggada' (local pronunciation). Ride costs .400 Dt in minibus, 1Dt in share-taxi, 2.5Dt in a taxi by yourself. There is also a bus leaving at 15 mins past the hr from Av Haffouz. Ask to be let off for the museum, which is a 15-min walk from the stop.*

There is a new **dam at El Haouareb** on the Oued Merg Ellil some 10 km west of Kairouan. This, in addition to providing extra, and always welcome, water for irrigation now protects Kairouan from the serious flooding previously caused by the irregular rainfall.

Essentials

Don't worry about the address, all the hotels are clearly signposted. There are perfectly adequate budget and medium-priced hotels south of the médina near Bab ech Chouhada and a new, top-of-the-range option, the *Hotel Kasbah*. (Kairouan's former best address, *Hotel Continental*, is now closed.) The problem might be to find a place in a budget hotel at busy times of year, so try to ring to reserve.

Sleeping
■ *on map, page 288*
Price codes:
see inside front cover

North of the médina B *Hotel Kasbah*, 97 rooms in a former barracks not far from the *Mobil* station, just north of the médina – coming from the Tunis direction, turn left on Av Ibn el Jazzar after the (closed) *Hotel Continental*. T237301, F237302, kasbah.kairouan@gnet.tn Part of the Golden Yasmin chain, Kairouan's most comfort-able address. Rooms overlook a tiny, unheated pool. At the back in the former store-rooms are a few shops and a café which gets animated when tour groups are around. Limited choice of drinks but hubbly-bubbly pipes available. **NB** The *Kasbah* fills up quickly with groups during winter and spring breaks. **B** *Hotel Amina*, Rte de Tunis, GP2, 300 Kairouan, T226555, F225411. 3 mins from city centre, 62 rooms, 5 suites, all with bath and balconies, telephone, a/c, 2 restaurants, coffee shop, bar, large pool, garden, near Tourist office and Aghlabid pools, disco each evening, good lunch for 7Dt served from 1230, hence popular with coach parties. Only convenient for sites if you have a car. Very much a second choice to the *Kasbah*.

D *Hotel Menema*, on R Moez Ibn Badis, not far from *Mobil* and *Hotel Kasbah*, T235033. 50 beds, rooms with 2 and 3 beds, some with showers. Some rooms have windows opening on to corridors. Heating very light. Used by 'travel adventure' groups. Slight smell of drains but helpful reception. Still, prefer the *Hotel Sabra* (below).

Médina **D** *Hotel Barouta* , near the Bir Barouta well just right off the main drag on your right as you come from Bab ech Chouhada. No phone, curious – presents itself as a hotel but maybe it's just a sort of poor men's hostel. Prices appear negotiable around the 5Dt mark. Must have been the first modern hotel in Kairouan. Well worn marble stairs lead up to 1st floor rooms off narrow corridor. Top floor rooms off large hall, view over minarets (not for light sleepers). Rundown, but no doubt too small to be turned into a carpet emporium. At the time of writing (spring 2002), the old **F** *Hotel Marhala*, on Souk El Bey in the médina near Bir Barouta, was closed for redevelopment.

Bab ech Chouhada and Av de la République **C** *Hotel Splendid*, R du 9-Avril (turn up a leafy street almost opposite *Restaurant Sabra* and *BNA* with ATM), T227522,

Central Tunisia

F230829. 1920s building, 35 rooms with renovated baths, a/c, clean, basic, bar and busy restaurant, slightly overpriced. Plus point: alcohol available. Minus: bathrooms a bit niffy. **C** *Hotel Tunisia*, Av Farhat Hached, not far from *UBCI*, T231855, F231597. 44 rooms with shower/bath, breakfast, comfortable, very clean, no a/c but fans on ceiling. Good heating in winter. *Restaurant Sabra* n ext door. Best rooms: 108 for a couple, 109 for a triple – big bathroom. Nice reception. Minor problem: all rooms street facing. On balance, probably preferable to *Le Splendid*. **D** *Hotel Sabra*, R Ali Belhaouane, by Pl des Martyrs, T230263. Clean, pleasant, friendly staff, roof terrace, 2 floors with total of 30 small, 2- and 3-bed rooms with wash-basin, on U-shaped corridors (echoing footsteps of early departures), hot showers on corridor, no heating, rooms at back are quieter, adequate breakfast in TV room, *hammam* next door highly recommended but men only. Handy for all sites and restaurants near hotels *Tunisia* and *Splendid*. Absolutely fine for a night.

Kairouan

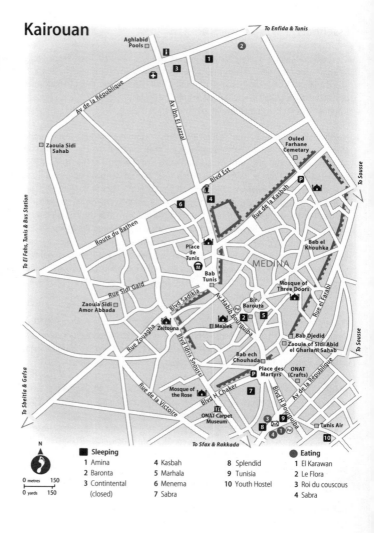

Sleeping		
1 Amina	4 Kasbah	8 Splendid
2 Baronta	5 Marhala	9 Tunisia
3 Contintental	6 Menema	10 Youth Hostel
(closed)	7 Sabra	

Eating
1 El Karawan
2 Le Flora
3 Roi du couscous
4 Sabra

0 metres 150
0 yards 150

Youth hostel Av de Fès, T228239. In the new town, kitchen, 70 beds, reports say noisy and dirty but a fairly cheap option for the night.

Expensive If you want alcohol, try the restaurants of the *Hotel Kasbah* or the *Hotel Amina*. **Mid-range** *Le Flora*, Rte de Tunis. *Restaurant El Karawan*, R Soukeina Ben El-Houssein, behind *Tunisia Hotel*, usual Tunisian fare, much used by small tour groups, clean loos, family run, open in the evening. If on R Hamada-Laâouani, locate *UBCI* – restaurant is nearby. **Cheap** *Restaurant des Sportifs*, Pl de la Victoire, couscous speciality. *Restaurant Fairouz*, signposted off Av Habib Bourguiba in the médina, good food. *Restaurant Sabra*, Av de la République, next to *Hotel Tunisia*, handy and perfectly acceptable. *Roi du Couscous*, Pl du 7 Novembre, Tunisian food at cheap prices, closes in late afternoon, best for lunch or early dinner. *Restaurant La Tabouna*, off Pl des Martyrs, another just about adequate cheap eating place, plenty of chips.

Eating
● *on map, page 288*

Kairouan is one of the major centres for **carpets** in the country. Visit first the display of old and new carpets at the **ONAT** on Av Ali Zouaoui to get an idea of real prices even though carpets can be cheaper elsewhere. Be careful when walking around, the term *musée du tapis* does not indicate a museum but rather a shop with carpets on display and the hard sell. For an experience of purchasing carpets try *Société Tapis Sabra*, R Sidi Abid, T223068, or *Centre Kairouanais du Tapis*, 35 Souk des Tamis, T226223. An arched doorway in a plain wall leads into what was once a private home. Sunlight filters down onto hundreds of carpets, spread on floors, hung on walls and piled in rolls at every turn. In one room there is a loom and a woman or women will appear to demonstrate how a carpet is woven. Seating is provided in the largest room where any carpet you would like to see is rolled out for inspection.

Shopping

If carpets are not your thing, then you could look out for some **beaten copper** kitchen pans and dishes for which Kairouan is also known. Items covered in zinc (*tekezdeer* is the technique) are attractive but expensive and can be found on the main drag in the médina. Otherwise, the best buy in Kairouan are **makroudh**, sweet date cakes basted in oil and coated in syrup and sesame seeds. Appropriately packaged in boxes labelled *pâtisserie tunisienne* they make a sticky, calorific gift.

Long distance Bus: the bus station is northwest of the town centre, a good 20-min walk from the médina. For information T300011. Departures to **Tunis**; **Kebili/Douz**; **Gafsa**; **Tozeur**; **Djerba**; **Zarzis**; **Medenine** and **Nefta**. **Louages**: departures from stand close to bus station. To **El Djem** possible by louage, requires changes and patience.

Transport

To walk from the bus station to the centre of town, turn left out of bus station, then right again at the first wide street. Shortly after, take street running left, slightly uphill, and then turn right at the first major junction. Keep going straight ahead: you are on the right track when you reach the roundabout with *Shell* and the *Agil* station (on right). Keep straight ahead and at the junction with the *Total* station go left on to R de Gafsa. After just over 200 m you will find *Hotel Sabra* on your right and Bab ech Chouhada on left. This is a long walk on a hot day, hence best advice is to get a taxi.

Banks Banks with ATMs on Av du Dr Hamda Laâouani and next to *Hotel Tunisia*. **Car hire** *Budget*, Av de la République, T220528; *Hertz*, Av Ibn el Jazzar, T224529, near hospital. **Communications** Internet: near to the *Agil* station, via R Zouagha, T231041. **Post Office**: Pl du 7-Novembre, R Farhat Hached. **Medical services** Chemist: all-night chemists near the centre on Av Ali Zouaoui, between junction with Av Hédi Chaker and Bab Jedid. **Doctor**: *Hotel Kasbah* recommends Dr Kharrat, T232160/233630, T98451426 (mob). Surgery located between Bab Tounes and *Hotel Kasbah*, opposite Chaussures de l'Etoile. **Hospital**: *Hopital Ibn Jazzar*, between the Aghlabid pools and the *Hotel Kasbah*, T230036. **Useful addresses** Police: T220577.

Directory

Central Tunisia

Hammam: *Sabra*, next to the hotel of the same name, close to the tourist office by Bab Ech-Chouhada. Immaculately clean. Men only, closes around 1600.

South from Kairouan to Gabès

Colour map 2, grid A/C4 If you want to get south fast, avoiding Sousse and Sfax, there is the busy GP2 running directly south to Skhira, where it joins the GP1 coast road for Gabès. Leaving Kairouan, you pass the National Museum of Islamic Art at **Rakkada**. Further south, where the GP2 crosses Oued Zeroud and the railway line and where the C86 cuts off to to the southwest, is **Zaâfrane**, a small settlement with a large clean café set back off the road. Eucalyptus trees provide welcome shade, although their number has been reduced by road widening. Further south, olives stretch as far as the eye can see.

Some 35 km south of Kairouan, **Bouhajla** is a small crossroads settlement. Here you will find the National Guard, yet another square-faced clock on a central pillar, chemist, bread shop, louage and bus stop. There is a café by the bus stop and a slightly better café to the north of the village by the new mosque and petrol station.

Djebel Khechem closes in on the west and Djebel Kordj on the east. At the road junction GP13 and GP2 are two fairly basic cafés. Sebkhet Mecheguig, to the west, in right conditions a very large expanse of water, supports a rich bird life.

Bir Ali Ben Khalifat, 49 km north of the Skhirat/GP1 junction, has developed from a government resettlement into a small town. If you need to overnight for some reason, there is the large *Hmaissa Relax Centre*, a new monster pink hotel, campsite opposite, occasionally used by tour groups steaming up from the South to Kairouan, also by returning émigrés heading south.

On the routes north of Kairouan

Colour map 1, grid A/C4 The road north from Kairouan towards Tunis (GP2) is in poor condition in parts, although there is a rolling improvement programme. (The Kairouan ringroad is reaching completion and means the town can now be circumvented.) Heavy weekend traffic can make the journey slow.

Bird watching at Lake Kelbia The wildlife reserve of **Lake Kelbia**, about 30 km northeast of Kairouan, spreads to the southwest of the GP2, the main road to Enfida which eventually merges with the GP1 for Tunis. Clear paths and viewing points are rare as the water level of the lake varies, falling dramatically in summer. Access is through fields or olive groves. However, at 25 km from Kairouan a small loop to the east takes one nearer to the water. In summer you may spot squacco herons, purple gallinules or the fantailed warbler. In the winter, migrating birds (flamingos and cranes) pass through.

Ksar Lamsa, a remote Byzantine fort A more interesting route from Kairouan takes you along the C99 towards Siliana, passing between the Djebel Ousselat and Djebel Bou Dabouss. At Aïn Djelloula, you pass a fine field of ruins. Before reaching remote Ouesslatia, turn right on the C46. The ruins of Ksar Lemsa lie some 23 km to the north. (After Ksar Lemsa, you can continue on to El Fahs, 50 km further north. Some fine scenery here.)

Like all Roman cities Ksar Lamsa was situated in a position of strategic importance. It overlooked the valleys of the Oued el Kebir and the smaller, nearer Oued Maarouf. It controlled movement from the plains of the west to the coast and was itself protected by its position on a low plateau backed by the

Djebel Bargou. The fortress (hence the modern Arabic name *ksar*) dates from the sixth century BC (the reign of Justinian) though reuse of older building stones complicate the issue. The battlements of the well-conserved fortress remain. Entrance was through a gate on the north side. Inside the fortress was a large, deep water cistern fed by a conduit from outside – a supply in times of siege. Around the fortress are many ruins, few excavated. On the opposite side of the road to the fortress is a pocket-sized amphitheatre. Even Ksar Lamsa must have had its entertainments.

Northwest of Kairouan: the road to Siliana

Following the same route out of Kairouan as for Ksar Lamsa, and eventually El Fahs, you could continue at Ouesslatia on the C73 northwards for Siliana. The road will take you past **Djebel Serj**, at 1360 m the second-highest mountain in Tunisia (Djebel Chaâmbi near Kasserine being highest at 1554 m). The road climbs up through the moutains to Siliana, now capital of a governorate.

Colour map 1, grid B3

West of Kairouan: La Kessera and Makthar

Driving west of Kairouan, head for Chebika (not to be confused with Chebika in the Djerid region), on the P3. Branch right off the P3 onto the the GP12 for Makthar and Le Kef. Here you are heading into *la Tunisie profonde*, the remote interior of Tunisia, although this was a region settled by the Romans too, as the number of ancient sites shows. It was also a region of settlement in prehistoric times. In contemporary Tunisian political jargon, large parts of the interior are the *zones d'ombre*, the 'regions in the shadow', untouched by the prosperity of the east coast in the first decades of Tunisian independence. Since the early 1990s, the government has made major efforts to develop the isolated parts of the interior, and the results are evident to even the casual visitor: pistes replaced by metalled roads, power lines, schools, post offices, the odd bit of light industry.

Phone code: 78
Colour map 1, grid C3

Heading for the northwest, you could combine the scenic drive from Kairouan to Le Kef with visits to the hillcrest village of **La Kessera** and the remains of Roman **Mactaris**, at **Makthar**, roughly halfway between Kairouan and Le Kef. Driving time to Le Kairouan to Makthar is roughly two hours, from Makthar to Le Kef 90 minutes.

Some 17 km before you reach Makthar, the village of La Kessera is up on your right on a loop off the GP12, in a magnificent defensive position. The houses are grouped below the plateau, sheltered by cliff from the prevailing winds. Originally built of local stone, the houses blended into the landscape, perfect protection from marauders. Although chosen for defensive reasons, the site had the additional plus of plentiful water (there is a spring in the middle of the village). Above the village, on the plateau, was grazing, and there was plentiful wood in the Aleppo pine forests.

La Kessera
Altitude: 1,078 m

The origins of La Kessera are lost, as you might expect, in the mists of time. Was there a settlement called Chusira, named for distant Chosroes, king of the Persians? Or does the name derive from the Latin 'caesar'? Some slight remains of a Byzantine watch-tower overlook the village. Stelae and stones of ancient origins can be found integrated into the walls of the houses. During the French protectorate, La Kessera was the seat of a caïdat, and its zaouia, Sidi Ameur, a place of local pilgrimage. In the 1960s, policy was to bring isolated communities into line. A new village was built below the village, with standard concrete

Central Tunisia

houses, facilities were moved down next to the main road. The village people refused to move, however, remaining attached to their homes. Whereas in many hillcrest villages – Zriba, near Zaghouan, for example – people moved down to the plain, the advantages of ancient La Kessera were too good be lost.

In recent years, signs of a new prosperity have appeared, with constructions in the usual concrete style being lodged on top of older stone dwellings. There has also been much new building down below the village. The village lives on agriculture, government employment, and some weaving. Heavy wool *kachabia* cloaks for men, essential gear for the cold winters of the interior, are a local speciality.

Sleeping Out on the Makthar side of La Kessera, you come to the only accommodation option here, the *Hotel des Chasseurs*, which may be open in the near future. The bar should be in operation.

Makthar

Altitude: 900 m
Population: 7,500

Next stop on the GP12, **Makthar** lies 114 km west of Kairouan. Though the new town was built by the French in 1887, the Roman city of Mactaris, dating from around AD 200, was built on the site of an earlier Numidian defensive position. Makthar town lies to the north of the site and is refreshingly cool. The town is built on the hillside and the buses stop at the lower end of the town while the louages stop higher up the main street. Market day is Monday. Make sure you don't miss the **dolmen**, a megalithic tomb near the town centre, on the left as you come in from Kairouan. (If you have a car, and have a yen for things prehistoric, you might want to head for **Ellès**, off the GP12 road north to Kef, see below.)

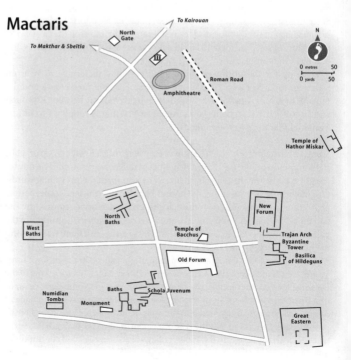

Mactaris

To Kairouan

North Gate

To Makthar & Sbeïtla

Roman Road

Amphitheatre

0 metres 50
0 yards 50

Temple of Hathor Miskar

North Baths

West Baths

Temple of Bacchus

New Forum

Trajan Arch

Byzantine Tower

Basilica of Hildeguns

Old Forum

Numidian Tombs

Baths

Schola Juvenum

Monument

Great Eastern

The ruins of ancient Mactaris are fairly scattered, so you will probably need at least an hour to visit them. Start with a look at the triumphal arch of Bab el Aïn right in the middle of town. You get tickets for the site at the museum. The remains of the **amphitheatre** lie to the left and further left, across the Roman road, are the remains of a **temple** dedicated to the Carthaginian god Hathor Miskar. Follow the Roman street towards the central section of the site where there is the main forum and the remains of Trajan's Arch, looking less triumphal than in its heyday of AD 115. Beyond are the foundations of the fifth-century **Basilica of Hildeguns** and after another 100 m are the **southern baths**, built around AD 200, considered among the best preserved in Africa. Much of the splendour is in the mosaics. The building was changed into a fort in the more troubled Byzantine times. The walls are 20 m high in places; unfortunately the vaulting failed to survive. To the west, lies the **Schola Juvenum**, one of the most charming ruins in Tunisia, once a sort of clubhouse come educational establishment for young men. Close by is the old forum, and just across the street, a temple dedicated to Bacchus. ■ *Winter 0830-1730, summer 0800-1200 and 1500-1900. Entry at museum 2Dt, photography 1Dt.*

Not too much choice at Makthar. Try **C** *Mactaris*, T78876014, 20 rooms, reasonable standard, bar.

Twice-daily **buses** from Tunis, Kasserine and Le Kef.

Ancient Mactaris

Sleeping

Transport

Central Tunisia

Makthar to Sbeïtla: across deepest Tunisia

The 75-km journey south from Makthar to Sbeïtla is along winding minor roads through the Dorsal region. Within 2 km of leaving Makthar, there is a magnificent view north to the mountains and as the P4 climbs through the **Djebel Skarna** (1,076 m), the Tunisia seen here is in sharp contrast to the level plains of the Sahel. As the road descends, the ruins of the ancient settlement of **Sufes** at Sbiba lie to the left and 40 km further on is the magnificent Roman site at Sbeïtla.

North of Makthar: routes to obscure funerary monuments

If you are on the look out for the more **obscure ancient sites**, then you have a sprinkling within easy driving distance of Makthar (or Le Kef), on much improved country roads leading off the GP12 which links the two towns. Heading northwest out of Makthar for around 25 km, you could start with the most ancient, the dolmens at **Ellès**, by taking a left (west) turn down a minor road off the GP12, at a junction with a school a few kilometres before you reach Le Sers. (Turning right takes you to Siliana, 26 km to the east, on the GP4 past a couple of later funerary monuments, namely the Numidian (?) **Kbor Klib**, a large mausoleum, rather like one at Chemtou, to the right/south of the road and **Ksar Toual Zammel**, an unrestored Numido-Punic mausoleum, to the left/north.)

For **Ellès**, having left the C12, head down the recent road for about 2 km and turn left at the first junction. The village soon comes into sight, a few kilometres ahead. Drive uphill, past the waterpoint on the right, and at a sort of junction go left. The great low-lying stone slabs of the main dolmen, set against a backdrop of young pines, come into view. A warden may emerge from the whitewashed building nearby. In fact, there are 63 dolmen-type tombs in the Ellès area. This one in the village has seven chambers, each about

1½-m high. Until recently it was the centre of the local market, being used as an abattoir. In 1985 a research group began working on the area, and since then our main dolmen has been given an annual sweep out. Other dolmens are scattered around the stony hillsides while in the village you may see Roman stone integrated into the houses. In the near future, it may be possible to drive south of Ellès on a soon to be improved piste to Hammam Zouekra, shown on the maps as Souk el Jemaâ (Friday Souk). From there, you could complete a circuit back to Makthar.

After Ellès, the next site in the region, at nearby **Zannfour** to the north, is there to delight enthusiasts of unexcavated Roman towns. Head back down to the junction and turn left (west). After a few kilometres, over to your right, you see a much-eroded triumphal arch, the most substantial construction still standing in what is Roman **Assuras**. This was clearly a pretty large place with splendid views over the surrounding plain and archaeologists have lots to discover here. Unless hectares of shard beds are your thing, you can then drive on via El Ksour to Kalaât el Khasba, from where you have just 18 km further to drive to Haïdra in the west.

If you are in need of petrol/coffee/food, head back to the GP12 and then north to **Vieux Sers**, a French-founded town with an old railway station and a truly outback feel. You are now just a few rapid kilometres south of Le Kef.

If you were coming from the Tunis direction, this region is best accessed by taking GP3 to El Fahs, then the GP4 to **Siliana**, total distance 126 km. Arriving in Siliana, go right at the tractor roundabout (*Agil* lead-free petrol). Then turn off left for Makthar at the roundabout with the wheat-ear monument down a wide avenue planted with new trees. (Consult your e-mails at the *publinet* on your left just before the *Esso* station.) Watch out for speed bumps. The site of ancient **Zama Minor**, modern **Zamna**, is signed right just before the lycée as you leave Siliana. A few kilometres further on, where the road forks, go right for Le Sers (29 km). Here the road narrows, although there are works underway. Where it climbs up hill, look out for **Ksar Toual**, isolated in the middle of the fields to your right. A couple of kilometres further on, just over the brow of the hill, **Ksar Klib** – left down a few hundred metres of piste – is easily missed. Here there are fine views westwards. Grain silos are an indication of the region's main source of wealth. At letting-out time, you will see kids with their satchels walking along the roadside, so keep your speed down. The junction with the GP12 is reached a few kilometres further on.

Across the steppe: routes for Le Kef, Kalaât Senam and Haïdra

From Makthar, there are a number of options for continuing your exploration of central Tunisia. The obvious choice is to overnight in Le Kef (covered in the previous chapter, Northern Tunisia). Then, if you have a car, you can easily cover the Roman site of **Haïdra** and **Kalaât Senam** in a day, pushing on south to overnight in **Kasserine** or **Sbeïtla** (for which see below). Without your own transport, getting to Haïdra will be fairly time consuming, requiring a louage or bus to Kalaât Khasaba, and then hitching or country minibus to Haïdra. For Kalaât Senam, you will need to take a louage or bus from Le Kef to Tajerouine, a minor town on the GP17, 37 km south of Le Kef. There you change louage for Kalaât Senam. An early start would be a good thing.

A more obscure route from Makthar would take you from the turn-off at Henchir Lorbeuss (left off the GP12, 38 km north of Makthar). A minor road takes you down to **Dahmani** (aka **Souk el Arbaâ**, Wednesday Souk) whence the C18 takes you across to the former mining town of **Jerissa** and the GP17 just south of Tajerouine. Between Dahmani and Jerissa you have another remote Roman site south of the road shown as Fej el Tameur on the maps.

Kalaât Senam, Senam's Citadel, is one of the more rewarding out-of-the-way **Kalaât Senam** corners of Tunisia. It is a strange, flat-topped mountain which rises up out of the surrounding steppelands. The settlement below has grown considerably in recent years, with electricity being brought in. From the village, a 90-minute hike takes you to the top of the citadel. Small children may offer to show you the way. The walk is not difficult, with one steep climb up a flight of steps carved out of the rock. After passing through an ancient gatehouse, you are on the plateau, which must have been one of the most impregnable sites in pre-modern Tunisia. There are remains of a village, some cisterns, and an eerie *zaouia*, white-domed, the interior blackened with candle smoke.

The tale goes that the table mountain is named after a brigand who lived in more heroic times. When the bey's army passed through these remote marchlands to collect taxes, Kalaât Senam was a port of call. The inhabitants of the region would shut themselves off with their flocks in their rocky citadel, flinging down a bit of rotting carrion to show their indifference to the tax-collecting army, which would go on its way empty handed. Local people still take goats and cows up onto the plateau to graze.

You might like to spend an hour exploring the desolation of Kalaât Senam. There are wonderful views, and even non-birdwatchers will be impressed by the number of birds of prey soaring around the cliff faces. Aleppo pine woods can be seen away to the south. At the western end of the plateau are some rock chimneys. The local story is that a few years ago, a lad from the village climbed to the top of one of these pillars for a bet. Unfortunately, he couldn't get down. Given the sheer drops on all sides, children shouldn't be left unaccompanied. In fact, the 'table' is not flat at all. It hollows towards the middle, and is actually quite large. One can easily lose sight of other members of one's group – the plateau takes on a mysterious feel – shades of the Blair Witch Project *à la tunisienne*.

Haïdra   حيدرة

Haïdra, ancient Ammaedara, is well off the main tourist track . It lies a short dis-   Colour map 3, grid A1
tance from the Algerian frontier, on the way to nowhere (at the moment),
although when Algeria reopens for tourism, you will be able to combine visiting
Haïdra with ancient Theveste. The site is lonely, the ruins scattered over an arid
hillside sloping down to a river. On the far side, Aleppo pines contrast green with
the stony ground. There are all the usual features, including triumphal arch and
basilicas, and the massive masonry of Byzantine forts. In Roman times, either the
climate must have been wetter, or the water infrastructure very efficient to sup-
port such a grand military base on this stony site.

Getting there   Haïdra can be easily reached by louage from Kalaâ Khasbah, about 18   **Ins & outs**
km northeast. **Getting around**   The main site lies southeast of the modern town of
Haïdra. The old Roman road runs parallel to the P4 from which many ruins can be seen.

History

Ammaedara stood at the western end of one of the oldest Roman roads in Africa, running inland from Tacapae, (modern Gabès) on the coast.

Central Tunisia

Inscriptions record it as having been built in AD 14. Later, a road from Carthage to Theveste, some 40 km to the southwest and a major military base, passed through Ammaedara. Theveste became the Third Augustan Legion's headquarters in the first century AD, under Augustus or Tiberius. Later, when the legionary base was moved west to Theveste, a colony of veterans was settled at Ammaedara at the end of the first century.

In Christian times, Ammaedara remained an important centre, and there are the remains of no less than five basilicas to visit on the site. Under Justinian in the sixth century, with Africa temporarily reconquered by the Byzantines, the town acquired a vast citadel, which in all probability continued in use under the early Arab rulers. It was in part restored and altered in Husseinid times.

Visiting the site

The remains at Haïdra are located to the north and south of the main road, the more spectacular sights being on the south side. For the moment there is no entrance charge, but someone might emerge into the sunbaked field of ruins to show you around (you will probably need about an hour). In summer, given the shadeless nature of the site, an early start is advisable. At the time of writing, a museum was planned for the site, to be housed in a former customs building.

Ruins south of the road Coming from the east, one first encounters the **Triumphal Arch of Septimius Severus** which once spanned the Roman road to Carthage. The arch was dedicated in AD 195 as can be seen from the frieze. Having been incorporated in a small Byzantine fort at a later stage, it is not exactly in pristine condition.

Southeast of the arch are the remains of a **Byzantine church** with three naves. Excavations show that this covers a more ancient church. In both the apse faced east. This church is dedicated to the martyrs who perished under the persecution of Diocletian.

Haïdra

Fortifying Africa: the Byzantine defences

In the 6th century, under the leadership of the energetic emperor Justinian, Africa returned to the Byzantine fold. The Vandals were defeated, and the province once more became part of the Eastern Roman Empire. But things could not be as they had been before. The Roman peace had been shattered forever. During the Vandal interregnum, security had been shaken, and a new factor had appeared: roaming nomad tribes, highly mobile on their camels.

Justinian wanted to see the restoration of the old Roman frontier of Hadrian's day. His governor Solomon realised that the enemy was now within, not in the lands south of the limes. A new approach to defence was necessary, it was no longer a matter of stationing a legion on the frontier. Forts and citadels were therefore put up wherever important towns needed protection. Some 80 fortified sites have been identified, and there are thought to be many more. Towns which once had no need of a garrison were heavily fortified – Dougga and Mactaris, for example.

Remote villages were given look out posts – see La Kessera, while even quite minor settlements received solid square forts (Ksar Lemsa).

Huge energies were put into protecting the reconquered province's settlements. There was a good deal of dismantling/ rebuilding, and at times, older Roman buildings were integrated into the new fortifications (the capitol at Dougga became part of the new walls). The aim was to ensure that Africa remained under Byzantine rule. Ultimately, however, Byzantium's efforts to maintain its hold on the province failed. Despite all the best efforts of the empire's military engineers, the province fell to the Muslim armies in the second half of the 7th century. The fortifications which survive are often spectacular – as can be seen at Haïdra, unequalled in scale and sophistication until the 16th century and the coming of Renaissance military technology (see the fort at La Goulette and 17th-century forts at Ghar el Melh).

Central Tunisia

About 300 m to the south, not far from the *oued*, is a beautiful **mausoleum** with portico. It is well preserved, still having a second storey. The upper floor is in the style of a small temple and the façade of four columns supporting a pediment gives it its name. Any statues which stood between the columns have long since been removed.

The building of greatest distinction at Haïdra is without doubt the **Byzantine Fort**, built at the time of Justinian (AD 527-565). It has claims to be the largest Byzantine fort in Africa. The massive fortifications measured 200 x 110 m, and had walls 10-m high. Nine square towers can be clearly seen. Halfway down the east wall was a circular tower. The main north-south route actually passed through this fortress and at the south end led to a bridge over the Oued Haïdra. A small chapel with three naves was incorporated into part of the west wall against one of the towers. There was a side aisle on the south side and a high tower, as high as the wall. Parts of the ribbed vaulting are still preserved. Renovations to the north elevation of this fortress were undertaken by the Turkish beys. And just outside the walls to the southwest is yet another small basilica.

On the north side of the main road, the ruins are rather less legible than the spectacular Byzantine citadel. At 200 m north of the road and in line with the **Church of the Martyrs** is the **square mausoleum** decorated with Corinthian pillars and stylized garlands. The **Theatre** is a great disappointment as the restorations of AD 299 have not prevented it from being now just a pile of stones on hard to distinguish foundations. The **Building with Troughs** (French:

Ruins north of the road

Church of Bishop Melleus

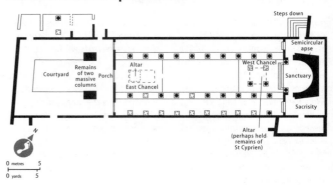

edifice à auges) has stone basins topped by arcades, the purpose of which may have been storage of grain. The nearby **Vandal Chapel** with three naves, refers to these invaders from the fifth century who left funerary inscriptions. Further west, the jumbled ruins are thought to be those of the Capitol. Between this and another basilica, the so-called Church of Bishop Melleus, a discernible square with miscellaneous stones was probably the market.

The **Church of Bishop Melleus** was a most distinguished building with two massive columns supporting an arch at the perimeter of the courtyard. Inside there were three naves, a semicircular apse on either side of which was a sacristy. It is said relics of St Cyprien were kept here in the sixth century.

Sbeïtla سبيطلة

Phone code: 77
Colour map 3, grid A2 *The golden-stone ruins of Sbeïtla have an other-worldly feel to them. The most distant major site from Carthage, it is also one of the best preserved. Whereas many Roman cities were quarried for building stone down the centuries, Sbeïtla was to remain relatively untouched, apart from a little refortifying under the Byzantines. For a short time, it was even an imperial Christian capital. In 646, the exarch Gregory had himself proclaimed emperor and moved from Carthage to Sbeïtla to better defend Africa against the Arab-Muslim invasions.*

Ins & outs   Nearby modern Sbeïtla, an unexciting minor agricultural centre, has all the necessary facilities and probably looks its best during the Wednesday weekly market. **Getting there**   The bus station is in the centre of the new town and the louages are next to it. Many buses come in from Kasserine, Gafsa, Tunis and Kairouan. The train station is on R Habib Thameur to the south of town.

History

The Roman town of Sufetula was probably built in the year 3 BC, but little is known about it until the period under the rule of Emperor Vespasian (AD 69-79). The town was very prosperous during the second and third centuries, judging by the remains of the public buildings.

It is in the early seventh century that Sbeïtla emerges into history. Byzantine Africa was supplying corn and olive oil to Constantinople, which under the leadership of the emperor Heraclius (died 641), defeated the Sassanid Persian

Empire in the East. But a new enemy was emerging, in the form of the tribes of Arabia, united by a new revealed religion, Islam. Egypt was invaded, leading to a flood of refugees. In 642, the Arabs took Cyrenaica, and in 643 they besieged Tripoli. In 646, the exarch Gregory, in a bold move, declared himself independent from Constantinople, called himself Emperor and moved his administration from Carthage to Sufetula, which he considered to be a better centre from which to defend the country against the new and energetic enemy from the east.

This proved not to be the case. Abdallah ibn Saâd launched an invasion in 647. Gregory's forces were annihilated by the mobile Arab cavalry, and Gregory himself was killed. The remaining Byzantine forces withdrew northwards, abandoning southern Byzacena. But the Arab forces were more interested in booty than siege warfare.

The Byzantines, however, made a fatal error after their defeat. They offered a huge bribe to the Arabs to leave. Abdallah ibn Saâd, surprised by the quantity of coins put before him, asked where all this wealth came from. The Byzantine representatives explained that it came from the sale of olive oil to Constantinople. Such a rich territory would clearly have to be conquered on a more long term basis. Though the Arabs headed back to Egypt, they were to return and conquer the whole of North Africa in the late seventh century.

No modern city was grafted onto ancient Sufetula, and the result is one of the best preserved Roman street layouts in Tunisia.

Visiting the site

The best time to visit this impressive ruined town is early in the morning or in the evening when the sunlight is softer on the stones of the temples (and there are fewer visitors). As you drive up from Sbeïtla town, the first evidence of the site is the **Arch of Diocletian** which formed part of the old walls to the south of the site. Opposite the ruins (adjacent to the drinks stall and coach park) is a recent **museum** which is worth taking in first in order to better appreciate the stones. ■ *0830-1730 winter, 0600-2000 summer, closed Mon. 2Dt, photo fee 1Dt. Most of the site is accessible in a wheelchair. Toilets next to museum.*

Sbeïtla

The recently constructed museum at Sbeïtla is well worth visiting. **Room 1** contains local material from Sufetula accompanied by maps and plans. The Libyan period is represented by megalithic tombs from Djebel Selloum and Thala and by an inscription from the region of Djediliane-Rouhia to the north of Sbeïtla. The early Roman period is represented here by a series of votive and funerary steles. In **Room 2**, there are marble statues and busts

The museum

Related map
Sufetula, page 302

Central Tunisia

Know your Romans – who was Emperor Diocletian?

Gaius Aurelius Valerius Diocletianus (AD 245-313) was Emperor of Rome 284-305. Co-emperor Numerian, at that time in charge of eastern areas, died in 284 and Emperor Carinus, in charge of western areas, was assassinated in 285, leaving Diocletian in full control. He was revered as an able soldier and an energetic ruler. Initially he split the empire into two,

then four administrative divisions, instituted domestic and fiscal reforms and reorganized the army. He is particularly remembered for his persecution of the Christians (303-305) having them thrown to wild animals, stretched on racks and burned during public demonstrations. He abdicated in 305 and retired to Yugoslavia.

including a statue found at Sufetula, Bacchus, god of wine, accompanied by a panther from whose open mouth once came a fountain of water. From Kasserine came the statue of a female figure, perhaps Diana the huntress. Look too for the female bust from Haïdra and a smaller statue from Sbiba. In **Rooms 3** and **4** there are two important mosaics, from Sufetula and Sbiba. The rest of the space is given over to the economic life of the region at that time which was firmly based on olive oil. There are presses, containers for carrying the oil, lamps, plates and dishes. The marble head of Mercury from Sufetula is on display here and a special piece of very ancient leather from Sbiba. **Room 5** is devoted to Christian and Byzantine exhibits. From the second century the Christian religion was expanding its influence. Here in Tunisia there were many churches, as many as six at Sufetula and Haïdra. The display attempts to give an idea of the richness of the period with photographs and artefacts. There are sarcophagi, bronze, and glass items.

Byzantine quarter Your visit to the site proper starts opposite the museum going into the Byzantine quarter where there are remains of three forts/dwellings constructed of materials taken from older buildings. The nearby **Byzantine church** is dedicated to Saints Gervais, Protais and Tryphon; and there are **baths** badly damaged and partially rebuilt with a mosaic of fish and crustaceans and an oil press (originally there were two presses and a windmill).

Turning right, down the street taking you towards the central area is a large cistern which supplied water to the city, the rainwater being perhaps supplemented by an underground canal. Close by are the remains of a large **public baths**, with hot and cold rooms and a geometric mosaic decorating the room dedicated to exercise. You can see evidence of the hypocaust underfloor heating system very clearly. The nearby fountain is one of three public fountains dating from the fourth century.

To the right here, overlooking the Oued Sbeïtla, is the **theatre**, a shadow of its glorious past. The tiers are in ruins but the orchestra pit is clearly visible as are the colonnades round the stage. Worth the detour if only for the magnificent view over the dry river course. Turn back to the baths and head towards the main temples. The **Church of St Servus**, built in the courtyard of a Roman temple, is on your right. Now only four columns of stone mark the corners of the building.

The capitol Head along the street, which originally had shops on either side, to the magnificent capitol entered through the **Arch of Antonius Pius**. This gateway was built in the style of a triumphal arch and formed part of the ancient walls. This arch can be dated AD 138-61 thanks to an inscription which refers to the Emperor

Antonius Pius and his two adopted sons, Marcus Aurelius and Lucius Verus. The **three massive temples** which stand side by side opposite this gate, across the vast, almost square, **Forum** are assumed to be dedicated (from right to left) to Juno, Jupiter and Minerva. The central temple, accessible only by steps from the side, was the more opulent of the three. The temple of Minerva has the more elegant columns. Under the temples are cellars. The Forum, paved with huge stone slabs, is surrounded by a wall which shows evidence of several restorations. The whole complex is highly impressive, and will provide you with some superb holiday snaps. Close to the Forum is another church constructed on the site of an older building. This is in poor condition but visible are the central aisle and the two smaller side aisles separated by a double colonnade.

The group of buildings to the northeast, known as the episcopal group, comprises two churches, a baptistery, a chapel and small baths. The **Basilica Bellator**, excavated in 1907 is named after a fragment of inscription found there. Measuring 34 x 15 m, the building has a central nave, two side aisles and a double apse. The mosaic floor in the choir still remains. The baptistery was converted into a chapel dedicated to Bishop Juncundus (fifth century) who is believed to have been martyred by the Vandals. The adjacent **Basilica Vitalis** is a later, larger building. It has five naves and double apses and like the Basilica Bellator has evidence of long occupation. A marble table decorated with biblical themes found here is now in the Bardo Museum. (The site museum has only a photograph.)

The **'episcopal group'**

If time and enthusiasm permit, you could explore the northwest of the site through the houses and unidentified temple to the amphitheatre and across to the much restored bridge.

Central Tunisia

Essentials

There are two hotels. **B** *Hotel Sufetula*, just before the ruins on the way to Kasserine, T465074, F465582. Pleasant, clean, nice pool (available to non-residents), the only good hotel in the town, and charges accordingly. Used by tour groups, 37 rooms and bungalow-type accommodation. **D** *Hotel Bakini*, R 2 Mars 1934, T465244. Has 80 beds. Adequate. Try also **D** *Motel* , T466528, close to the bus station on Pl des Martyrs. Small rooms with wash-basin opening onto courtyard.

Sleeping
■ *on map, page 299*

The Capitol at Sufetula

After H Saladin & A Merlin

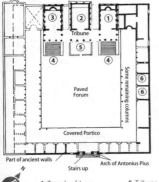

1 Temple of Juno
2 Temple of Jupiter
3 Temple of Minerva
4 Stairs up with wide steps
5 Tribune
6 Large room or hall

0 metres 10
0 yards 10

The *Hotel Sufetula* has fairly unexciting fare. Cheaper are *Restaurant Ambassadeur* in the Centre commercial Touati (sign in Arabic only). Visiting the archaeological site, you have *Restaurant Le Capitole*, T466880, in the complex opposite the site (view over the ruins), eat for around 7Dt. Snacks are available downstairs in the courtyard.

Eating

There are shops, a bank, téléboutique and post office at Sbeïtla. International telephone calls can also be made from the complex opposite the ruins.

Directory

A detour from Sbeïtla to Sbiba

Colour map 3, grid A2 Sbiba is really only a destination for enthusiasts who will find interest in the scattered ruins of **ancient Sufes**. Sbiba is a minor village 39 km north of Sbeïtla on a country road leading towards Dahmani. The site, close to the Oued el Hattab and protected by the Djebel Oust to the west and Djebel Mrihila to the south, survived into the early Middle Ages, probably due to its strategic position and the fertility of the soil. There are traces of strong Christian influence (two basilicas), the usual ramparts erected by the Byzantines, parts of which still stand, but perhaps the best remnants of this obscure site are to be found in the mosaics and statues on display at the museum in Sbeïtla.

Kasserine and ancient Cillium

Phone code: 77
Colour map 3,
grid A1/2

Kasserine lies 38 km southwest of Sbeïtla. Behind it to the west stands Djebel Chaâmbi (1,544 m), the highest peak in Tunisia. The ruins (very few) of the Roman town of Chaâmbi are here to the left of the road. **Chaâmbi National**

Sufetula

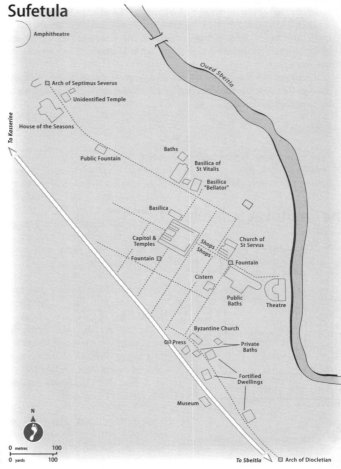

Amphitheatre

Oued Sbeïtla

Arch of Septimus Severus

Unidentified Temple

To Kasserine

House of the Seasons

Public Fountain

Baths

Basilica of St Vitalis

Basilica "Bellator"

Basilica

Capitol & Temples

Shops
Shops

Church of St Servus

Fountain

Fountain

Cistern

Public Baths

Theatre

Byzantine Church

Oil Press

Private Baths

Fortified Dwellings

Museum

N

Related map
Sbeïtla, page 299

0 metres 100
0 yards 100

To Sbeïtla

Arch of Diocletian

Golden oil

In the second and third centuries AD, while under Roman rule, the cultivation of the olive tree (oleo europeae sylvestris) spread through North Africa from Morocco to Libya. Oil 'factories' and stone olive presses can still be seen at certain Roman sites – for instance Sbeïtla.

In fact the method of harvesting and production has not essentially changed. Hitting the trees with sticks to make the fruit fall is harmful, and reminders are given on television at the harvest season. Tree-abuse harms the olives, letting in the air; the resultant oxidization reduces quality. The harvested berries are washed in tepid water then crushed. The oil is separated from the water by centrifuge, filtered, kept at a regulated temperature in airtight steel vats, then bottled. The older method incorporates rotating stone grinders, the resulting paste being fashioned into rings on esparto grass mats which are then squeezed by an animal turning the screw tighter and tighter. The resulting oils, dark and thick, are then purified.

In modern olive cultivation on the plains the trees are planted 10 x 10 m apart, leaving room for machinery, and yields reach 50 kg per tree. Traditional methods produce 15-20 kg per tree.

Around 90% of olive trees are in the Mediterranean Basin, leading oil-producers being Spain, Italy, Greece and Tunisia. Some of the finest table olives come from the Meknès region of Morocco. Tuscany considers itself to produce the best oil, Greece prides itself on Kalamat oil from the southern Peloponnese. Some oil is a clear yellow, some is thick and golden like honey. In some countries, they prefer to produce a more bitter oil.

In the 1980s, northern Europe woke up to the fact that olive oil, with its low cholesterol content, is good for the health, and bottles of the precious liquid marked 'extra-virgin' appeared on supermarket shelves. (Since when was anything, or anyone, been 'extra-virgin'?) It may be, however, that long, slow Mediterreanean lunches and siestas are indispensable to an olive oil-based diet, too.

Park protects the last of the mountain gazelles. Take the GP17 north from Kasserine and before the Oued Hattab turn left/west on the GP13. Five kilometres after crossing the railway look for a track to the left which skirts Djebel Chaâmbi and returns to the GP17.

The road from Sbeïtla to Kasserine takes you 38 km southwest across arid plateau lands. Esparto grass is all that really grows here and is the source of the region's livelihood – a cellulose-processing factory forms the industrial heart of Kasserine. More promisingly, the town stands at a very important junction and controls an important pass, a fact which didn't escape the Romans. In more recent times the American troops tried to hold the area from the German advance. The Oued Eddarb, tributary of the Oued el Hattab, is crossed between the junction and the town proper. There are plenty of banks, small and medium size shops, a chemist and a hospital. Kasserine is large enough to have two of the regulation issue square-faced clock monuments, confusing when getting directions, but the central monument is a hand clutching a few stalks of cereal (or is it esparto grass?). Bus and louages stop in middle of town. The main ruins are a good walk or a short taxi ride to the west, past two more interesting pieces of public art: an oversized concrete candle with garlands of apples, on a roundabout, and a Tunisian horseman, up on your left.

Cillium is the most important Roman site in this region, strategically located **Ancient Cillium** to control routes both north-south and east-west. Once the local nomads were subdued it was settled by the Romans. The site is on a plateau overlooking the Oued Derb, a tributary of the much larger Oued el Hattab. As the present town of Kasserine was built on the far side of the *oued* much of the site has been preserved though the necropolis was unnecessarily destroyed when the *Hotel Cillium* was built. So what is there to see? There are two mausolea which would seem to have given Kasserine its name (lit: 'the two palaces'). Next to the main road, there is the three-storey **Mausoleum of the Flavii**. On its main façade, Latinists will be able to pick out a long poem in memory of one Flavius Secondus. Further on is the distinctly ruined **Mausoleum of the Petroni**. Continuing on the road to Gafsa, just after the *Hotel Cillium*, you will see more confusing ruins (signposted), including the **Triumphal Arch** (third century AD) with a dedication mentioning the Colonia Cillitana from which the town gets its name. Also in the area is a **dam** on the Oued Derb and a number of small **Byzantine forts**.

Cillium was a fairly prosperous sort of place to judge from mosaics discovered there, some of which are now in the Bardo. These were found in houses which stood about 100 m west of the Triumphal Arch. Best known is a panel with Venus, surrounded by tritons, nereids on sea-monsters and putti on dolphins.

For those searching for finer details, the water for the baths was supplied from the *oued* and there is a small channel which leads from there to the baths. At present the water in the *oued* is some 50 m below the channel entrance, so no baths today.

Just 5 km south of Cillium, near the tiny settlement of Henchir el-Guellali, are the remains of a reservoir which supplied Cillium and the irrigation needs of nearby fields.

Sleeping
Kasserine has adequate accommodation for a one-night stopover

B *Hotel Cillium*, T474406, F473682. 5 km from town centre set among eucalyptus trees, just before the ruins en route from Kasserine, interesting 1960s circular design, 72 beds, large rooms have bath, 770 m above sea level, splendid views, pleasant (in an Eastern European sort of way) hotel, pool sometimes full, a/c, the prime address in Kasserine (although poorly maintained) and charges accordingly. Popular for lunches (7Dt), can organize wild-boar hunting in the vicinity. **C** *Hotel Pinus*, T470166, F470457, 13-room hotel near the *Total* station on the Gafsa exit from town. Rooms with shower and loo. Again, poorly maintained. **D** *Hotel de la Paix*, T471465, Av Habib Bourguiba, next to the *Shell* station. Just about acceptable. Washbasin in rooms, hot showers on corridor. **E** *Hotel Ben Abdallah*, next to the *Magasin Général*.

Youth hostel In *Kasserine*, 3 km from Kasserine centre, T470053. 92 beds, meals available.

Eating
If you're staying in town and don't want to head out to the *Hotel Cillium*, then you have the choice of cheap eateries in the town centre. Try *Restaurant Essnouber (Les Pins)* opposite the *Banque du Sud* on Av de la République. Standard Tunisian fare.

Transport
Moving on to Gafsa by louage will require changes at Fériana and Mejel Ben Abbès, each leg costing about 1.5Dt. Louages also run to Tunis, Sbeïtla, and Thala, but not as far as Le Kef. Tunis is a good 4½-5 hrs drive away, Le Kef about 2 hrs. The SNTRI has buses for Fahs, Gabès, Gafsa, Sbeïtla and Tunis.

Kasserine to Gafsa

Phone code: 77
The road runs across a high and lonely plateau, with Djebel Chaâmbi to the west/right. There are stretches of Aleppo pine, and occasional settlements. Before reaching **Fériana**, you pass faint traces of ancient Thelepte and some

pitched roof houses dating from colonial times. If you get stuck in Fériana try **E** *Hotel Mabrouk*, T485202, near bus and louage stop. In the future, if things continue to calm in Algeria, it may be possible to cross the frontier to visit the ruins of **Tébessa**, ancient Theveste, once an important legionary base.

Further on, **Mejel ben Abbès** has some interesting pieces of recent public art, including a wild grey leopard outside the municipality, and a sort of viking ship with an eagle prow and a giant figure seven in place of a sail.

Sfax   صفاقس

Sfax ought to be an entertaining Mediterranean city, and it certainly has all the right pieces: a historic old town with mosques and perfectly preserved walls, and a new town with boulevards and some fine pieces of neo-Moorish wedding-cake architecture. Once upon a time it was a multi-ethnic place, with large Jewish and European communities. But multiculturalism is not the buzz-word in today's Sfax. The city, second largest in Tunisia, is entrepreneurial and energetic. There are industrial zones, phosphate processing and olive oil plants – which give a characteristic odour to the air. None of this goes to make Sfax a magnet for tourists. The médina and the new town nevertheless merit a couple of hours on your way south (or north). And if you are heading for the Kerkennah Islands, the ferry runs from the port of Sfax.

Phone code: 74
Colour map 3, grid B6

Ins and outs

Sfax can be reached by rail and road. If you arrive in Tunis, and want to head south, the 4-hr train down to Sfax might be a good way to start your journey. Although slower than road, it avoids a trip down the autoroute in a lunatic louage. The airport, 6 km to the southwest, T241700, handles a few international and internal flights.

Getting there

The main SNTRI bus station is at the east side of Av Habib Bourguiba, in front of the train station. There is another bus station (SORETRAS) at the other end of Av Habib Bourguiba at Ibn Chabat, beyond the market, for services to Gabès and all destinations south. Louage station is nearby. Louages (Tunis-Sfax, slightly under 4 hrs) stop on Pl de la République. The airport is a 4Dt taxi ride, or take bus 14 from R Abou Kacem Chabbi, Bab Bhar (town centre). To get to the Kerkennah boat station, head down R Hédi Chaker, going away from the médina. Turn right, the boat station is 400 m on your left. If stuck in Sfax, you might want to go to the beach. Head for Chaffar, 13 km away from louage station at start of Rte de l'Aéroport.

Getting around

Oldest part of the new town is on a regular grid-iron pattern. Small cheap hotels are in the médina at Bab Diwan, easily reached on foot from train and SNTRI stations. It is a bit more of a trek from the louage station. Useful services: *UBCI* with ATM on R Abou Kacem Chabbi on new town grid, other key services on Av Bourguiba and around.

Orientation

Tourist office is just next to the ferry terminal for the Kerkennah Islands. More centrally, the **Syndicat d'initiative** is at Pl de l'Indépendence, in a little kiosk, T224606, often closed.

Tourist information

Those wishing, perhaps understandably, to avoid Sfax can use the clearly signed bypass (*rocade*) which skirts the town centre to the west. It is a dual carriageway with the main storm drain down the middle. There are numerous slow junctions with lights. In places it is three lanes wide and the turn to Sfax generally has a filter. Try to avoid getting into the wrong lane.

Bypassing Sfax

Central Tunisia

Background

With a population of well over 500,000, Sfax is the second-largest city in Tunisia and is an important agricultural, industrial and commercial centre. The older part of the city has, however, retained a lot of its charm. Sfax is a thriving city with a city centre composed of two distinct parts: the new town, built on a geometric pattern, and the médina, still surrounded by its original walls. It is a delight for tired visitors for it is absolutely flat.

The fact that the city is absolutely flat also explains the presence of mopeds. During the evening rush hour, thousands of these squealing mobylettes take their owners homewards. But by nine in the evening, the streets are empty. Sfax, a hard working city, goes to bed early. In the rest of Tunisia, the business sense (and the supposed avarice) of worthy Sfax's people are legendary. One of the country's biggest banks, the *BIAT*, is very much dominated by Sfaxians, and it is true to say that Sfaxians are active in all areas of the economy. Rumour has it that Sfax produces the best students although the cynics say that this is because, as soon as pupils show signs of failing, they are withdrawn from school to go into the family business. Solidarity across the extended family continues to play an important role in everyday life. So Sfax is not a town which offers much to the outsider. It has no pleasant eccentricities, no late night cafés or cabarets. Sure of its entrepreneurial capacities, the city of Sfax devotes itself to the making of money.

History

Sfax has its founding legend. The Arabic name of the town, Safakus, derives from the name of an Aghlabid prince's groom, Safa, and the Arabic verb *kus*, 'to cut'. "Cut, Safa," said the prince, "cut the cow hide into fine strips and mark out the limits of the city." This, of course, is a repeat of the myth which

Sfax Médina

	Sleeping				Eating
	1 Cheap Hotel Area		3 Habíb & Essaada		1 Café Diwan
	2 Ennaser		4 Médina		

Related map
Sfax, page 308

0 metres 100
0 yards 100

Very fishy

Today in Tunisia the sign of the fish is still a sign of a blessing. Look around now and see delicate pendants of gold and silver fishes in jeweller's windows, fish above shops, dangling fish rather than dangling dice in the taxi, fish-shaped amulets on babies' clothes, fish-shaped biscuits at a feast, fish motifs on mosaics and fish on every menu. After all, the fish was the symbol of early Tunisian Christians. In Sfax the bride and groom still step seven times over a large fish elaborately decorated with ribbons which is afterwards part of the wedding feast. Listen for the blessing Al hoot aleekum meaning the blessing of the fish be on you. For a country with 1,600 km of fishy coastline – why not?

recounts how Dido outsmarted the local tribes to found Carthage. More prosaically, however, it would seem that the name Safakus is of Berber origin.

There was an ancient town called Taparura on the site of present day Sfax, apparently with a strong commercial tradition. In the seventh century the town was already a trade centre, exporting olive oil to Italy. By the 10th century, Sfax declared itself an independent state, only to be conquered by Roger of Sicily in 1148. It later fought off the Venetians in 1785 and only surrendered to the French in 1881 after some fierce fighting, one of the few Tunisian towns to bother putting up any resistance at all. In the early years of French rule, the new Bab el Bhar neighbourhood replaced the old Rbat el Qibli, the Frankish and Jewish quarter A number of fine public buildings in the neo-Moorish style went up, including the town hall, with its minaret, the now-demolished municipal theatre, and the *Hotel des Oliviers*. A modern port was completed in 1891.

Bombardment during the Second World War destroyed a large part of the town centre. This created an opportunity to replan the city centre. Neighbourhoods close to the médina's walls were cleared. The resulting open spaces give central Sfax the feel of a Moroccan city, where new European areas were always built separately from the old médinas. The walls give a monumental feel to the boulevards.

Today, Sfax has Tunisia's second-largest port. Activities include exporting phosphates, and olive oil processing continues to be a major industry. The city has expanded far beyond the original dual core. Until the mid-20th century, Sfax was surrounded by orchards and market gardens, and every wealthy Sfax family would have its *saniya* or orchard, complete with summer residence (*borj*). The city is constantly expanding. To the north of the médina, the new quarter of Sfax el Jedida is nearing completion, dominated by the minaret of the Sidi el Lakhimi mosque.

Sights

Sfax probably has enough sites to keep you busy for a half a day, without rushing. In the new town, there is the Archaeological Museum and some nice bits of architecture; in the médina, likewise, there is a museum (Dar Jellouli), and more architecture, plus some interesting atmosphere and workshops.

The **Archaeological Museum** (T229744) is on Place Hedi Chaker, off Avenue Habib Bourguiba, housed in the town hall building with its mock minaret. This small museum of seven rooms displays Islamic, early Christian and Roman exhibits, mostly mosaics, manuscripts and pottery. There is a third-century Roman painted funeral artefact. ■ *0900-1200 and 1500-1830 summer, 1400-1730 winter, closed Sun. 3Dt.*

Central Tunisia

The **médina** is one of the best preserved and most authentic in Tunisia. Unlike the souks of Tunis and Sousse, it is primarily aimed at the locals, who do a lot of their shopping there. Many artisans and craftsmen still work here and earn a living in a traditional way. This all makes the médina very interesting for visitors, particularly as its walls are still intact and the difference in atmosphere between the old and new cities is clear. You should try to visit the **Dar Jellouli** museum, climb up onto the battlements at the **kasbah**, and have a look at the **Great Mosque** (from the outside).

Visiting the médina Entering the médina by the main gate, **Bab Diwan**, there are two roads leading straight ahead, the Rue de la Grande Mosquée to the left, and the Rue Mongi Slim, on the right. You could head straight up the Rue de la Grande Mosquée, and have a look at Sfax's oldest mosque, situated bang in the middle of the médina. You might catch some glimpses of the interior, closed to non-Muslims, then continue down Rue des Etoffes, which merges into Rue des Teinturiers. Within the Souks, one can find everything from clothes and meat to saddles for donkeys. At the end of this street are the city walls and the Rue des Forgerons (blacksmiths). Opposite is the **Bab Djebli**, a gate looking over a recently built market, where food is generally sold – worth a visit. In the Rue des Forgerons, artisans can be seen at work in cramped workshops. Go back in the direction you crossed the médina, but on the Rue Mongi Slim. There are some fine doorways here. This street takes you back towards

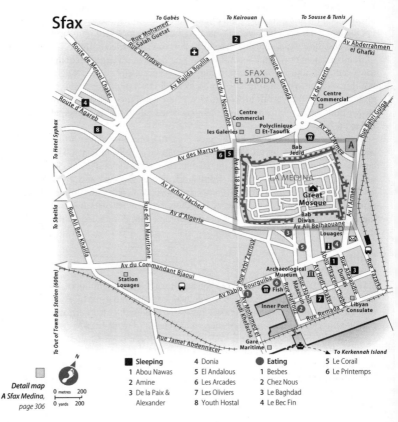

Sfax

Central Tunisia

Detail map
A Sfax Medina,
page 306

0 metres 200
0 yards 200

■ Sleeping	4 Donia	● Eating	5 Le Corail
1 Abou Nawas	5 El Andalous	1 Besbes	6 Le Printemps
2 Amine	6 Les Arcades	2 Chez Nous	
3 De la Paix &	7 Les Oliviers	3 Le Baghdad	
Alexander	8 Youth Hostal	4 Le Bec Fin	

Bab el Diwan. Take a left onto Rue de la Driba and on the left is the **Dar Jellouli Museum**.

Also of note is Place de la Kasbah, to the west of Bab Diwan. The **kasbah** itself is of no great interest, but there is a beautiful private building on the square. In the streets leading into the médina from here notice the iron grilles on the first floors of most houses. Also notable is a beautiful 17th-century private house on Place Barberousse.

The main gate of the médina, **Bab Diwan**, dates back to 1306. However, it was reconstructed in the 17th and 18th centuries. The last reconstruction was after the bombardments of 1943.

Médina monuments

Dar Jellouli, T221186, is a fine city residence dating back to the 17th century and now housing the **Regional Museum of Popular Arts and Traditions** at 5 Rue Sidi Ali Nour, off Rue de la Driba. On the ground floor the rooms are organized around a small courtyard. Each contains well-explained life-size pictures of traditional Tunisian living. In one room is a kitchen complete with implements, in another living rooms with all the furniture and so on. On the first floor is a display of traditional clothes and jewellery. ■ *0930-1630, except Mon and public holidays. 2Dt.*

The **Great Mosque** was built in the late ninth century, and altered in 988 and 1035. From the outside you can have a look at the minaret, made of three superimposed square sections. There are similarities with the minaret of the Great Mosque of Kairouan. There is far more decoration, however, including horizontal bands and religious inscriptions. Unfortunately, the interior is closed to non-Muslims. As elsewhere, there is a large courtyard, which is considerably smaller than it once was, part of it having been built upon during an extension of the prayer hall. On the eastern outside façade of the mosque are some niches decorated with a tooth motif. Can the influence of the Norman dog-tooth style be detected here?

Essentials

Sfax does not have a vast range of hotels. For the budget traveller, there are some cheap options located close to each other in the médina. Going slightly more upmarket, there is a scattering of handy places in the new town. **Médina** Cheap hotels here are grouped just inside the main gate, Bab Diwan, on R Borj Ennar (first street on your right after you enter via Bab Diwan) and on the R Mongi Slim running straight ahead into the old town. Many of these cater to an exclusively male, local clientele. A hot shower will cost extra in most of these places. **D** *Hotel Ennaser*, R des Notaires, inside the médina via Bab Jebli or Bab Jedid, T299919, F221037. Clean, renovated. Parking nearby outside the walls. **E** *Hotel El Habib*, R Borj Ennar, T221373, 22 rooms, clean, communal showers. Most rooms with washbasin, fan, some with loo. Downside? Noisy, not that clean. **E** *Hotel Essaada*, R Borj Ennar, T220892, opposite *El Habib*, 43 beds, small, clean. Communal showers. Just about OK. **E** *Hotel Médina*, 53 R Mongi Slim, T220354. 32 beds, small, clean, pay shower, on the noisy side.

Sleeping
■ *on maps, pages 306 and 308 Price codes: see inside front cover*

Ville nouvelle The *Andalous* and the *Arcades*, 2 useful mid-range hotels, are located northwest of the médina and are easily located as you drive in from the north. The remainder are south of the médina in the original ville nouvelle. Most charming address? Probably the renovated *Hotel Les Oliviers*. **A** *Hotel Abou Nawas Sfax*, Av Habib Bourguiba, T225700/1, F225521, abounawas.sfax@abounawas.com.tn 115 rooms, 8 suites, built 1987, very little character, all mod cons. Not the best the Abou Nawas chain has to offer. **B** *Hotel el Andalous*, Blvd des Martyrs, T 405406, F406425. A 1990s place

Central Tunisia

Visiting El Djem and Sfax in the 1920s

"About El Djem is no trace of the city that once sent its tens of thousands of shouting spectators to the games, that gave rise to the mighty coliseum that now alone remains. The gaunt relic stands, solitary, and native huts have nested in its broken columns and porticoes.

A little overwhelmed you turn toward Sfax – think of a city called 'Cucumber'. But cucumbers are a lordly vegetable in the East, quite worthy to name a town. Gardens spread about its walls. It is a merry town, this Cucumber, a garrison town, full of gay uniforms and their attendant brightly gowned ladies. No wonder there are beauty salons in the square, henna plantations close by, and groves of almonds for protection salves. A

garrison town where all the colourful Colonials are seen at their most resplendent. Chasseurs d'Afrique, in sky blue tunics and voluminous scarlet trousers. Swaggering Spahis with crimson capes to the ground. Black Tirailleurs from Senegal in high tarboosh and khaki – all the welter of savage tribes that serve the tri-color of France. Patrols just in from the desert mingle with their nomad friends in an irresistible jumble. Here, at his best and his worst, you may see the horse dealer and learn of the ways of that marvel, the Arab horse, for the army takes great pride in its cavalry and rightly so."

From a 1923 brochure entitled Tunisia, *produced by the French Line (Compagnie générale transatlantique).*

handily located for parking and exploring the old town. 90 a/c rooms, bar, 2 restaurants, on busy street but quiet inside and in rear rooms, free underground parking. **B** *Hotel Les Arcades*, Blvd des Martyrs, T400700, F405522. Next to the *Andalous* and equally practical and comfortable. **C** *Hotel Alexander*, 21 R Alexandre Dumas, T221911. Fairly well kept, 30 rooms, clean, good restaurant with lunchtime menu. Is there now a sign in Latin letters? **C** *Hotel Les Oliviers*, Av Habib Thameur, T225188. Charming, 50 rooms, old style, currently undergoing renovation – reopening soon? **C-D** *Hotel Etoile*, 9 R Mohamed Jamoussi T296091. West of médina, handy for gare routière and louage station. 16 well kept rooms, 5 with bath, remainder with washbasin. **D** *Le Colisée*, R Taieb M'Hiri, T277800, F299350. 40 rooms with bath, a/c, heating, restaurant. **E** *Hotel de la Paix*, R Alexandre Dumas, T296437/221436. In new town, 30 rooms, pay showers, very clean. Good value, next door to *Hotel Alexander*.

Elsewhere B *Syphax Novotel*, Rte Soukra, T243333, F245226. 127 rooms, 65Dt a night, low season. Recommended. **C** *Hotel Amine*, out of town centre on Av Majida Boulila (go right the first main ring blvd as you come in from Tunis), T245601. 40 rooms, has been recommended. **C** *Hotel Donia*, Rte de l'Aéroport, T247391, F223594. Used by tourist groups. Minus? A fair walk to the médina.

Youth hostel On the airport road, close to *Hotel Donia*, T243207, 126 beds, train station 1 km.

Eating
● *on map, page 308*
Note that most cheap restaurants are closed by 1900

Expensive *Le Baghdad*, Av Farhat Hached, T299173, F298108, fine Tunisian food, if a bit expensive. Around 35Dt a head. Sfax's number 2 restaurant. Try the *kamounia* or the fish soup. *Le Corail*, Av Habib Maazoun, T210317, F227301. The top address. Very comfortable restaurant, excellent seafood, very expensive, you could pay as much as 50Dt a head. Good value, nevertheless. *Le Printemps*, 55 Av Habib Bourguiba, T226973. Fish a speciality, a more European style cuisine. **Mid-range** *Chez Nous*, R Patrice Lumumba, near port, open Sun evening, alcohol served. Acceptable. For lunch try *Le Bec Fin*, opposite Hotel Abou Nawas, T221407. Clean, good Tunisian food served in large, simple restaurant. **Cheap** *La Renaissance*, 77 Av Hedi Chaker, T220439. Choice of fish and

Central Tunisia

meat dishes, clean. Other cheap eateries nearby. There are a number of very reasonably priced eateries just inside Bab Diwan.

For a **drink** go to Pl de l'Indépendence and the surrounding streets, or to the médina. **Cafés** Recommended is the *Café Diwan*, on the left after the main gates (Bab Diwan), following the walls. Nice terrace with views. Pleasant in the evening.

Markets Central Market on Av Habib Bourguiba. Fish markets at Bab Jedid, to south- **Shopping** west of town, and Rte de Gabès/Av Farhat Hached. *Monoprix*, 12 R Abou el Kacem, open daily 0800-1900.

Bahri Travel Agency, 32 bis Av Habib Bourguiba, T228654. *General Voyage*, Av Hedi **Tour operators** Chaker, T221067. *Siwar Voyages*, 26 bis R Habib Thameur, T226400. *Tourafrica*, Av Hedi Chaker, T229089. *Tunisia Line Service*, 16 R Habib Maazoun, T296983. *Univers Tours*, Av Habib Bourguiba, T222029.

Long distance Air: airport, T241700, is about 6 km southwest on the road to Gafsa. **Transport** **Train**: information on T222364, 221999. Departures for **Tunis** (via Sousse), **Gabès** and **Metlaoui** (via Gafsa) 0143. 2nd-class return Sousse 7Dt plus 650 mills fee each way. Takes 2 hrs. **Bus**: services for **Gabès, Djerba, Zarzis, Tataouine, Ben Ghardane** and **Tunis** leave from the bus station on Av Habib Bourguiba, by the train station. Information on T22355. All other destinations are served from the bus station at the other end of Av Habib Bourguiba. **Louages**: leave from Pl de la République. **Ferry**: information on ferries for the **Kerkennah islands** can be found in the back pages of *La Presse*. Departures more frequent in summer, 1st boat leaving at 0500. Winter 4 boats per day 0700-1700. Foot passengers 0.5Dt, motorbikes and cars 4Dt; crossing takes just over 1 hr. For further information contact *Sonatrak*, Av Hedi Khefacha, T222216.

Airline offices *Tunisair*, 4 Av de l'Armée, opposite Post Office, T228028, F299573; **Directory** *Air France*, R Taieb Mehiri, T224847. **Banks** *UBCI* (ATM) and *Banque du Sud*, R Abou el Kacem Chebbi. *STB* on Av Hédi Chaker has ATM for Visa and Mastercard users. **Car hire** *Avis*, R Tahar Sfar, T224605; *Budget Immeuble Taparura*, T222253; *Europacar*, 40 R Tahar Sfar, T226680; *Hertz*, 47 Av Habib Bourguiba, T228626; *Locar*, R Habib Maazoun, T223738; *Mabruk Car*, 46 R Mohammed Ali, T297064; *Rent a Car*, R Habib Maazoun, T227738; *Solvos*, R Remada, T229882. **Communications** Post Office: large building at east end of Av Habib Bourguiba, T224722. **Fitness centre** *Samorail*, Rte Sidi Mansour, near beach. **Medical services** SAMU: For emergencies contact the SAMU on 190 and 241894. Chemist: all night, *Rekik*, 25 R Alexandre Dumas. *Kilani*, Av Habib Bourguiba, T220740. **Hospital**: *Hôpital Hedi Chaker*, Rte d'El Aïn, T244422. *Polyclinique Ettaoufik*, T241105. **Places of worship** Catholic: 4 R Dag Hammarskjold, T210253, Sat 1830 and Sun 0930. **Useful addresses** Customs: R Mongi Bali, T229184. **Police:** R Victor Hugo, T229710.

Central Tunisia

The Kerkennah Islands

Phone code: 74
Colour map 3, grid B6

Little has happened in history to disturb the tranquillity of the Kerkennah Islands. They are flat, planted with palm trees, and somnolent. The legend goes that they are named for the nymph Circe who had a try at keeping Greek hero Odysseus here during his Mediterranean travels. Other famous exiles on Kerkennah include Hannibal and Habib Bourguiba. There are two main islands, Gharbi (western) and Chargui (eastern), a few hotels, and rumour has it that further tourist development is on the way. Until then, the Kerkennah Islands go quietly about their business. The people are welcoming in a reticent sort of way, and you could have a pleasant few days on the archipelago, cycling, birdwatching, and splashing in the shallows. Note that Kerkennah is one of the few places on the planet where you can buy stretches of sea.

Ins and outs

Getting there Daily crossings from Sfax, 6 in summer, 4 in winter (ticket 560mills). Crossings take 1¼ hrs. For information contact *SNTKS*, Av Hedi Khefacha, Sfax, T498216, F497496. Most hotels in Sfax have ferry timetables available, or you can look in *La Presse* (back pages). In Kerkennah the ferry lands at Sidi Youssef, at the southwestern end of Gharbi, about 20 km from the hotel zone. As you leave Sfax on the *loud* (ferry), you have a good view of the city, and you may even see some dolphins.

Getting around The 2 main islands are linked by a Roman causeway. A minibus service is provided and will meet the incoming ferries, though this costs more than the service bus. A bus will go directly to the hotels, so be sure to take the right one! All buses go to Remla. For El Attaya, there are a few buses a day, but they tend to stop early, so check the times. Buses for the ferries leave about an hr before ferry departure time. Times can be checked at the bus station in Remla, beside *Hotel el Jazira*. All other hotels should have this information. Otherwise, rent a bike (try *Hotel Farhat*) – the islands are very flat.

Central Tunisia (side margin)

Kerkennah Islands

Background and history

Just 20 km from the Tunisian mainland, the Kerkennah archipelago is made up of seven low-lying islands, none higher than 13 m, occupying a total area of 15,000 ha – 6,000 ha devoted to farming, 4,000 ha of palm trees and the remainder barren salt flats. **Gharbi**, to the west, and **Chergui**, to the east, are the twin large inhabited islands. The people live largely off fishing and, to a lesser extent, tourism which is just developing. The hotels are concentrated around the *zone des hôtels* in **Sidi Frej**, with a few in **Remla**.

The rest of the island is almost untouched, making it quite easy to 'get away from it all'. A good way to get around is to rent a bicycle from one of the hotels. Some of the beaches are difficult to get to without transport as the buses only go through the main villages. The inhabitants have the reputation of being the most hospitable in Tunisia. As there are few sights on Kerkennah, activity is restricted to lying on the beach and taking life easy. In Remla it is possible to visit a carpet factory, without the anxiety of sales pressure as here they don't sell, but ship them to the mainland for retail.

Beaches & islets

The Mediterranean round the Kerkennah Islands is extremely shallow. At low tide it is possible to walk for several kilometres out into the sea from the islands, the water lapping round one's ankles. At high tide, the water rises up to chest height – in places. So expect to do a lot of paddling rather than swimming. Unfortunately, the beaches are a little disappointing, tending to be made up of gravel and pebbles rather than sand. The more interesting beaches are at Sidi Fankhal, near Remla and Bounouma, between Abbassia and Chergui on the northwest side of Chergui Island. From **El Attaya**, at the northeastern end of Chergui, you could find a fisherman to take you over to the islet of **Gremdi**, aka Camel Island, as a local keeps his small herd of camels there from time to time.

Fishing on Kerkennah

The shallowness of the sea around Kerkennah has led its people to develop unique fishing techniques. The island's men have a great reputation as skilled fishermen, being recruited by mainland fishing fleets and also teaching apprentices sent to Kerkennah how to fish. When the men are out at sea, it is the women who continue fishing off the islands, using some unusual local methods – they also ensure that the land gets cultivated.

Kerkennians own sections of sea. Using palm branches and fronds, they construct fences out into the water which form a sort of hedge, curving or zigzaging away from the coast. At high tide, shoals of fish swim in between hedge and beach. When the tide goes out, it becomes impossible for them to swim back, and they are stuck in the increasingly shallow water, where they take refuge in special fish-traps (*drina* in Arabic, *nasse* in French). Another fishing technique, primitive but fairly efficient, involves a team of people and a sort of floating barrier made of *dhriaâ* sea weed (*Posidonia oceanica*). The team walks slowly through the shallows, moving away from the coast, each individual pushing a floating section of twisted seaweed. The frightened fish swim back landwards between the individual fishers. A kilometre from the shore, the team turns backwards, gradually moving closer together. The fish are trapped in the shallows. Fishing for octopus is another activity, the beasts unwisely taking up residence overnight in specially planted pot traps. Once, sponge fishing was important on the islands.

Fishing on Kerkennah has suffered considerably since the early 1990s. Pollution and competition from other regions are the main culprits. In the

Central Tunisia

early 1990s, pollution, possibly caused by phosphate processing in Sfax and Gabès, had severe side-effects, leading to a sharp reduction in the fish stock. It is also thought that the Cap Bon fishing fleet, under severe competition from Italian boats illegally fishing with more sophisticated methods in Tunisian waters, has begun to fish further south, in areas traditionally fished by Kerkennah's people. Modern trawling methods are harmful. The heavy weights used on trawler nets rake up the sea bottom, destroying the weed, source of food for the fish.

If you want to go out fishing, many fishermen, for a small fee, will take a passenger with them. It is also possible to rent a *felouka* (traditional fishing boat) with a captain and go either for a day trip round part of the island and probably a quiet lunch out at sea. ■ *Prices 12-15Dt for a half-day per person. Information for these trips at either El Attaya, a small fishing village in the north of the island, or at one of the two larger hotels, the* Grand Hotel *or the* Hotel Farhat, *in Sidi Frej.*

Sights

Kerkennah has little in terms of sights. Up at the northeastern end of Chergui, there used to be a small museum commemorating Bourguiba's escape by *loud* (traditional fishing boat) to Libya in 1945. You can see the shack he hid in and his boat. The *Festival des Sirènes* takes place in August.

Birdwatching Keen birdwatchers will find some points of interest on Kerkennah. It has a unique sub-species, Thekla's crested lark, or *cochevis de Thekla i*. There are lots of great grey shrikes but no birds of prey. It is also a place to observe migrant cranes (Fr: *grue cendrée*). Whereas this bird is practically never seen out of shallow water, on Kerkennah it can be seen among the palm groves.

Essentials

Sleeping **C** *Appart-Hotel Aziz*, Sidi Frej, T 215884. Self-catering an option. **C** *Grand Hotel*, Sidi
Many hotels are closed Frej, T281266, F281485. Large hotel, 114 rooms on 2 floors, half with sea view, a/c din-
in winter and those ing room, pool, tennis, organized watersports, cycle hire, nightclub, beach restaurant,
that remain open are open all year. Has the best stretch of beach at Sidi Frej. **C** *Hotel Farhat*, Sidi Frej,
often poorly heated T281240, F281237. Next to *Grand Hotel*, 308 beds, well decorated, pleasant, pool, tennis, beach virtually non-existent. **D** *Hotel Cercina*, Sidi Frej, T281228, F281262. Very
good, beach, 70 beds, half rooms have bath, most rooms are bungalows, some have
sea view, restaurant has typical Kerkennian fish specialities. **F** *Hotel el Jazira*, Remla,
T281058. Well kept, small, 24 rooms, communal bath/toilet, bar, good restaurant open
all year but cold in winter. Try also the unclassified *Aziz*, 88 beds, T259405, F259404;
and *Kastil*, 32 beds, T281212. **Youth hostel** Remla, just behind the stadium, T281148,
80 beds, meals available, family room. **Camping** El Attaya.

Eating **Mid-range** *Restaurant La Sirène*, T481118, by the bank in Remla, very good fish and
seafood, alcohol available, shaded terrace. **Cheap** *Le Régal*, at El Attaya, north of
Remla, by the harbour, very good simple, cheap food, welcoming owner. Try the special Kerkennah sauce of tomato and garlic which is excellent on shellfish.

Sport All **watersports** including windsurfing and octopus fishing, horse- and camel-riding
and tennis. Try a camel ride from Sidi Frej to the ruined tower at Borj el Hissar.
Yachting El Attaya has berths for 10 yachts, minimum-maximum draft 3-4 m.

Ferry Office on Av Hedi Khefacha, Sfax, T498216, 497616, F497496, frequent ferries **Transport**
summer 0600-2000 about every 2 hrs and winter 0700-1700 4 return journeys. Car 4Dt,
passengers 0.570Dt, motorbike 1.250Dt.

Banks *UIB* in centre of Remla, beside *Hotel el Jazira*. **Communications** Post Office: **Directory**
centre of Remla, T281000. There are a few other branches, the closest to the hotel zone
being in Ouled Kacem. **Medical services** Chemist:: *Behiri* in centre of Remla,
T281074. **Hospital**: Remla, T281119. **Useful addresses** Police: in Remla and El
Attaya, T281053. **Maritime police**: Mellita, T223615.

Northwards from Sfax to El Djem

Taking the much improved GP1, Sfax to El Djem is 64 km. The road runs   *Phone code: 74*
through farming land. At the ribbon settlements along the way (petrol sta-   *Colour map 3, grid A5*
tions, cafés and small shops), slow right down and look out for 'sleeping
policemen'. About two thirds of the way to El Djem, the village of **El Hencha**
has grown to a good size and even has a small industrial zone as well as the
usual shops and car repair outfits. Here and there, as the road rises, you have
views across vast olive groves. Note that slow moving heavy goods vehicles
can make this stretch of road fairly frustrating.

Routes southwards: Sfax to Gabès

Heading south of Sfax on the GP1, you enter road-movie territory, passing   *Colour map 3,*
through an industrial zone with a tentacular phosphate works covering the   *grid B4*
land between the road and the coast. Then it is flat landscape all the way to
Gabès. There is little dual carriageway, so if driving you will be faced with
thundering lorries and louage drivers with suicidal tendencies.

The saltpans of the region immediately south of Sfax are of interest to birdwatchers. At 10 km south of Sfax, the Roman ruins of **Thaenae** near present-day Thyna, fairly well signposted, are of minor interest. There is a sign at the
south end of Thyna pointing to the land between the coast and the road. Follow
the track through a small agricultural area to the coast beside the lighthouse.

Thaenae was at the coastal end of the line marking the limit between   **Ruins of**
Numidian and Roman territories. It has suffered from thoughtless pillage and   **Thaenae**
the necropoli on the town's periphery were 'turned over' for profit. Later
excavations produced evidence of a huge square enclosure having a side over
2 km long with semicircular towers. Baths were discovered nearer the coast,
and it was suggested that the bathing facilities, originally of individual ownership, had been changed into public use. Mosaics and painted frescoes are
recorded. The Baths of the Months, excavated in 1961, had walls several
metres high, roofing with groin and barrel vaults. There were some notewor-
thy mosaics but to cheer the workers a treasure hoard of gold coins was discovered dating back to the third century AD. The better objects were taken to
the Bardo and to Sfax Museum.

Maharès

The roadside town of Maharès, 24 km south of Sfax, has a reputation for pub-   *Phone code: 74*
lic art. From the four-lane main street (Avenue Habib Bourguiba, as usual),   *Colour map 3, grid B5*
metal fun structures can be seen on the beach-side gardens. On a long car
journey, children will appreciate a stop to have a look at the reconstructed

Central Tunisia

skeleton of a small whale in the sculpture promenade near the harbour. There are numerous petrol stations, car and tyre repairers, metalworkers, mini-supermarkets, chemists, and bakers. A new mosque is set back at the south end of town while the older mosque is right on the road.

Market day is Monday and the carpets for sale in large quantities are laid out along the harbour wall. All very colourful. Should you have time for a swim, prefer the beach at Chafaar, 15 minutes' drive away (head north out of Mahares, turn right after level crossing, follow the track).

Sleeping　**C** *Hotel Marzouk*, Av Habib Bourguiba, T290261, F290866. 20 rooms, pool, clean, good restaurant for evening meals, café, snacks all day, pleasant management. **C** *Hotel Tamaris*, Av Habib Bourguiba, T290950, F290494. Next to *Hotel Marzouk*, 60 beds, popular with safari tour groups.

Eating　Try the *Caféteria du Festival* for a break from driving, or eat at the *Hotel Younga*.

Transport　Public transport for Sfax leaves from next to *Hotel Younga*. There is a train station inland, with 2 trains a day for destinations north and Gabès, and 1 train to Gafsa/Metlaoui.

Skhira

Phone code: 74
Colour map 3,
grid C4
Skhira, 45 km down the GP1 (and 42 km north of Gabès), has southern Tunisia's largest oil terminal. The town is a major junction. For those heading north, there is the choice of the GP1 for Sfax and the coast, or the inland GP2 direct to Kairouan. (The latter is usually fairly clear and avoids the painful business of driving through the suburbs of Sfax.) Skhira has cafés and small shops on both sides of road. Petrol and car repairs available. The agriculture here consists of beans and moderate grazing land. Perhaps there is more money to be made out of selling food and drink to passing lorry drivers.

Southwestern Tunisia

7

Southwestern Tunisia

*In southwestern Tunisia, the landscapes are arid and often spectacular. There are canyons and a vast low-lying region of salt lakes, the **Chott el Djerid**. Beyond this is the colossal Sahara desert. At oasis towns with poetic names like **Tozeur, Nefta** and **Douz**, civilization's hold over nature becomes distinctly shaky. Once upon a time, life depended solely on the palm tree and pack animals, whose survival was possible thanks to painstakingly managed spring-water. From the palm tree, the region around Tozeur takes its name, 'El Djerid', 'palm' in Arabic. Like the Nefzaoua, to the south of the Chott el Djerid, this area is best visited in spring or autumn, when the great vault of the desert sky is clear and temperatures are lower. (In high summer, temperatures of 50°C are not uncommon.) The date harvest finishes in early winter, and there is a festival in Douz. Today, southwest Tunisia is easily visited by car and public transport. (There are also some ersatz 'safaris' by four-wheel drive running from the main coastal resorts.) But the peace of the desert is best experienced by travelling by camel. From remoter settlements like **Zaâfrane** it is sometimes possible to head off with a local guide to explore the white dunes of the **Grand Erg Oriental**.*

The Djerid and the Nefzaoua

Heading down from the Sahel, **Gafsa** is the first oasis town you come across. With its backdrop of arid hills, it provides a foretaste of the barren landscapes to the southwest. The Djerid and the Nefzaoua regions have a range of spectacular scenery a few hours' travel by road from the crowded towns of the Sahel. Vast salt flats, the **Chott el Djerid** and the **Chott el Fedjaj,** divide the area in two. The Djerid, to the north, centres on the important oasis town of **Tozeur,** strategically located at the western end of the Djebel Cherb and north of the Chatt el Djerid. A regional capital with an expanding tourist industry, Tozeur sits 22 km east of **Nefta**, important as a centre for the cult of Islamic saints until the mid-20th century. Here again there is an old oasis, set in a deep natural hollow surrounded by cliffs.

Hill villages & phosphate towns North of Tozeur and Nefta lies the **Chott el Gharsa**, and within an easy day trip distance of Tozeur (60 km north), close to the border with Algeria, is a hilly area, just west of the Djebel en Negueb, with the much touted mountain oases of **Chebika**, **Tamerza** and **Midès**. From Chebika there are superb views westwards. The old village of Tamerza has been abandoned but there is an upmarket hotel. Midès is perhaps the most attractive of the three, its abandoned village overlooking a deep gorge. The oasis is still very much under cultivation. You can continue east from the hill oases to the phosphate towns of **Redeyef** and **Moularès**, joining the main GP3 road at Metlaoui, from where it is 42 km east to Gafsa and 50 km southwest to Tozeur.

Douz & dune desert In the old days, crossing the Chott el Djerid was a risky business. Today the 86 km from Degache, close to Tozeur, to Kebili are fully tarmacked road. There is little risk of tourist buses being swallowed up in the great salt waste, as was the case for caravans in earlier times. South of the Djerid is the **Nefzaoua**. **Kebili** is the regional capital, **Douz** is the second largest town, scene of an annual Festival of the Desert in late December. The east-west range of the **Djebel Tebaga** separates the Chott el Fedjaj from the arid lands to the south. In the Nefzaoua, you are at the eastern edge of the **Grand Erg Oriental**, the true dune desert of heroic films. The oases appear as tiny spots of green in a white sand waste – a 'leopard skin' in the eyes of the region's poets.

Changing lifestyles Both the Djerid and the Nefzaoua have felt the impact of the modern world. The process began back in Protectorate days when the French made Kebili an important base. Today, the pure nomad lifestyle is very much a thing of the past. The attractions of a settled life are too great and the government has made efforts to stabilize the nomads and enable them to enjoy the benefits of modernity. Although you can still see old-style oasis cultivation with vegetables and fruit trees growing in the shade of great palms, the region has vast new agri-business oases, notably near Nefta and at Rejim Maâtoug, where the succulent Deglet en Nour, 'finger of light', dates are cultivated for export.

In the 1990s tourism arrived in a big way with new *zones touristiques* at Douz, Nefta and Tozeur. The expensive Saharan hotels have found it difficult to break even, however, as visitors come in overnight rather than stay a week. Nevertheless, the tourist is now very much part of the local scene. At the main sights, you are as likely to see large numbers of visitors, decked out in mock-Touareg dress, as you are to see real nomad tents. The desert lifestyle of the M'razig and the Adhara, perfectly adapted to a difficult environment, did

Things to do

- Near Tozeur, visit the cliff-top village-oasis of **Midès** and the sites where *Star Wars* was filmed.
- Bathe at the tiny hot spring of **El Hamma du Djerid** near Tozeur.
- Take a stroll in the village of **Old Kébili**.
- Travel out into the desert by camel from **Zaâfrane** near Douz.
- Visit the cave-dwellings of **Matmata**.

not survive the 20th century unadulterated, but it could yet provide the basis for a new, ecologically friendly tourism based in the local communities. For the moment, four-wheel drive safaris are the main 'product' on offer.

Gafsa قفصة

Gafsa may well be your first taste of a southern Tunisian town. Not quite the desert, it nevertheless has the midday somnolence of a desert settlement. You approach Gafsa from the northeast via a long straight road shaded with eucalyptus, followed by a view of the deep course of the oued Baïech. The modern town centre has an undistinguished Eastern Bloc feel to it, but the médina with its narrow streets and doorways feels suitably ancient, though decay and demolition have set in. However, there is the superbly restored Dar Loungo to visit, and the Piscines romaines. André Gide in crumpled linen suit can be imagined watching the local lads diving from a great height into the ancient waters if restoration work on the pools has been completed.

Phone code: 76
Colour map 3, grid B2
Population 60,000

Southwestern Tunisia

Ins and outs

Getting there Gafsa is very much a meeting of the ways, and coming from Sfax, Kairouan, Kasserine or Gabès, you will no doubt pass through Gafsa on your way to and from the Djerid. The train station is 3 km east of town in the new suburb of Gafsa Gare. Buses and louages come into the main square, in front of *Hotel Gafsa*. If you are driving, you are 369 km from Tunis, 149 km from Gabès, and 93 km from Tozeur. Once you get beyond Kairouan, the P3 is a quiet road. Note, however, that after heavy rains, there may be flooding on the plain around Bir el Hafey (30 km northeast of the P3/P13 junction), which could mean a detour, approaching Gafsa via Sbeïtla, Kasserine and Feriana, on the P13 and P15 over higher plateau lands to the west.

Getting around Shared taxis to and from the train station terminate in the town centre next to the *Hotel Maamoun*. The old town is easily explored on foot in an hr or less, depending on your level of interest in vernacular architecture.

Orientation Coming in from the Gabès or Tunis direction, after crossing the bridge, you hit a confusing sort of junction after the *Agil* petrol station. The bus station is on your left, followed by a small park. (Opposite the market is on the right.) First right takes you down to the R Ahmed Senoussi where there are some small eateries and the *Hotel Gafsa*. If you are driving on to the Djerid, head straight along the main drag, past a large mosque on left and *Hotel Khalfallah*, right, to a junction where you go left and follow straight through to leave Gafsa for Tozeur.

Tourist information The tourist office is by *Piscines romaines* at the end of Av Habib Bourguiba, T221664. Little written information, but very willing to talk, open 0900-1700 in winter, summer opening hours vary with siesta.

History

Gafsa (Roman Capsa), the most northerly of the oasis towns, is also the chief town of the southern steppe region. It stands at the junction of the P3, P14 and P15, the crossroads between southwestern Tunisia and the central plains. Gafsa has a long history going back to prehistoric times. A Proto-Mediterranean people left traces of a civilization referred to as Capsian by archaeologists. The main find in the Gafsa area has been mounds of waste composed mainly of snailshells – hence the French technical term *escargotière* for this kind of prehistoric remains. Capsian Stone Age tools can be seen in the Gafsa Museum.

Gafsa comes into written history with the Romans. Capsa was an important town on the road linking the III Augustan Legion's base at Haïdra to Gabès on the coast. Although some way back from the southern frontier or *limes* controlling tribal movements, it had a role as regional tax collection centre. Under the Byzantines, the fortifications were developed and Capsa was renamed Felicissima Justiniana (why not?). For a short while it was capital of the province of Byzacium. It fell to the invading Arabs in 668. Any trivia quiz on Gafsa should include a question on its 12th-century inhabitants: Arab historian El Idrissi reports that they spoke a Berbero-Latin, and that many were still Christian. This is surprising, given the supposed impact of the 11th century invasion by Hilali Arab tribes from Egypt.

Gafsa

■ Sleeping		■ Eating
1 Ali Pasha	4 Gafsa	8 Maamoun	12 Tunis	● Eating
2 El Bechir	5 Hedili	9 Moussa	13 Youth Hostel	1 Patisserie & Café
3 Ennour	6 Khalfallah	10 Oasis		2 Semiramis & Les
	7 La Lune	11 République		Ambassadeurs

Gafsa made the headlines with another rather more mysterious invasion in 1980. A commando troop of 300 exiled Tunisians came from Libya and captured the city. It took the army three days to dislodge them. The reasons for the choice of Gafsa remain unexplained. Was the town's seizure related to a general climate of unrest in early-1980s Tunisia? Did the organizers think that Gafsa was ripe for rebellion, its people discontented as they were not seeing any benefits from the phosphate industry? Suffice to say, the question is never discussed today, and only finds a mention in the pages of obscure guidebooks. Late 1990s Gafsa, like the other secondary towns in Tunisia, saw public money going into new infrastructure: a higher technology college was opened, and a conservation area plan for the old town was drawn up.

Sights

Gafsa is not the most picturesque of places and a lot of tourists heading south on landrover safaris just pass through. This is a working city, with a fair amount of employment in the phosphate industry – and a lot of unemployment, too. There is no artificial zone for tourists, built on tour operator money and state subsidy. Nevertheless, Gafsa has a small but interesting historic centre, largely abandoned by the original inhabitants, and a couple of attractions – the Roman pools and the restored Dar Loungo. It is interesting to see what an everyday southern Tunisian town looks like, especially if you are going on to the over-touristed oasis towns of Tozeur or Douz. For most visitors, a couple of hours will be enough to do the main sights of Gafsa.

If you just wander in the old quarter, you will eventually come across most of the historic sights of Gafsa. Proceeding in a more orderly manner, you could head down the Avenue Ali Belhaouane, passing the *Hotel de l'Oasis* on your right. Second turn right will lead you to Dar Loungo, on your left. Continue down the street and you will come to Roman pools, a museum, and the arcades of Dar el Bey. The Kasbah is just beyond, off the Avenue Habib Bourguiba. **Old quarter**

The restored **Dar Loungo** gives you an idea of what a patrician residence of the 18th/19th centuries looked like. There is an entrance passage, lined with seating, and no doubt the clients and tenant farmers of the master of the house would wait here to be received. Inside there is a large courtyard, and some splendid apartments upstairs. There are good views over the town from the roof terrace. Dar Loungo may become open to the public with tickets; for the moment, though, you need to hope that there is a warden around to let you in. (*Où est le gardien?/wayn el assas?* you could ask.)

To reach the **Piscines romaines** (Roman baths) turn left out of Dar Loungo. They are some 50 m away and consist of two deep rectangular pools. Nearby there is an ancient but none too salubrious hammam. These pools are the only major building to have survived from Roman Capsa. In the summer, youths jump from the side into the water. The diving used to be even more spectacular when there was a particularly tall palm tree overlooking the pools. Watch the diving, but remember that a tip may well be expected. Young Gafsans have played this game since the dawn of tourism. The square surrounding the pools has recently been carefully redeveloped and has a small café. The tourist information office and the small museum are also here. At the time of writing, there were works underway to improve the pools. The water level had fallen, so maybe they will be returned to their former glory. ■ *0800-1200 and 1500-1900 summer, 1930-1630 winter, closed Mon, 1Dt.*

The **Museum** of Gafsa has the sort of local artefacts you would expect, along with two absolutely superb mosaics of sporting activities. The better one shows an athletics tournament from start to the prize-giving ceremony. ■ *0930-1630, closed Mon.*

Near to the pools, on Avenue Habib Bourguiba, is the **Kasbah**, which from a distance looks like a splendid fortress. It was built by the Hafsids, on the foundations of the usual Byzantine fortress. Under the energetic Ottoman beys, it was partly rebuilt in 1663: artillery bastions were added, and the curtain walls adapted to firearms. There were further major works in the 19th century. Unfortunately, in 1943, ammunition stored in the Kasbah exploded, destroying one side. The **Palais de Justice**, which fits into part of the site, was built in 1963. Note that under the walls of the Kasbah, there is a tiny ancient hammam.

Oasis   The oasis starts just beyond the Kasbah, and has over 100,000 palm trees and numerous pomegranate and some citrus trees. Follow the extension of Rue Ali Belhaouane into the oasis. This is a pleasant ride/walk with numerous side turnings. The direct road through the oasis emerges at the P3 about 7 km west of town. The dates are of poor quality, and the oasis is better known for its fruit trees and vines. The pistachios and apricots are among the best in Tunisia.

Essentials

Sleeping   There is little choice in the way of accommodation in Gafsa. Cheap hotels are concen-
■ *on map,*   trated behind the bus station, Av Ali Belhaouane. If you have no pressing interest in the
page 322   town's limited sights, it is probably best to soldier straight on down to Tozeur.
Price codes:
see inside
front cover   **B** *Hotel Jugurtha*, 4 km west of town, in the oasis of Sidi Ahmed Zarroug which is now a built-up suburb of Gafsa. Still closed? An impressive site, 78 rooms, pool, tennis, to be upgraded after renovation.

C *Hotel Maamoun*, Av Taïeb Mehiri, T224441, F226440. Central, modern, relatively nondescript building, 46 a/c rooms, pool, restaurant used by tour companies, indifferent service but all mod cons. Very handy for louage station but little else to recommend it. **C** *Hotel Gafsa*, R Ahmed Snoussi, street behind cinema parallel to main street, close to market and louage station, T224000, F224747. Modern, East European style, 5-storey block, lift, a/c (check it works), some satellite TV. Handy for restaurant *Semiramis*. **C** *Hotel Khalfallah*, Av Taïeb Mehiri (the main drag), by police station, T221468, F229800 A little expensive for what is provided, some rooms with satellite TV and hot shower. Adequate.

D *Hotel Moussa*, Av de la Liberté, T221333. Clean and cheerful, on your right as you leave town in the Tozeur direction. Small brick-faced building, carpark. Street-facing rooms noisy. A long walk from bus station with lots of luggage. **D** *La Lune*, R Jamel Abdel Nasser, T222212. South out of town on left beyond *Maamoun*. Has a good reputation.

E *Ennour*, Av du 13 Février 1952, T220620. Very cheap, outside showers, close to bus station. **E** *Hotel de la République*, Av Ali Belhaouane, T221807. Quite new, clean, 20 rooms, probably the best of the cheap hotels, sig-posted in Arabic only. Other hotels worth trying are: **E** *Ali Pasha*, 4 R Ali Belhaouane, T220231, which is more than adequate. **E** *El Bechir*, 40 R Ali Belhaouane, T223239. Reported as 'cosy'. Rooms on the small side. **E** *Tunis*, Av 2 Mars, T221660. Overlooking Pl du 7 novembre and very near to bus station, perhaps a bit too near. Also try *Hotel de l'Oasis*, on Av Ali Belhaouane, T222338. Handy for the bus station.

Youth hostel *Centre d'hébergement pour jeunes*, 2 km from bus-station, T224468. Kitchen, meals provided, 56 beds, small 5-bed rooms, north side of Av de la Liberté, turning right beyond *Hotel Moussa* as you come from town.

Camping *Camping La Galia*, T229135, F229165, clean, modern campsite in the oasis, signposted from centre.

Eating
● *on map, page 322*

Mid-range *Restaurant Semiramis*, R Ahmed Senoussi, T221009. By *Hotel Gafsa*, one of the best places in town for French and Tunisian cooking, expensive for what it is. Opposite is the *Restaurant Les Ambassadeurs*, signs in Arabic only, dining upstairs. If all else is closed. **Cheap** *Pizza Tony*, down a side-street near the Semiramis. Has it kept its alcohol licence? *Restaurant de Carthage*, on the main square. Basic Tunisian fare. Try also the *Restaurant du Paradis*, Av Taïeb Mehiri, opposite the *Hotel Maamoun*.

Entertainment

Hammam There is a clean hammam on R Hassouna Ismaïl, women till late afternoon, men from late afternoon till 2000. Try also the hammams on or near the R Houcine Bouzaïane as you head for Pl Pasteur.

Shopping

Handicrafts The craft school set up by the ONAT to train people in the art of carpet making is signposted at the top of the Av Bourguiba. May be possible to visit the workshops. Gafsa has a reputation for flat-weave hangings with geometric designs.

Transport

Airport 3.5km southeast of town, T273700. No scheduled flights to Tunis. **Bus** Bus station is by the main square, just off the Av du 2 mars. Information on T221587. Frequent departures to **Tozeur** and **Nefta**, also buses to **Kairouan, Sfax, Sousse, Gabès** and **Sbeitla. Tunis** 0730, 1030, 1230 (4Dt). Bus info: SRTG, T220335, SNTRI, T221587. **Louages** Av Abou el Kacem Chabbi. (Turn left at the *Hotel Mamoun* coming from the town centre, the louage station is sort of behind the hotel.) **Train** The station is rather inconveniently situated 3 km outside the town in the suburb of Gafsa Gare, along the road to Gabès. One train daily at 2056 goes on to Tunis (via Sfax and Sousse) and 1 to Metlaoui at 0526. Information on T270482.

Directory

Banks On main drag, Av Taieb Mehiri. NB At time of writing, there were no ATMs in Gafsa. **Communications** Internet: Cyberspace, opposite police station, T227830. Post Office: Av Habib Bourguiba north of the kasbah. **Medical services** Regional Hospital: R Avicenne, T225055/177 **Places of worship** Catholic: Chez les Soeurs, Quartier Doualy, T223785. Ring for details of services.

Gafsa to Sfax

The road south out of Gafsa crosses the **Oued Sidi Aïch** and turns northeast. The road to Tunis continues in this direction while that to Sfax takes a right turn. Just at this junction is the **wildlife park**, very popular in the evening and at weekends. Visitors at other times may find the gates firmly locked. Here gazelle and ostriches roam in enclosures. There is a small café.

Colour map 3, grid B2-6 Gafsa to Meknassy, 85 km; to Mezzouna, 109 km; to Sfax, 190 km

The P14 runs adjacent to the railway for much of the journey. Around **Zannouch** is a richer, government settlement area with expanses of plastic greenhouses and wells at intervals for the irrigation. This availability of water encourages plasticulture which is not perhaps the most economic return for such an expensive commodity.

East of Gafsa, scattered hamlets enliven the flat landscape. Esparto grass grows on the poorer soil. Journey times have been shortened considerably by major road works in 2001.

Southwestern Tunisia

Mirages – illusions in the desert

A mirage is a type of optical illusion, caused by the refraction (bending) of rays of light as they pass through air layers of varying temperatures and densities. The most common mirage occurs in the desert where what appears to be a distant pool of water, perhaps surrounded by palm trees, turns out, to the disappointment of the thirsty traveller, to be only another area of dry sand.

The rays of light that come directly to the eye show the palm trees in their correct position. The rays of light that travel through the warmer, less dense air travel faster as they meet less resistance and change their direction. They bend nearer to the ground, but are assumed to have come directly to the eye so the brain records the trees and the blue sky as reflections in a pool of water.

The rays are real, just misinterpreted, thus a mirage can be photographed; but that does not, alas, make the shimmering 'water' available to quench the thirst.

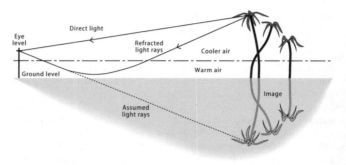

Sened **Sened Gare** is a ribbon settlement that has grown up along the road near the railway station. Djebel Majoura (874 m) stands to the north. Old **Sened**, aka **Sened Djebel**, is up in the hills about 10 km to the south. Coming from Gafsa, the turn-off is first right after the petrol station. Take the metalled road for about 100 m, then bear left, sports ground on left. After 70 m, with house with red tiled roof on left, bear right and follow track (not to be taken after rain) towards mountains. Drive should take no more than 20 minutes. Most of the traffic will be mule carts. Sened Djebel nestles into the north slope of the Djebel Biada (1,163 m). The village is quite scattered, seemingly semi-ruined at first sight. There are white-painted marabouts and stone enclosures, a water point as the road climbs. Some of the houses are part underground, making use of caves cut into the rock. Latest news on the road across the pass to **Sakket** and **Guettar** on the south side of the hills is that improvement works are underway. For the moment, this is not a route for small hire cars.

Back on the GP14, about 3 km east of Sened Gare, where change of governorate is indicated, look out for railway lines which are raised well above the level of the road. These could cost a tyre or two if the road hasn't been improved. The road continues through rolling country, with the line of hills to the south. Then it drops down to land planted with olive groves. There are a few small settlements on the road – don't run short of petrol – there are few buses and few louages.

Maknassy Maknassy, 85 km from Gafsa, is the first settlement of size. The main street, Avenue Habib Bourguiba, is a dual carriageway and the main square is Place

'Come explore the oasis, my gazelle'

Metaphor for grace and beauty in classical Arabic poetry, symbol of speed on the tailfins of national carrier Tunisair, the gazelle is a rare animal in North Africa today. The main species is the Dorcas gazelle, rim in Arabic, easily distinguished by the black stripe along its flank, separating fawn back from pale underbelly. Within living memory, the gazelle could be found in the central steppes. The spread of settlement and cultivation, and above all hunting, have limited its range to the southern wastes. The gazelle is easily frightened, taking flight at the approach of humans. It is also known for its ability to shake off hunters, who then get lost in the desert emptiness without capturing their prey. Hence the unattainable, graceful gazelle becomes a metaphor for female beauty. Courtly Arab poets often refer to the eyes, neck, nose and gait of the gazelle in

descriptions of exquisite concubines. (The beautiful tourist may be addressed with a bonjour, la gazelle.) From gazelle horns, as from ram's horns, fish tails and pointed pieces of red coral, emanates protective force. Today, the hunting of the Dorcas gazelle is strictly controlled. Once upon a time, the nomads would rear gazelles. Captured young enough, the gazelle fawn becomes very tame.

Today, there are two national parks east of Gafsa: Djebel Bou Hedma, south of Meknassy, and Hadaj, where an attempt is being made to reintroduce the Dorcas gazelle into an unusual micro-environment, the last surviving area of natural savanah in Tunisia. Also included in the reintroduction programme are the oryx and addax antelopes, and the ostrich. Gazelle can also be seen at the Orbata Zoo outside Gafsa on the Tunis road.

des Martyrs complete with blue square-faced clock, chemist, post office and *Agil* petrol. There is a bus station with a café. The reasonable C83 road goes north from here to Sidi Bouzid, and a track suitable only for walkers or mountain bikes goes south round Djebel Bou Hedma to Bou Hedma National Park, though this is better accessed from Gafsa via the C124.

Bou Hedma National Park is an area of pre-desert steppe, where Dorcas gazelles, sabre-horned oryx, Addax antelopes and ostriches have been reintroduced. To visit, permission must be gained from the Ministry of Agriculture. Really determined visitors to this national park will have arranged this in Tunis at the Direction des Forêts on Rue Alain Savary (near the Belvédère Park) and have suitable transport available. Although the Tunisian press occasionally runs features on the park, for the moment it is far from being a major tourist attraction.

The road climbs out of the basin onto the edge of Djebel Bou Hedma and down to the next basin of olive cultivation and almonds. The road is straight and level, the pointed summit of Djebel En Nedjilet a feature on the right. At **Mezzouna**, 93 km to Sfax, the C89 cuts down south to Gabès and north to Sidi Bouzid. There is a railway station and basic facilities. In fact, the main road will not take you into Mezzoun at all. Next main settlement, 31 km further on, is **Bir Ali Ben Khalifat**, whence it is a straight 42 km run east to Sfax. Bir Ali Ben Khalifat has expanded rapidly, being at the intersection of the main route south from Kairouan, the GP2, which runs on south to intersect with the GP1 near Skhira. Watch out for 'sleeping policemen' as you arrive from the Gafsa direction. If you need to overnight, go right (south) for the large **C** *Hmaissa Relax Centre*, a hotel and café, very popular at lunch times, clean toilets, welcoming staff, with campsite opposite.

Water technology of yesteryear

Tunisia, like other North African countries, benefited in the past from the introduction of the khattara *or foggara (or mkeil as they are known locally in south Tunisia), which is an underground water channel that taps the water table in alluvial fans of hill areas. The technology was brought probably from as far away as eastern Iran or western Afghanistan in the medieval period, though Roman systems with well-engineered and large diameter channels also exist in Libya. Water can be transported to fields and villages over considerable distances. The* mkeil *in south Tunisia was formed by a narrow diameter inclined channel, with 20-30 m deep vertical shafts spaced at 15-20 m intervals for the removal of detritus during building or maintenance and for*

ventilation afterwards (see illustration). In the villages in El Guettar, located on the GP15 between Gabès and Gafsa, the remnants of the mkeil *can still be seen but are sadly not in current use.*

The mkeil *illustrates the virtues of traditional technology. It has a generally long life cycle. Once it has been completed, it will keep flowing, given adequate maintenance. It will run continuously day and night and, except in a few cases, throughout the four seasons. The* mkeil *needs no power other than that provided by gravity. The* mkeil *is a friendly influence on the water table.*

Despite these major advantages, the mkeil *and its traces, as with so many other kinds of traditional technologies, are now at great risk of complete extinction.*

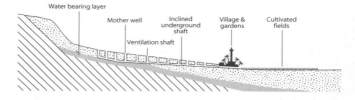

Water bearing layer

Mother well

Inclined underground shaft

Ventilation shaft

Village & gardens

Cultivated fields

Gafsa to Gabès

Colour map 3, grid C2-4 Running southeast out of Gafsa on the GP15, you reach Gabès after a drive of 146 km via El Guettar and Sidi Mansour. A possible stop is the oasis of **Lalla**, clearly signposted to the east of the road, 5 km out of Gafsa. Turn left after crossing the railway track. This thriving oasis community is a pleasant contrast to the bustle of Gafsa and very popular at weekends. **Lares**, 18 km from Gafsa (turn off south on a good surfaced road), is much quieter. The oasis is planted with a mixture of palm, olives, figs, almond trees and prickly pear hedges. The road through the oasis rejoins the main road after 5-6 km.

The C124 goes off east at **El Guettar**, taking advantage of the lower land between the Djebel Orbata and the Djebel Ank, and is a road of variable quality. There is a turn-off for the isolated village of **Sakket** 13 km from El Guettar. **Djebel Bou Hedma National Park** is 63 km from Gafsa.

El Guettar   El Guettar is a small settlement of about 15,000 inhabitants on the foothills of the Djebel Orbata (1,165 m). It owes its existence to the unusual (for Tunisia) system of water supply to the oasis. Water trapped within rock layers in the foothills was led by gravity to the oases. At one time 28 *khattara* were recorded providing 5-6 litres of water per second, and this supply was shared between the fields on a six-hourly basis. The system no longer functions, though in places remnants of the shafts to the underground channel can be seen.

At 37 km out of Gafsa along the GP15, there is a turning south to Kebili (68 km) across the Chott el Fedjadj. It is wise to check this road (C103) is open after the winter rains, some parts are very low-lying; 56 km across the Chott you reach the tiny oasis of **Stiftimia** where there are hot springs.

Gafsa to Kasserine

In Gafsa, at the junction with the square-faced clock, take the road north to Kasserine. At **Barroucka**, on the left, set well back off the road, is a huge ornate mosque. The road runs close to the Oued el Kebir, with open plain used as grazing land on the east and Djebel Bou Ramli (1,128 m) to the south-west. There are a few settlements on the road. At 32 km from Gafsa you cross the Oued el Kebir which is very, very wide. It is hard to imagine such a valley full of rushing water. The only settlement of any size is **Maajen Bel Abbès**, which has developed due to its position by the railway station. It has some spectacular pieces of public art, including a galley with eagle prow and a leaping leopard.

Colour map 3, grid A/B2

The road and rail now run parallel all the way north to **Fériana** (72 km from Gafsa), a long narrow rural settlement with petrol stations and the usual small shops.

Sleeping

F *Hotel Mabrouk*, T485202, in town centre, directly opposite bus station and adjacent to louages.

Fériana to Kasserine

There are Roman ruins on the west side of the road just south of Thélepte; the ruins and the village have the same name. There is not much to see except ruined walls of dressed stone. Thélepte itself has a splendid air of decay. Some of the original bungalows remain, and with their pitched roofs would not look out of place in a French suburb. From Fériana to Kasserine there are very few settlements, an expanse of sparse grazing land, cereal, fruit trees and olive plantations. Djebel Chaâmbi, Tunisia's highest mountain, can be seen to the west.

Into the Djerid: from Gafsa to Tozeur via Metlaoui

From the square-faced clock at the centre of Gafsa, take the road west to Tozeur, 93 km to the southwest. A junction to the north should indicate *Hotel Jugurtha*. At 7 km from town, the road from the oasis joins on the left. The route is pleasant, lined with stands of young eucalyptus trees. After crossing the Oued el Melah (Salty River), the major *oued* of the region, the railway accompanies the road and the *djebel* on the right and gradually closes in until Metlaoui is reached, 42 km from Gafsa.

Colour map 3, grid B2-C1

Metlaoui
Phone code: 76

Thanks to the phosphate industry, the village of Metlaoui has grown into a minor regional centre. Unless you chose to stop, you will see little more than ribbon development along the busy tree-lined main road. Elsewhere, in the shadow of conveyor belts and industrial buildings, the visitor can spot French-built staff houses with their pitched roofs. After the hospital, over the railway line up the Moularès road, there is the **National Mining Museum** (*Musée national des mines*), recently revamped, housing various fossils and prehistoric remains.

By the railway station, there is a restaurant and a number of small cafés used by tour buses and safari four-wheel drive vehicles. There is a large

Southwestern Tunisia

mosque with a striking bright green dome at the centre, and all the usual facilities, including petrol and chemists. The bus station and louages are in the town centre. At the square-faced clock is the junction with the road running north to the mining town of **Moularès** and the **hill oasis towns**, as well as to the station from which the Lézard Rouge/Red Lizard train departs. Here too you will find the STB bank, a chemist, the police and *Restaurant Ellafi*.

Sleeping Two newish hotels on main road. **D** *Hotel Ennacim* ('the breeze') is out of the town centre on the Tozeur side, T241920. 18 rooms, extra for a/c or heating. Restaurants and bar.

Eating At the *Hotel Ennacim* or the *Restaurant Ellafi*.

Transport **Louages**: run out of a station up the Moularès road. **Train**: the station is to the east of the town. One train daily to **Tunis** (via Gafsa and Sfax) at 2045; **Redeyef** at 1555. **Lézard Rouge/Red Lizard**: *Galilée Travel*, which deals with trips on this tourist train, is located left of the entrance to the main station, details below.

Seldja Gorges Once through the town the junction west to the **Seldja Gorges** is clearly signed by the *Mobil* petrol station. At this junction is *Café Seldja*, busy when the tourist coaches arrive.

The gorges, with their sandstone cliffs rising to 200 m in places, are best seen from the train to Moularès and Redeyef which departs daily from Metlaoui. You could take the ordinary train, advertised to leave at 1505 for Moularès and Redeyef at 1555. Far more appealing, though more expensive, is to take the **Lézard Rouge**, or Red Lizard, a restored former royal train complete with original fittings, now used for touristic purposes. ■ *It does the journey in about 2 hrs and leaves daily at 1100, except Mon, 20Dt. A fascinating trip, often booked-up in advance. Information from* Galilée Travel, *T241469, F241604, or Tunis office, T71799634. The train doesn't run if there aren't enough people. Both trains return to Metlaoui at 1830.*

You can also access the Gorges by car. Leave Metlaoui on the GP3 heading for Tozeur, and take the track right across the plain for 5 km until you reach a narrow defile called the *coup de sabre*, the 'sword cut'. Walk through into the Gorges. There are two narrow tunnels. It is best to do this in the morning before the temperature gets too high. Note, however, that this is a potentially dangerous activity – you don't want to be caught in a tunnel by a speeding phosphate train. The Oued Seldja is also subject to flash floods, so the gorges are best left alone after heavy rains.

Continuing south to Tozeur, the GP3 is a well surfaced road which does however have some bends and dips. Watch your speed, and do not overtake on a continuous line. The Garde nationale will be just around the corner ready to pull you over. This region is still used by the nomads and their black tents and grazing dromedaries can on occasion be seen out on the barren plain.

Tozeur توزر

Capital of the Djerid, Tozeur is everybody's ideal oasis. There are thousands of palm trees, and a chance to see a disappearing rural way of life in action. In the narrow streets of the old Ouled el Hadaf neighbourhood, the houses have patterned façades carefully executed in narrow mustard brick. Many of the women still wear an all-enveloping black wrap, decorated with a white band. Tourism has come to stay in Tozeur, with Landrover safaris from the coastal resorts and vast hotels overlooking the oasis. This is not Marrakech, however. It is all rather low key and few stay more than a couple of nights, but Tozeur is a good base from which to explore the region. With a hire car or by public transport you can reach Nefta and the hill oases, and at El Hamma du Djerid you can enjoy a bath with the locals at the hot springs.

Phone code: 76
Colour map 5, grid A1

Ins and outs

Tozeur is accessible by air and road. You can also get the overnight train from Tunis and Sfax as far as Metlaoui, then complete the remaining 93 km journey by bus or louage. The bus station on Av Farhat Hached is used by buses from Tunis, Nefta, Gafsa and Kebili. The louage station is opposite.

Getting there

The airport is 4 km out of town, with taxis generally available for the short run to the nearby *zone touristique*. Bus and louage stations are 800 m from the *Hotel Splendid*, other cheap hotels being nearer. Turn left out of the bus station onto Av Farhat Hached, then right onto Av Bourguiba.

The town is easily explored on foot. The central area (Av Bourguiba plus old quarter Ouled el Hadef) is linked to the upmarket tourist hotels by the 1,500-m long Av Chabbi, along which is a sprinkling of other hotels.

Getting around

The tourist information office is *ONTT*, Av Abou Kacem Chabbi, close to *Hotel Jerid*, T454088/503.

Tourist information

History and background

Tozeur is strategically located between two seasonal salt lakes or chotts, the vast Chott el Djerid, to the south, and the Chott el Gharsa to the north. Human settlement here goes back at least to Roman times, no doubt because of the abundant water close to the surface. The small oasis settlement of Bled el Haddar has a minaret built on Roman foundations, and is thought to be the site of Roman Tusuros. Tozeur was conquered by the Muslim Berber dynasties which came out of Morocco in the early Middle Ages. It was the key town in a region known as Kastiliya, perhaps from the number of abandoned Roman forts or *castella*. Tozeur basically remained an independent statelet, until brought under Hafsid rule in the later Middle Ages. The village was dominated by rivalry between different groups, which often erupted into open feuding. In the 18th and 19th centuries, Tozeur was the final stop on the bey's annual tax-gathering expedition or *mahalla*.

Under the Protectorate, Tozeur remained an independent minded sort of place. Charles Lallemand, propagandist for French rule in the late 1800s, noted that there was little interest in modern education, unlike the rest of Tunisia where demand was huge. Traditional forms of learning remained strong, and it is hardly surprising that the town produced Abou Kacem Chabbi, romantic

Southwestern Tunisia

poet who wrote of love and freedom and was adopted as Tunisia's national bard after independence. (See 30Dt banknotes for his portrait.)

Managing the oasis

Traditionally, the oasis was the mainstay of Tozeur life. Dates were the basic crop, while fruit trees and vegetables were grown in the shade of the palms. A carefully worked-out system ensured irrigation water for all. Written by one Ibn Chabbat back in the 13th century, the regulations were designed to avoid wasting the oasis's scarcest resource, water. Water was channelled from the spring into the palm groves to irrigate the trees and market gardens. Water flowed along hollowed-out palm trunks and out through holes which were blocked with clay when the allotted irrigation time was over. Time was calculated by means of a *kadouss*, a water container with a hole in it which took just over an hour to empty. Each landowner would be allotted so many *kadouss* units.

To support more modern lifestyles, water needs have grown dramatically – and the water table has fallen in the oasis. The precious fluid is thus pumped up from deep underground. Thanks to the increasing depth of the boreholes, the area of palms under cultivation has been expanded. The new *périmètres irrigués* (see the Ibn Chabbat area south of the Chott el Gharsa) are planted with high quality date palms. The traditional cultivation and labour systems have given way to advanced agri-business. Dates, harvested early, are now even ripened artificially in ovens to prepare them for export to the European Christmas market.

Tourism in Tozeur

Tozeur is now well established as the political and commercial centre of the Djerid. With its new international airport it is starting to develop a significant tourist industry, and hotel developers benefit from considerable state subsidies and preferential loans. Of course tourist development has a social dimension, too. Bringing large numbers of visitors to Tozeur, both local and international, is a way of showing the conservative oasis people that they are part of Tunisia's republic and its values, that women can actually go around unveiled outside films.

Tozeur centre

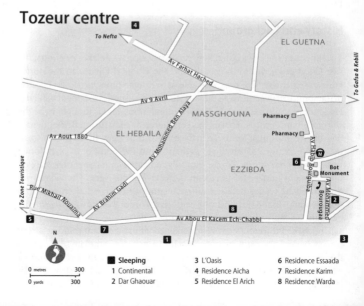

Sleeping		
1 Continental	3 L'Oasis	6 Residence Essaada
2 Dar Ghaouar	4 Residence Aicha	7 Residence Karim
	5 Residence El Arich	8 Residence Warda

The difficulty for the hotels is to try and build a clientele prepared to stay more than a couple of nights. Many of Tozeur's visitors at present just stay overnight as part of a four-wheel drive excursion round the South. To attract people with money and taste for the exotic, *à la Marrakech*, Tozeur will need some proper restaurants and smaller, classier hotels. The development of more intelligent, less tacky attractions would also be a step in the right direction. Developments such as the planned Jardin des 5 Continents – basically a themed oasis garden designed by top French landscapers – will help Tozeur build a reputation as something more than just a stopover.

Sights

To cover the sights of Tozeur, you will probably need little more than a day. Two days would allow you to really take in the atmosphere of the oasis, while with three days you could do a trip to the other main Djerid town of Nefta, 25 minutes down the road towards Algeria. Another day-trip, easily done with a hire car, takes you up to the hill oases (*les oasis de montagne*) of Chebika, Tamerza and Midès. Four days in Tozeur and you will really be unwinding, your body clock slowing to the rhythm of oasis life.

The town

Tozeur is a three-street sort of place. The Avenue Farhat Hached (bus and louage station) takes traffic through the town. The Avenue Abou Kacem Chabbi runs along the edge of the oasis, and has some of the older tourist hotels. The Avenue Habib Bourguiba, with its arcades and market, links the two. Here are the main cheap hotels and restaurants, and male Tozeuris come out for their evening paseo here. In Ramadan there is some mild animation on the market place.

Central Tozeur is rendered exotic by local **brickwork** on the arcades, strung here and there with colourful klims – and by the town council's recent improvement scheme. There are large onion-shaped wrought iron grills along Avenue Abou Kacem Chabbi, and some moderately dramatic pieces of **public art**, not least of which is an oversized fountain-type structure on the market place. Irrigation expert Ibn Chabbat, water-saver extraordinary, must be turning in his grave.

The Ouled el Hadaf neighbourhood

North of the Avenue Habib Bourguiba is the Ouled el Hadaf neighbourhood. (Turn left off Av Bourguiba before the market into Avenue Ibn Chabbat.) Down this street on the right, follow Rue de Kairouan (signposted to the museum) which passes under an arch. This is the oldest part of the town with many archways and intriguing side streets. Some of the houses date back to the 14th century. They are decorated with geometric patterns executed in earthen bricks in an elaborate style particular to this region. Notice that few houses have windows onto the street, light for the rooms coming from a central courtyard. The doors are decorated with nails and three door knockers. The explanation (for tourists?) is that the one on the left is for women, on the right for men and the lowest for children. Each knocker emits a different sound, that is deeper for men, enabling residents to recognize who is at the door. Sounds fair enough.

The small **Museum of Popular Arts and Traditions**, housed in the former Zaouia of Sidi Aissa in Rue de Kairouan, has some interesting displays. Everyday objects are on view, giving insight into daily life in Tozeur. There are diverse objects, including traditional clothes for celebrations, jewellery, oil lamps, cooking implements and weapons. Also on show are manuscripts written by Ibn Chabbat in the 13th century, setting out the complex water

Southwestern Tunisia

distribution system in the oasis. In the courtyard you can see one of the doors with the three knockers. The museum, though simple, has a certain charm, and shouldn't be missed. It certainly tells you more about a vanishing way of life than the ersatz Dar Cheraït. ■ *0900-1200 and 1500-1800 summer, closes 1700 winter. Closed Mon. 1Dt includes services of guide.*

The Oasis Tozeur's raison d'être is of course the oasis. It is beautifully fresh in summer, due to the large number of irrigation canals fed by more than 200 springs. Get there by following the signposts to the 'Jardin du Paradis' or take the road leading to the Belvédère, on the left after the tourist office. If the peace of the oasis is to be appreciated the well advertised tour by *calèche* is to be avoided. Problems with water supply and neglect have resulted in the loss of some of the palm trees.

One oasis activity is to take a dip in one of the springs. Ras el Aïn is well known, a spring emerging at 30°C at the foot of a low buff. (The water flow may have fallen off considerably with hotel development.) Water from the springs is subsequently diverted for irrigation. The oasis definitely merits exploration: vegetation is surprisingly dense and the palm groves large enough to enable you to escape the crowds.

The name the **Belvédère** suggests a large cliff overlooking the oasis. In fact, you are dealing with a couple of large boulders, which do however give you some nice views over the palms and the arid plain and salt flats beyond. At night the Belvédère boulders may be illuminated to provide a view for those in the *zone touristique* hotels. The road to the Belvédère (3 km) goes through one of the most picturesque parts of the oasis. It is a long, but nevertheless very pleasant, walk starting on the left along Avenue Abou Kacem Chabbi, beyond the tourist office, and following the oued.

Zoos Tozeur has three establishments with caged animals, **Le Jardin du Paradis**, the **Zoo du Désert** and the **Zoo de Tijani** (once a snake farm). The Jardin du Paradis is through the oasis (about 3 km), following the well-signposted road which starts just before the *Hotel Continental.* (The Zoo du Désert is just next door.) The Zoo de Tijani is near the old train station. At the Jardin du Paradis, the camel may perform, swigging Coke straight from the bottle. They also do some unique natural syrups. Flavours include pistachio, rose and pomegranate. Next to the Jardin is the Zoo du Désert (■ *0800 till dusk, entry 1Dt*), with examples of desert animals and reptiles including snakes and scorpions. Beasts in both places are kept trapped in minute cages. Hell for animals, basically, in the gardens of Paradise.
■ *0800 till dusk, entry 1Dt.*

Heritage sights At the end of the Av Abou Kacem Chabbi, the road veers to the right. The *zone touristique* begins here, and on your left is the **Dar Cherait Museum**. Dar Cherait is easy to find: look for the groups of parked tour coaches just beyond on the left or the tourist-trap shops on the opposite side of the road. This private museum is located in a mock-up of an upper-crust Tunis house, a sort of cross between Dar Lasram and Dar Ben Abdallah, the Museum of

Dar Cherait Museum

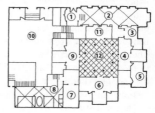

1 Entrance	7 Koranic school
2 Reception hall	8 Hamman
3 Wiseman's chamber	9 Ladies' chamber
4 Bey's chamber	10 Art gallery
5 Kitchen	11 Glassware room
6 Bridal chamber	12 Courtyard

Popular Arts and Traditions in Tunis. The displays are clearly inspired by those at Dar Ben Abdallah, and there are areas set up as kitchens, living rooms and even a hammam. There are some very flashy pieces of Damascus furniture with mother-of-pearl inlay, and some highly decorative firearms. There is also a small collection of modern Tunisian painting. ■ *0800-2400. 3Dt, photography fee 1.5Dt, video recorder 10Dt.*

The display rooms are located round a spacious central courtyard, complete with star-shaped fountain and an L-shaped hallway that opens onto a grand staircase. Grand houses in Tunisia's main cities had a number of vestibules, the greater the family's importance, the greater their number. Suppliers and tradesmen never progressed beyond the first, distant relatives would reach the second, but only very close friends and members of the family would reach the last which opened out on to the patio. Of the display rooms, the old-fashioned kitchen is of particular interest. Kitchens of this kind, with wood or charcoal used as a source of heat, were common 50 years ago. The red-copper utensils, each with a special role, were made in Kairouan.

In addition to the main museum area, Dar Cheriat has some Disneyfied attractions, including a tacky Arabian Nights grotto and a '3,000 years of Tunisian history' experience. Love it or hate it, nowhere else in Tunisia offers such a concentration of processed heritage. It is disappointing, however, that the same effort has not been put into presenting the culture and history of the Djerid region.

Essentials

In Tozeur, there is cheap accommodation in the town centre or along the R Abou Kacem Chabbi, or something altogether more plush in the recent *zone touristique (ZT)*. Budget travellers should try to reserve ahead, especially at end of year. In coming years, look out for new, discrete upmarket guest-house type accommodation in the *palmeraie* and the small Ouled el Hadaf neighbourhood.

Sleeping
■ *on maps, pages 332 and 336*

Zone touristique AL *Hotel Dar Cheriat*, T454888, F454472, 85 rooms, credit cards accepted. Too big to be intimate, but tacky decoration adds a certain charm. Styles itself as Tozeur's premier address. Good sized rooms, pool, tennis. **AL***Hotel Palm Beach Palace*, T453111, F453911, palmbeach.tozeur@gnet.tn Has neither beach nor that many palms for an oasis hotel. An upscale establishment, nevertheless, with entrance fountain decorated by artist Rachid Koreïchi. Impeccable. Highly recommended if you have the funds, all the top people who come to Tozeur stay here. **AL***Hotel Palmyre*, T452040, F453470, 101 rooms. At the far end of the ZT. Well decorated reception area, architecture uses local features. Terrace and pool with view, hammam, too. Services said to leave something to be desired for a hotel at this price. **A** *Hotel Abou Nawas*, T452700, F452686, tozeur@abounawas.com.tn With 93 beds, one of the nicest hotels in the reliable Abou Nawas chain. Good price reductions at quiet times of year. Pool, terrace overlooking palmgroves. **A** *Hotel Ksar Rouge*, T454933, F453163. On the right after the *Palm Beach* as you head uphill along the ZT road. 111 rooms large rooms. Definitely one of the best appointed ZT hotels, rather more tasteful than most. Built on 3 levels with views over the oasis. Few palm trees, however. Indoor and outdoor pools, tennis courts. A good address if there is a special seasonal offer. Managed by *Eldorador*. **A-B** *Hotel Ras el Aïn*, T452003, F452189. 63 rooms, heating and a/c. Hammam video room. Check out half-board rates. Is this still Club Med territory? Pleasant grounds with lots of green, next to the oasis.

B *Hotel Basma*, T452488, F452294. 88 rooms, one of the simpler hotels, rooms with showers, small pool. **B** *Hotel El Hafsi*, on the left as you head up the ZT road, first hotel after Dar Cherait, T452101, F452726. Pleasant reception, restaurant, small (8 x 12 m) unheated pool. Much used by groups and local families. Walls between rooms are very thin and hot water not always reliable. Acceptable if there is a special offer. Also has a *Centre d'animation* in the oasis, evening of folklore for 30Dt. **B** *Hotel Ksar Jerid*, T454357, F454515. One of the newest *ZT* hotels. All the usual facilities, including organized excursions. **B** *Hotel Sarra*, T453544, F454648, 120 rooms. Pool, large rooms with terrace, some overlooking pool and oasis.

Av Abou Kacem Chabbi (the road running parallel to the oasis linking town to *zone touristique*) **A** *Hotel de l'Oasis*, on Av Habib Bourguiba, T461300, F461153, 125 a/c rooms, very popular with tour groups. A good address, bookings essential. Clean and well-managed. Small pool and early morning call for light sleepers from nearby mosque.

C *Hotel Continental*, Av Abou Kacem Chabbi, on your left after the *Résidence Warda* as you head for the *ZT*, T461411, F452109. 150 rooms, 1970s hotel, part of the Fourati Hotels group, which must have been something in its day. The pool is surrounded by palms, and the back of the hotel abuts onto the oasis. Could be a fine place, but not well run. **C-D** *Hotel Karim*, past the *Hotel Continental*, on your right on a corner, T454574. Street-facing rooms noisy, others face onto small, tiled areas. Popular with French travellers. Adequate but prefer the *Warda* or the *Arich*.

D *Résidence El Arich*, on left at intersection just before *ZT* starts, T462644, F461544, New (2000) 3-storey building, views over the oasis, rooms include a furnished flat sleeping 5. Garden area with swings, sunny café terrace, pizzeria in summer, also big tent with chicha café where locals watch the football. Website underway, helpful reception But: rooms at back noisy in evening in summer with music from wedding parties. Management say not. **D** *Résidence Warda*, T460000, 452597, F452744. Coming from town, on your left after *Restaurant Le Soleil*. 2-storey unprepossessing building with simple, very clean rooms, some doubles very cramped (a squeeze once you've got your luggage in), some big rooms with bath. Tiny courtyard out the back, dry your laundry on the roof. Supplement for a/c or heating. Recommended, handy for oasis and town.

Town centre and around C *Hotel Dar Ghaouar*, R de Kairouan, behind the market, beside the *Hotel Splendid*, T452782, F452666. Opened 1993, 50 rooms, 116 beds, some 3- and 4-bed rooms, also a 6-bedder. Despite ugly entrance and reception, a good cheapish address. Chiefly famed for its bar. Large terrace area shaded by big eucalyptus trees round pool (to be filled?). Clean, a/c, TV.

E *Hotel Aïcha*, R Farhat Hached, T452788, F452873. Turn right (Nefta direction) out of bus station onto Av Farhat Hached, hotel is 300-m walk. Some rooms with bath and a/c (supplement). Cheap restaurant, hotel

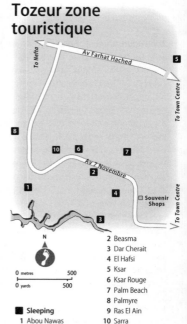

Tozeur zone touristique

To Nefta

Av Farhat Hached

To Town Centre

Av 7 Novembre

To Town Centre

Souvenir Shops

N

0 metres 500
0 yards 500

■ **Sleeping**
1 Abou Nawas

2 Beasma
3 Dar Cherait
4 El Hafsi
5 Ksar
6 Ksar Rouge
7 Palm Beach
8 Palmyre
9 Ras El Ain
10 Sarra

closed during Ramadan. Inconvenient for interesting part of town. **E** *Hotel Splendid*, behind central market, near the Post Office, T450053, extremely faded charm, requires some attention, clean, most rooms with bath, pool, restaurant. **E** *Hotel Essalem*, Av Farhat Hached, T462881. Turn left out of the bus station, then 1½ km walk straight along Av Farhat Hached. Cheapish but incovenient for oasis, although quite near old neighbourhood. Last choice in this price bracket. **E** *Résidence Niffer*, Bab el Hawa, T460555/460610, F461900, on the square at the bus station end of Av Habib Bourguiba. New in 1998. Clean and simple, although Av Farhat Hached facing rooms may be noisy. Extra rooms have been added, all with heating and washbasin, a/c 4Dt extra. Some 3- and 4-bed rooms. Best of the cheapies and only 300 m from bus/louage station. NB Some rooms have windows opening onto corridor. **E** *Hotel Essaâda*, Av Habib Bourguiba, on the right as you go down the slope, opposite *STB Bank*, look for small courtyard behind the arcades, T460097, a good, cheap choice. A warren of 32 small rooms overlooking patio and off corridors, some rooms with 4 beds, all with washbasin, hot showers (electric heating) on corridor. Noisy if there is a student group. 1Dt for a hot shower.

Youth hostel Av de la République in the Gafsa direction, close to the station, T452335. A fair trek – turn left out of bus station onto Av Farhat Hached, after 800 m, and mosque on right, go left at ten-to-the-hour onto Av de la République. 47 beds, noisy. The very last option for budget travellers.

Camping At Degache, 10 km north of Tozeur on the C106. *Bedouin Camping*, down the track opposite the *piscine municipale*, clean facilities, food available, shady sites. 5Dt for 2 people, 1 car and 1 tent – rates pro rata. *Camping les Beaux Rêves*, Av Abou Kacem Chabbi, after the winged-horse monument as you come from town, T453331, F454208. 5Dt/tent/per person, 40 sites, also very basic bamboo shelter type accommodation, 6Dt/night. NB Have mosquito lotion ready. Can advise on walks in the palm groves.

Tozeur's none-too-exciting restaurants are all on or around Av Habib Bourguiba and the Av Abou Kacem Chabbi. The gaudy *Dar Cheraït* serves as the upscale eatery. **Eating**

Mid-range *Restaurant Diamanta*, on Av Abou Kacem Chabbi. Opposite *Hotel Continental*. The usual traditional fare. *Restaurant Le Soleil*, almost opposite the *Résidence Warda*, T454220, closed Ramadan, has a cosy atmosphere in evening. Starters 2Dt, main courses 4Dt. Local specialities like camel-meat couscous, minimum 4 people, need to be ordered in advance. *Restaurant Le Petit Prince*, T452318, signposted off Av Abou Kacem Chabbi, near *Hotel Oasis*. Given the lack of competition, this passes for a good restaurant. Fairly pleasant surroundings with candlelit dining. Eat outside in summer. Just off the Deggache road, try *Restaurant Les Andalous*, T454196. Dear for this price bracket, service could be better. In need of an upscale place to dine, you might also check to see if there is a restaurant in the *Dar Cheraït* museum complex. **Cheap** *Restaurant de la République*, go downhill on Av Habib Bourguiba, restaurant is just after minaret, through arcade on right. Good standard fare, eat for 5Dt a head, main dishes approx 2.5Dt. *Restaurant du Paradis*, by the *Hotel Essaâda*, off Av Habib Bourguiba, very good, cheap, a few pleasant tables outside. Try also the no-name restaurant under the arcades opposite the market and the big bowl monument. They'll bring the food across the road to the tables in the square. Close to the bus station is *Restaurant des Sportifs*, cheap and cheerful.

Hammam Just next to *Hotel Essaâda*. Signposted. Some of the upmarket hotels in the *ZT* have their own hammams. **Entertainment**

In season, go for the fresh dates. In autumn and winter, stands selling dates are behind post office. If you are Tunis-based and can arrange transport, there is a small workshop **Shopping**

Southwestern Tunisia

Southwestern Tunisia

 ## The Talisman

The 'evil eye' is a powerful force in the local societies of North Africa. It is believed that certain people have the power to damage their victims, sometimes inadvertently. Even a camera can be considered as an alien agent carrying an evil eye – so only take photographs of country people where they are comfortable with the idea and be exceptionally careful in showing a camera at weddings and above all funerals. Envy too is a component of the evil eye and most conversations where any praise of a person or object is concerned will include a tabark allah ('blessing of God') as protection against the evil spirits that surround human kind. Likely victims of the evil eye are the young, females and the weak. Vulnerability to it is seen to be worst in marriage, pregnancy and childbirth, so that women in particular must shelter themselves from the evil eye. Uttering the name of Allah is a good defence against the evil eye. Alternatively amulets are used, this practice originating from the wearing of quotations from the Koran written onto strips of cloth which were bound into a leather case, which was then strapped to the arm. The amulet developed as a form in its own right, made of beads, pearls, horn or stone brought back from a pilgrimage. Amulets also have the power to heal as well as to protect against the occult.

The Romans too were keen to fend off the effects of the evil eye and incorporated in the mosaics at the threshold of their dwellings, 'good' components to fight off the 'evil'. The mosaic from Moknine and now in the museum at Sousse shows the 'good' fish and snake keeping an 'evil' eye in bounds.

For Tunisians particular talismans are the hand of Fatima, the five fingers known as the khamsa, and the fish symbol, which is regarded as very effective as a protection for women and new-born infants.

In contemporary North Africa, medicine, superstition and ornament combine to give a wonderful array of amulets and decorations worn for both everyday and specific use.

doing palm-branch furniture on the Av Abou Kacem Chabbi. Otherwise, most of the souvenirs are things you can find anywhere in Tunisia.

Sport **Hot-air ballooning** *Aeroasis Club*, T452361, does hot-air balloon flights every day of the year, weather permitting. Trips last 2½ hrs with lunch stop and are a very peaceful way to see the Sahara. The club has 3 balloons and can cater for 15-18 people at a time. Trip timing will probably be early morning when the air is cool. Have something warm to wear and to cover your head, as the flame flaring up to heat the balloon is hot on the back of the neck. Too little or too much wind and extreme heat prevent flying. Expect to pay about 85Dt and be as flexible as possible in your arrangements. (**NB** At time of writing, it seemed that the balloon company might eventually close down.) **Sand yachting** A fun activity for the flat, empty wastes of the Chott el Djerid. Check tourist office or upmarket hotels for information. Best season is Nov-May.

Desert excursions Day-long 4WD 'safaris' sold by the tour agencies along Av Abou Kacem Chabbi can be expensive. If cash is a problem try the management of the *Hotel Saâda* (see above). 30Dt gets you to Nefta and Ong Jemal out in the desert by 4WD or a half-day trip to the mountain oases. For 45Dt, you get the same plus an evening's 'Berber' entertainment. Try also *Sassi Tours*, Av Abou Kacem Chabbi, T462555, F463555.

Tour operators Most of these are to be found on Av Farhat Hached going out towards the airport. From the junction with Av Habib Bourguiba, they are in order on the right: *Tozeur Voyages*, T452439, F451440; *Cartours*, T450547, F451077; *Tunisair*, on the right beyond the stadium; then on the left *Meheri Voyages*, T450387, F451211; *Passion Voyages*; *Etoile du Sud*, T451055; *Carthage Tours*, T541300; *Europ Tours*. In addition there is *Abdelmoula Voyages*, Rte de Degache, T451130, and *Voyages Chaabane*, Av Abou Kacem Chabbi, T451011.

The Tourist Office, *ONTT*, organizes camel trips from Tozeur. There is an official price list for all excursions. *Pension Warda* and *Hotel de l'Oasis* offer 4WD tours to Nefta, Tamerza and Seldja Gorge.

Long distance Air: the airport is 4 km along the road to Nefta, T450345. Frequent **Transport** scheduled flights to Tunis, charter flights from European destinations. Check with *Tunisair*, Rte de Nefta, opposite *Magasin Général*, T452127, F452033; at the airport, T453388. **Bus**: frequent buses to **Tunis, Nefta, Gafsa** and **Kebili**. A few buses a day to **Gabès, Kairouan** and the north. Information on T451557. **Louages**: opposite the bus station. Louages have destinations marked only in Arabic, ask for your destination. Be early at the stop and be sharp, as locals with less luggage slip quickly into the seats. Plenty every day to Kebili, none direct to Chebika, go via Redeyef (or hitchhike).

Banks *STB* and *BDS* on Av Habib Bourguiba, *BNT* and *BIAT* on Av Farhat Hached. *STB* **Directory** has ATM (dinars) for Visa and Mastercard holders. **Car hire** Agencies located close together on Av Farhat Hached/Rte de l'Aéroport. *Avis* and *Car Tours*, 3 Av Farhat Hached, T453547; *Europcar*, Rte de l'Aéroport, T460119; *Hertz*, Av Farhat Hached, T/F463214. **Communications** Internet: Tozeur now has a *Publinet*, including close to the *Résidence Arich* junction on street perpendicular to Av Abou Kacem Chabbi. Turning right out of the bus station, there may be another one on the first right, almost opposite *Restaurant des Sportifs*. **Post Office**: on the main square off Av Habib Bourguiba. **Medical services** Chemists: on Av Abou Kacem Chabbi, T450491; Av Farhat Hached, T450370; Av Habib Bourguiba, T450153. *Doctor*: Dr Ramzi, T98450101 (mob) speaks some English. Ask also at the **Pharmacie de nuit** opposite the bus station. **Hospital**: *Hôpital Régional de Tozeur*, Cité de l'Hôpital, T453400. **Useful addresses** Police: T450126, 1 km down road to Gafsa.

Tozeur to the hill oases via Metlaoui

The much-advertised *oasis de montagne* provides a wonderful day's excursion *Colour map 5,* for those with own transport. (For those without, there are plenty of *grid A1* four-wheel drive excursions.) **Chebika**, **Tamerza** and **Midès** are at some of the most beautiful sites in the Tunisian south, and if you have time, should not be missed. An ideal circuit would be anticlockwise from Tozeur via Metlaoui, giving you some fantastic views and getting most of the boring driving out of the way first. Total distance: 185 km. Accommodation on this route is extremely limited, there being only two hotels in the oases, both at Tamerza: one upmarket (the *Tamerza Palace*), and the basic *Les Cascades*.

Leave Tozeur on the GP3 heading northeast for **Metlaoui**, where you turn left at the junction with the square-faced clock for Moularès. The area to the north of town is like a moonscape. Spin-offs from the phosphate industry include piles of dark gritty material, huge lorries, and dust. Driving here is dangerous, as the lorry drivers must be on piece-work and few give consideration to other road travellers. There is also much heavy industrial plant being moved. The road runs adjacent to the conveyor belt for a while, interesting but not scenic, and then winds up slowly into the *djebel*. The Michelin map has a green line on this road to indicate a scenic route, which is only part of the story. The road surface is poor in parts.

At the top, after 16 km of grime, everything changes. Turn left to Moularès going directly west through barren plain with Djebel Bou Ramli to the north, Djebel Mrata (948 m) and Algeria directly ahead. **Moularès** means 'mother of the bride'. The settlement grew up thanks to the phosphate industry, and today includes a collection of government buildings, small shops and petrol stations. Phosphate wagons trundle along the railway line running through the middle of town. A few palm trees struggle to brighten the environment. From Moularès to Redeyef is 18 km. There is a bypass round **Redeyef** which means you miss seeing the bus station and the regulation issue square-faced clock.

After Redeyef, the road gets more interesting. Although the road surface is quite rough, there is very little traffic apart from tourist four-wheel drives and the occasional Peugeot pickup truck. This road crosses many *oueds* and the engineering is erratic. At times the dip down to the *oued* bed is very steep – keep speed down. At **Aïn el Ouchika**, there is the turn-off for **Midès**, 5 km away, and, in normal times, you can get your papers checked before continuing into Algeria.

The road to Midès (ancient Madès), 8 km from Tamerza, is on a good surfaced road as it goes on to Algeria. You approach through a very beautiful, working oasis, the old system of tiered cultivation still in operation, with palm trees underplanted with pomegranates and vegetables. Park near the village, now essentially abandoned, and no doubt you will be greeted by kids hoping to take you to the canyon, round the old town, into the oasis. Merging into the rocks, atop a cliff and surrounded by canyons on three sides, the village is impressive. Flints and other traces of prehistoric occupation have been found nearby. The Imazighen who founded Midès really knew what they were doing – a site with better natural defences would be difficult to imagine. Rumour has it that *Club Med* was interested in developing the old settlement as a holiday village. Buying out the multiple-owners would be an estate agents' nightmare, however, so Midès looks safe for the time being.

There is no other road out of Midès so you backtrack to the junction and turn right for Tamerza, 8 km from Midès. Go carefully, the road dips down to the Oued el Horchane and four-wheel drive vehicles sometimes go faster than they really should.

Tamerza
Phone code: 76

Ancient Ad Turres, today's Tamerza, was part of the Limes Tripolitanus fortifications. Here again the old village has been abandoned. Tamerza, situated on lower-lying ground than Midès, suffered heavy flood damage. Now often used for film shoots, the walls have been restored in places. The *marabouts* are kept in good repair, too. In the old village walk down the deserted main street from the highest point, the *kalaâ*, to the lowest point around the mosque and *marabout*. The extensive oasis with abundant water produces excellent dates as well as vegetables. The valley is full of stands of giant cane which apparently provide a refuge for wild boar, unwelcome visitors to the oasis gardens. The new village is a standard Tunisian rural settlement. From new Tamerza you access the main attraction, the **cascades**. Given the shortage of such sites in the Tunisian south, they are a bit of a tourist trap, attracting lots of local visitors too.

A possible **walk** is back up to Midès via the canyon. Take plenty of water and provisions – there are no shops in Midès. Also work out how you're going to get back if you're not going to walk. It might be better to do this trip with a mule and guide arranged via the *Hotel des Cascades*. On no account attempt this excursion if rain looks like a possibility. Flash floods are extremely dangerous, and carry everything in front of them.

The Marabout

The North African landscape is dotted with small white painted buildings scattered about the hillsides, hilltops and cemeteries. These are the burial places of the holy men or marabouts (marabit in Arabic). The marabout was a religious teacher who gained credibility by gathering disciples around him and getting acknowledgement as a man of piety and good works. Marabouts were in many cases migrant preachers travelling to and from Mecca or were organizers of sufi schools. Place names of marabout sites are mainly after the names of the holy man interred there, usually prefixed by the word 'sidi'. Some sites are very modest, comprising a small raised tomb surrounded by a low wall, all whitewashed. Other marabouts have a higher tomb several metres square topped by a dome (koubba). In some instances, marabout tombs are large house-like structures acting as mausoleums and shrines. Most tombs in rural areas can carry stakes bearing flags in green cloth as symbols of the piety of their donors and as a token of continuing protection from the marabout.

In Libya annual processions are made to the marabout shrines for good luck, fertility and protection against the evil spirits. This is particularly the case where the area around is occupied by a tribe claiming descent from the holy man in question.

Sleeping The area's only hotels are here. **AL** *Tamerza Palace*, T/F485322, www.tamerza-palace.com Stone-built in a kasbahish style, 65 spacious rooms, a/c, heating, bar, good restaurant, panoramic views over old village, pool, conference room, tennis. Has a certain elegance. Staff have lots of little hotel-school touches like leaving a flower on pillow. Seems to make most of its money doing lunches for tour groups and safari tours overnight. Make sure your room has views over old Tamerza from its pleasant little balcony. Is the service up to par? **C** *L'Hotel des Cascades*, T485732, 150 beds, outdoor restaurant, pool, beautiful location to the east of the palm groves. Follow the signs to the cascades about 100 m from the main road, 50 individual 'bungalows' are made out of palm frond walls with concrete lining. Mosquitoes are a major presence, you need your jungle gel. A cheaper and more pleasant alternative is to rent a tent from the locals at the entrance to the village (5Dt per person) and spend the night in the oasis by the river. This is not an official camping area.

Eating *Tamerza Palace* is an adequate but expensive choice. Down by the *Hotel des Cascades* are a couple of cheap restaurants, including *Le Chedli* and *Restaurant Gelain*. Menus at around 6.5Dt. Arriving in Tamerza from the Chebika direction, try also the *Restaurant du Soleil*, on the left about 200 m before the mosque.

The road from Tamerza to Chebika has been improved considerably. There are splendid views over Chott el Gharsa and over the plain to Algeria. There are occasional service buses to Tozeur, but very little traffic otherwise. Between Tamerza and Chebika the waters of the Oued el Horchane actually run across the road.

Some 8 km on from Tamerza lies Chebika, Ad Speculum in classical times and also part of the Limes Tripolitanus fortifications, a small oasis of palms and vegetables in a narrow gorge. The name Ad Speculum derives from an ancient Roman communication method. Roman outposts and troops on the move could signal to each other by mirror (Latin: *speculum*). Later the village became known as Ksar ech Chems, 'palace of the sun'. Chebika has a beautiful

Chebika

Southwestern Tunisia

Change at Chebika

Reached by little more than a rough piste, Chebika was one of the remotest places in Tunisia in the mid-20th century. It wasn't until the early 1990s that the piste was turned into road. Back in the 1960s, Chebika was the focus of a study which was to become a classic of social anthropology. Academic Jean Duvignaud was looking for a place to undertake research into the impact of development on isolated rural communities. At Chebika, he and his team of young Tunisian researchers were to enter into the daily lives of a community with its own deep-rooted values. The messages of the modern world (and the new Tunisia) were only just beginning to arrive via the transistor radio.

Duvignaud and his team found an oasis community regulated by complex unwritten rules of conduct. There was little money circulating in the oasis, but a complex exchange economy, services and favours being constantly traded. Contacts with the outside world were limited, though certain Chebikans were working in the mines at Redeyef, and marriages were arranged with the sister village of El Hamma du Djerid. But it was oasis cultivation which was the centre of Chebika's existence. For the village's

people, the oasis was a divine creation, more than just land cultivated to produce profit. But the Chebikans had lost control over their palmgroves: acquiring sheep and goats from the nomads, they had been forced to exchange land ownership to cover their debts.

Chebika in the 1960s was already beginning to change. A local official declared that "the people of Chebika belong to the past, they will be swept away if they don't adapt."

While the older people saw themselves as part of fictional family trees going back to the land of the Prophet, the children, beginning to go to school, could place their village in the south of the new Tunisian nation state. Today, the old ways of thinking are gone for ever. Chebika has become picturesque, providing the rushed tourist with a place where 'the old ways of life continue unchanged'. But how are Chebika's people doing beyond the façade of 'desert serenity'?

Duvignaud's research was translated into English as Change at Chebika *(University of Texas Press), but is unfortunately out of print. A cheap paperback edition of the French original is available in Tunis bookshops, published by Cérès Editions.*

location looking out over arid plain to the west and south to Chott el Gharsa. The old, abandoned village clings to the rocky hillside, while its residents have moved out to the new village. New Chebika is a small village, just a mosque, shop and a post office. There is parking at the top with a café overlooking the palm trees and gorge. If you arrive at the wrong moment, there will be 20 or so four-wheel drives jostling for parking space. Walk up into the old village. Hordes of excited kids will probably accompany you, ready to sell various minerals and poor necklaces made of tiny coloured flour beads. The spring comes trickling out of a narrow defile below the old village.

Nefta نفطة

While Tozeur had a reputation for its men of letters, the sister oasis town of Nefta was famed across the Sahara as a spiritual place. Arriving in Nefta today, one's initial impression is more of a dust-blown outpost town. From the cliffs above the Corbeille (surely the only oasis to be set in what looks like a large crater), there is a panoramic view of Nefta. On its cliff top, there is the brooding mass of the Sahara Palace. Opposite, across the Corbeille, is the El Bayadha quarter. Here and there among the low sand-brown buildings are domes signalling the tombs of holy men. Explore the alleyways, still suffused by a certain spirituality, but better still, head off into the palm groves, where, at the right time of year, it will be possible to get a taste of the local 'palm wine' or the dates for which Nefta is famous.

Phone code: 76
Colour map 5, grid A1

Ins and outs

The bus station is on the north side of the main street, Av Habib Bourguiba. The louages stop opposite. Journey time from Tozeur, just 23 km down the GP3, is 20 minutes. Hazoua on the Algerian border is only 36 km away.

Getting there

The main tourist information office is on the right as you enter the town, T430236, almost opposite the *Mobil* station. It organizes *calèche* and camel rides around the oasis, and can also organize excursions into the desert and the dunes. Guides are available. Open daily 0800-1800.

Tourist information

History

Nefta was settled back in ancient times, when it was known as Aggersel Nepte. In the 11th century, the town was destroyed for refusing to pay taxes to Tunis. Rebuilt, Nefta became an important sufi centre by the 16th century. The cult of saints fell into disrepute after independence, and Nefta no doubt suffered.

Like other fringe areas of the Islamic world (Iran and Turkey), North Africa was to prove fertile ground for the cult of saints. Shrines of earlier animist Berber or Roman deities tended to take on Islamic identities, but why Nefta in particular should have proved such a centre for mystic Islam is something of a mystery. There are said to be over 125 shrines in the area. Some, such as the Zaouia of Sidi Bou Ali, were extremely important, attracting adepts from far afield.

It may be that sufism held a greater attraction for the peoples of the peripheral Islamic regions where there were deep rooted forms of religious practice. Sufism offers spiritual development through means other than the study of the Koran. Only a few adepts actually achieve the highest stages of sufi practice. Sufism was rejected by orthodox Islam but became quite popular due to the freedom it offered within the austere confines of mainstream Sunni Islam.

Sights

The oasis in Nefta has about 400,000 palm trees which produce some of the best dates in Tunisia. The **Corbeille**, a wide, deep basin which originally had springs flowing from its sides, must be seen as well as the old town. This large depression is situated to the north of Avenue Habib Bourguiba, and from the ridge surrounding it there is an excellent view over the **oasis** below and towards the Chott el Djerid in the distance to the east. The best view is from the *Café de la Corbeille*, which is reached by taking the road north from the tourist office or by foot through the old town north of the Place de la République. Walk down into the oasis. Natural springs used to flow from the sides of the Corbeille. Children will want to act as guides but this is not necessary. The tourist office provides guides who are both competent and friendly.

Nefta has two main neighbourhoods: **Ouled ech Cherif**, on your right as you arrive from Tozeur, and **El Bayadha** to the west side of the Corbeille. It is recorded as having 24 mosques. The neighbourhoods are well worth strolling around, particularly as not that many tourists make the effort. In the narrow streets, you may come across women wearing the traditional black wrap, here enlivened with a blue stripe.

The **Zaouia of Sidi Brahim** (his tomb) is at the head of the Corbeille adjacent to *Café de la Corbeille*. **Sidi Salem's Mosque**, also known as the Great Mosque, is on the ridge above the Corbeille.

Brickmaking On the western outskirts of Nefta, you may come across a rudimentary brick (*yajour*) factory. As in medieval Europe, bricks are handmade according to the needs of a building project. The craftsmen create good stodgy mixes of clay and sand, which is then used to make the bricks, shaped in rough wooden moulds and left to dry in the sun. The sun-dried bricks are then covered in ash and kiln-fired.

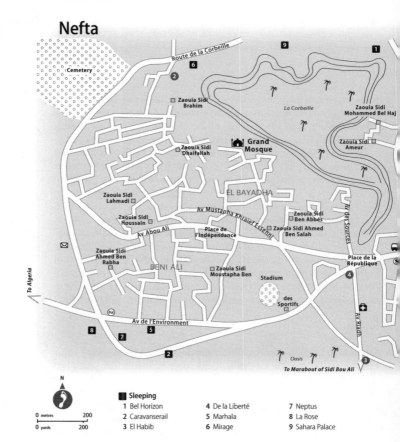

Nefta

Sleeping
1 Bel Horizon
2 Caravanserail
3 El Habib
4 De la Liberté
5 Marhala
6 Mirage
7 Neptus
8 La Rose
9 Sahara Palace

Southwestern Tunisia

Originally, brick must have been the perfect construction material for the region, given that other naturally occurring materials are poor. Today, hand-made bricks are increasingly in demand. Though concrete post construction with red-brick infill has pushed traditional brick into second place in the Djerid, the realization has grown that local brick provides far better insulation against the extremes of the desert climate. Yellow brick decorative work can be found in many of the new hotels, too, providing that essential 'traditional touch'.

How brickmaking technology reached the Djerid is unknown. Could it be a survival from classical times? The Romans, after all, were a dab hand at making thin bricks or *tegulae*. Or was it brought from the Middle East, where decorative brickwork was used for many buildings in Iraq and Iran? Maybe the skill filtered in from Europe thanks to some renegade converted to Islam. Whatever the case, the ochre imperfections of brickwork lend texture to a façade. When used to create patterning, geometric brickwork animates a wall with geometric detail. With so many Tunisian towns losing the last fragile vestiges of their local architecture, it is nice to see that at least one technique is still surviving down in the Djerid as people rediscover the benefits of brickwork.

The oasis

You might try a walk down into the oasis, heading for the **Zaouia of Sidi Bou Ali**. From the junction where the Avenue Bourguiba meets Avenue des Sources, head towards the hospital on Avenue Riadh. (Some 200 m after the hospital, the *Palmery Bar* is on your left.) Carry on for the Zaouia, some 300 m further on. This is a good chance to have a look at the palm gardens.

The Zaouia of Sidi Bou Ali is one of the most important in Nefta, mausoleum to a holy man who came from Morocco in the 13th century. The zaouia is visited to ask the saint's blessing on important family occasions: pregnancy, circumcision, marriage. The annual pilgrimage, the *dakhla*, attracts pilgrims from both the Djerid and across the border in Algeria. Unlike many other zaouias, that of Sidi Bou Ali has managed to maintain its prestige. The family guarding saintly prestige has managed to win the favours of the authorities. With the tourist industry in search of picturesque places, the folklorish side of zaouia life will no doubt become part of the tourist attractions of the region.

Southwestern Tunisia

● **Eating**
1 Café du Stade
2 La Corbeille
3 Palmery Bar
4 Restaurant du Sud

Essentials

Sleeping
■ *on map, page 344*
Price codes:
see inside front cover

Nefta is entering the age of mass tourism, albeit more slowly than Tozeur. New hotels are springing up along the *route touristique*, although given the financial difficulties facing the Saharan hotels which mushroomed in the mid-1990s, construction may be slower. Nefta's hotels come in 3 main areas. Large hotels are either overlooking the Corbeille or down on the inevitable *route touristique*, next to the oasis, on the road leading west out of town. There are only a couple of cheapies in the town centre. However, Nefta is near enough to Tozeur for you to nip back if you can't find a room.

Overlooking the Corbeille AL *Sahara Palace*, just behind the Corbeille, T431700, F431444, 100 a/c rooms and 9 suites, luxurious, large pool with panoramic view, disco, well situated overlooking the oasis. The hotel, now part of the Sangho group, has been beautifully refurbished and merits at least a look. The rooms are very smart indeed. Coach tours stop here for buffet lunch and a gaze out over the palms and village. **B** *Hotel Bel Horizon*, T430328, F430500. Close to the *Sahara Palace*. The decorators made an effort here, with Liberty lamps and Berber bits and pieces. Lacks the style of the *Sahara Palace*, however. Pool, hammam and a/c in rooms. Another good hotel. **B** *Le Mirage*, T430622, F430644, further round the Corbeille, close to the *Café de la Corbeille*. Acceptable but dull.

Next to the oasis, *Route touristique* **AL** *Caravanserail*, T430355, F430344. Part of a chain which also has a hotel in Douz. Quite attractive stone-built hotel, right next to the oasis. Very small pool. Has a standard and a *luxe* wing. (Showers not baths in the former.) **B** *Hotel Marhala*, T430027, F430511, an old address, with choice of accommodation in older wing or newer 3-star wing. Pool with view, restaurant, simple decoration. Plenty of parking. **B** *Neptus*, T430186, F430647. Not a first choice, home to groups. Some 6-person apartments. **B** *La Rose*, T430697, F430385.

Ouled ech Cherif neighbourhood and around E *Hotel Les Nomades*, at the entrance to town on the left, T430052. In its day, this must have been a fine address, just 'typical' enough. There are a couple of older wings with vaulted rooms and beds on built-in platforms, and a new block under construction. All rooms have shower. The hotel, about as far from the old town and its *marabouts* as you can get in Nefta, also has a bar, its main raison d'être. **D** *Hotel El Habib*, the 3-storey block on the main square in Ouled ech Cherif, signposted, T430497, F430522. Clean and very basic, some rooms with bath, rooftop rooms. Go for rooms giving onto the back, as the square can be noisy with traffic. Handy for early morning bus departures. **E** *Hotel de la Liberté*, eccentric little place built around a patio, at the heart of the Ouled ech Cherif neighbourhood. No sign. Not terribly clean, but if you have a sleeping bag, you can kip out on the roof terrace. Say 10Dt a night with breakfast. Fine if you're broke.

Eating
● *on map, page 344*

Mid-range *La Corbeille*, T430308. Near the *Hotel Mirage*, up the top, overlooking the Corbeille. The 'upmarket' address. **Cheap** *Restaurant du Sud*, Av Habib Bourguiba, good, cheap Tunisian food. *Restaurant Les Sources*, by the tourist office, on Av Habib Bourguiba where the buses come in near the *Mobil* station, recently renovated, Tunisian specialities, outside terrace.

Cafés

On the Pl de la Libération there's a 'local' café. Try *La Corbeille* and *Café Kazan*, near the *Hotel Mirage*, overlooking the Corbeille

Shopping

Best buys *Roses des sables*, 'desert sand roses', are found a few metres under the desert surface, are chunky objects looking for all the world like peculiar petrified sea creatures. They are formed through evaporation from the mineral barites. The biggest are enormous, but you'll probably need a small one to take home for the nature table.

Bus Departures to **Tunis** (takes 8 hrs), at 1030 and 2400; 5 daily buses to Tozeur and Gafsa; early morning departures for **Sfax** and **Kairouan**. Bus information (gare routière) on T430602. Also buses to Algerian border. Buses do not cross the border but taxis do, otherwise you are faced with a 5-km stretch of no-man's land to get to the Algerian border post. From the other side, it is 80 km to the first town, El Oued, but louages are available. **Louages** Depart frequently to Tozeur (takes 20 mins). There is a service to Hazoua and the Algerian border. **Transport**

Banks *Banque du Sud* and *UIB* on Av Habib Bourguiba. **Communications** Post Office: Av Habib Bourguiba, 150 m beyond the Tourist Office. **Medical services** Chemist: on Av Habib Bourguiba, T457159. **Hospital**: *Hôpital Local de Nefta*, R des Martyrs, T430193. **Useful addresses** Police: T457134. On Av Habib Bourguiba. **Directory**

West from Nefta into Algeria

The Tuniso-Algerian border is only 35 km west of Nefta and El Oued another 64 km. In the 1990s, Algeria was most definitely off-limits to tourists, who, like foreign workers, were a target for Islamist groups. In early 2002, the situation in Algeria had settled considerably in terms of violence. Time will tell, but maybe in a few years time southern Algeria will be a viable onward destination for travellers leaving from the Djerid. For the moment, the main option for travel in the mountain massifs of the Algerian Sahara is to go with a tour operator directly from Europe.

Southeast from Tozeur to Kebili

This is a worthwhile route to follow. It goes via the small oases of Degache and Kriz right through the centre of the massive salt lake, Chott El Djerid. It is a most impressive sight, a single black line of road cutting through the white salt deposits. Mirages and interesting optical illusions are frequent. The Chott begins about 20 km from Tozeur where the road dips down. The west side of the Chott is not so tidy, with abandoned vehicles, split tyres and old oil cans. There are occasional small palm thatched huts at the side of the road at about the centre point, all with the same facilities, selling *roses des sables* (some dyed garish hues), cups of tea and coffee, and providing a primitive toilet a few steps across the salt flat. These are frequented by coach tours.

Phone code: 75
Colour map 5,
grid A1/2

Where the chott is at its lowest salt is extracted. At each side of a road a channel, about one metre wide, has been dug in the white sand. In winter and spring this is full of water which will evaporate and leave a deposit of salt. Occasionally work with mechanical diggers is in progress lifting this salt.

About 40 km from Kriz, the land begins to rise and you come onto a peninsula sprinkled with small oases. The small settlement of **Souk Lahad** (lit: 'Sunday souk'), 75 km from Tozeur, has the usual services, banks, chemist, two or three cafés, of which *Café Salam* by the bus stop and the municipal garden is perhaps the best.

For an area sitting next to a salt sea, there is a gratifying amount of vegetation as you approach Kebili. There are recently planted palm groves to the south of the road, and elsewhere the trees are almost mature, with underplanting of olives and cereals. In less fertile places the scrub provides grazing land. Just after the Chott el Djerid, at **Zaouia**, 20 km before Kebili, is

Southwestern Tunisia

C *L'Hotel les Dunes*, T480711, F480563, 89 rooms, built 1991, exchange and boutique, very well decorated, pool, entertainment includes *mechoui* outside under the tents with traditional dancing and music. Turn off opposite the petrol station. **Menchia** has cafés for a rest en route.

At **Mansoura** (turn left off the main road at Tombar) there is another Roman outpost. Here was one of the key strong points on the southern frontier, the legionary base of Turris Tamalleni, controlling access to the narrowest point across the Chott el Djerid, just west of the Djebel Tebaga which provided a natural rampart running eastwards to El Hamma (Acquae Tacapitanae) and Gabès (Tacapae). All that survives are a couple of Roman pools. **Telmine** is another compact oasis 7 km before **Kebili**.

Kebili   قبلي

Phone code: 75
Colour map 4, grid A1

Never really more than a stop-off on the route to Douz, Kebili has a discrete charm. A late-19th-century French creation, the modern town has a pleasant shady central square. There are hot springs, too, on the Douz side of town. Abandoned old Kebili, a few kilometres from the new town, crumbling but still largely intact, is worth a look. The domed marabouts are perfectly preserved in the thick green shade of the palms; the fruit trees and vegetable patches are a gardener's delight.

Sights   Modern Kebili, founded 1892, is a small regional town which had considerable military importance under the French. Kebili's strategic location at a meeting of the ways from Tozeur, Gabès and the desert settlements further south obviously made it just right for a military outpost. There are few specific sights to see, but plenty of interest in the oasis surrounding the half-forgotten settlement of old Kebili. You could also relax at the **hot springs** to the left of the main road on the west side of town. Originally, the locals could bathe in splendid open air pools, said to go back to Roman times. The authorities decided that this was an unfitting spectacle, so they had the pool replaced with a large fountain, sometimes lit up at night with coloured, underwater lights. A truly fairy-tale spectacle. The concrete hammam buildings are a few metres back from the road, separate sections for men and women. If you are really enthusiastic about hot springs, you could head for obscure **Steftimia** on the road north to Gafsa crossing the Chott el Fejej.

Old Kebili   The old village of Kebili is decaying quietly in an oasis to the north of the road taking the four-wheel-drive brigade through to the dune desert and Douz. Follow the signs more or less opposite the fountain on the road to Douz and take the road and track winding through the oasis. The **market gardens** under the palm trees are carefully tended, the irrigation system apparently in good order. The oasis is said to produce a unique variety of fig. At the heart of the palm forest, the village is quiet, the house roofs falling in and walls collapsing. Only 30 years

Kebili

To Tozeur · To Telmine · To Gabes · To Douz

Garde Nacional
Place de l'Indépendence
Total · Clock · S · Flag · Esso · Chemist
Louages
Av Habib Bourguiba
Oued
Hotsprings & Hammam
OLD KEBILI

N · Not to scale

■ **Sleeping**
1 Ben Said
2 Fort des Autriches
3 Kitam

4 Oasis
5 Youth Hostel

● **Eating**
1 Lamazigh

ago, this was a busy centre but following floods, people moved en masse to the modern town nearer the main road. Still, on Fridays, men come to pray at the mosque. The blue-painted koubba in the village is in good repair.

B *Fort des Autruches*, signposted left off the road to Douz, about 300 m out of Kebili, T491117, F491295, 96 rooms, recently renovated, pool, bar on a terrace overlooking the oasis and the Chott, clean, views over oasis, can organize rides and tours, a good place as stop-over, advisable to book as used by groups. The hotel's derives from a time when ostrich feathers were in fashion and an abortive attempt was made to breed ostriches here. **C** *Hotel Dar Oasis*, also off the Douz road, close to the *Fort des Autruches*, T491436, F491295, 1 km from town centre, 256 beds in 124 rooms, all with bath, good view, telephone with direct line. Bureau de change, major credit cards accepted, 4WD trips, camel treks, car hire, restaurant, large pool, conference centre for 300, disco, mini souk, hammam, sauna, provision for disabled visitors. **D** *Hotel Kitam*, near town entrance on right as you come from Gabès, T491338, 32 rooms, a/c, telephone, restaurant, exchange, open all year. **E** *Hotel Ben Said*, Av Habib Bourguiba, T491573, on left of road to Douz, near centre of town and louage stop, 11 clean rooms, shared bathroom, café downstairs for breakfast, mosque nearby for early morning call. Recommended cheapie. **Youth hostel** T490635, 60 beds, bathrooms awful, meals available, catch bus in town centre in Tozeur direction to *Total* petrol station.

Sleeping
■ *on map, page 348*
Kebili is very short on hotels, although even it has an incipient zone touristique. Best to continue to Douz or Tozeur to overnight

Museum of Kebili near fountain on way to Douz is really a shop selling *kilims*. (Someone will demonstrate the working of a loom.)

Shopping

Buses to Kebili from Douz (35 km), Gabès, Blidet, Nouail, Tozeur (157 km) and Tunis. Two bus companies operate services: the *SRT* and the *SNTRI*. **Louages** run from all these towns, too. Note that buses from Tunis may run via Tozeur or Gabès. Buses come into the main street, stopping by the *Magasin Général*. The louage station is central, just behind the *Magasin Général*.

Transport

From Kebili to Douz

Bazma, 4 km south of Kebili on the east side of the road, has an old *ksar* and minaret among the palm trees, both abandoned. M'Said, 10 km south of Kebili, and a further 5 km from the road to the west, is a rather more pleasant place than Bazma, with the advantage of being on slightly elevated land and completely encircled by a cool and inviting palm oasis. The squat minaret, with a small cupola on the top, is in the centre of the new settlement, the old settlement of mud bricks being completely abandoned.

Colour map 4, grid A1

At **Djemma**, 16 km from Kebili, the road edges are painted, trees have been planted at intervals along the way and the settlement is just big enough to offer most services. Set back from the road, the newly settled areas still have a raw appearance. It is noted for the water in the public fountain which, unlike most water in the area, is not brackish.

El Golaâ is really a suburb of Douz, north of the main settlement. The town centre is marked by yet another square-faced clock, this time on brick pillars. The oasis covers a large area and it is possible to approach the town on a road through the palm groves parallel to the main road.

Douz دوز

Phone code: 75
Colour map 4, grid B1

Hard by the oasis town of Douz are the dunes you find in the Tunisian holiday brochures: rolling expanses of smooth sand, searing white in the day, golden-brown at sunset. Douz also has plenty of palm trees, camel rides, hot springs, an interesting desert museum – and a lot of charm. At year's end, there is even a folkloric festival. There are mammoth hotels lined up along the desert edge like so many UFOs – and some rough and ready places in town. Douz, or nearby Zaâfrane, could be your base for a couple of nights in the desert, crunching across the sand in the company of the dromedaries and a hard-bitten former nomad. Far from any urban glow, the desert sky at night is unbeatable for star gazers.

Ins and outs

Getting there Douz is 35 km south of Kebili and 122 km from Tozeur (via Chott el Djerid). Gabès is the nearest large town, 155 km to the east via Kebili and El Hamma. The town is easily accessible by bus and louage. By bus, journey time from Gabès is around 2½ hrs, from Tozeur 2½, generally with a change at Kebili. Louage times may be somewhat shorter.

Getting around You can do most things on foot. The dunes by the *zone touristique* are a 3-km walk from the centre. If you want to go down to Zaâfrane (12 km west), there are louages/rural transport running from just opposite the inter-city louage station.

Tourist information The tourist information office *ONTT*, Pl des Martyrs, Rte de Zaâfrane, T495350, is in the same building as the local tourist office. They are separated by a café. Local office, T470351, where Mr Amor Boukris has very little information to hand out but everything you want to know in his head. He is most helpful. Open 0830-1400 and 1500-1800 every day. They organize excursions into the desert on camels.

History

At the beginning of the 20th century, Douz was an isolated oasis. Today it is a small town, witness to the attractions of a settled life. The nomad lifestyle is an ancient one and tribal roots still run deep though. The main tribe in Douz are the M'razig. To the southwest, the Adhara are essentially based in Zaâfrane, and practise a form of seasonal nomadism, migrating with their flocks across to Ksar Ghilane to the west. Then there are the Sabria, centring on the village of the same name. Originally, the distinctions between the tribes would have been obvious from their tents and tatoos. (Until the 20th century,

Detail map
A Douz centre,
page 352

Douz

To Kebili, Tozeur & Gabès

To Zaâfrane, Sabria, Nouil & El Faouar

Av 7 Novembre

To Matmata & Ksar Ghilane

Total

Av Taieb Mehiri

Chemist

Place des Martyrs

2 Gazelles (Statue)

Av des Martyrs

Maison de la Culture

OASIS

OASIS

Camels for 'Safari'

To Festival Site

N

0 metres 50
0 yards 50

■ Sleeping	
1 Camping	5 Rose du Sables
2 El Mouradi	6 Sahara
3 Iberotel Mehari	7 Saharien
4 Marhala	8 Sun Palm
	9 Touareg

men as well as women had tatoos.) Today, however, true nomadism is more or less a thing of the past. French observers of 70 years ago report encampments of up to 30 tents, something never seen today. The nomad populations have been settled, giving up their ancestral myths. Sidi Marzoug, 15th century founder of the M'razig, is said to have declared "I will lead my sons far from the rainy lands which turn a man into a slave stifled under insults. Better to keep their honour, even if their stomachs be half-empty, rather than have full stomachs at the price of humiliation."

Today the settled way of life is gaining ground and the combined population of Douz and the villages in the region must be around 50,000. Douz is where nomads and oasis dwellers meet. But though there are very few purely nomadic families left, the desert is all around Douz and just a few kilometres out of town the road is hemmed in by dunes. The harsh environment maintains its hold on visitors' imaginations, no doubt through images maintained in Hollywood myth, of which *The English Patient* is the most recent example.

Sights

The centre of Douz does not have very many sights as such. The **Place du Souk** with its arcades somehow feels like 40 years ago with its small, locally run shops. Best buys are pretty desert boots and beautifully soft camel-wool cloaks and blankets. Central Douz has not been subject to a 'beautification' programme with unlikely pieces of urban street art that has afflicted Tozeur. There are a couple of pieces of statuary, handy for directions, notably the camel and rider at the north entrance to the town, and the twin gazelles on the road towards the oasis.

The **Ofra sand dune** is one of the largest easily accessible sand dunes. Take the road towards the hotels and park by one of them or, alternatively, hire a camel by the tourist office, where the official prices are posted. Further on is the village of **Glissia**, now largely covered by the shifting sands.

There is a **market** each Thursday attended by many nomads. (Douz is a centre for the now largely settled M'razig nomads.) There is also an animal market which sometimes has camels. Buyers and sellers collect in the designated area off Avenue des Martyrs, beside the oasis.

Douz International Festival, also known as **Festival du Sahara**, is generally held around Christmas. Lasting three days, the festival is centred on a large stadium overlooking the dunes a couple of kilometres down the road from the *Hotel Saharien*. Here there are horse races, demonstrations by acrobatic riders, camel races and mock camel combat, and the ever popular *sloughis* (desert greyhounds), only bred in the Douz region, who go racing after unfortunate hares. There will be finely turned out horsemen from Libya, and a *jahfa*, a camel topped with a bridal palanquin accompanied by musicians. In the evening, there may be poetic jousting in the nomad tradition at the **Maison de la Culture**. Various traders set up their stalls on the main road in the villages. There are some fierce contests for position and at times it's a problem to find a way through the throng. Douz families' friends and relatives swell the crowds. The posh hotels organize displays of traditional costume and the like, while downtown, some of the lads may get a bit excitable after a few too many beers. On the day after the festival, all along the road back to Kebili, are dromedaries, Arabian horses and their owners.

There is also a **Folklore Festival** in March. Check exact dates with the tourist office. At peak festival periods, be sure to have booked a hotel room. Cheap hotels in particular can fill up at popular times of year.

Douz International Festival

Museum of the Sahara The Museum of the Sahara is housed in a large building at the end of the village, just before you turn left onto Place des Martyrs and down towards the hammam. Recently revamped, the museum has displays on textiles and tents, desert plants (and their uses), domestic items and even tatoos. It illustrates the difficulty of making a good museum around what was a frugal way of life, perfectly adapted to a difficult environment. It would be nice to know how nomad life evolved as the French brought the Sahara into their orbit, and how life has changed in the last 20 years. An audiovisual display on nomad music and poetry might be a good thing, too. ■ *0830-1300 and 1500-1800.* (If you want to know more about nomads in southern Tunisia, try to get hold of Louis André's *Nomades d'hier et d'aujourd'hui dans le Sud tunisien* (Aix-en-Provence, Edisud, 1979).

Excursions

Desert trips Douz is an important point of departure for trips into the desert. In spring you could try a week's camping trip through the desert to **Ksar Ghilane** by camel. In summer the desert gets much too hot for these trips. ■ *Camel trekking is organized by Douz Voyages and by Abdelmoula Voyages (see Tour operators, page 354, for further details) – Douz to Ksar Ghilane (8 days) or Douz to Sabria (3 days). Price of 21Dt per day includes camels and drivers, cooks, blankets, sleeping bags, breakfast, lunch and dinner.*

Essentials

Sleeping
■ *on maps, page 350 and opposite. Price codes: see inside front cover*

Douz acquired large new hotels at a vertiginous rate in the late 1990s.They sit on the edge of the dunes the way hotels at Sousse are all lined up along the beach. The older, more modest hotels are in town or in the oasis. Although the big hotels are most comfortable, you might have more fun and find out more about the local people in one of the town centre cheapies.

Zone touristique (ZT) **A** *Iberotel Mehari*, T471088, F471589, elmouradi. douz@planet.tn 127 rooms, pool, opened 1999, built to look like a ribat, so plain stone exterior but inside a cool environment, luxury, rooms with phone, a/c, heating, 2 pools. The outside pool has sulphurous hot spring at a temperature of 25°C spilling down a sort of stone column. Hotel also has nightclub, boutiques, conference facilities. Recommended if you have the cash. **A** *Oasis El Mouradi*, T470303, F470905/906, meharidouz@ planet.tn Large hotel, used by safari tours, 342 beds in 180 rooms with a/c, outdoor pool and indoor covered pool with a solarium, hammam, sauna, and a 'fitness centre', conference facilities, well

Douz centre

To Kebili

Square Clock

Man on Camel Statue

Travel Agents

Chemist

Books & Cards Shop

To Zaafrane

Av Taïeb Mehiri

Louave Station

Rue de la Liberté

Av 7 Novembre

Rue Ghara Jawai

Christian / Craft Shops

Av des Martyrs

To Chemist, Post Office & Tourist Hotels

To Matmata, Ksar Guilane, Camping & Picnic Area

Secondary Market Area

Av Mongi Slim

Animal

Av Farhat Hached

Av 7 Novembre

OASIS

N

0 metres 50
0 yards 50

■ Sleeping	● Eating
1 20 Mars	1 Ali Baba
2 Bel Habib	2 Café 20 Mars
3 De la Tente	3 Café Amel
	4 Café Sahara
	5 La Rosa

appointed restaurant with a good choice of food. **B** *Le Sahara Douz*, T470864, F470566, 300 beds, opened in 1990, all with balcony, vast covered heated pool with hammam-type atmosphere. **B** *Sun Palm* (was *Caravanserai*), T470123, F470525, 130 rooms, pool, rather smaller establishment than others in the *ZT*. **B** *Touareg*, T470245, F470313, 315 beds. Built around a pool, restaurant and bar. **C** *Hotel Rose du Sable*, Rte touristique, T470597, not quite as nice a position as *Saharien*, recently renovated and enlarged, 200 beds in 90 rooms, all with bath and a/c and heating, pool, restaurant.

In the Oasis **B** *Hotel Saharien*, T471737, F470339. Turn left into the oasis, just before the corner with the Maison de la Culture. Accommodation in bungalows, most with bath, among the palms. Pool, delightful setting, rooms spacious but a little dusty, a/c and heating, hot water, not much choice for dinner. Bar lively with tour groups in evening. Continuing a couple of km down the road, you come to the stadium where the festival parade and displays are held.

In town **D** *Hotel Bel Habib*, on the Av du 7-Novembre near Pl du Souk, T471115, habibbek1@excite.com Clean, welcoming management, communal bath/toilet, large breakfast, dearer rooms have ensuite shower. Views from terrace over fruit and vegetable market. Owner will organize lifts – eg Ksar Ghilane in 4WD for 5Dt. **D** *Hotel du 20 Mars*, R du 20-Mars, behind the big square with the arcades, T470269. Unclassified, clean rooms off small patio. **D-E** *Hotel de la Tente*, R Gassi, T470468, F470978, next to louage station, reception on 1st floor, cheapest rooms 10Dt, sleep on the roof in a bedouin tent for 2Dt, nice manager. Recommended.

Camping *Camping du Désert*, in the palm groves, T/F470575. Modern campsite set up by Italians. Clean wash block, 70 camping spaces with lighting, restaurant with Italian food open to all.

Nothing to get very excited about here, although you should try the local 'desert pizza', *m'tebeg*. When eating in cheap restaurants, remember to calculate your bill. It may be tempting for an underpaid cashier to add on an extra 5Dt.

Eating
● *on map, page 352*

Expensive *Hotel El Mouradi*, good standard buffet evening meal in upmarket surroundings. **Mid-range** *Restaurant Ali Baba*, by the police station to north of town, keeps the backpackers happy. Hospitable son of the original owner runs the place with panache. Inside dining or outside in the sandy back courtyard. *Restaurant Le Petit Prince*, between the 2 tourist offices on Pl des Martyrs. *Restaurant La Rosa*, Av du 7-Novembre, in the town centre, friendly sort of place, has been recommended. **Cheap** *El Kods*, 100 m from tourist office, good simple food, cheap.

Stop in at the *Café du Théâtre* of an evening. This is where generations of amateur theatre groups have performed, and there are pictures on the walls to prove it. Generally, the place functions as a blokey chicha café. Pleasant service. Busy during the Douz Festival, but not with theatre.

Cafés

Hammam Unfortunately, a couple of the big hotels seem to have tapped most of the hot spring water for their clients. For the locals, there remains a small hammam located down the hill to the left after the museum. Mornings for men, afternoons for women. There is a covered pool to soak in, and individual cubicles with baths. Bring your own towels, no extras like massages.

Entertainment

Surprisingly perhaps, there are some really nice buys to be had in Douz. Have a look round the Pl du Souk. You could go for a pair of Douz shoes, which have some coloured

Shopping

embroidery and high backs, or a pair of *ni'al* sandals, very Ali-Baba with their pointed toes. Other good buys include camel-hair cloaks and blankets.

Tour operators *Douz Voyages*, Av Taïeb Mehiri, T470178/9, F470135, has various camel excursions as do *Abdelmoula Voyages*, Av des Martyrs, T495484, F459336. Try also *M'razig Voyages*, Av du 7-Novembre, T470255, F470515, and *Zaïed Travel Agency*, Av Taïeb Mehiri, T491918, F470584.

Transport **Bus**: from the station near the junction by the cemetery there are frequent buses to **Kebili**. Check times given here for buses: Tunis 0600 (via Kairouan) and 2030 (via Gabès and Sfax); **Gabès** 0700, 1000, 1430; **Tozeur** 0630; **El Faouar** (via Zaâfrane) 0645, 0800, 0900. The **local buses** can be absolutely jammed – a problem to get on and even worse to get off. **Louages**: are based near the bus station in the centre of town. Louages to Kebili 1.8Dt, to Gabès 6Dt. Almost opposite the louage station, you have the *nakl rifi* (rural transport) for Zaâfrane and places west.

Directory **Banks** Douz has the *STB*, just opposite the bus station on Taïeb Mehiri. At the time of writing, there were no ATMs. **Communications** Internet: on R el Hanin, near the market square, T472777; **Post Office**: in the centre of the town. **Medical services** Chemist: *Pharmacie Barnous*, R du 7-Novembre, T470369, near the market place. **Doctor**: T470213; **Hospital**: T470323/012.

From Douz into the desert

Southwest from Douz The metalled road from Douz takes you to Zaâfrane, about 10 km away, and on to the once remote oases of Sabria and El Faouar. You head out through new concrete housing and small palm gardens, neatly laid out, carefully irrigated, protected from the elements and the blowing sand by palm-frond fences. But soon the barren land appears and small salt lakes, which may provide birdwatchers with some interest. Lines of palm fronds stick out of the top of the dunes, the sand gleams almost white due to the high salt content, the road is a thin black line and the sky an amazing blue. Young eucalyptus trees line the road.

Zaâfrane
Phone code: 75

Zaâfrane is easily reached by public transport from Douz. The abandoned old village, west of the modern settlement, is slowly returning to the sands. New Zaâfrane stretches out along the road with palm groves to the north. Features include a police station, a water tower, a school, two bakeries, a butcher, taxiphone and post office. Modest housing was provided by the government to settle the nomads. Each property starts off consisting of a small square block with vaulted roofing for humans, plus a storeroom, opening onto a courtyard. According to their resources, individuals then build on as they can.

Tourist activity takes place on the El Faouar (west) side of the town, where there are photogenic dunes and the remains of the original village. The tourist office is open only in 'the season', unspecified, and is situated by the café and the dromedaries. There are many dromedaries here, already harnessed to take the tourists on a very short ride to see the sand.

Sleeping **C** *Hotel Zaâfrane*, T491720, small, simple hotel, café, beers, rooms with a/c, heating in winter. Excursions by camel are available, 25Dt per day, following a circuit around the water-holes, picnic with desert bread, cooked in the sand. Hotel also has a campsite out in the dunes.

The tribes of Nefzaoua

The region is called the Nefzaoua region and in it there are five tribes. These are the M'razuig *of the Douz area numbering around 29,000; the* Adara *of the Zaâfrane region numbering around 5,000; the 7,000* Sabria *in the region of the same name; the* Ghribs *of the Faouar region numbering* *3,000; and a final 3,000* Aoulad Yaghoub. *While to the visitor they may seem all alike there are obvious distinctions, clear to themselves, and each tribe can be recognized by the clothes, the bags, the tents and domestic objects and, on the women, their head and face coverings.*

Camel trips There are plenty of camels available for short rides into the desert from opposite the *Hotel Zaâfrane*. More interesting would be a few nights in the desert, walking/riding camels. One way to organize this is via the tourist office in Douz. Another option could be to ask in the local shops on the Douz side of Zaâfrane. This is very much at your own risk, however. The best times of year are spring and autumn. Remember to have a warm sleeping bag, as desert nights can be bitingly cold. The really courageous might want to travel south to isolated oases with magical names like Aïn Mansour, Bir Bel Kacem, Bir Touil el Adhara and Tembaïn.

Zaâfrane to Sabria and El Faouar

The land south of Zaâfrane is very flat, the bed of a dried lake. You could turn off left to visit Sabria, 3 km south off the C206. The palms begin 1 km off the main road. The road which bends sharply through the palms to the village soon deteriorates into a track. Although the settlement has spread the palm trees have been retained beside the houses, tempering the starkness of the settlement. Sabria goes about its daily rural business, there are chickens in the streets, goats by the houses, women by the well. Though a poor sort of place (hence investment by the National Solidarity Fund in the late-1990s), it has a certain charm. The children here are less used to tourists and if you come by car may lob the odd stone or follow you around.

Colour map 4, grid B1

Approaching El Faouar, the flat dried lake bed gives way to small dunes which have been stabilized with palm fronds and planted with mimosa and acacia. Moving the ever-encroaching sand seems to be a major occupation here, either with bulldozers or shovels and mule carts.

El Faouar
Phone code: 05

El Faouar is also accessible by bus, louage or hitchhiking. (In the winter there is a steady stream of four-wheel drive vehicles on the road west of Douz.) This is the last major village on the road. Try to see the **market** on Friday when any nomads and locals assemble. It is at its most interesting when dates are in season. Go early in the morning as many goods have disappeared by 1000. El Faouar is surprisingly large and busy with a police station, a clinic, a large school and oasis. The *Café de Tunis* stands at the entrance to the town on the south of the road, the chairs and tables are set up across the street. The central square, from which the buses and louages leave, is marked by the mosque and a square-faced clock. Here stands *Restaurant Salam*. The first bus of the day (good quality but exceedingly crowded) leaves about 1000 from El Faouar.

Sleeping B-C *Hotel El Faouar*, T460531, F460576, international telephones, satellite TV, 106 rooms with 300 beds, a/c and heating, comfortable shady lounge area, bar (with alcohol), sand skiing, folklore during dinner under tents, is virtually built in the desert,

Southwestern Tunisia

The Roman frontier

*In the second and third centuries AD, the Roman province of **Africa** prospered in peace. While the northern provinces of the empire faced invasion from Germanic tribes, the Rome's southern African frontier was a different matter. The pre-Saharan and Saharan regions were peopled by Berber nomads, who no doubt moved northwards in the summer when the scarce desert pasture for their flocks ran out. They may also have participated in the annual grain harvest, much as nomads continued to do well into the 20th century. To keep a check on the nomads, the Romans, with their usual efficiency, developed a frontier defence system referred to as the* limes. *Unlike massive works like Hadrian's Wall in the province of Britain, it was designed more as a filter than a linear frontier.*

Part of the more extensive limes *Tripolitanus, a defensive zone varying from 50 km to 100 km in width, the* limes *in Africa had two main parts. The northern line of defence ran east-west from **Tacapae** (**Gabès**), via **Thelepte** to **Haïdra**. Eventually, as Romanization advanced, it was extended to **Teveste** (**Tebessa**) and **Lambaesis**, both in*

*contemporary **Algeria**. The southern limit of the* limes, *completed under the Severan emperors, ran from **Leptis Magna** (in **Libya**) across to **Turris Tamalleni** (**Telmine**), just north of modern **Kebili**. The frontier was designated by forts and camps, watchtowers (equipped with mirrors for signalling) and short sections of wall and ditch (fossatum). The whole system made good use of natural features such as the chotts, which became impassable in winter and spring after the rains. Scholars believe that the whole point was to regulate pastoral tribes, ensuring that their beasts did not stray into Roman farmlands when the crops were young. The* limes *was practical, no doubt permitting the taxing of the nomads as well.*

More than 140 sites forming part of the limes *have been identified. Some of the most important ones – **Turris Tamalleni**, **Talalati** (**Ras el Ain Tlalit**, near **Tataouine**) – are little more than heaps of stones today. The outpost of **Ksar Ghilane** has survived, witness to Roman tenacity.*

with pool, restaurant. The hotel organizes 4WD and camel trips (2-3 hrs) in the desert and you can learn dune skiing! The palm groves close round the village to the west.

West of El Faouar Until recently, the surfaced road ended at El Faouar. By 1999, the road had been surfaced all the way round the western end of the Chott el Djerid, enabling the visitor to complete a circuit to Tozeur. The state has ploughed considerable sums of money into developing the oasis at **Rejim Maâtoug** to the west, with the army involved in land preparation and construction work.

Another possibility from El Faouar is to return to Kebili (54 km) via the isolated settlements of **Blidet** and **Touiba**. Returning up the main Zaâfrane to Douz P206, you would turn off left on the metalled road which runs to Blidet via Noueil. There are regular daily buses from Kebili to Blidet and Noueil. The old settlement of Blidet, visible from the road, has been abandoned to crumble away around its whitewashed marabout. In the school holidays, hordes of children will emerge to show you round the ruined village.

On Nefzaoua desert roads

There was a good deal of road improvement in the Nefzaoua in the late 1990s. Unfortunately, the maps available in Tunisia (Geo-Center and Freytag and Berndt) are not always accurate, especially for the area west of Douz. The maps show the P210 from Blidet as joining a road between Sabria and El Faouar. This is not the case – unless it was completed in late 1999. Sabria is shown as being on the P952 Douz to El Faouar road, when it is actually 3 km south of the road, etc. Be aware of the official map deficiencies when travelling in the area, and be prepared to ask. (Ettarik mekeyyes walla piste? *Is the road tarmacked or track?*)

If you pick up a hitchhiker at a remote settlement, they may advise you to take shortcuts across sandy piste. Such shortcuts are not to be attempted lightly in a hire car. You need to have confidence in your skills as an off-road driver and a spade. Getting stuck in the middle of nowhere with night coming on is tedious, to say the least. And you will probably be in breach of your hire car contract.

East to Ksar Ghilane

Remote Ksar Ghilane is a long uncomfortable slog across the desert. A four-wheel-drive safari from Djerba will probably take you there via Matmata and Tamezret. The short stretch from Matmata to Tamezret is a little rough, while from Tamezret, you take a rough track for 18 km to join the pipeline track. With the pipeline on your right, head southwards for 59 km. Then turn right for Ksar Ghilane, which is 13 km down a rough track. Another possible approach is via a piste from Chenini. This is not to be recommended unless you are a very good navigator and have a tough four-wheel drive. The route from Douz, 124 km, really does not warrant doing unless you have a yen for flat stony landscapes. Note that the Douz to Matmata route is now fully surfaced. *Colour map 4, grid B3*

Ksar Ghilane (Roman Tisvar) is the most isolated of the oases, a small settlement right out in the desert, recently discovered by tourism. There are numerous tamarisk trees, a little cultivation, a few nomad shacks, and three camp-type hotels. The outstanding feature of Ksar Ghilane, however, is the nearby remains of an ancient fort. **Ksar Ghilane**

The Roman fort or *castellum* of Tisvar is on a low rise looking out over the dunes. The scenery is totally Beau Geste; the military objective was control of an important watering point mid-way between the Nefzaoua and the *castrum* (camp) at Remada (ancient Tillibari), in the far south of modern Tunisia. The fort is thought to have been built under the emperor Commodus in the second century AD. It may well have continued in use into the Middle Ages, and was excavated by the French, who discovered an altar to the spirit of Tisvar. The fort was an outpost of the main *limes* which lay further north. No doubt its solid construction and Roman garrison effectively intimidated the nomads. The commander would have been responsible for providing intelligence on nomad movements.

Sleeping Until the 1990s, the drive to Ksar Ghilane was the ultimate adventure of the Tunisian south. It is still sold as such by the four-wheel-drive safari operators. Today there are three tourist campsites, including the extremely pricey **AL** *Pansea* which even has a pool. Reservations via *SITH* in Tunis on T71893275, F71846129. Also via Paris office of *Pansea CIRH* on T1-42275431, F1-42275434, www.pansea.com The *Pansea* is

Southwestern Tunisia

sold as a harbour of peace and tranquillity. There is a watchtower for looking out over the oasis, and the reception areas and bar are built with vaults like the *ghorfa* granaries of the Tunisian south. People from the other campsites will not hesitate to come trooping through, however, just to have a peek at the rising sun. The catering has had some very mixed reports. NB Credit cards not accepted.

Camping Try the the **Campement Le Paradis** close to the spring, reservations via Tunis on T71752108, in France T03-26554160, F03-26578708. Prices around 20Dt per person on half-board. Excursions organized.

Southeastern Tunisia

8

Southeastern Tunisia

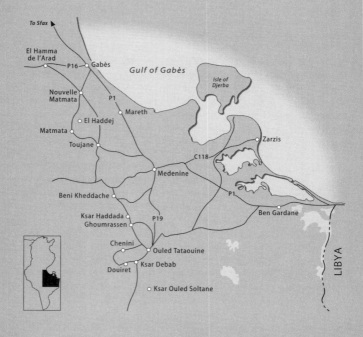

*Heading south from Sfax, the olive plantations gradually give way to an arid monotony. At **Gabès**, the visitor has a first taste of the South. Right next to the sea is a great oasis. Inland, the landscape soon turns mountainous, and here at the northern end of the **Djebel Dahar** are villages of pit homes at **Matmata** and hilltop Amazigh outposts. On the road south, the battles of the Second World War are commemorated at **Mareth** in a military museum. The burgeoning town of **Tataouine** is the gateway to the citadel villages of **Chenini**, **Guermessa** and **Douiret**. The region is also home to numerous ksour, fortified granaries which once played such a key part in the lives of the region's tribes. East from **Medenine**, the coast is quickly reached again. **Zarzis** has pleasant hotels and sandy beach, while towards the Libyan frontier, the remote **Bhiret el Bibane lagoon** will provide opportunities for birdwatching.*

Background

Under the French protectorate, Tunisia was seen as a land which divided into a rich, fertile, well-watered North, around Tunis, Sousse and Sfax and the cereal growing lands of Béja, and an arid South which had to be administered, in part, to keep Italian colonial ambitions at bay. In the decades following independence, there was considerable migration from the arid South to the northern cities and on to France. Investment in modern agriculture and industry tended to be on the northeastern seabord, reinforcing the pull. In the 1990s, tourism and petroleum-based manufacturing slightly redressed the balance, though almost all of this kind of employment has tended to be on the coast. One unexpected factor did help the development of southeast Tunisia, however – the UN-imposed embargo on Libya, which created a huge amount of business. The result today is a scattering of increasingly developed towns – industrial and military Gabès, desert Tataouine, regional centre Medinine, tourist-oriented Zarzis – and inland areas left with low productivity agriculture.

1990s prosperity The bustling air of incipient prosperity in the southern towns is based on a number of factors: phosphate processing, petroleum exploration, tourism and new agricultural ventures. Petroleum exploration is mainly offshore but workers in the industry come mainly from the South, basically because they can stand the heat and have no qualms about spending long periods working away from home. In the late 1990s, a large number of new hotels went up along the northeast coast of Djerba, catering mainly for the European package market (see next chapter). These hotels – and the building sites – on Djerba are an important source of employment, too. Inland from Gabès too, new hotels at Matmata have made this a comfortable overnight stop, and the completion of the direct road from Matmata to Douz has created a southern tourist circuit in the desert for European visitors, most of whom would never have found their way to this region. Even once sleepy Tataouine is getting in on the act, with several new hotel ventures. Four-wheel drive tourism is getting (perhaps unfortunately) to be a major source of income for local people.

Agriculture The changes in agriculture in the South are less dramatically visible than the convoys of four-wheel drive vehicles. In addition to the age-old export of dates, the warm, sunny winters of the South are now used to grow crops demanded out of season in prosperous industrialized states of the EU. Recently, melon and soft fruit have been grown for the French market. New technology and newly found underground water supplies may allow further development, especially with the opening of EU markets thanks to the Association Agreement of 1995. And the waters of the Mediterranean too contribute to the region's economy. King prawns, octopus, squid and cuttlefish found in the region of Gabès are all valuable exports.

Effects of the Libyan embargo For most of the 1990s, the UN embargo on Libya injected much cash into the region's economy. Libyans travelling abroad were obliged to transit either via Djerba (or Malta). The black market in the Libyan currency made products subsidized by the Libyan State incredibly cheap, and large amounts of electrical goods, foodstuffs and household essentials found their way into Tunisia to be sold in the informal 'Libyan souks' on the outskirts of the main towns. The embargo ended in 1999, and it remains to be seen how this will effect the informal Libyan trade that gave a boost to so many households' incomes. Libyans

★

Things to do

- View the market of **Tataouine**. Can you find a *bakhnoug* (traditional bordeaux-coloured weaving with fine white embroidery)?
- Take a trip out to the mountain villages of **Chenini** and **Douiret** or the best preserved fortified granary at **Ksar Ouled Soltane**.
- Have a look at the mini-fossil museum near Tataouine.
- Using a 4WD, cross arid landscapes to **Ksar Ghilane**.
- See how the black market in imported products from Libya operates at **Ben Gardane**.

from the Tripoli region still look set to enjoy weekends in Djerba (and Malta) as a break from their country's somewhat austere atmosphere, and there is a well established tradition of Libyans travelling up to Sfax for medical treatament.

The south of Tunisia, including the Djerid, is growing in importance in the overall Tunisian economy. Djerba has changed from being a somewhat exclusive and sleepy island resort into a major package destination, especially popular with Germans. The knock-on effects of the jobs generated are felt across the South - witness the vast amount of new building. It remains to be seen whether tourism in the south of Tunisia is sustainable and this depends principally on the development of something more challenging for the tourist than being driven across stoney wastes in an air-conditioned four-wheel drive vehicle.

Visitors heading to southeast Tunisia do so mainly for the landscapes. There are some extraordinary forms of local habitat to see, too. With plenty of time, you would want to have a look at the the **pit-dwellings** and **Amazigh villages** of the **Matmata region**, 40 km west of Gabès (say one day, though two would be better), and some of the **hillcrest villages** and **fortified granaries** (*ksour*) in the Tataouine region. Here again, two days would be best. Note that Gabès to Tataouine is 135 km, say 2½ hours driving time. Another worthwhile if small attraction is the **Mareth Line military museum**, some 40 km south of Gabès.

What to see in Southeast Tunisia

The Land Rover safari packages are organized to cover the main villages and most striking landscapes. For the full desert experience, you could take a package to one of the tent hotels out in the desert at Ksar Ghilane (see previous chapter). Whether the hours of piste driving are really worth it is another matter.

Basically, in the Matmata region, you should see old **Matmata** and **Tamezret**, and if there is enough time, Toujane and Techine (rough tracks to these destinations). South of **Tataouine**, **Douiret** and **Chenini de Tataouine** should not be missed, along with isolated Ksar Ouled Soltane (perhaps the best preserved *ksar*). Guermessa, Ghomrassen and Ksar Haddada are worth a look if there is time. Most of the remaining *ksour* are for enthusiasts only.

Note that although the distances are not enormous, in the summer, the hot sun takes it out of you, meaning that not as much gets covered as you would like. If you are driving down from Tunis to Gabès, a good journey time (without stops) is 5¼ hours, Sfax to Gabès, just over 2 hours, and Sousse to Gabès, 3¾ hours, in clear road conditions. Matmata is well under an hour from Gabès on a much widened and resurfaced road. 75 km separate Gabès from Medenine, the main road junction town for the Southeast. From Medenine, distances to main towns are: Tataouine, a fast 40 km; Zarzis, similarly, a fast 60 km on a good road. The ferry to Djerba from Djorf is a short drive north of Medenine.

Driving times to Southeast Tunisia

Southeastern Tunisia

Gabès   قابس

Phone code: 75
Colour map 4, grid A4

As you head south from Sfax, Gabès is the first town where you really feel 'the South'. The pace seems slower, the traffic more erratic. Despite much industry both north and south of the town, the oasis, in fact only seabord oasis in Tunisia, remains an important presence. There is a garrison, a reminder that Gabès sits strategically on the easiest north-south route. Tourism is a minor activity – there is a small souk catering for the four-wheel drive trade. But Gabès merits more than just a cursory halt. It is also well situated for day trips to troglodyte Matmata and reminders of the Second World War Mareth line.

Ins and outs

Getting there
See Transport, page 371, for further details

Strategically located Gabès can be reached by road and rail. It is a transport hub with buses coming in from all over the country. Journey time from Tunis by louage, if the motorway is not too crowded, is around 6 hrs, including short stops.

If you are driving, the GP1 Sfax to Gabès road (138 km) is single lane all the way. Journey time around 2¼ hrs. Heavy traffic in Sfax's southern suburbs and lorries will slow you down. Remember to slow at roadside settlements – the Garde nationale may be lurking. 95 km from Sfax, Bou Saïd with its numerous butchers is a good place for a pause and a barbecue lunch. Next 'main' settlement with mechoui restaurants is Akarit, 106 km out of Sfax, prominent features being a metal railway bridge over deep oued, mosque and Garde nationale waiting under the gum trees.

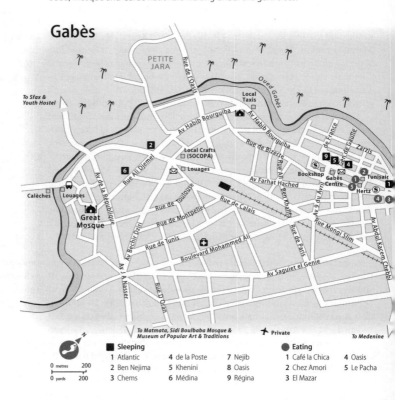

Gabès

■ **Sleeping**	● **Eating**
1 Atlantic 4 de la Poste 7 Nejib	1 Café la Chica 4 Oasis
2 Ben Nejima 5 Khenini 8 Oasis	2 Chez Amori 5 Le Pacha
3 Chems 6 Médina 9 Régina	3 El Mazar

0 metres   200
0 yards   200

To Matmata, Sidi Boulbaba Mosque &
Museum of Popular Art & Traditions

✈ Private

To Medenine

Coming in from the north (Kairouan), you will have headed down the single-lane but fairly empty GP2 via Bir Ali Khalifa (road restaurants, hotel in the form of the monster *Hmaissa Relax Center*, small campsite opposite) to intersect with the GP1 at Sekhira, 160 km from Kairouan. Sekhira to Gabès is just over 60 km. Coming in from Gafsa to the northwest, the GP15 intersects with the GP1 at Oudref, some 20 km northwest of Gabès.

Other distances to Gabès: Matmata 40 km, Mareth 35 km, Djorf (for Djerba ferry) 90 km, Kebili 116 km, El Hamma 29 km.

The bus station is on the main street, Av Farhat Hached, at the west end, where the Sfax road comes into town. Walk east to the town centre. There are a number of louage stations, the main 1 being next to the main bus station. Louages for local destinations like Mareth and Matmata leave from next to the Great Mosque opposite the tourist souk. Louages for Matmata also leave from the Av Farhat Hached, almost opposite the Hotels *Ben Nejma* and *Marhaba*. Trains from Tunis and the coastal resorts, Gafsa and Metlaoui, arrive at the station on Av 1er Juin, in the centre of town. **Getting around**

The tourist information office is at Pl de la Libération, T220254, open 0830-1300 and 1500-1745, closed Fri, Sat and Sun afternoon. **Tourist information**

Coming in from the north, the GP1 narrows. Busy with traffic, it reaches a roundabout set with a strange golden palm tree monument. Take 2nd exit after *Agil* for Av de la République, the main north-south inner ring-road. Follow through. Matmata is signed right at the clock roundabout. If you need to overnight, there is the new *Hotel Anis*. The ribbon development south of the town now extends all the way down to Teboulbou (3 petrol stations, including *Agil* for unleaded petrol, pharmacy, publitel). **Driving through Gabès**

To Tunis ▲

Harbour

Customs

Casino (Closed)

Av Hedi Chaker

Av Habib Thameur

Promenade

[Pol] Place de la Libération

Coming down from Kairouan or Sfax, you may be tempted to avoid Gabès altogether and head on south. The town can be bypassed by a route to the west. There is a turn-off 16 km north of Gabès near Oudref, signposted to Kebili. This turning is alongside the military zone (guard posts with armed guards – definitely not the place to take photographs.) You will know you are on the right road if you almost immediately cross the railway. Take a right turn to Oudref (a bit confusing when you know you want to be going south) and then left on to the C208. On the road south ignore the industrial pollution from the cement works to the west of Gabès and note the ruined ksar up on the hillside to the east of the road instead. In this area you may see a number of black tents, depending on the season and the grazing available. The nomads are not fully settled and these tents are erected adjacent to pasture for the herds. Very little of this route is lit at night. **Bypassing Gabès**

Southeastern Tunisia

History

Thought to be of Phoenician origins, by 161 BC Gabès was part of the Carthaginian domains, an important trading link with the South. Under Roman rule, it was known as Tacapae Destroyed during the Arab invasions, the rebirth of the town was linked to the arrival of Sidi Boulbaba, the Prophet's companion, in the seventh century. He is now revered as the town's patron saint. Gabès later became an important halt on the caravan routes from the South.

The French turned Gabès into a garrison town. Concerned about potential Italian interference from neighbouring Libya, they set up their largest base in the south. During the Second World War, the Afrika Korps had its headquarters in Gabès, using it as a strategic point on their supply lines back to Libya. The town was retaken in March 1943 by British and French troops, but only after extensive damage had been done.

Modern Gabès is a relatively new city, much of it having been rebuilt after the Second World War and the serious floods in 1962. Despite the long beaches and fine sand, the coast is not very appealing. Today, apart from traditional industries such as fishing and agriculture based on fruit from the oasis and the 300,000 palm trees, Gabès has become highly industrialized with a massive cement and brick factory, an oil refinery, harbour and projects for petro-chemical industries. Oil and gas wells have been drilled offshore in the Gulf of Gabès. Fortunately, though, the industries are dispersed over the surrounding suburbs, making them less conspicuous. There are two ports, the small harbour in town and the industrial port 6 km away.

The amount of industry probably means that the sea at Gabès is polluted, but it is nevertheless worth a stop to enjoy the coolness of the oasis. In summer, local people tend to head south of town to Teboulbou to swim.

Sights

Despite having a population of nearly 100,000, Gabès has a sleepy small-town feel. The main attraction is the large oasis which comes right down to the sea. A full day should be enough to explore the main sights and take in the atmosphere.

Downtown Gabès can seem a confusing place to the first time visitor. There is no readily comprehensible distinction between the walled old town and new 19th-century neighbourhoods. Traditionally, there were two rival quarters: **Menzel**, basically the area south of the present bus station; and **Jara**, which divides into two parts: Petite Jara, north of the Oued Gabès, and Grande Jara. The French established a small new town and a large military base east of Jara, towards their new port.

Practically no ancient monuments remain in Gabès. Nonetheless, up in the oasis there are traces of the Roman dam across the Oued Gabès, several pillars and column capitals that have been incorporated in the mosque of Sidi Idris and the mausoleum of Sidi Boulbaba. Some other fragments of lesser value have been used in buildings in the older quarters.

North of the Oued Gabès: Petite Jara One of the most important old buildings is the **Mosque of Sidi Idris**, over the oued in Petite Jara. The building goes back to the 11th century and although you will not be able to see the interior, a considerable amount of Roman masonry was recycled into the building. Unfortunately, many of the Jara neighbourhood's older buildings disappeared during the bombardments of the Second World War.

Henna for the future husband

"Traditionally, the bride's henna ceremony would involve elaborate geometric designs being placed on hands and feet. The future husband, too, might have a finger tip dyed with henna, or designs placed on the inside of the hand. The henna ceremonies

would be accompanied by much rejoicing and singing."

From Nomades d'hier et d'aujourd'hui dans le Sud tunisien *by André Louis (Aix: Edisud, 1979)*

In the Menzel district, you might look out for the **Great Mosque** at the junction of Avenue de la République and Avenue Bechir Dziri, dating back to 1938. The neighbourhood has its own market on Rue Omar el Mokhtar. The **Zaouia of Sidi Ben Issa** is another interesting old building to look out for in Menzel.

Menzel

More spectacular is the **mosque** on Avenue Bourguiba in Grande Jara, recently heavily expanded. Opposite the mosque is a **souk** which attracts plenty of tourists. Local handicrafts include basketwork items and hats made of plaited palm. There are stalls selling jewellery, food and spices. Both spices and plaited items are very good buys. However, Gabès's real speciality is **henna** and you can see powdery green volcanoes of this powerful dye in the souk. There are three strengths, 'neutral', red and black. The strength of the henna depends on how long the leaves were left on the plant. Neutral henna strengthens the hair. Red henna is used as hair dye, while black is used for geometric temporary bridal tatooes. In the souk, you may find a stall able to do you a quick scorpion design.

The maritime **oasis** of Gabès, area 10 sq km, has an estimated 300,000 palm trees sheltering hundreds of olive and fruit trees, plus numerous vegetable gardens. To get to the more attractive parts of the oasis you can go by car towards the village of **Chenini** by taking the main road towards Sfax, turning left in the direction of Kebili, then left again, signposted Chenini. Alternatively, go on foot from the other end of the oasis, by the bus station, crossing the little bridge. Following the road it is 7 km to Chenini, but it is not necessary to go that far since there are pleasant walks along the small, shaded paths between the palm trees, especially in summer. A more picturesque way to see the oasis is to take a *calèche* from the end of Avenue Farhat Hached. A good tour takes around 1¼ hours.
■ *The price, 12Dt, for up to 4 people, is set by the Tourist Office.*

The Oasis

The oasis has a couple of sights in the form of a small **zoo** (entrance 0.5Dt) complete with crocodiles and scorpions. At the end of the oasis, towards the source of the river, are located the **Sidi Ali el Bahloul Mausoleum** and a very small waterfall. The area attracts a very high proportion of tourists but the oasis is large, and it is easy to get away from the crowds.

South of town, about 30 minutes on foot, is the third of Gabès historic areas, the Boulbaba neighbourhood. The elegant **Mosque of Sidi Boulbaba**, dating back to the seventh century, is one of the most important religious monuments in the area. This is the burial place of Sidi Boulbaba, who was the Prophet's barber after he came from Kairouan. Only the inner courtyard is open to visitors. The saint is still the object of much veneration, and on Friday afternoon the smell of incense wafts around the mausoleum. The portico is crowded by people drinking tea kept hot on small charcoal braseros. Women come to ask Sidi Boulbaba's intercession for success in exams, a happy marriage or to bring about a much-awaited pregnancy.

Boulbaba neighbour-hood

Southeastern Tunisia

Also in the Boulbaba neighbourhood is the **Museum of Popular Arts and Traditions**, housed in a former medersa next to the Sidi Boulbaba mosque. Built during the reign of Mohammed Bey, the medersa once provided student accommodation. Today, the rooms contain a collection of everyday objects demonstrating the traditional way of life in Gabès. Although information is a bit lacking, there may be a guide on hand to add explanations. There are four sections: domestic crafts, marriage, oasis cultivation, food preparation and storage. Nevertheless, the building is the prime attraction.

Inside the building, the first room on the left begins with **domestic crafts**. This section focuses on women's traditional home-based handicrafts, notably weaving and embroidering. There are different kinds of wool on display, together with the spinning, combing and dyeing tools, jars with different vegetable dyes (tannin, henna, et cetera), a vertical loom and examples of typical textiles (*hambel*, *bettaniya* and *ferrashiya*). Also on display are different veils: on the right the white veil typical of Gabès, in the centre the veil decorated for wedding ceremonies at Gabès, on the left the Matmata veil. There are also displays of cushions, blankets, kilims and a selection of embroidery.

In the room opposite the main entrance, originally the prayer hall of the medersa, **marriage** is the theme. Here the trousseau, traditionally given to the bride by the groom, and the dowry are on display. In the middle of the room, three different bridal dresses are on show; the first to be worn during the ceremony, the second when the bride was introduced to relatives, the third for the seventh and last day of the wedding feast.

In the section on **agriculture in the oasis** there are displays of different tools, jars to transport foodstuffs, along with information on irrigation and cultivation patterns. The section on **food preparation and storage** has jars and boxes with vegetables and cereals, photographs of 10 different types of dates, oil-press, mortar, millstones, jars and pots.

Leaving the display areas, turn right into the small garden where, among the fruit trees, you can find Roman and Punic capitols. At the end of the garden it is possible to see the old minaret of the medersa. ■ *Daily 0800-1300 and 1600-1900 summer, 0930-1630 winter, closed Mon. 1.10Dt plus 1Dt photograph fee, flash prohibited. T281111.*

Essentials

Sleeping
■ *on map, page 364*
Price codes:
see inside front cover

C *Hotel Chems*, end of Av Habib Thameur, 1st on the right after the railway line, 5-mins walk from the centre, just beyond *Hotel de l'Oasis*, T270547, F274485, 1 min to beach. Over 200 a/c rooms with telephone, each with a small terrace, some with sea view, small pool, childrens' pool, 500-seat restaurant. A standard 3-star hotel, clean but dull. Ugly tiles and 1970s décor, obliging reception but pitiful breakfast. The hotel is situated right next door to the *Foire Internationale de Gabès*, much used for weddings in summer. Heavily amplified music means you will be sleeping with windows closed and a/c on – unless you go and invite yourself to a wedding. **C** *Hotel de l'Oasis*,

Museum of Popular Arts & Traditions

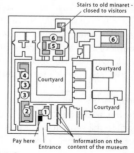

Displays of
1 Wool & associated crafts
2 Veils
3 Cushions, blankets, kilims & embroidery
4 Embroidered blouses & embroidered motifs
5 Wedding dresses & finery
6 Agriculture in the Oasis

Fingers of light – or the dates of Tunisia

In Tunisian cities, the feathery foliage of the date palm waves majestically over squares and avenues. In the southern oases of Tunisia, it is the tree of life: its fruit, leaves and wood the basis of the local economy. The Swedish naturalist Carl Linnaeus rendered homage to the beauty and generosity of the palm tree when he classified it in the order of Principes. The Latin name of the date palm, Phoenix dactylifera, *may be translated as "the Phoenician tree with fruit resembling fingers" and Tunisia's top variety of date, the famed* Deglet Nour, *are also referred to as* doigts de lumière.

The date palm is a close relation of the grasses. Its trunk is in fact a stem with no branches. It has no bark, being simply covered by the base of the old fallen leaves. A cross section of a palm trunk reveals a multitude of rigid tubes containing sap bearing vessels, rather than annual growth rings.

In the wild state, the young palm tree tends to resemble a hedgehog due to the uncontrolled development of buds at the base of the initial trunk. If severed with skill, these buds can be planted elsewhere. There are both male and female trees. Broadly speaking, a male tree can pollinate some 50 female trees but to ensure maximum fruit production, the farmer will place a sprig of male flowers next to the female flowers.

In March or April, the tiny green date is round like a marble. Its future is uncertain

for if the sand winds are too fierce, it may be blown from the tree before its time. During the summer, the date reaches full size, becoming smooth and yellow, rich in vitamins but bitter to taste. In the heat of the summer and autumn, the fruit slowly matures on the tree, softening and turning an amber colour, deep brown or black, depending on the variety. The date sugars change as well and little by little, the date dries out and becomes a preserved fruit while still on the tree.

Each country has its top varieties of date. As well as Deglet Nour, *Tunisia produces the Kuwat, a rather dry dessert date; Kentra which is very sweet; Menakher, the robust Allig and Ftimi; and Kentichi, a dry date stored in jars and which does not harden.*

The date is no longer a providential food for oasis dwellers. The date palm orchard, now limited to the top producing varieties, has become more fragile. The market economy now regulates the palm grove with all that this implies in terms of processing and packaging. Whereas in the traditional palm grove, apricots, pomegranates, figs and oranges were grown in the shade of the palms, newly planted groves are laid out to permit greater mechanization. Whereas once there were tiny allotments between the irrigation channels, the modern palm grove is devoted to dates alone.

at the end of Av Habib Thameur, 2nd turn right after railway line, T270381, F273834, just 5 mins walk from town centre and 1 min from beach. 112 a/c rooms with bath, private terrace, telephone, sea view, also 9 luxury apartments, safe car parking, conference facilities for 20-200 persons, small pool and some garden. Gabès' number one address, which must have been very stylish in the 1970s, now needs a low-key facelift.

D *Chellah Club* (Village de Vacances), in Chenini in the oasis, 20 mins from the beach and 300 m from the zoo, T270442, T/F227446, clearly signposted. Accommodation in 50 small bungalows (damp in winter and spring), ask for hot water as heating runs independently in each bungalow, indoor restaurant only fair, outdoor restaurant under vine arbour marred by overamplified music, pool small and mucky, no credit cards, no money change, from Gabès yellow taxi to Chenini around 1.5Dt. Must have been very pleasant in its day, but basically now functions as locals' drinking den. Nothing wrong with that – but the food could be improved. Bungalows have pitched roofs, and are hot in summer, though they provide you with a fan. Bring your insect repellant.

Southeastern Tunisia

D *Hotel Anis*, about 3 km from town on road to Medenine, T278744. Very new. **D** *Hotel Nejib*, corner of Av H. Bourguiba and Av Farhat Hached, T271686. 56 rooms, all mod cons, a/c, noisy due to main streets on both sides, slightly overpriced but very comfortable and convenient, showing signs of age.

E *Hotel Atlantic*, 4 Av H. Bourguiba, T220034. Old hotel retains some charm but needs decorating, clean, all 64 rooms have bath, restaurant, good value, recommended. **E** *Hotel Khenini*, Blvd Mohammed Ali, T270320. 34 rooms with bath, breakfast only 1.5Dt. **E** *Hotel Médina*, near Great Mosque, T274271. 40 rooms. **E** *Régina*, 135 Av H. Bourguiba, T272095. Only 14 rooms with bath, arranged around central courtyard back from the street, clean, restaurant, food is served on the patio, best of the cheap hotels. However, in summer the patio is used for weddings, which means no sleep until the small hours. A good opportunity for a free invitation.

F *Ben Nejima*, 68 R Ali Djemel, near train station, T271591. Clean, quite pleasant and very simple, hot communal showers, rooms at front rather noisy, acceptable cheap restaurant; **F** *Hotel de la Poste*, 116 Av H. Bourguiba, T270718. Very cheap but not really very clean, communal bath and toilets.

Youth hostel Known as *Sanit el Bey* or *Centre de stages et de vacances*, R de l'Oasis, T270271, F275035. In Petite Jara quarter north of the souk. Small rooms, 80 beds, clean, 4Dt per night, breakfast 1Dt, dinner 3Dt.

Camping On main road, follow sign opposite *Agil* petrol station. Cheap and adequate, also at Youth Hostel, 2Dt per person, 1Dt per tent, per car and per van. Palm trees here provide some shade.

Eating
● *on map, page 364*
Note also several very cheap, very small, restaurants beside the vegetable market off Av Farhat Hached

Expensive *Restaurant Chez Amori*, 82 Av H. Bourguiba. Has good, simple Tunisian food, choose the fish before it is cooked, very friendly. *Restaurant l'Oasis*, 15-17 Av Farhat Hached, T270098. A very popular restaurant especially for locals at lunch time, evenings are quieter, more expensive than the others. *Restaurant* in *Hotel Chems*, serves international and some Tunisian food, buffet 11Dt, menu 7.5Dt. Try also restaurant *El Mazar*, Av Farhat Hached, T272065. **Mid-range** *Restaurant A la bonne table*, Av H. Bourguiba. Very reasonably priced. *Le Pacha*, Av Farhat Hached. Filling food, served by welcoming people. *Pizzaria Pino*, 114 Av H. Bourguiba, T272010. Standard Tunisian version of Italian grub. Clean, no booze. **Cheap** *La Ruche*, on the road to Sfax, T270369. *El Khalij*, Av Farhat Hached, T221412. *Chez Amori*, 82 Av H. Bourguiba. Is not quite as good as it used to be, choose the fish before it is cooked. The restaurant in *Hotel Ben Nejima* has good, well presented food.

Shopping
Bargains *SOCOPA* (part of ONAT) on Blvd Farhat Hached by post office has a range of quality goods. Open 0900-1300 and 1600-1900 summer, 0830-1230 and 1500-1830 winter, closed Sun afternoon. Gabès is well known for its woven palm-frond products (see souk). **Books** The bookshop marked on map has a very good selection. **Crafts** The ONAT school/workshop on Av Farhat Hached, T270775, is worth a visit to see all the local handicrafts on display, closed Fri and Sat afternoons. This is where the various craft techniques are taught. The course lasts 2-3 years for jewellery making, with some of the young artisans opening their own shops on completing the course. There are courses, too, on palm-frond weaving and carpet-making and the demonstrations show how these skills are taught. **Food** In the area of the Sidi Boulbaba mosque and the museum, on the corner on the right, there is good bakery. **General** The *Gabès Centre* on Av H. Bourguiba has a selection of small and noisy boutiques, plus a public internet centre on the 1st floor.

Sailing 20 yacht berths min-max draft 2-4½ m, T270367. **Sport**

It is possible to get a round trip visiting all the villages and the area surrounding Gabès. **Tour operators**
Tour operators offer a variety of options, including travel by 4WD with a group of 5-10
people. *Etoile du Sud*, Av Farhat Hached (same office as *Express Rent*), T650244,
F651076. *Voyage Najar Chabane*, Av Farhat Hached, T272158, F277555. *Europtours*,
12 Av Farhat Hached, T274720. *Sahara Tours*, Av Farhat Hached, T270930. *Gabès Voyage*, Av Farhat Hached, T270797. *Carthage Tours*, Av H. Bourguiba, T270840.

Local Car hire: Hire here as there are no facilities in Medenine or Foum Tataouine. **Transport**
Avis, R du 9 Avril, T270210; *Budget*, 57 Av Farhat Hached, T270930; *Europcar*, 12 Av
Farhat Hached, T274720; *Economic Rent-a-Car*, 159 Av Farhat Hached, T257515;
Express, 154 Av Farhat Hached, T274222, F276211; *Hertz*, 30 R Ibn el Jazzar, T270525.
Cycle hire: enquire at the Youth hostel or at *Hotel de la Poste*.

Long distance Air: nearest airport is Sfax 137 km north or Houmt-Souq on Djerba 106
km east. *Tunisair*, Av H. Bourguiba, T270697; *Tunis Avia*, Rte de Sfax, T272501. **Train**: the
train station is off R Farhat Hached. Information on T270744. Departures as follows: Tunis
(via Sfax and Sousse) 1535, 2310. **Bus**: the bus station is at the end of Av Farhat Hached,
by the entrance to the oasis. Information, T270008. In Gabès there are 3 bus companies,
all in the same place. *Sotregames* (timetable only in Arabic) **Tunis** via **Sfax** and **Sousse** at
0600, 0945, 1230, 1235, 2115, 2200, 2215, 2250 and 2350; **Medenine** 0600, 0730, 0800,
1000, 1700, 1730; **Matmata** 1015, 1100, 1200, 1400; **Djerba** 0930, 1345, 1530. *Entri* **Tunis**
0600, 0945, 1230, 1235; **Sousse** 0815, 0915; **Djerba** 0930, 1345, 1530; **Zarzis** 1345;
El Hamma 1400; **Sfax** 1500; **Tataouine** 1615; **Ben Gardane** 1735. *STE* **Tataouine** via
Medenine 1000; **Zarzis** via Medenine 1100, 1330; **Djerba** via Djorf 0945; **Ras Ajdir** and
Libyan border via Medenine and Ben Gardane 1145, 1530. **Louages**: the louage station
is close to the bus station. Sample fares Tunis 14Dt, takes 6 hrs; Djerba 5Dt; Sousse 10Dt;
Medenine 3.5Dt; Tripoli (Libya) 25Dt.

Banks *BCT*, R Mohammed Ali, T271203. *BIAT*, Av Farhat Hached, T270459. *BNA*, Av H. **Directory**
Bourguiba, T272323, with ATM. *BS*, 131 Av H. Bourguiba, T271499; *BT*, Av H. Bourguiba,
T270093. *UIB*, Av H. Bourguiba, T274881, 0800-1200 and 1400-1700. On Sat and Sun
there is always one bank open at 0930. *STB* has an ATM (dinars) for Visa and Mastercard
holders. **Communications** Internet:*Publinet Gabès* on Av H. Bourguiba, Gabès Centre building, 1st floor, unit 146-7, T275724. Quite easy to find in a large shopping precinct. One of the few places for you to check your email in southern Tunisia.
Post Office: T270544, Av H. Bourguiba, opposite *Hotel Régina*, exchange available.
Hammam There are 4 to try, in the souk, on Av Mohammed Ali, by the *calèche* station
and close to the Sidi Idris mosque. Open morning and evening for men, afternoon for
women, entrance 1dt. **Medical services Chemist**: all night, 2 in Av H. Bourguiba.
Hospital: *Hôpital Universitaire*, Cité M'Torrech, T282700. *Clinic Bon Sécours*, 10 R
Mongi Slim, T277700. *Dialysis Centre*, 112 R Mongi Slim, T273200, F275822.
Places of worship Catholic: 25 R d'Alger, T270326, service Sat 1830.

Gabès to Medenine via Mareth

Driving southeast to Medenine there is little of major interest to keep the traveller. Military history buffs will want to take a look at a small Second World
War museum south of Mareth, scene of fierce battles in 1943.
  Just 4 km from Gabès, on the right in Teboulbou, is the *Restaurant Les
Lanternes*. Gabès people tend to head out to the shore at Teboulbou to swim.
Some 20 km further is the village of Kettana on the Oued El Ferch. On the right

*Colour map 4,
grid A/B4*

Southeastern Tunisia

under the shadow of the palm trees, a permanent market of small shops sells local handicrafts – all-night opening too! The main market day is Wednesday.

Mareth
Phone code: 75
Colour map 4, grid A4

Mareth is 37 km from Gabès and 39 km from Medenine. The name survives in the annals of military history. If you have time, take a look at the **Military Museum of the Mareth line**, located east of the main road, shortly before the turn off for Djorf after an avenue of gum trees. ■ *0900-1645, closed Mon. 1Dt, photography 2Dt, free entrance for students, children (under 8 years old) and disabled.*

The **Mareth Defensive line** was built between 1936 and 1940 by the French forces in response to a possible Italian armoured offensive into Tunisia from Libya, that time an Italian colony. (Italy, only involved in the colonial race from the late-19th century, had always felt that the French had acquired their protectorate over Tunisia in 1881 unfairly.) Called the 'desert Maginot line', 45 km of concrete bunkers alongside the Oued Zigzaou in the Mareth region defended a strategic gap between the mountains (Jebel Tebaga) to the west and the Mediterranean, the easiest place for tanks to swarm up from Italian Tripolitania to overrun French Tunisia and Algeria. There was fierce fighting here during the Tunisian Campaign of November 1942 to May 1943. The final version of the line, as repaired by the Germans after the Battle of El Alamein in late 1942 comprised 40 infantry emplacements, 8 large artillery bunkers, 15 command posts and 28 support points.

The Mareth Defensive Line

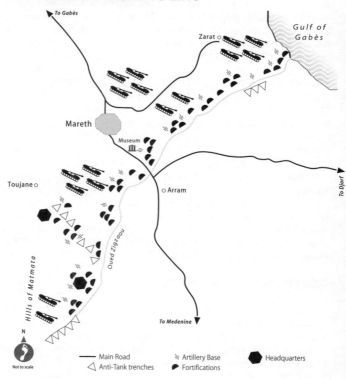

The Battle of Mareth, March 1943

After the occupation of French territories by the Germans in 1940 and the Franco-German and Franco-Italian armistice treaties, a German-Italian commission proceeded to demilitarize the Mareth line. The German-Italian troops commanded by Field Marshall Rommel withdrew from Tunisia via Tripolitania as a consequence of their defeat against the British Eighth Army led by General Montgomery (4 October 1942, Battle of El Alamein). In order to enable Rommel's forces to hold up the British advance, the Mareth line was rearmed and reinforced by the Axis High Command. This rearming took place between November 1942 and March 1943. As a result, the Mareth line became an insurmountable obstacle, especially during the flood season.

The Battle of Mareth took place in March 1943. The Allies were winning sea and air supremacy in the Mediterranean, the Axis forces in central and northern Tunisia under General Von Arnim were under heavy pressure. By early 1943, the Allies had brought
up 160,000 men, 750 tanks and 535 planes. Opposing them, the Italo-German forces had 76,000 men, a mere 150 tanks and 123 planes. The Axis-held Mareth Line, with its bunkers, anti-tank trenches and 100 km of barbed wire had to be taken to speed the Allied advance north.

The battle began on 16 March 1943 when the British attacked the Mareth line on two fronts, the first along the coastal area between Mareth and the shore, the second across the Dahar plateau. On 20 and 21 March the British attempted to cross the Oued Zigzaou, but met fierce Axis resistance led by General Messe. The Oued Zigzaou, in full flood, further hampered the Allied advance. Ultimately, the Axis were forced to withdraw northwards from Mareth on 28 March 1943 after the British successfully crossed the the El Hamma-Tebaga gap to the west. The Axis forces were forced to abandon their defensive positions on the Mareth line and withdrew northwards to new positions on the Oued Akarit, whence they were soon dislodged.

The museum, run by the military, has cases of uniforms and arms and displays of fuzzy black and white photographs. The wall map of the Mediterranean and the scale model showing troop movements during the 1943 campaign give you a good idea of how the Battle of Mareth was fought.

With your own transport, after visiting the museum, you could always head out to inspect the territory fought over by Allied and Axis armies. Head south on the Toujane road, and at the village of **Lazaiza**, you will be in Mareth line territory. Rommel's command post is a couple of kilometres from the village.

Should you need to stay overnight in Mareth, there is not too much choice. Try the **F** *Hotel du Golfe*, T236135. There are some restaurants and banks, notably the *BNA* (on the right arriving from Gabès) and the *STB* (on the left).

Mareth to Medenine

Moving on from Mareth, you pass through the village of **Koutine** (24 km) (handy cafés on the main road). A few kilometres before Medenine, **Metameur** is signposted to your right. Coming from the North, you will see your first *ghorfa* or fortified granary here, a hive of vaulted cells built around three courtyards. One section is used for tourist accommodation, the personably run **C-D** *Hotel des Ghorfas*, T646458, say 25Dt the double, reasonable food, very simple accommodation. The manager is very talkative and knowledgeable on local culture. Arrive early or reserve, as custom can be sparse and manager lives a distance from the hotel and might leave before you arrive. Only worth an overnight if you are too tired to drive on to Gabès/Matmata or Tataouine region.

The pistes in the region have been much improved. The rough piste from Metameur northwest to Toujane, extremely slow and painful going in a

Tunisia and Libya in the Second World War

The physical marks of the destruction wrought by the Second World War are still very apparent in Tunisia and Libya – if mainly now in the large cemeteries of war dead.

Italy, the colonial power in Libya at the outbreak of the Second World War, invaded British-held Egypt in the closing weeks of 1940, mistakenly believing that the campaign there would be brief and successful. In reality, the war raged, with many changes of fortune for the combatants, until May 1943. The prize of winning Egypt from the British was the destruction of British lines of communication to the Middle East, India and the Far East, together with access for the Italian and German commands to the rich oil fields of Iran and the Arabian peninsula. Great Britain and the Commonwealth countries, for their part, desperately needed to hold their grip on

Egypt, their lines of communication such as the Suez Canal and the natural resources of the region. Scarcely surprising, therefore, that the battle for control of North Africa should be so protracted and bitter.

The local populations were for the most part unwilling spectators of the desert war, though their suffering was considerable. In Libya, the Senusi movement backed the British against the colonial Italy, and Libyan troops did ultimately have a hand in the re-conquest of their country. In Francophone North Africa there was uncertainty and confusion in the ranks of the French colonial authorities and their colonial peoples as a result of the Pétain régime's accommodation with the Nazis.

Although the Italian armies made some progress in Egypt in 1940, they were soon expelled. Faced with what appeared to be an Italian collapse, German troops and

War in the desert 1940-43

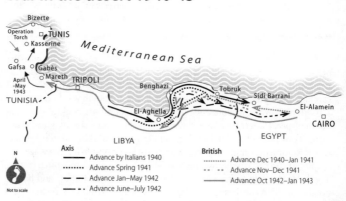

standard hire car, but feasible by four-wheel drive, may have been upgraded to minor road standard by the end of 2002.

Gabès to Kebili via El Hamma de l'Arad

Colour map 4, grid A1-4

Four kilometres north out of Gabès, the P16 west to Kebili is clearly signed. This first part is through the pleasant oasis region. At Maqsef, where the C208 'Gabès bypass' crosses, the route is a government-subsidized agricultural estate with surprisingly large grain silos, large areas under plastic, olives and a few date palms. About 5 km before El Hamma on the north side is an area used by coaches and safari tours, *Station Chincou Tourisme*, a good place for a

armour were moved into Tripolitania in February 1941. The combined German and Italian army pushed back the British to the Egyptian frontier by April. The Axis army was led by General Rommel with skill and audacity, supported by a strong air force. Rommel's eastwards advance was slowed by the protracted resistance of the garrisons – first Australian, then British and Polish – at Tobruk. Meanwhile, the main armies fought pitched battles around the Libyan-Egyptian frontier until Rommel withdrew temporarily in December 1941. Once back in Libyan territory, Rommel reorganized and, taking advantage of improved lines of communication, prepared a counter attack which pushed the British back as far as Gazala, near Derna, in January and February 1942 and, after a pause, into Tobruk and deep into Egypt in June, though this advance was finally held at El-Alamein after a fierce battle. Rommel made a final attempt at Alam Halfa, east of El-Alamein, to push aside British and Commonwealth forces and break through to the Nile Valley in August 1942, but failed in the face of a strong Allied defensive effort and his own growing losses of men and equipment.

The balance in the desert war changed in mid-1942. The Allies gradually won superiority in the air and gained freedom of movement at sea. The Germans and Italians increasingly lacked adequate armour, reinforcements and strategy as Rommel's personal health also deteriorated. On the Allied side, General Montgomery took over leadership and began a build-up of the Eighth Army sufficient to overwhelm the well-trained and experienced Afrika Korps. Montgomery opened his attack at El-Alamein on 23 October 1942 and, after 11 days of hard fighting, the Axis army was beaten back and retreated by rapid stages to the west to make a last stand in Tunisia.

The German attempt to hold on in North Africa was made difficult by sea and airborne landings by Allied, including American, troops in Morocco and Algeria in November 1942. These two countries were liberated with comparative ease when French Vichy units, formerly collaborating with the Germans, were brought round to support the invasion. German and Italian reinforcements were rushed to Tunis, and a battle began to stop the advance of Allied units from the west as they fought their way in from Algeria and from the south through Libya. German attacks in the Battle of Kasserine in the hills north of Gafsa during January and February 1943 almost succeeded in halting the Allied progress. Rommel's final assault against Montgomery's advancing Eighth Army arriving from Libya failed in early March. Axis troops retreated northwards behind the Mareth Line on the Gulf of Gabès, before being outflanked and being forced to withdraw by Montgomery's troops. A concluding series of battles in northern Tunisia saw the Allies push through the Medjerda Valley to Tunis and Bizerte in May 1943, effectively ending Axis resistance in North Africa.

Southeastern Tunisia

coffee. This is decorated with huge desert roses and is impossible to miss. It is here that the gas pipeline crosses the route and where a number of tracks lead out north across the sebkha.

The settlement of El Hamma de l'Arad, 32 km west of Gabès, has grown up round the hot springs. (Note that there is another El Hamma, also with hot springs, near Tozeur, called El Hamma du Djerid.) The town is situated between the salt flats to the north and the foothills of Djebel Tebaga to the south. The Romans called it *Aquae Tacapitanae*. The hot water in the springs which feed the hot baths is very sulphurous. The road in through the triumphal arch just beyond the *oued*, by the hospital and the grain stores, leads past

El Hamma de l'Arad
Phone code: 75
Colour map 4, grid A3

a few villas to the date palm oasis. The road into the oasis turns off north and the dual carriageway, complete with smart double globe lights, goes right through the town. Here you will find plenty of shops (try *Ulysses* for size), tyre and car repairs, patisseries, chemist, petrol, calor gas, cafés, three banks near the square-faced clock and even the opportunity for photo development. The souk has a good selection of spices, market day is Monday. The louages gather near the *Shell* station while the post office is opposite the road to Matmata.

In El Hamma there are several thermal springs and three **hammams**. Unlike many hammams which use the same facilities and divide out the time, here the bathing areas and entrances for men and women are quite separate so no timetable is needed. The hammams here differ in condition of the buildings, some less pleasant than others. Hot showers are available in all.

From Place 7 Novembre go towards the banks and turn right. On the left is **Hammam Aïn el Borj**, entrance 0.250Dt, four pools for women and four for men. This is probably the most friendly and most colourful hammam. At the women's entrance, soaps, underware, combs, shampoo, henna and *suak* (walnut bark to clean the teeth) are sold.

The hammam on the road to Gabès is not clearly signed, though there is a white label with a red arrow and the name of the bath house in Arabic script. Turn right before the hospital into a nameless and dusty road. At the very end there is the **Hammam Esghaier**, entrance 0.500Dt. This is the cleanest and the most expensive hammam in town and also the least crowded, probably because it is a 15-minute walk from the centre. The building is well kept, with blue columns and a light blue ceiling. Both the women's and the men's areas are provided with lockers, one big and one small pool, and a hall with benches for resting before leaving. The toilets are pretty unpleasant, however.

Situated near the souk is **Hammam Abd el Kader**, entrance 0.12Dt. This is the most crowded hammam. There are two big pools for women and one for men, high ceilings but unpleasant atmosphere and the usual grotty toilets.

El Hamma de L'Arad

Sleeping **F** *Hotel Hammam*, 80 Av H. Bourguiba in front of *Banque de Tunisie*, 8 rooms small and mostly dark, extremely cheap (3Dt without breakfast). The only hotel in town, management don't speak much French, so smile and do your best.

Eating **Mid-range** *Restaurant de Tunis*, Av H. Bourguiba/Pl 7 Novembre near *Bank de Tunisie*. Couscous with lamb is better than elsewhere. For dessert try *makroudh* (date cakes) from the nearby patisserie. **Cheap** *Restaurant Amel*, in the commercial centre. Has food on display, good chicken kebab, very cheap, no tables.

A 19th-century tourist at the baths of El Hamma

"It was late in the evening, near ten o'clock, and I was about to retire to rest, when Ali noticed that I had caught a slight cold. He insisted that I should at once go down to the wonderful healing waters of the warm spring, declaring that in a quarter of an hour I should be perfectly well.

It was pitch dark when Hamed, Ali and I, carrying lanterns, strolled through the village to the spring near the ruined old 'Borj'. We descended a stone stair which ended in a dark, paved lower room, from the opening into which steam issued into the cold outer air. By the light of the lantern I saw that the water rose within the room, through which it flowed, and was discharged through a small opening into a basin outside. In the centre of the room stood a clumsy pillar supporting the roof, and surrounding the fountains were tanks built of stone.

The room was full of choking hot steam, as in a Roman or Moorish bath; I began to perspire before I got into the water. Counting 1, 2, 3, I scrambled in. Over my whole body I felt an icy sensation, just as though I had plunged into cold water, but immediately after followed a feeling as of being scalded, and I sprang back to the stone verge. Twice I repeated my endeavours to bear the burning heat of the water, but each time had to jump out quickly; so I remained seated on the stones, throwing the water over my body, and even that I could hardly bear.

With Hamed it was the same, but he was able to remain longer in the water. But Ali astonished us by quietly enjoying himself sitting in the water, the temperature of which was at least 113° Fahrenheit."

From The Cave Dwellers of Southern Tunisia *by Daniel Bruun, (London, 1898).*

Southeastern Tunisia

There are some other cheap eateries at the western end of town. Coffee shops and restaurants are found on both sides of the main street.

Bus: plenty of buses to Gabès, just 30 mins away, and 6 to Kebili (1hr 45 mins). Also **louages** from Av H. Bourguiba.

Transport

Banks *BT* and *BNA* in Av H. Bourguiba near *Restaurant de Tunis*. **Communications** Post Office: on Pl 7 Novembre. **Hammam**: see above. **Festival** of the *hammam* each Mar. **Medical services** Chemist: on Pl 7 Novembre. **Hospital**: on road to Gabès in a very new building, T234127. **Useful addresses** Police: T234141.

Directory

Just after El Hamma de l'Arad, **Sembat** is basically a continuation of the main settlement with the same central reservation with double globed lights. There is low-income housing with half cylinder roofs and a huge brickworks colouring everywhere around bright red. In contrast, immediately after the *oued* is the oasis, with good quality soil and adequate water providing good crops, particularly pomegranates. From here to Kebili it is a very long straight road, with the serrated summits of the **Djebel Tebaga** visible across scrub land to the south. To the north is low grade grazing land. Watch out for the white posts with red writing. The sign says 'danger, death' but only in Arabic script. **Don't check**. **Don't enter**. The few small settlements in this region can be spotted by their tall water towers.

El Hamma to Kebili

Keep a watch at 57 km from Kebili for a restaurant on the north side of the road, and reward yourself with a coffee. The 'feature' marked on the Michelin map at **Saïdane** was a fort, then a hotel and now a police post, so no photographs. Finally the road turns south and cuts up through the Djebel Tabaga to take you to Kebili.

El Hamma to Nouvelle Matmata Rather than get to the Matmata on the direct, newly resurfaced road from Gabès, Matmata Nouvelle can be reached from El Hamma via a track (34 km) clearly signposted in the town centre. A normal car will do it (very slowly) in good weather conditions and with daylight. At the 6 km crossroad, go straight ahead. In El Magcem, at 12 km, drive carefully as there is a school and children usually try to get a lift. At 15 km, El Magcem ends, there are some houses on the left and a crossroads with a fountain in the centre. Take the road on the left. From here the route to Nouvelle Matmata is straightforward.

Matmata مطماطة

Phone code: 75
Colour map 4, grid A3
Population: 3,500

Nothing really destined the Matmata, southwest of Gabès, to become a major daytripper destination: there was merely the mild curiosity of the underground pit-homes and some arid hills, and many of the villagers moved to Nouvelle Matmata in the 1970s. Then came Star Wars, and the famous bar scene with bizarre denizens of the galaxy, enough to put Matmata firmly on the tourist trail. Roads across the area have been improved, and it is now possible to cut westwards right across to Douz via the outpost village of Tamezret. Tracks to other villages – notably scenic Toujane – look set to be improved in the near future, too. Although sometimes swamped by herds of four-wheel drive vehicles, the landscapes of Matmata nevertheless merit more than just a flying visit.

Ins and outs

Getting there
See Transport, page 381, for further details

Matmata is most easily accessed from Gabès, 44 km away. There are buses and louages, from next to the big minaret by the tourist market in downtown Gabès. Journey time, depending on traffic and roadworks, just under 1 hr. Note that most louages only go to Nouvelle Matmata. You have to take a 2nd louage or minibus for the final leg of the journey from the main street of Nouvelle Matmata. This leaves when it is full.

The Gabès to Matmata road is being upgraded, and eventually the section Gabès to Nouvelle Matmata (28 km) will be very good indeed. After Nouvelle Matmata, the road begins to wind up into the hills. You pass Tijma and the turn-off for another troglodyte village, Haddej, 10 km after Nouvelle Matmata. A further 6 km on you climb over a small col and into the Matmata Valley.

With your own transport, Matmata can also be approached from Douz to the west on a newly built road. Journey time is around 2¾ hrs, depending on traffic. The approach to Matmata from Medenine (via Toujane) to the east is only to be contemplated with a good 4WD.

Getting around
From the main road junction, you can have a good wander around Matmata on foot, discovering the underground *Hotel Sidi Driss* and the nearby museum (market day is Tue). Without your own transport, things get more difficult if you are pressed for time and want to get to the nearby villages such as Tamezret (13 km on metalled road) and Toujane (23 km on rough piste). Neither has accommodation, and both are too far for a

Matmata

To Gabès

Chemist

Bread Shop

To Toujane

To Tamezret

■ **Sleeping**
1 Kousseïla
2 Ksar el Amazigh
3 Les Berbères
4 Marhala
5 Matmata
6 Sidi Driss

● **Eating**
1 Café
2 Café Hamadi
3 Ouled Aziz
4 Pâtisserie
5 Rim

N
Not to scale

comfortable day walk in the heat. There is a minibus once a day to Tamezret from the centre of Matmata. For Toujane there is no public transport.

Should you have your own transport, there is a poorly surfaced road to Toujane from Nouvelle Matmata via Beni Zeltene and Aïn Tounine.

The tourist information office (*Syndicat d'initiative*, T230114) is right on the crossroads in the middle of Matmata. They are helpful, and will allow you to leave your rucksack in the office while you explore. Closes at 1715. **Tourist information**

Background

The appearance of the Matmata Valley is generally described as 'lunar', the arid yellow landscape being scattered wth numerous pit-dwellings. Until 15 years ago, the only visible signs of habitation above ground were the TV aerials. But increasing prosperity and new means of construction have enabled the people of Matmata to build themselves concrete houses next to their troglodyte homes. The other features of the area are the numerous *marabouts* or saints' tombs, speckling hillside and valley with their white domes.

As in many poor southern Mediterranean communities, there is a tradition of migrating to the cities of Europe for work. At one time, many Matmatans would set up as bakers in northern Tunisia's towns. Money earned elsewhere funds new building. A section of the population still live in the underground dwellings, but their number is slowly decreasing. If you want to see the inside of one of the underground houses it isn't really necessary to take a guide, but doing so is one way of obtaining entry. The fee should be negotiated but is generally very reasonable, about 1-2Dt.

The people of Matmata have been living in these houses for over 700 years. The population may originally have lived in more defensible hill villages like the ones at Tamezret and Toujane. When times became more secure, the underground home was the ideal building solution in a region of great extremes of temperature. The soft ground made the construction of homes underground possible. Provided there was no excssive rainfall, troglodyte living provided the best protection from heat and marauders.

There is little scope for agriculture in Matmata due to the climate and the lack of water, which explains the tendency to migrate. Traditionally, each family would have olive and almond trees and date palms, as well as a few animals and fowl. There was a little dry farming. Water was carefully husbanded in cisterns. A carefully constructed system of terraces (the *jessour*), visible here and there off the road as you approach Matmata from Gabès, increases the area available for agriculture. Today, however, jobs in the ever-expanding tourist sector provide a new source of income for low-skilled labour.

Sights

Matmata has few sights. Obviously, you will want to see one of the famous **underground dwellings.** On arriving in Matmata it is unclear where to go since nothing is visible, but walking around will reveal one of the 700 underground houses. Many of these can be visited in return for a small payment at the end of the tour. You could start with a look in at the underground **Hotel Sidi Driss**, down the road to the right just after the café at the central crossroads. Sort of 'behind' the hotel is a small **museum** in a typical, though rather tumbledown, troglodyte dwelling. There is a bridal chamber with a rather stylish built-in bed made from white-plastered branches. In another

A bridal baton

"One custom is universal amongst these people; it is that at the wedding the bridegroom shows his bride a heavy stick, of which one end that he holds to her nose is thoroughly and sweetly scented. The interpretation of this custom being that so long as she conducts herself *properly, her life will be mild and pleasant like the scent; but, on the other hand, should she misbehave she may be sure of being well punished. I saw one of these sticks at Tatauin."*

From The Cave Dwellers of Southern Tunisia *by Daniel Bruun (London, 1898).*

chamber, you can see some local girls at their looms weaving mergoum carpets. Note also the way the tunnelled entrance passage is carefully roofed with supporting flat stones. ■ *Opening hrs and entry fee (say 1Dt a head) are erratic.*

And of course there are **camel rides** to be had from just by the *Hotel Sidi Driss*. Probably best to pay all the fee when you get down or it may cost you more. More camels and guides can be found on the way to Toujane.

The **underground dwellings** really are rather special. The basic layout centres on a large excavated area or *houch*, in the local parlance, which will have a tunnel or occasionally stairs leading to the surface. The houch is often as much as 7 m below ground level, with a diameter of 10-15 m. It functions like the courtyard in the Tunisian townhouse, providing light and air for the rooms joining onto it. Large dwellings for an extended family will have several *ahouach*, connected by tunnels.

Troglodyte dwellings are kept impeccably clean. Traditionally, they would have whitewashed walls, shelving cut out of the soft rock and tiny excavated cuboards. Sleeping rooms would have small curtained niches for washing. In the village of Techine, near Matmata, the houses have built-in furniture, constructed from branches coated with a white plaster finish. Some dwellings have been modernized, and have electricity and water. With the successful conversion of some underground homes to hotel use, the troglodyte dwelling in Matmata looks set to survive well into the 21st century.

Overlooking the village, off the Toujane road, is a small fort which unfortunately cannot be visited because it is occupied by the military.

Excursions **Nouvelle Matmata**, 15 km away, is often ignored, but a visit here will help explain the reasons why the villagers moved. By car there is a variety of places to visit. Going southeast towards Medinine, you can reach Toujane via a poorly metalled road.

Essentials

Sleeping
■ *on map, page 378*
There are some nice comfortable hotels and some cheapish underground places much used by student excursions. Ask at *Syndicat d'initiative* about accommodation in Toujane and Tamezret. The hotels are quite scattered, so you'll have to walk a bit if you arrive by bus.

B-C *Hotel Diar el Barbar* on the Douz road out of Matmata, T230074, F230144, 162 rooms, partly dug out of the ground, resembles a huge troglodyte dwelling. Pool with view. Most expensive option, underground authenticity – at a price. **B-C** *Hotel Ksar el Amazigh* (ex-*Hotel Les Troglodytes*), T230062, F230173, 1 km down road to Tamezret on left. Small but pleasant pool, 50 pleasant a/c rooms, opened 1993, during the late evening and night water is not very hot, no credit cards, private parking, most expensive hotel in the village, but reasonable nevertheless. Views over the fierce sunburnt hills. Best upmarket option. **B-C** *Hotel Kousseïla*, arriving from Gabès take Toujane exit at Matmata's central roundabout. The hotel, a large brown concrete structure with some vaguely 'Berber' designs, is on your right, T230303, F230265. 35 rooms, 100 beds, a/c, no pool, no credit cards, clean. Opened 1995. Not a very inspirational place, but would do for an a/c night. Makes its money by feeding tour groups in a viewless restaurant. Slighlty cheaper than the *Ksar el Amazigh*.

D *Hotel Les Berbères*, T230024, F230097, on Tamezret road, on left before *Ksar el Amazigh*. Most recent and smallest underground hotel, communal bath/toilet, restaurant, book in season, a curious experience, 13 rooms, 120 beds (some rooms have 9 beds), the holes in which the hotel is built are less deep than usual and are therefore less impressive. Watch your head! **D** *Hotel Matmata*, F230177, beyond the *Kousseïla*, turn right off the Toujane road. Quite small, above ground (so no troglodyte charm), all 32 rooms have bath, a/c, comfortable, clean, small pool, restaurant, management offers large discounts to groups of over 10, be warned. **D** *Hotel Marhala*, T230015, slightly out of the village, up the Toujane road towards the fort. The best of the 3 underground hotels, very clean, very basic (bed, door without lock, light bulb), communal bath/toilet, quiet, Tunisian food in restaurant, book in summer, composed of 5 holes around which the rooms are located, neither humid/cold in winter, nor hot in summer, cheap, friendly management. **D** *Hotel Sidi Driss*, T230005, F230265, close to the centre of the village. Turn right immediately after Toujane exit on main roundabout by café. Largest (35 rooms, 145 beds) and most touristy of the underground hotels, endless corridors and courtyards, communal bath/toilet, bar, restaurant, fairly clean, not all the management can speak English or French. Claim to fame? That short bar scene in *Star Wars* was filmed here. Does the bar still have alcohol?

Eating
● *on map, page 378*

For a reasonable feed, it is probably best to eat in the hotels, open to all visitors, although there are a few restaurants in the market place. **Mid-range** *Hotel Ksar el Amazigh*. Try the warming barley soup (winter only) and as a dessert the *mehchi Tataouine*, a pancake filled with almonds, sesame seeds and peanuts, lunch 7.5Dt. **Cheap** *Café Restaurant Ouled Aziz aka Chez Abdoul,* at the centre of Matmata almost opposite the tourist office. Has the traditional Tunisian restaurant staples (salade tunisienne, chicken or lamb couscous, etc). Full meal (salad, main course, dessert or fruit) is 5Dt. No menu on display, so check prices when you order. You might be able to find a local guide here to take you round the region. (NB Negotiate prices firmly first.) *Café Hamadi*, near *Restaurant Ouled Aziz*. Has reasonable cakes. Try also *Café Restaurant Rim*, arriving from Gabès at the beginning of Matmata on the left, T230023. Opened 1996. *Café de la Victoire* has only coffee, tea and soft drinks.

Transport

Bus the buses come to a halt in Matmata's main square, on the Toujane road just below the main junction. No buses to Medenine. Tunis 1930 running via Sousse; Gabès 0530, 0730, 0900, 1100, 1230, 1330, 1400, 1600, 1730, 2000; check varying times of Tamezret service. Also a couple of minibuses to Techine. Check whether there is a public bus service running across to Douz (unlikely). **Louages** on main road in town centre but very few cars. Matmata to Matmata Nouvelle is 15 km.

Directory

Banks In Matmata Nouvelle, 15 km towards Gabès. **Communications** Post Office: in the centre of town, changes money. **Medical services** Chemist: on the main road in front of bus station. **Useful addresses** Police: on road to Medenine, T270390.

Around Matmata

Phone code: 75
Colour map 4, grid A3

If you have time, there are a number of small villages to visit around Matmata. Without your own transport, getting to these settlements, although not especially difficult, takes time with waits for louages or buses. **El Haddej**, off the main Matmata Nouvelle to Matmata road, is similar to Matmata, though much less visited. West of Matmata, stone-built hillcrest **Tamezret** and **Taoujout** are different kinds of village altogether, as are **Techine** and **Toujane** to the east. **Beni Aissa** and hilltop **Beni Zelten** are probably for enthusiasts only.

El Haddej
Many of the troglodyte houses are inhabited. Tourists will only be welcome with a guide

Inconveniently, El Haddej is not very clearly signposted off the Nouvelle Matmata to Matmata road. Coming up from Matmata, look out for signs for **Tijma**, a tiny roadside settlement with some troglodyte dwellings. This village is located on the road to Gabès. After 6 km north from Matmata, turn right where the tourist shop and the *Relais Touristique des Troglodytes* are situated. The *Relais* is a restaurant with a circular courtyard and, around it, 10 small dining rooms, T230129, prices 4-6Dt (better to book as in low season they do not cook every day, suitable for groups). After the *Relais* the paved road goes on, full of curves and ups and downs, for 2 km to El Haddej. (Takes one hour to walk.)

El Haddej is made up of cave dwellings hidden in the ground. Many have partly collapsed, some have been abandoned. Going around El Haddej may seem familiar as this landscape was used to great effect in famous films such as *Star Wars* and *Raiders of the Lost Ark*. Though similar to Matmata, El Haddej has been less involved with tourism so it is possible to see what Matmata must have been like before the tourist influx. Nonetheless, guides are easy to find. There are three main things to see: the oil-press, the marriage cave and the typical troglodyte house. Bargain and arrange the tour price in advance.

The **oil-press** is made of a huge stone trough and an enormous mill wheel once turned by a camel. The **marriage cave** is a troglodyte dwelling used only for wedding ceremonies. Around the courtyard are several rather derelict rooms. One of them was the bridal kitchen, where the food for the guests of the marriage ceremony was prepared. Another was the wedding room, where the bride and the groom consummated their marriage. In this room there was a hole in the ceiling connected to the upper surface. Through this hole the groom threw a foulard and some sweets. The bride waited here, sitting below the hole in the wedding room and if the foulard and the sweet touched her, it was considered good luck. In the wedding room there was a window from where the groom shot his rifle, signifying the bride was a virgin. The rifle fire meant that the wedding feast could start and that dinner

Haddej: rooms set aside for the wedding ceremony

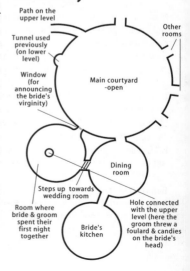

- Path on the upper level
- Tunnel used previously (on lower level)
- Window (for announcing the bride's virginity)
- Main courtyard -open
- Other rooms
- Dining room
- Steps up towards wedding room
- Room where bride & groom spent their first night together
- Bride's kitchen
- Hole connected with the upper level (here the groom threw a foulard & candies on the bride's head)

could be served to the guests waiting in the courtyard. Watch your head when you enter the rooms.

Northwest of Matmata to Beni Aissa

Beni Aissa is a sleepy troglodyte settlement 7 km from Matmata. Few tourists come here, and it could give you a feel for what the area was like before the arrival of the four-wheel-drive brigade. To get there, take the Tamezret road from the centre of Matmata. Measure the journey. After 1 km turn right towards El Hamma. After another 500 m you pass a troglodyte dwelling on the left. After a few hundred metres more the road condition becomes very poor and there is, unfortunately, a lot of litter here. After 6 km, turn left at the crossroads and on both sides are troglodyte houses almost hidden (of course) and still inhabited, although their owners might be with their sheep and goats. At 7 km on the right there are two *marabouts*. The track ends here.

West of Matmata: Tamezret, Taoujout & Zeraoua

Try if possible to visit **Tamezret**, just 12 km from Matmata, an easy drive along the much improved road running through to Douz. The village has a striking position above stoney hills to the east, while to the west the arid land levels off into desert. Drive carefully on the first section out of Matmata, past the *Hotel Ksar Amazigh*: the narrow road winds and you may meet speeding tourist buses and all-terrain vehicles. There is a morning bus from Matmata to Tamezret, return journey 1600. Make sure you show up on time, as otherwise you will have to hitch or run the risk of being charged well over the going rate by a local driver spotting for tourist dinars.

Ignoring utility cables, the scenery on this route is a mixture of the moon and the Grand Canyon. The presence of troglodyte houses can be detected at 3 km and 4½ km on the left, and, if you look down, at 6½ km on the right. Eventually the road runs up to Tamezret (small Berberish shop on the left, modern concrete café building on right). The stone-built houses blend in perfectly with the scenery. Though many houses have been abandoned, the village seems to be enjoying a minor revival, thanks to its position on the new Matmata to Douz

Southeastern Tunisia

Around Matmata

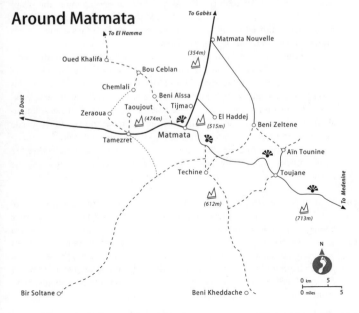

With the Khalifa of Haddej in the 1890s

"Said-ben Mansur-Fatush, as Khalifa of the mountains, exercises authority over the villages of the Matmata range. His is born of the tribe of Uled Sliman, of which his son is a tribal sheikh.

The Khalifa is between 60 and 70 years of age, and has three wives, Mena, Fatima and Sasia. By the first he has two sons, Amar and Mansur. By the second, one son, Mohamed ... the Khalifa's family, therefore, consists of about a score of souls, who, as will be seen further on, live together; but to these must be added other members of the household, negroes and servants with their children, and a number of near relatives and a number of men who attach themselves to the Khalifa's service. Many of the latter have homes of their own, and possess palms, olive trees and cattle, which they farm on their own account, but being dependants of

the Khalifa, must help him sow and reap his corn, prune his palms, gather the dates and olives, press the oil, and, in short, do any work of which they are capable.

The Khalifa is very rich. He owns many underground dwellings, barns, stables and oil mills, but a large proportion of the profits of all these must be expended in providing food and shelter for the infinity of people whom he protects. The Khalifa's property is valued at some 200,000 francs – a pretty penny for a mountaineer living amongst barren hills devoid of either springs or wells, but where the cliffs and valleys are furrowed with channels to conduct the rain water to cisterns, and where every tree must have earth banked about it that the water may lie at its foot."

From The Cave Dwellers of Southern Tunisia by Daniel Bruun (London, 1898).

road. The state has put money into paving the narrow streets and repairing once tumbledown walls. Tea stop at the most touristic *Café Mamou le Berbère*, on your left on the main road as you arrive from Matmata. Stroll around the narrow, winding streets and walk up to the top of the village. To reward your efforts, there is a small chicha café and marvellous views across the desert. Tamezret, along with neighbouring Taoujout, is one of the few places in Tunisia where a variety of Amazigh is still spoken. The relative isolation of the village enabled the language to survive the 20th century. Although it is not politically correct to mention ethnic difference in contemporary Tunisia, the language has been the object of recent ethnographic research.

Taoujout, 4 km on from Tamezret, and also a hilltop community where Amazigh has survived, is more a destination for enthusiasts. The black top goes as far as the village, but no further. With a four-wheel drive or motorcycle, plus good navigating skills, it might be possible to drive from Taoujout to Beni Aïssa.

Finally, just 6 km by piste northwest of Tamezret, lies **Old Zeraoua**, an abandoned Amazigh village. The inhabitants have moved to Nouvelle Zeraoua. Feel free to wander through the streets and look into the houses which have survived better than those at, for example, Tamerza as they are stone constructions. Many have vaulted roofs and it is possible to climb the outside stone stairs for a view over the region.

East of Matmata: Techine & Toujane To the east of Matmata is another area ripe for exploration should you have the time. There are two interesting villages, **Techine** and **Toujane**, the latter having superb views east over the plain towards the sea. There are two approaches to Toujane from Matmata, the poor quality metalled road from Nouvelle Matmata, and the very rough piste from Matmata. (There is also a piste in from the east, 35 km of difficult driving from Medenine, four-wheel drive enthusiasts only.) There are no buses along this route. At Toujane, there is one simple accommodation option (see below).

Heading east out of Matmata, **Techine**, another troglodyte settlement, could be your first destination. The road is metalled most of the 12 km to Techine. After 1 km on the right is a military fort while to the left is a panoramic view over the plain below. On a clear day it is apparently possible to see as far as Djerba! (**NB** No photographs here, as this is all a military area.) Look out for the birds of prey and the ground squirrels. After 5 km on the right is a *marabout* and, 2 km further on (on the right again), some troglodyte houses. At Km 8 is a crossroads, left for Toujane and straight on for Techine, which is noted for the built-in furniture in the dwellings, carefully constructed out of branches which are covered in decorative plaster. This furniture looks fragile, but no doubt replacement is not a problem as all the materials are close to hand

After visiting Techine, the track is not very easy (be sure to have a good spare tyre) but a normal car could just about do it. The asphalt returns at a T-junction 1 km from Toujane. At 10 km more crossroads (right to Zriba, Techine and Beni Kheddache): go straight on here and also at the next crossroads (left to Beni Zelten and Mzata). Keep an eye on the track as its condition gets worse and worse, and look down on the right at the small lakes (during spring) or at the *oued* (during winter and autumn). The landscape is gorgeous. At 14 km on the right is a troglodyte house. At 20 km you will be on the edge of the mountain.

At 24 km is another T-junction where you can turn right to Cheguine or left to start the descent to **Toujane**, which will suddenly appear, apparently clinging to the mountain side. It is a beautiful village on an exceptional site. Wander around – there may be locally made carpets and weavings for sale. Purchases can be made at *Chez Laroussi* on the road. At the end of the village, after Chez Laroussi, on the left is the *Relais Mohammed Esnani*, selling kilims, *smen* (cooked butter used on couscous), honey and tea herbs. Drinks, coffee and tea available, too, but unpleasant toilet. For an overnight, try **D** *Auberge Chambala*, three small rooms, one underground, hot water, simple meals. No phone.

To avoid repeating the boneshaking piste from Matmata to Toujane, you could head for Nouvelle Matmata, following a poorly surfaced road which runs via Aïn Tounine (6 km from Toujane) and Beni Zelten.

Toujane to Nouvelle Matmata

After the café in Toujane take the C104 towards Medenine. After 7 km is the new village of Dekhilet Toujane. This is not an interesting place but has *Café du 7 Novembre* on the left and a post office on the right. After 5 km a paved road goes north to Mareth (36 km), while the main road (unsurfaced) goes on to Medenine (25 km). The truly adventurous, equipped with four-wheel drive, could turn right and head for Ksar El Hallouf and Beni Kheddache. The track is good at the beginning but soon deteriorates. There are some herders' huts, magnificent views and plenty of holes in the road. Really a trek for the desert navigator with plenty of time.

Toujane to Beni Kheddache

There is now a fully metalled road from Matmata to Douz, running via Tamezret. This is 60 km shorter than the route via El Hamma-Kebili, although not necessarily faster. From here on it is more or less a straight 43 km to Douz.

Matmata to Douz via the desert road

Southeastern Tunisia

Medenine مدنين

Phone code: 75
Colour map 4, grid B4
An important crossroads in the South, through which you will probably pass on your way to Tataouine and the ksour, Medenine has little of interest for the visitor. Of the once vast fortified granary complex, only a rump courtyard remains. With the usual concrete buildings, Medenine bears witness to the huge changes in the life of the Tunisian South in the last quarter of the 20th century.

Ins & outs **Getting there** Medenine is accessible by bus and louage. Journey time from Gabès (73 km) is about 1½ hrs. There are overnight buses from Tunis, 7¾ hrs away, and plenty of buses from Tataouine (55 km) and Ghoumrassen, Djerba, Zarzis (62 km) and Ben Gardane. **Getting around** The bus station is on R du 18 Janvier and the louages stop in a small street opposite. All the main hotels are within walking distance of these. If you want to go to Beni Kheddache, once an important ksar, there are louages leaving from near the *Agil* station on the Av Bourguiba.

Market day: Thu Medenine is at the northern end of what might be called the **ksour** area, a region whose economy once centred on nomad stock raising and some cereal cultivation. The harvests were stored in characteristic fortified granaries or *ksour*. The region is a frontier between two cultures, the nomads and the settled people. Once the area was totally controlled by nomads, but today the tents have been replaced by small concrete houses and the camel by a Peugeot or Isuzu truck.

Medenine once had the largest ksar in the South, a primitive but efficient 'silo' for the Ouerghama tribal confederation. Early photographs show a vast network of interlinked courtyards. After independence, however, everything changed. Settlement was the order of the day; the *ksour* of Medenine were almost completely demolished. What remains – a single courtyard – is an attraction for day-trippers.

Medenine is not a bad place for the start of excursions towards Metameur and the surrounding area, where there are some *ksour* in a far better state of preservation than in Medenine. Nevertheless, given the choice, Tataouine, 55 km further south, is a much better choice as a base, being close to both hillcrest villages and *ksour*.

Sleeping Medenine has a poor choice of hotels given its location at a meeting of routes from
No need to overnight in Medenine, unless you are very weary or unlucky with bus connections Libya, Djerba, the South and northern Tunisia. **B** *Etape Sangho*, formerly the *Hotel Ibis*, Pl du 7 Novembre in the centre of town, 200 m from the *ksour*, T643878/9, F640550. 44 rooms, all a/c, some rooms with terrace, conference room, clean, sometimes lively as sports teams usually stay here, recently taken over by Sangho. **D** *Hotel Hana*, T640690, in Av H. Bourguiba, opposite the market arcades, climb up a few steps. Quite noisy, but well placed, central and more or less clean. Has carpark for 2Dt. **E** *Hotel Essaâda*, Av H. Bourguiba, small sign easily missed, T640300. 28 rooms, 6 with shower but none with toilet. Basically clean and handy for cheap eateries. **Youth hostel**: located in the *Maison des Jeunes/Dar ech Chebab* on R des Palmiers, on road to Djorf, 500 m after the *ksar*, on the left. T640338. 60 beds.

Eating **Mid-range** *Restaurant of the* Etape Sangho. Acceptable but unexciting. **Cheap** *Restaurant de la Liberté*, opp. *Etape Sangho*. Good and cheap. *Pizzeria Plaza*, Av H. Bourguiba. *Restaurant Carthage*, R du 18-Janvier-1952, across the road from the bus station. *Hotel Hana*, Av H. Bourguiba also has a restaurant. Out of town, you have the *Restaurant l'Olivier*, road to Gabès (km 14, Koutine), T630017.

Jouant à la Kherbga or playing draughts Tunisian style

This popular game requires no board or manufactured counters. Everything required is readily available. A small pile of earth, sand or roadside dust is scraped together with the foot and patted flat with the hand. Seven rows of seven holes are impressed into the surface and the playing area is ready. Pieces used in the game are small pebbles, date stones or dried dates, all to hand.

The aim of the game is to eliminate the

pieces of the other player in a style similar to draughts. Although this is a 'game for two', everyone around takes part with well-meaning advice or noisy criticism about the mode of play.

The game can be set up so that the players and spectators can also watch the activities in the village street, while the shepherds organize their games in a position from which they can watch over their flocks.

Bus Medenine has 2 bus stations. The *SNRTI* terminal, 3 km out of the centre on the Gabès road, handles long distance destinations, including Tunis. The *SRTMI* station, information T640020, on R du 18-Janvier-1952, opposite *Tunisair*, is for nearer destinations, including Djerba and Zarzis, Ben Gardane and Beni Khaddache, information T640070. — **Transport**

Airline offices *Tunisair*, R du 18-Janvier-1952, T640817, F642490, 0830-1730. **Banks** *Amen Bank*, behind *Etape Sangho* in Pl du Festival. *STB*, R 2 Mai, T640053. *BNT*, Av H. Bourguiba, T640088. NB By the time this goes to press, there may be an ATM in Medenine. **Communications** Internet: just off Pl du 7-Novembre, in the ODS building, T640781, open early to 0200, around 3Dt/h. **Post Office**: on Pl des Martyrs, off Av H. Bourguiba, near the crossroads towards Foum Tataouine, where the Gouvernorat and public gardens are to be found. **Tour operators** 52 R de 18 Janvier, T640817. **Useful addresses** Police: T640033. — **Directory**

Around Medenine

If heading north to Djerba, the ancient site of **Gightis** (*Colour map 4, grid A5*) will attract archaeology enthusiasts. Located on the coast 27 km north of Medenine on the road to Djorf, Gightis has remains of Romano-African style buildings, capitol, forum, temples, and baths. ■ *Museum 0830-1730 winter and 0900-1300 and 1500-1900 summer, closed Fri, entrance 1Dt.* — **On the Djerba road**

Heading southwest from Medenine, the C113 takes you to the ksar villages of **Djoumaa** and **Beni Kheddache**. Located 36 km southwest of Medenine, Djoumaa is composed of a new village and the original ksar. Situated at the top of a hill, old Djoumaa is crumbling back to nature. There are buses here from Medenine at 0815 and 1000, returning at 1000 and 1400. It is worth a trip to this most attractive hill top village with splendid views. The *ksar* has only recently been abandoned. — **The ksour west of Medenine** *Phone code: 75*

Beni Kheddache, beyond Djoumaa, 65 km from Ksar Guilane and 14 km from Ksar Hallouf, can be reached by the same buses from Medenine at 0815 and 1000. The village is of little interest in itself except on Thursday which is market day, but from here you can take the road south to Ksar Haddada and on to Tataouine (see below). From Ksar Haddada there is occasional public transport on to Ghromrassen and Tataouine. South of Beni Khaddache is surprisingly fertile area planted with olive groves and fig trees.

Southeastern Tunisia

Sleeping If you want to stay the night out this way, the only option is at Zamour, where there is the **F** *Hotel Zamour*, on a track a few km after the Beni Kheddache post office and the hospital (better ask), T647196, F647197, 13 rooms, 40 beds, very basic (bring your own sleeping bag and be prepared to sleep on a mattress on the floor), built in a cave structure therefore no windows, communal toilets and showers, clean, very quiet as you are surrounded by the mountains, excellent restaurant (best to ring to book).

Directory Beni Kheddache has basic facilities. **Hospital**: T647010. **Post Office**: in centre of town, close to hospital and behind louage. **Police**: T647025.

Medenine to Ben Gardane

This 77 km of road is very busy as goods go into Libya this way. You could hitch, but there are plenty of louages and 3-4 buses daily. The chaps with the plastic jerricans and funnels at the side of the road are selling cheap Libyan petrol. Other local produce for sale at the roadside includes live turkeys and chickens, their legs well tied, local olive oil (in a good year) and even the occasional fossil or carpet. As you approach the Libyan border, gentlemen will wave bundles of green banknotes at drivers. The devaluation of Libyan currency to a more realistice exchange rate may, however, put an end to these roadside black-market practices.

Medenine to Tataouine

From Medenine, Tataouine is an easy 49 km drive south. Although Medenine, like many small towns in southern Tunisia, can seem a little confusing for the foreign driver, the route south to Tataouine is easily found. For the first few kilometres out of Medenine, the road is protected by new plantations. At Bir Lahmar, 29 km from Tataouine, an expanding ribbon settlement, there is a handy publinet on the main road. Still heading south, there is a turn-off right (west) for Ksar Haddada (27 km) and left (east) for Guermessa (32 km). Approaching Tataouine, the road widens to smooth dual carriageway with numerous splendid new official buildings. After this administrative zone, the first big junction with a giant 7 and an upside-down pyramid-carpet monument has a turn-off for Guermessa. Also just north of the town is a *Shell* (unleaded petrol) station. Taking the Medenine to Tataouine road at night, drive with care. It is easy to pick up speed on the straight parts, to your peril, for there are some unexpected dips and slow-moving mopeds and local pick-up trucks without lights.

Tataouine   تطاوين

Phone code: 75
Colour map 4, grid B4

Established by the French as an administrative centre for the villages and nomad tribes, Tataouine still has something of a frontier feel to it. Though fleets of four-wheel drives pass through on their way to picturesquely abandoned villages and ksour, life goes on unperturbed, with local people, settled, semi-nomads or government employees, coming in for the jolly weekly markets. The area has gained in prosperity – witness the amount of new construction – and tourism may yet bring benefits in the form of a rural life museum. Tataouine makes a good base for exploring the hill villages to the west and ksour of the Djebel Abiadh.

Ins and outs

Getting there
See Transport, page 391, for further details

Tataouine is accessible by public transport from Medenine (49 km). There are direct buses morning and evening from Tunis (530 km) via Gabès. Journey time from Tunis about 9 hrs, from Gabès 2½ hrs. If you are driving from Medenine to Tataouine, be

Homes and citadels in southern Tunisia

Southern Tunisia has a characteristic selection of local architectures – and a precise terminology in Arabic to name the different forms of building. A **kalaâ** is a citadel, the fortified village in a mountain strongpoint. A **ksar** (pl. **ksour**) is also a fortress, the Arabic giving the modern Spanish Alcazar. In southern Tunisia, the term refers to a courtyard made up of **ghorfat**, vaulted cells built to store grain, oil and fodder. Each tribe would have its ksar, inhabited only by a caretaker and family. As times became more settled, **ksour** were constructed on the plains.

The nomads and semi-nomad family would spend the spring and autumn months living in a tent or **khayma**. In summer, when the tent was too hot, they might live in a roughly constructed hut or **zriba**. Eventually, the hut would turn into something more permanent, a **raguba**, a stone-walled enclosure roofed over with olive branches and alfa grass – preferable to the zriba as the fire risk was less.

In the citadel villages, homes may be composed of a **houch** (courtyard) and a **ghar**, a cave-like inner area excavated out of the hillside. In coastal areas, homes are different again. On Djerba, the **menzel**, a courtyard building surrounded by fields, was the typical home. In the orchards round Sfax, city families traditionally had a **borj** (lit:'a tower'), a place where they could spend the hot summer months. Matmata has the most original form of housing in the South, the famous pit-dwellings – the only place where 'the living live below the dead', to quote the local saying.

---

prepared for numerous police checkpoints – unsurprising given the security problems in Algeria. Slow right down and be prepared to smile and show your papers.

Getting around

Buses from Tunis arrive at the *SNTRI* station on Av H. Bourguiba. Buses from Medenine, Zarzis, Houmt Souk, Ghoumrassen and other southern places arrive at the *SRTGM* bus station on the corner of Av du 1 Juin 1955 and Av Ahmed Tlili. The louage station is on Av du 1 juin as well. For getting out to Chenini and Douiret, pick-ups run from R du 2 Mars, a street parallel to Av du 1 Juin.

RHP Orientation

Clambering out of a hot louage, Tataouine can seem a bit confusing at first. In practice, it is a small place built on a grid-iron pattern, the focus point being a large market square. The main upmarket hotels with bars are a few km south of the town. Cheap hotels and eateries are all just a couple of blocks from the bus stations.

Tourist information

The **ONTT** has an office on Av Bourguiba, and there is a **Syndicat d'initiative** on Av Hedi Chaker, almost opposite the *Hotel Hamza*, T850850. The *Hotel Sangho* has numbers for companies organizing camel treks (*randonnées chamelières*) and 4WD excursions.

History

At first glance, Tatouine is not the most interesting of towns. It is more charming than Medenine, and there is a lively market on Monday and Thursday. Discussions with locals will give you some insight into the way the area has changed.

In fact the changes wrought by the 20th century were enormous. Nothing really destined Tatouine to become centre for the most southerly inhabited region of Tunisia. The town's name points to Amazigh (Berber) origins, however. (Tataouine is the plural of the Amazigh *tit*, meaning 'spring', and the town used to be referred to as Foum Tataouine, 'mouth of the springs'.)

Southeastern Tunisia

In 1881, on the declaration of the French Protectorate over Tunisia, the southern tribes initially accepted the new authorities' rule. As there was only a small garrison left in Medenine, dissident tribes were not slow to revolt in 1882. In 1883, the tribes submitted once more, with the Touazine and Ouderna being given the status of *makhzen* tribes, that is, exempt from taxation provided they protected the South from outside incursions and rebellion. In 1888, the French created a *bureau de renseignement* at Douiret, the largest settlement in the region. But Douiret was too isolated, and the office was moved to Tataouine, where there was a military camp. After discussion with local leaders, a market was set up in 1892. An infirmary followed in 1914 and a primary school in 1916. A recruitment centre for the French *goumier* regiments was set up. The French military authorities asked tribal notables to settle at Tataouine – which the cheikhs did. They built houses which they then entrusted to Jewish or Muslim traders, preferring to live close to their *ksour* as they had always done. Later Tataouine was a garrison for one of the penal regiments, the *bataillons d'Afrique*. Originally set up in Algeria, the *bat d'Af* recruited men condemned for minor felonies. As their marching song put it: "De Gabès à Tataouine, de Gafsa à Medenine/Sac à dos dans la poussière, marche bataillonaire".

Tataouine thus started life as a military town, and like many southern towns, it still has a major garrison. The UN-imposed embargo on Libya undoubtedly brought prosperity to the region, and in the late 1990s, the Tunisian government invested heavily in new infrastructure – witness all the splendid new administrative buildings on the Medenine road north of the town.

Tourism may also become an important source of prosperity. With four-wheel drive excursions from Djerba now popular, Tataouine is now an established lunch stop. Dinosaur fossils were discovered recently, leading to the creation of a tiny museum (just opposite the entrance to the *Hotel Mabrouk*, south of the town). The Tourist Board plans a 'Jurassic Tour', the first stage of which is the lifesize stegosaurus on the hill above the museum. There is even a *Festival des Ksours* in April – not terribly spectacular, but an occasion for local people to gather. Desert culture does not lend itself to public display, but visitors will probably get to observe a mock marriage procession complete with bride riding in a *jahfa*, a camel-back palanquin heavily covered with cloth. This tradition is still alive and well in rural communities like Douiret.

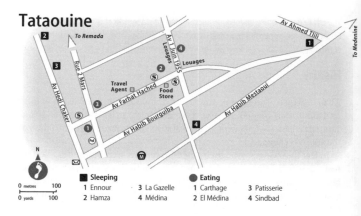

Tataouine

■ Sleeping		● Eating	
1 Ennour	3 La Gazelle	1 Carthage	3 Patisserie
2 Hamza	4 Médina	2 El Médina	4 Sindbad

Essentials

South of Tataouine The expensive hotels are located a few km south of the town in an incipient *zone touristique*. The *Sangho* is easily the best, both in terms of service and aesthetically. **A** *Hotel Dakyanus*, 6 km from Tataouine on the road to Chenini. Turn right at the crossroad towards Ghoumrassen, the hotel is low earth coloured building on the left next to the Oued El Ferch, T832199, F832198. Heating, no TV, bar with alcohol, 100 beds, pool with water if supplies permit. **A** *Sangho*, T860102, F862177, 86 rooms, 3 km south of Tataouine near the turn-off for Chenini and Ghoumrassen. Heading south turn right towards Ghoumrassen el Bled. The hotel is clearly signed, spotlessly clean, tastefully decorated. Good-sized rooms in low stone buildings which merge into the hillside. Pleasant pool (unheated), restaurant terrace next to pool, bar with alcohol. Recommended, if you can afford it. **B** *Hotel Mabrouk*, T852852/3, F850100, just after the turn-off for the *Sangho*, next to the road on the left opposite the small Musée de la Terre. 30 rooms with a/c, heating. A la carte restaurant (no booze), 15-20Dt/head. Pool on the way (they say). Big conference room, 400 seats, used by locals for wedding parties. Stone accommodation block, vaulted rooms, a bit grim (no view), touristy décor. Restaurant does lunch for large tour groups.

In Tataouine In contrast to the hotels south of the town, those in town are pretty low grade. **B-C** *La Gazelle*, 11 Av Hedi Chaker, near the post office, opposite Garde nationale, T860009, F862860. A/c (sometimes), all 23 rooms have bath, needs better maintenance, same hotel would be much cheaper in coastal resort, unfortunately few hotels in this price bracket in Tataouine. Used by groups. **E** *Hotel Médina*, Pl du 18 Janvier, T860999, in 3-storey block overlooking small square in centre, family-ish atmosphere. Rooms on 2nd/3rd floors, restaurant/reception on 1st floor. 20 rooms with sink, hot showers, breakfast 1.5Dt. Handily located near souk and bus station. Very basic, rooms a bit noisy. **F** *Hotel Ennour*, Av H. Bourguiba, T860131, by the main road to Remada. Not very clean and quite noisy. **F** *Hotel Residence Hamza*, Av Hedi Chaker, not far from *Hotel La Gazelle*, T863506. 9 rooms, communal toilet and shower every 3 rooms, cheap and fairly clean, ask for hot water because the heating has to be switched on, nice management. The woman on duty in the morning speaks only Arabic, in the afternoon somebody can speak French. Recommended. If all else fails, may let you sleep on roof-terrace.

The restaurants of the hotels *Gazelle* and *Mabrouk* cater mainly for tour groups. If eating à la carte in such places, check the bill. If you need a beer, head for the *Hotel Gazelle* or the *Sangho*. **Mid-range** *Relais Le Borj*, on the Remada road south of town, T851236, take 4th turn left after the 'globe' roundabout. Say 10Dt a head for a full feed. Has views over Tataouine and a few local animals the kids might like. **Cheap** *Restaurant Carthage*, R 20 Mars, T863167. Cheap, *méchoui* (grilled meat) the main dish, owner speaks only Arabic but his young son can get by in French. Recommended. *Restaurant El Médina*, near louage, T861978. *Restaurant Sindbad*, 13 Av 1 Jun 1955, near bus station and louage. Varied menu.

The **market** is held Mon and Thu on Av Farhat Hached. Among the stands selling plastic goods and clothing, you might just find a bargain in the shape of a piece of locally woven cloth. Shop for the rather nice slippers made in Tataouine, combining leather and pieces of klim-type wool or plastic weaving. The main square also has some jewellery shops, and you might just be lucky and pick up an old silver ankle-bracelet.

Bus Intercity buses to Medenine at 0630, 1000, 1300; to Gabès at 0630 and 1000. Rural buses (*naki-rifi*), 8-seater minibuses, run out to Douiret, 1Dt a head. **Louage** On the corner between Av Farhat Hached and Av 1 Jun 1955. Fare to Medenine 2Dt, to Gabès 5Dt.

Sleeping
■ *on map, page 390*
Limited choice – book ahead in upmarket hotels as they can fill up with tour groups

Eating
● *on map, page 390*

Shopping

Transport

Southeastern Tunisia

Directory **Banks** *Banque du Sud*, close to Post Office, in the centre of town. *Amen Bank,* on the corner between R Farhat Hached and Av 1 Jun 1955. **Communications** Post office: in the centre of town, close to *Café de Paris*. **Medical services** Emergencies: Infirmary behind Garde nationale on Av Hedi Chaker, T860902. **Hospital**: on the road to Medenine, T860114. **Private clinic**: near *Hotel Hamza* and *Hotel La Gazelle*, T860710. **Useful addresses** Police: R 20 Mars near *Restaurant Carthage*, T860871, ask here how to apply for permission to drive from Remada onward in the desert (the *Gouvernorat* is the authority that gives such permits).

Hillcrest villages and fortified granaries around Tataouine

The region around Tataouine has two main draws for the tourist: the landscapes and some surprising vernacular architecture, some of it in impressively good condition. Happily, the two attractions combine rather well and some of the best views can be had from the once isolated hillcrest villages. A couple of good day-trips, easily done with own transport, will give the visitor a feel for the region: one day could be spent exploring the villages of **Ksar Ouled Debab**, **Douiret** and **Chenini**, while another could be devoted to a circuit south and east of Tatatouine, taking in one of the best preserved *ghorfa* complexes, Ksar Ouled Soltane. A third possibility is to do **Guermessa**, **Ghomrassen** and **Ksar Haddada**, all of which lie to the northwest of Tataouine.

If you have limited time, then Douiret and Chenini are a must, even if the former is now pretty heavily visited. Without your own transport, one possibility is to get an early-morning pick-up truck out to the villages. There is also a twice daily local bus to Chenini.

South & east of Tataouine – the Ksar Ouled Soltane circuit
Colour map 4, grid B4

If you have your own transport, then there is an interesting tour to do into 'ksar land' south of Tataouine. The road is blacktop all the way, and there are well-preserved ksar at Ksar Ouled Soltane and at Ezzahra. If doing this excursion by public transport, there is no link between Ksar Ouled Soltane and Ezzahra. If you have to choose, go for Ksar Ouled Soltane, served by at least a couple of daily buses from Tataouine and by the odd pick-up.

Take the road directly south of Tataouine, to the left of the main road to Remada, in the direction of Maztouria where on the right are three *ksour*, and overall some splendid views.

On the way to Ksar Ouled Soltane there are some small villages in which it is possible to buy bread and drinks. In **Tamelest**, on the right, you have a small shop (bread, vegetables and drinks) and, after the mosque on the left, another one stocking bread and yoghurt. There is a café in the square in Ksar Ouled Soltane, but neither a hotel nor a restaurant as the inhabitants apparently have been opposed to catering for mass tourism. People are, nonetheless, very nice and knowledgeable about the history of their *ksar*.

Ksar Ouled Soltane is one of the best preserved *ksour* in Tunisia. The circular outer wall of the *ksar* is still virtually intact. The *ksar* is built on a slight rise allowing good views across the desert towards Libya. The people stored their grain in *ghorfas*, and two superb courtyards of them survive, the older dating from the 15th or 16th century. Standing on the hillside below this ksar, you can understand how easily defensible it must have been, at least against pillagers armed only with light firearms.

From Ksar Ouled Soltane the blacktop road snakes off across the arid land. After Ksar Ouled Soltane, you come to **Mghit**, where you need to go right at the junction. Next on the road is **Ezzahra**, 10 km from Ksar Ouled Soltane, which used to be called Ksar Retbet or El Krachaoua. It is an impressive village on the top of a hill. The village itself is a *ksar* built around a square in the middle of which two eucalyptus give shade. From the main square pass through the arch which joins a second square, which looks rather like a courtyard and where the third and fourth floor *ghorfas* are still in use. The people of Ezzahra voted against a tourist development project which would have meant the opening of restaurants, cafés and hotels.

From Ezzahra to Tataouine is a further 21 km drive. Leaving Ezzahra, after 500 m on the right there is a *marabout*. At 3 km on the right is the tiny village of Bir Yekzer, at 5 km Khatma, and at 6 km on the left Maaned. More interestingly, at 10 km from Ezzahra you come to the villages of **Beni Blel** and **Guettoufa**. Ksar Jelidat on the left is worth a look. After 500 m, turn left at crossroad (Beni Mhira 23 km away on the right) to admire the *ksar*. After 300 m, there is another crossroad, turn right for a panoramic view. Drive carefully as the road is up and down and there are many curves. Just keep to the surfaced road and Tataouine will appear.

The hillcrest villages of **Chenini** and **Douiret** lie to the south and west of Tataouine. Once home to self-sufficient Amazigh communities who lived in close contact with the Arab nomads, they are now on the tourist trail. Nevertheless, their impressive hilltop positions make them among the most impressive sights in the Tataouine region. Visiting them with your own vehicle is easy enough, Douiret being only 17 km from Tataouine, Chenini around 20 km. The 'back route', once a rough track, has now been fully replaced by blacktop road with signs. From Tataouine, both villages can also be reached by minibuses (rural transport - *nakl rifi*) running from the Rue du 2 Mars. If you are pushed for time, you could hire a taxi to take you to Douiret at around 15Dt plus waiting time. If you take a louage to Douiret, you'll have to wait until the car fills up for the return journey – or pay for the extra places.

For Douiret, leave Tataouine on the P19 and head out in the Remada direction. **Ksar Ouled Debbab** is about 10 km south along the road. Arriving in the new village at the foot of the hill, walk left towards the mosque. You will find a path on the left. If you have your own transport it is possible to drive up to the hill. This beautiful hilltop *ksar*, now abandoned and falling into ruin, blends into the surrounding landscape. Steps and arches can still be identified. It looks like a lonely place, but local lads spend time hanging out on the top of the *ghorfas*, their days rhythmed by the passage of tourist four-wheel drives.

The road to **Douiret** heads west from the centre of Ksar Ouled Debbab, running for 9 km through land cultivated after the winter rains but barren in the summer. Drive with care as the road has many bends and drivers may be looking at the view. The old, almost abandoned village is perched on the hillside 2 km further along the track. Only five families remain here. Even with tourists, the place feels quite eerie and has a faint mystical air with its white mosque and dun-coloured, half-ruined houses blending into the hillside. There is a small *marabout* on the left on the way into the village. Watch out for dogs. Notice the inscriptionless tomb stones. In the 19th century, before colonial boundaries, Douiret must have been quite a prosperous place with the trans-Saharan trade. In the early days of the French occupation, it was home to the *Bureau des renseignements*, subsequently moved down to more accessible Tataouine.

The scenic back route from **Douiret** to **Chenini** has now been fully surfaced and equipped with signposts. Cross the new village of Douiret and follow through to the west. (In winter, check road conditions with locals in any case as rain may spoil things.) There is another direct road to Chenini, south of Tataouine. Heading south out of Tataouine, turn right after 2 km on the

Southwest of Tataouine: Ksar Ouled Debbab, Chenini & Douiret
Colour map 4, grid B4

C207 to Ghoumrassen el Bled. Opposite the *Hotel Mabrouk* is the new **Musée Mémoire de la Terre**, dedicated to dinosaur fossils and other geological finds from the region. No need to stop in the new town, follow the road round the hill to the only restaurant, the very touristy *Relais de Chenini* (same management as the *Hotel Mabrouk*), see below.

On foot, Chenini is only 5½ km (about 1½ hours) from Douiret over the top past the highest houses. Seek a guide for at least the first half of the walk as the only people en route will be girls herding goats. Leave Douiret early and wear strong shoes since the path is, in some parts, rocky. You will arrive in Chenini Nouvelle, where it is possible to visit the old mosque on the top of the hill. Near the mosque on the right there are a *marabout* and graves covered by stones and grass. If you do not have your own transport don't leave it too late to look for a lift back.

Located high above the arid plain, **Chenini** is an impressive sight. The houses which are built into the rock have a small courtyard, where animals are kept. There are some *ghorfas* at the top of the village, but few are still in use. Like those of the other Amazigh villages, Chenini men began to migrate to the cities in the 20th century, where they became established as newspaper sellers. Visit the underground Mosque of the Seven Sleepers with its particularly intriguing long tomb stones. Chenini has become part of the tourist route but, despite the crowds climbing up and down the village, it is worth seeing for the extraordinary setting. The streets here are just ledges, scarcely wide enough for two people to pass! The restaurant *Relais de Chenini* at the bottom of the hill has reasonably priced food but lunch (5Dt) service can be slow as many groups call in here. With a packed lunch and a drink you will have more time for the sights.

Northwest of Tataouine: Ghoumrassen, Guermessa & Ksar Haddada
Colour map 4, grid B4

Another 'ksar circuit' takes you through the arid landscapes northwest of Tataouine. **Ghoumrassen** is a largish market centre with much modern building and some underground dwellings. **Guermessa** is the least visited of the hillcrest villages, while at **Ksar Haddada** a small hotel has been fitted into the old ghorfa complex.

Travelling by public transport, there are buses from Tataouine and Medenine to Ghoumrassen. Ksar Haddada, just 5 km north of Ghoumrassen, is served by local bus, or you could try hitching. There is blacktop road to Guermessa, 8 km south of Ghoumrassen. Try to get a local pick-up truck out to the village, or again, hitch.

With your own transport, heading out of Tataouine, you can take either the direct route to Ghoumrassen (north along the GP19 for Medenine, then turn left onto the C221) or the scenic route. For the latter, head south out of town on the GP19 and take the C207 on the right. You will be looking for a left hand turn-off for **Guermessa**. The new village is of no interest but behind it, along a dirt track to the west, is the old village. It is similar to Chenini, but without the tourists. From the top (half an hour climb up a paved path), the panorama of the surrounding area is breathtaking.

For those with a four-wheel drive vehicle and good navigation skills, it is possible to head due west from Guermessa to the desert outpost of Ksar Ghilane (see chapter 7). This is a route **not** to be taken lightly. (Whether it is actually worth going to Ksar Ghilane like all four-wheel safaris from Djerba is another matter.)

Ghoumrassen is only 8 km further on to the north from Guermessa. The most interesting part is towards the centre of the town. Behind the town, to the north, you can see the old abandoned village clinging to the cliff topped by a small mosque, as if watching over the inhabitants. If you have the energy, it is worthwhile going up to the mosque. From here you will see the old *ghorfas*

Ghorfas

Throughout the south of Tunisia grain was stored in small stone cells known as ghorfas. *They were each about 2 m high and 6-10 m in length. More units were added as required both at either side and above, sometimes reaching up to five units in height. Eventually the whole formed a courtyard, the blank outside walls deterring raiders.*

A skill you might just require – how to make a ghorfa:

1. Build two walls of rock and mud about 2 m apart and 1½ m high.

2. Place vertically between the walls two straw grain baskets packed with earth. These must fit exactly between the walls to support them. Place a third straw grain basket of earth horizontally on top of the first two.

3. Over this place a previously manufactured plaited reed/straw mat to make an arch.

4. An arched roof of rocks held by a fine clay and gypsum mortar can then be gradually constructed, using the matting and grain baskets as support.

5. Construct a rear wall if necessary. Remove the supporting baskets and plaster the internal walls with lime and mud. Decorate if required with figures and handprints or fish to ward off the evil eye.

6. Construct a front wall with a wooden access door of palm.

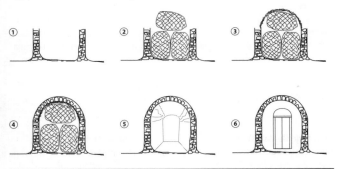

and the rest of the old town. There has been a considerable amount of new building. To walk to the top to the old mosque on top of the hill, ask in the centre of town where the path starts. It is not very clear. It is a stiff climb and rather dangerous. The mosque is small and its plan is quite irregular. On Thursday evenings many people walk up to the old mosque. Friday is market day.

The story goes that the people of Ghoumrassen are famous throughout Tunisia for their **fritters**, *ftayer* in Arabic. (Note also the Tunis saying, *wajhek kee fatira*, 'fritter face'.) Despite this culinary skill, there aren't too many restaurants in Ghoumrassen. Nonetheless, the patisserie in Avenue H. Bourguiba and, in the same road, the baker can provide some basic food. Avoid the restaurant in the small road close to the police station as it is neither good nor cheap.

Sleeping If you want to spend the night in this area, there are as yet no hotels in Ghoumrassen. Your option (apart from back-tracking to Tataouine) is to stay in **Ksar Haddada**, a small settlement just 5 km north along the road after Ghoumrassen el Bled. The only *ghorfas* left have been beautifully conserved and transformed into a hotel. The **E** *Hotel Ksar Haddada*, T869605, is very cheap, 26 simple rooms, with bath/toilets which could be cleaner, restaurant serving good, traditional meals at reasonable prices. Even if the comforts are limited and the management not very cordial; a night in the hotel could be an experience.Some rooms have 3 floors and up to 7 beds. Anti-mosquito gel will come in handy. In the main square by the hotel, there is the rather touristic *Café Etoile*.

Taking out a contract at the ksar

The ksar region was a complex mosaic of nomad and semi-nomad tribes, some Arab, some Arabised Berbers and sedentary communities, some Berber. These groups had to make use of the scarce resources of the region to the best advantage, and there was a sort of ethnic division of labour. The Berbers were not nomads, having neither horses nor camels. Living in their citadel villages, they cultivated their ghabat, meagre parcels of land, maximizing water resources by constructing jessour dams. They grew olives, figs. The Berbers 'cut their hair, wear the burnous and eat couscous', went the saying. If they had herds, they would entrust them to an Arab neighbour.

The desert Arabs were always on the move, following their herds. They were masters of both grazing areas and cultivated land on the plains. But given their nomadism, they needed Berber produce – olives, dried figs and dates – and above all, woven cloth for garments. The nomad women, being always on the move, were unable to produce fine weavings. Thus the nomads would give the wool from their flocks to the Berbers who would produce cloth for them.

A sort of service-exchange system had developed over time, formalized by sahaba ('friendship') contracts. The nomad Arab needed the Berber – and vice versa. Times were often unsettled – as the Berber villages' locations show. The nomads thus offered to protect the Berbers from raids. The Berber would pay a sort of fee in kind, while the Arab would provide protection and bring an annual gift, either wool from the flock or smen (salt melted butter).

After the arrival of the French in the southern regions, 'protection contracts' gradually fell into disuse. Raiding became a thing of the past, life became more settled. Today, they are very much a thing of the past. The distinction between the different groups remains, however. Marriages in isolated areas are often still within the tribal community.

Directory Banks: *BS*, Av H. Bourguiba, T869147. *STB*, Av H. Bourguiba, T869115. **Communications**: Post Office: Av H. Bourguiba. **Useful addresses**: Police: R Ibn Arfa (in front of post office), T869175.

North of Ksar Haddada North of Ksar Haddada, the road runs on for 22 km (soon to be fully surfaced) towards **Beni Kheddache**. There is as yet no public transport between these two settlements. Real ksar enthusiasts might want to try for **Ksar Kerafcha**, which lies east of the Ksar Haddada to Ben Kheddache road.

Into the Deep South

Colour map 5 In Tunisia's southern cone, the only major settlement is **Remada,** a military town 78 km south of Tataouine. This can be the starting point for travelling west 41 km to the military posts of **Borj Bourguiba** (ex-Fort Saint, also shown as Borj el Hattaba on some maps) or southeast to **Dehibat**, where there is a border post with Libya (50 km). Heading south, you come to Lorzot (75 km), Bir Zar, still further south on the Libyan border. Travelling on from Remada, either in the desert or to the Algerian or Libyan borders, requires special permission. The competent authority is the Governorate in Tataouine. Tents and sleeping bags are required, as there are no hotels in the area. However, the Governorate is unlikely to grant the necessary papers to everyday travellers – at least, not without prolonged consultations with the Ministry of the Interior in Tunis. Should you wish to go on into Libya, the border post up at Ras Ajdir is by far the easiest option. **Borj el Khadhra** is the southernmost point in Tunisia.

Medenine to Zarzis

Medenine to Zarzis is a fast 62 km. The wide, smooth C118 road out of Medenine runs through an undistinguished landscape scattered with small, newish homesteads. The first useful settlement is Hassi Amor (*Agil* station, unleaded petrol), 14 km out of Medenine. The next settlement, 6 km further on, is Souitri. There is a major junction where the GP1 runs off southeast for Ben Gardane. At 29 km from Medenine, coming up to Grabat, the C118 dips and winds and you should expect to find the Garde nationale waiting to catch speeding motorists in the shade of the eucalyptus trees. Khalfallah, 43 km out of Medenine, is the first 'major' settlement. Shortly after, a junction indicates a turn-off left for Djerba, 35 km to the north. The usual concrete sprawl indicates that you are reaching an important town, namely Zarzis. At the junction with the turn-off south for Ben Gardane, last town before the Libyan frontier, there is a handy *Agil* (unleaded) petrol station.

Watch out for Garde nationale patrols on this route

Zarzis جرجيس

On the mainland a stone's throw from Djerba Island, Zarzis is Tunisia's most southerly resort town. Nothing remains of the town's previous life as a Roman outpost. Under the French, the town had a small military garrison and there was much planting of olive trees in the region. In recent years, a few more hotels have sprung up along the beach, and there is now a tax-free industrial zone. A Zarzis hotel could make a nice base camp before driving off round various remote southern villages. Local antiquities: the ruins of ancient Zitha.

*Phone code: 75
Colour map 4, grid A6*

Ins and outs

Zarzis can be reached by public transport from Djerba (8 buses a day) and Medenine (8 buses). There are buses and louages from certain northern towns too, journey time from Tunis, with stops, around 9 hrs. There are buses from Ben Gardane and Gabès, too, and 1 daily bus from Tataouine.

Getting there
See Transport, page 400, for further details

Buses and louages arrive some 300 m from the central square, at a station off the Av Habib Thameur. If you need to get out to the *zone touristique* and its beach, and the outlying resort area of Sangho, then bus No 1 from the town centre will get you there.

Getting around

The tourist information office is a fair way from the centre, on Rte des Hotels, close to the *Hotel Zarzis* and the *Restaurant Abou Nawas*, T694445. Opening hours Jul-Sep 0730-1300, rest of year 0730-1300, 1500-1745.

Tourist information

Background

The town has long been associated with Djerba as a tourist resort, and there are certain similarities. The architecture is quite similar and the landscape, with large olive groves and long, white beaches, is indeed very reminiscent of Djerba. The town, originally the market town for the area, is highly developed for tourism and generally well organized. The main point of interest in the town, apart from the market on Monday and Friday, is the **Sponge Festival** (15 July-15 August) which is celebrated with traditional dances and music, fishing boat competitions and, of course, sponge fishing. Zarzis is probably best enjoyed as a low-key beach resort, with the additional plus of being near the **Bahiret el Bibane** lagoon to the southeast, a little awkward to get to without your own transport, however.

Southeastern Tunisia

Zarzis is close to the road access to **Djerba**, across the causeway which was originally built by the Carthaginians and later rebuilt by the Romans. The road as it stands today was rebuilt in 1953. (The only other access to Djerba is by the Djorf ferry.) Given this easy access to Djerba and its airport, plus the good beaches, Zarzis looks set for major hotel development in the near future, particularly as further hotel construction on Djerba has been stopped.

Essentials

Sleeping
■ *on map below*

Accommodation in Zarzis comes in three categories. Town centre hotels, cheap and nothing special; older tourist hotels on the Rte des Hotels, a couple of km out of the town centre; and finally, the new places (and the *Club Sangho*) in the beachside Sangho area, 12 km from Zarzis.

Town centre *Hotel Nozha* About 1 km from centre, near the barracks, T681593, F694355. Good-sized rooms with sea view, check if a/c works, cheap out of season. Libyan clientele. **D** Hotel Corniche, Av Tahar Sfar, T682833. Pleasant cheap hotel **D** *Hotel Médina*, T691909. 40 beds, right in the centre, down the street on the right after the *Café de Paris*. Rooms with shower and loo. Small restaurant. More than acceptable. **E** *Hotel Afif*, T684639. 1980s block close to centre on Djerba road, 20 rooms, shower on corridor, a 'metal bed frames and blankets only' type place. Some rooms 5 beds. Grim. **E** *Hotel de la Station*, R Abou Kacem Chabbi, large building with a tower. T684661. 51 beds. Handy for the SNTRI bus station, as its name suggests. Cheap, loos just about acceptable. **E** *Hotel du Sud*, 18 Av Farhat Hached, almost opposite the *Hotel Médina*. 20 beds. **F** *Hotel de l'Olivier*, close to the bus station, T694637. 20 beds, simple, clean, probably the best of the cheap hotels. **Youth hostel**: R de l'Algérie. 30 beds in 3 blocks, acceptable, T681599.

Prices for the large hotels vary hugely according to season

Route des Hotels B-C *Club Oamarit*, T705770, F705685. 375 rooms. Calm, pleasant, much used by tour groups. **B-C** *Résidence Sultana*, T682206, 681115, F683167. 16 rooms, direct access to beach. Heating, nice small restaurant. **B-C** *Zarzis Hotel*, T684160, F694292. 600 beds. Large package hotel. **B-C** *Hotel Zita*, T694246, F684350.

Zarzis

N
Not to scale

■ **Sleeping**
1 Afif
2 Amira
3 Corniche
4 De la Station
5 De l'Olivier
6 Du Sud

● **Eating**
1 El Bibane

Ralia of Zarzis

The independent-minded E Pellissier had a North African career in the 1830s and 1840s. France was interested in building a picture of all things North African, and Pellisier, who had a reputation as a historian, was a member of the Commission for the Scientific Exploration of Algeria. From 1843 to 1848, Pellissier was French consul in Sousse, a post which gave him the leisure to gather the material for his Déscription de la Régence de Tunis, *published in 1853. Here are his reflections on Zarzis.*

"Zarzis is a small maritime town with fairly fertile land producing lots of palms and olive trees. It has a small castle with a few men to garrison it. It has a cheik, like all the other villages, but, at the moment, this authority is effectively exercised by a woman. She is called Ralia. At the height of her youth and beauty, the remains of which are still remarkable, this woman played a certain role in the troubles at Tripoli. Brave as a man, she was often seen in the midst of the fighting, displaying the greatest courage. However, immoral as a woman of the Orient who has thrown down her veil, she had many lovers, whose generosity provided her with a fortune which she has managed well. Retiring to Zarzis, she married a quiet man there, who is known merely as Ralia's husband, as is the common destiny of all those who marry famous women. I met Ralia, who was a generous host in her village, where she has the influence which a strong and resolute mind can always exercise over the Arabs, no matter what the sex. Her manners are polite and quite distinguished, her conversation interesting and her good sense remarkable. Finally, she was of enough interest for me to devote these few lines to her in a book where all kinds of observations must find a place."

From Déscription de la Régence de Tunis *by E Pellissier (Paris: Imprimerie Impériale, 1853).*

Vast 1970s hotel, 13 ha grounds, 600 rooms, a/c, adequate restaurant, closed Nov to mid-Mar. **C** *Hotel Amira*, T694188. 22 beds, small beach hotel. **C** *Hotel Zephyr*, T681027, F681026. 652 beds. One of the older package hotels. Not one of the best – visitors have noted noisy building works at the height of the season.

Sangho AL *Odyssée*, T705705, F705190, odyssee.resort@planet.tn 340 rooms, credit cards accepted. Vast new hotel, worth taking a look at the interior, de luxe Matmata pit-dwelling style. Thalassotherapy and sports activities, kids club, too. Double 200Dt in high season, but prices can be much lower. **B** *Club Sangho*, T705124, F705715. 722 beds. The oldest and still probably the nicest of the Zarzis beach hotels. Simple whitewashed buildings in extensive grounds on sloping site overlooking sea. Each room has a small balcony. Animated village-street feel in centre of hotel. Lots of activities for children. Popular all year round.

Lots of eateries in the *zone touristique* with menus in German, open high season only. Standard steak or fish, pizzas or pasta type places.

Eating
● *on map opposite*

Expensive *Restaurant Abou Nawas*, Rte des Hotels, T650583. Said to be the best restaurant in Zarzis. Fish.

Mid-range *Restaurant El Bibane*, Av Farhat Hached near Pl de la Jeunesse, T684344. Good fish cooked for locals, cheap and clean. Recommended. *Restaurant El Borj*, Rte des Hotels, T680928. *Restaurant Nozha*, Rte de Sonia, Plage municipale, T681593. *Restaurant l'Oasis*, on the road to *Club Sangho*, T680124. *Restaurant Le Pacha*, Rte des Hotels, T680497. Has a good name. *Restaurant Les Palmiers*, town centre, T694114. *Restaurant Le Pirate*, Rte des Hotels, T683352, tables outside overlooking street, fine, alcohol. *Restaurant République*, town centre.

Restaurant Le Typique, opposite entry to *Club Sangho*, no alcohol but reasonable food nevertheless. *Restaurant Yasmina*, Rte des Hotels, next to *Le Pirate* , but no alcohol.

Cheap *Restaurant l'Olivier*, Av Farhat Hached after *Restaurant El Bibane* on the same side of the road. Try lamb steak or chicken. *Restaurant La Station*, Av Abou Kacem Chabbi, in the centre, near the hotel of the same name. Simple, cheap food.

Sport In season, there is windsurfing and water-skiing, jet-ski and inflatable banana rides at beaches of large hotels. Working harbour not really for pleasure craft, min-max draft 2-4½ m. Zarzis used to be famous for sponge fishing (may be advertised). Best tennis courts at *Club Sangho*, T705124.

Tour operators *Agency Globus*, T/F668288. *Majus Voyages*, T694666. *Syndabad Tours*, Zarzis, Av Moham-med V, T681896. *Tunisirama* at *Club Sangho*, T694124. *Zarzis Loisirs* at *Hotel Zita*, T694246. *Zarzis Travel Service*, Rte de Djerba, T681072. *Zarzis Voyage*, Rte de Ben Gardane, T694654.

Transport **Local** **Car hire**: For car hire, contact *Hotel Sangho* or *Hotel Ulysse* who will put you on to a reliable agency. **Long distance** Long distance buses and louages come into the new station near the port, a good 20 mins' walk from the town centre. **Bus**: **Tunis** 2100; **Sousse** 1300 (via Medenine); there are about 4 buses a day to Medenine and Ben Gardane, 1.7Dt, more frequent departures towards Djerba, 2.1Dt. Information, T680661. **Louage**: Av Farhat Hached, T680078. **Taxi**: Av Mohammed V, T680063.

Directory **Banks** *STB*, town centre, T694082; *BNT*, R de Palestine, T694020; *BT*, R de Palestine and R d'Algérie, T694024; *Banque du Sud*, T694318, town centre, Av Mohamed V, in the Djerba direction; *Bank el Amen*, ex-CFCT, Av Mohammed V, T680818. There are also bureaux de change along Rte touristique, 100 m beyond the tourist office. **Communications** Post Office: Av H. Bourguiba, T680125. There is another post office/telephone centre in the hotel zone, about 1 km north of the Tourist Office.**Medical services** Chemist: all night, Av Farhat Hached, T694124. **Clinique de l'Olivier**: on the road to Djerba, T682240. **Hospital**: Av du 20 Mars, in town centre, T680302. **Supermarket** Downtown Zarzis has a *Magasin général*. For alcohol, look for the salespoint next to the *Sahara Confort* shop. **Useful addresses** Police: Av du 20 Mars, T694063/017 and Av Farhat Hached, T694745. **Port**: Rte de Porte, T681827.

Zarzis to Ben Gardane

Phone code: 75
Colour map 4, grid B6

If you have your own transport, drive on the C109, which follows the coast, skirts the salt lakes and reaches Ben Gardane 46 km away. Otherwise take the bus (the bus station is near the port). The ticket costs 1.7Dt and the trip should take one hour, but it might take more as stops are on request. As you arrive in **Ben Gardane**, the market, held on Saturday, is on the right. The bus station is 100 m from the louage stand.

Sleeping, eating & transport Should you need to spend the night in Ben Gardane, there are a good few hotels, including the **E** *Pavilion Vert*, T665103; **E** *Hotel de l'Algerie*, R 20 Mars, T665279; **E** *Hotel El Ouns*, R de Medenine, T665920, 20 rooms, most with bath, fairly clean, good views over town from ter-race on upper storey; **F** *Baghdad*, R de Zarzis, T05-666123, next to bus station, clean, shared toilet facilities. For food in Ben Gardane, try the *Restaurant de l'Espoir*, in front of *Hotel Baghdad*, R de Zarzis. A very good unofficial exchange rate for Libyan dinars is available here, and you are now just 33 km away from the Libyan border. Going to the Libyan border at Ras Ajdir by louage costs 10Dt, and there are plenty of buses doing the run as well.

Djerba

Djerba

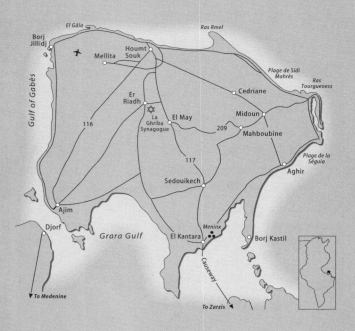

A low-lying expanse of sand and palm trees moored off Tunisia's southern coast, Djerba is the perfect holiday island. It is a slow-moving, seductive place – you can feel that life pulses quite a few beats slower than on the mainland. There are long stretches of sandy beach, mainly along the northern and eastern coasts, fringed with palms and backed by tourist hotels.

Coming to Djerba on a package, you could quite easily spend the entire holiday between beach and hotel compound. The island does, however, merit some exploring. Architecture buffs will find the white vernacular building of the countryside fascinating (there are some nice walks to do near **Midoun** and **Mahboubine**), while birdwatchers could nip out to **Ras Rmel** to see the wading birds. There is an ancient community of potters at **Guellala** in the southwest of the island, a large synagogue at **Hara Kebira** and some scattered Roman remains at **Meninx**, in the southeast, close to the causeway.

Djerba

Ins and outs

Getting there There are 3 points of access to the island. There is a 6 km causeway leaving the mainland near Zarzis, or the ferry from Djorf to Ajim. Coming from Gabès, the ferry saves a lot of driving time but in summer be prepared to queue. The crossing only takes 15 mins. The ferry runs every 30 mins until 2000. From then it sails hourly through the night. Free for foot passengers and motorbikes, 1Dt for cars by day and 1.5Dt at night. All buses arrive at the bus station in the centre of Houmt Souk. The 3rd way in is via Djerba's international airport (T75650233) in the northwest of the island, near Houmt Souk. It receives scheduled flights from Frankfurt, Lyon, Geneva, Zürich, Brussels and Paris, and regular internal flights from Tunis (1 way 46Dt), Sfax and Tozeur.

Getting around You will probably be staying in a hotel either in Houmt Souk or the *zone touristique* on the northeast coast. Distances are not great – the beach hotels start 6 km to the east of Houmt Souk with the massive *Robinson Select Athénée Palace* and run round the coast for over 12 km. The energetic could hire a bike or moped to get around the villages of 'the interior', otherwise there are taxis and local buses. A taxi ride from Houmt Souk to hotels should cost around 3.5 to 4Dt, 50% more after 2100. Most of the 2-wheel transport hire places are along the main hotel zone road. More tend to open in summer.

Background

History Djerban history begins in mythic times with Greek hero Odysseus. In the Homeric epic, Odysseus lands in Djerba and has great difficulty in leaving again, not least because of the attractions of the lotus flower he found on the island. Back in real history, Djerba was in turn Phoenician, Carthaginian and Roman. To the Carthaginians, it was the island of Meninx, much appreciated for the safe anchorage it offered. The Romans were not about to leave such a pleasant island unsettled and they established a city in the southeast part of the island, close to where their causeway touched land. Djerba was finally conquered by the Arabs in 667, but was later involved in the rivalries between the Kharijite sect and the orthodox Muslims.

By the 15th century, Djerba had become a den of pirates. Efforts were made to dislodge them, the most fateful being in 1560 when an attempt was made to fight off the pirate Dragut. This failed and Dragut built a tower with the skulls of the slain Christians. The unpleasant monument was demolished in 1848, though images of it survive in early prints. In the late 19th century, the French arrived. In fact, the commercially minded Djerbans were actually quite happy to see the French come, fearing attacks from rebellious inland tribes which would upset trade and the making of money. The arrival of French authority imposed a new form of order on the southern regions and created more stable souks. Djerbans were quick to seize the opportunities for commerce.

Djerba's people The population of Djerba has always been quite isolated from the mainland. The effect has been the development of a unique style of life and architecture. The population is now mostly Berber in origin but, until recently, there was also a significant Jewish population on the island, one of the oldest communities in the world, dating back to 566 BC and the fall of Jerusalem to Nebuchadnezzar. Now there are only about 1,000 Jewish people left here, a large number having emigrated to Israel and France. The Muslim population numbers over 100,000, and a small percentage belong to the Ibadite branch of

Things to do

- Discover all things traditional and Djerban in the **Guellala Museum**, a purpose-built complex on the hill above the village of Guellala, once famed for its pottery.
- Try a seawater cure at the *Centre de thalassothérapie* in the Hotel Ulysse, T75758777.
- Visit **El Ghriba** one of the oldest synagogues in the world, at Hara el Kebira, just outside Houmt Souk. (The annual pilgrimage in late April/early May takes place on the 33rd day of Jewish Easter.)
- Djerba was once famed for its Jewish silversmiths. Look out for heavy silver bracelets by artisans such as Nemli in the **jewellers' shops** of Houmt Souk.
- Rent a bike anc cycle down the narrow roads between cactus hedges in the middle of the island, you may come across simple whitewashed mosques and *menzahs*, as the old island houses are called in Arabic.

Islam, which derives from the rigorous and austere Kharijite sect, established shortly after the Arab invasion. It is possible that the Djerban Berbers adopted this form of Islam in order to keep some independence from the mainstream Islam preached by the Arab invaders.

Today, the population is faced with the new problems of tourism. Having lived for so long in isolation, Djerbans were perhaps less well equipped than other places for the large influx of tourists. The industry has had considerable impact on the population's lifestyle. In many families, work in traditional farming and fishing continues alongside easier and better paid jobs in tourism. Other residents have been forced to change jobs or leave due to the ever increasing cost of living, making Djerba an island with a very high emigration rate. In major French towns, the ever open corner grocer is often *un Djerbien*. However, after years abroad, this grocer will usually return to his native island to live out retirement among family and friends.

Traditional activities

Traditionally, Djerba's main resources were agriculture, fishing and handicrafts, including in particular weaving and pottery. Given the lack of rainfall, agriculture required the cultivation of a drought-tolerant trees (date palm, olive and pomegranate), and the careful management of water. Every farmstead has both wells and cistern. Though there are many palm trees, they produce poor quality dates, due to the high salinity of the water. Olive trees are more successful and olive oil production used to be an important industry. Traditional fishing is slowly declining, however. Hotel employment, though seasonal, is easier and better paid. Of the crafts, some pottery making continues at Guellala, although here, as elsewhere in Tunisia, most of ceramics on sale will be from Nabeul.

Tourism on Djerba

The arrival of mass tourism since the mid-1980s has brought about a huge change in the life of the island. In the second half of the 1990s, development outpaced expectations. There are now close on 100 hotels and 35,000 beds, usually occupied mainly by Germans. (German tour operator Neckerman is set to buy hotels.) The authorities have tried to encourage a more upmarket form of tourism than that at Hammamet and Sousse. The most recent hotels are all four or five star, and there are a number of new attractions, including a 27-hole golf course and a casino. The austere Ibadite ancestors of today's Djerbans must be turning in their graves at such tack. On a more heritage level, an upscale guest house has opened at Erriadh, an attempt to imitate the plush *hotels de charme* of Marrakech. Thalassotherapy is another area in which Djerba's hoteliers have invested their money, and there is an elaborate centre at the *Hotel Ulysse*.

Whether Djerba will be successful in attracting the upscale traveller remains to be seen. Many hotels were built by investors attracted by the tax breaks for putting money into the tourist industry. Hotel investment companies need to fill beds and pay back loans, and the major European tour operators have huge leverage on prices, being able to buy large numbers of bed nights at very cheap rates years in advance, or take over the management of whole hotels. The result is of course that while the overall standard is good, service is often poor.

In early 2002, with the Middle East and Islamic countries shaken by the American bombing of Afghanistan and the brutal Israeli reoccupation of the Palestinian autonomous territories, Djerba witnessed its first ever terrorist attack in which around 20 tourists, mainly German, were killed. A lorry containing explosives was parked next to the synagogue at Hara Kebira, with terrible results. Initially, the Tunisian government denied that terrorists could have been at the root of such an act, asserting that the lorry contained a faulty gas-bottle. Germany, Tunisia's biggest source of tourist euros, pushed for an real investigation, and it emerged that there was a connection with a wider Islamic-extremist terrorist network, though to what extent was unclear at the time of writing. Whatever, security on the island was stepped up with elaborate controls on the ferry and causeway.

An island changed for ever? One-off terrorist attacks aside, Djerban tourism faces other, more basic problems. The island produces very little, so everything the tourist (and those working for them) needs has to be imported. Further State investment in infrastructure will be essential. The airport, which saw traffic grow with the embargo on Libya, is being extended, the causeway will need widening, further water and waste treatment plants will have to be built. The tourist industry has created a huge demand for unskilled and semi-skilled labour, almost all of which has to come from outside. If large numbers of outsiders settle, they could change the face of island society. The hotels which line the northern and eastern coast have already changed the landscape. Elsewhere, the new generation of Djerbans prefers to live in concrete houses with verandas, much like the houses going up everywhere else in Tunisia. The discrete *menzels*, the simple whitewashed homesteads of the past, are left abandoned among the olive groves. Sign of the times, there is no longer any need to explore the island for traces of a vanished rural way of life. Up on the hill at Guellala, there there is a new 'Djerba Island experience', a museum complex with buildings half-mosque, half-menzel containing a concentrate of all things traditional and Djerban.

Routes to Djerba

Mareth to Djerba Coming down from Tunis and Gabès, or across from the southwestern oases, the best way to Djerba is the **Mareth** to the tiny port of **Jorf** route. At Jorf, you pick up the ferry for **Ajim**. (Foot passengers go free, car only 1Dt, motorcycles 800 millimes.) Distances: Gabès to Jorf 90 km, Mareth to Jorf 50km. From Mareth, you drive south for a few kilometres on the fast GP1 before turning off left (east) a few metres after the Mareth Line Museum to head for Jorf. After an avenue of eucalyptus trees, the road runs across rolling arid land with occasional olive plantations. Drive carefully at night when locals are tempted to speed on the smooth but winding, unlit road to catch the ferry. Driving time from junction on GP1 to Jorf, around 30 minutes.

Ajim was once an important sponge-fishing harbour although this activity is now virtually abandoned, due to overfishing and the dangers of the job. Today, cormorants do a lot of the fishing. Cars queue for the *transbordeur*. The wait can sometimes be long, anything up to 1½ hours. There are the usual small cafés and eateries at both Ajim and at Jorf on the other side, a few minutes' sail away. From the Jorf to **Houm Souk** is a distance of 20 km. Since the bomb explosion at the Ghriba Synagogue on Djerba, security checks have been stepped up on the mini-ferry. These may not remain in force for long.

Coming from Tataouine or from Zarzis to the east, take the C108 north from **Medenine**. Where the C108 reaches **Bou Grara** on the coast, some 20 km before Jorf, you will pass the sparse ruins of ancient **Gightis**. Set at the bottom of the Gulf of Bou Grara, basically a shallow inland sea south of Djerba, the ancient town was a Punic trading post before becoming an important port under Roman rule. Today, the best preserved features are traces of a temple to Jupiter and the usual Byzantine fort. Enthusiasts only, site open 0800-1200 and 1500-1900 in the tourist season, 0900-1700 out of season. After the isolated attractions of Gightis, continue north for Ajim and the ferry to Djerba.

Medenine to Djerba

Houmt Souk   حومة السوق

Up in the northwest of Djerba, Houmt Souk is the only real town, and is therefore referred to as the island's capital. Its 20,000 inhabitants strive to avoid being too swamped by visitors and, and a certain charm is just about maintained. The Association Sauvegarde de Djerba is ever vigilant, limiting the lurid neon signs. Nevertheless, traffic is becomgin a problem. In the gaudy souks an enthusiastic lad will dress you up as an Arab for a photograph while venerable traders and craftsmen sell textiles and silver. Some of the old fondouks where merchants would spend the night have been tastefully turned into small hotels. (The town's name means 'market quarter'.) And to return to Djerba's traditions, there is a small museum of traditional life.

Phone code: 75
Colour map 4, grid A5

Djerba

Ins and outs

As above for Djerba. The airport is a short taxi ride from Houmt Souk (around 3Dt by day, 4.5Dt at night). Most buses coming to Djerba terminate at Houmt Souk. There are direct buses from Tunis. Travelling by louage, you may need to change at Medenine.

Getting there
See Transport, page 412, for further details

The main bus-station is a good 20 mins' walk from the Borj (old fort) on the coast and hotels *Dar Faiza* and *Lotos*. The main Av Bourguiba has all the essential services (pharmacies, ATMs, *Tunisair*, internet) near the section with the tree-lined central reservation. Where this ends, you reach 2 planted squares. On the left one, in front of the municipality, is a tourist information office. Going right, the square is called the Pl Farhat Hached. You wander on into two more squares, the Pl M. Attia and Pl Hédi Chaker, then a confusing but small neighbourhood of pedestrian streets with tourist shops, cafés and restaurants. Just north of this area, the main fondouk hotels and youth hostel are all close together.

Orientation in Houmt Souk

At Houmt Souk you are well placed for exploring the Jewish centre of Hara Kebira (bus 14, also goes to Guellala). Bus 11 runs to the big hotels at Sidi Mahres and to Midoun.

Getting around

You could also rent a bike or scooter to get around. In practice, the best way to get back and forth between Houmt Souk and the beach hotels is by taxi. Infrequent bus 12 takes you back to Ajim and the ferry.

Tourist information The helpful **Syndicat d'initiative** is on Av Habib Bourguiba in a small pavillion in a very small park, on your left, just before the Post Office as you head north towards coast, T650157. Closed on Sat afternoon, Fri, Sun and public holidays. Nice staff, maps of various kinds available. English of a sort usually spoken.

Houmt Souk

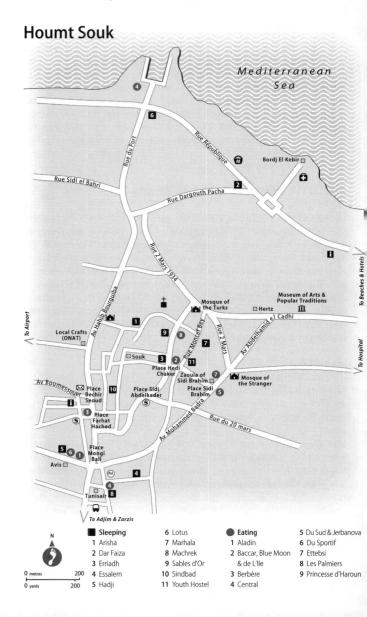

Sleeping				
1	Arisha	6	Lotus	
2	Dar Faiza	7	Marhala	
3	Erriadh	8	Machrek	
4	Essalem	9	Sables d'Or	
5	Hadji	10	Sindbad	
		11	Youth Hostel	

Eating			
1	Aladin	5	Du Sud & Jerbanova
2	Baccar, Blue Moon	6	Du Sportif
	& de L'Ile	7	Ettebsi
3	Berbère	8	Les Palmiers
4	Central	9	Princesse d'Haroun

N

0 metres 200
0 yards 200

Sights

The central souk area has small shops targeting tourists with silver, brass, leather **The souk**
goods, shoes, material and clothes. Prices are on the high side. Djerba is noted
for its alfa mats (originally made for olive oil presses) and pointy straw women's
hats, blankets and silver jewellery (until recently, much was Jewish-made). Pottery, chiefly from Guellala is unglazed and made for practical use, for storing
water, oil or foodstuffs. A street market is held around the souk every Monday
and Thursday. Large doorways indicate an old *fondouk* or merchants' hostel.
Many of these have been converted for use as hotel accommodation.

The austere 17th-century **Zaouia of Sidi Brahim** (works started in 1674) was a **Religious**
centre of religious learning. It still contains the saint's tomb, and is off limits to **buildings**
non-Muslims. Across the road is the **Mosquée des Etrangers** (the **Outsiders'**
Mosque), distinguished by the large number of small domes around the main
one. The **Mosque of the Turks**, further north, is interesting due to its splendid
pointy minaret, recalling those built by the Ottomans further round the coast in
Tripoli. Unfortunately, all these monuments are closed to non-Muslims. You
could, however, have a look in at the **catholic church**, down a side-street near the
cinema. In the 19th and first half of the 20th centuries, Djerba, like other southern
ports, had a fair-sized European population, of Greek, Maltese and Sicilian origin, who were involved in fishing (for both sponges and fish) and trade.

On the seafront by the harbour north of Houmt Souk is the **Bordj el Kebir** (the **The Fortress**
Great Tower). This largely 16th-century fort goes back to the 13th century **(Bordj el Kebir)**
(although it is likely that there was a Roman construction here), when Roger de
Lluria, King of Sicily, then extending his influence along the Ifrikiyan coast,
needed to build his forces a strong point on Djerba. Later, in the 16th century,
with Habsburg Spain and Ottoman Turkey fighting for Mediterranean
supremacy, the fort was occupied by the Spaniards. In 1560, Ottoman sea sup-
remo Dragut wiped out a Spanish fleet, and a large number of Spanish troops
were left defending the fort. When the *bordj* fell, the Turks massacred the Spaniards, building a tower with their skulls – now marked by a small monument – as
the tower was demolished in 1848. The fort is sometimes referred to as Bordj
Ghazi Mustapha, after the Turk who supervised its reconstruction.

Inside the fort it is possible to see the ruins of an earlier fort built in the 13th
century, though the site goes back further to Roman times. ■ *0800-1200 and*
1500-1900 summer, 0830-1730 winter, closed Fri, 3Dt. From the top of the fort
there is a view over the sea and harbour. There is the **market** by the harbour
held every Monday and Thursday.

The **Museum of Popular Arts and Traditions** on Avenue Abdelhamid El Cadhi **The musuem**
is set in an old *zaouia*, dedicated to Sidi Zitouni who used to come here and heal
the mentally ill. The collection is interesting and well labelled. The first room displays traditional Djerban costumes and jewellery and explains the history of the
island. Another room shows a pottery workshop, the instruments used and the
production process. The last room is particularly special, as it was once a place of
pilgrimage. This room is known as *koubbat el khyal* ('the ghost's dome').
■ *0800-1200 and 1500-1900 summer, 0930-1630 winter, closed Fri, 2Dt*.

The beaches close to Houmt Souk are not very pleasant. The nearest to be rec- **Beaches**
ommended is 6 km east along the road towards the hotels, either a short taxi or
bus ride away. Turn left along a track just before the *Hotel Ulysse*.

Djerba

Essentials

Sleeping
■ *on map, page 408*

Accommodation prices are generally higher on Djerba than in the rest of Tunisia and there is little budget accommodation. Houmt Souk is the best bet for cheaper accommodation but note that there is nothing in the rock bottom category bar a rather good youth hostel. If you have come for the beaches, then you will be taking buses and taxis out to the *zone touristique*. (See page 417). Budget accommodation, especially in the converted *fondouks*, is much in demand with groups, so try to book in advance.

AL *Dar Dhiafa*, T671166/7, F670793, dar.dhiafa@gnet.tn Although not in Houmt Souk, included here for convenience. Hidden away in nearby village of Er Riadh (ex-Hara Sghira), about 1 km from La Ghriba. 14 rooms in 5 old houses completely restyled and transformed into a very pricey *hotel de charme*. 2 tiny unheated pools, hammam, well reputed restaurant. Rooms too small for price. Fine if not too many guests, otherwise a bit cramped.

B-C *Hotel el Machrek*, Av Habib Bourguiba, very handy for the bus station, T653155/6, F653157. 40 a/c rooms, some with terrace, parking, very clean, fairly new. A reasonable choice if you can't get into one of the converted *fondouks*. Doubles vary seasonally from 35Dt to 60Dt. **B-C** *Hotel Dar Salem*, in the Sidi Mahres area, managed by same people as *Dar Faiza*, T757667/8, F757677, 22 rooms. **B-C** *Dar Faiza*, R Ulysses, T650083, F651763. Heavily converted villa housing small hotel near Borj el Kebir. 25 rooms around courtyards, small unheated pool, restaurant. Has loyal following so reserve. Bus 11 for the beaches east of Houmt Souk stop nearby.

C *Hotel Erriadh*, off Pl Hedi Chaker on R Mohammed Ferjani, just opposite El Bitan *'La Coupole'* jewellers, T650756, F650487. An old *fondouk*, 28 simple rooms with bath arranged around a central courtyard, very clean, lots of charm, important to book in season. Probably the best of the *fondouk* hotels. NB 20 rooms with a/c 4Dt extra (new split system), other rooms have fans, heating included. Lots of bright flowering bougainvillaea and tiles. **C** *Hotel Hadji*, off Av Bourguiba, T650630, F651963. Handy for bus station, early 1980s building, not much charm but practical. All 45 rooms with bath, 17 have a/c (5Dt extra), TV (5Dt extra). Street-facing rooms sunny but noisy. Locale clientele, some 4 single bed rooms. Helpful reception. **C** *Hotel Lotus*, 18 R de la Republique, close to beach, T650026, F650127. 14 rooms with bath, shaded courtyard for outside eating. Fans but a/c planned. Reserve for Jul-Aug. **C** *Hotel Sables d'Or*, R Mohammed Ferjani, T650423. Charming old house transformed into a small hotel, some of the 12 rooms rather dark. Ensuite bath, toilets shared. Not a bad choice.

C-D *Hotel Marhala*, beyond Pl Hedi Chaker on R Moncef Bey, T650146, F653317. 38 rooms off pretty patio with bougainvillaea and palm trees. Ground floor rooms ensuite basin/shower/wc, upstairs shared bathrooms and w/c. More basic than *Erriadh*, would suite student groups (some rooms with 7 beds). Bar/restaurant, menu 7Dt, big carpark at back. **D** *Hotel Arisha*, 36 R Ghazi Mustapha, T650384. Hidden away near the chapel converted into a library. Heading seawards from the post office, go right at the junction before the ONAT craft centre. Clean, simple rooms in a converted *fondouk*. **D** *Hotel Sindbad*, Pl Mongi Bali, T650047, in town centre, across the square from the post office, on your right coming down Av Bourguiba from the bus station. Old *fondouk* with simple rooms, shared, cleanish bath/toilet. Not the prime choice. **D** *Hotel Essalem*, R de Ramada, T651029. On a side-street near *Tunisair*, on your right as you come from the bus station. Recommended as cheap, clean and friendly. Reception on 1st floor.

Youth hostels 11 R Moncef Bey, T650619, near the *Hotel Marhala*. 90 beds, 38 2-bed and 4-bed rooms. 6Dt with breakfast, 9Dt500 half-board, 13Dt full board. Full from mid-Jul to end Aug, when YHA card is required. Cool, dark vaulted rooms (once used for storage?), beds (proper mattresses) on masonry platforms. Courtyard with flowering plants. Good value.

There is a small but good range of restaurants to suite all budgets. The larger hotels all have the usual à la carte restaurants, which tend to be expensive for the level of service provided.

Eating
● *on map, page 408*

Expensive *Restaurant La Princesse d'Haroun*, T650488, by the harbour. Specializes in fish, has a reputation for being the best restaurant on the island, although this is now challenged by the *Dar Dhiafa* in Er Riadh/Hara Sghira. Busy in summer with groups. Anything up to 40Dt a head. Fish couscous a speciality. *Restaurant Ettebsi*, Av Abdel Hamid El Cadhi, T651399. Close to the Pl Sidi Brahim, not far from the *Marhala* and the Youth Hostel. Pleasant, no credit cards. Folklore-type entertainment some evenings.

Mid-range *Restaurant Baccar*, Pl Hédi Chaker, T650708, specialities fish and couscous. Has a good reputation, not far from the central *Café Ben Dammech*. *Restaurant Blue Moon*, Pl Hédi Chaker, T/F650559. Tables in both the big inner courtyard and inside. Pleasant, one of the better restaurants in this category, claims it has the best fish on the island. Meal with ½ bottle of wine and two starters, around 30Dt. Their *mezze* at 15Dt a head are a good feed. Wine: bottle of red 10Dt, rosé 8Dt. *Pizzeria Dar*, 161 Abdel Hamid El Cadhi. Good value pizzas. *Restaurant Dar Faïza*, R de la République, T650083. Good, reasonably priced set menu. Perhaps the best of the hotel restaurants, has a loyal clientele. *Restaurant El Hana*, Pl Mohamed Ali, T650568, near one of the entrances to the central market. *Restaurant de l'Ile*, Pl Hédi Chaker, T650651. Go for the upstairs dining room. Alcohol. Set menu or à la carte. *Restaurant Les Palmiers*, R Mohamed el Ferjani, almost opposite the *Hotel Sables d'Or*, T621324, popular restaurant, but no alcohol, try their couscous with calamari. *Restaurant Jerbanova*, Pl Sidi Ibrahim, next to the *Restaurant du Sud*. Menu at 10Dt. Not a bad choice, alcohol.

Cheap *Restaurant Aladin*, Av Mohamed Badra. Small and cheap. *Restaurant Berbère*, Pl Farhat Hached, T650884. Small eatery with good couscous. No alcohol. *Restaurant Le Carthage*, 11 Av Mohamed Badra. Tunisian home cooking, including dishes like *kamounia* (meat in a tomato and onion stew with cumin) and an excellent couscous. *Restaurant Central*, 128 Av Habib Bourguiba. Good, cheap food. Handy for the bus station, closes late. *Restaurant du Sud*, Pl Sidi Ibrahim. A bit touristy but the food is good. *Restaurant Chez Salem*, central market near the sea and the fish auction. Buy your fish or meat at the market, then head for *Chez Salem* who will cook them for you. Get there before midday. Lunches only, local clientele. *Restaurant du Sportif*, 147 Av Habib Bourguiba, on the tree-lined section under the arcades. Tunisian food at budget prices, stays open late. Cheap eats also available in the Jewish neighbourhood around the Hara Kebira.

Cafés Houmt Souk goes to bed quite early and for a café with some ambience in the small hours, you are better of going to the new museum complex at Guellala or *Le Pacha* on the *zone touristique* road. Central Houmt Souk has some big leisurely old-style Tunisian cafés, including the *Café Ben Dammech* on Pl Mokhtar Ben Attia (vines, frenetic domino players, mint tea, football on TV) and the *Café Pingwin* on the nearby Pl Hédi Chaker. For ice-cream, try the *Café Pâtisserie Ben Yedder* on Pl Farhat Hached, just off the Av Habib Bourguiba, not far from the Syndicat d'initiative. Part of the Ben Yedder chain of pâtisserie shops. Popular with locals is the newer glacier *La Fontaine*, opposite the Turkish Mosque. Ice-cream and pizzas. **Patisseries** Best address is *Café Pâtisserie Mhirsi* near the central market. Also does sandwiches.

Cafés & patisseries

Djerba

Shopping **Handicrafts** The main ONAT craft shop is on ave Habib Bourguiba, where the workshops and training centre are open for viewing.

Entertainment **Casino** The *Pasino de Djerba*, so named after its owner, one M. Partouche, is in the Zone touristique de Midoun, T757537. Slot machines and gaming tables, restaurants and floor-shows. Open 1200-0400. A mint is made out of gullible tourists in a temple of tackiness. Surely hapless Djerba could have been better served than this? Luckily for them, locals cannot legally go gambling. (Tourists must become members for a nominal rate.) Other plus point: close to the island's best night clubs, the *Sun Club* and the imaginatively named *Holiday Beach Club*.

Sport **Aerobics** The bigger hotels all have mini-gymnasia which may run aerobics classes in season. Some hotels also do early morning aqua-gym. **Diving** Try the Merry Land Beach, *Hotel Golf Beach*, T600250. **Fishing** See box, page 413. **Golf** In the *zone touristique* near Midoun, 27 holes, T659055, F659051. See Golf, page 55, for further details. How is it that such a heavily watered facility can be justified in terms of the island's meagre water resources? Sustainable tourism this is not. **Harbour** 10 yacht berths, min-max draft 1-3 m. **Thalassotherapy** See below in listings for the *zone touristique*.

Tour operators All tour companies and travel agents can organize 2-4 day tours of the desert and into the towns and villages of southern Tunisia. *Carthage Tours*, centre of town, T650308. *Djerba Voyage*, Av Habib Bourguiba, T650071. *Evatour*, 653172, on airport road. *Malik Voyagec*, R Habib Thameur, T650235. *Sahara Tours*, Av Taleb Mehiri, T652646, F652822. *Tourafricac*, 146 Av Habib Bourguiba, T650104, F653240. *Voyages Najor Chabane*, Av Habib Bourguiba, T652633, F652632.

Transport **Local Bus**: Djerba has a good public bus service to most parts of the island. There is also a bus link with most major Tunisian towns. The bus station, through which all buses pass, is in the centre of Houmt Souk. Information on T650076. Buses 10 and 11 go hourly round the island, along the coast past the major hotels; 12 goes to Ajim and the Djorf ferry; 13 to Beni Maquel; 14 to Guellala and 16 to Sedouikech. **Car hire**: although cars can be rented they are expensive and there is a minimum 24-hr rental. However it is a good idea if you intend to go down to the south. Be careful in Houmt Souk when you park, as the police have clamps (same problem as in Tunis: the difficulty is not the fine but finding the person with the keys to come and remove the clamp!). *Avis*, Av Mohammed Badra, T650151; *Budget*, R du 20 Mars 1934, T650185; *Europacar*, Av Abdelhamid el Cadhi, T650357; *Hertz*, Av Abdelhamid el Cadhi, T/F650039, highly recommended; *Topcar*, R du 20 Mars 1934, T650536. **Cycle hire**: the island is small and flat making bicycles, which can be rented at most large hotels and in Houmt Souk, an attractive means of transport. In the tourist area to the east of Houmt Souk try *Holiday Bikes Tunisie*, close to *Hotel Médina*. At *Hotel Arischa* half day hire (0900-1300 or 1400-1900) is 6Dt, all day is 10Dt. Check the insurance when you hire: are you insured against theft? **Moped**: from *Location Cycles*, Av Abdelhamid el Cadhi, in front of *Shell* petrol station, T650303, 15-20Dt per day. **Taxis** are a good way of getting around but can be hard to find, particularly at night, on market day or away from main routes. Taxi to airport from Houmt Souk, 5Dt. Taxis from airport to Tripoli, Libya take 4-5 hrs. The route to Libya is from Djerba to El Kantara, Zarzis, Ben Gardane, Ras Ajdir and over the border, 100Dt.

Long distance Air: T650233/650408, *Tunisair*, centrally located on Av Habib Bourguiba, T650586; *Air France*, Av Abdelhamid el Cadhi, T650461. The airport is 8 km from Houmt Souk, served by a bus from town, but be sure to check the times beforehand. Flight information on T650233. **Bus**: the bus station is in the centre of Houmt Souk. Information on T650399/650475/652239. Departures to: Sfax; Gabès; Medenine;

Fishing in Djerba

Djerba's coastline is composed of rocky shallows, sandy ledges and clay banks. It is occasionally cut by oueds which meander through vast fields of eelgrass. There are approximately 86 fish species living off the shores of Djerba. Generally speaking, bass and mackerel can be found off the northern coast (Borj Jellij, Houmt Souk, Ras Rmel and Ras Tourgueness), made up of limestone tables and sandbanks constantly beaten by waves and by the eastern Barrani wind. There are mullet, carangidae and flat fish off the south coast (Ajim, Guellala, El Kantara and Aghir), deep and sandy, where the Ghibli wind blows. The east and west coasts are both rocky and dotted with lagoons. Off the east coast are perch, bass and dace. Off the western coast are weevers and dogfish. Fishing methods widespread in the island of Djerba are hook fishing, la palangrotte (hook fishing from the shore), rod fishing, troll fishing (nocturnal and winter only), long line fishing, fishing à la lenza in shallow waters, net fishing and fishing à la sautade.

Tataouine (2½ hrs); Zarzis and Tunis. **Louages**: by the bus station. **Ferries**: the transbordeur aka le bac between Ajim to Djorf run by CTN.

Banks Plenty of banks in the centre of Houmt Souk, on Av Bourguiba and around. **Directory**
STB, Pl Farhat Hached, T650140. BNT, Pl Ben Daamech, T650025. BT, R du 20 Mars, T650004. There are also a number of bureaux de change which accept credit cards and have more flexible opening hours. There are 3 ATMs within 20 m of the Syndicat d'initiative, at Banque de Tunisie, Banque du Sud and UIB (the latter 2 are on the pedestrian square opposite the Syndicat.

Communications Internet: for the moment, the only cybernet seems to be in the whitewashed 1920s building (Einkauf Zentrum) on the main Av Bourguiba on same side as Syndicat d'initiative. Building houses the Restaurant Fondouk and a pharmacy. Cybernet (signs on façade) is on 1st floor. If out in a zone touristique hotel, there may be new publinets opening up in the shopping centres sprouting along the main road. **Post Office**: Av Habib Bourguiba, after the main square. **Telephone**: international exchange, on the side of the Post Office. **Hammams** Try the 1 next to the zaouia on Pl Sidi Ibrahim in Houmt Souk (men mornings, women afternoons). **Medical services** Hospital: main hospital on Av Habib Bourguiba, T650018. Private hospital El Yasmin on Av Mohammed Badra, T652032. Try also the Clinique Dar Echifa, T653326, F652215. **Places of worship** Catholic: 2 R de l'Eglise, Houmt Souk, T650215, service Sun and holy days at 1000.

Exploring Djerba

Southwest Djerba

If you opt to head north from Medenine or east from Mareth, you will be crossing over to the island from **Djorf,** departure point for ferries to **Ajim.** (See Routes to Djerba, page 406, for further details.)

Ajim village itself is of minimal interest, but there are a few cafés and restau- **Ajim**
rants with large terraces and rows of street stalls. Arriving from Houmt Souk or Borj Jellij, in Avenue Habib Bourguiba, on the left is the medium priced Restaurant Ouled-M'barak serving fish. Make sure you know what you are paying when you make your order. Towards the port are more cheap eateries.

Djerba

The Jews of Tunisia: ancient community, modern diaspora

The Jews were the first non-Hamitic people to settle in the Maghreb, their presence going back 26 centuries to the time of King Solomon. After the Arab conquest in the eighth century, the Jews remained important in the region: across the Maghreb there were Jewish communities, and Hara Sghira was founded in 586 BC on Djerba after the destruction of the first temple in Jerusalem (see page 416). In the 16th century, Testour became a leading centre of the megorashim, the Jews expelled from Andalusìa.

In the 17th and 18th centuries, with Tunisia a regency of the Ottoman Empire, the Jews came to play an important role in the developing trade with Europe. In the 18th century, numerous Jews of Iberian origin, established in Livorno, took up residence in Tunis, forming the core of the Grana community, as opposed to the Twansa or Tunis Jewish community. As of 1741, each community had its own synagogues and institutions. An 1846 agreement with Tuscany allowed the Grana Jews to settle in Tunisia while retaining their original nationality.

As elsewhere in the Mediterranean, the Jews were quick to understand the importance of modern education.. The coming of the French Protectorate in 1881 opened new possibilities for an increasingly educated, energetic group. As they prospered they left their insalubrious quarters in the médina for new areas like Lafayette – where the community's wealth

is reflected in the great Art Déco synagogue on Av de la Liberté. Unlike Algeria's Jews, who received French nationality en masse, Tunisia's Jews remained subjects of the bey in their great majority – which by no means stopped them from joining the Communist Party and the Nationalist Movement. By 1950, the community was at its peak with 120,000 members, 25,000 of whom had foreign nationality.

After independence in 1956, Tunisia's Jews voted to elect the Constituent Assembly on equal footing with their Muslim fellow citizens. Again in contrast with Algeria, most felt secure enough to remain in their newly independent country, even if the new government aimed to remove any trace of separatism. Hence, in 1957, the Rabbinical Courts were dissolved, followed by the Community Council in 1958. More serious, however, was the transformation of the main Jewish cemetery into a public park, today's Jardin Habib Thameur.

A spiritual people, deeply attached to their traditions, the Tunisian Jews were almost too well prepared to receive the ideology of the 'Promised Land'. Some 50,000 opted for Israel, in the years after independence, a further 35,000 for France. Today, the community numbers a few thousand, Nevertheless, the sacred books are still carried in procession during the annual pilgrimage to the El Ghriba Synagogue on Djerba, the oldest synagogue in the world.

Guellala   Guellala, called Haribus in classical times, is the first point of interest in south-western Djerba. Once, it was renowned for its **pottery**, both large white utilitarian clay pots and more delicate shiny terracotta ware. The latter, ressembling cheap Roman tableware, has practically disappeared and much of the pottery now on sale is standard Nabeul issue. Outside the sleepy village, a number of old-style potters continue to work from semi-underground workshops. The huge clay amphorae, once used for storing barley and oil, have found a new market among French interior decorators and landscapers. The clay for the pottery comes from galleries cut into the ground rising above the village, on the road to Sedouikech. After a brief soaking in seawater the clay goes white. Another village once well known for its pottery is **Sedouikech**, 3 km east of Guellala on the road to Midoun. Today all that remains of this craft are long underground stores. Other crafts still plied include alfa-grass plaiting for baskets and mats for the olive press.

The main attraction at Guellala is now the **Musée de Guella**, set outside the town on the hill above the road to Sedouikech. The turn-off is well signposted, the whitewashed buildings and their central minaret are clearly visible. Without a vehicle, it is about 2½ km up to the top from Guella village, a fair trek in summer. The museum complex also has a small restaurant and popular café which stays open into the small hours in summer. Old style Djerbans would never have built a village on such an obvious (and waterless) site. Nevertheless, traditional Djerbans, in dummy form, are what it's all about. You will see lots of interiors with waxwork models showing locals preparing to get married, including the *barboura*, a rite during which the future husband would walk around a sacred olive tree to the squeal of the bagpipes (*mizoued*) to gain protection and a women's hair removal session. Look out too for the bridal gear – particularly spectacular with all its gold and sequins is the costume from Bizerte, the traditional healer with a chameleon in his claws, and Yacoub Bchiri, the lutist, marked as Jewish by the black ribbon in his baggy pantaloons or *siroual*. More interesting is the working underground olive press, driven by a blinkered, soft-drink consuming camel. (Local Hamadi Hmid may be on hand to explain the process.) There is also a threshing floor where ancient technology (the 'Berber Mercedes'), also camel-powered, will be enthusiastically demonstrated. The last section of waxworks is devoted to Typical Tunisia. Here the glassed-in waxwork dummies figure a lonely desert shepherd playing his flute, a Zlass tribal horseman, a nocturnal Ramadan drummer waking the faithful for their pre-dawn meal, and a courting couple in a Sidi Bou Saïd street. In fact, the fine views from the café terrace at the museum have given it the nickname 'the Sidi Bou Saïd of Djerba'. Opened in November 2000, it has quickly achieved popularity, especially among locals and returning expatriates looking for a pleasant place for a sociable night out with friends. ■ *Adults 3Dt, children 1.5Dt, 1Dt extra to go up the minaret.*

Eating If the food in the museum complex doesn't appeal, try the *Restaurant El Kobry*, speciality grilled fish, on your left as you go up the hill in the Sedouikech direction. (To get there, turn left onto the main road as you come down from the museum.) The views are pretty good here, too. Next to *El Kobry* is a large pottery sales area with lots of terracotta jars, mostly far too large to take on a plane. The other 'formal' eating option is *Restaurant La Goulla*, back in Guellala. No alcohol, fish menu 9Dt, à la carte eating at around 15Dt.

The west coast

The west coast of Djerba is still untouched by tourism – and looks set to remain this way as it is rocky and there are few beaches. It is, however, ideal for walks, or a trip along the coast. To get there, take the road to the airport and continue straight on towards **Borj Jellij**, until the road goes right. Here you should take the track to the left. You can follow it south, all the way to Ajim. A few kilometres along the track, on the right, there are a few beautiful houses and a mosque by the sea. Allow half a day to Borj Jellij and all day to Ajim. At Borj Jellij there is a small port with a few simple fishermen's houses and a small lighthouse. The fishermen spend 3-15 days here in the huts and then return to their village and their family elsewhere on the island. There is no organized transport here, no facilities and certainly nowhere to buy food. If you have made an arrangement with a taxi, make sure the driver knows where and when to pick you up.

On your way out of Houmt Souk heading for the coast, you might stop off in **Melita**, a village near the airport. There is a white block-shaped mosque with a very low minaret. Most of the older houses in the village have vaulted roofs. There are two cafés here and the usual takeaway.

South of Houmt Souk

A few kilometres south of Houmt Souk, there are some final examples of Djerban religious architecture. El May has a fine mosque, while at Er Riadh, formerly Hara Esseghira, is a major Jewish shrine. Hara Kebira, the other main Jewish village, is within walking distance from Houmt Souk.

El Ghriba Synagogue

Er Riadh was originally known as **Hara Sghira** or 'Little Neighbourhood'. It was here that most Jews moved after the introduction of Islam to the area. They were treated with tolerance and became famous for their jewellery. In the village a signposted road on the left leads to the **Synagogue of El Ghriba**. The original synagogue is said to have been built at the time of the first Jewish settlement in 586 BC, shortly after the destruction of King Solomon's temple in Jerusalem. The story goes that the place for the first synagogue was marked by a sacred stone falling from heaven and by the arrival of a strange woman to supervise the construction. Should the Jews ever abandon Djerba, then the key to the Synagogue will be hurled back up to Heaven.

Ghriba means 'miracle' and there is an annual procession on the 33rd day after the Passover – called *Lag be Omer* to commemorate the miracles. The congregation, including many pilgrims, bear the holy books through the streets on a covered platform. The Synagogue has become a spiritual centre for the study of the Torah and makes an interesting stop in an Islamic country. Inside the synagogue heads will have to be covered (head covers provided).

The Ghriba synagogue is a smart building, freshly whitewashed each year. The present building was constructed in the 1920s, and is neither really beautiful nor wholly kitsch. The huge studded wooden doors open into the large, rectangular main room. The marble-paved floor is covered with rush matting. The walls are faced with blue tiles, the columns have had a good dose of pale blue gloss paint, and there is coloured glass in the windows filtering the sun onto dark, heavy wooden furniture. Aged men recite from the holy books. Some of the older men wear baggy trousers which fasten at a black band below the knee. The black signifies mourning for the destruction of Solomon's temple. The second room holds what is said to be one of the oldest Torahs in the world. ■ *0700-1800 except Sat. A small contribution (say 1Dt) is appreciated.*

The **Jewish population** on Djerba today is down to a couple of thousand, although numbers are said to be on the increase. They practise their religion unhindered. Attitudes are tolerant. Although there is latent anti-Jewish prejudice in some everyday sayings, this never spills over into violence. Many older Tunisians have fond memories of departed Jewish neighbours. The Tunisian Muslim viewpoint includes a respect for local Jews (accepted as part of a way of life now almost vanished) and a strong opposition to continued Zionist occupation and colonization of Palestine.

After visiting El Ghriba, you might want to continue south to **El May**, home to the Mosque of Um Etturkia, a vernacular, fort-like building with thick walls and a low, rounded minaret. On Friday afternoon and Saturday morning, a small local **market** takes place here. *Restaurant Aladin*, Rue Salah ben Youssef in front of the market place, is small and cheap.

Heading northeast from El May towards the Plage Sidi Mahres, you pass through **Cedriane**, also spelt **Cedghyène** or even **Sedghiene**. Going straight through the village, you reach the main Houmt Souk to Midoun road after about 2½ km. Note that south of Cedriane is a ruined 18th-century palace, the

Djerba

Looking for lotus fruit

George Woodberry goes looking for lotus fruit on Djerba:

"Yes, there was a jujubier in the neighbourhood. The old man, who had an alert, breezy way about him ... seemed to wonder that I had come to see it, but said nothing; he was for the time more intent on rites of hospitality, and I went about examining the curiosities. His wife and a little girl came in with a great pitcher and tall glasses and set them down before us, and the old man poured out generous draughts of bright-brown cider. I smiled to think into what a vintage my dreamed-of juice of the enchanted stem had resolved itself – a glass of russet cider ... It was excellent cider ... On inquiry I found it was not even of the fruit of Djerba, but brewed from a preparation made at Paris, somewhat as root beer is with us. Meanwhile, we had tales of the sea and old adventures on 'the climbing wave', pleasant talk, till I brought the conversation round to the jujubier. It bore a hard, brown fruit, I learned, sweetish, and a drink was made from it, like lemonade; and, yes, it had a sleepy effect. No, it was not bottled. So, talking incidentally of many things, my host showed me the rest of the house, the little bedroom with his photograph of other days, and with a last health we went out into the garden, where the little girl was waiting with a bunch of spring flowers, and we walked off to see the jujubier.

It was at the end wall of a small, shut-up Arab house near by, against which it was trained. It was shoulder-high, and grew in stout, hardy stocks. The blithe old man told me it must be more than two hundred years old. I said it was very small for its age; but he added that its growth was very slow, almost imperceptible. It was just showing signs of leaving out; a naked, rough, shrub-like tree, with neither leaf, nor flower, nor fruit; but it was alive, and I still have hopes that in the case of a tree so long-lived I shall some time find it in its season, and eat of it, and perhaps drink of its sleepy soul. I went back to the garden and said goodbye to my kind and gentle host, and I was really almost as glad to have had this tranquil hospitality and Crusoe memory as if I had met with better luck in my search. I walked back over the rough fields content; and as we drove slowly through the sand in the wide prospect of scattered palm and olive, with the little white domes, quiet in the universal sun, I thought the lotus land was very good as it was."

From George Woodberry's North Africa and the Desert, scenes and moods (London, 1914).

Qasr Hamida Ben Ayed. East off the road to Midoun are palm groves where the huge *menzels* (now abandoned and in disrepair) can be seen.

Plage Sidi Mahres and Plage de la Séguia: the tourist coast

Hotel development has been concentrated on the island's two best stretches of beach, the Plage Sidi Mahres, running from Ras Rmel to Taguermess, and the Plage de la Séguia, running from Taguermess to Borj Kastil. The beaches are kept clean – but can get very crowded in summer. Surfboards can be rented and various other watersports are organized in all the major hotels. If you want some peace, however, head for the west coast.

Outside summer, there is a longish beach walk, taking around three hours, from Aghir to Borj Kastil, a fort falling slowly into ruins on the southeast point of the island. There are interesting views, especially south across the mainland and the causeway. A very primitive overnight stop, if necessary, is available at the fisherman's cottage at the end of the walk.

Many of the large beach hotels are run by foreign tour operators, including the large German TUI group. The *Club Med*, with 2 very high standard holiday villages, is another

Sleeping
Phone code: 75

Djerba

important presence. *Club Robinson* is a sort of *Club Med* run by TUI. The best rated hotels are on the beach and many now have thalassotherapy centres in addition to the usual sports activities. There is now almost a complete '2nd line' of hotels off the beach in the Sidi Mahres part of the *zone touristique*. The present listings give a range of the better establishments, all in the upper price brackets. Note that some of the most expensive foreign-run establishments may be **restricted** to clients who have bought their package holiday abroad. In terms of restaurants, the à la carte places in the big hotels are often a weak point, the catering being organized around providing copious breakfasts and solid buffet-format evening meals for a Teutonic clientele.

AL *Hotel Athénée Palace*, T600600, F601601. A truly luxurious place, closest to Houmt Souk on the Plage de Sidi Mahres. **A** *Hotel Hasdrubal*, T657650, F657730, asdrubal.djerba@gnet.tn Another well reputed luxurious establishment, one of the oldest, on Plage de Sidi Mahres, towards Ras Taguermes end. Good-sized rooms with balcony, thalassotherapy centre, nice reception. **A** *Hotel Movenpick Ulysse Palace*, T758777, F757850, hotel.djerba@movenpick.com 270 rooms all a/c, on beach, pool, restaurant, thalassotherapy, sports activities, business centre with conference rooms. Incentive groups. 10 km from Houmt Souk. **A** *Hotel Sofitel Palm Beach*, T757777, F758888, palmbeach.palace@gnet.tn The usual splendid reception area. Good-sized, pleasant rooms, restaurants – snack bar next to pool good. **A** *Hotel Yadis* T747235, F747223, hotel.yadis@planet.tn Next to the beach, accommodation in local style buildings, thalassotherapy, good-sized pool, tennis courts. Recommended.

A-B *Abou Nawas Djerba*, T657022, F657700. On the beach, central section of Sidi Mahres beach, a reliable address, like all the hotels of this company. Impressive central reception area, small, heated swimming pool, efficient reception. Good deals possible out of season. **A-B** *Hotel Ithaque*, T658168, F658169. The luxuriously revamped Dar Midoun. Rooms still spacious. Right on the beach, nice grounds, usual facilities. **B** *Aquarius Club*, T657790, 600 beds beach hotel at Taguermes 28 km from Houmt Souk. **B** *Hotel Djerba Orient*, T657440, opposite *Hotel Ulysse*, 56 beds, 10 km from Houmt Souk, not on beach. **B** *Hotel Djerba Plaza*, T658230, F658229. A large hotel, close to golf course at Ras Taguermes end of Sidi Mahres.**B**Palm Azur T750700, F750710, palmazurdjerbatryp.hotel@planet.tn Over 300 rooms, some overlooking large pool. Bars, nightclub, shops, etc.

B-C *Djerba Haroun* T758562, F758560. Though located 200 m from the beach, this hotel is popular with groups. Rooms with a/c, TV, mini-bar. Some mini apartments. **B-C** *Les Sirènes* T757266, F757267, hotel.sirenes@gnet.tn 120 rms, a/c, large pool and some sports activities. **C** *Dar Ali*, T658671, F758045, 20 room family-run establishment near the Sidi Mahres beach, best known for its restaurant *El Besskri*. **C** *Hotel El Djazira*, T657300, F657015. Plage de Sidi Mahres, on the beach after the *Hotel Ulysse*. One of the oldest hotels in the *zone touristique*.

Holiday **B** *Club Méditerranée Djerba La Douce*, T657129, F657161. On the Plage de la Séguia.
villages Very comfortable *Club Med* holiday village. Never a dull moment. Nicely appointed by tiny rooms, but then that doesn't matter as you'll be involved in sports and entertainment the whole time. **B** *Club Méditerranée La Nomade*, T746842, F745939. Architecturally tasteful holiday village, close to beach. All usual facilities. **B** *Eldorador Aladin* T750180, F750184, large holiday village in extensive grounds, right next to beach. Pool, children's club and tennis among the offerings. Reasonably priced. **B** *Palma Djerba* T750830, F750833. Has a strong reputation for its organized activities (mini-club for kids, tennis, mini-golf). Accommodation in small chalets, some with sea view. Useful shopping area. **B-C** *Sidi Slim* T750450/1, F750449. Simple maisonette-type accommodation. Not close to beach but lots of activities.

Three suggestions if you don't want to go into Houmt Souk but want a change from your hotel buffet. **Mid-range to expensive** *Le Phare*, pricey Tunisian cooking in agreeable setting, T745382. *Le Rendez-Vous*, T659119, outside terrace, on the main Midoun round-about, close to *Le Pacha* café on main beach hotel road. Also try *Da Mario*, T757822, Italian restaurant on the beach near the *Hotel Palm Beach*. Recommended.

Eating
Phone code: 75

Evening entertainment is in short supply on Djerba. The night clubs are all in the *zone touristique* and the best is said to be the *Royal Golden* (free entry for tourists, 4Dt a beer or soft drink). Also said to be good are the *Sun Club* and the *Holiday Beach*. Only way there from Houmt Souk, or indeed all but the closest hotels, is by taxi. Another option is 10-pin bowling. Try the one at the *Hotel Dar Djerba*.

Nightclubs & bowling

In the late 1990s, Djerba began to try to build itself a reputation for sea-water cures. All the new hotels had their sea-water spas, older hotels being refurbished added in thalassotherapy centres. Try sea-water treatments at any of the following hotels: *Athénée*, T757600; *Club Med Marina Beach*, T750430; *Dar Djerba*, T745181; *Hasdrubal*, T657650; *Ulysse*, T758777; and the *Yadis*, T747235.

Thalasso-therapy

Midoun

Djerba's second largest town, Midoun, is 12 km from Houmt Souk. (The term 'town' is being a little generous perhaps for a sort of road-junction village.) A large black community, descendants of slaves brought from sub-Saharan Africa, still exists here. Midoun has a weekly **market** each Thursday afternoon and Friday. To see an **olive press** take the road towards Houmt Souk and turn right at the crossroads, R Salah Ben Youssef. The press is about 400 m on the left by the well and hidden by an olive tree. A mule or camel was used to turn the stone roller to crush the olives which were then transferred to a sieve where a large palm tree trunk squeezed out the oil into a jar underneath. All around are chambers once used for stocking olives. This particular piece of ancient technology is said to be more than 300 years old.

The only hotel is the **E** *Hotel El Jawhara*, completely refurbished, T600467. Midoun is close to the beach hotels, however.

Sleeping
Phone code: 75

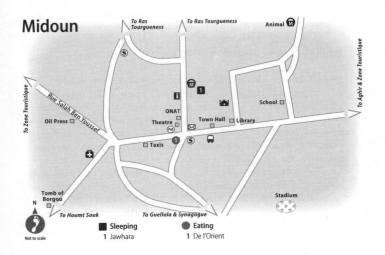

Midoun

To Ras Tourgueness
To Ras Tourgueness
Animal
To Aghir & Zone Touristique
To Zone Touristique
Rue Salah Ben Youssef
Oil Press
ONAT
Theatre
Town Hall
Library
School
Taxis
To Zone Touristique
Tomb of Borgou
N
To Houmt Souk
To Guellala & Synagogue
Stadium
Not to scale

■ **Sleeping**
1 Jawhara

● **Eating**
1 De l'Orient

Djerba

Eating **Expensive** *Restaurant Le Khalife*, Rte du Phare, Midoun. Tunisian specialities. **Mid-range** *Restaurant El Guestile*, T657724, 21 R Marsa Ettefah, near the Pl du Marché. Typically Tunisian, eat on the terrace, on the verandah or the upper floor in one of the small dining rooms. Fish specialities. Menzel-type building. **Cheap** *Restaurant de l'Orient*, on central roundabout. Tunisian food. There is also the cheap *Restaurant Constantine*, Av Badra, less smart, food good.

Directory **Banks** *STB*, T657723, *Bank El Amen* (ex-CFCT), T657493, both in town centre.

Around Midoun

From Midoun, there are some pleasant excursions to be done, either by bike or on foot, into the countryside of central Djerba. Heading south or west of Midoun, you are in a landscape of olive and palm groves dotted with *menzels*, the fortified farmsteads typical of the island. The tracks, perfect for walking or cycling, run between high earth banks planted with agaves and prickly pears.

One option is to explore the countryside west of Midoun, heading for **Mahboubine** and **Khasroun**. The aim is to keep off the roads as far as possible, following the sandy tracks. Mahboubine lies 3 km west of Midoun. From there, a track will take you north towards Khasroun. Take the blacktop road east from Khasroun and, after 1 km, turn right. After a further kilometre, a piste leads to the left to take you back to Midoun.

If walking, you could always break at **Mahboubine**, which is half an hour by bus from Houmt Souk. The village has an interesting mosque, a pictur-esque and peaceful village square, and could provide an opportunity to become acquainted with the real people of Djerba. Said a taxi-driver, 'At Mahboubine there is nothing' – or at least nothing more enjoyable than this visit. Certainly don't expect to find a hotel or a restaurant. There is only the café in the main square, alongside the mosque and the bus stop.

Another option is to explore the area south of Midoun, heading for the village of **Arkou**. Leaving Midoun on the road for El Hdada, turn right down a piste after 500 m. A piste runs south for 2 km. As you approach Arkou, there is a small gro-cer's on your left. At the crossroads, go right. After 5 km you cross the main Midoun-Aghir road. You are on the track for Mahboubine. After about 2½ km, head right down another track crossing an area of farmsteads. Eventually, you reach the main Mahboubine to Midoun road. Head right for Midoun. This is a particularly good route if you want to have a look at the *menzel* farm buildings.

Heading for the causeway: Meninx

Leaving Djerba (or arriving) from the southeast you will drive over the 7 km of causeway originally built by the Romans. At the Djerba end of the causeway is **El Kantara** ('the bridge'). If you are coming from El Aghir and the Plage de la Séguia, then you will see the remains of ancient Meninx on the left (eastern) side of the road. The settlement, first established by the Carthaginians, was re-founded in Roman times, and was no doubt an important trading post, especially given its proximity to the great city of Leptis Magna, near modern Tripoli in Libya.

For drivers, there are *Agil* petrol stations at both ends of the causeway. Go carefully and slow down for the Garde nationale checkpoints at both ends of the causeway. From the mainland end, it is 21km to **Zarzis**. At **Chamakh**, 14 km northwest of Zarzis, there is a turn off left for the *zone touristique* and an *Esso* petrol station.

Background

10

Background

History

Greeks, Phoenicians and Carthaginians

Like other parts of the Mediterranean, the North African coastal regions became an area for competition between the Greeks and the Phoenicians. The power of both peoples was based on their maritime technology. In order to trade in the commodities of Africa, they established settlements on the coast of present day Libya, entering into relations with the nomadic communities of the desert, notably the Garamantes around the Fezzan. The **Garamantes** appear to have specialized in warfare based on charioteering and they began to raid the new coastal settlements. At the same time, they also controlled trans-Saharan commerce, one of the major reasons why the Phoenicians, at least, were so interested in North Africa.

The **Greeks** had begun to colonize the Egyptian and eastern Libyan coastline as part of their attempt to control Egyptian maritime trade. Cyrene, the first of five Greek colonies in Cyrenaica, Libya, was founded about 625 BC and, a little earlier, three **Phoenician** colonies were created in western Libya, on the coast of what is today Tripolitania, in order to exploit new commercial opportunities – the Phoenicians were first-and-foremost traders. Eventually more important, however, was the major Phoenician settlement at **Carthage**, on the coast of northern Tunisia, close to the modern capital of Tunis, founded in the late ninth century BC, in order to control access to Sicily and the western Mediterranean basin.

Greeks and Phoenicians competed for control of the coastal areas in Libya and eventually created an uneasy division of the region between themselves. The Greeks took over Egypt after the creation of the **Ptolemaic Kingdom** on the death of **Alexander the Great** in 323 BC and incorporated Cyrenaica into the new kingdom. The Phoenicians, harried in their original Lebanese home of Tyre by the Assyrians and Persians, created a commercial empire based on Carthage, with outlying colonies to the west, right round to the Atlantic coast near Larache in present day Morocco. Traditionally, Carthage was founded in 814 BC when princess Dido led part of Tyre's population to settle in a safe place on the North African coast, founding Qart Hadasht, the 'new city', which was to become the leading maritime power in the western Mediterranean.

The rise of Carthage

In the seventh century BC, Carthage had trading posts in the Balearic Islands, Sardinia and the western end of Sicily. In the sixth century BC, they achieved footholds in Corsica, with Etruscan aid. In 481, they organized a great expedition to extend their influence in Sicily – with disastrous results. At the Battle of Himera, the Carthaginian forces were crushed by the rulers of Agrigentum and Syracuse. It was a huge disaster for the ruling Magonid family. (Carthaginian compensation payments probably funded a Hellenic renaissance in Sicily.) Henceforth, Carthage restricted her efforts to maintaining her valuable network of trading posts. From the fifth to the third centuries BC trade flourished, with Punic merchants providing the link between Africa and the Mediterranean. They traded in gold, ivory (highly prized for statues of the gods), and slaves from Africa, silver from Spain, copper from Sardinia and olive oil from Sicily, exchanging them against manufactured products from the eastern Mediterranean: Greek pottery and textiles. Explorers were sent to prospect distant coasts: Himilcon reached Finistère, while Hannon sailed along the western coast of Africa, possibly as far as the Gulf of Guinea. Commerce with remote peoples was based on barter – the Carthaginians first struck coins in the late fourth century.

The late fourth century was a time of strife in Sicily as the Syracusan state fell apart. In 310-308, Syracuse's ruler Agathocles took an army into the Carthaginian heartlands,

Background

The Tophet, centre of Carthaginian child sacrifice

From the mid-1800s, numerous ancient stelae ('stone markers') were discovered at Carthage around the Punic harbours and near Byrsa Hill, many incorporated into Roman or Byzantine structures. The discovery of the sacred precinct, known today as the Tophet, in 1921, was an important archaeological event. Initial excavations were supported by one Count Byron Kuhn de Prorok, a Maecenas figure who sponsored various archaeological projects in Carthage in the 1920s.

All those who excavated the site have supported the view that the Phoenicians practised child sacrifice. A Greek writer, the 3rd century BC Alexandrian Clitarchus, tells us how the Carthaginians would sacrifice a child to Cronus every time they needed a big favour. Other ancient sources say or imply that child sacrifice was a feature of Carthaginian religious life. Centuries later, the sources appeared to have been vindicated with the discovery of a sacred precinct in Carthage. Dedicated to Tanit Pene Baal and her consort Baal Hammon, the area contained numerous stelae and burial urns, filled with the cremated bones

of infants, lambs and kids, along with amulets, beads and jewellery.

Biblical evidence also attests to child sacrifice among the Canaanites, as the Bible calls the Phoenicians. Both children and animals were votive offerings, made because the sacrificer's wish had been fulfilled ('Because the gods heard my voice and blessed me', Carthaginian inscription formula). It may be that the first born was sacrificed – see the near sacrifice of Isaac by Abraham. Another possibility is that Carthaginian child sacrifice functioned as a ritual method for disposing of unwanted children. Digs in the 1970s suggest that in the later Carthaginian city, the number of cremated infants increased, and animal sacrifices decreased. The practice seems to have survived into Roman times, if Christian author Tertullian, writing around AD 200, is to be believed. In any event, the similarity of the literary sources suggests that child sacrifice was a very real part of Carthaginian religious practice. Today the Tophet, hidden away in the suburb of Salammbô, remains a place of morbid fascination.

landing on the Cap Bon and causing considerable damage. (The round town of Kerkouane may well have been abandoned after being sacked by his army.) When Carthage attempted to make the most of the situation, extending her hold by setting up a garrison at Messina in 270, she found herself faced with a new enemy, Rome.

Roman Africa

The Roman conquest Conflict between Carthage and the expanding Roman state was inevtable. Both had interests in Sicily which, for Rome, was of vital strategic importance. Three conflicts between the two powers ensued: the **Punic Wars**. Although Carthage was expelled from Sicily in 201 BC, Rome still feared Carthaginian power and the city was eventually razed to the ground in 146 BC, after three years of warfare. The fertile plains around the city were then converted into a Roman province. A hundred years after the fall of Punic Carthage, **Julius Caesar** defeated the last of his political adversaries at Thapsus (modern Ras Dimas), an event which signified the end of the Roman republic as well as the end of the independent Numidian states. The Kingdom of Juba I was annexed and renamed as the province of Africa Nova. Subsequently, **Augustus** was to rebuild Carthage as a Roman colony. The city became headquarters of the proconsul and capital of Africa Proconsularis.

Roman administrators in the new North African province faced a problem of border security, with nomad tribes and local dynasties constantly threatening stability. The problem was solved by creating the *limes*, a border region along the desert edge which was settled with former legionaries as a militarized farming population. Thus, although the border region was permeable to trade, resistance to tribal incursion could be rapidly mobilized from the resident population, while regular forces were brought to the scene. As Roman power and influence grew, the *limes* spread westwards from Egypt as far as the Moroccan Atlantic coast. In southern Tunisia, the frontier was reinforced by a ditch – the *fossa regia*.

The Roman peace

Under Roman rule, Carthage quickly became one of the most important cities of the empire. In the first century AD, the twin African provinces were a major source of wheat for Rome. From the reign of Nero, two-thirds of Rome's total grain supply came from Africa, with the remaining third coming from Egypt. Other farming activities developed, notably the cultivation of olives and vines, thanks to the establishment of irrigation programmes. Indigenous villages and Roman settlements (*coloniae*) became prosperous towns. The most fortunate became fully fledged *municipiae*, managed by Roman magistrates and embellished with fine temples, baths and market squares.

Towards the end of the second century AD, a number of men of African origin reached important posts in the empire: 15% of the knights and senators were from Africa, and the province produced several emperors too, notably **Clodius Albinus** (AD 196-197) and **Septimius Severus** (AD 193-211). The African provinces also produced intellectuals, including **Fronto**, tutor to the Emperor Marcus Aurelius, and the poet **Apuleius**, author of *The Golden Ass*.

By the beginning of the Christian era, North Africa had been organized into five Roman provinces: Africa Vetus and Africa Nova, Numidia, Mauritania Caesariana and Mauritania Tingitania. The sedentary Berber populations were largely Romanized in the coastal and agricultural regions and North Africa, in cultural terms, was now part of the Mediterranean world, its gods and goddesses assimilated to imported Roman deities: Baal Hammon had become Saturn, Punic Tanit was Caelestis, and fertility god Shadrapa was the dionysiac Liber Pater.

In addition to the commercial and cultural interpenetration of North Africa and Rome, this cultural interaction was intensified by two other factors. First, the region had long been in contact with **Greek culture** and, indeed, through the Phoenicians, with **Levantine culture**. Secondly, as a result of the destruction of the Kingdom of Judea in AD 70, large numbers of Jews migrated into North Africa and **Judaism** intermixed with **Berber culture** to a significant extent, as the surviving contemporary Jewish traditions in Tunisia show.

Early Christianity

The eastern part of North Africa, and in particular the provinces of Africa Vetus and Africa Nova (Byzacium in the late Roman period), was the site of major developments in the early history of the Christian church. In the early days, the church was much persecuted by the Roman emperors, who had a tendency to blame the Christians for the various problems facing their vast empire. But Christianity spread across the empire. There were invaders threatening on all sides, and the gods of the Roman pantheon seemed to have abandoned the people.

By the mid-third century AD, Carthage had become the seat of an important bishopric. The forceful **Cyprian**, one of the great figures of the early church, became bishop there in AD 249. Cyprian led the African church at a time when Trajan had increased the level of persecution. He was eventually to die a martyr in AD 258. The church, however, continued to attract numerous new adepts and to divide into warring factions supporting different theological positions.

Under **Diocletian** in the early fourth century, the empire was split up to be ruled by four leaders, a tetrarchy. Africa Proconsularis was divided into two, the southern and southeastern areas being renamed Byzacenium. The province became the

Background

theatre of the **Donatist** heresy – far too complicated to go into here. However, the emperor **Constantine** came to believe that the only hope for the survival of the empire was for Christianity to become the official religion – and he became the first emperor to embrace it. In AD 313, his **Edict of Milan** proclaimed religious tolerance throughout the empire. He also relocated the capital from Rome to Constantinople.

By the late fourth century, the problems created by the Donatist heresy had largely disappeared. One of the great figures of the early church, **St Augustine** rose to prominence in Africa. Son of a pagan father and a Christian mother, he misspent his youth at Carthage, where he studied and taught, before leaving for Milan. In his *Confessions*, he wrote of his life as a young man in the cosmopolitan capital of Africa, describing it as 'a hotbed of sinful desires.' He had a mistress and a thoroughly hedonistic time – but once converted to Christianity he criticized the licentiousness of Carthage's student population. The town was obviously a highly entertaining place, both a fun city and a centre of scholarship and high learning.

The Vandals and the Byzantine reconquest

Augustine died in AD 429. In hindsight, the early fifth century was to prove the high point of the Christian presence in Africa. The Roman Empire was crumbling under external threats, and North Africa was invaded by a Teutonic tribe based in Spain: the **Vandals**, who by AD 429 had conquered as far as eastern Cyrenaica. The Vandal ruler Gaiseric's aim was clear: a rich homeland for his people and independence from the Roman Empire. The Vandals' capture of Africa deprived Rome of corn supplies – and created a dangerous precedent: the Vandal Kingdom was the first independent state actually within the borders of the empire. Feeble attempts at liberating the North African provinces were launched from Constantinople in the 440s, but to little avail. The Vandals were able to use the captured Byzantine fleet for raids on Italy and Sicily, and in 455 **King Gaiseric**, benefiting from the chaos left behind in northern Italy and Gaul by Attila and his Huns, succeeded in looting Rome itself, carrying off empress Eudoxia and her daughters. The eastern emperors feared that the Vandals would expand into the vital corn-growing lands of Egypt. However, the Byzantine expeditionary force launched against them in 468 was a total disaster. As a result, Gaiseric was able to take Sicily, Rome's oldest province. In fact the end of the Roman Empire in western Europe was nigh (in 476 to be exact). Central power collapsed, and Roman populations came to co-exist with Visigoth and other Germanic settler populations.

However, the Vandals were not efficient managers in their new North African homeland. Although they have gone down in history as the most destructive people of the ancient Mediterranean world, certain contemporary writers left a rather different image. Wrote Byzantine historian Procopius: "Of all the nations I know, the most effeminate are the Vandals. They spend all their days in the baths and in consuming sumptuous repasts ... Covered with gold ornaments and clothed in Oriental silks, they pass their time in spectacles, circus games and amusements. They especially like to hunt. ... They like to locate their homes in the middle of well-irrigated orchards with abundant trees. Finally being lovers of the earth, they deliver themselves without reservation to the pursuit of love making."

All of which gave the Byzantines time to get organized. The Eastern Empire re-asserted its control under Emperor **Justinian** and his general, Belisarius, in AD 533. However, this was to prove unpopular, not least because of the onerous taxation system necessary to cover Byzantium's heavy military expenditure as it tried to confront the Sassanids in Asia as well as maintain its position in the Mediterranean. A little more than a century later, when Byzantine rule in Africa was threatened once more, this time by the expansion of Islam, local populations showed little enthusiasm for supporting Constantinople's continued hegemony in the region.

St Augustine and the decline of Rome

The future St Augustine of Hippo was born in the province of Numidia. In his early 30s, he converted to Christianity, and by 395 he had become the Bishop of Hippo (Annaba, ex-Bône, in modern Algeria, close to the Tunisian frontier). Like most Romans, he was horrified by the sack of Rome in 410 by Alaric and the Goths. He had a deep-felt belief that the Roman empire had been created by God as an instrument for the spread of Christianity. He thus sought to understand how God had allowed such terrible things to happen to the empire.

This is the theme of his work, The City of God. For Augustine, history moves forward according to the purposes of God. However, he came to consider that God's instrument on earth was not a city or an empire. Rather it was the community of believers; it was they who formed 'the city of God.' Unbelievers were of course excluded. Thus it was that the decline and fall of the Roman empire did not really matter in the long run, for the community of believers would survive. St Augustine was to live long enough to see North Africa ravaged by Vandal invaders.

Despite the supposedly destructive presence of the Vandals, there are numerous remains in contemporary Tunisia from the period of the third to seventh century. Carthage has the ruins of one of the largest early churches, the great Damous El Karita basilica, while up and down the country are the remains of Byzantine fortresses – see for example Aïn Tounga, near Dougga, Oudna and Ksar Lemsa, south of El Fahs. Sbeïtla, ancient Sufetula, where Byzantine prefect Gregorius made a stand in 646 against the invading Arabs, has basilicas too.

The Islamic conquest

In the first half of the seventh century, Semitic tribes of the western Arabian desert, under the sway of a new revealed religion, Islam, were able to make considerable conquests in the Fertile Crescent. The tribes' sudden unity under the charismatic leadership of the Prophet **Mohammad** came at a time when the two great powers of the region, the **Sassanian Empire** (centring on what is now Iran and Irak), and the **Byzantines** in Syro-Palestine, were weak after years of fighting. The Muslim Arabs were not to stop at the Middle East, however, and continued their conquests westwards into Byzantine North Africa.

In AD 642, 10 years after the death of the Prophet Mohammad, Arab armies, acting as the vanguard of Islam, conquered Egypt. To secure his conquest, the Arab commander, Amr Ibn al-As, immediately decided to move westwards into Cyrenaica where the local Berber population submitted to the new invaders. Despite a constant pattern of disturbance, the Arab conquerers of Egypt and their successors did not ignore the potential of the region to the south. Nubia was invaded in AD 641-42 and again 10 years later. Arab merchants and later, bedouin tribes from Arabia were able to move freely throughout the southern regions. However, until AD 665, no real attempt was actually made to complete the conquest, largely because of internal problems within the new Islamic Empire. Then, after two feints southwestwards towards the Fezzan, an army under **Okba Ibn Nafi'** conquered what is now Tunisia and set up the first Islamic centre there at **Kairouan** in AD 670. Four years later, the Arabs in Kairouan were able to persuade **Kusayla**, the leader of the Berber confederation which spread right across Tunisia and into modern Algeria as far as the Oued Muluwiya in Morocco, to convert to Islam. Shortly afterwards, Okba Ibn Nafi', in a famous expeditionary raid to scout the unvanquished areas to the west, swept across North Africa along the northern edge of the Sahara desert as far as the

Atlantic coast of Morocco, into the land of the Sanhadja Berbers who dominated the major Western trans-Saharan trade routes.

These early conquests were ephemeral, being based on two mistaken assumptions: the first was that the new conquerors could afford to ignore the isolated Byzantine garrisons along the North African coast, because they would eventually collapse due to their isolation (the Byzantine navy, in fact, supplied them by sea); the second was that the Umayad Arab commanders and administrators now imposed on North Africa ignored the promises of equality of treatment given to Berber converts and thus encouraged a major rebellion, led by Kusayla. Arab control of Kairouan was lost and the Arabs had to reconquer the **Maghreb**, the Land of the West, as they called North Africa.

The first Arab move was against Kusayla, who was killed in AD 688 or 689. Then after a further delay caused, once again, by unrest in the Levant, a new army moved northwards against Byzantine centres in Carthage and Bizerte, where the last remaining garrison was defeated in AD 690. The Arab conquest came up against determined Berber resistance, this time in the Algerian Aurès where the core of the Berber Zenata confederation was led by the **Kahina**, a Judaized or Christianized Berber priestess. Once again the Arabs retreated to Cyrenaica, returning to the attack only in AD 693. In AD 697, the Kahina was killed and her forces defeated in a battle at **Tubna** in the Aurèsm, marking the start of a permanent Arab presence in North Africa.

The city of **Tunis** was founded to prevent further Byzantine encroachment at neighbouring Carthage and, under **Musa Ibn Nusayr**, Arab armies swept westwards to conquer **Tanger** in AD 704. There they came to terms with the sole remaining Byzantine governor in North Africa, **Julian of Ceuta**, a Christian potentate who paid tribute to the new Muslim governor of neighbouring Tanger, Tariq Ibn Ziyad, in order to be confirmed in his post. Seven years later, Ziyad, with help from Julian, who had maintained links with the Visigoth rulers of Spain, organized the Muslim invasion of the Iberian peninsula. By AD 732, Muslim forces had conquered virtually all of Spain and Portugal and had even crossed the Pyrenees. The Muslim advance was stopped near Poitiers by **Charles Martel**. Although for the next four years Provence was ravaged by marauding Muslim armies, the Muslim presence in Europe had reached its limits at the Pyrenees.

Early Islamic rule   As it was the governors of Egypt who had piloted the conquest of the Maghreb, these areas remained initially attached to that province. In 704, the eastern Maghreb was constituted as a separate province, the **wilaya of Ifrikiya**, an Arabic version of the Latin Africa. The term was initially used to cover what is now Tripolitania, Tunisia and eastern Algeria. With the conquest of Morocco, the wilaya extended right across to the Atlantic, and its capital was at Kairouan. The emirs of Ifrikiya thus represented the person of the caliph, the leading authority in Islam, across a vast expanse of territory. Unfortunately, authority was not easily imposed, and the Arabs, by imposing extensive taxes beyond what Islam allowed on the Berbers, created much resentment. Heavy taxation was no doubt levied because of an exaggerated idea of the wealth of the Maghreb held in the Middle East. The inferior status given to Berber warriors in the Arab armies which conquered Spain was another factor in fuelling resentment.

In the event, major **Berber rebellions** broke out. In the seventh century, Islam was yet to develop the set of all-encompassing set of rules for an ideal, pious society which it was to have thanks to the great theological and legal scholars of later centuries. A challenge arose in the Maghreb in the form of the **Kharijites**, who rejected the hereditary succession of the caliphate, insisting that an imam should be chosen by the community on the basis of his learning and religiosity. They also adopted a severer approach to sin than mainstream Muslims. The movement grew out of Berber feelings of resentment. In 741, a Kharijite Berber army defeated an Arab army in a

North Africa and Shi'ite Islam

Islam, one of three great revealed religions emanating from the Middle East, remained solidly united only for the brief period, AD 632-661, under the rule of the early Caliphs. The succession was contested, however, after the reign of the prophet's son-in-law Ali (656-661) and led to a divide in Islam. The followers of Ali and his son Hussein became known as shi'at Ali *('the party of Ali'). They believed that Ali, as nephew and son-in-law of the Prophet Mohammad, was the true heir to the Islamic Caliphate. They held that only his direct male descendants could be supreme religio-political leaders or* imams *for the Muslim community. The Umayyad rulers of the early Islamic empire (late seventh/eigth centuries) were usurpers for these Shi'ites.*

The development of Shi'ism is complex. The Shi'ites held their imams to be divinely inspired – and hence infallible. Things got complicated when sixth imam Ja'far el Sadik died. His son, Ismail, had died before him, and a group of Shi'ites held that Ismail had not died, but merely been occulted. As the Mahdi ('rightly guided one'), he would return from his hiding place to lead the Islamic world and restore justice.

The Shi'ites also understood that communication with God could be done in individual ways, and importantly, through God's interpreters on earth – the eminent authorities of the Islamic teaching schools at Karbala, Najaf, Qom and Meshed. The Shi'ites rejected the formal teachings of the Islamic jurists and the religious consensus

of Sunni Islam. One reason for the survival of Shi'ism in the face of an all-powerful Sunni tradition and military supremacy was that the Persians adopted Shi'ism and incorporated it into their cultural and political resistance to the Arabs and gave the religion a geographical base in what is present day Iran.

It is strange to reflect that present-day Tunisia could have been one of the main Shi'ite centres. The Ismaili Shi'ites sent preachers across the Abbasid empire to convert people to their cause. The creed of these Ismailis was one of humanity and equality, and proved attractive to the North African Berber communities. In AD 893 one such preacher, Abu Abdallah, converted the powerful Katama Berbers of what is now eastern Algeria. This eventually led to the Ismaili leadership's move to North Africa. A certain Ubaydallah Saïd claimed the imamate for himself and founded the Fatimid state (so-called because of the succession in the caliphate from Fatima, the prophet's daughter).

Tunisia served as a base for the Fatimids for the period 909-973 after which time their ambitions to convert the Islamic world back to Shi'ism led them successfully to attack Egypt, found Cairo in 969 and give up their hold on Mahdia. Tunisia was thus a mere stepping stone for the Fatimids. Shi'ite Islam all but died out in North Africa under the impact of Arab invasions by the Beni Hilal and Beni Sulaim beginning in AD 1050.

Background

major battle. In 742, the position was reversed when the Umayyad governor of Egypt defeated the Kharijites in two battles near Kairouan.

In political terms, much of the remainder of the seventh century in Ifrikya was dominated by clan rivalry. The **Fihrids**, descendants of Okba Ibn Nafi', created a principality based on the interests of the Arab warriors. In 750, a new dynasty assumed the caliphate in the Middle East. The **Abbasids** were open to non-Arab cultures, Greek, Persian, and other, and during their rule, the Maghreb became a full part of the Islamic cultural domain. The Fihrids were overthrown, an Ibadite (Kharijite) state came into being for a short while – and then an Abbasid army imposed its authority on the eastern Maghreb in 761. Further west, three autonomous dynasties appeared, the most important of which was the **Idrissids** who were eventually to found Fès and enable Islam to take root in the western Maghreb. Ifrikiya thus gradually shrunk back to the eastern segment of the Maghreb, ruled from Kairouan by a series of able governors with the co-operation of the Arab warrior caste.

The Aghlabids

The clan rule which typified North Africa in the late eighth century was ended in AD 800 when **Ibrahim Ibn Al-Aghlab** was made the ruler of the Muslim province of Ifrikiya, based in Tunis. He came from the Middle Eastern lands of the central Caliphate and had been a successful governor for the Abbasid Caliphs in Baghdad. His brief was to manage Abbasid possessions in North Africa without relying on Baghdad for financial support. In practice, granting Ifriqiya to Ibn Al-Aghlab was to lead to the establishment of a local dynasty.

Ibrahim Ibn Al-Aghlab began his reign by imposing peace on the turbulent Berber and Arab tribes of Tunisia. There was a great deal of opposition, not least from the vested interests of the Islamic jurists in Tunis and Kairouan and the Arab garrisons in the main towns who had grown slack and oppressive. In a short time, regional groups were put down and order restored.

The Aghlabid contribution Ibrahim Ibn Al-Aghlab's successors kept up the peace and there began a period of **artistic** and **architectural development**. Under Abu Ibrahim Ahmad (AD 856-863) the great mosque in Tunis was restored. In water storage and irrigation the Aghlabids were particularly active, the large storage pounds at Kairouan were their work and are still known as the *Bassins aghlabites*. The pools were fed by springs 36 km to the west. Impurities were allowed to settle in a first pond before the water was transferred into elaborate and ornate long term storage pools. The royal city of **Rakkada** near Kairouan was the work of the Aghlabids, built in the tradition of Islamic dynasties, as a strongly fortified palace complex complete with water pools, mosques and housing areas.

The Aghlabids retained independence from Baghdad but eventually fell to the rising power of the Berber Katama tribes, converted to Shi'ism, and the emergence of the Fatimid state. The Aghlabid contribution to Tunisian technology and welfare was considerable, bringing artistic and architectural techniques from the eastern Caliphate to mix with Mediterranean and local traditions.

Local dynasties like the Aghlabids were able to dominate the Maghreb from a few small cities, and much of the population was converted to Islam. Nevertheless, **Christian** and **Jewish** communities survived, the former until the 11th century, the latter until the present day. Arabic only took hold slowly, and 10th-century writers observed that the bulk of the population spoke no Arabic.

Fatimids, Zirids and the Beni Hilal

The 10th to the 11th centuries in Tunisia were a period of complex dynastic manoeuvrings, with the creation of new royal capitals and a great nomad tribal invasion which was to have long lasting ethnic and linguistic impact on the eastern part of North Africa.

The beginning of the 10th century saw the arrival in the Maghreb of one **'Ubaydallah**, arch enemy of the Abbasid caliphs in Baghdad and leader of a dissident branch of Islam, the **Ismaïli** sect. (The Ismaïlis were a branch of Shi'ite Islam, that of the *shi'a* or party of 'Ali, the prophet Mohammad's son-in-law.) Aghlabid rule in the eastern Maghreb collapsed, and in 909 'Ubaydallah made a triumphant entry into the royal capital of Raqqada. He immediately proclaimed himself the *mahdi*, and the dynasty he founded was to be called the **Fatimid**, after the Prophet's daughter Fatima from whom all Shi'ite religious leaders claim descent. In 915, 'Ubaydallah moved to the coast, and began work on a new royal capital at **Mahdiya**, indicating the start of a new political leadership.

The relations between the Shi'ite Fatimids in their Mahdiya stronghold and the Sunni Muslim majority in cities like Tunis and Kairouan were strained, not only for

The curse of the Fatimids: two tribes go to war

Both Tunisia and Libya were deeply affected in ethnic origin, religion and culture by two invasions of Arab groups from the east – the Beni Hilal and the Beni Sulaim. The Beni Hilal confederation consisted of the three tribes, the Atbeg, the Riah and the Zoghba, which originated in central Arabia before moving to Egypt. A parallel tribal group, the Beni Sulaim, had similar origins and structure. Both tribes had created security problems in southern Egypt, being constantly involved in uprisings against central authority. When in 1047 the Zirid successors to the Fatimid rulers in Tunisia changed their allegiance from the Shi'ite branch of Islam to Sunni and recognized the Abbasid Caliphs, the Fatimids retaliated by bequeathing their former territories in North Africa on the unruly tribes.

The Beni Hilal began their journey west in AD 1050-51 and first settled in Cyrenaica before moving, first, into Tripolitania where the Zoghba took control, then second, into Tunisia in the 11th century. They defeated the Zirid governors of Tunisia at Gabès in 1052 and by 1057 Kairouan fell to the nomadic invaders. The Beni Hilal fought the ruling Muslim rulers in North Africa, fought amongst themselves and were a thoroughly

disruptive force in the eastern Maghreb. It took the tough Moroccan Almohads to contain both them and the Beni Sulaim.

It appears that both tribes were essentially marauders looking for loot and land rather than soldiers of Islam. Little was done on behalf of the Fatimids in the religious domain and the two tribes remained as nomads and herders entirely unabsorbed into the city and its civilization, often making bedouins of the more settled populations.

The Hilalian invasion is celebrated in the Saga of the Beni Hilal, which tells of love, conquests and tales of derring-do. On the other hand, Arab historians remember the two tribes of nomadic invaders as 'no better than a cloud of locusts.' After the invasions, the surviving cities in the eastern Maghreb were foreign bodies in a sea of nomadic backwardness. Cultivation was largely abandoned and irrigation systems fell into disrepair.

But though the Fatimid curse on North Africa destroyed urban life, it didn't do the Fatimids much good either. It took many years before the towns were repeopled, and in many cases it wasn't until Hafsid rule in the 13th century that some degree of prosperity was re-established.

theological reasons. Taxation and money from the sale of government posts was spent on numerous campaigns against the Sunnite caliphate. Eventually, however, in 969, the Fatimids successfully conquered Egypt, leaving behind a tribal chief named **Buluggin** as viceroy. He was to create a dynasty of viceroys, referred to as the **Zirids**, who came to view themselves as the rightful rulers of Ifriqiya. They took up residence in yet another palace-city, **Sabra al Mansouriya**, located just outside Kairouan. Sunnite influence was growing all the time, however, and in 1016 there were major anti-Shi'ite riots. Eventually, in 1044, the Zirid ruler, **Al Mu'izz** (1016-51) broke with the Fatimids – with disastrous results.

As a punishment, the Fatimids directed two great tribal groups, the **Beni Hilal** and the **Beni Sulayman**, against the Maghreb. (Both tribes had been creating considerable problems in Egypt.) Fatimid caliph Al Mustansir actually 'granted' towns and provinces to these tribal groups. Over 50,000 tribal warriors headed northwestwards into Ifriqiya, pillaging the countryside. The Zirid state collapsed, and a large number of local emirates – the Khorassanids in Tunis, for example – emerged to fill the power vacuum. **Malikite Islam**, centring on the Kairouan school of legal theology, had emerged as a strong force, underpinned by the belief that the life of the Muslim community should be governed according the principles of Islamic law. Such a concept was to be crucial to the success of the great tribal based dynasties which emerged in the late 11th and 12th centuries.

Background

Almoravids and Almohads

And now over to the High Atlas, the mountains dominating the western part of North Africa. The Saharan gold trade, in the 11th century, was to be dominated by a nomad Berber group, based in fortified religious settlements or *ribat* – hence their name, *el-murabitoun*, which transposes as **Almoravid**, as the dynasty is called in English. Based in the northern Sahara, they founded a capital at **Marrakech** in 1062. Their empire was to expand to include much of Spain and present day Algeria.

A second tribal group, also given cohesion by a strong sense of religious mission, was to unite the Maghreb. In the 12th century, the Almoravids were overthrown by the **Almohads**, *el-muwahhidoun* or 'unitarians', whose power base lay in the Berber tribes of the High Atlas. United by their common religious cause, the Almohads took Sijilmassa, the 'gold port', and their empire expanded to include the whole of present day Morocco, Algeria and Tunisia, along with Andalusia. This political unity, lasting from c.1160 to 1260 brought cultural and economic development. The cities expanded and distinctive mosques were built, along the lines of the Koutoubia at Marrakech (see the mosques at the Kasbah and Bab Jazira in Tunis). Trade grew with the merchant cities of Europe. Arabic took root as the language of urban areas.

The Almohad Dynasty disintegrated towards the end of the 13th century. The ruling tribal élite lost its sense of cohesion – and the feudal Christian lands of Spain were quick to react: Seville fell to the Christians in 1248, and Granada became a sort of protectorate. The Almohad Empire split into three separate kingdoms – roughly corresponding to the independent states of today's central Maghreb. Ifrikiya (presently Tunisia), was ruled by the Hafsids, who initially ruled in the name of the Almohads; other regional kingdoms were centred on Tlemcen and Fès.

The Hafsids

The new Hafsid state saw itself as the legitimate successor to the Almohads and its ruler as caliph. The claim was widely accepted, even in the Middle East, because the strength of the Hafsids coincided with the Mongol invasions which destroyed Baghdad and the last vestiges of the Abbasid caliphate in 1250. But in reality, the Hafsid state lacked the social and political cohesion of its predecessor. Thus its long history was marked by the constant interplay of internal conflict between different members of the Hafsid family and with Arab and other tribal leaders who sought supreme power. Like the Merinid state, based in Fès, it also had to integrate increasing numbers of Muslims and Jews emigrating from Al Andalus.

The Hafsids had to deal with an ever greater **Christian threat**. This came in two forms: direct aggression, such as the eighth crusade, led by the French King Louis IX, which besieged Tunis unsuccessfully in 1270, and commercial penetration. In the early part of the 13th century, the great Italian trading cities of Pisa, Genoa and Venice, together with the French of Provence, obtained trading and residence rights in Ifriquiya. The most important dynamic trading state was Aragón. The Aragonese had created a major commercial empire in the western Mediterranean and, after 1246, Aragón had an ambassador in Tunis, the Hafsid capital. Mercantile representation was established in 1253. After Aragón annexed Sicily in 1282, this commercial hegemony was backed by military dominance as well.

By 1318, Aragonese influence was on the wane and Hafsid fortunes revived. The Hafsid state was, nonetheless, a Mediterranean state rather than one with its attention directed towards Africa or the Middle East – in part, its finances increasingly depended on piracy. By the end of the 15th century Hafsid influence had declined once again. Spain, the new threat to the Mediterranean Muslim world, annexed Tripoli in Libya and Bejaïa in modern Algeria in 1510, as the first move in a widening penetration into the Maghreb. The Hafsids lingered on until 1574, when Tunis and its lands were integrated into the Ottoman Empire.

Hafsid rule left an important socio-religious legacy, however. Their predecessors, the Almohads, had been reforming crusaders, conquering Spain and North Africa in the name of a puritan doctrine. The first Hafsid ruler at Tunis, **Abdul Wahid**, son of Abu Hafs Umar, a governor for the Almohads. His successors developed an independent state in Ifriqiya while retaining the strong religious bent of their ancestors. In conjunction with native Tunisian scholars, this led to the development of **Malikite law** as the foundation for the social life of Tunis. This trend became particularly marked under three strong rulers from the late-14th to the late-15th centuries (Abu Al Abbas, Abu Faris and Abu 'Amr Othman). Malikite scholars in official posts legitimized Hafsid authority in the eyes of the city populations. The developing Malikite religious awareness also counterbalanced the influence of saints, which although it led to stability in rural areas, could also create centres of dissidence. The Hafsid rulers thus founded numerous *medersas* (colleges), which although at first intended for the study of Almohad doctrine, later came to give instruction in Malikite law. This strong interest in the law, and the idea that *'urf*, local customary law, could have legal validity as long as it did not contradict the *shari'a*, was to prove a distinctive and longlasting trait in Tunisian Islam.

Ottoman rule

The Hafsid Dynasty came to an end in the middle of the 16th century. A succession of weak rulers proved no match for the ambitious Habsburgs and Ottomans, for whom the Mediterranean with its ports and islands was to be the setting for an imperial struggle for most of the 16th century. Tunis was captured by a Turkish-Algerian pirate, Kheïreddine Barbarossa (Red Beard) in 1534. The city subsequently fell to Charles V of Spain in 1535, who was to reinstate the Habsburgs as puppet rulers. Then in 1574, the Ottomans finally retook La Goulette and Tunis (Tunis suffered considerable destruction during these mid-16th century conflicts).

Once the Spaniards had been driven out of Tunisia and the remnants of the Hafsid Dynasty had been eliminated, the Ottoman commander, **Sinan Pasha**, was given a mandate to organize the administration of Tunis and its region. From the conquest until the 1620s, the Ottoman military controlled government and army. A corps of often rowdy janissary troops was stationed in the city, while leadership often came from the renegades, dynamic Christians who converted to Islam in order to be able to rise to positions of importance. The task of bringing nomad tribes to heel and collecting of taxes from the countryside was entrusted to the *bey*, a post which was to rival the power of the military leader, the *dey* by the late 17th century. The political subordination of Tunis and other cities to the Ottoman Empire took the form of payment of annual tribute to Istanbul and the important place given to the Hanefite school of Sunni Islam (the dominant form of Islam at court at Istanbul.)

The early 1600s in Tunis were marked by two soldiers of fortune, **Othman Dey** (1598-1610) and **Youssef Dey** (1610-37). (Dey was an Ottoman military title, and the deys based in Tunis elected one of their number as leader.) As neither Othman nor Youssef had much taste for luxury, the influence of Tunis was reinforced. The turbulent soldiery was disciplined, and Djerba, run by Tripoli, was brought under Tunis' authority. Mosques, fortifications and barracks were constructed. Under Youssef Dey in particular, piracy became an important source of revenue, and the Tunisian fleet had around 20 ships.

More importantly in the long term, large numbers of Andalusians fleeing Catholic persecution in the Iberian peninsula were allowed to settle in Tunisia. Othman Dey gave favourable treatment to the new arrivals. Unlike earlier Andalusian immigrants, many were poor folk. They were given tax exemption for three years, and land grants in the Medjerda River valley and the Cap Bon, where they established their own villages. They contributed greatly to the development of agriculture, as well as to the *chéchia* or felt cap industry. The export of this characteristic piece of headgear, so useful for winding a turban on, was to become an important source of revenue for Tunis.

A further source of dynamism were the European Jewish immigrants, the *Yahoud el Grana*. (The term is a corruption of the Ladino/Hebrew term *Gornim*, itself a corruption of Livornese.) The first wave of these Sephardic Jews, originally pushed out of Spain to settle in Livorno and Ancona, migrated to Tunis in 1675.

In the mid-17th century a renegade of Corsican origin, one **Murad Bey**, rose to prominence, building a power base by using local troops to collect taxes in rural areas. His son Hammouda was to rule from 1631-66. Both these beys received the title of pasha from Istanbul, in recognition for their capacity to maintain order in the countryside. Their capacity to mobilize taxation revenue enabled them to reduce the power of the deys, and after 1665, they controlled customs revenues from European trade as well. **Murad II** (1666-75) succeeded his father, further reinforcing the hereditary principle. The situation in the late 17th century deteriorated, however, with often bloody struggles for influence between deys and beys.

There is no space here to go into the complex political infighting of the first years of the 18th century. The last Muradite bey, Murad Ben Ali, was assassinated in 1702. In 1705, the exasperated notables of Tunis requested one Hussein Ben Ali, a local member of the Ottoman military caste of Greek origins, to take control. He had been deputy bey, and understood the weakness of the situation. Through the creation of a local military force, part Tunis citizens, part tribal warriors, he was able to stabilize the situation, and eventually turned out to be the founder of a hereditary dynasty, the Husseïnids, around whom some semblance of a nation state was to begin to take shape in the late 18th century.

A strong hereditary dynasty: the Husseïnids

After defeating an attempt by the Regency of Algiers to conquer Tunisia in 1705, Hussein Ben Ali acquired considerable prestige, and was able to reorganize the adminstration and army to suit him. The Turkish military group or *jund* ceased to have any governmental authority, becoming an army corps providing ultimate protection for the bey. The dey became just another official post. Leading Tunisian families and Malikite religious leaders were brought into the spheres of government. The rural areas were administered by local notables or *qaids*, a sort of mix between governor and tax-farmer.

Tunisia was now effectively independent and came to be referred to as the *Iyalet Tunis*, generally translated as the Regency of Tunis to denote the fact that allegiance was still owed to the Sultan-Caliph in Istanbul. The Ottoman Empire, covering vast territories with often poor communications, was a loosely organized sort of affair, and could easily tolerate such arrangements.

Thus, in the course of the 18th century, the Husseïnids, despite a certain amount of strife, appeared as hereditary rulers of a nascent Tunisian state. Djerba marked the southeastern limit of their domains, while the northwestern limit was somewhere up in the Khroumirie Mountains. This region of the eastern Maghreb had a number of advantages for an emerging dynasty: fertile agricultural lands and a series of well-fortified coastal towns, within a couple of days' horse ride of each other; the population was relatively homogeneous, comprising a settled Malekite urban Muslim population and nomad tribes; minorities (Jewish, Kharijite in Djerba) were small and unlikely to threaten the dynasty. Thus the Husseïnids were able to carve out a role for themselves as intermediaries between the rural and urban subsistence economies and the expanding trade of the Mediterranean. The only people who could have really opposed the Husseïnids, the urban populations, benefited from the prosperity brought by this trade, especially in the latter half of the 18th century.

Under Ali II (1759-82) and more especially his son, Hammouda Bey (1782-1814), the **Regency of Tunis** emerged as something of a Mediterranean power, albeit only a minor one. The encroachments of the restive and powerful Regency of Algiers was resisted as necessary, the Ottomans' wishes regarding Tripolitania were defied, and annual tributes were extorted from various minor European states by using the threat of piracy. Hammouda Bey inherited a prosperous state, and fully intended things to stay that way. (An indication of the prosperity of Tunis at the time are the large palatial homes of government officials like the Dar Lasram in the Médina of Tunis.) He encouraged subordinates to express opinions, and came to rule with the assistance of a super-minister, the vizir and lord of the seal, Youssef Sahib al-Tabi'a. Hammouda also spent considerable time and energy in reinforcing his Turkish and Zouawa army corps.

The 19th century: rising European influence

Hammouda Bey's reign was the last during which the Regency of Tunis was treated as an equal of the European powers. No one in Tunis seems to have foreseen the coming change. The context, of course, had been favourable to an increasingly inde- pendent Regency. The Europeans were too embroiled in the Napoleonic Wars to be bothered about North Africa. Their military and administrative technologies were developing, however. France was finally defeated in 1815, and eventually was to turn a colonizing gaze southwards, partly as a way of rebuilding smashed prestige. Dying in 1815, Hammouda Bey was not to live to see the change.

In the 17th century, and right up to the 1740s, it had been the custom for visiting European dignitaries to kiss the bey's hand at audiences. However, in the early 19th century, there was a huge shift in the balance of power. A series of new factors weakened the Regency of Tunis' position in the Mediterranean and strengthened the European powers of the northern shore. In 1816, **Lord Exmouth** and his fleet had successfully put pressure on the Algiers' beys to end Christian slavery. A similar concession was exacted from Tunis. In 1827, the Greek War of Independence was at its height. The Ottoman fleet, with Tunisian ships, was destroyed at the **Battle of Navarino**. In 1830, the French took Algiers; Constantine fell in 1837. To the south- east, the Ottomans re-conquered Tripoli from the Karamanlis. Tunis now had strong and potentially dangerous neighbours.

Internally, things were little better. The Turkish army corps revolted twice, in 1811 and 1816. The second revolt left the Husseïnids with reduced military support. A ter- rible plague epidemic swept the country in 1829. France was strengthening her presence. In 1829, Hussein Bey signed a capitulation treaty giving the French consul the right to try cases involving French nationals in Tunisia. The government was increasingly forced to borrow from foreign banks, and manufactured goods were beginning to appear, sold far more cheaply than the handmade goods produced in Tunisia. In short, by the 1830s, the writing was on the wall.

In 1837, an energetic ruler, **Ahmed II**, came to the throne. Son of a Sardinian mother, Ahmed Bey (who ruled to 1855) was determined to reform his country. He sought to reduce European domination in trade. Institutional reforms aimed at increasing taxation on agricultural produce were introduced, monopolies were established, and soap and tobacco factories built in Tunis.

Reacting to the increased military strength of the European nations Ahmed Bey was the founder of the modern Tunisian army based on the Ottoman model. Keen on all things military, he had headed the army under his father Mustapha Bey's short

Why the Tunisian monarchy was abolished

Ruler from 1859 to 1883, Sadok Bey and his mamlouk ministers (some of considerable incompetence) proved incapable of preventing the country from passing under French "protection". From 1881, the beys lived a rather pleasant bourgeois existence, moving with the seasons from one suburban palace to another. The uprisings and murders of 18th century court life gave way to Ruritanian ceremonial. No longer did a mauvais café sort out the succession. Rubber stamping the decisions of the resident general, the bey (and his entourage) benefited from the prosperity generated by France's 'informal colonization'. The Bardo Palace was heavily remodelled at the beginning of the 20th century, Nasser Bey built himself a new palace at Sidi Bou Saïd.

However, living in settings worthy of an exotic opera, the beys proved unable to follow the rising demands of Tunisia's nascent independence movement. (The 1930 eucharistic congress at Carthage, partly sponsored by the bey, helped fire nationalist sentiment). Moncef Bey, the one ruler who openly challenged the power of the residence, exploiting French weakness during the Axis occupation of 1942-43) was exiled by the victorious allies, accused of collaboration with the Nazis. His successor, Sidi Lamine, was a kind old man who was no match for the nationalist leader, the wily Monastir lawyer, Habib Bourguiba. Unlike the Moroccan sultan who returned in triumph from exile as liberator of his people, the bey had lost all legitimacy. Undefended, the monarchy was eventually abolished on 25 July 1957. Its fall was lamented by very few.

reign (1835-37). He was very close to the troops, which enabled him to see where changes were needed. On coming to power in 1837, he implemented a number of reforms: the move from a small army of Turks and Zouaves to a larger professional army was accomplished. In 1840, the Bardo military academy was opened. By the end of the first decade of Ahmed's reign, a *nizami* or regular army with a strength of 27,000 men had been created. There were seven infantry regiments, and a Tunisian expeditionary force was participating in the Crimean War (1855-56) at the time of Ahmed's death in 1855.

The schemes, very much in line with the *tanzimat* reforms taking place in Mohammad Ali's Egypt and in the Ottoman Empire, were unfortunately not very successful. The tax farmers turned out to be unscrupulous, and massive spending was needed for the steamship fleet and a large new palace complex at Mohamedia, south of Tunis. The agricultural sector, heavily dependent on the vagaries of Tunisia's rainfall, could not always produce harvests good enough to meet extortionate tax demands. Thus the following year's activities could not be financed, and farming went into decline. Major epidemics – cholera and smallpox – took their toll. In 1853, a new burden appeared. As an Ottoman vassal, the Regency of Tunis was obliged to contribute an expeditionary force to fight alongside the Turks (and France and Britain) in the Crimean War – 10,000 troops were sent, of which 4,000 died from sickness (but none in the fighting).

Ahmed Bey's successor, **Mohammad** (1855-59) attempted legislative reform too. It was during his reign that the *Ahd al Aman*, the Pledge of Security, a sort of constitutional pact, was drawn up, a unique document for the time.

The 1860s were a difficult decade for Tunisia: the doubling of the poll tax in 1864 led to a rebellion which was fiercely suppressed; there followed drought, a cholera epidemic in 1865 and typhus in 1868. Burdened with debts, the country was reduced to a state of misery which the reforming minister Kheïreddine was to find difficult to overcome. The general depression was reflected in the situation of the country's armed forces, for example. The Bardo military academy was disbanded, the supply factories closed, and the number of soldiers (and their salaries) reduced. Increasing debts brought Tunisia's finances under the control of an international financial commission, an early version of the IMF. The events of the 1870s which eventually brought the Regency of Tunis under French 'protection' in 1881 are too complicated to recount here, but involved corrupt super-ministers, scheming European consuls jockeying for influence, and unscrupulous banking houses.

The cosmopolitan regency of Tunisia

From 1881 and until around 1960, the cities of Tunisia were cosmopolitan places. When the protectorate was declared, the country's cities already had sizeable Italian and Maltese populations. This was swelled by an influx of civil servants from France. In the early 20th century, there were further arrivals fleeing the wars of Europe. After the Russian Revolution, a small White Russian community arrived at Bizerte aboard Admiral Wrengel's fleet, escaping the Bolsheviks. There were Greeks involved in sponge fishing. Later came Italians and Spaniards fleeing fascism in their homelands.

In numerical terms, the **Italian** community was initially the most important. As the largest European group, they had to be handled carefully by the French administration, especially as Italy considered Tunisia as *terra perduta*, the colony which should have been. In the 1930s, to counteract the growing influence of fascism, French nationality was granted extensively to Italians resident in Tunisia. The Tunisian Jewish community also became increasingly gallicized during the 75 years of the French protectorate. Education spread rapidly, and the growing wealth of both Twansa and Grana Jews was reflected in a move from the médinas to new, well-planned neighbourhoods.

Today, the cosmopolitan towns of the 1950s are a memory of the older generation, recalled with nostalgia in films like Férid Boughedir's *Un été à La Goulette*, memorial to a Mediterranean mix of peoples. On a tree-lined avenue, the visitor may come across a synagogue; the cafés and the bi-lingual street plaques, the grand old apartment buildings and the surviving terrace tables of a restaurant speak of a Mediterranean sociability. French politicians, comics and artists born in Tunisia now return for visits, as the tensions of the decolonization period have receded from the public memory. The 1990s official slogan *Tunisia, Land of Tolerance*, no doubt owes much to a multi-religion, multi-cultural period which with hindsight seems like a cosmopolitan interlude.

Moving to independence

In the immediate aftermath of the installation of the French Protectorate, Tunisian resistance was confined to tribal groups in the south of the country. Opposition to colonial occupation gradually began to gather strength reflecting popular opposition to the growing, and predominantly Italian, European settler colony in Tunisia, a colony totalling around 100,000 people and controlling some 800,000 hectares of Tunisia's best agricultural land.

Initially, the opposition was diffuse, with a focus on the **Destour** or Constitution party, which reflected the thinking of the educated urban intelligentsia. The Destour was founded in 1919 by one Abdelaziz Thaâlabi. Its basic idea was that Tunisia should become a constitutional monarchy based on on the 1861 *destour* or constitution. The fact that there was a French protectorate was no reason for not applying a valid local code of law. In 1921, the Destour Party proposed a reform package, including the creation of a Franco-Tunisian assembly.

All this was to little effect. French commercial interests had become too important, and the depression and strikes of the 1930s meant that no one was willing to give way. The poorer members of the French community, minor officials and government employees, and the poor Italians had too much to lose.

A more radical current was taking shape in the Destour Party, however, under a bright, charismatic French-trained lawyer, **Habib Bourguiba**. At a conference held in the movement's regional fief of Ksar Hellal in 1934, the Destour split, with Habib Bourguiba taking over the more radical wing, now renamed the **Neo-Destour**. This part of the movement had its power base in the small towns of the Sahel and the growing urban proletariat of Tunis. Many of its leaders had risen thanks to the Franco-Arab schools and university education in France, where they had studied law and medicine. The old urban élite of Tunis, the *beldia*, were little represented. For the first time, a political movement was taking shape independently of both the beylical establishment and the leading city families.

The French authorities did their best to stamp out the Neo-Destour, but to no avail. Time and the general trend of history was on the nationalists' side. The early 1930s was a time of poor harvests. The Depression led to a huge fall in the price of olive oil, Tunisia's staple agricultural export. Much marginal land was abandoned; drought had terrible effects on nomads, who had lost their ancestral grazing rights, as land was enclosed for modern agriculture. The mechanization of farms also put many out of work. There was a drift towards the towns – severely repressed by the police.

A package of reforms was put forward in 1938, but too late. Developments in Europe meant that such schemes had to be shelved, and the Neo-Destour's leaders were imprisoned. A chance for France and Tunisia to move towards a working relationship had been missed.

When the Second World War came, France lost considerable face, and the monarchy under Moncef Bey was not slow to exploit this weakness. Tunisia came under Axis occupation from 1941 to 1942. When the French returned with Allied support, however, nationalist bey Moncef was exiled and replaced by Amine Bey, an elderly be-spectacled monarch unlikely to provide a figurehead for the nationalist cause. Moncef Bey died in exile in Pau, fate was clearly on the side of the Destourians. In the wake of the war and growing agitation, it became clear that some concessions to nationalist sentiment would have to be made.

Before this was done, France tried to enforce its position in Tunisia by requiring the Bey to accept the idea of 'co-sovereignty', whereby France would gain permanent rights to Tunisian territory. Following this attempt by France in 1950 to gain a firmer foothold inside North Africa, the nationalist movement under Habib Bourguiba took on the characteristics of a mass movement. As a result, Habib Bourguiba was able to negotiate autonomy for Tunisia in 1955 and in 1956, when Morocco was granted Independence, Tunisia soon followed suit. The situation elsewhere in the French Empire was favourable to such a development. France had been defeated in Indochina and was facing simmering disturbances in Algeria, then considered as an integral part of France. The mid-1950s were clearly the wrong time to become bogged down in some sort of guerrilla warfare in a minor possession like Tunisia. In any case, France's economic interests and influence could be protected by other means.

Modern Tunisia

The kingdom of Tunisia which became independent in 1956 was very different from the Beylicate of the 1861 Destour (Constitution.) The new constitution, the type of state (a republic was proclaimed in 1957), administrative organization and practice made it firmly a modern state, very much in the French centralizing tradition. Further huge changes were on the way, however, to produce the prospering little North African nation that Tunisia had become by the end of the 1990s. Many commentators have seen these changes as being largely due to the energy and ambition of one man, Habib Bourguiba, Tunisia's leader from independence until 1987. The dynamism built up in the first decades of independence was continued under the country's second (and current) president, Zine el Abidine Ben Ali. Both figures led/lead the country as wise and enlightened father figures. However, this is a superficial similarity, for there are in fact considerable differences in their leadership styles.

Recent history

Post-independence Tunisia, unlike neighbouring Algeria (independent in 1962), had the advantage of having a strong, single-minded leadership with a clear vision of the future. For Habib Bourguiba, Tunisia had fallen under French domination thanks to the decadence and corruption of the beys. Radical changes, if necessary removing the country's traditional institutions, would be necessary to bring about progress to the benefit of all. Bourguiba made use of his immense personal prestige and the fact that the constitution was being revised to push forward major reforms in the period 1956-59.

Post-independence changes: 1956-59

Tunisia prides itself on having the most progressive attitude towards gender relations of the Arab states. In 1956, a **Personal Status Code** became law, replacing Islamic law and the Rabbinic courts in all matters of personal status. The new unified code abolished polygamy and introduced equality before the law between the sexes with regard to divorce. Minimum marriage ages were introduced, the marriage of non-Muslim men to Muslim women was legalised.

In hindsight, the vast expansion of **education** in the 1960s was a key element behind Tunisia's later economic success. The principle of free and universal primary education was accepted. The Sadiki College model, with sciences taught in French and humanities in Arabic, was extended to the rest of the educational system. The University of Tunis was set up in 1960. Tunisia, unlike her neighbours, had a small core of educated, urban women in the 1950s. Women's education was expanded rapidly, and by 1961 there were over 200,000 girls in school.

Land reform was a further key area. The country had large amounts of property, and notably agricultural land, held under the traditional Islamic mortmain system or *habous*. (The use and product of land could be left for future generations by the founder of the *habous*.) The system was abolished, and 175,000 ha of land was sold off between 1956 and 1961. Choice property went to reward loyal party followers. A futher 150,000 ha went into the cooperative system introduced in 1963.

Background

Bourguiba faced considerable pressure to achieve results for the poorer members of Tunisian society, and it this pressure which may have led him to introduce a rather limited version of socialist development in the 1960s. The concept of socialism entered Bourguiba's speeches, and the party was renamed the *Parti Socialiste Destourien* (PSD) in 1964. Agricultural cooperatives were set up to manage the former habous lands – and the farms confiscated from French and Italian farmers in 1964. The socialist experiment was managed by Ahmed Ben Salah, one time secretary-general of the UGTT, the

The 1960s: Ben Salah & the socialist experiment

main labour union, who gradually became a sort of super-minister, and for a time seemed to be being groomed to succeed Bourguiba.

But Ben Salah ran up against well established interests. When it began to look as though privately owned estates, (some belonging to members of old Tunisois families close to the presidency), might be nationalized, opposition began to Ben Salah began to grow. Sahel landholders were unhappy about risking the loss of their profitable olive groves, while other families in trade had suffered from import restrictions. The final straw was a World Bank report in 1969 criticizing Ben Salah's management of the economy. Bourguiba decided that the cooperative movement had had its day – and dismissed Ben Salah. He was charged with treason and condemned to 10 years imprisonment. (Three years later he was to escape and fled into exile.)

The 1970s:
the return to
capitalism

The year 1970 saw the old guard of the party under the leadership of the new premier, Bahi Ladgham, regain ground. Bourguiba was suffering from ill health, and spent increasing periods of time abroad for treatment. Ladgham was in office for barely a year, replaced by technocrat Hédi Nouira. A new constitution was promulgated in 1976, reflecting the leader's increasing inability to control all areas of policy. The new constitution entrusted executive authority to the cabinet headed by the prime minister, although the President retained the ultimate veto on policy.

The end of the socialist experiment coincided with a notable improvement in Tunisia's economic situation. Older Tunisians look back on the 1970s with nostalgia. It was a time of technocratic rule, when business became legitimate. Hédi Nouira, in his cold, efficient way, presided the liberalization of the Tunisian economy. Fortunes were made – not all of them honestly, and consumer goods returned to the market. Education continued to expand, and there were plenty of jobs in the civil service and new import substitution industries. Incentives were set up to bring investment into Tunisia, including the famous Loi 72, which offered a range of tax breaks to foreign investors willing to put money into export-oriented businesses.

During the 1970s, Nouira and his cabinet effectively governed, and came to replace Bourguiba in the Tunisian public's mind. This situation was not to last, however. Victim of a heart attack, Nouira was forced to retire from public life in 1980. One of his decisions was to have far-reaching effects years later: a hardworking military man from Hammam Sousse, one Zine el Abidine Ben Ali, was put in charge of national security .

The 1980s:
Mzali &
Arabism

The 1980s saw prime minister **Mohammad M'zali** emerge as President Bourguiba's successor until his spectacular fall from grace in 1986. The period was marked by growing domestic unrest, with the Islamic fundamentalist movements gaining ground in the suburbs. Official rhetoric was marked by a strong pan-Arab line.

Tunisia's performance during the Vth Economic and Social Development Plan (1982-86) was mediocre, to say the least. M'zali, a former Arabic teacher, proved to be a demagogue and was nicknamed 'Bozo le clown' on account of his haircut. The government gained a reputation for corruption and nepotism. (The premier's wife, Fathia M'zali became Tunisia's first Minister for Women.) In such a political climate, there was no room for the opposition in the National Assembly. Left wing groups, which during the 1970s had been under considerable repression, were replaced by a growing radical Islamic movement as the main source of opposition to the régime.

The crisis was at its most acute by August 1986, when a carefully worked out structural adjustment plan was adopted. The aim was twinfold: the reduction of macro-economic imbalances and the creation of a stable basis for growth.

The World Bank sponsored structural adjustment plan put forward a number of fast-working remedies, as well as providing for a number of long term strategies to help the Tunisian economy on its way to achieving faster growth. Shortly after the reforms had been launched, there was a change of president. Habib Bourguiba, increasingly out of touch with the mood in the country, demanded the retrial of some Islamic revivalist dissidents, in an attempt to ensure their conviction. It was clear that the president had lost his grip. The prime minister, **Zine el Abidine Ben Ali**, stepped in, and on 7 November 1987, President Bourguiba was declared medically unfit to govern. Ben Ali took over as president until elections could be organized.

The early Ben Ali years, broadly speaking 1987 to 1994, were devoted to ensuring stability, implementing the structural adjustment programme and making major institutional reforms, notably in education and investment legislation. The challenge from the revivalist Islamic movement was removed, and a number of major political reforms implemented. Life presidency was abolished, parties with a regional or religious basis outlawed. Political exiles were allowed to return. National reconciliation was the order of the day, in order to ensure favourable ground for *et taghyir*, *le Changement*, as the shift in social, economic and political life is referred to in Tunisian newspeak.

Simplifying greatly, by the mid-1990s, Tunisia had come through the period of structural investment successfully. There was no longer any risk of violent internal political upheaval. The process of building an investment-oriented economy was well under way, based on closer links with Europe. A friendly business environment and improved legislation was attracting investors. Whether incoming foreign capital flows will be sufficient for Tunisia's ambitions remains to be seen. As compared with its North African neighbours, Tunisia was easily the least problematic state of the region.

1986-94: structural adjustment & a big change

The Maghreb

Tunisia forms part of a block of North African countries generally referred to in Arabic and French as the Maghreb, the Arab west, as opposed to the Middle East, known as the Machrek. Four of the Maghreb countries, Algeria, Mauritania, Morocco and Tunisia, were colonized by France, while Libya came under Italian rule for a brief but fraught period. A United Arab Maghreb, free of outside domination, was a dream of those working for independence back in colonial days. In February 1947 the Committee for the Liberation of the Maghreb was set up. In 1958, at the time when th European Community was being established, Algerian, Moroccan and Tunisian representatives met at Tanger to discuss the prospects for Maghreb unity. On 17 and 18 February 1989, a united Maghreb seemed to be on the way to becoming reality. At Marrakech, the leaders of the five states, HM King **Hassan II** of Morocco, President **Chedli Bendjedid** of Algeria, President **Zine el Abidine Ben Ali** of Tunisia, Colonel **Muammar Gadhafi** of Libya and President **Ould Sidi Ahmad Al Taya** of Mauritania signed the founding act of the Union du Maghreb Arabe, whose acronym, UMA, recalls the Arabic word *umma* or nation. The new union was to be presided by each nation in turn for six month periods. The Moroccan political capital, Rabat, was to provide a building for the secretariat, to be headed by a Tunisian. Algiers was to be home to a future parliament (150 deputies, 30 per country), with Mauritania getting the supreme court and Libya an eventual university academy. In October 1990, a document was drawn up providing for the creation of a free exchange zone before the end of 1992 and the establishment of a customs union in 1995.

Very quickly, however, the new union ran into problems. With Bendjedid removed from power in Algeria, there was a cooling of Algero-Moroccan relations. Libya proved to be a difficult member of the team, and neither Morocco nor Tunisia were keen on Gadhafi's unpredictable style in international relations. The security situation

Slow progress in the 1990s

deteriorated rapidly in Algeria, with guerrilla warfare and appalling massacres in certain regions. Thousands of Algerians began looking to emigrate. In 1994, after a terrorist attack on a Marrakech hotel, Morocco sought to limit any risk of Islamic fundamentalist contagion and introduced a visa for Algerian visitors. Algeria replied by closing the frontier. In response, Morocco put its activities in the UMA on hold. While relations between Algeria, Tunisia and Libya remained generally good, there was little move to develop things at UMA level. Tunisia was increasingly drawn in the orbit of the European Union, while maintaining good relations with Libya. The borders between the two countries were defined.

Relaunching the UMA, 2002 Today, the UMA seems to be about to come out of a period of stagnations. Bilateral contacts began to improve as of 1999. Good personal relations would seem to have been established between the new king of Morocco, **Mohammad VI**, and Algerian president **Bouteflika**. In 2002, the Tunisian Habib Boularès, a former chair of the Tunisian National Assembly was designated secretary-general, while the new headquarters in Rabat was finally completed. A seventh summit was scheduled for 2002 to get the organization off to a new start.

Future of the UMA Any progress in the UMA will have to be based on the settlement of Algero-Moroccan differences over the latter's Saharan provinces. Without this, there seems little hope for any advance. Perhaps in any case it doesn't matter too much for Tunisia (and Morocco) since commercial relations with the European Union have taken on such great importance. And then there is the question of the name, Union du Maghreb Arabe. Given that a large percentage of the population in the two most populous countries, Algeria and Morocco, does not see itself as Arab at all, the Union is hardly likely to have much popular interest and support. Grandiose projects like the Trans-Maghreb autoroute and the Tunis to Rabat TGV look set to remain on the drawing-boards for a long time to come.

Tunisia and the European Union

As of the late 1980s, Tunisia opted to intensify its ties with Europe, although never going so far as Morocco, which in 1987 requested membership of the EEC, perhaps more as a symbolic gesture than anything else. Relations are generally excellent, for Europe and Tunisia have too much in common for the two sides not to work together. Algerian gas transits over Tunisian territory on its way to the Italian peninsula, European companies – and notably French, German and Italian ones – have relocated to Tunisia in recent years, benefiting from the favourable tax legislation. The current privatization programme and the recent, albeit timid, development of the Tunis stock exchange will no doubt maintain European business interest. Tunisia's credentials as a stable country, close to Europe, will doubtless continue to make it favourable terrain for business relocation.

Continuity and trends

Tunisian political life since independence has shown a remarkable degree of stability, notably in terms of the direction and application of policy. In Tunisia, as in neighbouring Libya, the political leadership, right from independence, has always followed the line that the improvement of the majority's living conditions was the way forward. Education and health, infrastructure and housing, and in recent years, leisure facilities have always been the focus for investment. (The army, which in both Morocco and Algeria, for different reasons, absorbed large amounts of state finance, has always been a negligeable factor.) The result has been the creation of an educated work force, able to

On being a good Tunisian

Coming to Tunisia, the visitor from the anglophone world is immediately struck by how responsive Tunisians are to friendly greetings. The polite Tunisian walks into the local shop and says sabah el khir ('good morning') or a more formal salam alaykum ('peace be upon you'), and a long exchange of greetings and hand shaking will follow. You certainly can't leave the country without learning the phrase ça va la bes? ('How are you, OK?'). Plenty of time is taken to greet friends and acquaintances, and being skilled in the niceties of greetings and small talk is a key part of being a good Tunisian.

Greetings and ways of thanking often include a religious formula (yaishek, 'may God give you long life', rebbi fadhlek). Tunisians are not however austerely religious. During Ramadhan, almost everyone fasts during daylight hours – but mosque-going is not a majority activity. Many Tunisians learn some of the Koran by heart at the local kuttab, when they are small. All will know the basic precepts of Islam, and newspapers run articles on the difficulties of certain points of observance. Islamic rules provide a valued basis for daily conduct.

Other valued characteristics include being metrebbi (well brought up), 'akil (calm) and ndhif – literally 'clean' but used to mean something approaching 'of good family'. A son of a long established family is an ould 'aila. Memories run deep, and belonging to a dar kebira, a big family is another plus point. Tunisians are very much family people. They adore children, and fathers can be frequently seen proudly showing off their children to their friends at the café. Everyone seems to know everyone somewhere along the line, even in Tunis. Knowing all your relations –

and being au fait with the intricacies of family politics – is another skill the good Tunisian naturally masters.

Getting on well in Tunisia calls for ability to manipulate the family links when necessary. You will have ktef (lit: 'shoulder') or piston to help you get essential papers or a job for a cousin. (The system roughly approximates the British old boy network). You have to be a little hallouf (lit: 'a pig'), ie sharp and a bit roguish. (The phrase inti hallouf, depending on context, means 'you're a clever bastard – and I know what you're at'). Tadbir ra's, 'getting by', is crucial. The effective Tunisian – and in particular the male – is a fixer, someone who is able to yakdhi, to use the verb, equally able to command good service from a tired café waiter or make sure that the dossier is in the right place for the right signature at the right time. Even if money is short, Tunisians appear as immaculately turned out as possible. Women, who shoulder most of the domestic tasks, have to be able to conjure up good meals out of whatever is in the kitchen or come up with magnificent garments from the friperie, the second hand clothes market.

Above all, the good Tunisian is generous, karim, able to give time to help out relatives, stand a round in the café or ferry friends around. This, along with a seemingly ready friendliness is perhaps the characteristic which will stay in the visitor's mind longest. In most of Europe, no-one seems to have the Tunisian generosity with time anymore. Hopefully, this characteristic, along with the vivaciousness of the children and a general staunch humanity will survive the damping effects of globalization.

satisfy the needs of relocating manufacturing industry. Islamic fundamentalism has little attraction for this large and stable group in society, content to work and enjoy the prosperity brought by the policies of the technocratic élite.

Under the country's first president, Habib Bourguiba, there was little room for public debate on government policy. Bourguiba had himself referred to as al Mujahid al Akbar, translated into French as le Suprême Combattant. In Arabic, the term carries a hint of jihad or holy war. Bourguiba considered himself to be leading a jihad against ignorance and poverty; only the application of reason could bring about development and well-being. The leadership style was paternalist, to say the least. The National Assembly essentially functioned as a forum for announcing decisions already taken at presidential level, the country was run by a growing body of university graduates who supported the modernizing policies of the Bourguiba's prime ministers because they were a product of them. The improvement in living conditions was apparent to all, essentially the result of work conducted by ministries answerable directly to the President.

But the '**Bourguiba system**' also had a very personal, and often flamboyant touch. The Tunisian people came to know all the details of their president's life, the influence of his mother, the oft-declared poverty of his childhood. And then there was the issue of the succession. A succession of ministers – notably **Ahmed Ben Salah**, **Hédi Nouira** and **Mohamed M'zali** – were groomed to take over. They would be raised to dizzy heights by Bourguiba. And then, when things began to go wrong, for whatever reason, political or economic, they were disgraced and unceremoniously removed from office. The rise and spectacular downfall of Tunisia's prime ministers were part of a saga that kept Tunisia entertained for decades. Then in 1987, when things had finally got seriously out of hand in both political and economic terms, Bourguiba basically senile and unfit for office, was removed by prime minister Ben Ali (see above).

Under **Zine el Abidine Ben Ali**, the leadership style altered radically. Speculation about manoeuvrings for influence in the Carthage Palace disappeared. President Ben Ali, surrounded by a team of steady technocrats, is a discrete figure. The policy options, marked by equally strong concerns for economic development and the well-being of low-income groups, are broadly the same. But whilst Bourguiba came from a family of upwardly mobile Sahel landowners, Ben Ali had a more difficult start in life – hence the interest in improving conditions for the poorest members of society. The question of Ben Ali's successor remains on hold, and in 2002, no clear favourite figure had emerged, although the names of technocrat **Mohammad Jegham**, a former minister, and **Hédi Jilani**, a leading industrialist close to Carthage, had been mentioned. A major constitutional reform was approved by national referendum in May 2002. Stability and continuity were the watchwords of public life. Given the state of the country's neighbours, it was in nobody's interest to rock the boat.

Gender issues

The **status of women** in Tunisia underwent huge changes after independence, although the debates had begun back in the 1930s, notably through the writings of Tunis intellectual Tahar Haddad. In the early 20th century, Tunisian women of enlightened Muslim families began to go to the Jewish and Catholic schools, and at independence there was already a small core of literate urban women – unlike Morocco, for example, which has had great difficulties in building female literacy.

Advanced legislation For the moment, Tunisia is the most advanced Muslim country in terms of legislation aimed at removing discrimination against women – and is a model often referred to by people in other Arab and Muslim states working for women's rights. The Tunisian *Code du statut personnel*, promulgated on 13 August 1956, was part of a package of reforms pushed through by Tunisia's first president, Habib Bourguiba, who considered that a radical improvement in women's status was vital for achieving progress and material wealth. The code was a great step forward, a single piece of legislation creating a unified personal status system applicable to all Tunisians, Muslims as well as Jews. It abolished both **polygamy** and *talaq* (Islamic repudiation by the male partner), a step which women's movements elsewhere in North Africa would still like to see taken. The Tunisian code did not, however, touch the issue of Islamic **inheritance** rules which favour male over female descendants, although laying down strict rules for the division of property. It did set a minimum age for marriage though: 18 for men and 15 for women.

The *Code du statut personnel*, like other codes in the North African states, affirms the importance of the family as the basis of society. The family is **patrilinear**, that is to say, takes its name from the father, although maternal filiation is recognized. Although permitted by the Code, practice means that a Muslim woman may not marry a non-Muslim man. He must convert to Islam, even if this is only for form's sake, and the process is a long one. Non-Muslim women marrying Tunisians do not have to convert, however. **Divorce** can be initiated by both parties, and both can be accused of adultery.

The availability of **education** was perhaps the key factor in improving women's conditions. In 1959, a 10-year programme was launched with the aim of achieving universal primary education by 1969. Educated women can better understand reproductive health issues, and Tunisia early on launched mass birth-control campaigns. This continues today through the work of specially trained health workers who cover even the most isolated rural areas.

Education & improved conditions

With the number of educated women increasing year by year, attitudes will continue to develop, and the coming generations will no doubt demand further changes. Back in the 1970s, there was an active women's movement with its own magazine *Nissa'* ('Women'.) Urban based, it had little reach into the countryside. Today, a government-sponsored organization, the Crédif (*Centre de documentation et information sur la femme*), provides a focus for research on women's issues.

Long established practices went overboard surprisingly quickly in the post-independence period, even though Tunisia, like the rest of the Maghreb and much of southern Europe, is in many ways a macho land, and the young girls of the house are the object of jealous surveillance. Although the Koranic texts are basically clear on the principle of equality between men and women, certain *souras* and *hadith* stress women's weakness, the need for women to serve men, and mention the need for male protection. The way ordinary daily relations between the sexes run is the result of a long history in which economic, religious and traditional social factors are interlinked. While essentially regulated by Islam, the nature of women/men relations differs between social classes and regional groups. And very often, in traditional areas, it is the women who seem to be the most vigilant guardians of the status quo.

However, in this system, although women rarely have direct authority, they have very definite space of their own. All is not repression – far from it. While weddings are still very often a matter of alliances between families, loving marriages certainly develop in this traditional context. Women are now present in most areas of the country's economic and professional life. There are frequent television programmes on women who have succeeded in new domains, as train drivers, pilots and physicists, in stockbroking, advertising, the catering business and the like. Although the legal status has improved since the 1950s, it will have to change even more to keep up with the new responsibilities taken on by women. The reduction of inequalities links in with the image which Tunisia wishes to project for itself and for the outside world. Women's quest for new identities is a legitimate one – and probably inseparable from the evolving identity of the modern nation.

Entering the public domain

Background

Prospects and ambitions

Tunisia has changed enormously since independence. The time when it was a pictur-esque French protectorate with a Ruritanian monarchy and an interesting ethnic-jig-saw population seems an age ago. Reforms in the late 1950s and early 1960s launched Tunisia in a direction on which there seems to be no going back. Clear symbols of national unanimity – religion, social solidarity – have been established. The govern-ment is only too aware of the divides which could arise if socio-economic divisions became too pronounced, and throughout the 1990s, adopted a gradualist approach to introducing the market economy, an approach which has been vindicated with time. Tunisia has some enormous advantages over its North African neighbours. It is a small country where consensus is carefully constructed. Unlike Algeria and Morocco, it does not have a complex set of geographic and linguistic identities waiting to surface. The military are not a force ever likely to enter the political scene, the ground has been cut away from under political, revivalist Islam.

The economy: privatization & diversification In terms of the economy, Tunisia has put its house in order. The rather adventurous financial policies of the 1970s are a thing of the past, and the budget deficit is mini-mal. Today growth, with an average of around 5% during the 1990s, is well above the birth rate. Of course, there are still challenges. Striving to move upmarket and diversify, the tourist industry, is making progress, not an easy task in the current con-text of the USA's self-proclaimed 'global war on terrorism'. There are still large num-bers of graduates in need of employment. The privatization process continues discretely – but how will local Tunisian companies fare when tarif barriers are fully removed? Will the arrival of multi-national companies compensate for an eventual loss of jobs in local firms?

An improved geopolitical context Things have moved forward hugely since the 1970s, and on the whole, the situation in the early 21st century was a positive one. Tunisia, with little oil resources, benefits from any fall in the price of oil, and its proximity to Europe and an expanding internal market make it an ideal base for relocating manufacturing industry. (Probably no other Arab country has made such efforts to attract foreign investment as Tunisia.) Education has been modernized, and is increasingly adapted to the needs of the job market. Poverty has been pushed back extremely effectively. The question over the first decade of the 21st century will be how to continue the fight against social inequality – and so avoid any risk of Algerian-type fundamentalist destabilization and strife. In the event, the immediate geo-political situation is improving: Algeria under President Bouteflika seems to be heading for national reconciliation, Libya, now free of the damaging embargo, will no doubt head for more stable forms of development.

Stability & consensus Modern Tunisia, helped by compact size and a mono-ethnic population, displays a degree of internal stability and consensus rare in the Arab world. This is definitely a factor which has allowed much to be achieved. The country has been touted by some has 'the new Switzerland' of the Arab world, taking over where the Lebanon of the 1960s and 1970s left off. But Tunisia is not in the Middle East, and has more prag-matic ambitions. With the current government's emphasis on social policy and opening up to the outside world, maybe 'the Arab Denmark' or 'the North African Portugal' are more appropriate comparisons. Will the European Union provide appropriate support to help Tunisia maintain social cohesion? Speculating further, will the country eventually request membership of the European Union, as Morocco has done in the past? Will it become the lead country working for the creation of a North African common market? Time will tell.

Economy

Tunisia has seen steady economic development and reconstruction since the damage created during the the country's brief, but destructive period (1941-42) as a setting for Allied-Axis conflicts during the Second World War. Since independence, development strategy has broadly speaking been constant, despite a flirtation with a form of state socialism in the 1960s. Changes in the economy are controlled by a series of five-year development plans. Major economic reforms were launched in 1986 in the form of the IMF-sponsored structural adjustment plan, and bore fruit in the 1990s.

Compared with other North African countries, Tunisia has a more diversified economy. Its modest oil resources have been an advantage in providing funding for non-oil development but have never been sufficient to encourage reliance on petroleum. There is, nevertheless, a certain vulnerability to external economic pressures including the vagaries of international trade, foreign aid flows, variation in tourist numbers and access to the EU for Tunisia's trade and labour. A youthful and fairly fast-growing population creates an added need for economic growth. The governments of the 1990s have worked hard to tackle these weak points in the Tunisian economy, to their credit with a great deal of success.

Agriculture

Farming until recently was the basis of the economy, and still employs 23% of the labour force and produces about 18% by value of all national output. Chief crops are cereals, citrus fruit, olives, dates and grapes. Approximately 20% of the value of agricultural production comes from cereals. Olive oil is an important export accounting for 4% of the total but suffers heavy competition from Spain and Italy in the main European market. Fishing provides about 6%t of the country's food supply with a catch of around 84,000 tonnes per annum. Esparto grass is collected to export for papermaking and the cork oak forests of the north provide timber and cork.

Energy

Tunisia's oil industry by no means compares with that of Libya or Algeria, it produces only 0.2% of the world total. Production comes from the El Borma field in the south, the Sbeïtla field in the centre and the Itayem fields close to Sfax, all of which feed to a refinery and export complex at Skhira. The Ashtart field offshore in the Gulf of Gabès is also productive and recent discoveries have been made both offshore and in the Cap Bon areas. In the early 1990s, crude and products sales account for 10% of exports.

Gas has become important to the Tunisian economy. Miskar gas field in the Gulf of Gabès was brought on stream by British Gas in 1995 enabling Tunisia to export more oil and to use less Algerian gas. Elf Aquitaine has made considerable investments in developing the Ashtart field.

Phosphates

Phosphates were discovered in southwestern Tunisia in 1885. A mining concession was granted in 1896, and the *Gafsa Phosphates and Railway Company* set up in 1897. Exports began when the Metlaoui to Sfax railway was completed in 1897.

Today, the *Compagnie de phosphates de Gafsa* remains a large producer and exporter of phosphates with annual production running at around 5.5 million tonnes. Phosphate and its products of phosphoric acid and fertilizer provide about 5% of all exports. The vast majority of CPG production is sold on the national market for processing, much of it to the *Groupe chimique* which has developed plants to produce superphosphates and sulphuric acid.

Manufacturing

Tunisia has made remarkable steps in effective industrialization, most of it small scale and private sector. Manufacturing now accounts for 18% of the work force and 17% of national production. Industry is located principally along the northern part of the east coast, main products being cement, flour, steel, cables, textiles, and beverages. The cement industry has undergone extensive privatization, and there are numerous Loi 72 companies working exclusively for the export market. Successful companies include Chakira (cables) and El Fouladh (steel). The **textile industry** is the great success story however, with piece-goods being made up in Tunisia for re-export back to manufacturers in Western Europe. *Levis*, for example, sub-contracts extensively in the Monastir region, exporting finished goods back to its main European headquarters in Belgium. In recent years the textile trade has provided 30% of Tunisia's total export earnings. In particular, French garment manufacture companies have closed their operations in Europe, relocating production in Tunisia.

Tourism   The tourist industry is a major employer and foreign exchange earner. Considerable investment in new hotels has come partially from abroad. The number of tourists rose from a mere 56,000 in 1961 to 4 million in 1995 and around the 5 million mark in 1999. These figures for foreign visitors include 2.5 million arrivals from Libya and Algeria, many visitors from the latter country coming in to buy consumer goods. Receipts from tourism are estimated annually at US$1,114 million.

The industry is developing from its traditional east coast strongholds (Hammamet, the Sahel) to the south where Djerba is proving a popular destination. Desert tourism has been encouraged with considerable subsidies to spread the benefits of the industry wider and change the conservative mentalities of the South. Tunisians are aware of the negative social effects of tourism and deal fairly and sensibly with foreigners so that the country retains a good name and many visitors return. Although 1991 was a difficult year for tourism because of the Gulf War, the market soon recovered, helped in part by troubles in former Yugoslavia, Turkey and Egypt. Inevitably, the events of autumn 2001 had their impact on south Mediterranean tourism. Happily, Tunisia has few tourists from the USA and the fall in demand appeared to be short lived. As ever in a crisis, the government reacted by encouraging local demand for holidays in resort hotels and by slowing progress on new infrastructure, including in particular Tunisia's projected third airport, to be built near Hergla, on the coast between Hammamet and Sousse.

The informal sector   International norms do not really concern Tunisia's flourishing informal sector. This is the most difficult part of the economy to evaluate – despite its high visibility in everyday life. A multitude of people get by selling second hand clothes, magazines and fruit in the street, doing some gardening or working as domestic help – even the odd bit of tourist guiding or the so-called *commerce de la valise* (selling clothes and consumer goods from places like Morocco and Turkey.) In the big cities, the big weekly souks are thought to account for as much as 20% of consumer expenditure. Large quantities of manufactured goods are imported from East Asia and Europe via Libya, where they are highly subsidized.

Improving economic performance in the 1990s   A number of Third World countries, which at the time of independence where at the same stage in their development as Tunisia, have now moved well ahead. In the early 1990s, awareness of this led the Tunisian government to adopt a wide ranging series of reforms touching on agriculture and industry, trade, investment and education.

As elsewhere, the basic reforms included a progressive reduction of import restrictions, convertibility of the dinar for current operations, and privatization. Despite the effects of the Gulf War, economic growth was steady in the early 1990s, reaching a high of 8.2% in 1992. GNP per inhabitant in 1990 was US$1,440, as compared with US$950 for Morocco. As Tunisian GNP approaches the threshold of US$1,500, multinationals are beginning to set up shop – Pepsi Cola arrived in 1995 with an advertising blitz, McDonalds may well follow, although why anyone in

Tunisia would want to swap the magnificent local food for such pap is anyone's guess. Most spectacular incomer in 2001 was Carefour which opened a hypermarket near La Marsa.

In the decade 1985-95, Tunisians saw a remarkable improvement in their living standards. The shops are full of consumer durables, the newspapers full of job advertisements, around 80% of Tunisians own their own homes. Basic foodstuffs continue to be subsidized, and rural development programmes are taking electricity and telephones to the remotest areas. The National Solidarity Fund (generally known as the 26-26 after its post office account number), closely supervised by the President, has done much for the poorest in society.

Although the cost of economic transition will be high, the future for the Tunisian economy is promising on the whole. Tunisia has been fortunate in not being an oil-dependent economy – like Jordan, linked to the fortunes of the Gulf. The fact that Tunisia only had a brief flirtation with socialism at the end of the 1960s has made the whole privatization process much easier. In terms of Africa, Tunisia is number two after Mauritius in terms of jobs created by industries relocating from Europe and elsewhere.The question remains whether the recent changes will actually produce results, turning Tunisia into a fast growth economy, a 'Mediterranean dragon' to use a cliché much bandied about in the local press.

A Mediterranean dragon?

Culture

People

Tunisia's population has undergone enormous changes since independence. In 1961, the population stood at just over 4 million. In 1994, it topped the 8.7 million mark. The growth rate has slowed dramatically, however, from 2.75% per annum in 1961 to 1.85% per annum in 1993. This is the result of sustained family-planning programmes. In a part of the world where population growth rates of 3% and above were current, Tunisia exercised a rare control over its population, with an average 2.2% growth for the period. A real improvement in purchasing power, nutrition, and a move by women into formal employment has accompanied this demographic slowdown. In 1994, average annual income was 23 times higher than in 1961, 1,706Dt as against 74Dt.

Population

So what does a typical Tunisian look like? The question is not an easy one to answer, as the population of contemporary Tunisia is the result of a long history during which various settlers passed through the country. While the earliest populations of northwestern Africa were probably of Hamitic stock, the ancestors of today's Berbers, there have been numerous other inputs (including Phoenicians and Romans, and in particular the **Arabs**, who first began to arrive in the eighth century.) The mid-11th century Hilalian invasions strengthened the Arab component, arabizing the **Berber**-speaking countryside, and removing the Arab/Berber divide which has remained so important in Algeria and Morocco. Until the mid-20th century, there was an important and ancient **Jewish** community, based in Tunis, Kairouan and the southern island of Djerba. This was reinforced, particularly in the 18th century, by highly educated and talented groups Jews from Livorno in Italy. Many Jews left Tunisia after the foundation of the State of Israel in 1948. As of the late 18th century, a **European** population settled in the coastal towns, and was particularly numerous in the mid-20th century. This population was mainly of French, Italian and Maltese origin, with a few Greeks and even the odd White Russian. There is a **sub-Saharan** African component to Tunisia's population, originally the result of the slave trade. In physical terms, then, an average room full of Tunisians at, say, a business meeting will not look very different from Brazilian or Spanish counterparts.

European travellers to Tunisia in the 19th century distinguished between three groups: the **Turks**, the **Moors** and the **Arabs**. The Turks were the ruling and military élite, and Ottoman Turkish was their prestige language. In court circles, it was practice to take wives of southern European origin, often captured in pirate raids on Italian islands or brought over from Istanbul. Travellers wrote of the Moorish population of the cities, who were described as being refined and polite. Seventeenth-century immigrants from Andalusia were a component of this population, but had been absorbed into the mass of Arabic-speakers.

The most important divide, however, was that between **townspeople**, sedentary countryfolk, and **nomads** ('the Arabs'.) There was a clear split in ways between the city people, the *beldia* (a term meaning 'people from the *balad* or town') and the nomads (*el 'arab*). Mannerisms, speech, and dress were highly different.

These socio-ethnic divisions have long since disappeared with the abolition of the monarchy and massive rural exodus after independence. Certain regional types can still be distinguished, however. The inhabitants of Sfax tend to be pale skinned, and have a distinctly Iberian look. People from coastal towns like Kélibia, Haouaria and Bizerte tend to look very Mediterranean, too. There are certain faces which to the insider look very Sfaxi or Djerbian, and others which are distinctly *'aroubi* ('from the country') – something in the shape of the face, perhaps. The older generation of Tunisians, particularly the country people, are shorter than their European counterparts. However, lifestyle for the urban middle classes differs little from that of southern Europeans. The rural regions, until recently fairly behind, are catching up fast. There are now very few parts of the countryside without electricity. Basic infrastructure is being put in everywhere, and as a result, life expectancy will rise.

Tunisians differ greatly from northern Europeans in the way their lives are focused, however. The **family** is of primary importance, determining a person's life chances to a great degree. Family loyalty is of great importance, with the father seemingly the dominant figure – although very often wives rule the roost. Islam is a strong force, laying down the limits of what can and cannot be done. The home is a private place – but strangers, when a friendship forms, are readily invited in. On the whole, however, men meet their friends in cafés, while women socialize in each others' homes. In some of the larger cities, there are places where young people of both sexes mix in cafés and restaurants – the Makni Centre and the Arcades in the El Manar area of Tunis, for example.

Tunisian society is changing rapidly. Today, just over 60% of the population is urban. The main cities have expanded enormously over the last 20 years. Tunisia's old families, and the brightest and best connected of the university educated élite, have done very well for themselves since independence from France in 1956. The second generation urban populations have new aspirations, however, and expect (and indeed are getting) some part of the national cake. Affluence is growing and Tunisia's people have seen their society transformed in the 45 years since independence. Education, some form of health care and consumer goods are available in a way unthinkable a couple of generations ago. Tunisia is well on the way to achieving the egalitarian society of which those who fought for its independence dreamed.

Arts and architecture

It is undoubtedly the great museums of Carthage and the Bardo which have the finest collection of objects from ancient times

Tunisia has a rich and diverse archaeological heritage along with a wealth of characteristic buildings and craft forms. There are over 40 museums under state management and another 15 or so managed by a number of official and private institutions. Exhibits are housed in old palaces (Rakkada), in forts (Monastir), government buildings (Sfax), purpose-built mansions (Dar Cherait, Tozeur) and on Punic/Roman sites (Kerkouane, Sbeïtla).

Prehistory

The earliest traces of human settlement in Tunisia go back to 800,000 BC. Towards 5000 BC, new populations, probably the ancestors of today's Berbers, are thought to have arrived. They brought with them a nomadic form of pastoralism. There are prehistoric remains at **Ellès**, near **Makthar** (tombs), and in the **Oueslatia** region west of Kairouan (a few isolated rock paintings and tombs). For information, neighbouring countries have some very fine prehistoric rock art, notably the Jebel Akakus and the Messak Settafet regions of the Fezzan, Libya's south-western province.

Carthaginian & Numidian period

When Rome was founded in 753 BC, the coast of Tunisia was already on the trade routes of Phoenician merchants. Inland areas were inhabited by a people called the *Numides* by the Romans – hence the name Numidia for the Roman province covering part of what is now Tunisia. There were a number of Berber kingdoms with zones of influence, and there were alliances and conflicts with the Numidian people during the Punic Wars which pitted Rome against Carthage. Important Numidian towns included the settlements which were to become Roman **Chemtou**, close to Jendouba, and **Dougga**. Evidence of Numidian artistic skills has survived in the form of a funerary monument at the latter site, the famous Libyco-Punic mausoleum, dating from the first half of the second century BC. The building features Egyptian cornices and Greek-style Ionic columns.

Little has survived of Punic building – apart from the remains of some sturdy housing on Byrsa Hill, **Carthage**, and ground floor walls in the round town of **Kerkouane**. History has looked on the Carthaginians with a rather cruel eye, partly because of anti-Punic Roman propaganda, partly because they left little in material terms, unlike the Greeks with their temples and the elegant Etruscans. Carthaginian pottery bears no comparison with Greek black figureware, and there is practically no statuary. Nevertheless, Carthaginian graves have produced numerous funerary offerings: small plates, jars and containers, incense burners, jewellery and amulets of various kinds. Among the more intriguing items discovered are ostrich eggshells with painted faces, probably a symbol of new life. Tiny glass pendants featuring human faces were also popular. Sacred razors, incised with varied motifs and scenes, and also part of the offerings left with the deceased, bear witness to Carthaginian skill in metal working, as does the display of Punic jewellery in the Bardo Museum.

Roman period

In contrast to Punic times, the Roman period has left the visitor to Tunisia with a wealth of sites to visit – and the finest collection of Roman mosaics in the world, housed in the Bardo Museum. The Romans were a practical lot, and so careful was their engineering that some of their greatest buildings – sections of the **Zaghouan to Tunis aqueduct** (originally 80 km long), the great amphitheatre of **El Djem** – have survived in an amazingly intact state down to the present day.

Some of the remains of the Roman towns in northern Tunisia are truly impressive. To the Romans, as later on to the Muslim Arabs, the city represented the home of civilization, and across their African territories the Romans laid out new towns on a grid iron pattern (see Haïdra) or overbuilt existing settlements – as at **Dougga** and **Carthage**.) The typical town which the visitor can see today centres on a forum and temples, and has extensive public facilities, including baths, a circus, a theatre and basilicas. There is also generally a triumphal arch or two, reminder of some benefactor emperor.

Temples The temples are generally the most impressive feature – especially at Dougga and **Sbeïtla** – and were derived from Greek and Etruscan models. Greek columns were the fashion from the second century onwards, but only covered the front of the temple, not all four sides, as in the Hellenic world. Accessible by steps, set at the heart of the Roman towns, the temples are the most striking buildings to have survived, even in their ruined state. Initially, temples were built to a trinity of gods, Jupiter, Juno and Minerva. Later in the empire, they were dedicated to deified emperors. When Christianity took root, they fell into disuse, as they were too small to house congregations, being built for ceremonies carried out by leading citizens and a priesthood. Great basilicas took their place, and remains of these can be seen in many of the Roman cities.

Statuary The influence of the Greek-speaking eastern Mediterranean was marked in another domain, that of statuary, samples of which (often minus head and limbs) can be seen in museums and archaeological sites across Tunisia. Perhaps we are a little blasé today when we look at Roman statuary. It is easy to forget that the Romans lived in a world without the instant images of today. Statuary, in stone and clay, played important social functions.

The **bust** was one of the most widespread forms of statuary. Portraits in stone were a way of spreading one's influence, of building family prestige. It was through statues that emperors could make their authority felt. The great families of the empire, old and *nouveaux riches*: any leading member of a major family would be immediately portrayed after his death. A **death mask** would be made, to be carried in procession at the funeral – along with the death masks of other members of the family. Thus ancient lineage could be displayed and a pecking order of important families maintained.

The emperors used busts and other statuary for propaganda purposes. Statues of Augustus and his successors, often larger than life, showed them as athletic men in the prime of life. Examples of such statuary can be seen in the museums at the Bardo and Carthage. Growing Greek influence can be observed at work in the fashions here as well. In earlier times, emperors are shown clothed. Later, with the mode for all things Greek, they were portrayed nude, with bodies that suggest gym workouts on a regular basis. The truth of the matter? Sculptors had a range of models, and practice was to add a lifelike portrait head to a standard body.

Street furniture: the honorific arch Statuary would have been displayed in niches on the triumphal arches which were very much a feature of Roman towns, and Africa is the province where the largest number have survived Good examples can be seen at **Dougga**, **Haïdra**, **Macthar** and **Sbeïtla**, while at **Tripoli**, (ancient Oea) in Libya, an arch to Marcus Aurelius survives on the edge of the old town. Although both the Egyptians and Greeks were familiar with the arch, they made no wide-scale use of it in building. The Romans, with their well-honed engineering skills, were able to build large arches without using mortar.

Urban arches of triumph were originally built to celebrate great military achievements. They were not related to the city walls, but were generally built on the street along which the victor's procession was to pass. Sometimes they are located outside the city. Later, arches would be dedicated by a city to an emperor who had been particularly generous. Basically, the Roman triumphal arch was a spectacular piece of street furniture – functioning rather like the Arc de Triomphe on the Champs Elysées, or the Porte de France in Tunis, an 18th-century arch which is all that remains of the walls on the east side of Muslim Tunis. One of the most spectacular arches is in Libya at

Leptis Magna, a great four-way construction decorated with reliefs commemorating the imperial family and military successes. In out of the way archaeological sites across Tunisia, very often the arch is the most spectacular piece of Roman building to have survived in some sort of intact form – see the arch at **Zanfour**, for example.

The Roman villa, built to a courtyard plan with colonnades and tiled roofs, was a cut above the Carthaginian dwelling in elegance and comfort. Wealthy citizens of Roman Tunisia liked to impress their neighbours, as the mosaics and statuary found in their villas clearly indicate. They also had elegant furniture including couches, bronze oil lamps and tripods and objets d'art, although little of this has survived and in all likelihood, there were wall paintings, although none of these have survived.

Villas

   It is the mosaics which are the clear indicator of the existence of disposable incomes for elaborate interior decoration in second and third century Africa.

In modern Tunisia, the finest survival of ancient times is undoubtedly the mosaic. The earliest mosaics go back to ancient Greece. In its most primitive form, mosaics of pebbles were used to cover floors. The **earliest figurative mosaics** date from fourth century BC Greece. The first mosaics made from specially cut stone cubes (*tesselae*) date from the early second century BC. The new more refined technique – known as *opus tessellatum* – created a smoother, more compact surface and meant that objects could be portrayed in much greater detail. It quickly became popular right across the Greek-speaking lands of the eastern Mediterranean. It also became increasingly sophisticated: fine lines of coloured stone allowed the artists to reproduce a huge range of tone and colour, to the point that certain ancient writers referred to the technique as *opus vermiculatum*, literally 'worm-style technique' (from the Latin *vermiculum*, 'little worm'), so fine were the lines.

The art of the mosaic

   The mosaic became popular in Italy, and fine mosaics dating from the second and first centuries BC have been discovered at Pompei. By the first century AD, the mosaic was a decorative technique used right across the empire, used along with the painted wall-fresco and statuary of Greek inspiration to decorate private homes and public buildings. Local schools of mosaic work grew up. Italy, for example, was known for its black and white mosaics. Africa, however, was to develop large and elaborate multi-coloured mosaics.

   The oldest figurative mosaics in Tunisia date from the beginning of the second century AD. The early figurative mosaics were composed by artists who were brought over from the Hellenistic regions of the eastern Mediterranean. These mosaics have a number of Hellenistic traits: they rival wall paintings in their subtle tones and detail; the themes – Nile landscapes, rural idylls, and the post-banquet 'unswept floor' motif – were popular in the East. Later, towards the end of the second century AD, strong **regional schools of mosaic work** emerged. New themes became popular, generally inspired by daily life in Roman Africa: hunting, the sea, the amphitheatre games and life on the farm. Sometimes these mosaics have captions. In the later third century, technique declines, becoming cruder. Mosaics become more abstract, and some, executed for early Christian buildings, have a strong symbolic charge, only obvious to the initiated observer, given that the Christian communities were initially persecuted. In the mid-fourth century, **Christian mosaic work** emerges. From this period date a fine portrait of a female saint (today in the Museum of Carthage) and more naïve work such as that from certain Tabarka Christian tombs.

   It is generally thought that mosaic work largely disappeared in the sixth century under the Vandals. However, recent finds at Thuburbo Majus contradict this view. After the Arab invasions of the seventh century, mosaic work disappeared from Africa, although the Fatimid caliph of Mahdia called in mosaicists to decorate his palace in the 10th century.

Background

Mosque terminology

jami' *mosque*

minaret *tower from which the call to prayer is made*

mihrab *door-sized niche in wall of mosque, indicating the direction of Mecca*

minbar *preacher's chair, often elaborate*

midha *ablutions area*

muezzin *the man who performs the call to prayer from the minaret*

medresa *institute of higher education in classical Islam*

taleb *student*

The buildings of Islam In 682, the Arab general Okba Ibn Nafi' and his army crossed the Maghreb, bringing with them a new revealed religion, Islam. This religion was to engender new architectural forms, shaped by the requirements of prayer and the Muslim urban lifestyle. The key building of Islam is of course the mosque, which evolved considerably from its humble beginnings as a sort of low platform from which the call to prayer could be made, becoming an elaborate tower designed to demonstrate the power and piety of ruling dynasties.

Mosques Mosques cannot generally be visited in Tunisia by the non-Muslim visitor, with some notable exceptions, including the colonnade of the Zitouna Mosque in Tunis and the Great Mosque of Okba Ibn Nafi' in Kairouan. Minarets, visible from afar, are not always easy to photograph close to, being surrounded by narrow streets and densely built up areas. Tunisian minarets are generally a simple square tower, with a small 'lantern' feature on the top, from which the muezzin makes the call to prayer. There are unusual exceptions, however, including the octagonal minarets of the Hanefite mosques (see Yousef Dey and Hamouda Pacha mosques in Tunis) and some of the simple whitewashed vernacular structures on Djerba (see El May near Houmt Souk). Some mosques bear witness to Almohad origins – the Kasbah Mosque in Tunis, for example – and are characterized by an interlinked lozenge pattern, executed in stone. (The Giralda tower of the Cathedral of Seville started life as an Almohad minaret.) Minarets tend to feature blind horseshoe arches and a small dome on the topmost 'lantern' room. On top of the dome is an ornamental feature resembling three metal spheres on a pole, topped by a crescent. This is the *jammour*: tourist guides have several entertaining explanations for this, for example, that the spheres represent the basic ingredients of bread (flour, water and salt).

Mosques tend to have large covered prayer halls, comprising a series of narrow transepts, created by lines of arches supporting flat roof terraces or, more rarely, pitched roofs (see Testour). There will be a main 'aisle' leading towards the *mihrab* (prayer niche) which indicates the direction of Mecca, and for prayer. The main nave in the traditional Tunisian mosque does not however have the same dimensions as the main nave of a Christian cathedral. Note that Islam does not favour representation of the human form. The oldest mosques make extensive use of masonry, including columns and their elaborately carved capitals, recycled from Roman sites. Later mosques, (18th and 19th century) may have much elaborate marble marquetry, carved plaster work and ceramic tiling. (See the beylical tombs, Tourbet el Bey, in the Médina of Tunis.) There is no religious pictorial art. The same dense decoration can be found in upper class 18th and 19th century domestic architecture too. A mosque will also have an open courtyard, occasionally with a decorative fountain. Modern mosques often adopt hybrid styles. In the Cap Bon, tall space rocket minarets are popular.

Medersas The non-Muslim visitor can get a very good idea of Muslim sacred architecture by visiting one of the medresas, the colleges which were an essential part of the Tunisian Muslim education system from mediaeval times onward. Perhaps the most spectacular are at the three medresas complex near the Zitouna Mosque in Tunis: the oldest medresa, the Nakhla or Palm Tree Medresa is simple; the latest in the series, the Slimaniya (mid-18th century) features tiles, stucco and black-and-white horseshoe arches. Here the austere students' rooms come as something of a shock after the elaborate decoration of the courtyard.

Perhaps the most easily photographed of the old mosques is the Mosque of Okba Ibn Nafi' in Kairouan, set close to the walls of the old town. However, this great building, one of the finest early mosques, is an exception in that it stands towards the edge of the city. Mosques and medresas are generally surrounded by buildings. The visitor to Tunisia quickly has to learn to navigate through the narrow streets of the médinas or old towns to reach the monument or museum to be visited.

Historic médinas

In much 19th-century writing, the médinas of the Maghreb – and of the Arab world in general – were seen as chaotic places, which although harbouring exotically clothed populations, were also home to disease and ignorance. The médina was taken as a metaphor for the backwardness of the *indigène*. In fact, the tangled streets of the average Tunisian médina are no more disorganized than many a European mediaeval town. Today's visitor will immediately be struck by the external walls in *pisé* (sun-dried clay, gravel and lime mix). Disorientation due to narrow alleys and high walls sets in later, perhaps after leaving the main souks.

The médinas of Tunisia do, however, obey a logic, satisfying architectural requirements arising from climatic and religious factors. The climate is hot in summer, but often very cold in winter. In the coastal towns, damp sea air is a problem, while inland there are hot summer winds from the South. The city therefore has to provide protection from this climate, and networks of narrow streets are the ideal solution. Streets could be narrow as there was no wheeled transport, there being plenty of pack animals for carrying goods around. Narrow streets also ensured that precious land within the city walls was not wasted.

Logic of the médina

For housing the Muslim family, the courtyard house was the ideal solution. This of course is an architectural model which goes back to Mesopotamia, Greece and Rome. For Islamic family life, with its insistence on gender separation in the public domain, the courtyard house provides a high level of family privacy. In densely built up cities, the roof terraces also provided a place for women to perform household tasks – and to share news and gossip. The biggest houses would have several patios, the main one having arcades on two levels. Thus extended families could be accommodated in dwellings with large open areas. Old Tunisian courtyard homes are not generally easy to visit, however. In Tunis and Sousse, there are houses which have been restored and altered to function as upmarket restaurants or retail spaces (in the Kasbah district of Tunis, for example see the nineteenth century residences like the **Dar Jeld** and the nearby **Dar Chahid**, aka **Dar Hammouda Bacha**) or private museums (lovingly restored **Dar Essid** in Sousse.) In Tunis, the visitor can discover a good concentration of Tunisian artefacts in a lovingly restored patrician house, the **Dar Ben Abdallah**, in the central Médina. You may well be invited into ordinary homes, however, where fridges and pressure cookers are in use alongside traditional braseros in the main courtyard.

The traditional city house

The **courtyard home** is the most characteristic building in Tunisia's cities, discrete and anonymous to all but a neighbourhood's inhabitants from the outside, spectacularly decorated in its patrician form on the inside. There are other, more rustic, building traditions which have only recently fallen out of use, however, the best known being the **fortified granaries** or *ksours* of the areas south and east of

Vernacular architectures

Tataouine, and the stone-built citadel villages (*kalaât*) in the same region and over in the Matmata Hills. The latter region also has the **underground dwellings** made famous by the Star Wars films. Tozeur has its characteristic yellow brick work, while the Djerba countryside is dotted with the austerely beautiful *menzels*, whitewashed courtyard dwellings totally in harmony with the natural environment.

Beautiful though they often are, the vernacular building styles are under threat. They are often more vulnerable to the weather than modern buildings, and despite excellent qualities in terms of temperature regulation, they need maintenance. Reinforced concrete building is becoming popular, and carries the prestige of being 'modern'. However, in the southern regions, mock vernacular architecture is often used for hotel buildings. Vaults and decorative detailing of vaguely Berber inspiration can be found on hotels and restaurants. The tourist industry may yet fuel some sort of return to traditional – and more ecological – building typologies.

Coastal strong-points On the coasts of Tunisia can be found interesting forms of military architecture. **Monastir** and **Sousse** have their *rbats*, early mediaeval fortresses built to defend the Muslim communities of the Sahel. And at coastal towns, there are numerous fortifications of early modern European inspiration. In the 16th century, the southern Mediterranean coasts were targets for expansionist Spain. Coastal strong-points such as **Bizerte**, **La Goulette**, **Porto Farina**, and **Tabarka** were occupied, all the better to control the Mediterranean. In the 16th century, Hapsburg Spain was still at the height of its glory as an imperial power, and the Nova Arx, a particularly elaborate piece of military architecture, was erected outside Tunis, equipped with all the most up-to-date features of the military architecture of the day. There were monumental gateways, cannons, watchtowers and sharp-angled bastions. When the Ottomans finally triumphed in Tunis, they continued to build and extend existing fortifications, notably at **Kélibia**, **Le Kef** and **Porto Farina**, as well as on **Djerba**.

20th-century architecture The heart of the contemporary Tunisian city is very much a late 19th century achievement, and there is a good variety of interesting architectural styles to observe. Except in the case of Tunis, old city walls were not totally demolished and re-used as development land, but kept as part of a buffer zone between old and new. The new areas had large open spaces planted with regular rows of trees, while a system of avenues in the new neighbourhoods (*villes nouvelles*) provided a grid for new apartment building and villa developments, as well as linking into a system of highways leading in and out of the city. After the destruction of the Second World War, the French became interested in preserving the aesthetic face of the city – witness the replanning of the area around the walls of Sfax.

In Algeria, the French had caused considerable destruction in the old cities, demolishing and pillaging entire neighbourhoods. In Tunisia, they wished to present themselves as protectors of the former Ottoman regency. Part of this policy was to display a respect for traditional building styles and crafts – hence the development of the *style arabisant* or neo-Moorish style for public buildings. The style, which involved extensive use of mock minarets, domes and horse-shoe shaped windows, originated in Algeria, were it was known as the *style Jonnart*, after the prefect who promoted it. In Tunisia, the *style arabisant* appeared in private villas, mainly the work of one Victor Valensi, and official buildings, designed by **Raphaël Guy**. Tunis and its suburbs, Sfax, Sousse and Bizerte all have fine examples of the style.

In the 1930s, most official commissions for buildings tended to go to French architects – which meant that architects from Tunisia's big Italian community had to look to the private sector. The result was some very fine Art Déco and modernist apartment buildings in the Lafayette and Passage districts. Among the architects active at the time were **René Audineau** (Hotel Ritza, 1929-30), the **Maltese Joss G.**

Ellul (Villa Boublil, rue d'Autriche, 1931-32), and **Georges Piollenc** and **Marcel Royer** (the Colisée cinema complex in downtown Tunis, also dating from the early 1930s.) **Victor Valensi** designed the Synagogue Daniel Osiris on avenue de la Liberté. One of the most surprising buildings of this period is the **Villa Zodiac**, a modernist country house built to a perfectly radiocentric plan situated in the countryside south of Grombalia near Hammamet. The story goes that the villa was built as a present from a leading member of the Italian community to **Mussolini**.

The post-Second World War period in Tunisia produced some interesting building. All construction materials were in short supply, and for a short period, 1943 to 1948, a strong team of architects, many of whom had started their careers in Morocco, were in charge of seeing that the country got new public buildings. The vernacular building style of the **Sahel**, with its whitewashed courtyard houses with their vaulted rooms was the model adopted for schools, training centres and administrative buildings across Tunisia, many of which can still be seen today. One of the team's leading architects, **Jacques Marmey**, was to stay in Tunisia where he continued to build. The former presidential palace at Rakkada, Kairouan is a Marmey building.

In the 1960s, Tunisia was proving to itself and the world that it was a modern nation. **Olivier Clément Cacoub** emerged as the leading architect, favoured by the President Bourguiba – and a number of other African presidents too – for the design of official buildings and hotels. The Hotel Aïn Oktor is a Cacoub building, as are many buildings in Monastir, President Bourguiba's hometown which was also redesigned by Cacoub.

In the late 1990s, new official building and hotels across Tunisia often incorporated features of traditional architecture in a throw-back to the neo-Moorish style of the early 20th century. The attention to the styling of more workaday buildings which was such a feature of protectoral architecture seems to have disappeared. Much of the new building in Tunisia's town centres relies on marble or mirror glass for effect. In the suburbs, very little building is architect-designed at all. Local builders make use of their imaginations, often with surprising results – for example the pagoda roof atop suburban villas in the Cap Bon towns.

Contemporary painting and photography

Given Tunisia's proximity to Europe, easel painting soon took root after the arrival of the French protectorate. (A stay in North Africa had already been a popular source of inspiration for numerous European painters, for whom Algiers or Tangiers was all exotic street scenes, cavalcades in movement, and sharp, often violent colour contrast.) A number of European artists passed through, the most important being **Paul Klee** and **Auguste Macke**. Struck by the light of the intense light and the forms and colours of St Germain (today's Tunis suburb of Ezzahra) and Kairouan, Klee was to draw on his experience in Tunisia for the rest of his career. **Alexandre Roubtzoff**, a White Russian who chose to settle in Tunis, documented local life with his line drawings and oils, while **Rodophe Baron d'Erlanger** painted oils of his adopted village, Sidi Bou Saïd, and its people. In the 1940s and 1950s, a number of self-taught Tunisian painters emerged, the so-called Ecole de Tunis. Some of these artists were self-taught, others trained at the Tunis Ecole des beaux arts or abroad. Some chose to imitate European styles, while others opted to illustrate the rich heritage of oral literature and the streetlife of their hometowns.

After independence in 1956, a generation of Tunisian painters came to the fore, working in a number of registers – calligraphic, abstract, naïve. **Nja Mehdaoui** produces vast expanses of calligraphic signs, while **Rachid Koreïchi**, an Algerian until recently based in Tunis, works with a repertoire of talismanic symbols and Arabic script in a variety of materials. **Adel Megdiche** produces scenes of strangely distorted voluptuous figures, often inspired by ancient Arab myth. **Rafik El Kamel** tries to capture daily life, the street scene, in a semi-abstract form while self-taught **Ahmed El Hajeri** creates a dream-like universe of swelling, supple forms where humans have an almost feline, animal appearance. **Gouider Triki** and **Abderrazak Sahli**, both of whom have withdrawn to their home villages, produce canvases filled with objects and figures of a strong hieroglyphic quality. Among the younger generation of painters, born in the 1960s and now coming to the fore, are **Meriem Bouderbala**, **Rim Karaoui** and **Asma M'naouar**. One of the strongest of contemporary painters is undoubtedly **Tahar M'guedmini** whose strong rounded forms executed in oil present figures and dreamscapes drawn from the painter's home island of Djerba.

Tunisia also has some interesting contemporary photographers, including **Jacques Perez**, best known for his colour work and **Jellel Gasteli**, whose primary focus is black and white. The wide-open rocky spaces of the Tunisian South and the subtle play of light on whitewashed walls have been recent sources of inspiration.

Unfortunately, there is as yet no museum of contemporary art, but there are frequent exhibitions in galleries in Tunis, Sousse and Hammamet. The plan to open a national gallery of contemporary art in the restored Palais de l'Abdaliya in the upmarket Tunis suburb of La Marsa has been shelved. (The ANEP, the heritage promotion body is to get the premises.)

Urban and rural crafts

Although Tunisia does not have the same reputation as Morocco for its craft industry, the visitor will find much of interest. In the souks of the historic cities, interesting ceramics and vivid carpets can be found. There is the delicate tracery of wrought iron, painted wood products and some fine basket work. Basically, the traditional arts divide into two categories, rural and urban. Urban crafts are generally taken to be more refined, displaying an Andalusian influence, while rural crafts, especially textiles, are very popular with visitors.

But rural and urban crafts are different in many other ways too. Rural craft items – carpets and woven items such as saddle bags and tent strips, pottery, jewellery – were, and still are, to a great extent produced in very different conditions to urban items. Rural craftwork is solid, practical, made to stand up to long years of use in places of harsh climatic extremes. Carpets and pottery are made by women, while jewellery and metal utensils by men in small country settlements. The signs and symbols used to decorate these items are generally geometric, arranged in simple, repetitive combinations to pleasing effect. Lines, dots and dashes, lozenges and squares are combined to cover surfaces made from clay, metal and wool. Sometimes these decorative forms are linked to the tribal marks tatooed on women's faces and arms. The isolation of rural communities meant that the peoples of different areas could develop very individual styles of craftwork. This is apparent in weaving, clothing and women's jewellery. But given the fact that craft-made items were subject to harsh conditions of use, few pieces can be safely said to be more than 100 years old.

Striking colour and form are often features of rural crafts. The *bakhnoug* and the *ta'jira* were the traditional veils woven by rural women. Dyed deep bordeaux or indigo, these pieces of textile may be decorated with dense white geometric forms or naïve silk embroidery. Flat weave carpets from the Gafsa region often display strong colourful forms. The jewellery of southern communities was once made by Jewish craftsmen based in Djerba. It is always silver; necklaces include silver tubes and spheres, mixed in with rings and sometimes amber. Pottery once varied greatly from region to region, each area having very individual forms. With the spread of cheap plastic and hard-wearing enamelled utensils, most of the local forms have disappeared.

Where to see (and buy) tiles and pots

After a visit to the potters of Kallaine, Georges Duhamel wrote "I looked for potters, I found poets". The traditional ateliers and kilns of the Médina of Tunis have long since vanished, and there is not much poetry about a visit to Nabeul, although this is definitely the place with the most ceramic showrooms – something for all tastes. In Tunis, some of the shops on rue de la Zitouna have good selections of contemporary Tunisian pottery, ranging from the neo-Habitat to the natural browns and reds of Sejnène pottery from the North. For fans of old ceramic panels, the Café Mnouchi (at the intersection of souk es-Sekkajine and souk el-Kebabjiya) has a fine collection, many with figurative designs. Older collectors' pieces may

sometimes be found at the antique dealers on the rue des Glacières (street to the right of the British Embassy) and in any of the antique shops in the La Marsa/Le Kram zone. (Look out for work by the Chemla brothers). Perhaps the most reliable craft emporium is Driba, near the TGM station and opposite Arthé restaurant in Marsa Plage. On occasion they also have some interesting contemporary pieces.

Some of the finest tiled interiors are in the Médina of Tunis, notably at Dar Lasram (rue du Tribunal), Dar Husseïn and Dar Ben Abdallah, which also houses museum displays of traditional life in the Médina. Fine tile detailing can also be seen on many buildings in parts of the city dating from Protectorate (1881-1956).

In contrast, urban craft items are generally produced by men, often working in structured corporations. While the women folk of nomad tribes produced for their own use, men in towns were working to sell their produce. They did not, however, build up sufficient capital to develop production on a large scale. City craftsmen produced carpets, jewellery, pottery, leather items, and metal utensils. They worked the raw materials for their production. Urban jewellery is in gold, often set with precious stones, and very finely worked. Pottery was enamelled and decorated with designs flowing and floral as well as geometric. The leather workers produced footwear (*belgha*) and high quality bindings for the sacred texts. Traditional copper work included cooking pots and trays. Wooden items were often very elaborate in their decoration – witness the painted marriage chests and *porte-armes*. Mahdia had a great reputation for fine quality silk weaving.

Within living memory, Tunisia's cities had very locally specific forms of craft production. Today, certain craft items are mass-produced for the tourist market. However, older items can only be found in the antique shops of Tunis, where they go for very high prices – the aesthetic qualities of the finest Tunisian craftwork are much appreciated by collectors. Unfortunately, there is little new craft production of any great quality – with some notable exceptions, one of which is the art of ceramic tile making, a craft which has been established in Tunis since the 16th century and possibly earlier.

Multi-coloured ceramic tiles or *zlliz* were traditionally used to decorate the walls of the Tunisian city home. The fashion probably came from Andalusia in the 17th century – or possibly with the 'integration' of Tunis into that most loosely articulated of empires, the Ottoman Empire, as of the late 16th century. (The great Sidi Mehrez mosque in the Médina of Tunis had red, green and blue Iznik-type wall tiles until its restoration in the late 1970s.)

In folk memory, the holy man named **Sidi Kacem Ezzilizi** (the tilemaker) is generally cited as having brought tilemaking to Tunis. Little is known about him except that he was a tile maker for part of his life and that he was highly esteemed by the Hafsid sultans. In 1496, he was buried at his home on the western edge of the Médina, overlooking the Sedjoumi saltflats. Today it houses a small museum of

Tiles from Tunis

Background

Tunisian ceramics, with a fine collection of both urban and rural pottery. Transformed into a museum with Spanish help in the 1970s, the building, situated on the place du Leader, is instantly recognizable with its pyramid-shaped green-tiled roof, recalling the palaces of Morocco and Andalusia.

From the late 16th century, **Tunis'** potters and tilemakers set up their kilns and workshops close to Bab Souika on the eastern side of the Médina, in an area which even today is still known as *Kallaline* (the plural form of *kallal*, potter.) Three influences were at work in Kallaline pottery – Andalusian, Ottoman and Italian, and the result was a uniquely Tunisian style. The *cuerda seca* or dry cord technique was used to imitate the geometric designs of Hispano-Moorish ceramic mosaic: fine lines of manganese and oil were used to define a pattern on the tile and isolate areas to be filled in later with coloured ceramic. **Cuerda seca** tiles are rather rare (the technique must have required considerable skill and was therefore expensive.) In the eighteenth century homes which have survived with their decoration intact – notably Dar Lasram, the preference is to cover large surfaces with small (12 x 12 cm) tiles in two or three colours. The result, cool to the touch in hot weather, would have provided an ideal solution to the dilemma of what to use on walls instead of flakey whitewash.

Exuberant floral motifs, stylized cypresses, minarets and domes, and occasionally animals too, feature in large panels executed in harmonious shades of green, blue and yellow on a white ground. Tile manufacture at **Iznik** in Turkey was at its apogee in the 16th century and the stylized yet fluid lines of the tulips and carnations of the Perso-Turkish decorative vocabulary came to feature in Kallaline tiles. Some of the best examples can be seen at the 17th-century palace **Dar Othman**. The craftsmen of Kallaline were never able to imitate the celebrated Iznik red, however.

In the 18th century, Kallaline products were in high demand. The increasing prosperity of Tunisia under two strong Husaynid rulers, Ali II (1759-82) and Hammouda Pacha (1782-1814) saw the development of a pronounced taste for richly decorated interiors which was to the great benefit of the ceramic tile industry. Great expanses of interior walls were covered with tiles in luminous shades of green and blue, egg yolk yellow contrasted with black and white, the whole set between the grey white of marble flooring and bands of elaborately carved white stucco.

In the early 19th century, Tunisois or *beldi* taste was to move towards the more naturalistic leaves and flowers of Italianate tiles. Large quantities of *zelliz* were imported from Italy, and to satisfy market demand, Hammouda Pacha created new workshops at Gammarth on the coast north of Tunis, employing foreign artisans.

To deal with the Italian competition, the artisans of Kallaline were to make use of Italianate motifs, adapting them to local taste. Times were changing, however, and large Italian and Spanish 18 x 18 cm tiles came to be used before giving way to modern industrial tiles with a fine biscuit, more suitable for the modern apartment. As the way of life changed, the demand for traditional pots fell as well. Kallaline was unable to compete, and by the 1960s, the workshops and kilns had disappeared.

The Tunisian ceramic industry is still very much alive in the holiday town of **Nabeul**. As tourism developed, some bright spark realized that large quantities of blue and white plates and dishes were what the visitor wanted to buy in a Mediterranean resort. (Observing the mountains of pots sold to tourists, Jean Genet expressed the fear that in a few decades time there would be nothing left of Tunisia.) Today, the traditional subtle greens, yellows and aubergine have practically disappeared – except for a few of the larger *khabia* type jars. The higher quality traditional pots, often with metal decoration, are imported from Morocco. However, there is some rather nice contemporary Nabeul stoneware, and German expertise has established *La Rose des sables*, a company manufacturing fine porcelain for the upmarket dinner table.

Language

Who speaks what language? when? and to whom? The visitor to Tunisia will quickly become aware of the range of languages on offer. Street signs and official notices are in Arabic, French and occasionally in English, people talk to each other in Tunisian Arabic, but seem to throw in a bewildering number of French terms. In tourist areas, souk salesmen can blarney their way in English, German, Spanish and many other tongues.

The use of different language styles depends upon social, professional and geographic factors. **Spoken Arabic** is the everyday language of the cities, with the dialect of Tunis the most prestigious. Classical or **formal written Arabic** is the language of law, religion, official government activities and political speeches. A 'halfway form' of Arabic, **_darija muhadhaba_** ('educated dialect') is spoken in the school room to facilitate communication. Dialect is also used in advertising. **French** is the language of business, science and higher education, and while a mixed language, **Franco-Arabe**, is used by much of the urban educated élite on many occasions. **Italian** – in part thanks to the availability of Italian television – is often understood in the north. **Berber** is spoken in tiny rural communities in the Matmata region (Tamezret), near Tataouine (Douiret) and in some villages on Djerba. It is not a linguistic hot potato in the way it is in Algeria and Morocco – reference is never made to Berber identity in the other North African states in Tunisian media. When relations are tense with France, then shopfront signs in Latin letters may be temporarily painted out or covered in black plastic bags, generally part of a knee-jerk reaction to criticism of Tunisian internal policy in the French press.

Historically, Berber is the oldest language in North Africa. Latin was obviously the educated urban language in Roman times, and before that Punic, a Semitic language, was in use in Carthage and its satellite trading posts. In the 10th century, a characteristic Maghrebi form of spoken Arabic appeared. Fourteenth century historian Ibn Khaldoun tells us that the mixing of Berbers with the Arab invaders led to the development of a form of Arabic very different to that current in the Middle East. Present day spoken Tunisian Arabic goes back to the linguistic interaction between Arabs and Berbers in early medieval times. Arabic has a huge word stock, and the choice of basic lexical items, including the main verbs, is often completely different to those in use in Egypt and the Near East. Added to this, Tunisian urban Arabic took on massive numbers of French and Italian terms from the 19th century onwards. While Tunisians will easily understand educated Middle Eastern Arabic dialects, especially Egyptian, thanks to the film industry, the reverse is not true.

Today the Tunisian language situation is complex – and changing. Behind the multi-lingual screen lie a range of personal attitudes and aspirations. How you get on in life is linked to your language ability, and few Tunisians have any doubt that mastery of at least one European language is essential for access to science and technology. French is certainly vital for achieving a useful university degree and indispensable for a well paid job. At the same time, there is an oft expressed will to 'Arabize', cultivated by the generation which passed through the university system in the 1970s and early 1980s. (The future of the Berber-speaking communities will be interesting to observe.) Arabization has become bogged down in the process of creating terminology, and several competing national language academies, notably in Baghdad, Cairo and Damascus, are involved in trying to keep up with the flood of new words in the main world languages. The truth is that Arabic has lacked the effective language policy which updated Hebrew, for example, and transformed it into the language of the State of Israel in a generation. In any case, Tunisians are a pragmatic lot, and a Gadhafi style Arabic-only stance is unlikely: it would interfere with the making of money far too much. For the moment basic literacy in classical

Hannibal, national hero

Today, no-one really knows what Hannibal looked like. Carthage was not a state which put up statues to glorify its leaders – that practice came later under the Romans. Nevertheless, as a tribute to a national hero, the Banque nationale de Tunisie shows a helmeted, rather sad-faced Hannibal in profile on the green five dinar note.

Hannibal was born in the flourishing city of Carthage around 246 BC. Aged nine, he accompanied his father, Amilcar Barca on a long campaign against the Romans which took him to Spain, over the Pyrenees and on to the Alps. However, before taking over command of the Carthaginian forces from his brother-in-law Asdrubal in 221 BC, Hannibal received a humanist Mediterranean education from Greek tutors. For military instruction, he shared the life of the soldiers in the barracks and on the battlefield.

During the Second Romano-Carthaginian War (218-201 BC), Hannibal was to win great victories, notably the Battle of Lake Trasimene, in 217 BC, and the Battle of Cannae on 2 August 216 BC. Hannibal's master strategies for both battles are still taught to officer cadets today. Once back in Africa, Hannibal set up camp in the Sahel region of present-day Tunisia. Battle was joined with the Roman general Scipio at Zama in 201 BC. (The location of this battle is unknown, some think that it was fought at Jama near present day Siliana). The Roman army was to win over the Carthaginians thanks to the Numidian cavalry commanded by Massinissa, an ambitious prince in search of a kingdom. In 196 BC, Hannibal had himself elected as suffete in Carthage. His aim was to reform the government of a city-state undermined by infighting and corruption among its ruling class. But his political career was cut short, his ideas were too dangerous. In 195 BC, he was forced into exile in Asia Minor, an unwise choice as it turned out. In 183 BC, Hannibal's host, the king of Bythinia, betrayed him. Besieged in his residence at Libyssa on the shores of the Sea of Marmara in present day Turkey, Hannibal realized that there was no escape. He committed suicide, taking the poison he had had secreted in the setting of his ring. He was buried in a plain stone sarcophagus, with a simple but fitting epitaph: 'Here lies Hannibal'. Much later, the Emperor Septimius Severus, he too a North African, had a mausoleum in white marble erected to the legendary Carthaginian general.

Arabic, al 'arabiya al fusha, the language of Islam, looks set to maintain its position in the education system, especially at primary level, alongside French for technical and commercial purposes.

Contemporary society

In late 1990s Tunisia, institutions were being modernized, industry upgraded, the civil service reformed. Tunisian society is in a period of change – and it can be difficult for the Tunisian to explain to the outsider the factors, both historical and social, which have led the country where it is today.

Education & language
In 1956, Tunisia already had literate educated Muslim men – and a few literate women. The overwhelming majority of Muslim Tunisians were illiterate, however. Independent Tunisia had to put a comprehensive education policy together. In the the enthusiastic, 1950s, the Sadiki College, Tunisia's leading school was the model. From the mid-19th century, this top Tunis secondary school had provided quality bilingual education in Arabic and French, and many of the post-independence élite had been schooled there. (The leaders of the Jewish community had been through the French system.) The Sadiki model proved difficult to generalize, and in the 1980s,

the use of Arabic was extended to subjects previously taught in French. Pragmatically, however, scientific subjects were left in French – thus avoiding the disasters of the Moroccan educational system were the Arabization of all subjects led to parents pulling their children out of state schools and a huge growth in private sector education. Tunisia spends large sums on education, around 7% of GNP, and seems set to continue to do so.

Under the education minister Mohammad Charfi, Tunisia's school system underwent extensive reforms in the early 1990s. School textbooks and the curriculum were redesigned. Images which showed women solely in subordinate positions were removed, civic instruction was introduced. Religious education, which had been based on a very conservative understanding of Islam, was reformed, and is now based on the principle of *ijtihad*, 'interpretation', i.e. modernist re-readings of the sacred texts. The history curriculum was reformed to reduce the emphasis on the Arabo-Islamic side of Tunisia's history. *Tunisianité*, 'Tunisianess' became important, with Carthage and Rome, Hannibal and St Augustine in the school history books along with Ibn Khaldoun and Kheireddine. The teaching style, which had often favoured rote learning rather than developing creative skills and a critical mind, was reformed. The language issue seems to have been resolved.

The curriculum is in Arabic, with French used for teaching scientific subjects in secondary school. English, German, Italian and Spanish are all available as foreign languages in secondary school. The Arabic used is modern standard Arabic, a version of the Arabic of the Koran modernized in lexical terms in the 19th century. This language differs considerably in grammar and vocabulary from the spoken language. Children with Tunisian Arabic as a mother tongue have to learn a new range of verb and adjectival forms, rather as if the English speaking child had to learn to use Old English verbs with modern English vocabulary. This is manageable, although given translation and terminology problems, there is a severe shortage of reading material in Arabic.

At university level, the vast majority of subjects are in French, bar family and criminal law and Arabic literature and some of the humanities. Parents with means put their children in bilingual primary schools with greater resources and more modern teaching methods. At secondary school level, the children with a bilingual background have much better chances of passing the more difficult science and mathematics baccalauréats. And after secondary school, public-sector technology colleges and numerous private institutes provide training in secretarial skills, IT, management and accounting, mainly in French.

It remains the case, however, that both standard *fusha* Arabic and French are effectively foreign languages for most Tunisian children going into primary school. No six year old speaks these languages as a mother tongue. Although a more extensive use of Tunisian Arabic in the education system was mooted in the late 1950s, standard Arabic looks set to maintain its place. As it stands, the education system serves the needs of both nation and economy. The language option reinforces a certain conception of the national identity, while ensuring that a steady stream of graduates, operational in French, and increasingly in other European languages, come on to the jobs market to satisfy the needs of finance, industry and technology.

The Media

Since the early 1990s, the Tunisian news media have undergone some changes. Newspapers have been brightened up with new layouts, and a number of leisure magazines have appeared like women's magazine *Nuance*. Other magazines to look out for, if you read French, include the weeklies *Réalités* and *L'économiste maghrébin*. The French press, both newsmagazine and newspapers, sells in Tunisia, although not as well as a couple of decades ago. At over 1Dt, an imported newspaper is a luxury well above the

The musical baron

One of the most extraordinary sights in Tunisia is the Dar Nejma Ezzahra, an orientalist fantasy palace at Sidi Bou Saïd. The story of this building is inextricably linked with the life and enthusiasms of one Rodolphe d'Erlanger, musicologist and gifted amateur artist. The first d'Erlanger to rise to prominence was a French banker of German origin, born in Frankfurt in 1832. Emile d'Erlanger settled in Paris in 1858. Business boomed in the prosperous atmosphere of Napoleon III's Paris, and Emile was soon to acquire a Second Empire noble title. Married to an American, the first baron had four sons, including the Baron Frédéric, born 1868, a composer who was to build a career in London, and the Baron Rodolphe, born 1872, of Sidi Bou Saïd fame.

Rodolphe d'Erlanger studied in Paris and London. He showed an aptitude for painting, exhibiting in Paris at the 1903 Salon des artistes français. A further major exhibition followed in London in 1908. A number of his works can be viewed at the Dar Nejma Ezzahra today. But it is as a scholar of Arab music that the baron is chiefly remembered. Between 1930 and 1959, his six volume La musique arabe, ses règles, leur histoire was published by Paul Geuthner in Paris. In 1931,

King Fouad of Egypt named the baron president of the organizing committee of the first congress of Arab music, held in Cairo in the spring of 1932. Unfortunately, the baron was to ill to attend, and died shortly after on 23 April 1932.

The love of Rodolphe d'Erlanger's life was his wife Elisabeth, Bettina to the family, daughter of an Italian aristocrat and an American wife. It was during a visit to Tunisia that they acquired the cliff-top site on which they were to build their orientalist dream palace. (The Erlanger banking house had had important interests in Tunisia since the mid-19th century, making large loans to Sadok Bey's government in the 1860s).

Rodolphe and Bettina had a son, Léo, (died 1978), whose wife English wife, Edwina, was the last d'Erlanger to inhabit Dar Nejma Ezzahra, maintaining grounds and interior as her father-in-law would have wished. When the palace eventually passed into the hands of the Tunisian state, it was as the Centre for Arab and Mediterranean Music. Concerts are regularly held in the patio, and a specially designed display room houses the baron's collection of Tunisian musical instruments.

means of most people. Tunisians are not great readers and the news and current affairs programmes now available on satellite television channels fill the need for information.

In terms of the audio-visual media, Tunisia has one and a half TV channels, the rather stodgy ERTT and a second channel, Canal 21, also broadcast by the national TV organization for a couple of hours in the evening on the same wavelength as France 2. Canal 21 aims at the youth market. There is a huge demand for quality tele-vision – hence the massive sales of satellite dishes in Tunisia, clear proof that the local television stations have a market waiting for them. The challenge is there for Tunisian TV professionals to produce a wider variety of programmes of real national and local interest. For the moment, satellite television, and pay-channels such as Canal Plus Horizons, seem set to expand their share of the market.

Music

What sort of music do Tunisians listen to? Walking past a cassette stall, your ears will be assailed by unfamiliar tunes and voices. With technology for the mass-pirating of music so easily available now, Moroccan musical tastes have become increasingly catholic. Tapes are cheap too, between 1Dt 500 and 2Dt 500. Among young women, top-selling cassettes are by Arab singers, like the Iraqi **Kazem Essaher** and **Diana Haddad**, whose videos are shown on satellite TV. Algerian raï music is popular too;

Further listening

The most colourful introduction to Tunis's musical heritage is H. Abbassi and illustrator Slah Hamzaoui's Tunis chante et danse, 1900-1950 (Tunis: Alif, 2nd ed. 2000). The book comes complete with CD and takes you from the beginning of the gramophone era to just before independence – although don't expect any political manifesto songs. The Paris-based Club du disque arabe has published CDs of Tunisia's musical heritage, including La Malouf tunisien (ref AAA 054) and Musique judéo-arabe vol.2 La Tunisie (ref AAA 072). The latter includes songs by great singers of the 1900-50 period, including Habiba Msika, Louisa Tounsia and Raoul Journo. Other great voices from the past to look out for include Hédi Jouini, Chafia Rochdi and Le Kef's greatest singer, Saliha.

At present, the country's top divas, available in any cassette shop, are Cairo-based Latifa Arfaoui and Sofia Sadek. In a more classical vein, Sonia Mbarek comes a close third. Tunisia's 'Pavarotti' is the moustachioed Lotfi Bouchnak. At the arty-jazz end of the market, there is lute player Anouar Braham who has recorded several albums (all with ECM Records Munich) with other musicians. In Tunis, the better bookshops stock Braham CDs like the 1998 Thimar (combines lute, sax, clarinet and double bass), and the 2000 Astrakan Café (lute, clarinet and Tunisian percussion). If Anouara Braham is too cerebral, then try some mizoued (bagpipe) music, a rural sound with sounds that set the trend in the cities. Best known representatives are Hédi Habouba and Faouzi Ben Gamra. Tunisia's best musical export of recent years has been the Hadhara, a show bringing together religious chants from the country's main traditional tarika-s, as the brotherhoods which gather round Muslim saints are known. Pirate and copy-cat versions of the Hadhara can be found on cassette stalls.

Good places to buy Tunisian music are the cassette stalls on the Rue Zarkoun, Tunis, or Librairie Le Diwan, Rue Sidi Ben Arous, Tunis.

---

top stars include **Khaled**, **Mami**, **Cheb Zahouani**, **Cheb Hosni**, **Cheb Amro** and **Faudel**. Local mizoued (bagpipe) music is in fashion in some quarters. Once upon a time, mizoued was considered vulgar, associated with a down-market atmosphere of boozy wedding parties ending in late night brawls. (The worst mizoued has the same spine-searing quality as a chainsaw heard at a distance.) Today, in a big turn around, leading mizoued stars like **Faouzi Ben Gamra** and **Hédi Habouba** get on national television. Still at the downmarket end of the musical spectrum, musical kitsch reaches new heights with trash diva **Fatma Bousaha**.

The 'politically committed' sound of the leading 1970s and 1980s Moroccan groups like **Jil Jilala**, **Nass el Ghiwane** or **Lmachaheb** or the Lebanese **Marcel Khalifa** still has some fans. Western music is popular too, and not only with the urban middle classes. Adolescents and students go for Bob Marley and Dr Alban, Madonna and The Spice Girls, 2 Be 3 and other boys' bands. 'Romantic' singers like Quebec's Céline Dion and Witney Houston (whose songs also exist in Arabic cover versions) also have a big following in Tunisia.

There is of course a more classical taste in music. Tunisian traditional urban music is called malouf. During Ramadhan, Tunisian television broadcasts music by the **malouf** choirs. Maybe the violons and lutes, and mix of solo and choral singing aids the digestion. Also in a traditional vein, singers of the 1950s and 1960s have found new popularity, thanks to their wide availability on disc. Look out for in particular for **Hédi Jouini**, **Ali Riahi**, **Saliha** and **Oulaya**. In this tradition, contemporary individual singers such as **Lotfi Bouchnak**, **Sofia Sadok** and Amina Fakhet have great popularity. Their concerts at the Menzah Coupole (sports dome) or the Carthage amphitheatre draw audiences of thousands – and they can command huge fees for singing at upscale weddings. **Amina Fakhet** has a huge following – perhaps because people identify with her rags-to-riches tale and her frankness. At the arty end of the scale, lutist **Anouar Braham** has won international recognition with his contemplative jazz – Arab crossover style.

Also still popular in Tunisia – as elsewhere in the Arab world – are the great Egyptian and Syro-Lebanese singers who had their heyday in the 1950s and 1960s. **Um Kalthoum**, peasant girl from the Nile Delta who became diva of the Arab world is popular everywhere. Her songs have probably done more for promoting classical Arabic poetry than any school book. Other great names you may want to look out for from this period include Druze princess **Asmahane**, **Mohammad Abdewahab**, **Farid El Atrach**, the Lebanese divas **Fayrouz** and **Sabah**, **Najet Es Saghira** and the brown nightingale, **Abdel Halim Hafez**, who died tragically young of bilharzia. Concerts by singers and musicians, both Tunisian and Middle Eastern are regularly broadcast by the ERTT, the national broadcasting corporation.

Television   As you might expect, television is the most widely available form of entertainment, much watched at both home and in cafés. The long running South American soap operas, dubbed into classical Arabic, are popular, as are Egyptian soaps and films. The annual Tunisian Ramadhan soap operas have a loyal following. And of course sport is popular viewing among men, especially in cafés with satellite television. International football competitions are the big draw.

Increased wealth and almost universal availability of satellite television since the late 1990s has created a revolution in Tunisian viewing habits. When **France 2**, then Antenne Deux, was made available in Tunisia in the late 1980s, there was a mass-migration of francophone viewers to the French public channel. The late 1990s saw the rise of Arabic-language satellite television. Tunisian viewers can mix and match, catching episodes of the latest mini-series on Egyptian television, game-shows on Lebanese TV, then switching to Qatar-based news channel **Al Jazeera** for animated debate and the latest on Palestine, and over to European culture channel **Arte** for art-house film and cosmopolitan trends.

Cinema   Back in the 1950s, the ingredients for a good Arab film were a dose of kitsch, lots of sentimentality and plenty of singing under the stars on the banks of the Nile. Things changed in the 1970s with the return to Tunisia of young European-trained directors brimming with ideas. In the late 1980s, a clutch of Tunisian films won international prizes. The big factor in putting Tunisian cinema on the map was the success of Moufida Tlatli's 1994 **Les Silences du Palais**, a maid's-eye view of a mid-1950s Tunis aristocratic home.

Independent Tunisia set up its first film laboratories, the SATPEC, in 1967. However, it was President Bourguiba's wife's nephew, the flamboyant Tarak Ben Ammar, who got Tunisia on the international directors' circuit. In the ex-president's home town of Monastir, he set up a studio complex where Polanski filmed part of **Pirates** and (curiously) a number of films figuring Christ were made, including **Life of Brian** and Zeffirelli's **Jesus of Nazareth**. A further stimulus to the nascent Tunisian film industry was the creation of the Carthage Film Festival in 1966, which provides a bi-annual meeting point for the African and Arab film industries.

In the mid-1970s a few Tunisian films were taken on by international distribution companies, including Naceur Ktari's **Les Ambassadeurs** (1976), a sharp critique of the conditions of migrant workers in Europe, and Rida Behi's sardonic look at the side effects of tourism, **Le Soleil des Hyènes** (1977). In the 1980s a new generation of local film makers and production companies like Carthage Film and International Monastir Film reached maturity, putting the experience from international

Background

Further viewing

If you want to return to the beginnings of Tunisian cinema, Guillemette Mansour's 1998 book Samama Chikly *documents the early days. Developing from an earlier activist tradition, by the late 1980s and early 1990s, Tunisian directors had a growing reputation for quality work, based mainly on the films of Nouri Bouzid (*L'homme de cendres, Les Sabots en or, Bezness*), Mahmoud Ben Mahmoud (*Chichkhan*) and Férid Boughedir (*Halfaouine, Un été à La Goulette*). Mohamed Zran's* Saïda, *a tale of contemporary childhood in a tough Tunis suburb and Moufida Tlatli's* Les Silences du Palais *(secret loves and hypocrisy in a 1950s Beylical palace) seemed set to maintain the trend. Recent films (*La Saison des hommes, Satin rouge*) are disappointing lacking the poetry of much African and Iranian cinema or the creative edge and pace of Latin American films. Dance and theatre seem to have assumed the creative place once held by Tunisian cinema.*

The best place to buy Tunisian films on video is the Institut du monde arabe *in Paris.*

productions to good use. A series of highly individual films gained the respect of the local public, among them Nacer Khemir's aesthetic reworkings of the theme of lost Andalucía, **Les baliseurs du désert** (1984) and **Le Collier perdu de la colombe** (1991)) and Mahmoud Ben Mahmoud's **Traversées**.

At the end of the decade, producer Ahmed Attia's Cinétéléfilm came up with three highly successful art house films: **L'Homme de cendres** in 1986, **Les Sabots en or** in 1989 (both by Nouri Bouzid), and Férid Boughedir's **Halfaouine** in 1990. With 500,000 entries, **Halfaouine**, a loving and sometimes whimsical portrayal of growing up in Tunis in the 1960s beat all the records for a film in Tunisia. The sensitive treatment of sexuality and the separation of the sexes in the still codefied world of an old part of the city ensured the film's success.

For its bold treatment of prostitution, the effects of child abuse and the relations between the Muslim and Jewish communities, Bouzid's **L'Homme de cendres** was condemned by critics. (Tolerance and the coexistence of different communities is central to Mahmoud Ben Mahmoud's symbolic **Chichkhan** and Férid Boughedir's 1996 film **TGM**). Bouzid's **Les Sabots en or** grew out of his experience as a political prisoner in the 1970s. The subject matter, imprisonment and the effects of torture, drew in the audiences, and the public clearly wanted more. In his third film, **Bezness**, Bouzid went on to attack 'sexual tourism' while **Une fille de bonne famille** tackles that old chestnut, marital breakdown.

Tunis seems unlikely to become the Hollywood of the Mediterranean, though, even though parts of **Star Wars** were filmed near Tozeur and Matmata. Morocco has more spectacular and varied landscapes, plus major studios at Ouarzazate in the south. For many years, Tunisian cinema came somewhere between the private Moroccan film industry and the state-dominated Algerian industry. It is not easy producing for a market of only nine million people, and in the early 1990s co-productions between European TV stations such as Channel 4 and Tunisian companies dominated. Will the production of the *films d'auteur* which have made Tunisia's name on the international festival circuit continue? Various forms of French government funding directed at African cinema can no longer be taken for granted, and Canal Horizons, the African version of French pay-channel Canal 4, folded in 2001. Little mourned, it was clearly killed off by the variety available of television coverage available on satellite. The country's cinemas specialize in Hindi melodramas, soft porn and Jean-Claude Van Damme. Art house films need ideas, and what passes for an original idea in Tunisia is often a cliché elsewhere. Tunisia's films please the local public and seduce festival juries. Whether the laws of international distribution will allow them to reach a wider audience is another

Background

question. While Mahmoud Ben Mahmoud **Les siestes grenadine** and Mohamed Zran's **Saïda** seemed to indicate a renewal in the late 1990s, the latest productions such as the 2002 **Satin rouge** are a clear illustration of a recent sub-genre of Tunisian film, 'oppressed Muslim woman finds freedom', seemingly made to confirm the stereotypes held by French audiences.

Sport (especially football)

While Tunisia has volleyball and handball teams which have been very successful in African and Arab competitions, football remains the number one spectator sport. At age six or seven, the little lads are out in the street or on a piece of rough ground, kicking a football around. Their heroes are teams like Tunis rivals **Espérance** (known as **Taraji** in Arabic) and **Club Africain**, and players like Ronaldo and Zinedine Zidane, captain of the French team which won the 1998 Mondial. In 2002, the Tunisian team participated in the Japan-Korea World Cup, although being in a difficult group, it was eliminated in the first round. Football, as in the other North African countries, is a great unifying factor. If local politics is dull, then football gives people – or rather men – something to debate. The deeds and doings of football stars can be read about in detail in the local press.

Dress & fashion: from chéchias to Nike

In old Tunisia, city men and women covered their heads when they went out, the latter with a *sefsari*, an ample sheet-like wrap (in cream coloured silk in Tunis), the former with a turban. However, to wrap a few metres of fabric on top of your head, you need a base, and this was provided by a wool felt cap, generally red, called the *chéchia*, the production of which was a whole craft industry in Tunis in the 17th and 18th centuries.

A symbol of national resistance in the Thirties and Forties (and part of postmen's uniform), the *chéchia* today is really only worn by older men. Arab specialist Jacques Berque, writing in the late Fifties, observed the end of traditional dress in his work *French North Africa*: "Head and loins resist longest: floating tunics, wide trousers and turbans persist". European-style shoes had become acceptable for "there was never any quarrel about shoes, whereas traditionalists long continued to consider narrow trousers obscene and hats or caps an outrage against religion". Today's Tunisian youth prefers the baseball cap, whereas sefsari wearing is limited to older or less-educated women – for younger women it is considered a *cache misère*, or just practical for nipping out to the corner shop if you can't be bothered to dress properly.

Tunisian traditional dress was a mixture of influences. The city gent would wear lose-fitting pantaloons or *serwel*, a tightfitting *sedria* or shirt and *fermela* waistcoats. Over this would be worn a lose fitting sleeveless tunic or *jebba*, woollen for winter, linen or raw silk for summer. (When the modern shirt appeared in the 19th century, it was called a *souriya*, a Syrian garment, as it was first introduced by Levantine merchants and dragomans.)

As in other cultures, dress had a high symbolic charge. Imams of the two main Muslim communities of Tunisia, the austere majority Malekites and the more aristocratic Hanefites could be distinguished by their turbans. At certain periods in North Africa, the Jews were required to adopt the *ghiar* (distinctive dress): in Tunis this was colour-based – light blue clothing with a black chéchia. However, after the abolition of the ghiar with the 1859 Fundamental Pact, the Jews were quick to adopt European dress. In the late 19th century, young reform minded Muslim Tunisians adopted the *chéchia mejidi*, the taller 'fez' type headgear popularized by the Young Turks.

In the 1990s Tunisia acquired an annual traditional dress day. Civil servants and ministers appear in full rig, and local TV runs features on tailors and weavers. However, as with other things, this new interest in tradition is a sign of change in society – change that it may be difficult to acknowledge. Any form of fundamentalist type dress is highly frowned upon, and if they have the means, today's young Tunisians want to wear Nike sweats and trainers, (real and imitation), and the latest MTV fashions.

Tunisia's population is moving towards a 75/25% urban rural divide. The land no lon- **Daily life**
ger provides the living it used to, expectations are higher, parents want their children to have some chance of an education – and this is most easily available in the
towns. In the country life is often hard, with women obliged to carry water, firewood
and animal fodder over long distances. But even this is changing, as rural development projects, often sponsored by the Fonds national de solidarité, bring electricity
to isolated *dachras*. Improved roads follow, then drinking water.

In the cities, life has improved for the inhabitants of the self-build housing areas,
the *quartiers spontanés* of city planning jargon. Essential infrastructure is being put
in, the streets no longer fill with water when it rains. As the formal economy pros-
pers, the city centres and tourist zones offer many employment opportunities for the
low-qualified. There are plenty of people with money to buy from a street stall selling cigarettes, chewing-gum or fruit, there is work on building sites and in factories.
And there is a chance of better housing, as government projects 'restructure' areas of
crude concrete housing, bringing in water and electricity.

For the middle classes, opportunities have never been better, even though
recruitment into government service has been cut back. There are, however, jobs in
multinational companies, the banking sector and the new service economy. Tunisia's
cities have a prosperous air. The tree-lined down-town streets, though increasingly
traffic ridden, are lined with shops with smart clothes and consumer durables. For
those with salaries, there are car and home loans. Domestic help is available for two
career families, there is a enormous range of consumer goods on offer, although
often at European prices. For the bright and energetic, the prospects are good –
although good connections and inherited family wealth do help.

Religion

The people Tunisia, and of North Africa, for that matter, follow Islam in the main, a
religion similar to Judaism and Christianity in its philosophical content. Muslims
recognize that these three revealed religions have a common basis, and Jews and
Christians are referred to as *ahl al-kitab*, 'people of the book'. (Both Moses and
Jesus are prophets for Muslims.) There are considerable differences in ritual, public
observance of religious customs and the role of religion in daily life between the
revealed religions, and when travelling in Tunisia it is as well to be aware of this.
Note, however, that although the Islamic revivalist movement has in recent years
been a force in neighbouring Algeria, in Tunisia, the situation, for historic and
social reasons, is very different.

Islam is an Arabic word literally meaning 'submission to God'. As Muslims often
point out, it is not just a religion, but a way of life. The main Islamic scripture is the
Koran (often also spelt Quran in English), again an Arabic term meaning 'the recita-
tion'. Islam appeared in the desert oases of western Arabia in the early seventh century AD. The isolated communities of this region were Jewish, Christian or animist,
existing on oasis cultivation and the trade in beasts of burden. There was considerable inter-tribal warfare. It was in this context that the third great revealed religion
was to emerge. Its prophet Mohammad was a member of the aristocratic Meccan
tribe of Quraysh, born c.570.

The **Koran** divides into 114 souras or chapters, placed in order of length running from the longest to the shortest. Muslim and western scholars disagree on
the nature of the Koran. For the true Muslim, it is the word of God, sent down via
the Prophet Mohammad. The Koran appeared in this way in segments, some in
Mecca, some after the Prophet was forced to leave Mecca for Médina. The later
souras tend to have a more practical content, and relate to family and inheritance

Special couscous

The end of the Hijra or Muslim year, Ra's el 'Am el Hijri, comes about 20 days after Aïd el Kebir, the main annual Muslim festival. Ra's el 'Am commemorates the Prophet Mohamed's departure from Mecca, where he was persecuted by the leaders of the tribe of Qureysh, for Médina, where he was to lay the basis for the new Muslim community. This anniversary is celebrated by Tunisian families in an almost ritual manner with a favourite dish, kuskusi bil-qadeed, couscous prepared with lamb dried and salted after the Aïd, and beans.

Traditionally, the right shoulder of the sacrificial lamb is not cut up. It is spiced with harissa, black pepper and garlic, then left out in the sun to dry. Then it is boiled well in olive oil, and placed in oil, in a large terra cotta jar or khabia. According to a religious tradition, the sacrificial lamb is to be divided into three parts, one to be eaten, one to be preserved, and one to be given to the poor. Another tradition runs that the destiny of the Muslim pater familias is inscribed on the shoulder bone of the sacrificial lamb. Thus it would be unfortunate if this bone were broken, as it would harm this future.

Times have changed, of course, and not all families actually prepare qadeed today. Nevertheless, many Tunisian families will bring the Muslim new year in with kuskusi bil-qadeed, along with rich green mouloukhia, (a sort of stew) to ensure that the coming year will be prosperous, and a fish dish, to bring good luck. In Tunisia, as in many Mediterranean countries, fish (hout) wards off the evil eye, so it is a good idea to yuhawit (prepare fish) on important occasions.

law, for during the period in Médina, an embryonic Muslim community was taking shape. Western scholars, however, have opened up more critical approaches to the Koranic text and the way it was assembled. During the Prophet's lifetime, nothing was written down. After his death, fragments of the text, noted in simple script on parchment or flat bones, were assembled at the order of Abu Bakr, Mohammad's successor or khalifa. In fact, the Arabic script was not fully codified at the time. the language of the Koran was to eventually to become the base reference point for the Arabic language.

The Koran does not cover all aspects of the Muslim's life – and it became apparent to early Islamic rulers that they would need another source. The hadith, short statements which recount what the Prophet is supposed to have said about various issues, were assembled to provide a crucial supplement to the main scripture.

The practice of Islam is based on five central points, the **Pillars of Islam**, namely the shahada or profession of faith, salat or prayer, sawm or fasting during the month of Ramadhan, zakat or giving charity, and the hajj or pilgrimage to Mecca which every Muslim is supposed to accomplish at least once in their lifetime. The **mosque** is the centre of religious activity. There is no clergy in Islam, although major mosques will have an imam to lead prayers. In principle, the mesjed, a small neighbourhood mosque, will have someone chosen from the area with enough religious knowledge to conduct prayers correctly.

The **shahada** is the testament of faith, and involves reciting, in all sincerity, the statement, "There is no god but God, and Mohammad is the Messenger of God." A Muslim will do this at **salat**, the prayer ritual performed five times a day, including at sunrise, midday and sunset. There is also the important Friday noon prayers, which include a sermon or khutba. When praying, Muslims bow and then kneel down and prostrate themselves in the direction of Mecca, indicated in a mosque by a door-sized niche in the wall called the qibla. The voice of the muezzin calling the faithful to prayer five times a day from the minaret provides Muslim cities with their characteristic soundscape. Note that a Muslim must be ritually pure to worship. This involves washing in a ritual manner, either at the *hammam* (local bathhouse) or the *midha*, the ablutions area of the mosque.

A third essential part of Islam is the giving of **zakat** or alms. A Muslim was supposed to give surplus revenues to the community. With time, the practice of *zakat* was codified. Today, however, zakat has largely disappeared to be replaced by modern taxation systems. The practice of *zakat al fitr*, giving alms at 'Id El Fitr, the Muslim holiday which marks the end of Ramadan, is still current, however.

The fourth pillar of Islam is **sawm** or fasting during Ramadan. The daytime month-long fast of Ramadan is a time of contemplation, worship and piety – the Islamic equivalent of Lent. Muslims are expected to read 1/30 of the Koran each night. Muslims who are ill or on a journey, as well as women breast-feeding, are exempt from fasting. Otherwise, eating, drinking and sexual activity is only permitted at night, until "so much of the dawn appears that a white thread can be distinguished from a black one".

The **hajj** or pilgrimage to the holy city of Mecca in Arabia is required of all physically-able Muslims at least once in their lifetime. The *hajj* takes place during the month of Dhu al Hijja. The 'lesser pilgrimage' to the holy places of Islam is referred to as the *'umra*, and can be performed at any time of year. Needless to say, the journey to Mecca is not within every Muslim's financial grasp – fortunately, perhaps, as the mosques would probably be unable to cope with the millions involved, despite the extension works of recent years.

The Koran and the hadith also lay down a number of other practices and customs, some of which are close to the practices of Judaism. Sexuality, provided it is within marriage, is seen as positive, and there is no category of religious personnel for whom marriage is forbidden. Sensuality and seduction, between the married couple, are encouraged, without any guilt being involved. Eating pork is out, as is drinking alcohol and gambling. In the matter of dress, habits have changed hugely in recent years. Young women no longer automatically cover their heads as their mothers did. (The veil disappeared after independence.) Even the 'headscarf and long dress', the modern version of Islamic dress, widespread in Egypt, for example, is rarely seen. Tunisian Islam, and indeed North African Islam as a whole, is a long way from the more extreme forms practised in Saudi Arabia, where women are forbidden from driving and are all but invisible in the public sphere. While in traditional families the women's domain is most definitely the home, Islam does not stop the overwhelming trend for Tunisian women to get themselves educated and into jobs once thought of as being exclusively for men. In any case, with the rising cost of living in the 1990s, urban professional families came to consider two salaries essential.

Background

Land and environment

Geography

The Republic of Tunisia has a surface area of 163,610 sq km. It measures 750 km from north to south and averages 150 km from west to east. The Gulf of Tunis is included in the northern coastal (330 km) zone while to the south, forming part of the east facing coast (1,270 km), are the Gulfs of Hammamet and Gabès, the latter lying between the islands of Djerba in the south and Kerkennah in the north. Tunisia is far from being a mountainous land: less than 1% of the land is over 1,000 m and more than 65% is under 350 m; the highest land is in the north and west. Nor is this a land of rivers: the one major river is the Oued Medjerda, in the north.

Borders Tunisia has a long land border with Algeria, with a multiplicity of crossing points. It has a short land border with Libya, the crossing point at Ras Jedir being well used at present – although this may change since air links were resumed in 2000 with the ending of the embargo. The Tunisia/Libya offshore boundary dispute over the El Bouri oilfield in the Gulf of Gabès was arbitrated in favour of Libya. Tunisia and Libya are, however, contemplating joint development of other oilfields lying across their offshore boundary. Relations with Algeria, neighbour to the west, are generally cordial and border disputes here are unlikely. On the other hand, the maritime boundaries with Malta and Italy have yet to be settled and may prove a source of difficulties in the future. Should offshore oil be found in what tiny, resource-poor Malta considers to be its territorial waters, problems may well arise.

Main regions Tunisians tend to be deeply attached to their home regions, and even when they move away for work, they return home frequently. The most populated area is the economically dominant eastern seabord. Regions with strong identities include Tunis, the Cap Bon, the Sahel, the Djerid and Djerba, all of which are well defined in geographic terms.

Three main physical regions can be distinguished. **Northern Tunisia** has a rugged north-facing coastline – an extension of the mainly sandstone Algerian Atlas which rises into a distinctive range known as the Northern Tell. In places these uplands with altitudes exceeding 1,000 m are covered with cork oak and pine. The southern flanks of the Tell in the Béja region are lower, more open and more fertile. To the east are the rich alluvial plains around Bizerte. The Oued Medjerda, Tunisia's only major perennial flow, cuts a wide fertile valley to the south of these ranges flowing northeastwards to enter the sea in the Gulf of Tunis. This is the major agricultural region noted particularly for cereals. Further south, aligned southwest-northeast, is an extension of the higher, broader and mainly limestone Saharan Atlas. This forms the distinctive Dorsal/High Tell region with its harsher climate and sparser vegetation. The Dorsal range, includingTunisia's highest point, Djebel Chaâmbi at 1,544 m, ends in the northeast at the Cap Bon peninsula, Tunisia's richest region, with a mild climate, fertile soils and a dense population.

Central Tunisia is a lower central plateau of semi-arid steppe land. Its harsh environment renders the area bleak and barren, especially in the west. Only the lower, eastern steppe offers opportunities for stock raising and cereal cultivation. The Sahel, a low-lying and flat westward extension of the coastal plain, has seasonal salt lakes and sandy soils with a widespread, dense cover of olive groves which are supported by light rainfall, heavy dews and the tempering influence of the Mediterranean Sea.

Southern Tunisia, lying south of the steppes and stretching from the Algerian border to the sea, is an area of low-lying salt lakes or *chotts*, some below sea level, which are flooded during the winter and which dry to give extensive seasonal salt flats. Other depressions, where the water table is exposed or very close to the surface, produce the spectacular green oases of date palms. The depressions in the north and the level summits of the Djebel Dahar to the east give way to the sand dunes of the Great Eastern Erg and rocky wastes.

Tunisia's largest river is the **Oued Medjerda**, the Bagrada of the Romans, which runs across northern Tunisia from the Souq Ahras area in Algeria to the Gulf of Tunis. It has been heavily engineered for irrigation purposes and carries only a moderate flow in its easterly reaches. Elsewhere the streams are short *oueds* which often drain internally into seasonal **salt lakes**, the largest complex being in the Chott El Djerid, south of Gafsa. *Oueds* in spate are dangerous and in recent memory heavy floods in the south have carried away whole villages. Travellers should not attempt to cross *oueds* in flood and should certainly not camp in stream beds. **Rivers**

Climate

The climate of northern Tunisia is archetypically Mediterranean with hot dry summers and warm, wet, westerly winds in winter. Moving southwards, Saharan influence increases and the landscape becomes progressively more arid. Rainfall is irregular and decreases progressively to the south with annual averages ranging from 1,000 mm in northern regions to 200-400 mm on the central plateau and less than 200 mm in the south. Rainfall, nowhere reliable, is most regular in the north. Although there was heavy rainfall in the 1995-96 winter season, subsequent years have been dry, with winter 2001-02 being particularly hard for farmers. Humidity is generally low, especially away from the coast and towards the south. In July and August, high temperatures and humidity combined can prove a trying combination in the coastal areas.

The prevailing wind is from the west, though in summer northeast winds also occur. A fierce, hot sirocco-type wind from the Sahara, the *shihili*, takes temperatures into the mid 40°C range, relative humidity to 10% and has serious effects on human and plant life. Temperatures are influenced by proximity to the coast. Average temperatures increase to the south and extremes of temperature between day and night occur in the desert. For the visitor, summers can be hot by day and over warm at night on the coast and unbearably hot (45°C) by day and surprisingly cool (10°C) by night inland. Winters are pleasantly mild in the north in the lowlands but temperatures fall quickly with altitude, while high daytime desert temperatures plummet at night making it 'too cold to sleep'.

Flora and fauna

Tunisia has a wide variety of natural habitats. The **Mediterranean coastline** is varied, with rugged inaccessible cliffs and smooth sandy bays. Coastal wetlands include deltas, salt marsh and estuaries, while inland lakes and reservoirs provide freshwater sites. The **maquis** and the **garrigue** contrast with the agricultural areas, while **mountain ranges** such as the Atlas provide their own climate, delaying flowering and shortening seasons. Even the **desert** areas provide contrasts with the sands (erg), gravels (reg) and rock (hammada) set with the occasional oasis.

However, many habitats are under threat, either from pollution, urbanization, desertification or advanced farming techniques. Conservation issues are beginning to attract interest, and a number of National Parks and Nature Reserves have been set up. It is probably too late to save many wetland sites, the greatest casualty being Lac Ichkeul near Bizerte. Once a wintering site for thousands of waders and geese, it

Background

Scorpions – the original sting in the tail

Scorpions really deserve a better press. They are fascinating creatures, provided they do not lurk in your shoe or shelter in your clothes. They belong to the class Arachnida as do spiders and daddy longlegs. There are about 750 different kinds of scorpions. The average size is a cosy 6 cm but the largest, Pandinus imperator, the black Emperor scorpion of West Africa, is a terrifying 20 cm long. The good news is that only a few are really dangerous. The bad news is that some of these are found in North Africa.

They really are remarkable creatures with the ability to endure the hottest desert climates, revive after being frozen in ice, and survive for over a year without food or water. They have a remarkable resistance to nuclear radiation, a characteristic yet to be proved of great use.

Scorpions are nocturnal. They shelter during the heat of the day and to keep cool wave their legs in the air. They feed on insects and spiders, grasping their prey with their large claw-like pincers, tearing it apart and sucking the juices. Larger scorpions can devour lizards and small mammals.

Their shiny appearance is due to an impervious wax coating over their hard outer shell which protects them from any water loss. They have very small eyes and depend on their better developed senses of touch and smell. The sensitive bristles on the legs point in all directions and pick up vibrations of movements of potential prey or enemies. This sensitivity gives them ample warning to avoid being seen by heavy-footed humans.

The oft reported 'courtship dance' before mating is merely repeated instinctive actions. The grasping of claws and the jerky 'dance' movements from side to side are a prelude to copulation after which the male departs speedily after the 'dance' to avoid being attacked and devoured.

Most scorpions retreat rather than attack. They sting in self-defence. The sting is a hard spine and the poison is made in the swelling at the base. The sole of the bare foot, not surprisingly, is most often the site of a sting, and the advice in the section on Health (see page 63) is not to be ignored. The African fat-tailed scorpion is described as aggressive and quick-tempered. It is responsible for most of the reported stings to humans and most of the human fatalities in North Africa. The beautifully named Buthus occitanus, the small Mediterranean yellow scorpion, and Leirus quinquestriatus, the African golden scorpion, also have neurotoxic stings that can be fatal.

now attracts barely a hundred greylag geese. Nevertheless, in the future the environmental education programmes in schools may have an impact on wider awareness of the environment.

In both the Mediterranean and desert regions, wildlife faces the problem of adapting to drought and the accompanying heat. The periods without rain may vary from four months on the shores of the Mediterranean to several years in some parts of the Sahara. Plants and animals have, therefore, evolved numerous methods of coping with drought and water loss. Some plants have extensive root systems; others have hard, shiny leaves or an oily surface to reduce water loss through transpiration. Plants such as the broom have small, sparse leaves, relying on stems and thorns to attract sunlight and produce food. Animals such as the addax and gazelle obtain all their moisture requirements from vegetation and never need to drink. Where rain is a rare occurrence, plants and animals have developed a short life cycle combined with years of dormancy. When rain does arrive, the desert can burst into life: plants seed, flower and disperse within a few weeks, or even days.

Many animals in the desert areas are nocturnal, benefiting from the cooler night temperatures, their tracks and footprints revealed in the morning. Another adaption is provided by the sandfish, which is a type of skink (lizard) which 'swims' through the sand in the cooler depths during the day. Perhaps the most remarkable example of adaption is shown by the camel. Apart from its spreading feet which enable it to walk on sand, the camel is able to adjust its body temperature to prevent sweating, reduce urination fluid loss and store body fat to provide food for up to six months.

Mammals have a difficult existence throughout Tunisia, due to human disturbance **Mammals** and the fact that many of the species are not well adapted to drought. Many have, therefore, become nocturnal and their presence may only be indicated by drop-pings and tracks. Some mammals common in northern Europe can, nevertheless, be seen in the Mediterranean environments and these include fox, rabbit, hare, Red, Fallow and Roe deer and at least three species of hedgehog. Despite wide-spread hunting, wild boar are common wherever there is enough cover in decidu-ous woodlands. Hyenas and jackals still thrive in many areas but the attractive fennec, whilst still fairly common in Tunisia is frequently illegally trapped. Typical woodland species include the red squirrel (the grey variety from North America has not been introduced), garden dormouse, which readily hibernates in houses, pine and beech martens and the polecat. The cat family, once common, is now rare, but the lynx hangs on in some areas. The leopard, formerly common, is now extinct. There are at least three species of gazelle in North Africa, the Dorcas gazelle preferring the steppes, the mountain gazelle inhabiting locations over 2,000 sq m especially where there is juniper forest, and the desert gazelle locating in the region of the northern Sahara. The latter is often hunted by horse or vehicle, its only defence being its speed. There are also many species of bat, all of them insectivorous. Recent ringing has shown that bats will migrate according to the season and to exploit changing food sources. Many species have declined in recent years due to insecticides and disturbance of roosting sites. Desert rodents include the large-eyed sand rat, the gerbil and the jerboa.

Tortoises are widespread in North Africa. The best distributed is Hermann's tortoise **Reptiles &** which can reach a maximum size of 30 cm. Pond terrapins are small freshwater tor- **amphibians** toises and can be found in all the Mediterranean habitats. Both tortoises are unfortu-nately taken in large numbers for the pet trade, and may be seen, along with chameleons, on sale in the souks. There are over 30 species of lizard, the most common being the wall lizard, which often lives close to houses. Sand racers are frequently seen on coastal dunes, while sand fish and sand swimmers take advantage of deep sand to avoid predators and find cooler temperatures in the desert. The ocellated lizard is impressive in size, growing to 20 cm. Geckoes are plump, soft-skinned, nocturnal liz-ards with adhesive pads on their toes and are frequently noted on house walls.

There are some 30 species of snakes in the Mediterranean areas alone, but only the viperine types are dangerous. These can be identified by their triangular heads, short plump bodies and zig-zag markings. The horned viper lies just below the sur-face of sand, with its horns projecting, waiting for prey. Sand boas stay underground most of the time, while other species twine themselves around the branches of trees. Most snakes will instinctively avoid contact with human beings and will only strike if disturbed or threatened.

The Mediterranean is a land-locked sea and it is only in the extreme west that there **Marine life** is any significant tidal range. Without strong tides and currents bringing nutrients, the Mediterranean is somewhat impoverished in terms of marine life. Fish and shell fish, nevertheless, have figured prominently in the diet of the coastal people for cen-turies, with sardines, anchovies, mullet, sole, squid and prawns being particularly popular. Tuna and swordfish are also widely caught. Over-fishing, leading to the depletion of stocks, has become increasingly problematic, especially with incursions

Background

by the well-equipped Italian fishing fleet into Tunisian waters. Of the sea mammals, Tunisia has a small colony of Mediterranean monk seals on the outlying northern archipelago of La Galite. Dolphins are also occasionally seen off the coast.

Butterflies & moths Because of the lack of vegetation on which to lay eggs, butterflies are scarce in the steppe and desert areas. The Mediterranean fringe, in contrast, is often rich in species, some quite exotic. The life cycle – mating, egg production, caterpillar, pupa, butterfly – can be swift, with some species having three cycles in one year. Some of the butterflies are large and colourful, such as the swallowtail and the two-tailed pasha. The most common butterflies in the early spring are the painted ladies, which migrate from North Africa northwards, often reaching as far as Britain. Other familiar species include the Moroccan orange tip, festoon, Cleopatra and clouded yellow. Moths are also widely represented, but as they are largely nocturnal they are rarely seen. Day flying moths include the Burnet and hummingbird hawk moths. The largest moth of the area is the giant peacock moth, with a wingspan of up to 15 cm.

Birds Neither the Mediterranean nor the desert areas is particularly rich in resident bird species, but both can be swollen temporarily by birds on passage. Four categories of birds may be noted. Firstly, there are the **resident** birds which are found throughout the year, such as the crested lark and the Sardinian warbler. Secondly, there are the **summer visitors**, such as the swift and swallow, which spend the winter months south of the Equator. **Winter visitors**, on the other hand, breed in northern Europe but come south to escape the worst of the winter and include many varieties of wader and wildfowl.

Passage migrants fly through the area northwards in spring and then return southwards in increased numbers after breeding in the autumn. Small birds tend to migrate on a broad front, often crossing the desert and the Mediterranean Sea without stopping. Such migrants include the whitethroat, plus less common species such as the nightjar and wryneck. Larger birds, including eagles, storks and vultures, must adopt a different strategy, as they depend on soaring, rather than sustained flight. As they rely on thermals created over land, they must opt for short sea crossings such as the route running via Tunisia, Malta and Sicily, where birds run the gauntlet of the guns of so-called 'sportsmen'.

Tunisia has a number of **typical habitats** each with its own assemblage of birds. The Mediterranean itself has a poor selection of sea birds, although oceanic birds such as gannets and shearwaters will enter the Mediterranean during the winter. Wetland areas may be home to varieties of the heron family such as the night heron and squacco heron, while spoonbill, ibis and both little and cattle egrets are common. Flamingoes breed in a number of locations when conditions are right. Waders such as the avocet and black winged stilt are also typical wetland birds. Resident ducks, however, are confined to specialities such as the white-headed duck, marbled teal and ferruginous duck. On roadsides, the crested lark is frequently seen, while overhead wires often contain corn buntings, with their jangling song, and the colonial bee-eaters. Mountain areas are ideal for searching out raptors. There are numerous varieties of eagle, including Bonelli's, booted, short toed and golden. Of the vultures, the griffon is the most widely encountered. The black kite is more catholic in its choice of habitat, but the Montagu's harrier prefers open farmland.

The desert and steppe areas have their own specialist resident birds which have developed survival strategies. Raptors include the long-legged buzzard and the lanner, which prefer mountain areas. Among the ground-habitat birds are the Houbara bustard and the cream coloured courser. Dupont's lark is also reluctant to fly, except during its spectacular courtship display. The trumpeter finch is frequently seen at oases, while the insectivorous desert wheatear is a typical bird of the erg and reg regions.

Flora

Most of northern Tunisia, as mentioned above, is in the Mediterranean region, and was covered by evergreen forest. Man has intervened extensively since then and there is a variety of plant life for the visitor to discover – many of the larger species having been imported from elsewhere in the world. The spring flowers which cover the fields, hillsides and ancient ruins of the north are a particular attraction for people from lands where farming relies more heavily on pesticides.

Hotel & villa gardens

The visitor's first contact with Tunisian plant life will probably be the hotel garden. Here there will be plants introduced from other Mediterranean climate regions, but now firmly established in North Africa. That great and colourful climber, the **bougainvillaea**, smothering walls with its sprays of purple, red, yellow and white 'paper flowers' will inevitably make an appearance. Bougainvillaea was introduced to Europe from Brazil in 1829, and in fact it is the papery bracts which surround the tiny white flowers which provide the colour. Hotel and villa gardens are also home to **hibiscus**, an import from China particularly popular for hedges. Among the climbers there will be pale-blue flowering plumbago, and various red and orange 'trumpet-flowering' climbers from the USA. **Datura**, originally from South America, and easily recognized by its great white bell flowers is elegant – and poisonous. Both datura and *Cestrum parqui* are highly scented. The latter, called *misk el lil* ('musk of the night') in Tunisian Arabic, has highly perfumed creamy yellow flowers. **Jasmine** is also essential to hotel and private gardens. Two pinkish-white flowering varieties are popular, *Jasminum officinale*, and the *Jasminum grandiflorum*, which – as its name indicates – has big flowers and larger, more rounded leaves. Both are used to make the *mashmoum*, the jasmine bouquet which is an indispensable fashion accessory for a Tunisian summer evening, worn jauntily behind the ear or in a corsage. Making a mashmoun involves carefully inserting jasmine buds on fine stems of alfa grass. The stems are bound together with a cotton thread, an orange or fig leaf provides a cradle for the unopened buds, which are held together with another thread, which, once removed, allows the flowers to open during the evening.

Streets & roadsides

Tunisia's city streets are planted with shade trees doing daily battle with the vehicle pollution. Varieties of hardy **ficus** are popular, which cut into a box shape on maturity, provide shade. They also provide an evening roost for great flocks of starlings (*asfour ez zitoun*, 'olive tree birds') in winter, unpopular with the local authorities for the large amounts of guano they leave behind. Palm trees are also popular for urban avenues, where both the ordinary date palm and the elegant *Washingtonia*, which grows to great heights, can be seen. Look out too for the **Norfolk Island pine** (*Araucaria heterophylla*), a relative of the monkey puzzle tree from Chile, with its distinctive frond-like branches. It gives an exotic touch to residential neighbourhoods by the sea. Its original home, Norfolk Island, is way down in the Pacific, between New Zealand and New Caledonia. Back on the city streets, there are plane trees, which provide leafy shade in summer, but let in the light in summer, and purple flowering **jacaranda** with delicate foliage and great sprays of pale mauve flowers.

Of the roadside trees, the eucalyptus is the most popular, although sadly many have been ripped out due to road widening schemes. **Eucalyptus** originally come from Australia, where they grow in open savannah. Tunisia has some old stands of eucalyptus forest (see the approach to Sidi Mechrig in the north), but most eucalyptus are roadside trees (see the M'saken to Sfax road). The tree grows fast, and many species have two types of leaves, broader on saplings, slender, green and dangling on the mature tree. Another characteristic tree is the rapid growing black poplar, seen in the north.

Background

The rarest fruit (and some veg)

*In any large Tunisian city, it is worth taking a look at the main fruit and vegetable market to see what's on offer. In May, the soft, apricot-coloured **bousa'a**, as the medlar-fruit is called in Arabic, are ready. Easily bruised, quick to soften, they are rarely seen in northern European markets. In late June, a special delight can be found, the **boutabguia**, an unusual flat peach (**pêche de vigne** in French). When ripe, the **boutabguia** has wonderfully juicy white flesh. In July, crunchy little pears appear, known as **inzas bouguidma**, literally, 'bite-sized'. Still in high summer, there are numerous varieties of melons and grapes, the most evocatively named being the long, translucent green **bazoula** (breast-shaped) grapes. Autumn finds the markets full of citrus fruit: look out for*

*lemon-like bergamotes (the taste approximates to soapy Earl Grey tea) and tiny green **lime beldi**.*

*On the vegetable front, Tunisian markets are full of greens much used in the preparation of stews and salads. Broad-leaved parsley or **ma'adnous**, essential for flavouring many dishes is always available, and no decent couscous sauce will be made without **klefs**, a sort of celery. In summer, the small fleshy leaves of **badalika** are used to make cooling salads. And if you want something to take home? Try dried bay leaves (**rand**), cheap and aromatic, a sachet of dried mint (**na'na'**) or even a bushel of lemon verbena (**trunjiya**), ideal for making a soothing, sleep-inducing infusion when you return to your hectic, everyday life.*

Approaches to towns and autoroute verges are often planted with **oleander**, (Arabic: *defla*) an attractive shrub which flowers white and pink, and can grow to some height in the right conditions. It is highly poisonous to beasts. In spring, you may notice low-growing flowering shrubs on the roadside. These may be **acacias**, another Australian import. The blue-leaved wattle has hanging branches and strong-smelling flowers, while the silver wattle, better known as the **mimosa**, has long branches of tiny yellow pompom flowers. A rarer species is the Persian acacia, easily identified by the long, silky, reddish stamens of its flowers. All the wattles are tough and drought resistant, and some can be found on sandy land close to the sea, like the tamarisk, used also as an ornamental tree in the southern oasis settlements. The tamarisk has delicate feathery branches with tiny leaves, and its flowers, pink or white, grow in dense bouquets.

In the interior, the **prickly pear cactus** (*Opuntia ficus indica*) is much used along with the **agave** to hedge in olive and almond groves. Both are naturalized imports from the Americas. With its wide flat thorny 'leaves', the prickly pear forms great barriers which dissuade foraging goats and sheep. You may see the new plantations of prickly pear where chunks of the plant have been pushed into the earth to take root. The pear shaped fruit, an attractive yellow-orange colour, is collected by small boys with long canes. Ripe at summer's end, it is known as *sultan el ghilla*, the 'sultan of fruit', and is both delicious and constipating.

Orchards The Cap Bon region and the Mornag plain, south of Tunis, have some of Tunisia's
(sweni) most fertile fruit growing regions. The orchards or *sweni* can easily be picked out: very often they are surrounded by lines of slender, dark **cypress** trees which protect the trees in blossom time from spring winds and driving rain. **Almond** are the earliest trees to flower, followed by **pear** and **peach**. Then come the citrus trees, filling the air with fragrance. The Beni Khaled area, lowlying land close to the sea, is famed for its citrus trees. In fact, **oranges** and **lemons** were unknown in the ancient Mediterranean, and were probably brought from China in the early Middle Ages. Today, Tunisia produces a large number of citrus fruits, and is especially known for the

Gnarly, resilient and productive : the olive tree

The olive branch, synonymous with peace, was Noah's first indication of the receding flood. It is a phoenix among trees. Gnarly and dead-looking, it will quickly produce fresh sprouts when cut back. It was Athena's gift to ancient Athens, the mother of all trees. When the Athenians climbed up to the Acropolis in 480 BC, the day after the Persians had sacked their city, they found that the remains of Athena's sacred olive tree had already sent out a new branch.

The olive is a subtropical, broad-leaved, evergreen tree, both fire and drought resistant. It grows 3-12 m high and many trees are said to be between 50-100 years old. The leathery, lance-shaped leaves, growing in pairs are dark green above and silvery underneath. From the tiny white flowers the green olives develop, later maturing through shades of purple to black.

The toughness of the olive tree is one of its most notable features. The tree can survive the odd frost, and grows right down on the edge of the Sahara, drawing its moisture from the dew. Modern archaeology has shown that in Roman times, the tree's southern limit was much further south than it is today. During its lifetime, the tree is often roughly treated, pruned and shaken, even beaten to bring
down the fruit, though this is not recommended. In some places, the pickers claw through the trees with goats' horns on their fingers to take off the olives.

Although table olives are a great delicacy, it is the oil which is the glory of the tree, a rich liquid which ranges from the cloudy green to the smooth golden. Its value is esteemed by all the peoples of the Mediterranean – in the Koran, it is referred to as "oil so luminous it seems to shine, though no fire has touched it." But the oil is as fragile as the trees are resilient. If the crushing and filtering process is too rough, the delicate smell of the oil is in part destroyed. The oil also quickly takes on surrounding aromas, which makes it ideal for cooking, but implies great care in the processing.

The olive tree carries much symbolism. For northern Europeans, its oil is synonymous with southern cuisine and the sunfilled landscapes of the Mediterranean. In Tunisia, the well-planted groves symbolize the wealth of an entire region – and this was the case back under the Romans, when olive trees were planted in their thousands, more profitable and less labour intensive than wheat. Visiting El Djem and Sfax, you have the strong impression that the landscape has not changed in a very long time.

Maltaise juice orange. Rarer citrus fruits include the *lime beldi*, a small green lime, the *bergamote*, a small sweet lemon with a slightly soapy taste, and the grapefruit (Fr: *pamplemousse*, Ar: *zimba'*).

Older residential areas often have some interesting fruit trees. The **mulberry** is often grown. Black mulberry is a sweet, deep mauve *fruit*, while the white mulberry was originally planted both for fruit and as food for silkworms. The production of **silk** was a Chinese state secret until the mid-sixth century. Then the Emperor Justinian managed to get two Persian monks to smuggle silkworms out of the Celestial Empire in their hollow bamboo walking sticks. Silk production then took root in the Middle East and Europe. Unfamiliar to European eyes is the **loquat** (*Eriobotrya japonica*) or **medlar tree** (*neflier* in French). Found in residential areas where it is grown for its orange, plum-like fruit, the medlar is easily recognized by its coarse dark green leaves.

Evergreen forest can be found in the Khroumirie Mountains south of the coastal resort of Tabarka. Evergreen **holm oak** and **cork oak** are the characteristic trees, and there is a dense undergrowth, home of the wild boar amongst other animals, of

Northwestern forests

Background

various thorn trees and juniper. In places, this forest grows quite high, and there are small areas of **sweet chestnut** trees. Another tree found in the north is the **carob** or locust tree (*Ceratonia siliqua*), which like many Mediterranean trees has coarse foliage and waxy leaves. The tree produces long, chocolate-coloured pods containing three or four big seeds, which are used for cattle fodder and as 'country chocolate'. Carob pods are also an ingredient in a Boga Cidra, a Tunisian fizzy drink with a passing resemblance to Pepsi or Coke.

Further south, in the mountainous parts of the interior (the Dorsal Range), the climate is drier, and the forest is mainly composed of **Aleppo pines**. This tree thrives on dry hillsides, regenerating after fire. It has long needles, which make great splashes of bright green on the landscape in the spring. The La Kessera region south of Makthar has particularly fine pine forest.

Brush *(maquis)*, garrigue & steppe lands

In many areas once covered with Aleppo pine, overgrazing and wood cutting have destroyed the forest. Vegetation becomes a dense, fragrant brush a few metres high, referred to in French as the *maquis*. **Tree heather**, **juniper**, **lentisc** and **broom**, along with **rosemary**, **sage** and **thyme** are the main plants. In such dry regions, the only plants to survive have special adaptive features: some have extensive root systems; others have hard, shiny leaves or an oily surface to reduce water loss through transpiration. Plants such as the broom have small, sparse leaves, relying on stems and thorns to attract sunlight. The herbs all smell strongly, which seemingly makes them less attractive to animals. (Maquis regions produce splendid **honey** on account of these herbs.) Where the maquis is overused by people, the vegetation becomes sparse and stunted, rocky outcrops more pronounced as the soil is eroded away. This plant cover is the ***garrigue*** in French, bright with annual flowers in spring, but an arid place in summer. Further south in central Tunisia, the garrigue turns to **alfa grass** steppe land. Salt bushes and the grasses which come up after the spring rains provide seasonal grazing. In the steppes too, modern agriculture is at work. Thanks to the irrigation water available from tiny hill dams and bore holes, there are new fruit orchards and plantations of prickly pear, acacia, and eucalyptus. Efforts are being made to upgrade the open grazing lands, the *terres de parcours*, with new varieties of artemisia. The process of reversing the impact of several thousand years of deforestation would seem to be underway at last.

Books

There is a severe shortage of reading material on Tunisia in English but if you read French, you will be spoiled for choice.

Moscati, Sabatino, *L'Empire de Carthage* (1995) Editions Paris Méditerranée, Paris. Covers the Punic side of things thoroughly.
Raven, Susan, *Rome in Africa* (1993, third edn) Routledge, London. An excellent background account of Roman Africa.
Slim, H and **Fauqué, N**, *La Tunisie antique, de Hannibal à Saint Augustin* . Coffee-table format, a good visual overview of the country's prime ancient sites.
Soren, David et al, *Carthage, uncovering the mysteries and splendours of ancient Tunisia* (1990) Simon and Schuster, New York. Very general and rather chatty.
Wells, Colin, *The Roman Empire* (1992, 2nd edn) Fontana, London. Highly readable.

Ancient history

In Tunis, you will find expensive coffee-table books on the ancient mosaics published by Cérès Productions and Alif. The ANPE, Tunisia's national heritage board, has a range of publications on sale at the main archaeological sites. You might take a translation of **Virgil**'s *Aeneid* with you, to have a read of Book IV (Dido and Aeneas in Carthage), **Sallust**'s *Jugurthine War*, or a heavier read in the form of **Flaubert**'s *Salammbô*. All are available as Penguin Classics.

Annabi, H, *Itinéraire du savoir en Tunisie* (1995) CNRS/IMA, Paris. In French, an interesting and beautifully illustrated collection of articles on Tunisian history.
Brown, LC, *The Tunisia of Ahmed Bey* (1974) Princeton University Press. A truly scholarly account of the modernizing work undertaken by an early 19th century ruler.
On a more specialized level, there are books on quite a few corners of Tunisian history in English, including:
Latham, JD, *Towards a study of Andalusian immigration and its place in Tunisian history* (1957) Cahiers de Tunisie, Tunis.
Lloyd, C, *English Corsairs on the Barbary Coast* (1981) London.
Messenger, Charles, *The Tunisian Campaign* Ian Allen, London.

History

There is very little available in English for the generalist reader.
Hopwood, D, *Habib Bourguiba of Tunisia – The tragedy of Longevity* Macmillan, London. On the first president, thorough.
Murphy. Emma, *Economic and Political Change in Tunisia: from Bourguiba to Ben Ali* (1999) Macmillan. Too dependent on official information to be really useful.
Zéraffa, Michel, *Tunisie* (1957) G. Lang, coll. Petite Planète, Paris. A small but perfect portrait of post-independence Tunisia.

Contemporary Tunisia

Background

Tunisia has produced few contemporary novelists of any standing – cinema and theatre are the country's strong points and local publishers publish the texts of plays in Tunisian dialect. In French, readily available titles include **Albert Memmi**'s *La Statue de sel* and **André Gide**'s *Amyntas*. The second-hand bookshop on Rue d'Angleterre in Tunis may produce a few finds.
Béji, Hélé, *L'Oeil du jour* (1993) Cérès, Tunis. Evocative writing on 'growing-up with granny' in the Médina of Tunis.
Bey, Faycal, *La Dernière Odalisque* (2001) Stock, Paris. A recent media success – the popularity of the escapist theme, intrigue and decadence in the palaces of Tunisia's failing monarchy, probably has as much to say about contemporary politics as about anything else.

Contemporary Tunisian authors

Fellous, Colette, *Avenue de France* (2001) Gallimard, Paris. A family tale rooted in Tunisia's recent past recounted with central Tunis as its backdrop.

Azza Filali, *Monsieur L.* (2000) Cérès, Tunis. New writer, following theme of roots and identity quests.

Moati, Nine, *Les Belles de Tunis* (1984) Le Seuil, Paris; (2000) Cérès, Tunis. Saga of three generations of women in a Tunis Jewish family.

Naccache, Gilbert, *Cristal* (2000, 2nd edn) Ed. Salammbô, Tunis. For left-wing militancy in late-1960s Tunis.

Travel writing Given that Tunisia was a battle ground for Allied and Axis armies, there was a fair amount of travel writing post-Second World War. Although most is now out of print, look out for reissues by London-based Sickle Moon Books.

Fielding, Xan, *Corsair Country: the diary of a journey along the Barbary coast* (1958) Travel Book Club, London. A piece that started as an attempt to 'rediscover the harbours and towns of the Barbary Coast pirates'.

Martin, Dahris, *Among the Faithful* (1937); (2001, new edn) Sickle Moon Books, London. The adventures of a young American woman in the holy city of Kairouan in the 1930s. Dahris is taken in by the roguish kalipha and his family. The tone is given by chapter headings like 'A Djinn party', 'Harlots' and 'Fatima becomes a problem'.

Moorhead, Alan, *African Trilogy* (1944) Hamish Hamilton, London. Chronicles of the Second World campaigns in 'one of the great battlegrounds of history', as Field-Marshall Viscount Wavell put it in his foreword.

Desert **Louis, André**, *Nomades d'hier et d'aujourd'hui dans le Sud tunisien* (1979) Edisud, Aix-en-Provence. The lost nomad way of life. A little confusing at times, as the book was put together after the author's death. Good bibliography if you are interested in the ways of the desert.

Scott, Chris, *Sahara Overland* (2000) Trailblazer Publications, Hindhead. For desert information, the best basic book in English.

Footnotes

11

Footnotes

Language

Arabic is the official language of Tunisia, but nearly all Tunisians with a secondary education have enough French to communicate with, and a fair smattering of English. In the North, Italian maintains a presence thanks to TV and radio. Outside education, however, Tunisian Arabic is the language of everyday life, and attempts to use a few words and phrases, no matter how stumblingly, will be appreciated. Those with some Arabic learned elsewhere often find the dialect difficult. It is characterized by a clipped quality (the vowels just seem to disappear), and the words taken from classical Arabic are often very different from those used in the Middle East. In addition, there is an admixture of French and Italian terms, often heavily 'Tunisianized'. The following word lists might help you get started, or leave a café waiter or garage attendant totally bewildered. French terms are given mixed in with the Tunisian Arabic – in many situations the French is understood and often used.

For the English speaker, some of the sounds of Tunisian Arabic are totally alien. There is a strong glottal stop (as in the word 'bottle' when pronounced in Cockney English), generally represented by an apostrophe, and a rasping sound written here as 'kh', rather like the 'ch' of the Scots 'loch' or the Greek 'drachma'. And there is a glottal 'k' sound (as in the word 'souq', generally represented as 'k'), which luckily often gets pronounced as the English hard 'g', and a very strongly aspirated 'h' in addition to the weak 'h'. The French 'r' sound is generally transcribed as 'gh'. The English 'th' sound as in 'three' is represented here as 'th', while 'dh' represents 'th' as in the word 'this'. Anyway, worry ye not. Tunisian acquaintances will have a fun time correcting your attempts at pronouncing Arabic.

English	French	Tunisian Arabic

Essentials

English	French	Tunisian Arabic
yes	oui	*na'm / ee-na'am / aywa*
no	non	*la*
please	s'il vous plaît	*min fadhlek / b'rrabi / ya'eeshek*
thankyou	merci beaucoup	*barak Allahou feek / shukran / ya'eeshek*

Greetings

English	French	Tunisian Arabic
Hello	Salut	*Sellam*
Good morning	Bonjour	*S'bah el khir*
Good afternoon/ evening/night	Bonsoir / Bonne nuit	*M'sa el khir / Tesbah ala khir*
Pleased to meet you	Enchanté	*Netsherrefou*
How are you?	Comment allez-vous?	*Shneeya el ahwal / La bes*
Fine, thankyou	Très bien, merci	*La bes*
How's things?	Comment ça va?	*Shneeya el ahwel? La bes?*
Everything's fine	Tout va bien	*El hamdou lillah (lit. Praise be to God) / Kull shay la bas*
Goodbye	Au revoir/Ciao	*Bisslema*
See you later	A tout à l'heure	*Ciao, Enshoufuk min ba'd / nitkablou ba'd*
Good luck!	Bonne chance	*Rabbi ma'ak*

Polite requests

Excuse me	S'il vous plaît/Excusez-moi	*Samahnee*
One minute, please	Un instant, si'il vous plaît	*Dkika, samahnee /*
		Dkika ya'eeshek
I do not understand	Je ne comprends pas	*Ma fehemtiksh*
Speak slowly,	Parlez lentement,	*T'kellem bishweyya,*
please	s'il vous plaît	*min fadhlek*
Do you speak some English?	Parlez-vous un peu l'anglais?	*T'arif shewyya bil-anglay?*
What is your name?	Comment appellez-vous?	*Shi-smek?*
How do you say...	Comment est-ce qu'on dit...	*Keefaysh taqoul...*
in French/Arabic?	en français? en arabe?	*bissouri? bil-'arbi?*
What is this called in	Comment ça s'appelle	*shi-sm hadha bissouri?*
French/Arabic?	en français? en arabe?	*bil-'arbi?*

Common expressions

I don't know	je ne sais pas	*ma n'arifsh*
How much?	C'est à combien?	*Qaddaysh?*
free (of charge)	gratuit	*bilesh*
no problem	pas de problème	*femmesh hatta mushkila*
OK/that's fine	d'accord	*d'akkordou*
It doesn't matter	Ce n'est pas grave	*Ma selesh*
Watch out!	Attention!	*Rud balak!*
Look!	Regardez!	*Shouf*, plural *Shoufou!*
Go away!	va-t-en!	*barra!*
Where are the toilets?	Où sont les toilettes?	*feen et-toilette?*

Handy adjectives and adverbs

NB French and Tunisian adjectives have masculine and feminine forms, which correspond to noun genders. Tunisian Arabic, unlike French, has only one definite article for singular and plural (el).

cheap	pas cher	*r'khees/r'kheesa*
expensive	cher	*ghalee/ghaleeya*
ready	prêt/prête	*hadhir/hadhira*
near	proche, près	*qreeb/qreeba*
far	loin	*ba'eed/ba'eeda*
hot	chaud	*sekhoun* (liquid) *ettaqs*
		sekhoun (weather)
cold	froid	*berid/berida*
beautiful	beau/belle	*tahfoun/tahfouna*
good	bien	*behi/behiya*
happy	content (e)	*farhan/farhana*
That's great	C'est super	*Tahfoun barsha!*
		behi yasser!
new	nouveau/nouvelle	*jdeed (a)*
old	vieux/vieille	*kdeem (a)*
clean	propre	*ndheef (a)*
in a hurry	pressé	*mazroub*
quickly	vite	*feesa feesa*

Quantities

a lot	beaucoup	*barsha*
a little	un peu	*shwaya*
half	la moitié	*nesf/shtar*

Shopping and other basics

bank	la banque	*el banka*
bureau de change	bureau de change	*mekteb sarf* (rare)
cash	du cash / du liquide	*cash, sarf belhadher*
notes/coins	billets de banque/ pièces de monnaie	*awrak / sarf*
do you have change?	est-ce que vous	*'endek sarf?*
post office	les PTT, la poste	*el bousta, el bareed*
stamps	des timbres poste	*tnebir (sing. timbree)*
corner grocery	l'épicerie	*el attar*
market	le marché	*essouk, el marshay*
restaurant/fast food	le restaurant/le snack	*el mat'am*
hotel	hôtel, auberge	*el hoteel*
youth hostel	auberge de jeunesse	*l'auberge / madheef esh shebab*
toilet/bathroom	les toilettes/la salle de bain	*el mirhadh/el beet bano*
customs	la douane	*ed diwana*
police/policeman	la police/le policier, le gendarme	*el bouleesiya/el boulees*

Eating

breakfast	petit déjeuner	*ftour essabah*
lunch	le déjeuner	*ftour*
dinner	le dîner	*'asha*
meal	le repas	
without meat	sans viande	*blesh lham*
drink	la boisson	*mashroubet* (pl)
dessert	le dessert	*dessert*

At the restaurant/café

a glass of tea	un verre de thé	*ka's tay*
teabag tea	thé infusion	*thé bissashay*
weak milky coffee	un crème	-
half espresso, half milk	un (crème) direct	*un direct*
without sugar	sans sucre	*blesh sukar*
a small bottle	une petite bouteille	*dabouza sgheera*
a large bottle	une grande bouteille	*dabouza kbeera*
still mineral water	de l'eau plate	(brands Safia and Marwa)
fizzy mineral water	de l'eau gazeuse	(brands Bulla Regia and Garci)
ashtray	cendrier	*taktouka*
bill	l'addition	*l'hseb*
fork	une fourchette	*falguita*
knife	un couteau	*sikeena*
spoon	une cuillère	*m'gharfa*
glass	un verre	*ka's*
bowl	un bol	*sahfa*
Excuse me (calling the waiter)	s'il vous plaît	*ya ma'lem, ya shef*
Could you bring us some more bread	encore du pain s'il vous plaît	*sahfa*
Please could I have …	S'il vous plaît, donnez-moi	*Birrebee, 'ateenee*

Food

beef	du boeuf	*lham bagri*
bread	du pain	*khubz*
butter	du beurre	*zebda*
chicken	du poulet	*djej*
chips	des frites	*batata maklya*
eggs	des oeufs (un oeuf)	*'adham (sing. 'adhma)*
fruit	des fruits	*ghilla*
lamb	de l'agneau	*alloush*
olive oil	de l'huile d'olive	*zit zitouna*
rice	du riz	*rouz*

Drink

a bottle of water	une bouteille de eau	*dabouza ma*
mineral water	l'eau minérale	*ma dabouza*
fizzy drink	une boisson gazeuse	*gazouza*
milk	du lait	*hleeb*
wine	le vin	*shreb*
beer	la bière	*birra*

Sleeping

room	une chambre	*el beet, esh shembre*
with two beds	avec deux petits lits	*ma' zouz afresh*
with private bathroom	avec salle de bain	*ma' beet banou*
hot/cold water	de l'eau chaude/froide	*ma sekhouna/barda*
to make up/	arranger/nettoyer la	*ykhemel el beet*
clean the room	chambre	
sheet/pillow	un drap/des oreillers	*el melhafa/el mukhada*
blanket	une couverture	*el gh'ta*
clean/dirty towels	des serviettes propres/sales	*fouta (pl. fut)*
loo paper	du papier hygiénique	*ndheef/mwessekh*

At the hotel – a few requests and complaints

Can I see the room?	J'aimerais voir la chambre	*mumkin nshouf el beet*
The water's off	L'eau est coupée	*El ma maqtouqa'*
There's no hot water	Il n'y a pas d'eau chaude	*Femmesh ma skhouna*
Excuse me,	S'il vous plaît, est-ce que	*Femma fut?*
are there any towels?	vous avez des serviettes?	
Could you bring	Est-ce que vous pouvez	*Mumkin tjeebilna fut?*
us some towels?	nous apporter desserviettes?	
The washbasin's blocked	Le lavabo est bouché	*El lavabo masdoud*
The window doesn't close	La fenêtre ne ferme pas	*Esh shubek ma yet'sekersh*
Toilet flush doesn't work	La chasse ne marche pas	*La chasse ma tekhdemsh*
The lightbulb has blown	L'ampoule est grillée	*El unbouba mahrouka*
Would you mind awfully	Auriez-vous l'extrême	*Rebbi fedhlek, mumkin*
changing the lightbulb?	amabilité de changer	*tebedil el unbouba*
		l'ampoule?
There's a lot of noise	Il y a beacoup de bruit	*Femma barsha hiss*
Can I change rooms?	J'aimerais changer de	*Mumkin nebedil el-beet*
	chambre	

Getting around

on the left/right	à gauche / à droite	*'al yasser/al yameen*
straight on	tout droit	*direct, toul*
first/second street	la première/deuxième rue	*awal/theni nahaj 'al*
on the right	à droite	*yameen*
to walk	marcher	*yimshee*
bus station	la gare routière	*el mahatta*
town bus/inter city coach	le bus/le car	*el bus/el car*
city bus stop	l'arrêt (des buses)	*el mahatta*
ticket office	le guichet	*el guishay*
train station	la gare (de l'ONCF)	*la gare*
train	le train	*el treenou*
airport	l'aéroport	*el eropor*
airplane	l'avion	*et-tayyara*
first/second class	première/deuxième classe	*dereja oula/theniya*
ticket (return)	le billet (aller – retour)	*el beeyay (meshee ew ja'ee)*
ferry/boat	le ferry/le navire	*el ferry*
a hire car	une voiture de location	*kerheba mekreeya*
road	route	*tareek, kayess, thniya*
bridge	pont	*kantra*
toll gate	péage	-
wheel/tyre	roue/pneu	*'ajla/pneu*

Health

chemist/all-night chemist	la pharmacie/pharmacie de garde (de nuit)	*es saydaliya*
doctor	le médecin	*et tabib*
emergency medical services	la SAMU	les urgences
Where does it hurt?	Où est la douleur?	*Feen youja' feek?*
stomach	l'estomac	*el ma'da*
fever/sweat	la fièvre/la sueur	*es skhana/el 'araq*
diarrohea	la diarrhée	*el kirsh yejree*
blood	le sang	*ed damm*
I have a headache	J'ai mal à la tête	*ra'see youja'a*
condoms	les préservatifs	*Rifel* (brand)
contact lenses	les lentilles de contact	

Numbers

one	un	*wahid*
two	deux	*ithnayn*
three	trois	*thelatha*
four	quatre	*arb'a*
five	cinq	*khamsa*
six	six	*sitta*
seven	sept	*saba'a*
eight	huit	*themaniya*
nine	neuf	*tissa'*
ten	dix	*ashra*
eleven	onze	*ihdash*

twelve	douze	*ithnash*
thirteen	treize	*thelathatash*
fourteen	quatorze	*'rb'atash*
fifteen	quinze	*kh'msatash*
sixteen	seize	*settash*
seventeen	dix-sept	*sb'atash*
eighteen	dix-huit	*t'mentash*
nineteen	dix-neuf	*ts'atash*
twenty	vingt	*'ashrine*
thirty	trente	*thlatheene*
forty	quarante	*'arba'eene*
fifty	cinquante	*khamseene*
sixty	soixante	*sitteene*
seventy	soixante-dix	*saba'eene*
eighty	quatre-vingts	*thamaneen*
ninety	quatre-vingt-dix	*tiss'eenne*
one hundred	cent	*miya*
two hundred	deux cent	*miyatayn*
three hundred	trois cent	*thlatha miya*
thousand	mille	*alf*

Days and months

Monday	lundi	*nhar el ithnayn*
Tuesday	mardi	*nhar eth thelatha*
Wednesday	mercredi	*nhar el arbi'a*
Thursday	jeudi	*nhar el khamees*
Friday	vendredi	*nhar el juma'*
Saturday	samedi	*nhar es sebt*
Sunday	dimanche	*nhar el ahad*

French only. Tunisian Arabic pronunciation similar to French

January	janvier
February	février
March	mars
April	avril
May	mai
June	juin
July	juillet
August	août
September	septembre
October	octobre
November	novembre
December	décembre

Asking questions

straight on	tout droit	*direct, toul*

SNCFT: Handy train times

As the SNCFT network is small, many of the train times vary only slightly. (Look out for variations during Ramadan). The following times are given as an example to help you plan. Obtain an up-to-date timetable (*horaire des trains grandes lignes*) at any station. Not all services are shown here.

Services between Tunis and Nabeul via Bir Bouregba

Tunis to Hammamet / Nabeul via r Bouregba

Destination/ time	Direct, a/c, Omni- bus	Direct, a/c, Omni- bus	Direct a/c	Omni- bus Omni- bus	Direct, a/c,	Omni- bus	Direct, a/c	Direct, a/c
Tunis	0625	0910	1305	1425	1540	1805	2050	2120
Bir Bouregba	0716	1001	1355	1531	1632	1910	2140	2210
	0718*	1005*	1418*		1635*			
Ham'met	0726	1013	1426	1539	1643	1918		
Nabeul	0748	1035	1448	1600	1705	1940		

NB *There are only two direct services from Tunis to Nabeul a day, at 1425 and 1805. Otherwise it is necessary to take a main line train to Bir Bourregba and then change for the Bir Bouregba to Nabeul shuttle train, shown *. There is no ongoing shuttle to meet the last Tunis to Bir Bouregba services on the main line at 2050 and 2110.*

Nabeul/ Hammamet to Tunis via Bir Bouregba

Destination/ time	Omni- bus	Omni- bus a/c	Direct a/c	Direct, a/c	Direct, a/c	Direct, a/c	Direct, a/c	Direct, a/c
Nabeul	0550				1335	1525	1900	
Ham'met	0610				1358	1548	1923	
Bir Bouregba	0618	0700	0758	0830	1405	1555	1930	2210
					1417*	1559*	1938*	2059
Nabeul	0722	0756	0848	0919	1507	1649	2028	2148

NB *There is only one direct Nabeul to Tunis service, the 0550 out of Nabeul. Three shuttle trains (1335, 1525, 1900) running Nabeul to Bir Bouregba are shown. Here you change for a main line train running up to Tunis (marked *). All the other departures require you to take a taxi to Bir Bouregba.*

Footnotes

Trains on the Tunis to Sfax route

Tunis to Sousse, El jem and Sfax

Destination/ Time	Express	Direct a/c	Direct a/c	Express	Direct a/c
Tunis	0800	1305	1415	1630	2120
Sousse	0948	1457	1611	1818	2312
El Jem	-	1552	1701	-	0002
Sfax	1118	1635	1744	1948	0046

Sfax to El Jem, Sousse and Tunis

Destination/ Time	Express	Direct a/c	Direct a/c	Express	Direct a/c
Sfax	0210	0650	1225	1440	1820
El Jem	0255	0823	1309	1613	1907
Sousse	0347	-	1402	-	1959
Tunis	0536	1008	1551	1758	2148

Trains on the southern and southwestern routes

Sfax to Gabès, Gafsa and Metlaoui

Destination/ time	Direct, a/c,	Direct, a/c,	Direct a/c	Direct, a/c,	Direct, a/c	Direct, a/c
Tunis	0625	-	1415	-	2120	-
Sfax	0956	1305	1744	1225	0038	0155
Gabès	0215	1635	2005	1309	0217	0405
Gafsa	-	2020	-	1402	1454	-
Metlaoui	-	2055	-	1551	1527	-

NB There are two different routes given here:

1. Tunis to Gabès via Sfax north-south route. (One train does just Sfax to Gabès);

2. The slow Sfax to Metlaoui via Gabès **and** Gafsa

Metlaoui to Gafsa, Gabès and Sfax

Destination/ time	Direct, a/c,	Direct, a/c,	Direct a/c	Direct, a/c,	Direct, a/c	Direct, a/c
Metlaoui	2110	-	1325	-	0850	-
Gafsa	2158	-	0413	-	0940	-
Gabès	-	2350	-	1000	-	1605
Sfax	0056/ 0110*	0210	0716	1210	1244	1820
Tunis	0436	0536	-	1551	1649	2148

*Connecting train

NB There are three different routes given here:

1. Metlaoui/ Gafsa to Sfax and Tunis (avoiding Gabès);

2. South - north Gabès/Sfax/Tunis route;

3. The long Metlaoui/Gafsa/Gabès/Sfax Tunis route

Index

Shorts index

Advertisers' index

Map index

Acknowledgements

The groundwork for the book was done by Anne and Keith McLachlan (authors of the original edition), with the help of Derek Alderton. Thanks are due to numerous people across Tunisia who shared thoughts and ideas about their country. The following travellers took time to write with ideas and experiences about their travels: David Halford, Jennifer Jasper and Brendan McGrath.

The health information was put together by Dr David Snashall, Senior Lecturer in Occupational Health at the United Medical Schools of Guy's and St Thomas' Hospitals in London and Chief Medical advisor of the British Foreign and Commonwealth Office, London.

It is extremely difficult to maintain a comprehensive coverage on the large number of areas that need regular updating – something which makes letters from travellers highly appreciated. The information contained in this third edition is, as far as possible, correct at the time of going to print. However, details change, inflation rears its ugly head, meaning that transport, hotel and restaurant costs increase. Some establishments change hands and improve – or even decline. All useful comments and corrections for future editions are welcome.

The present guide was produced without the assistance of official tourist boards and other State agencies.

Tunisia

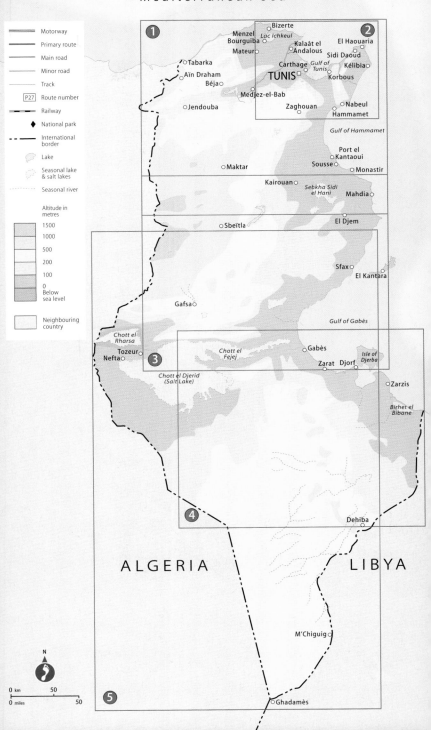

Mediterranean Sea

1

2

Tabarka

Aïn Draham

Béja

Jendouba

Menzel Bourguiba

Mateur

Medjez-el-Bab

Lac Ichkeul

Bizerte

Kalaât el Andalous

Carthage

TÚNIS

Gulf of Tunis

Zaghouan

El Haouaria

Sidi Daoud

Kélibia

Korbous

Nabeul

Hammamet

Gulf of Hammamet

Maktar

Kairouan

Sebkha Sidi el Hani

Port el Kantaoui

Sousse

Monastir

Mahdia

Sbeïtla

El Djem

Sfax

El Kantara

Gafsa

Gulf of Gabès

3

Chott el Rharsa

Tozeur

Nefta

Chott el Jerid (Salt Lake)

Chott el Fejej

Gabès

Zarat

Djorf

Isle of Djerba

Zarzis

Birhet el Bibane

4

Dehiba

ALGERIA

LIBYA

M'Chiguig

N

5

Ghadamès

	Motorway
	Primary route
	Main road
	Minor road
	Track
P27	Route number
	Railway
◆	National park
·–··–	International border
	Lake
	Seasonal lake & salt lakes
	Seasonal river

Altitude in metres

1500
1000
500
200
100
0
Below sea level

Neighbouring country

0 km 50
0 miles 50

Map 1

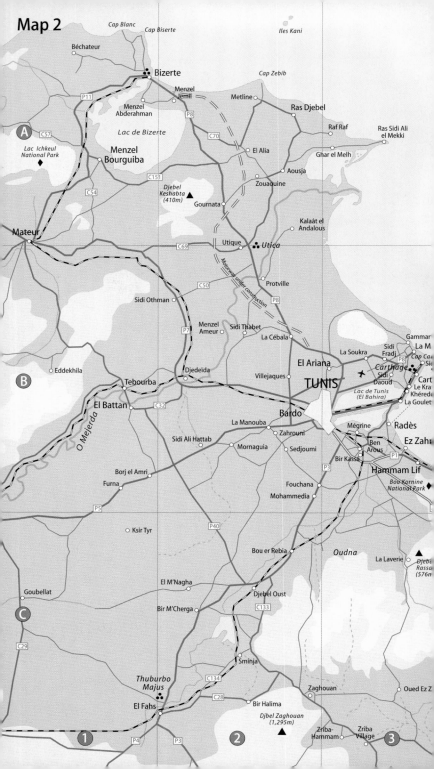

Map 2

Cap Blanc
Cap Biserte
Iles Kani

Béchateur

Bizerte

Cap Zebib

Menzel Jemil
Metline
Ras Djebel

P11
Menzel Abderahman
P8
Raf Raf
Ras Sidi Ali el Mekki

A C57
Lac de Bizerte
C70
El Alia
Ghar el Melh

Lac Ichkeul National Park
Menzel Bourguiba
C151
Aousja
Zouaquine

C54
Djebel Keshabta (410m)
Gournata

Kalaât el Andalous

Mateur
C69
Utique
Utica

C50
Protville
P8

Sidi Othman

P7
Menzel Ameur
Sidi Thabet
La Cébala
Gammar
La M
Sidi Fradj
Cap Ca
Sid
La Soukra

Eddekhila
Djedeïda
Villejaques
El Ariana
TUNIS
Sidi Daoud
Cart
Le Kra
Khéréde
La Goulet

B
Tebourba
Bardo
Lac de Tunis (El Bahira)

El Battan
C32
La Manouba
Zahrouni
Mégrine
Radès
Ez Zah

Sidi Ali Hattab
Mornaguia
Sedjoumi
Bir Kassa
Ben Arous
Hammam Lif

Borj el Amri
Fouchana
P3
Bou Kornine National Park

Furna
Mohammedia

P5
Ksir Tyr
P40
Bou er Rebia
Oudna
La Laverie
Djebe Rassa (576m

C
El M'Nagha
Djebel Oust

Goubellat
Bir M'Cherga
C133

C29
Sminja
Thuburbo Majus
C134
Zaghouan
Oued Ez Z

El Fahs
C28
Bir Halima

1 P4 P3
2 Djbel Zaghouan (1,295m)
Zriba-Hammam
Zriba Village
3

Mejerda

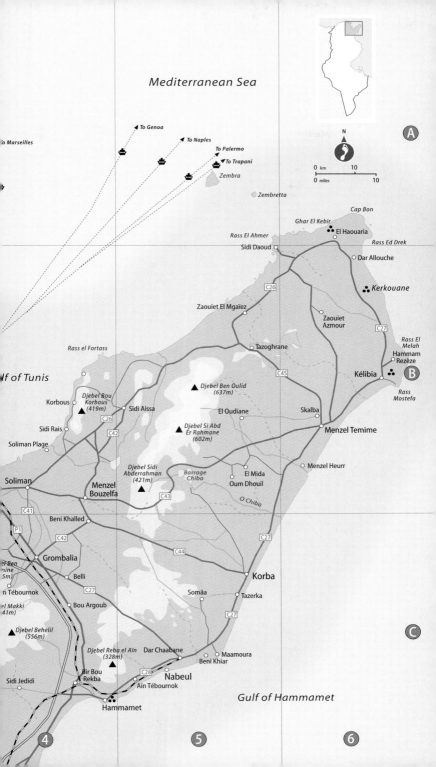

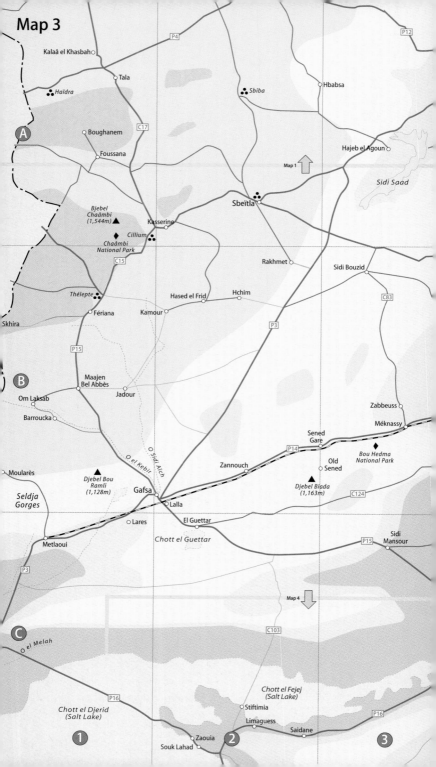

Map 4

C103

Oud
Gan

C2

Chott el Fejej
(Salt Lake)

Sembat   El Hamma   Ch

P16

A   P16   Steftimia

Limaguess   Map 3

Saidane   Nouve
Matm

Zaouia   Tombar   Beni Aissa   El Hadde

Souk Lahad   Telmine   Kebili   Zeraova   Taoujout

Chott el Djerid   M'Said   Bazma   Tamezret   Matm
(Salt Lake)

Djemma   Techine

Blidet   C206

Touiba   C114

Nouil

El Dergine   Douz

El Faouar   Zaafrane

Sabria   Bir Soltane

B

Ksar Ghilane   *Monument de la*
Colonnel Leclerc

C211

Zemlet el Borma
(250m)

O Nka

C

A L G E R I A

1   **2**   **3**

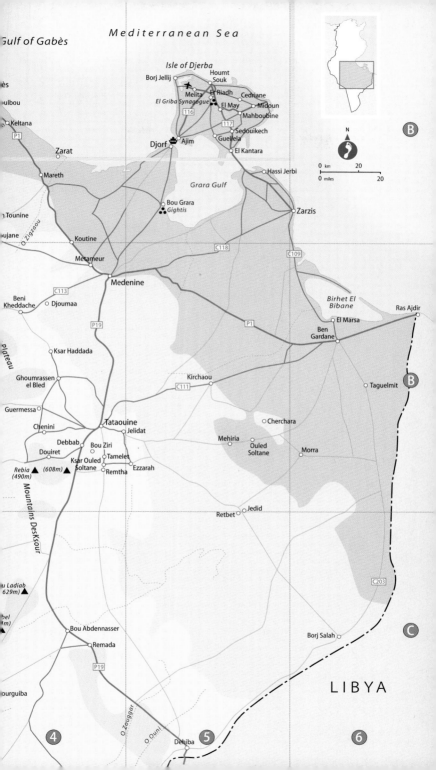

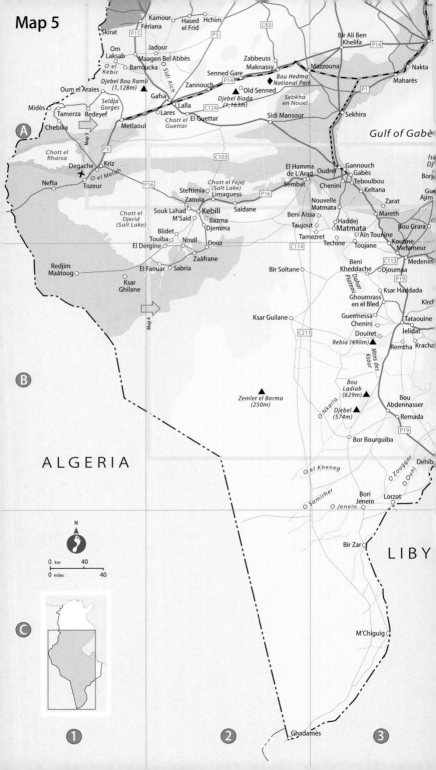

Footprint feedback

We try as hard as we can to make each Footprint Handbook as up-to-date and accurate as possible but, of course, things always change. Many people email or write to us with corrections, new information, or simply comments. If you want to let us know about your experiences and adventures – be they good, bad or ugly – then don't delay; we're dying to hear from you. And please try to include all the relevant details and juicy bits. Your help will be greatly appreciated, especially by other travellers. In return we will send you details about our special guidebook offer.

email Footprint at:
TUN3_online@footprintbooks.com

or write to:
Elizabeth Taylor
Footprint Handbooks
6 Riverside Court
Lower Bristol Road
Bath   BA2 3DZ
UK

www.footprintbooks.com
70 travel guides, 100s of destinations,
5 continents and 1 Footprint...